00

00
05
3

2004

PICTURE QUILTS

For Mum and Dad

PICTURE QUILTS

JOAN MASTERS

THE MAIN STREET PRESS
PITTSTOWN, NEW JERSEY

ACKNOWLEDGEMENTS
Permission to reproduce the
Paddington Bear cushion on
pp. 33–34 is granted by
Paddington and Company,
© Copyright Paddington and
Company 1986. Thanks also to
Bovril Ltd, The Ryvita Company
Ltd, and United Biscuits (UK)
Ltd for allowing us to reproduce
images on pp. 87 left and right
and 43 respectively.

First American Edition 1986

Copyright © 1986 by Joan Masters
All rights reserved. No part of this
publication may be reproduced,
stored in a retrieval system, or
transmitted in any form or by any
means, electronic, mechanical,
photocopying, recording or otherwise,
without prior permission of the
publisher.

Published by
The Main Street Press, Inc.
William Case House
Pittstown, NJ 08867

Published originally in Great
Britain by Bell & Hyman Limited

Designed by John Grain
Drawings by Hilary Evans
Printed in Portugal by Printer Portuguesa

Library of Congress Cataloging-in-
Publication-Data

ISBN 1-55562-012-4 **Paperback**
ISBN 1-55562-013-2 **Cloth**

Contents

Introduction

Over the last few years many people have become interested in the traditional crafts of patchwork and quilting. I suspect it's a reaction against all those mass-produced candlewick bedspreads and duvet covers! They're very practical of course, but rather dull and we'd all prefer something that's pretty and personal. Nowadays, however, few people have the time or patience to sew quilts by hand—mine ran out well before I'd covered a dog basket, let alone a double bed. Picture quilts can take even longer to make than the geometric patterns, and with all those fraying edges to turn under, a round sun may finish up looking as though it's been drawn with a ruler.

So thank goodness for the swing-needle sewing machine—making a picture quilt has suddenly become as easy as sewing a buttonhole, and I defy anyone to say that it's cheating. When I first began to sell my work at craft fairs elderly ladies would approach, full of admiration, but when they realized it was all done by machine they'd back away in horror! It was as if the Crown Jewels had turned out to be paste! Well I think that's nonsense. It's simply a modern version of a traditional craft—it's quick and it's fun, as I hope the following pages will show.

A lot of the fun comes from making up your own, personal designs. I started by making presents for friends, including pictures of all their favourite things; tea and Digestive biscuits, a dart board and a pint of stout, and a few things that are probably best left unmentioned! Later on customers sent me pictures of their houses or their pets and wrote long letters about their lifestyles and colour schemes. It was fascinating—like peering in through other peoples' windows—but my favourite commissions are still those from friends. When you know the details of someone's life you can create a picture that's witty as well as attractive, as much fun to make as to receive.

But don't forget yourself. If you can't afford a Picasso, make one in fabric, or if you just need a tea-cosy make one that says something about *you*!

INSPIRATION

If you want to make a quilt that reflects your own interests or lifestyle, think of all the things you like—favourite foods, flowers, an animal, your car, a picture of your house and so on—and if you can't draw them from life, trace or copy the pictures from magazines. You'll find advertisements can be especially useful.

There are lots of other sources of inspiration: children's books have simple, easy-to-copy illustrations, or look at birthday or Christmas cards for ideas. Work your way through the art and craft section of your local library. While you'll find it hard to capture the subtleties of Renaissance *chiaroscuro* in fabric, more stylized art-forms translate well: Greek, Romanesque and medieval painting; Indian, African and Islamic art; mosaics, stained glass or oriental carpets.

If that sounds a bit daunting, just sit down with a pile of fabric and a pair of scissors and experiment. Your picture will just grow. Never mind whether it's 'artistic'— simple shapes like a cat sitting on a mat or a rainbow can look so effective that I sometimes think being 'good at art' might be a positive disadvantage!

HOW TO USE THE BOOK

I've tried to keep instructions to a minimum. Read through the sections on materials and techniques and the sample cushion project which contain all the information you'll need on basic techniques. Finishing techniques are described on p. 119. On later projects I've suggested suitable fabrics and the best order for putting your picture together. I've also pointed out any details which may need extra care, but these are very few and mistakes are rarely critical. If you accidentally cut a hole in the picture or your sewing machine chews up the fabric, don't worry—just sew another flower, rabbit, wine bottle, or whatever seems appropriate over the top, and no one will ever know!

Materials

QUILT TOPS

As far as possible I like to use natural cotton because it's firm and easy to sew but your choice of fabrics will depend on your design as well as on your taste. Choose your textures and patterns carefully and the fabric will do a lot of the work for you, more than compensating for a lack of artistic talent!

For example, use a selection of flowery prints for meadows and leaves, a mixture of plain blues and blue and white patterns for sky and clouds. Scraps of lurex or satin are useful for bee's wings, giving them a translucent quality, while a fine velvet is ideal for birds or furry animals.

If you use fabrics like these you will need to have your quilts dry-cleaned but I think the effect repays the expense.

INTERFACING

Iron-on interfacing is a *far* better invention than sliced bread as far as I'm concerned. Applied to the back of fine fabrics it stiffens and strengthens them and prevents them from fraying. And, because it's white, you can draw clearly around your pattern pieces in ball-point pen, and identify them with notes such as 'top left feather' or 'third leg'.

WADDING

Courtelle or polyester wadding is available in various thicknesses and widths from most handicraft shops. It's very light and warm and washes well, but melts if it comes into contact with a hot iron.

BACKING FABRICS

Use a firm cotton or polyester/cotton mix. For a wall hanging or cushion front almost anything will do, but for a bedspread choose a soft fabric which will tone with the quilt top.

SEWING THREAD

Do use a good quality thread—remember this is decorative as well as functional. It *is* expensive because you may have to use up to a dozen reels in various colours for a cushion cover but a cheap thread that constantly breaks under tension really is a false economy.

Remember you can use any colour thread on your bobbin, so buy up peculiar, discontinued colours at reduced prices.

Cushions

BASIC TECHNIQUES

Materials:

**2 pieces of firm cotton backing fabric, at least
   3in/7.5cm larger than cushion**
1 piece courtelle wadding, the same size
Selection of coloured fabrics to create the design
Iron-on interfacing
Cotton thread
Spray-on starch

Method:

1. Press all the fabrics thoroughly. Using spray starch makes fine fabrics much easier to handle.

2. Iron interfacing onto the back of the fabric you intend to use for the pattern shapes (as opposed to the background).

3. Using one piece of backing fabric as a base, lay out the background of your picture, using appropriate colours. For instance, if the background shows grass and sky, use green fabric for the lower part of the picture and blue above. It is quite easy to do this without a pattern. Starting at the top of the picture, cut pieces out in any shape you like, move them around, add a cloud here or there—remember, this is *your* picture! Make sure they overlap by at least $\frac{1}{2}$in/1cm to prevent them parting as you sew.

4. When you are happy with the way they're arranged, pin and tack them to the backing.

5. Press and starch again—this will be your last chance. Courtelle wadding melts when it comes into contact with a hot iron, so once it's in place the work should not be pressed again.

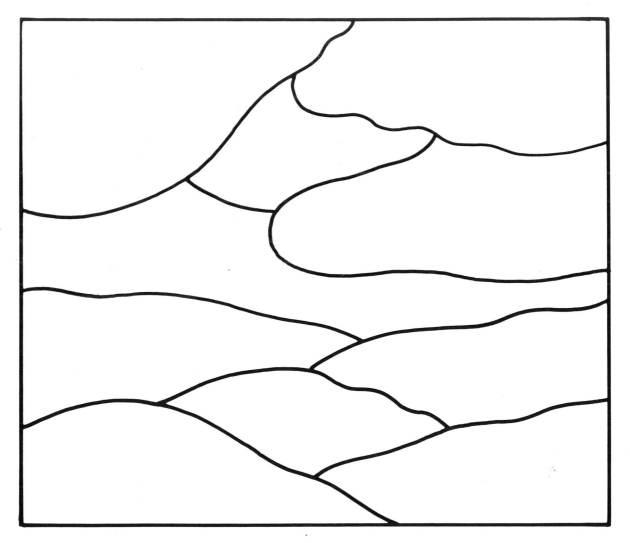

6. Make a sandwich with the second piece of backing fabric as the base, the wadding as the filling and the composite background as the top layer.

A cutting guide for a typical quilt background.

7. Pin through all thicknesses at regular intervals.

8. Using a close zig-zag stitch and matching or toning thread, machine over all the raw edges.

9. Remove the pins and tacking thread. Trim and tack around the four sides.

10. Trace off or scale up from this book the pattern shapes for the cushion you are making onto pieces of paper. Cut out the paper patterns.

11. Place the paper pattern pieces onto the correct coloured fabrics. They should be placed face down on the interfaced side of the fabric (see point 2 above).

12. Draw round the pieces with a ball-point pen and cut them out. NB It is important that all the paper patterns are put down facing the correct way–it is all too easy to cut out a bird with two left wings, just when you are running out of fabric!

13. Purists will be horrified, but I often use glue rather than tacking stitches to hold small pattern pieces in place. If you do decide to follow my (bad) example, *do* be careful—use only a trace of glue, otherwise it may go through the interfacing and mark the fabric.

14. Stick or tack the central pieces in place and machine stitch (zig-zag) around them. When sewing round curves try to ease the fabric round while continuing to sew slowly. Lifting the foot and turning the fabric can result in a broken, uneven line.

15. Place the next set of pieces on the background and stick or tack them in place.

16. Mark in details such as flower-stems, either with a line of tacking stitches or by drawing them faintly in ball-point pen—another bad but time-saving habit!

17. Machine around the unsewn pieces and down the tacked or drawn details in matching cottons.

18. Remove any tacking stitches and then check to see if your cushion front is still square! This may sound strange but areas covered by several close lines of stitching will tend to shrink. Starching the fabric before sewing and holding it taut as you sew will minimize the problem.

13

19. If you find that your cushion front looks rather like this:

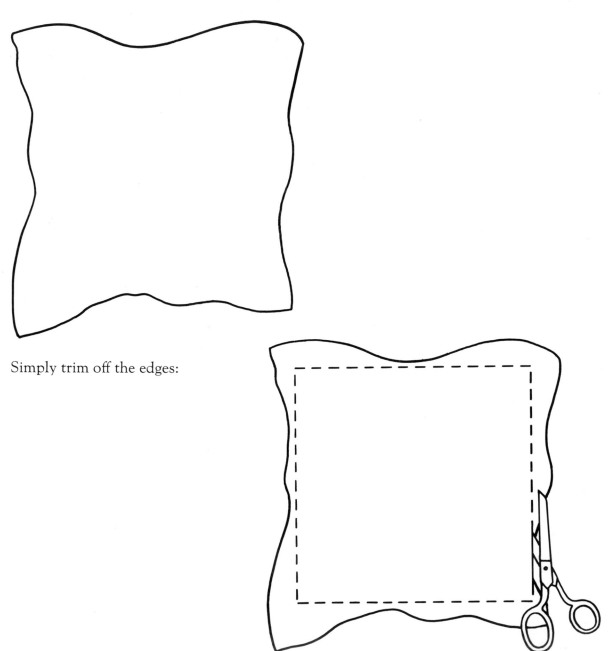

Simply trim off the edges:

If you allowed those extra few inches when cutting your backing fabric and wadding, you should still have a cushion front the size you wanted.

20. Tack once again round the four sides and then continue to make up your cushion cover in the normal way (see Finishing Techniques section, pages 119–23).

SCALING UP THE PATTERNS

The patterns given for the patch quilts are actual size, so you can trace them straight from the book and then, using carbon paper, transfer them to firmer paper and cut them out.

The other patterns can be enlarged in the following way. Trace the pattern from the book and then transfer your tracing to squared or graph paper. You can then enlarge the pattern by making a larger grid and carefully drawing in the larger squares what you've traced in each small one.

For the quilts illustrated you will need to make the patterns approximately two and half times bigger, so everything traced in a 1in/2½cm square on the original must be redrawn in a 2½in/6cm square. Of course, if you *really* want a six-foot rabbit or to enlarge an illustration from a book or magazine the principle is just the same.

Remember to mark your grid in *ball-point pen* and draw your pattern in *pencil*. Then, if you need several goes before it looks right, you can rub out the pencil lines without losing the grid too.

PIG
(approx. 20in/51cm)

A close friend of mine has a thing about pigs! I've no idea how it started but she collects pigs of all shapes, sizes and materials. This cushion and the nightdress case on p. 39 were both designed as additions to her collection.

For a cushion cover approximately 20in/51cm square, make up the background as in the Basic Techniques above.

Make up your paper pattern. This is a good one to begin with as there's only one piece, although you could use a lighter fabric for inside the ear.

Cut your pig from interfaced pink fabric (I used a fine velvet), and work the eye in black and white thread.

Place the pig in the centre of the cushion front and stick or tack it to the background.

Machine stitch (zig-zag) around all the edges and along the lines for the mouth, ear and wrinkles.

Make up your cushion cover in the usual way.

Poppy heads (red fabric)

Leaves (dark green fabric)

Flower centres (black, pale green fabric) (cut 3)

POPPY CUSHION
(approx. 20in/51cm)

For the background you will want a selection of red and green fabrics, and for the picture itself some fabrics in red, green, black and pale green. Make up the background and cut out your pattern pieces using the basic method. Then start by machine stitching the flower centres in place. Next glue or tack down the flower heads and leaves, and mark in the stems. Machine around the heads and leaves and down the stems in matching cottons, and then remove any tacking stitches.

18

RABBIT

(approx. 20in/51cm)

For an animal shape made up of several pieces, sew the sections together before sewing the *whole* animal to the quilted background. If you sew the sections down individually your rabbit may look more like an armadillo! Again, velvet gives the right silky feel for the rabbit's fur.

ST. BERNARD
(approx. 20in/51cm)

Sew together the face sections; the back/tail sections to the rest of the body and complete the barrel decorations before placing them on the background. Complete by stitching around the outline of the barrel, the dog's head and body and finally a line separating the back leg from the tail.

I've used chenille for the head and back—it suggests the woolly quality of the dog's thick coat.

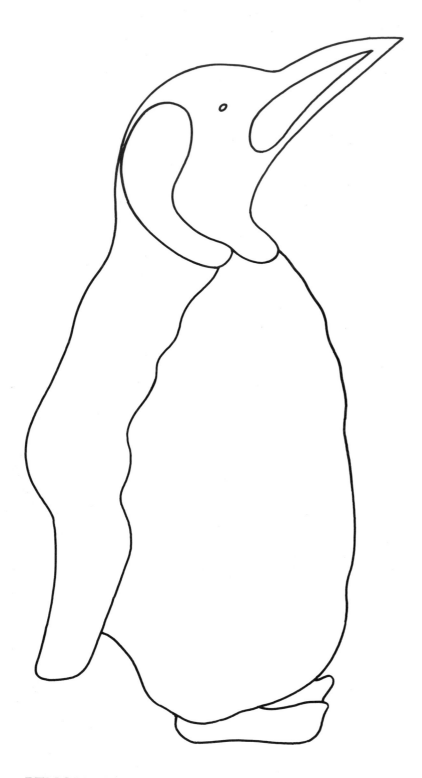

PENGUIN
(approx. 20in/51cm)

With the same icy background as the St. Bernard, this King Penguin was designed as a present for another friend, who—you guessed—collects penguins!

24

COW

(approx. 20in/51cm)

Sew the brown markings to the body before sewing the whole animal to the background.

For the trunk just cut a straightish strip of velvet and shape the end to look like roots. Add extra stitching to suggest bark, or you could use a thick corded velvet which will do the work for you!

MOUSE AND CHEESE

(approx. 20in/51cm)

This cushion was for a flatmate often found raiding the fridge at midnight! Where the pieces of cheese are made from two sections sew these together first. The 'blue veins' are lines of close zig-zag stitching. Move the stitch width gauge backwards and forwards as you sew to vary the thickness of the lines.

28

29

OWL

(approx. 20in/51cm)

Make the owl up in one piece before sewing it to the background. Use a mixture of plain and patterned velvets or add extra feathers with stitching lines. When the owl is complete place it in the centre of your cushion front and then cut about 25 leaves from a selection of green prints. Arrange most of these around the owl. Take up the owl and sew the leaves and some red berries in place.

Replace the owl and sew it down. Finally sew a few more leaves to cover the owl's toes.

ELEPHANTS

(approx. 24in/62cm)

Cut a 13in/32cm square of fabric and place it in the centre of a 26in/65cm square. Make a sandwich with wadding and backing fabric as in the Basic Techniques (p. 11). Machine stitch (zig-zag) around inner square and tack around the outer edges.

You can cut the three-elephant centre-piece from a single fabric, defining the elephants with lines of stitching as you sew it down or choose a different shade of grey for each elephant. In either case sew the tusk before sewing the elephants to the centre square.

Cut eight border elephants and attach them, trunk to tail, to the background. Machine around the edges of all the elephants in matching thread.

© *Paddington and Company 1986*

PADDINGTON BEAR
(approx. 36in/92cm)

I've made this up as a large cushion but it would be just as effective as a hanging for a child's bedroom wall. Make up the background as in the Basic Techniques section. Make Paddington up complete. Fill his pockets, paint his picture and label his marmalade jar before sewing the pieces to the background.

33

34

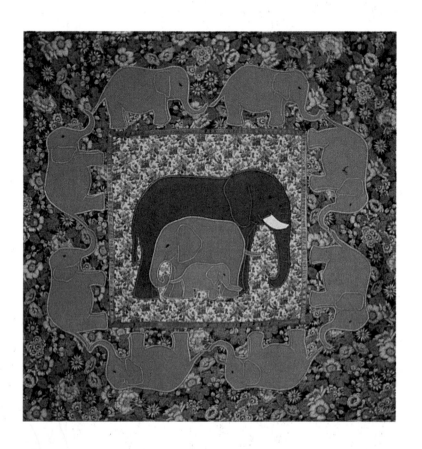

ANTELOPES

(approx. 36in/92cm)

This was designed for a friend who had just returned from a holiday in Crete and is based on wall-paintings she had photographed there. It could be made up as a wall-hanging (see p. 99) or the centre-piece of a quilt.

Make up the background more or less as suggested but you can simplify the design if you wish or cut it free-hand—don't let *my* pattern dictate *your* picture.

The antelopes themselves do need a little more precision. If you are using a very fine fabric, applying *two* layers of interfacing will make these intricate pieces easier to handle. Cut the two animals, minus tails and horns, from a single piece of white or cream fabric.

35

Cut the markings, horns and tails from black fabric and stick them to the animals' bodies. (This is definitely an occasion when the *judicious* use of fabric glue saves both time and temper!)

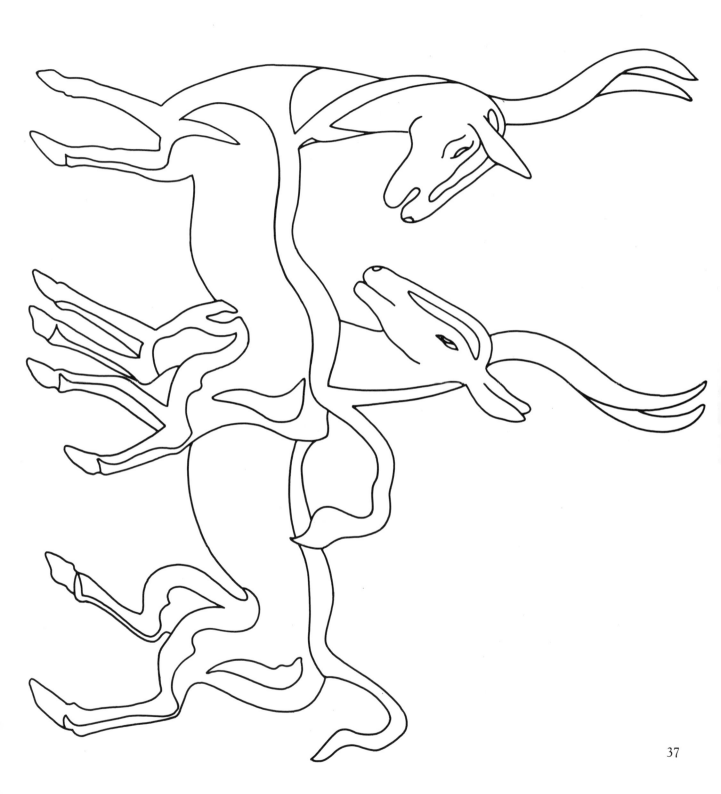

Machine around those edges that fall within the main
body outlines.

NB If the narrowness of the legs makes this tricky, blame
it on your machine and not your skill! They can be just as
effective all black, or all cream, outlined in black stitching.
Practise on scraps before you cut your pattern.

When you've assembled the antelopes, place them on
the background and machine around all the edges in black
thread. 'Draw' in the ears, eyes and back leg with lines of
stitching.

NIGHTDRESS-CASE
(approx. 16in/40cm diameter)

Make a paper pattern for a circle approximately 17in/43cm
in diameter either by drawing around a large platter or with

a piece of string tied to a pencil. Holding the string 8½in/22cm from the pencil, place your finger in the centre of your sheet of paper and swing the pencil round to describe a full circle.

You could cut the background from a single piece of fabric, in which case use the pattern as it is.

If you want a sectioned background, cut a second paper circle (you'll need the first to cut the back of the nightdress-case). Fold it in half and then in half again to give a quarter circle. By measuring around the circumference, mark it into three equal sections and draw lines from these marks to the centre of the circle. Cut out one section.

Adding a seam allowance to each side, cut twelve sections from a selection of toning prints.

Sew the sections together and press open the seams. Don't worry of they don't match perfectly in the middle—no-one will see!

Layer this top circle with wadding and a toning backing fabric and quilt them by machining (straight stitch) along all the seams.

If you've used a single piece for the top, mark in stitching lines with chalk and sew along these to give a sectioned effect.

Make the pig up complete before sewing it to the background. Trim the edges of the nightdress and night-cap with lace and ribbon and use scraps of fur fabric for the slippers and hot-water bottle cover.

Complete as for a piped cushion (see Finishing Techniques section). Either insert a zip opening across the centre back or leave one-third of the edge seam open, neatening the edges and attaching ribbon ties to either side of the opening.

Patch Quilts

If you doubt your talents as a quilt-maker, why not begin with one of these? A single 12in/30cm square with the addition of a 3in/7.5cm border can be made up into a small cushion cover, while four or nine squares sewn together will make either a larger cushion or a wall-hanging. If you get really ambitious, you can turn twenty squares into a double quilt!

BASIC TECHNIQUES

If you intend sewing several patches together they *must* all be the same size, so when you cut your squares remember to allow extra fabric to 'square up' the sides when you've finished the appliqué and for your seam allowance. Choose fabrics of a similar weight and texture in colours which will tone or contrast well in the finished quilt.

Unlike the method used for making cushions (see pages 11–15), here the wadding is only introduced at the final stage, so you can carry on pressing and starching as you sew. Choose from the designs below, but, when you can, try to personalize them—put *your* number on the telephone, *your* favourite wine in the bottle, use *your* birth-sign.

When you've copied or traced off the drawings cut out the individual pattern pieces and continue as for the basic cushion technique—iron interfacing to the back of your fabrics, *reverse* your pattern pieces, draw around them and then cut them out, allowing a small overlap where one pattern piece joins another.

It's a good idea to make several copies of the pattern so that you can cut out the smaller pieces and still keep the larger ones intact to use again.

When your patches are finished, press them once again on the reverse side to remove wrinkles and then trim to 12in/30cm square plus a seam allowance.

43

MAKING THE SQUARES INTO A QUILT

1. Arrange the patches so that the colours balance well. The illustration given here is for a nine-patch quilt, but the method is the same for 4 or 20 patches.

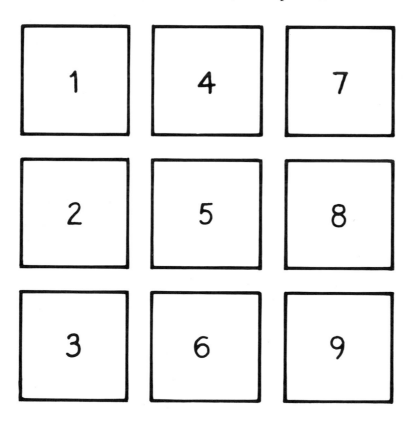

2. With right sides together, pin 1 to 2, and 2 to 3. Machine the seams and press open. Repeat for patches 4-5-6 and 7-8-9 (see top right).

3. Pin the strips together, matching the horizontal seams exactly by pinning through them at right angles to the edge (see bottom right).

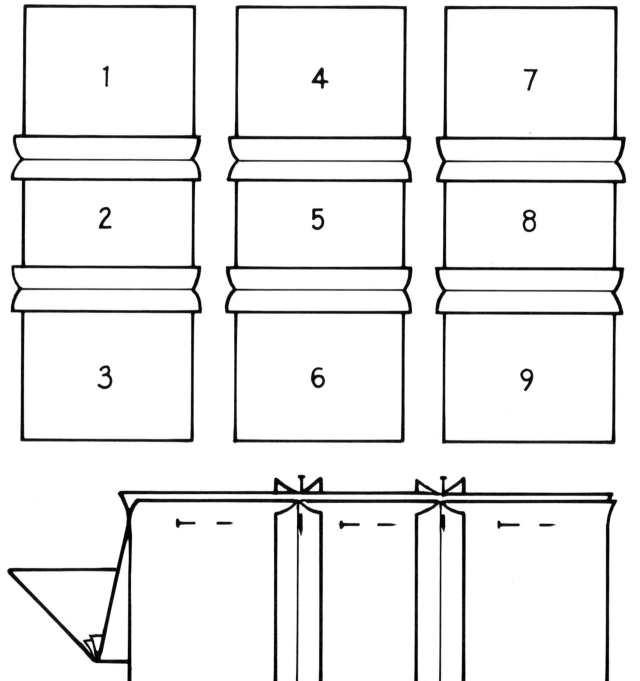

4. Machine the strips together to form the nine-patch
   square. Press the seams open (see below).

If you want to add a border do it at this stage (see Finishing
Techniques section).

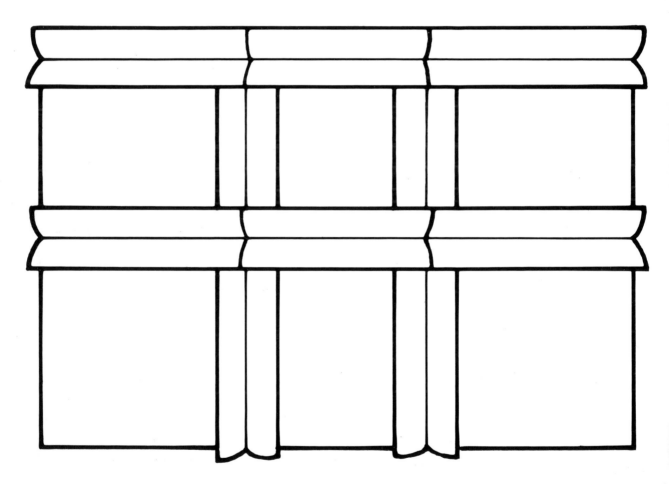

QUILTING

1. Cut a piece of Courtelle wadding, slightly larger than
   the patch square and a piece of backing fabric slightly
   larger again.

2. Make a sandwich as for the cushion technique—
   backing, wadding, patches on top.

3. Lay the sandwich on a flat, preferably hard, surface and working from the centre, smooth the seams out towards the edges, putting pins across the seams and through all three layers at regular intervals.

4. Working from top to bottom and then left to right, machine carefully down all the seams with a straight stitch. You may find that you need to adjust the pins slightly as you sew. If you've added a border do the same with those seams.

5. Tack round the four sides and trim off the excess wadding and backing fabric.

6. Continue with the instructions for making up into cushion, hanging or quilt (see Finishing Techniques section).

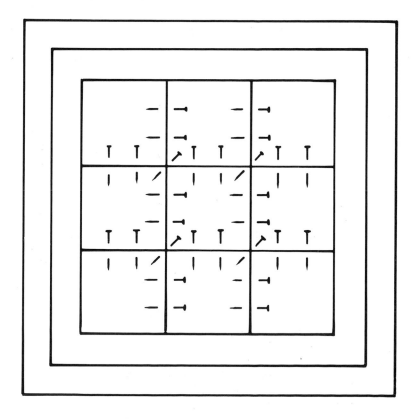

HAMBURGER AND CHIPS

The milkshake is made in one piece but outline the 'froth' in white or a pale shade, the glass in the same colour as the fabric.

Add your own stripes to the straw with lines of stitching.

Tuck scraps of red and green fabric into the bun for an extra salad filling. Make your chips from strips of yellow or gold fabric, piled up and overlapped. (Or try crinkle-cut!)

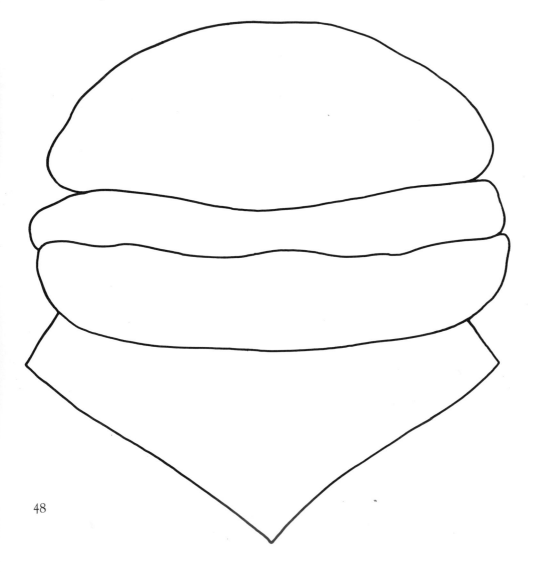

COW

Cut the body out in one, (a fine velvet would be ideal) and then stick the brown patches on with a spot of glue. The pattern is on p. 25.

SHIP

This looks as effective without the decorative stitching.

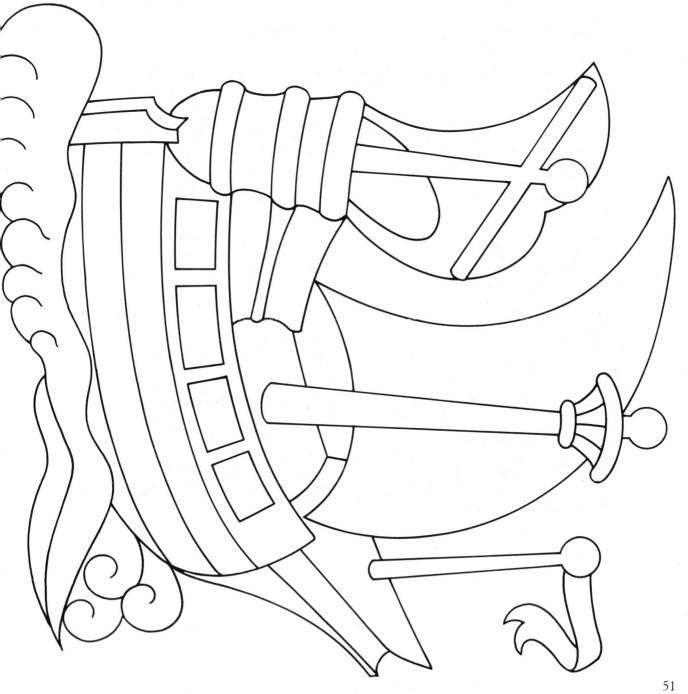

ELEVENSES

Make the clock face before sewing it onto your base fabric.
Use a full circle of brown fabric under the cream—this will
give a good firm base for stitching the figures. These could,
of course, be hand-embroidered, or, as a last resort, drawn
in ink!

RAINY DAY

Cut the umbrella out in one piece and lay the contrasting middle section on top. Cut the soles of *both* wellingtons out in one piece, the uppers in another. Mark the division between boots with a line of stitching.

WINE-GLASSES

Cut the bottle out in one piece and then place the labels on
top. Draw the outline of the glasses straight onto the base
fabric and stitch. Iron-on interfacing applied to the back of
the base fabric will help to prevent it from puckering. Use
fabric with a slight sheen for the bottle and the glasses—it
will look more drinkable!

LAMP

Again, a shiny fabric used for the shade will make the lamp look as if it is lit.

ASPIDISTRA

All these rows of stitching make this design especially prone to shrinkage and puckering. To minimize this, use lots of spray starch and/or apply interfacing to the wrong side of the base fabric.

59

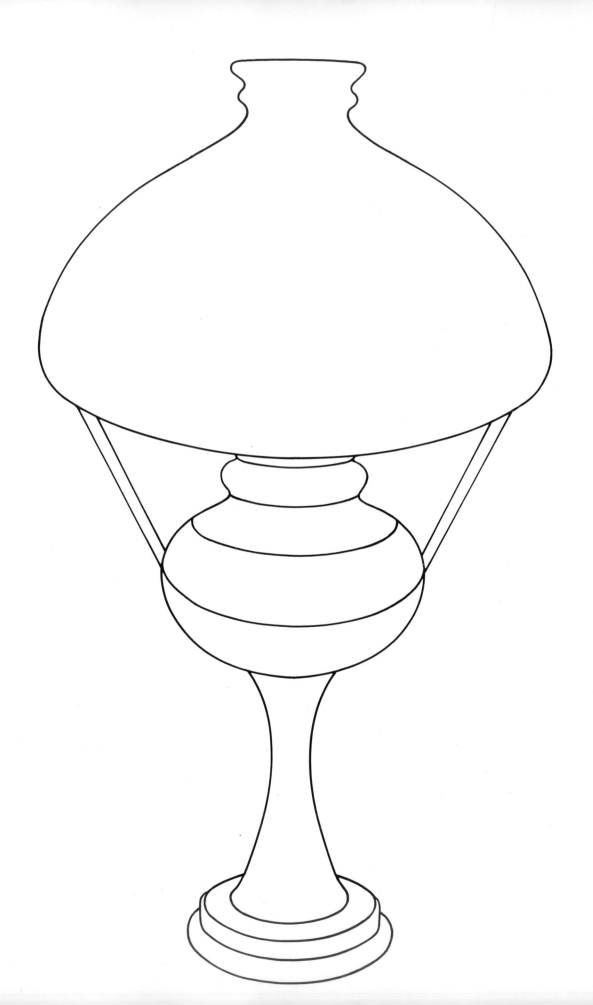

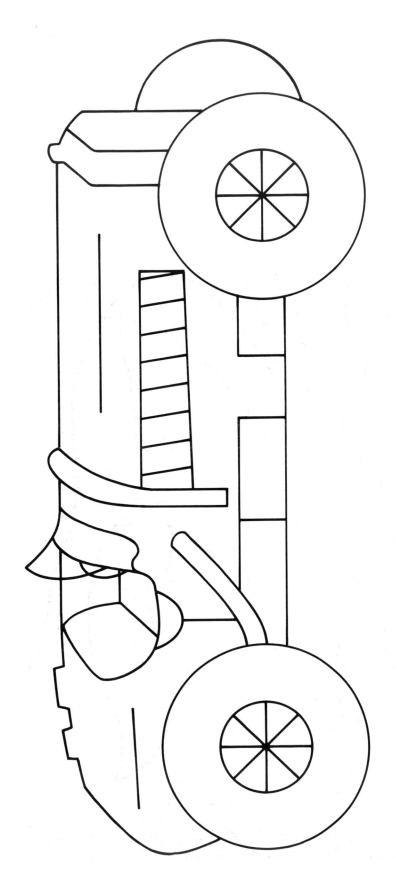

CAR

Use lurex or satin for the wheel hubs and the radiator, black needlecord for the tyres.

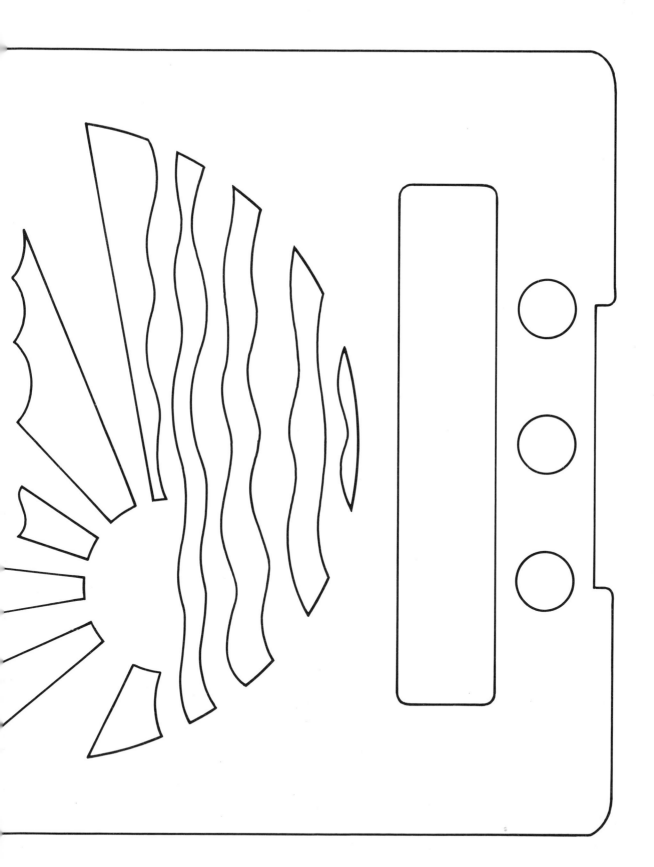

65

RADIO

This is easier than it looks! When you've made your paper pattern, cut out and discard those sections which appear in the lighter colour. Then carefully draw around the pattern on the reverse of the brown fabric and again cut and discard the light sections. Place a piece of light coloured fabric behind the radio speaker and carefully machine over all the edges. On the tuning panel, machine two thick lines in a light colour to represent the wave bands.

BOOKWORM

If you don't wear glasses, make the book larger and use that on it's own. Add a bookmark of ribbon or a fine strip of leather.

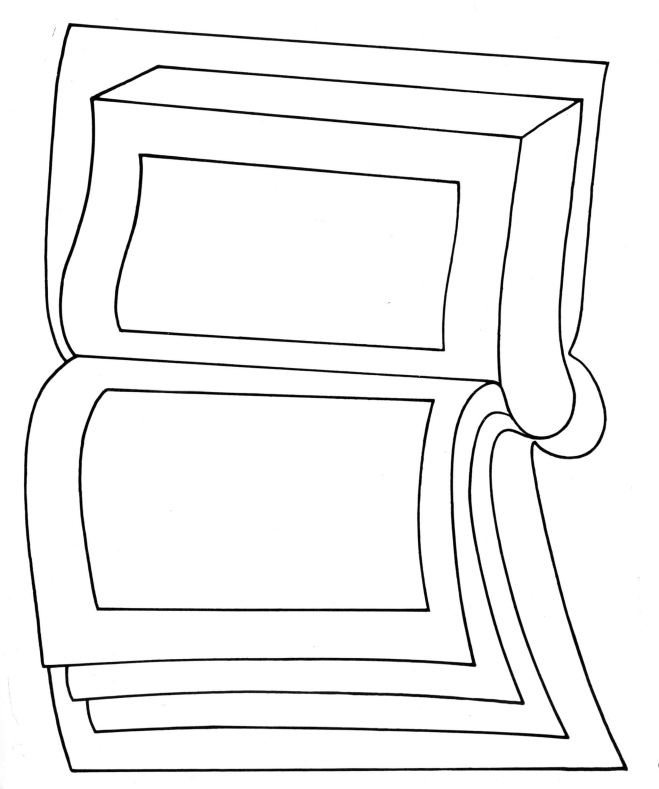

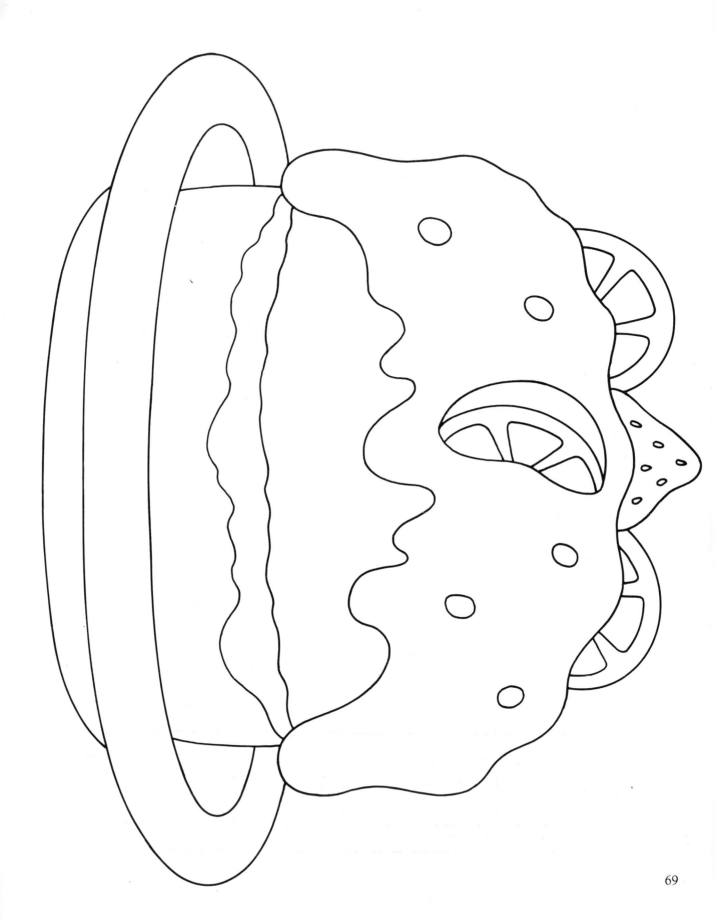

69

BEDTIME

Cut the bedhead and footboard out like stencils (as with the radio) and place the quilt underneath in one piece.

CAKE

Cut the sponge part of the cake in one piece and place the strip of filling on top. Use shiny fabric for filling and icing—make it a chocolate gateau or a Victoria sponge, according to your fabrics, and your taste!

A NIGHT AT THE OPERA

If you have a favourite opera or play, put it on the cover, otherwise use contrasting stitching to decorate.

NAKED LADY

Probably the simplest design in the book! Make the garter from ruched ribbon and lace.

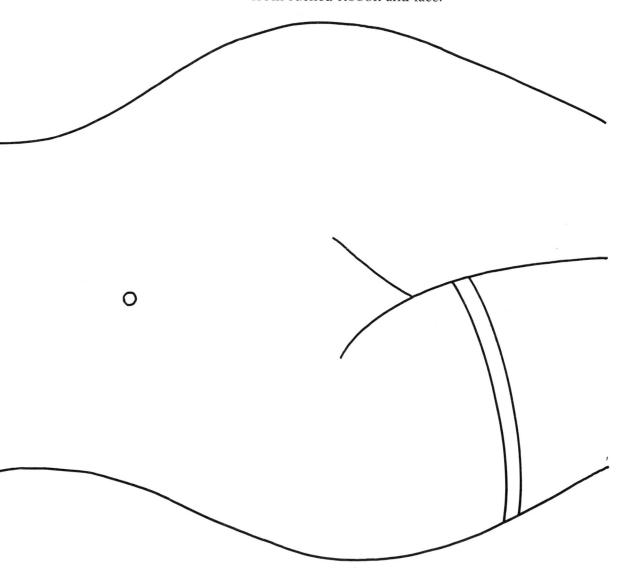

BREAKFAST PAN

Build the design up from a base of the whole pan, cut from red fabric, then the grey inner pan and finally the individual items. Outline the bacon fat in brown if you like the rind left on, and if you prefer streaky to back, lines of contrasting red and cream stitching will give that effect.

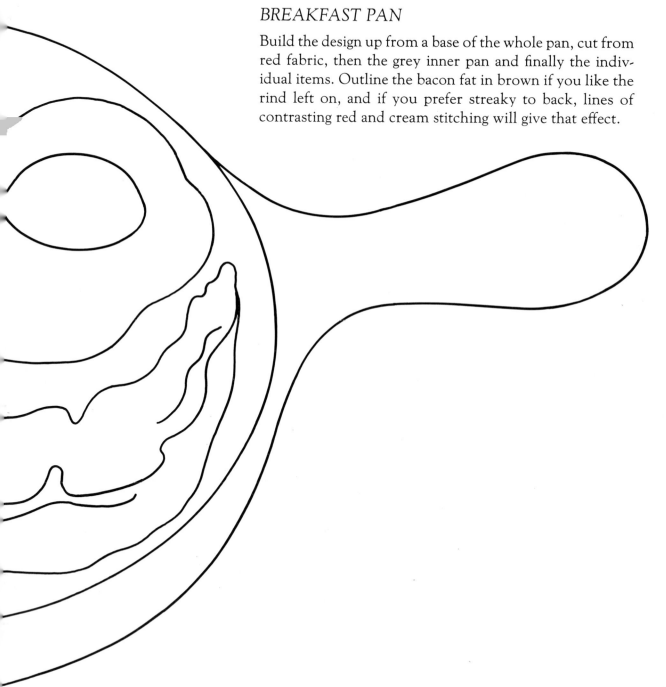

75

BUMBLE-BEE

Cut the bee's wings from lurex if possible and cut them in *one* piece, placing the upper body section over the top. The stripes on the lower body could be lines of stitching or fabric. Velvet would be the best fabric for both body and feet.

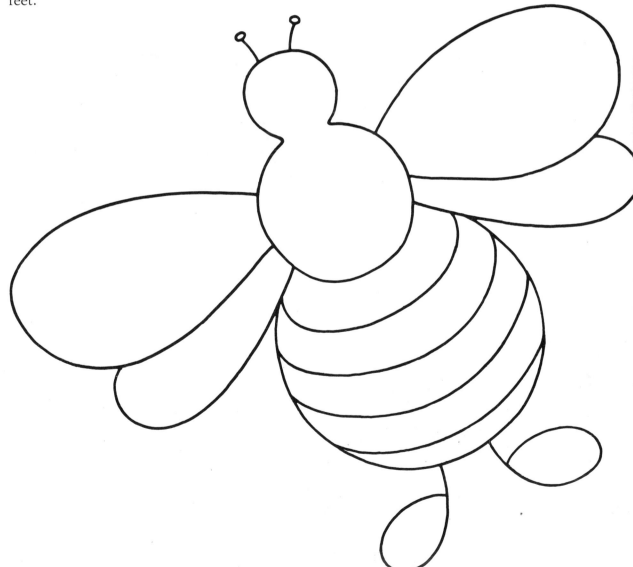

TEATIME

Add some wavy lines of stitching to represent steam rising from the cup.

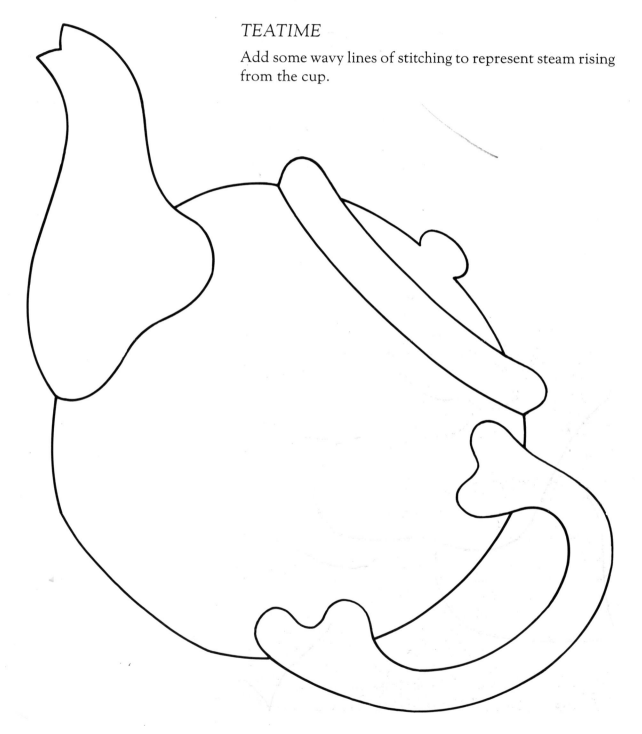

DIGESTIVES

Don't attempt to copy *tiny* lettering on packages but where it's large enough to form a part of the design draw it carefully and then embroider by hand or machine.

TELEPHONE

Cut a full circle in lurex or satin for the chrome dial and smaller cream circles for the numbers and centre-piece. Machining round these small circles and embroidering the numbers themselves needs patience but it does look effective, so persevere.

PIERROT

This was based on a pierrot doll. If you have a teddy bear, a rag doll, even an 'E.T.' use that for your design.

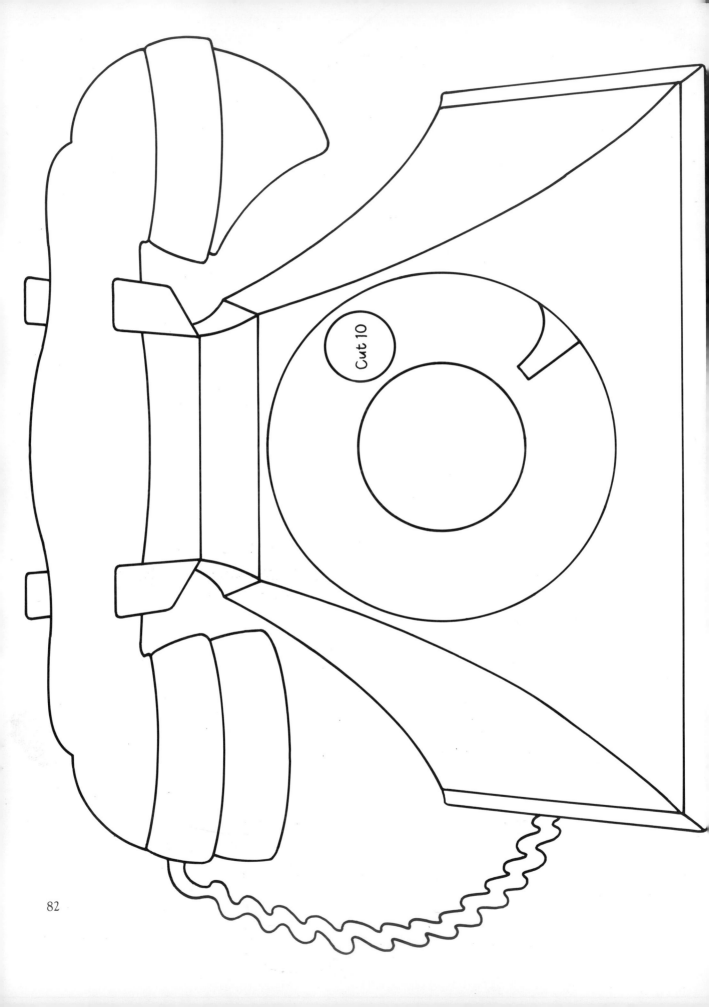

Cut 10

82

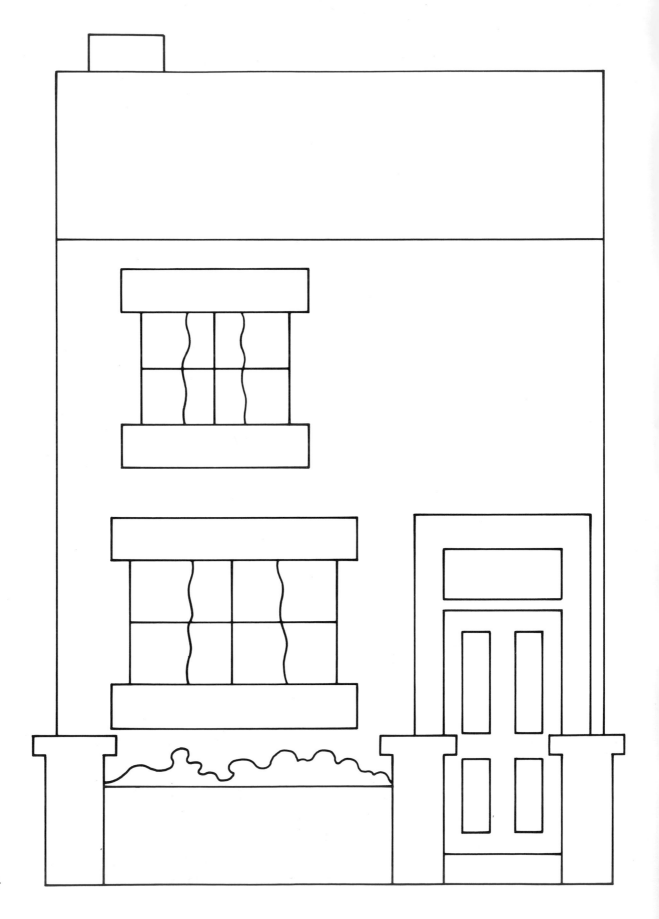

HOME SWEET HOME

Using the whole house as a base, apply the smaller pieces on top, and stitch around the windows and doors in a contrasting colour to represent their frames. You could add a cat or some milk bottles on the doorstep, or a window box perhaps. Better still, draw your *own* house.

MARMITE JAR

Familiar packages can be very effective and, again, you don't need to worry about the small print.

RYVITA PACKET

Turn your diet into a work of art!

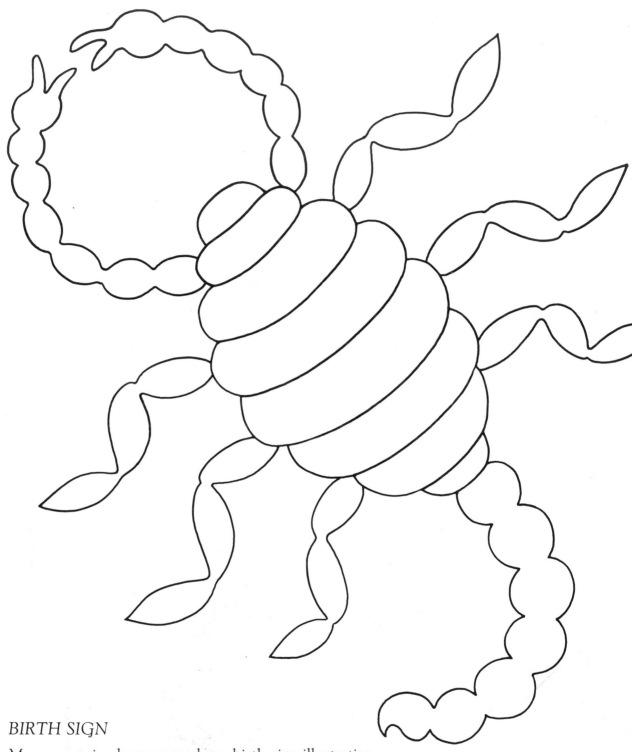

BIRTH SIGN

Many magazine horoscopes have birth sign illustrations.
Copy your own and incorporate it in your design.

COFFEE POT

Again, use your own as a model.

Hangings

HEN AND CHICK

(approx. 20 × 24in/51 × 61cm)

Make up the background using the cutting guide opposite and the method described in the Cushion Techniques section (page 11).

Use a single piece of fabric for the foreground and mark in diagonal lines as shown with tailor's chalk. Machine along these lines to give a quilted effect. Use the patterns

already given for the poppy heads and leaves and for the bee (see patch patterns, pages 19 and 78).

Cut the egg-shells in two pieces, using a slightly darker fabric for the insides and sew these together. Use either fur fabric or velvet for the chick and sew beak, eyes and contour lines.

Make up the hen complete, adding extra feathers with stitching lines if you're using plain, flat fabrics.

Attach and sew all these pieces to the background and finally add some leaves to balance the picture.

Trim and square up the edges, lay the picture on the backing fabric and tack around the edges. Finish off the edges (see page 121).

91

SHIP

(approx. 20 × 24in/51 × 61cm)

Make up the background in the usual way (see page 95, above). Use a selection of blue, turquoise and lilac prints for the waves and pick out the crests in white.

Use the ship pattern from the patch quilts (page 53) and make it up complete before sewing it down.

I cut my water lilies from a lilac print with darker violet centres but they can also be blue, yellow or white. Use more or less, smaller or larger flowers just as you wish.

Sew all the pieces down, and trim and square up the edges. Then tack the picture onto the backing fabric and finish as in the instructions on page 121.

MOUSE AND FLOWERS

Make up the background in the usual way.

Use the mouse from the 'Mouse and Cheese' cushion (page 28) and sew on the inner ears. Cut out a variety of flowers and leaves using the patterns given, or make up your own. Arrange these on the background, framing the mouse, and sew all the pieces down. Lightly mark the flower stems in ball-point pen and stitch. Finish as for the ship hanging above.

MINOAN WOMAN

(approx. 24 × 48in/61 × 122cm)

Having said that I like to make quilts which reflect the personality of the owner, I made this one for myself. *I* like to think that it reflects my interest in colour, texture and stylized design and has nothing at *all* to do with my figure!

Flower heads for Ship Hanging
Mermaid Quilt
Mouse Hanging

Flower heads for Mouse Hanging
Cow Quilt
Fox Cottage Quilt

95

One thing that you *can't* do in fabric collage is 'paint' a portrait. However careful you may be, your sewing machine will probably take over and determine the expression of the eyes, the shape of the mouth. So very stylized representations of the human figure such as icons, medieval paintings or even cartoon characters provide better inspiration than Rembrandt!

Once again the figure can be made up complete before it's applied to the background. For the skirt, cut out the basic shape in a piece of backing fabric. Using this as a base, cut and sew the individual stripes in place. Don't worry about following the pattern precisely. You can make them narrower to use up tiny scraps of fabric or you can use decorative bands of stitching on wider stripes.

Sew the figure to the *unquilted* background fabric—if this is fine, starch it well or use interfacing. Use additional rows of stitching on the hair and for the jewellery and take particular care with the face.

Then make up the complete background using a selection of prints, stripes and plain fabric for the top and bottom sections. Layer with wadding and backing fabric and then quilt with either a close zig-zag or a straight stitch used decoratively. For background, see page 95 below.

WINGED LION
(approx. 27 × 42/70 × 108cm)

The inspiration for this hanging comes from the medieval Book of Kells manuscript and shows the winged lion, symbolizing Saint Mark. The rich colours and patterns used by medieval illustrators translate well into fabric—providing you have the patience!

Scale up the pattern, marking and numbering the individual pieces, (e.g. LW2 = left wing, second stripe). Then trace a second pattern from the first. If you don't do this before you cut out the individual pattern pieces you'll have an impossible jigsaw to deal with.

As always, you can simplify the design by working some of the decoration in bands of contrasting stitching.

Keep the pattern pieces *large* where possible. For example, I cut each wing from one piece of gold fabric onto which I sewed the smaller pieces. In the same way, cut a full circle for the halo. Use this as a base for the face and mane.

When you've completed the wings, body and head sections place these on the background with the remaining pieces and pin or tack them in place. Finish by machining (zig-zag) around all the edges.

Layer the picture with wadding and backing fabric cut to the same size and tack round the edges. Finish in the usual way, as explained in the Finishing Techniques section.

ANTELOPES
(approx. 36in/92cm)

This hanging is made from the same design as the antelope cushion (see pp 36-7). Follow the instructions for the cushion, and finish as in the Finishing Techniques section.

BIRD
(approx. 36in × 24in/90 × 60cm

I based this design on a poster of which I was very fond. The poster itself had become very tatty and dog-eared, so now, instead of a reproduction, I have an original 'work of art' hanging on my wall!

Make up the background in the usual way and then make up the bird complete with extra stitching lines for the feathers. If you can beg old pattern books from furnishing shops a range of velvet samples in toning colours will be perfect for the wings. Arrange the bird, leaves and flowers on the background and sew down.

103

Quilts

BASIC TECHNIQUES

The methods used are the same as for the patch quilts and wall-hangings, except that you are working with a larger size. I must admit that when I start a quilt I don't always know what size it will turn out. For a single quilt I usually work the picture to a finished size, (allowing for squaring the edges) of approximately 2ft × 3ft 6in/61 × 108cm and 3ft × 4ft/92 × 122cm for a double. With the addition of two 6in/15cm borders and a narrow binding this gives a finished size of 4ft × 5ft 6in/122 × 168cm (single) and 5ft × 6ft/168 × 184cm (double). This will lie on top of the bed like an eiderdown with a few inches to spare at each side.

However, sometimes an extra border seems to give a better balance to the picture, and of course, if you suddenly decide to turn an intended hanging or cushion cover into a quilt the number and width of the borders will vary considerably. For instructions on adding borders see the Finishing Techniques section.

If you want to extend the sides and bottom of a quilt so that it falls to the floor, simply add more borders. Alternatively, you could make the quilt exactly the size of the mattress and gather a length of fabric around the sides and bottom to act as a valence.

To do this, measure from the top of the mattress to the floor to give your *depth*—remember it will be slightly deeper at the pillow ends—and add seam and hem allowances. To find the *length* of the fabric required, measure from the pillow end, down the side, along the bottom and up the other side and then multiply by three.

COW QUILT

(approx. 4ft × 5ft 6in/122 × 168cm)

This was one of the first quilts that I ever made and has proved to be one of the most popular.

By now you'll be familiar with the method—and with most of the pattern pieces! The only additions are the rabbits, the robin, and the foxgloves. The cow pattern is on p. 27. For the rabbits use velvet if you can and sew the cream patches and the eyes before placing them on the background. Then sew round the edges in matching thread and mark the noses in black or pink thread. Add whiskers with a few lines of straight stitching.

Foxgloves
Cut larger for bottom of flower decreasing in size towards the top

Make up the robin and sew to the background. Mark in the beak with yellow thread, tapering your stitching line towards the point of the beak.

For the foxgloves, cut twelve or fourteen flowers of various sizes and arrange them against the background. Begin at the base with the larger flowers, using smaller ones towards the top. Finish off with a few buds cut from the darker fabric.

Add borders, quilt and bind as described in the Finishing Techniques section.

107

'FOX COTTAGE' QUILT
(approx. 4ft × 5ft 6in/122 × 168cm)

This quilt was a birthday present for a little girl whose parents had, reluctantly, moved from 'Fox Cottage' to a new home. As the little girl still missed living there her mother sent me a photograph of the cottage and asked me to make this for her.

At first glance the house may look rather complicated but the basic shapes are very simple. Remember the window frames are 'drawn' with lines of stitching. When you've completed the house place it on the background. Using a selection of green prints, cut out 'shrubs', 'bushes' and 'climbing roses' and stick or pin them on top of the house.

Sew down the house and the vegetation and complete the rest of the picture as described in previous projects.

Finish as in the Finishing Techniques section.

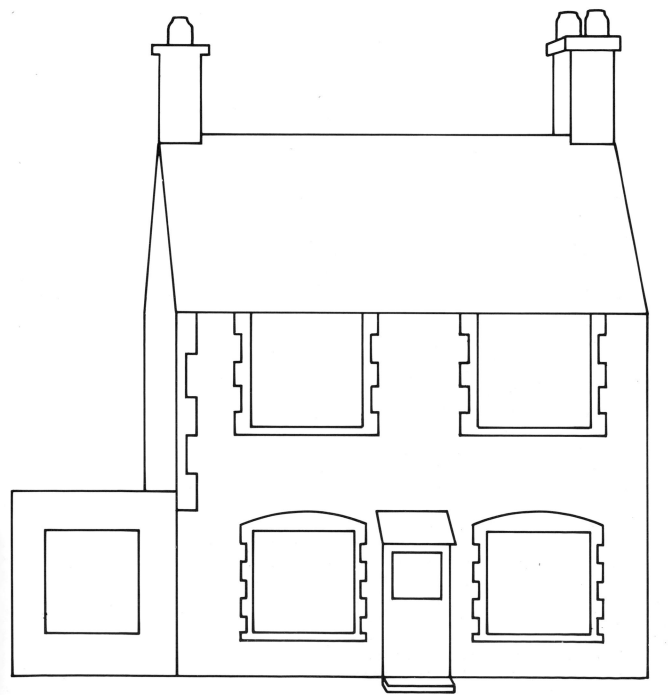

109

HEN AND CHICKS QUILT

(approx. 4ft × 5ft 6in/122 × 168cm)

This is an 'expanded version' of the Hen and Chick wall-hanging (see page 90). Make up the picture as described in that project and finish as in the Finishing Techniques section.

MERMAID QUILT
(approx. 5ft × 6ft/168 × 184cm)

This was my first commissioned quilt and so it was one of the rare occasions when I had to produce a design for approval before I started work. (Normally I only have a rather vague idea of how the finished picture will look, they just seem to grow.) It was for a hairdresser who approved most of the design but had very definite ideas about the hairstyle. The customer, of course, is *always* right! So I made up the quilt as he wanted but *I* still prefer the original. Take your choice by working either from the photograph or from the pattern.

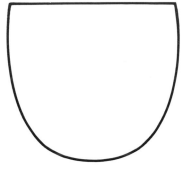

Scale for mermaid's tail.

As you'll see, the background is the same as for the ship wall-hanging (p. 94 above) with the addition of a large rock. I used satin to make it look wet, and a fine velvet for the strands of sea-weed but you could use satin for those too.

Whichever design you decide to use for the hair, use a mixture of fabrics. Break up the large areas with 'strands' of print, velvet, brocade, even scraps of lurex, and add extra interest with stitching lines once you've sewn the pieces down.

Make up the tail in one piece. Cut the whole shape from a firm backing fabric and then cut plenty of shell-shaped pieces. I used moiré, velvet and satin in plain colours, interspersed with cotton prints. Arrange them in overlapping rows and then sew them to the backing fabric. Trim away any edges that extend beyond the outline of the tail. The scales for the tail can be as large or small as you wish. Smaller ones will look better but require more patience!

Once the strands of hair are in place, arrange, and sew down the mermaid's body and tail, taking care with the face—sailors are not drawn onto the rocks by scowls!

Finish the quilt as in the Finishing Techniques section.

Cot Quilts

BASIC TECHNIQUES

Because cot quilts need frequent cleaning, I think it's wise to use cotton *only* here, and before you begin, check that your colours won't 'run' in the wash by testing samples of them for colour-fastness.

For these two quilts I made up a patchwork background by machining together squares of cotton fabric, 5in/13cm squares for the Duck Quilt, and 3in/8cm squares for the Elephant Quilt. (You can, of course, keep it simpler by using a single panel of fabric for the centre of the quilt and adding straight borders.)

Work out your background design on squared or graph paper, turned diagonally. Colour in the squares to represent the fabrics you intend to use and then work out how many of each you'll need and cut them out.

Lay the squares out on a flat surface, following your design. Working diagonally, stitch rows of squares together to form strips and then sew the strips together to form the rectangle.

Now apply your figure to the centre panel. Use lots of spray starch to keep the fabric firm as you sew.

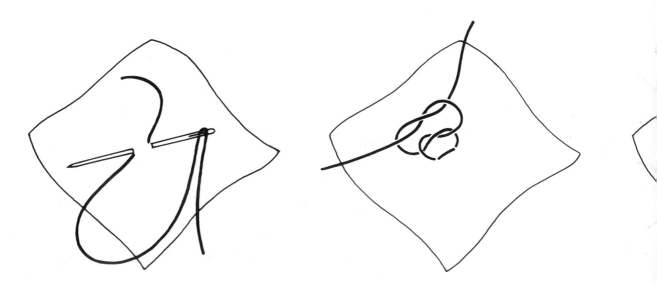

QUILTING

You can quilt by machine stitching along the seams as described earlier, but for a softer finish try hand-knotting.

Layer the quilt top with the wadding and backing fabric as usual. Starting from the centre and working outwards, pin through all the layers at regular intervals, smoothing out any wrinkles as you go.

Using a double length of strong cotton thread, make knots at the corners and centre of each square if using the larger size squares, at the corners only on the smaller ones.

To make a knot: Starting at the centre of the quilt, make a stitch and pull the thread through, leaving a tail of about 1½in/4cm. Take a second stitch over the first and pull it tight. Tie the two ends together firmly in a reef knot and snip them to about ½in/1cm.

Cut the edges of the quilt straight and bind them in the usual way.

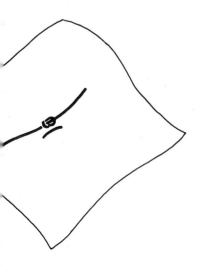

DUCK QUILT

Cut out the body in one to provide a base for the smaller pieces. If, as here, you're using strong colours next to white, the colour-fast test is especially important. Stick or tack the pieces down and machine stitch around them in the usual way.

ELEPHANT QUILT

I used a thick brushed cotton for the body which was soft but provided a firm base for the smaller pieces—pink moiré silk for the inner ears and feet and linen for the hat (all washable). The flower I cut complete from the fabric on which the elephant is sitting. Mark in the wrinkles with ball-point pen and then stitch.

117

Finishing Techniques

The techniques for making your quilt picture have been covered in the earlier part of the book. Now you must decide how to make it up. The most obvious choices are bedspreads, wall-hangings and cushion covers, but you could use the same method for making bags, tea-cosies, waistcoats, etc.

ADDING A BORDER

Finishing the edges of your quilt with a binding strip (see below) will give a narrow border. However, if you want to extend the quilt, one or two wider borders of toning or contrasting fabrics are easy to apply. A light border within a darker one can be particularly effective, acting as a mount and a frame for your picture.

1. Make your borders from straight strips of fabric the required width plus seam allowances on both sides. If you have to join several pieces, try to ensure that your seams come in the centre of each side.

2. There are two ways to finish the corners, straight or mitred. I always use the first method because it's quicker and easier. Simply cut border strips the exact length of the two sides and sew right sides together. Then add borders across the width of the top and bottom. As I always use patterned fabrics, the seams are barely noticeable.

3. However, for the true professional and for those who prefer a plain border, mitred corners are *de rigeur*. Let the side borders extend beyond the length of the quilt top. Sew the end borders across the quilt top *only*, having the ends extend by the same amount. Open out the end border and fold the extensions under, forming a 45 degree angle. Handstitch the diagonal fold in place and repeat for each corner.

FINAL QUILTING

If you've added a border to your picture you must now re-quilt the whole piece.

1. Cut a piece of wadding slightly larger than the quilt top and a piece of backing fabric slightly larger again. (See Materials Section on page 9 for choice of backing fabric.)

2. Lay the backing fabric right side down on a large table or on the floor. Taking care to smooth out any creases, place the wadding on top and finally the quilt top, right side up. Smooth out all the layers.

3. Working from the centre of the top border seam, pin horizontally across the seam at short intervals. Continue down the side border (fig. 1).

4. Pin the other half-top and side seam in the same way. Finally pin across the bottom seam.

5. Repeat for a second border.

6. Pin around the four edges and then turn the quilt over to check for any creases that may have crept in. If any have you'll have to smooth them out and re-pin.

7. With the quilt top facing you, carefully machine with a straight stitch following the seam lines.

8. Square up the edges and tack the layers together.

EDGING A BEDSPREAD

1. Cut straight binding strips approximately 2½in/6cm wide, joining them as necessary.

2. Machine these to the tacked edges as for a border using either straight or mitred corners.

3. Turn over and hand sew to the backing fabric.

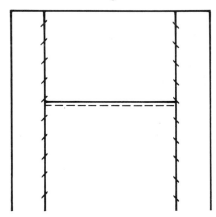

Fig. 1

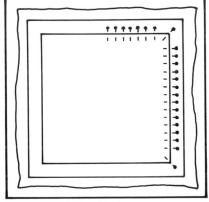

Fig. 2

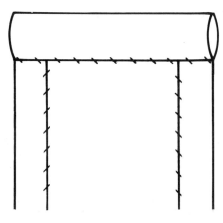

Fig. 3

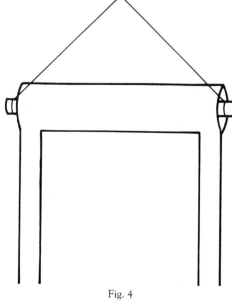

Fig. 4

Fig. 5

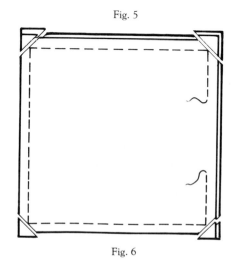

Fig. 6

FINISHING A WALL-HANGING

1. Cut 2½in/6cm strips for the sides, and 5in/13cm strips for the top and bottom, and attach using the *straight* corner method.

2. Fold over and hand sew the side edges as in the bedspread (fig. 2).

3. On the top and bottom strips turn the seam allowance under and hand sew to the backing fabric just below the machine stitching, leaving the ends open (fig. 3).

4. Cut two lengths of bamboo (available from gardening shops), and insert into the casings so they protrude slightly at either end. You can then hang your picture with a cord or by resting it between two nails (figs. 4 and 5).

PLAIN CUSHION COVERS

1. Measure your picture and cut a piece of fabric the same size for the cushion back.

2. Place the right sides of the two pieces together and pin, tack and sew around three sides, leaving ½in/1.5cm seam allowance.

3. Stitch about 2in/5cm along each end of the fourth side. Clip corners (fig. 6).

4. Turn the cover right side out and poke out the corners.

5. Put your cushion inside the cover and slip-stitch the open edges together.

PLAIN CUSHION COVERS WITH ZIP

1. With right sides together, stitch 2in/5cm along each end of the bottom edge (fig. 7).

2. Insert a zip in the opening. Open zip (fig. 8).

3. With right sides together again, stitch the remaining three sides. Clip corners. Turn right side out.

PIPED CUSHIONS

1. A plain piping picking up one of the colours in your picture will set it off well. Cut a piece of piping cord slightly longer than the total length of the four sides of your picture.

2. For a perfect finish you should cut *bias* strips of fabric to cover your piping cord but this is not essential. Cut your strips wide enough to cover the cord with a generous seam allowance. Sew them together to make one continuous strip, slightly longer than the cord.

3. Fold the covering over the cord and machine down the strip as close to the cord as possible, using the zipper foot on your machine. Trim the seam allowance to ½in/1.5cm.

4. Leaving ½in/1.5cm of the piping free, sew it around the edges of the cushion front, notching the corners to ensure a smooth curve (fig. 9).

5. Join the ends of the piping by opening out the casing, cutting the cord to exactly meet the free end, and then cutting the casing to allow for a turning and ½in/1.5cm overlap. Fold casing together again and finish sewing (fig. 10).

6. You can now continue as for the plain cover above, closing the opening by hand stitching. For a zip closing I find the following method easier with a piped cushion.

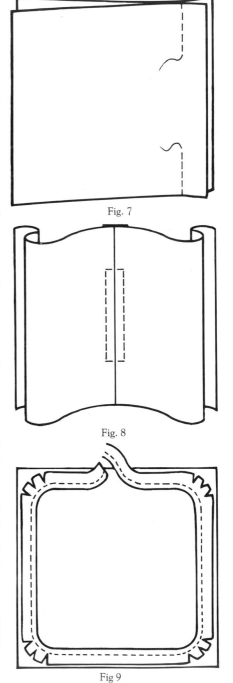

Fig. 7

Fig. 8

Fig 9

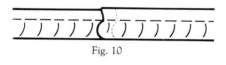

Fig. 10

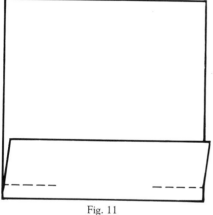

Fig. 11

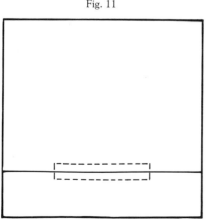

Fig. 12

PIPED CUSHION WITH ZIP

1. Cut the cushion back 1in/2.5cm *longer* than the front, then cut across the width of the fabric approximately 4in/10cm from the bottom.

2. With the right sides together stitch 2in/5cm at each end (fig. 11).

3. Press the seams open and insert the zip (fig. 12).

4. Open the zip and then, with right sides together, sew cushion back to cushion front. Clip corners and turn right side out.

5. NB This method is also useful for circular cushions.

CUSHION PADS

1. If you cannot buy a pad exactly to fit the finished size of your cover you will have to make your own. Simply cut two pieces of fabric the same size as your cover plus seam allowances.

2. Machine around the four sides leaving an opening of about 8in/20cm on one side. Turn right side out.

3. Fill with either kapok, which is soft but tends to flatten after a time, or foam chips.

4. Sew the opening together by hand or machine.

Study Guide for

Porth's Essentials of Pathophysiology

Third Edition

Wolters Kluwer | Lippincott Williams & Wilkins
Health

Philadelphia · Baltimore · New York · London
Buenos Aires · Hong Kong · Sydney · Tokyo

Acquisitions Editor: Hilarie Surrena
Product Manager: Katherine Burland
Editorial Assistant: Shawn Loht
Design Coordinator: Joan Wendt
Manufacturing Coordinator: Karin Duffield
Prepress Vendor: Aptara, Inc.

3rd edition

9 8 7 6 5 4 3 2 1

Printed in the United States of America

ISBN: 978-0-7817-7779-7

Care has been taken to confirm the accuracy of the information presented and to describe
generally accepted practices. However, the authors, editors, and publisher are not responsible for
errors or omissions or for any consequences from application of the information in this book
and make no warranty, expressed or implied, with respect to the currency, completeness, or accuracy of the contents of the publication. Application of this information in a particular situation remains the professional responsibility of the practitioner; the clinical treatments described
and recommended may not be considered absolute and universal recommendations.

The authors, editors, and publisher have exerted every effort to ensure that drug selection
and dosage set forth in this text are in accordance with the current recommendations and practice at the time of publication. However, in view of ongoing research, changes in government
regulations, and the constant flow of information relating to drug therapy and drug reactions,
the reader is urged to check the package insert for each drug for any change in indications
and dosage and for added warnings and precautions. This is particularly important when the
recommended agent is a new or infrequently employed drug.

Some drugs and medical devices presented in this publication have Food and Drug Administration (FDA) clearance for limited use in restricted research settings. It is the responsibility of
the health care provider to ascertain the FDA status of each drug or device planned for use in his
or her clinical practice.

Preface

This Study Guide was written by Brian Kipp, PhD, to accompany the third edition of *Essentials of Pathophysiology: Concepts of Altered Health States* by Carol Mattson Porth. The Study Guide is designed to help you practice and retain the knowledge you've gained from the textbook, and give you a basis for applying it in your practice. The following types of exercises are provided in each chapter of the Study Guide.

ASSESSING YOUR UNDERSTANDING

The first section of each Study Guide chapter concentrates on the basic information of the textbook chapter and helps you to remember key concepts, vocabulary, and principles.

- **Fill in the Blanks:** Fill-in-the-blank exercises test important chapter information, encouraging you to recall key points.

- **Labeling:** Labeling exercises are used where you need to remember certain visual representations of the concepts presented in the textbook.

- **Matching:** Matching questions test you knowledge of the definition of key terms.

- **Sequencing:** Sequencing exercises ask you to remember particular sequences or orders, for instance of normal or abnormal physiologic processes.

- **Short Answers:** Short-answer questions cover facts, concepts, procedures, and principles of the chapter. These questions ask you to recall information as well as demonstrate your comprehension of the information.

APPLYING YOUR KNOWLEDGE

The second section of each Study Guide chapter consists of case study-based exercises that ask you to begin to apply the knowledge you've gained from the textbook chapter and reinforced in the first section of the Study Guide chapter. A case study scenario based on the chapter's content is presented, and then you are asked to answer some questions, in writing, related to the case study. The questions could cover lab values, next steps in treatment, anticipated diagnoses, and the like.

PRACTICING FOR NCLEX

The third and final section of the Study Guide helps you practice NCLEX-style questions while further reinforcing the knowledge you have been gaining and testing for yourself through the textbook chapter and the first two sections of the study guide chapter. In keeping with the NCLEX, the questions presented are multiple-choice and scenario-based, asking you to reflect, consider, and apply what you know and to choose the best answer out of those offered.

ANSWER KEYS

The answers for all of the exercises and questions in the Study Guide are provided at the back of the book, so you can assess your own learning as you complete each chapter.

We hope you will find this Study Guide to be helpful and enjoyable, and we wish you every success in your studies and future profession.

The Publishers

Contents

Cell Structure and Function

SECTION I: LEARNING OBJECTIVES

1. State why the nucleus is called the "control center" of the cell.

2. List the cellular organelles and state their functions.

3. State four functions of the cell membrane.

4. Trace the pathway for cell communication, beginning at the receptor and ending with the effector response, and explain why the process is often referred to as *signal transduction*.

5. Compare the functions of G-protein–linked, ion-channel–linked, and enzyme-linked cell surface receptors.

6. Relate the function of adenosine triphosphate (ATP) to cell metabolism.

7. Compare the processes involved in anaerobic and aerobic metabolism.

8. Discuss the mechanisms of membrane transport associated with diffusion, osmosis, endocytosis, and exocytosis and compare them with active transport mechanisms.

9. Describe the function of ion channels.

10. Describe the basis for membrane potentials.

11. Explain the relationship between membrane permeability and generation of membrane potentials.

12. Explain the process of cell differentiation in terms of development of organ systems in the embryo and the continued regeneration of tissues in postnatal life.

13. Describe the characteristics of the four different tissue types.

14. Characterize the composition and functions of the extracellular components of tissue.

15. Explain the function of intercellular adhesions and junctions.

SECTION II: ASSESSING YOUR UNDERSTANDING

Activity A *Fill in the blanks.*

1. _____ is composed of water, proteins, neutral fats, and glycogen.

2. All _____ cells have a nucleus, whereas _____ cells do not.

3. The nucleus contains _____, which serves as the template for making all the _____, which is later used to direct the synthesis of _____ in the cytoplasm.

4. Ribosomes serve as the site for _____ synthesis in the cytoplasm.

5. _____ endoplasmic reticulum is studded with ribosomes attached to specific binding sites on the membrane.

6. The _____ complex modifies proteins and packages them into secretory granules bound for the membrane.

7. _____ contain powerful hydrolytic enzymes that are used to break down excess and worn-out cell parts as well as foreign substances.

8. Peroxisomes contain a special enzyme that degrades _____.

9. Mitochondria are the site of cellular _____, the product of which is the formation of _____.

10. Transport along the axon of neuronal cells takes place along the primary cytoskeletal component _____.

11. Actin and myosin are examples of functional _____ within muscle cells.

12. Integral proteins span the entire lipid bilayer, whereas _____ proteins are bound to one side of the membrane or the other.

13. The four tissues of the body are _____, _____, _____, and _____.

14. The differences in permeability of _____ is responsible for the generation of membrane potential. Permeability is regulated by ion channels.

15. Of the four tissue types, only _____ and _____ tissue is excitable.

Activity B *Match the key terms in Column A with their definitions in Column B.*

1.

Column A

___ 1. tRNA
___ 2. Flagella
___ 3. Tubulin
___ 4. Glycocalyx
___ 5. G protein
___ 6. Smooth ER
___ 7. Mitochondria
___ 8. Centrioles
___ 9. Proteasomes
___ 10. First messenger

Column B

a. Site of synthesis of lipid molecules
b. Transfer RNA
c. Hormone or neurotransmitter
d. Second messenger that mediates cellular responses
e. Site of aerobic respiration
f. Protein subunit of microtubules
g. Sperm motility

h. Division of cells following mitosis
i. Organelle that metabolizes misfolded proteins
j. Carbohydrate and protein layer that participates in cell recognition

2.

Column A

___ 1. Diffusion
___ 2. Osmosis
___ 3. Active transport
___ 4. Passive transport
___ 5. Cotransport
___ 6. Facilitated diffusion
___ 7. Primary active transport
___ 8. Secondary active transport
___ 9. Counter transport
___ 10. Symport

Column B

a. Secondary active transport in which substances are moved in the same direction
b. Any type of transport across the cell membrane that requires energy as it moves material against the concentration gradient
c. Secondary active transport in which substances are moved in the opposite direction
d. The coupling of the transport of one solute to a second solute
e. Transport across the cell membrane through a protein channel that does not require ATP
f. The diffusion of water
g. Any type of transport across the cell membrane that does not require energy
h. Direct use of ATP in the transport of a solute
i. Utilization of the energy derived from the primary active

transport of one solute for the cotransport of a second solute

j. Passive movement of solute down the concentration gradient

Activity C *Consider the following figure.*

1.

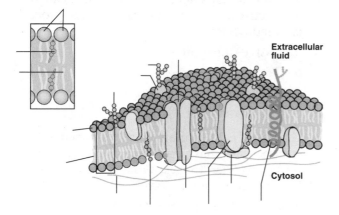

Extracellular fluid

Cytosol

In the figure above, label phospholipid by layer, an individual phospholipid, an integral protein, a peripheral protein, a channel protein, a glycoprotein, and a glycolipid.

Activity D *Briefly answer the following.*

1. In many diseases, the root cause is ischemia (low blood flow) or hypoxia (decreased delivery of oxygen). Using what you know about aerobic metabolism, explain how alterations in oxygen delivery to the tissues are detrimental.

_____

_____

_____

2. Tissues must maintain their shape and integrity in order to function. Explain from the cellular level to the tissue level what is responsible for maintaining tissue shape and structure.

_____

_____

_____

3. Signal transduction is a complex and varied process. Describe the process starting at the first messenger and ending in a physiological response. Be sure to include the various possibilities at the receptor level as well as the second messenger level.

_____

_____

_____

4. Large molecules or particles are ingested or released from cells. Describe the basics of ingestion and release.

_____

_____

_____

SECTION III: APPLYING YOUR KNOWLEDGE

Activity E *Consider the following scenario and answer the questions.*

Fourteen-year-old Thomas Kirk is brought to the clinic for a routine physical before starting to play sports in school. He is 77 inches tall and weighs 200 pounds. Tom states, "I have tried to lose weight so I can wrestle at a lower weight and I just don't understand why I still weigh 200 pounds. My science teacher said it's because I have white fat and not brown fat." How would you explain to Tom about the two kinds of adipose tissue in his body?

SECTION IV: PRACTICING FOR NCLEX

Activity F *Answer the following questions.*

1. There are two forms of endoplasmic reticulum (ER) found in a cell. They are the rough and the smooth ER. What does the rough ER do in a cell?
   a. Produces proteins
   b. Combines protein with other components of the cytoplasm
   c. Exports protein from the cell
   d. Destroys ribosomes

2. The Golgi complex, or Golgi bodies, consists of stacks of thin, flattened vesicles or sacs within the cell. These Golgi bodies are found near the nucleus and function in association with the ER. What is one purpose of the Golgi complex?

   a. Produce bile

   b. Receive proteins and other substances from the cell surface by a retrograde transport mechanism

   c. Produce excretory granules

   d. Produce small carbohydrate molecules

3. In Tay-Sachs disease, an autosomal recessive disorder, hexosaminidase A, which is the lysosomal enzyme needed for degrading the GM_2 ganglioside found in nerve cell membranes, is deficient. Although GM_2 ganglioside accumulates in many tissues, where does it do the most harm?

   a. Brain and retinas

   b. Retinas and heart

   c. Nervous system and retinas

   d. Nervous system and brain

4. The mitochondria are literally the "power plants" of the cell because they transform organic compounds into energy that is easily accessible to the cell. What do the mitochondria do?

   a. Make energy

   b. Form proteasomes

   c. Needs DNA from other sources to replicate

   d. Extracts energy from organic compounds

5. The cell membrane is also called what?

   a. Plasma membrane

   b. Nuclear membranes

   c. Receptor membrane

   d. Bilayer membrane

6. Some messengers, such as thyroid hormone and steroid hormones, do not bind to membrane receptors but move directly across the lipid layer of the cell membrane and are carried to the cell nucleus. What do they do at the cell nucleus?

   a. Transiently open or close ion channels

   b. Influence DNA activity

   c. Stabilize cell function

   d. Decrease transcription of mRNA

7. The Krebs cycle provides a common pathway for the metabolism of nutrients by the body. The Krebs cycle forms two pyruvate molecules. Each of the two pyruvate molecules formed in the cytoplasm from one molecule of glucose yields another molecule of what?

   a. FAD

   b. NADH + H$^+$

   c. ATP

   d. H_2O

8. When cells use energy to move ions against an electrical or chemical gradient, the process is called what?

   a. Passive transport

   b. Neutral transport

   c. Cotransport

   d. Active transport

9. Groups of cells that are closely associated in structure and have common or similar functions are called tissues. What are the types of tissue in the human body?

   a. Connective and muscle tissue

   b. Binding and connecting tissue

   c. Nerve and exothelium tissue

   d. Exothelium and muscle tissue

10. Endocrine glands are epithelial structures that have had their connection with the surface obliterated during development. How are these glands described?

    a. Ductile and produce secretions

    b. Ductless and produce secretions

    c. Ductile and release their glandular products by exocytosis

    d. Ductless and release their glandular products by exocytosis

11. Each skeletal muscle is a discrete organ made up of hundreds or thousands of muscle fibers. Although muscle fibers predominate, substantial amounts of connective tissue, blood vessels, and nerve fibers are also present. What happens during muscle contraction?

    a. When activated by GTP (guanosine 5'-triphosphate), the cross-bridges swivel in a fixed arc, much like the oars of a boat, as they become attached to the actin filament.

    b. During contraction, each cross-bridge undergoes its own cycle of movement, forming a bridge attachment and releasing it, the same sequence of movement repeats itself when the cross-bridge reattaches to the same cell.

    c. The thick myosin and thin actin filaments slide over each other, causing shortening of the muscle fiber.

    d. Calcium–calmodulin complexes produce the sliding of the filaments that form cross-bridges with the thin actin filaments.

12. The three main parts of a cell are the nucleus, the _____, and the cell membrane.

13. Bilirubin is a normal major pigment of bile; its excess accumulation within cells is evidenced clinically by a yellowish discoloration of the skin and sclera, a condition called _____.

14. Cells in multicellular organisms need to communicate with one another to coordinate their function and control their growth. The human body has several means of transmitting information between cells, what are they? (Mark all that apply.)

    a. Direct communication between adjacent cells

    b. Express communication between cells

    c. Autocrine and paracrine signaling

    d. Endocrine or synaptic signaling

15. The human body has nondividing cells that have left the cell cycle and are not capable of mitotic division once an infant is born. What are the nondividing cells? (Mark all that apply.)

    a. Mucous cells

    b. Neurons

    c. Skeletal muscle cells

    d. Cardiac muscle cells

16. Smooth muscle is often called _____ muscle because it contracts spontaneously or through activity of the autonomic nervous system.

CHAPTER 2

Cellular Responses to Stress, Injury, and Aging

SECTION I: LEARNING OBJECTIVES

1. Cite the general purpose of changes in cell structure and function that occur as the result of normal adaptive growth and differentiation.

2. Describe cell changes that occur with atrophy, hypertrophy, hyperplasia, metaplasia, and dysplasia and state general conditions under which the changes occur.

3. Cite three sources of intracellular accumulations.

4. Compare the pathogenesis and effects of dystrophic and metastatic calcifications.

5. Describe the mechanisms whereby physical agents such as blunt trauma, electrical forces, and extremes of temperature produce cell injury.

6. Differentiate between the effects of ionizing and nonionizing radiation in terms of their ability to cause cell injury.

7. Explain how the injurious effects of biologic agents differ from those produced by physical and chemical agents.

8. State the mechanisms and manifestations of cell injury associated with lead toxicity.

9. Identify the causes and outcomes of mercury toxicity.

10. State how nutritional imbalances contribute to cell injury.

11. Describe three types of reversible cell changes that can occur with cell injury.

12. Define *free radical* and *reactive oxygen species*.

13. Relate free radical formation and oxidative stress to cell injury and death.

14. Describe cell changes that occur with ischemic and hypoxic cell injury.

15. Relate the effects of impaired calcium homeostasis to cell injury and death.

16. Differentiate cell death associated with necrosis and apoptosis.

17. Cite the reasons for the changes that occur with the wet and dry forms of gangrene.

SECTION II: ASSESSING YOUR UNDERSTANDING

Activity A *Fill in the blanks.*

1. Cells may adapt to the environment by undergoing changes in _____, _____, and _____.

2. Atrophy is seen as a decrease in cell _____.

3. Denervation will result in cellular _____.

4. Hypertrophy is an _____ in cell size.

5. An increase in muscle mass associated with exercise is an example of _____.

6. An increase in the number of cells in an organ or tissue is known as cellular _____.

7. Liver regrowth is an example of _____ hyperplasia.

8. _____ or _____ hyperplasia is due to excessive hormonal stimulation or excessive growth factors.

9. _____ represents a reversible change in which one adult cell type is replaced by another adult cell type.

10. Metaplasia usually occurs in response to chronic _____ and _____ and allows for substitution of cells that are better able to survive stressful or harmful conditions.

11. Deranged cell growth of a specific tissue that results in cells that vary in size, shape, and organization is known as _____.

12. Dysplasia is strongly implicated as a precursor of _____.

13. Intracellular _____ represent the buildup of substances that cells cannot immediately use or eliminate.

14. _____ radicals are highly reactive chemical species having an unpaired electron in the outer valence shell of the molecule.

15. _____ deprives the cell of oxygen and interrupts oxidative metabolism and the generation of adenosine triphosphate (ATP).

16. Reversible cellular injury is seen as either cellular _____ or _____ accumulation.

17. _____ differs from apoptosis in that it involves unregulated enzymatic digestion of cell components, loss of cell membrane integrity with uncontrolled release of the products of cell death into the intracellular space, and initiation of the inflammatory response.

18. The increased _____ levels may inappropriately activate a number of enzymes with potentially damaging effects.

19. Acidosis develops and denatures the enzymatic and structural proteins of the cell during _____ necrosis.

Activity B *Consider the following figure.*

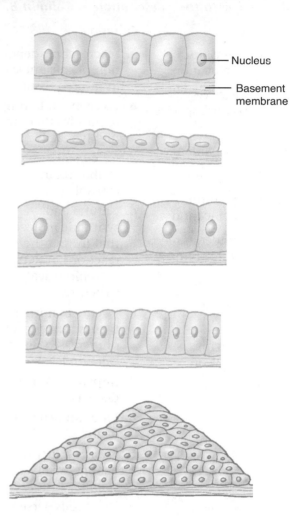

Nucleus

Basement membrane

The figure pictured above represents cellular adaptation. Label each adaptation and state whether it is a physiologic, pathologic, or if it could be both types of adaptations.

Activity C *Match the pathologic process in Column A with their description in Column B.*

Column A

_____ **1.** Metastatic calcification

_____ **2.** Reactive oxygen species (ROS)

_____ **3.** Antioxidants

_____ **4.** Apoptosis

_____ **5.** Dystrophic calcification

_____ **6.** Temperature-induced injury

_____ **7.** Ischemia

_____ **8.** Caseous necrosis

_____ **9.** Ionizing radiation

_____ **10.** Gangrene

Column B

a. Macroscopic deposition of calcium salts in injured tissue

b. Oxygen-containing molecules that are highly reactive

c. Ice crystal formation in cytosol

d. Natural and synthetic molecules that inhibit the reactions of ROS with biological structures

e. Occurs in normal tissues as the result of increased serum calcium levels

f. Impaired oxygen delivery

g. Programmed cell death

h. Causes injury by changes in electron stability

i. Dead cells persist indefinitely as soft cheeselike debris

j. Term applied when a considerable mass of tissue undergoes necrosis

Activity D *Briefly answer the following.*

1. Why does chronically damaged tissue result in calcification?

_____

_____

_____

2. List the five categories of cellular injury.

_____

_____

_____

3. Lead has been found in paint used to give children's toys their brilliant colors. Why is this a concern?

_____

_____

_____

4. List and describe the three major mechanisms of cellular injury.

_____

_____

_____

5. Oxidative stress has been implicated as the causative agent in numerous disease states as well as the cause of physiological aging. Explain how oxidative stress can cause damage and why it is a concern.

_____

_____

_____

6. Explain why one of the complications of hypoxia is the development of acidosis and how the acidosis will damage the tissue.

_____

_____

_____

7. Apoptosis takes place under normal stimulation or as the result of cellular injury. There are two pathways for apoptosis to occur. What are they and what major protein is involved?

_____

_____

_____

SECTION III: APPLYING YOUR KNOWLEDGE

Activity E *Consider the scenario and answer the question.*

Your child is acting more clumsy than normal and is not communicating well. In the doctor's office you are told she has lead poisoning.

1. How does lead affect the nervous system?

_____

_____

_____

SECTION IV: PRACTICING FOR NCLEX

Activity F *Answer the following questions.*

1. Many molecular mechanisms mediate cellular adaptation. Some are factors produced by other cells and some by the cells themselves. These mechanisms depend largely on signals transmitted by chemical messengers that exert their effects by altering the function of a gene. Many adaptive cellular responses alter the expression of "differentiation" genes. What can cells do because of this?
   a. A cell is able to change size or form without compromising its normal function
   b. A cell incorporates its change in function and passes this change on to other cells like it.
   c. A cell is able to pass its change on to a "housekeeping" cell
   d. A cell dies once the stimulus to change has been removed

2. Hypertrophy may occur as the result of normal physiologic or abnormal pathologic conditions. The increase in muscle mass associated with exercise is an example of physiologic hypertrophy. Pathologic hypertrophy occurs as the result of disease conditions and may be adaptive or compensatory. Examples of adaptive hypertrophy are the thickening of the urinary bladder from long-continued obstruction of urinary outflow and the myocardial hypertrophy that results from valvular heart disease or hypertension. What is compensatory hypertrophy?
   a. When the body increases its major organs during times of malnutrition
   b. When one kidney is removed, the remaining kidney enlarges to compensate for the loss
   c. When the body controls myocardial growth by stimulating actin expression to enlarge the heart
   d. When the body stimulates gene expression to begin a progressive decrease in left ventricular muscle mass

3. Metastatic calcification takes place in normal tissues as the result of increased serum calcium levels (hypercalcemia). Anything that increases the serum calcium level can lead to calcification in inappropriate places such as the lung, renal tubules, and blood vessels. What are the major causes of hypercalcemia?
   a. Diabetes mellitus and Paget disease
   b. Hypoparathyroidism and vitamin D intoxication
   c. Hyperparathyroidism and immobilization
   d. Immobilization and hypoparathyroidism

4. Mercury is a toxic substance, and the hazards of mercury-associated occupational and accidental exposures are well known. What is the primary concern for the general public in regard to mercury poisoning today?
   a. Amalgam fillings in the teeth
   b. Mercury from thermometers and blood pressure machines
   c. Mercury found in paint that was made before 1990
   d. Fish such as tuna and swordfish

5. Small amounts of lead accumulate to reach toxic levels in the human body. Lead is found in many places in the environment and is still a major concern in the pediatric population. What would you teach the parents of a child who is being tested for lead poisoning?

   a. Keep your child away from peeling paint.

   b. Keep your child away from anything ceramic.

   c. Do not let your child read newspapers.

   d. Do not let your child tour a mine on a school field trip.

6. In a genetic disorder called xeroderma pigmentosum, an enzyme needed to repair sunlight-induced DNA damage is lacking. This autosomal recessive disorder is characterized by what?

   a. Patches of pink, leathery pigmentation replace normal skin after a sunburn.

   b. Extreme photosensitivity and a greatly increased risk of skin cancer in skin that has been exposed to the sun

   c. White, scaly patches of skin that appear on African American people after they have a sunburn

   d. Photosensitivity and a decreased risk of skin cancer in skin that has been exposed to the sun.

7. While presenting a talk to the parents of preschoolers at a local day care center, the nurse is asked about electrical injury to the body. She would know to include what in her response?

   a. In electrical injuries, the body acts as a deflector of the electrical current.

   b. In electrical injuries, the body acts as a magnifier of the electrical current.

   c. The most severe damage is caused by lightning and high-voltage wires

   d. When a person touches an electrical source, the current passes through the body and exits to another receptor.

8. A man presents to the emergency department after being out in below zero weather all night. He asks the nurse why the health care team is concerned about his toes and feet. How would the nurse respond?

   a. Cold causes injury to the cells in the body by injuring the blood vessels, making them leak into the surrounding tissue.

   b. After being out in the cold all night your toes and feet are frozen and it will be very painful to warm them again, and the health care team is concerned he might be a drug addict.

   c. It is obvious that you are a homeless person and we were wondering how often this has happened to you before and when it will happen again.

   d. Your toes and feet are frozen and there is a concern about the formation of blood clots as we warm them again.

9. Clinical manifestations of radiation injury result from acute cell injury, dose-dependent changes in the blood vessels that supply the irradiated tissues, and fibrotic tissue replacement. What are these clinical manifestations?

   a. Radiation cystitis, dermatitis, and diarrhea from enteritis

   b. Dermatitis, diarrhea from enteritis, and hunger

   c. Diarrhea from enteritis, hunger, and muscle spasms

   d. Radiation cystitis, diarrhea from enteritis, and muscle spasms

10. Biologic agents differ from other injurious agents in that they are able to replicate and can continue to produce their injurious effects. How do Gram-negative bacteria cause harm to the cell?

    a. Gram-negative bacilli excrete elaborate exotoxins that interfere with cellular production of ATP.

    b. Gram-negative bacilli release endotoxins that cause cell injury and increased capillary permeability.

    c. Gram-negative bacilli enter the cell and disrupt its ability to replicate.

    d. Gram-negative bacilli cannot cause harm to the cell; only Gram-positive bacilli can harm the cell.

11. When confronted with a decrease in work demands or adverse environmental conditions, most cells are able to revert to a smaller size and a lower and more efficient level of functioning that is compatible with survival. This decrease in cell size is called _____.

12. Match the pigments (Column A) with what they cause in the body (Column B).

Column A

____ **1.** Icterus

____ **2.** Lipofuscin

____ **3.** Carbon

____ **4.** Melanin

Column B

a. A yellow discoloration of tissue

b. A blue lead line along the margins of the gum

c. A brown or dark-brown pigment that is found in the skin and hair

d. A yellow-brown pigment that accumulates in neurons

13. Match the type of agent causing cell injury (Column A) to the agent (Column B).

Column A

____ **1.** Physical agent

____ **2.** Chemical agent

____ **3.** Biologic agents

____ **4.** Nutritional factors

Column B

a. Submicroscopic viruses

b. Mechanical forces that produce tissue trauma

c. Free radicals

d. Vitamin B deficiency

14. You are a nurse preparing an educational event for a group of single parents. You are going to talk about drugs and the damage they can cause to the body. You would know to include which of these? (Mark all that apply.)

a. Acetaminophen and aspirin

b. Immunosuppressant drugs

c. Alcohol and cigarettes

d. Vitamin supplements and antineoplastic drugs

CHAPTER 3

Inflammation, the Inflammatory Response, and Fever

SECTION I: LEARNING OBJECTIVES

1. State the five cardinal signs of acute inflammation and describe the physiologic mechanisms involved in production of these signs.

2. Describe the vascular changes in an acute inflammatory response.

3. Characterize the interaction of adhesion molecules, chemokines, and cytokines in leukocyte adhesion, migration, and phagocytosis, which are part of the cellular phase of inflammation.

4. List four types of inflammatory mediators and state their function.

5. Contrast acute and chronic inflammation.

6. Describe the causes of chronic inflammation and the role of granuloma formation.

7. Define the systemic manifestations of inflammation, including the characteristics of an acute-phase response.

8. Describe the normal mechanism of body temperature regulation.

9. Characterize the inflammatory initiation of a febrile response.

10. Explain how age and fever are related.

SECTION II: ASSESSING YOUR UNDERSTANDING

Activity A *Fill in the blanks.*

1. _____ is a protective response intended to eliminate the initial cause of cell injury, remove the damaged tissue, and generate new tissue.

2. The cardinal signs of inflammation are _____, _____, _____, and _____.

3. In addition to the cardinal signs that appear at the site of injury, _____ manifestations may occur as chemical mediators produced at the site of inflammation gain entrance to the circulatory system.

4. _____ inflammation is of relatively short duration, lasting from a few minutes, whereas _____ inflammation is of a longer duration, lasting for days to years.

5. Acute inflammation involves two major components: the _____ and _____ stages.

6. Increased circulating white blood cells are a condition known as _____.

7. _____ produce prostaglandins and leukotrienes, platelet-activating factor, inflammatory cytokines, and growth factors that promote regeneration of tissues.

8. _____ changes that occur with inflammation involve the arterioles, capillaries, and venules of the microcirculation.

9. The selectins function in adhesion of _____ to endothelial cells.

10. The integrins promote _____ and cell-to-extracellular matrix interactions.

11. Chemotaxis is dynamic and energy-directed process of directed _____.

12. Groups of proteins that direct the trafficking of leukocytes during the early stages of inflammation or injury are known as _____.

13. The _____ pathways generate toxic oxygen and nitrogen products.

14. The plasma-derived mediators of inflammation include the _____ factors and the _____ proteins.

15. Histamine causes _____ of arterioles and increases the _____ of venules.

16. The _____ family inflammatory mediators consist of prostaglandins, leukotrienes, and related metabolites.

17. The _____ induce inflammation and potentiate the effects of histamine and other inflammatory mediators.

18. Aspirin and the nonsteroidal anti-inflammatory drugs (NSAIDs) reduce inflammation by inactivating the first enzyme in the _____ pathway for prostaglandin synthesis.

19. Eating oily fish and other foods that are high in _____ results in partial replacement of arachidonic acid in inflammatory cell membranes, which leads to decreased production of arachidonic acid-derived inflammatory mediators.

20. _____ fragments contribute to the inflammatory response by causing vasodilation, increasing vascular permeability; and enhancing the activity of phagocytes.

21. Activation of the _____ system results in release of bradykinin, which increases vascular permeability and causes contraction of _____, dilation of blood vessels, and _____.

22. _____, a cytokine that will induce endothelial cells to express adhesion molecules and release cytokines, chemokines, and reactive oxygen species, is released from mast cells.

23. The _____ radical, _____, and _____ radical are the major free oxygen radicals produced within the cell.

24. At higher levels, free radicals mediators can produce _____.

25. The acute inflammatory response involves the production of _____; they can be serous, hemorrhagic, fibrinous, membranous, or purulent.

26. Agents that evoke chronic inflammation typically are low-grade, persistent infections or irritants that are unable to _____ or _____.

27. The function of the acute-phase protein _____ is thought to be protective, in that it binds to the surface of invading microorganisms and targets them for destruction by complement and phagocytosis.

28. _____ is one of the most prominent manifestations of the acute-phase response.

29. Virtually all biochemical processes in the body are affected by changes in _____.

30. There are numerous _____ under the skin surface that allow blood to move directly from the arterial to the venous system.

Activity B *Consider the following figure.*

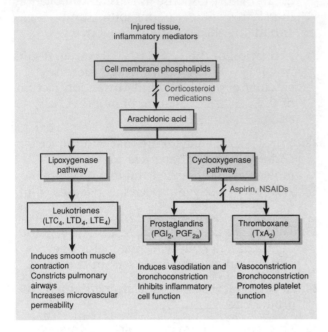

1. What does this figure represent? Explain the process that is depicted.

Activity C *Match the key terms in Column A with their definitions in Column B.*

Column A

____ 1. Endothelial cells

____ 2. Eosinophils

____ 3. Edema

____ 4. Neutrophils

____ 5. Exudate

____ 6. Nitric oxide

____ 7. Margination

____ 8. Thrombocytes

____ 9. Mast cells

____ 10. Basophils

Column B

a. Increase in the blood during allergic reactions

b. Leukocyte accumulation

c. Regulate leukocyte extravasation

d. Stimulate inflammatory reaction in response to injury or infection

e. Circulating cells similar to mast cells

f. Primary phagocyte that arrives early at the site of inflammation

g. Stimulator of vasodilation

h. Activation affects vascular permeability, chemotactic, adhesive, and proteolytic properties

i. Swelling due to movement of fluid from vasculature into tissues

j. Outpouring of a protein-rich fluid into the tissue and extravascular space

Activity D *Put the following events into the proper order.*

_____ → _____ → _____ → _____

• Chemotaxis

• Margination and adhesion to the endothelium

• Activation and phagocytosis

• Transmigration across the endothelium

Activity E *Briefly answer the following.*

1. The cardinal signs of inflammation result from the physiologic processes of the inflammatory cells and protein systems. List the signs and give a brief explanation as to its cause.

_____

_____

_____

2. Describe and differentiate between acute and chronic inflammation.

_____

_____

_____

3. The vascular response of inflammation follows one of three patterns. Describe these patterns and explain why it is necessary to have multiple responses.

_____

_____

_____

4. Many leukocytes have the ability to phagocytose foreign material and dispose of it. The process involves three steps. List and explain these steps.

_____

_____

_____

5. There are many mediators of the inflammatory system. They may be grouped by function. Describe each group and give a brief example of each.

_____

_____

_____

6. Explain and describe the two types of chronic inflammation.

_____

_____

_____

7. What is the purpose of the acute-phase response of inflammation?

_____

_____

_____

SECTION III: APPLYING YOUR KNOWLEDGE

Activity F *Consider the scenario and answer the questions.*

You are the nurse caring for a burn victim who has sustained second- and third-degree burns over 50% of the body. The family is asking you questions about the care that is being given to the burn victim.

1. A family member asks about the drainage they see on the bandages. What would you tell them?

_____

_____

_____

2. Several days after injury, a family member asks why the client isn't eating. What kind of information would you give the person?

_____

_____

_____

SECTION IV: PRACTICING FOR NCLEX

Activity G *Answer the following questions.*

1. The cardinal signs of inflammation include swelling, pain, redness, and heat. What is the fifth cardinal sign of inflammation?
    a. Loss of function
    b. Altered level of consciousness
    c. Sepsis
    d. Fever

2. The cells that are associated with allergic disorders and the inflammation associated with immediate hypersensitive reactions are known as what? (Mark all that apply.)
    a. Macrophages
    b. Eosinophils
    c. Mast cells
    d. Neutrophils
    e. Basophils

3. Inflammation can be either acute or chronic. The immune system is thought to play a role in chronic inflammation and may be one of the reasons chronic inflammation may persist for days to months to years. Why is the risk of scarring and deformity greater in chronic inflammation than it is in acute inflammation?
    a. Chronic inflammation is the persistent destruction of healthy tissue.
    b. Fibroblasts instead of exudates proliferate in chronic inflammation.
    c. Typically, agents that evoke chronic inflammation are infections or irritants that penetrate deeply and spread rapidly.
    d. Chronic inflammation is often the result of allergic reactions.

4. All wounds are considered contaminated at the time the wound occurs. Usually the natural defenses in our bodies can deal with the invading microorganisms at the time the wound occurs; however, there are times when a wound is badly contaminated and host defenses are overwhelmed. What happens to the healing process when host defenses are overwhelmed by infectious agents?

   a. The inflammatory response is shortened and does not complete destruction of the invading organisms.

   b. Fibroblast production becomes malignant because of hypersensitization by invading organisms.

   c. The formation of granulation tissue is impaired.

   d. Collagen fibers cannot draw tissues together.

5. During the acute inflammatory response there is a period called the transient phase, where there is increased vascular permeability. What is considered the principal mediator of the immediate transient phase?

   a. Histamine

   b. Arachidonic acid

   c. Fibroblasts

   d. Cytokines

6. Inflammation can be either local of systemic. What are the most prominent systemic manifestations of inflammation?

   a. Fever, leukocytosis or leukopenia, and the acute-phase response

   b. Fever, leukocytosis or leukopenia, and the transition-phase response

   c. Widening pulse pressure, thrombocytopenia, and the recovery-phase response

   d. Widening pulse pressure, thrombocytopenia, and the latent-phase response

CHAPTER 4

Cell Proliferation and Tissue Regeneration and Repair

SECTION I: LEARNING OBJECTIVES

1. Distinguish between cell proliferation and differentiation.

2. Describe the phases of the cell cycle.

3. Explain the function of cyclins, cyclin-dependent kinases, and cyclin-dependent kinase inhibitors in terms of regulating the cell cycle.

4. Describe the properties of stem cells.

5. Define the terms *parenchymal* and *stromal* as they relate to the tissues of an organ.

6. Compare labile, stable, and permanent cell types in terms of their capacity for regeneration.

7. Describe healing by primary and secondary intention.

8. Explain the effects of soluble mediators and the extracellular matrix on tissue repair and wound healing.

9. Trace the wound-healing process through the inflammatory, proliferative, and remodeling phases.

10. Explain the effects of malnutrition; ischemia and oxygen deprivation; impaired immune and inflammatory responses; and infection, wound separation, and foreign bodies on wound healing.

11. Discuss the effect of age on wound healing.

SECTION II: ASSESSING YOUR UNDERSTANDING

Activity A *Fill in the blanks.*

1. Cancer is a disorder of altered cell _____ and _____.

2. The process of cell division results in cellular _____.

3. _____ is the process of specialization whereby new cells acquire the structure and function of the cells they replace.

4. Proteins called _____ controls entry and progression of cells through the cell cycle.

5. Kinases are enzymes that _____ proteins.

6. Continually renewing cell populations rely on _____ cells of the same lineage that have not yet differentiated to the extent that they have lost their ability to divide.

7. _____ cells remain incompletely undifferentiated throughout life.

8. _____ *stem cells* are pluripotent cells derived from the inner cell mass of the blastocyst stage of the embryo.

9. Body organs and tissues are composed of two types of structures: _____ and _____.

10. _____ are those that continue to divide and replicate throughout life, replacing cells that are continually being destroyed.

11. Cells that are capable of undergoing regeneration when confronted with an appropriate stimulus and are thus capable of reconstituting the tissue of origin are termed _____.

12. _____ tissue is a glistening red, moist connective tissue that contains newly formed capillaries, proliferating fibroblasts, and residual inflammatory cells.

13. The elderly have reduced _____ and _____ synthesis, impaired wound contraction, and slower reepithelialization of open wounds.

14. The _____ is often born with immature organ systems and minimal energy stores but high metabolic requirements—a condition that predisposes to impaired wound healing.

Activity B Match the key terms in Column A with their definitions in Column B.

Column A

____ 1. Endothelial cells

____ 2. Proliferation

____ 3. Edema

____ 4. Differentiation

____ 5. Renewal

____ 6. Nitric oxide

____ 7. Margination

____ 8. Thrombocytes

____ 9. Mast cells

____ 10. Cellular potency

Column B

a. Process of cell division

b. Leukocyte accumulation

c. Regulate leukocyte extravasation

d. Stimulate inflammatory reaction in response to injury or infection

e. Defines the differentiation potential of stem cells

f. Process of cell specialization

g. Stimulator of vasodilation

h. Activation affects vascular permeability

i. Swelling due to movement of fluid from vasculature into tissues

j. Stem cells' undergoing numerous mitotic divisions while maintaining an undifferentiated state space

Activity C *Put the following events into the proper order.*

_____→_____→_____→_____

- Chemotaxis
- Margination and adhesion to the endothelium
- Activation and phagocytosis
- Transmigration across the endothelium

Activity D *Briefly answer the following.*

1. Not all cells in the body can re-enter the cell cycle, but some will do so continuously. In terms of regeneration and differentiation, which types of cells will or will not re-enter the cell cycle?

_____

_____

_____

2. Explain the concept of wound healing by first and second intent.

_____

_____

_____

SECTION III: APPLYING YOUR KNOWLEDGE

Activity E *Consider the scenario and answer the questions.*

You are the nurse caring for a burn victim who has sustained second- and third-degree burns over 50% of his body. The family is asking you questions about the care that is being given to the burn victim.

1. A family member asks about the drainage they see on the bandages. What would you tell them?

_____

_____

_____

2. Several days post injury a family member asks why the client isn't eating. What kind of information would give them?

_____

_____

_____

SECTION IV: PRACTICING FOR NCLEX

Activity F *Answer the following questions.*

1. A class of student nurses is hearing a lecture on wound healing. The professor explains about primary and secondary healing. The professor continues to talk about the phases of wound healing and states that in both primary and secondary healing the phases of wound healing occur at different rates. What are the phases of wound healing? (Mark all that apply.)
   a. The activation phase
   b. The proliferative phase
   c. The nutritional phase
   d. The inflammatory phase
   e. The maturational phase

2. Hyperbaric treatment for wound healing is used for wounds that have problems in healing due to hypoxia or infection. It works by raising the partial pressure of oxygen in plasma. How does hyperbaric oxygen treatment enhance wound healing?
   a. Destruction of anaerobic bacteria
   b. Increased action of eosinophils
   c. Promotion of angiogenesis
   d. Decrease in fibroblast activity

3. Wound healing is more difficult for persons at both ends of the age spectrum, although the reasons differ. In the elderly, wound healing is impaired or delayed because of structural and functional changes in the skin that occur with aging and the chronicity of wounds the elderly have. Why do neonates and small children have problems with wound healing?
   a. Their body is not yet capable of an inflammatory response
   b. The fragility of their skin
   c. They don't have the reserves needed
   d. Their immune system is hypersensitive to infectious agents

4. All wounds are considered contaminated at the time the wound occurs. Usually the natural defenses in our bodies can deal with the invading microorganisms at the time the wound occurs; however, there are times when a wound is badly contaminated and host defenses are overwhelmed. What happens to the healing process when host defenses are overwhelmed by infectious agents?
   a. The inflammatory response is shortened and does not complete destruction of the invading organisms.
   b. Fibroblast production becomes malignant due to hypersensitization by invading organisms.
   c. The formation of granulation tissue is impaired.
   d. Collagen fibers can't draw tissues together.

5. In normal tissue the size of the cell population is determined by which of the following?
   a. Balance of cell proliferation
   b. Death by apoptosis
   c. Emergence of newly differentiated cells

CHAPTER 5

Genetic Control of Cell Function and Inheritance

SECTION I: LEARNING OBJECTIVES

1. Describe the structure and function of DNA.

2. Relate the mechanisms of DNA repair to the development of a gene mutation.

3. Describe the function of messenger RNA, ribosomal RNA, and transfer RNA as they relate to protein synthesis.

4. Cite the effects of posttranslational processing on protein structure and function.

5. Explain the role of transcription factors in regulating gene activity.

6. Define the terms *autosomes*, *chromatin*, *meiosis*, and *mitosis*.

7. List the steps in constructing a karyotype using cytogenetic studies.

8. Explain the significance of the Barr body.

9. Construct a hypothetical pedigree for a recessive and dominant trait according to Mendel's laws.

10. Contrast genotype and phenotype.

11. Define the terms *allele*, *locus*, *expressivity*, and *penetrance*.

12. Differentiate between genetic and physical maps.

13. Briefly describe the methods used in linkage studies, dosage studies, and hybridization studies.

14. Describe the goals of the International HapMap Project.

15. Describe the process of recombinant DNA technology.

16. Characterize the process of RNA interference.

SECTION II: ASSESSING YOUR UNDERSTANDING

Activity A *Fill in the blank.*

1. Our genetic information is stored in the structure of _____ acid.

2. _____ acid serves as the template for protein synthesis.

3. The complete set of proteins encoded by the genome is known as the _____.

4. A precise complementary pairing of _____ and _____ bases occurs in the double-stranded DNA molecule.

5. DNA replication is semiconservative, meaning the parental DNA strands dissociate and pair with _____ strands to complete mitosis.

6. Human somatic cells contain _____ pairs of different chromosomes.

7. In the nucleus, DNA is in the form of _____ and during mitosis, it condenses into _____.

8. The genetic code is _____ repeat of bases.

9. Errors in DNA duplication are known as _____.

10. A _____ represents the variations in the genetic code that are responsible for the differences between individuals.

11. Messenger RNA is formed in the process of _____.

12. The coding sequence of an mRNA molecule is known as _____.

13. _____ undergoes the process of _____ to form a protein in the cytosol.

14. Molecular _____ assist in the folding of proteins into their three-dimensional conformation.

15. The degree to which a gene or particular group of genes is activated is termed *gene* _____.

16. DNA determines the type of biochemical product that is needed by the cell and directs its synthesis, but it is _____, through the process of transcription and translation that is responsible for the actual assembly of the products.

17. _____ occurs in the cell nucleus and involves the synthesis of RNA from a DNA template.

18. The pattern of gene expression and the outward presentation is the _____.

19. The position of a gene on a chromosome is called its _____, and alternate forms of a gene at the same locus are called _____.

20. A _____ is a graphic method for portraying a family history of an inherited trait

Activity B *Match the key terms in Column A with their definitions in Column B.*

1.

Column A	Column B
____ 1. tRNA	a. Used to align amino acids with ribosomes for the formation of protein
____ 2. Transcription factors	
____ 3. Penetrance	b. Ability of a gene to express its function
____ 4. mRNA	c. Initiate and regulate transcription
____ 5. Mitosis	d. Manner in which the gene is expressed
____ 6. Meiosis	e. Template that is copied from DNA
____ 7. Expressivity	f. Replicating germ cells
____ 8. Chromosomes	g. Multiple alleles at different loci affect the outcome
____ 9. Multifactorial inheritance	h. Organized and condensed DNA
____ 10. Single gene inheritance	i. One pair of genes is involved in the transmission of information
	j. Duplication of somatic cells

2. Gene-gene interactions are interesting and complex. Match the term with the description.

Column A

_____ 1. Collaborative genes

_____ 2. Multiple alleles

_____ 3. Complementary genes

_____ 4. Epistasis

_____ 5. Alleles

Column B

a. More than one allele affects the same trait

b. One gene masks the phenotypic effects of another nonallelic gene

c. Each gene is mutually dependent on the other

d. Two different genes influencing the same trait interact to produce a phenotype neither gene alone could produce.

e. Alternate forms of a gene at the same locus

Activity C *Sequencing.*

1. The processing of genetic material involves many well-organized steps. Put the following in order, starting at transcription and ending with the three-dimensional protein.

□→□→□→□→□→□→□→□→□

a. Transcription
b. Translation begins
c. mRNA moves to cytosol
d. mRNA is read by ribosome complex
e. Posttranslational processing
f. tRNA moves to ribosome
g. Ribosomal subunits come together
h. Formation of peptide bonds
i. Final 3D protein structure

Activity D *Briefly answer the following.*

1. Gregor Mendel was the first to study and characterize inheritance. Explain what he did and what he discovered.

_____
_____
_____

2. Genetic mapping is done to allow us to know the position of certain genes and sequences on the chromosomes. Explain the difference between genetic maps and physical maps. In your explanation, describe the basic methodology used to construct these maps.

_____
_____
_____

3. During meiosis, a process occurs that increases genetic variability. Explain how this occurs. Is it a good or bad thing?

_____
_____
_____

4. Humans have both somatic and sex chromosomes. How many of each do we have and where do they originate?

_____
_____
_____

5. Only about 2% of the genome encodes instructions for synthesis of proteins; the remainder consists of noncoding regions that serve to determine where, when, and in what quantity proteins are made. Explain how this occurs and describe its significance.

_____
_____
_____

SECTION III: APPLYING YOUR KNOWLEDGE

Activity E *Consider the scenario and answer the question.*

Jessica Jones, an adopted child, has been searching for her parents for many years. She believes that she has finally found her father but wants to be 100% sure before she approaches him.

1. Is there any way for her to absolutely identify her father before she meets him? Discuss the use of DNA fingerprinting to identify familial relationships.

_____

_____

_____

SECTION IV: PRACTICING FOR NCLEX

Activity F *Answer the following questions.*

1. It is the proteins that the genes encode that make up the majority of cellular structures and perform most life functions. What is the term used to define the complete set of proteins encoded by a genome?

  a. Proteome

  b. Protogene

  c. Nucleotomics

  d. Chromosome

2. Below are the steps in cell replication. Put them in the correct order.

  A. Complementary molecule is duplicated next to each original strand.

  B. Separation of the two strands of DNA

  C. Mitosis occurs

  D. Two strands become four strands

  a. ACBD

  b. BADC

  c. BDAC

  d. DBCA

3. Chromosomes contain all the genetic content of the genome. There are 23 pairs of different chromosomes in each somatic cell, half from the mother and half from the father. One of those chromosomes is the sex chromosome. What are the other 22 pairs of chromosomes called?

  a. Ribosomes

  b. Helixes

  c. Autosomes

  d. Haploids

4. On rare occasions accidental errors in duplication of DNA occur. What are these called?

  a. Codons

  b. Ribosomes

  c. Endonucleases

  d. Mutations

5. Most human traits are determined by multiple pairs of genes, many with alternate codes, accounting for some dissimilar forms that occur with certain genetic disorders. What type of inheritance involves multiple genes at different loci, with each gene exerting a small additive effect in determining a trait?

  a. Polygenic inheritance

  b. Multifactorial inheritance

  c. Monofactorial inheritance

  d. Collaborative inheritance

6. Two syndromes exhibit mental retardation as a common feature. Both disorders have the same deletion in chromosome 15. When the deletion is inherited from the mother, the infant presents with one syndrome; when the same deletion is inherited from the father, Prader-Willi syndrome results. What is the syndrome when the deletion is inherited from the mother?

  a. Turner syndrome

  b. Angelman syndrome

  c. Down syndrome

  d. Fragile X syndrome

7. Homozygotes are what people are called in whom the two alleles of a given pair are the same (AA or aa). Heterozygotes are what people are called who have different alleles (Aa) at a gene locus. What kind of trait is expressed only in homozygous pairing?

   a. Dominant trait

   b. Single-gene trait

   c. Recessive trait

   d. Penetrant trait

8. The International HapMap Project was created with two goals. One is the development of methods for applying the technology of these projects to the diagnosis and treatment of disease. The other is to map the (what) of the many closely related single nucleotide polymorphisms in the human genome?

   a. Codons

   b. Triplet code

   c. Alleles

   d. Haplotypes

9. DNA fingerprinting is based in part on recombinant DNA technology and in part on those techniques originally used in medical genetics to detect slight variations in the genomes of different individuals. These techniques are used in forensic pathology to compare specimens from the suspect with those of the forensic specimen. What is being compared when DNA fingerprinting is used in forensic pathology?

   a. The banding pattern

   b. The triplet code

   c. The haplotypes

   d. The chromosomes

10. There are two main approaches used in gene therapy: transferred genes can replace defective genes or they can selectively inhibit deleterious genes. What are the compounds usually used in gene therapy?

    a. mRNA sequences

    b. Cloned DNA sequences

    c. Sterically stable liposomes

    d. Single nucleotide polymorphisms

11. The human genome sequence is almost exactly (99.9%) the same in all people. What is thought to account for the differences in each human's behaviors, physical traits, and the susceptibility to disease is the small variation (0.01%) in gene sequence. This is termed a _____.

12. Like DNA, RNA is a long string of nucleotides encased in a large molecule. However, there are three aspects of its structure that makes it different from DNA. What are these aspects? (Mark all that apply.)

    a. RNA's double strand is missing one pair of chromosomes.

    b. The sugar in each nucleotide of RNA is ribose.

    c. RNA is a single-stranded molecule.

    d. RNA's thymine base is replaced by uracil.

13. One of the first products to be produced using recombinant DNA technology was human _____.

14. Cytogenetics is the study of the structure and numeric characteristics of the cell's chromosomes. Chromosome studies can be done on any tissue or cell that grows and divides in culture. What are the characteristics of a chromosomal study? (Mark all that apply.)

    a. The completed picture of a chromosomal study is called karyotyping.

    b. Human chromosomes are divided into three types according to the position of the centromere.

    c. Special laboratory techniques are used to culture body cell. They are then fixed and stained to display identifiable banding patterns.

    d. Complementary genes and collaborative genes are easily recognized.

15. Genetics has its own set of definitions. Match the word with its definition.

1. Genotype
2. Phenotype
3. Pharmacogenetics
4. Somatic cell hybridization
5. Penetrance

a. Traits, physical or biochemical, associated with a specific genotype that is recognizable.

b. How drugs respond to an individual's inherited characteristics.

c. The genetic information contained in the base sequence triplet code.

d. The ability of a gene to express its function.

e. The fusion of human somatic cells with those of a different species to yield a cell containing the chromosomes of both species.

Genetic and Congenital Disorders

SECTION I: LEARNING OBJECTIVES

1. Define the terms *congenital, allele, gene locus, gene mutation, genotype, phenotype, homozygous, heterozygous, polymorphism, gene penetrance,* and *gene expression.*

2. Describe three types of single-gene disorders and their patterns of inheritance.

3. Explain the genetic abnormality responsible for the fragile X syndrome.

4. Contrast disorders due to multifactorial inheritance with those caused by single-gene inheritance.

5. Describe three patterns of chromosomal breakage and rearrangement.

6. Trace the events that occur during meiosis and explain the events that lead to trisomy or monosomy.

7. Describe the chromosomal and major clinical characteristics of Down, Turner, and Klinefelter syndromes.

8. State the primary mechanism of altered body function in mitochondrial gene disorders and relate it to the frequent involvement of neural and muscular tissues.

9. Cite the most susceptible period of intrauterine life for development of defects due to environmental agents.

10. State the cautions that should be observed when considering use of drugs during pregnancy, including the possible effects of alcohol abuse, vitamin A derivatives, and folic acid deficiency on fetal development.

11. List four infectious agents that cause congenital defects.

12. Cite the rationale for prenatal diagnosis.

13. Describe methods used in arriving at a prenatal diagnosis, including ultrasonography, amniocentesis, chorionic villus sampling, percutaneous umbilical fetal blood sampling, and laboratory methods to determine the biochemical and genetic makeup of the fetus.

SECTION II: ASSESSING YOUR UNDERSTANDING

Activity A *Fill in the blanks.*

1. _____ defects, also known as birth defects, abnormalities of structure, function or metabolism that are present at the time of birth.

2. Genetic disorders are caused either by an alteration in _____ that disrupts the single-gene sequence or _____ rearrangements.

3. Genes either are expressed in an individual in a dominate, recessive, or in pairs of _____.

4. A gene _____ is a biochemical event such as nucleotide change, deletion, or insertion that produces a new allele.

5. Genetic disorders arise in two ways: (1) _____ from parents or (2) _____ due to an acquired mutation.

6. Someone who carries a gene responsible for a disease but does not manifest the disease is said to be a _____.

7. _____ syndrome is an autosomal dominant disorder of connective tissue.

8. X-linked inheritance patterns are predominantly _____.

9. Specific chromosomal abnormalities can be linked to more than _____ identifiable syndromes.

10. Chromosomal disorders may take the form of alterations in the _____ of one or more chromosomes or in an _____ number of chromosomes.

11. _____ occurs when there are simultaneous breaks in two chromosomes from different pairs, with exchange of chromosome parts. In the reciprocal type, there is no loss of information.

Activity B *Consider the following figures.*

1.

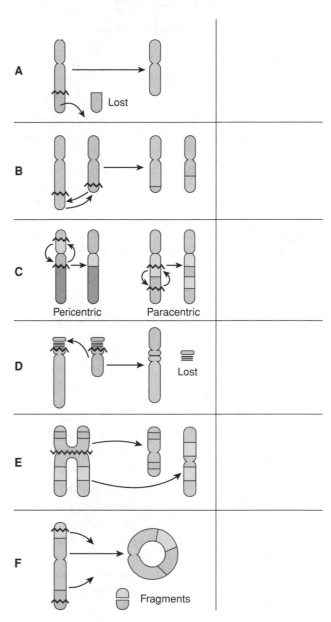

In the figure above, label the abnormality (deletion, reciprocal translocation, Robertsonian translocation, inversion).

2.

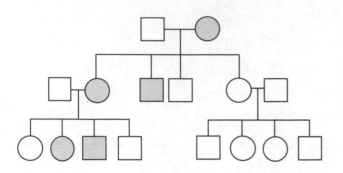

Is the pedigree shown in the preceding figure for an autosomal dominate, autosomal recessive, or sex-linked disease?

Activity C *Match the key concepts in Column A with their descriptions in Column B.*

Column A

_____ 1. Single-gene disorders

_____ 2. Multifactorial inheritance

_____ 3. Autosomal dominant disorder

_____ 4. Haploid

_____ 5. Chromosomal abnormality

_____ 6. Autosomal recessive

_____ 7. Polymorphism

_____ 8. Phenotype

_____ 9. Mutation

_____ 10. Mitochondrial disorders

Column B

a. Single set of chromosomes

b. Disorders are manifested only when both members of the gene pair are affected

c. Traits carried by multiple genes and influenced by the environment

d. The outward expression of a gene

e. Affected parent has a 50% chance of transmitting the disorder to each offspring

f. Follow a nonmendelian pattern of inheritance

g. Trisomy

h. Disorders are caused by a defective or mutant allele at a single-gene locus

i. A biochemical event such as nucleotide change, deletion, or insertion

j. Genes have more than one normal allele at the same locus

Activity D *Briefly answer the following questions.*

1. Inheritance of a genetic disease depends on the location of the mutation within the karyotype. What are the potential methods of inheritance? What will determine the likelihood of the offspring developing the disease? Does the sex of the offspring make any difference?

_____

_____

_____

2. Multifactorial inheritance patterns involve many different genes and their interactions with the environment. Predicting such disorders is more difficult than others are, but they do display several characteristics. Explain these characteristics.

_____

_____

_____

3. Chromosomal abnormalities are among the most common reasons for first-trimester spontaneous abortions as well as over 60 different diseases. Structural changes are a common form of chromosomal abnormalities. Explain what a structural change is and list the potential causes.

_____

_____

_____

4. Why are alterations in sex chromosomes better tolerated than alterations of autosomal chromosomes?

_____

_____

_____

5. Mitochondrial genetic abnormalities are not transmitted via mendelian genetics. In addition, they tend to affect the brain and muscle tissue. Explain why these two characteristics of mtDNA inheritance are true.

_____

_____

_____

SECTION III: APPLYING YOUR KNOWLEDGE

Activity E *Consider the scenario and answer the questions.*

A woman aged 37 is 2 months pregnant and has a history of alcohol intake of one to two drinks a day. She states, "My co-worker told me that drinking alcohol can harm my baby."

1. She asks you how having a drink or two every day can harm her baby. What would you respond?

_____

_____

_____

2. Discuss the effects of fetal alcohol syndrome.

_____

_____

_____

SECTION IV: PRACTICING FOR NCLEX

Activity F *Answer the following questions.*

1. Chromosomes carry 46 genes, 23 from the mother and 23 from the father. These genes are paired, and if both members of the gene pair are identical the person is considered homozygous. What is the person considered if both members of the gene pair are not identical?
   a. Heterozygous
   b. Phenotypic
   c. Codominant
   d. Mutant

2. An adolescent presents at the clinic with complaints of pedunculated lesions projecting from his skin on his trunk area. The nurse knows that this is a sign of what?
   a. Marfan syndrome
   b. Neurofibromatosis−1
   c. Down syndrome
   d. Klinefelter syndrome

3. The parents of an infant boy ask the nurse why their son was born with a cleft lip and palate. The nurse responds that cleft lip and palate are defects that are caused by many factors. The defect may also be caused by teratogens. Which teratogens can cause cleft lip and palate?
   a. Mumps
   b. Pertussis
   c. Rubella
   d. Measles

4. Sometimes an individual that developed from a single zygote is found to have two or more kinds of genetically different cell populations. These individuals are called what?
   a. Mutant
   b. Monosomy
   c. Aneuploidy
   d. Mosaic

5. With increasing age, there is a greater chance of a woman having been exposed to damaging environmental agents such as drugs, chemicals, and radiation. These factors may act on the aging oocyte to cause what in a fetus?
   a. Down syndrome
   b. Marfan syndrome
   c. Patau syndrome
   d. Turner syndrome

6. The embryo is most susceptible to adverse influences during the period from 15 to 60 days after conception. This period is referred to as what?
   a. The period of susceptibility
   b. The period of organogenesis
   c. The period of fetal anomalies
   d. The period of hormonal imbalance

7. Teratogenic substances cause abnormalities during embryonic and fetal development. These substances have been divided into three classes. These classes are called what?

   a. Period of organogenesis, third trimester, second month

   b. Outside environmental substances, inside environmental substances, internal environmental substances.

   c. Radiation, drugs and chemical substances, and infectious agents.

   d. Drugs and chemical substances, smoking, bacteria and virus

8. Infections with the TORCH agents are reported to occur in 1% to 5% of newborn infants in the United States and are among the major causes of neonatal morbidity and mortality. Which of these are clinical and pathologic manifestations of TORCH?

   a. Microcephaly, hydrocephalus, spina bifida

   b. Pneumonitis, myocarditis, macrocephaly

   c. Hydrocephalus, macrocephaly, thrombocytopenia

   d. Microcephaly, hydrocephalus, thrombocytopenia

9. The birth of a child with a defect brings with it two issues that must be resolved quickly. The traumatized parents need emotional support from the nurse and guidance in how to resolve these two issues. What are these issues?

   a. The immediate and future care of the affected child, and the possibility of future children in the family having a similar defect.

   b. The immediate and future care of the affected child, and the possibility of the child's death.

   c. The possibility of future children having a similar defect and the possibility of this child's death.

   d. The need for financial resources and the possibility of this child's death.

10. Genetic counseling and prenatal screening are tools both for the parents of a child with a defect and for those couples who want a child but are at high risk for having a child with a genetic problem. What are the objectives of prenatal screening?

    a. To detect fetal abnormalities and to provide information on where they can have the pregnancy terminated if they choose to.

    b. To detect fetal abnormalities and to provide parents with information needed to make an informed choice about having a child with an abnormality.

    c. To provide parents with information needed to make an informed choice about having a child with an abnormality and to assure the prospective parents that any defect in their hoped for child can be identified.

    d. To allow parents at risk for having a child with a specific defect to begin a pregnancy with the assurance that knowledge about the presence or absence of the disorder in the fetus can be confirmed by testing and to provide information on where they can have the pregnancy terminated if they choose to.

11. Match the genetic disorder (Column A) with its kind of disorder (Column B).

Column A	Column B
Marfan syndrome	Single-gene disorder
Huntington's chorea	Autosomal dominant
Tay-Sachs disease	Autosomal recessive disorders
Fragile X syndrome	Sex-linked disorders

12. Although multifactorial traits cannot be predicted with the same degree of accuracy as the mendelian single-gene mutations, characteristic patterns exist. What are these characteristic patterns? (Mark all that apply.)

    a. Multifactorial congenital malformations tend to involve a single organ or tissue derived from the same embryonic developmental field.

    b. The risk of recurrence in future pregnancies is for the same or a similar defect.

    c. The risk increases with increasing incidence of the defect among relatives.

    d. Multifactorial congenital malformations are always present at birth.

13. _____ is a rare metabolic disorder that affects approximately 1 in every 15,000 infants in the United States. The disorder is caused by a deficiency of the liver enzyme phenylalanine hydroxylase. Without a special diet these children will die.

14. After conception, development is influenced by the environmental factors that the embryo shares with the mother. Some of these factors can act on the developing fetus and cause defects. These factors might be what? (Mark all that apply.)

    a. Drugs

    b. Weather

    c. Air pollution

    d. Radiation

15. The U.S. Food and Drug Administration passed a law in 1983 classifying drugs according to their proven teratogenicity. Listed below are the classes of drugs in random order. Put them in order according to their teratogenicity.

    A. Class X

    B. Class A

    C. Class C

    D. Class B

    E. Class D

    a. BDCEA

    b. ABCDE

    c. BCDAE

    d. AEBCD

CHAPTER 7

Neoplasia

SECTION I: LEARNING OBJECTIVES

1. Define *neoplasm* and explain how neoplastic growth differs from the normal adaptive changes seen in atrophy, hypertrophy, and hyperplasia.

2. Distinguish between cell proliferation and differentiation.

3. Describe the phases of the cell cycle.

4. Describe the properties of stem cells.

5. Cite the method used for naming benign and malignant neoplasms.

6. State the ways in which benign and malignant neoplasms differ.

7. Relate the properties of cell differentiation to the development of a cancer cell clone and the behavior of the tumor.

8. Trace the pathway for hematologic spread of a metastatic cancer cell.

9. Use the concepts of growth fraction and doubling time to explain the growth of cancerous tissue.

10. Describe various types of cancer-associated genes and cancer-associated cellular and molecular pathways.

11. Describe genetic events and epigenetic factors that are important in tumorigenesis.

12. State the importance of cancer stem cells, angiogenesis, and the cell microenvironment in cancer growth and metastasis.

13. Explain how host factors such as heredity, levels of endogenous hormones, and immune system function increase the risk for development of selected cancers.

14. Relate the effects of environmental factors such as chemical carcinogens, radiation, and oncogenic viruses to the risk of cancer development.

15. Identify concepts and hypotheses that may explain the processes by which normal cells are transformed into cancer cells by carcinogens.

16. Characterize the mechanisms involved in the anorexia and cachexia, fatigue and sleep disorders, anemia, and venous thrombosis experienced by patients with cancer.

17. Define the term *paraneoplastic syndrome* and explain its pathogenesis and manifestations.

18. Cite three characteristics of an ideal screening test for cancer.

19. Describe the four methods that are used in the diagnosis of cancer.

20. Differentiate between the methods used for grading and staging of cancers.

21. Explain the mechanism by which radiation exerts its beneficial effects in the treatment of cancer.

22. Describe the adverse effects of radiation therapy.

23. Differentiate between the action of direct DNA-interacting and indirect DNA-interacting chemotherapeutic agents and cell cycle-specific and cell cycle-independent drugs.

24. Describe the three mechanisms whereby bio-therapy exerts its effects.

25. Describe three examples of targeted therapy used in the treatment of cancer.

26. Cite the most common types of cancer affecting children.

27. Describe how cancers that affect children differ from those that affect adults.

28. Discuss possible long-term effects of radiation therapy and chemotherapy on adult survivors of childhood cancer.

SECTION II: ASSESSING YOUR UNDERSTANDING

Activity A *Fill in the blanks.*

1. Cancer is a disorder of altered cell _____ and _____.

2. The process of cell division results in cellular _____.

3. _____ is the process of specialization whereby new cells acquire the structure and function of the cells they replace.

4. Proteins called _____ control entry and progression of cells through the cell cycle.

5. Kinases are enzymes that _____ proteins.

6. Continually renewing cell populations rely on _____ cells of the same lineage that have not yet differentiated to the extent that they have lost their ability to divide.

7. _____ cells remain incompletely undifferentiated throughout life.

8. _____ *stem cells* are pluripotent cells derived from the inner cell mass of the blastocyst stage of the embryo.

9. The term _____ refers to an abnormal mass of tissue in which the growth exceeds and is uncoordinated with that of the normal tissues.

10. _____ do not usually cause death unless the location interferes with a vital organs function.

11. Malignant neoplasms are less well _____ and have the ability to break loose, enter the circulatory or lymphatic systems, and form secondary malignant tumors at other sites.

12. Tumors usually are named by adding the suffix -_____ to the parenchymal tissue type from which the growth originated.

13. A _____ is growth that projects from a mucosal surface.

14. The term _____ is used to designate a malignant tumor of epithelial tissue origin.

15. There are two categories of malignant neoplasms, _____ and _____ cancers.

16. The term _____ is used to describe the loss of cell differentiation in cancerous tissue.

17. A characteristic of cancer cells is the ability to proliferate even in the absence of _____.

18. With homologous loss of _____ gene activity, DNA damage goes unrepaired and mutations occur in dividing cells, leading to malignant transformations.

19. The types of genes involved in cancer are numerous, with two main categories being the _____, which control cell growth and replication, and tumor _____ genes, which are growth-inhibiting regulatory genes.

20. _____ is the only known retrovirus to cause cancer in humans.

21. Tumor cells must double _____ times before there will be a palpable mass.

22. A common manifestation of solid tumors is the cancer _____ syndrome.

23. As cancers grow, they compress and erode blood vessels, causing _____ and _____ along with frank bleeding and sometimes hemorrhage.

24. _____ is a common side effect of many cancers. It is related to blood loss, hemolysis, impaired red cell production, or treatment effects.

25. A tissue _____ involves the removal of a tissue specimen for microscopic study.

26. _____ therapy uses high-energy parti-cles or waves to destroy or damage cancer cells.

27. _____ is a systemic treatment that enables drugs to reach the site of the tumor as well as other distant sites.

Activity B _Consider the following figure._

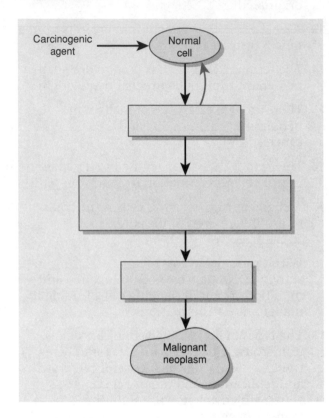

1. In the flow chart above, fill in the missing steps using the following terms: _DNA damage, alterations in genes that control apoptosis, unregu-lated cell differentiation and growth, inactivation of tumor suppressor genes, activation of growth-promoting oncogenes, DNA repair,_ and _failure of DNA repair._

Activity C _Match the key terms in Column A with their definitions in Column B._

Column A

_____ **1.** Malignant mass

_____ **2.** Cellular potency

_____ **3.** Renewal

_____ **4.** Proliferation

_____ **5.** Tumor-initiating cells

_____ **6.** Tumor

_____ **7.** Apoptosis

_____ **8.** Benign mass

_____ **9.** Differentiation

_____ **10.** Oncology

_____ **11.** Protooncogene

_____ **12.** Growth fraction

_____ **13.** Tumor suppressor gene

_____ **14.** Genetic instability

_____ **15.** Epigenetic effects

_____ **16.** Anaplasia

_____ **17.** Anchorage dependence

_____ **18.** Doubling time

_____ **19.** p53

Column B

a. Defines the differen-tiation potential of stem cells

b. Undefined or less differentiated cellular mass

c. Mass of cells due to overgrowth

d. Process that removes senescent and or damaged cells

e. Stem cells undergo-ing numerous mitotic divisions while maintaining an undifferentiated state

f. Cancer stem cells

g. Process of cell spe-cialization

h. Well-differentiated mass of cells

i. Study of tumors and their treatment

j. Process of cell divi-sion

k. Loss of cell differentiation

l. Changes in gene expression without DNA mutation

m. Normal gene that can cause cancer if mutated

n. Promote cancer when less active

o. Ratio of dividing cells to resting cells

p. Tumor suppressor gene

q. Marked by chrom-osomal aberrations

r. Epithelial cells must be anchored to either neighbor-ing cells or the underlying extracellular matrix to live and grow

s. Time it takes for the total mass of cells in a tumor to double

Activity D *Put the following terms for cellular potency in order from the least differentiated to the most differentiated.*

a. Pluripotent

b. Totipotent

c. Unipotent

d. Multipotnet

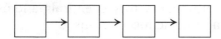

Activity E *Briefly answer the following.*

1. Not all cells in the body can re-enter the cell cycle, but some will do so continuously. In terms of regeneration and differentiation, which types of cells will or will not re-enter the cell cycle?

_____

_____

_____

2. Compare and contrast benign tumors and malignant tumors.

_____

_____

_____

3. List the five factors used to describe benign and malignant neoplasm.

_____

_____

_____

4. Describe the process and routes of metastasis.

_____

_____

_____

5. Explain how a diminished immune system may play a role in carcinogenesis.

_____

_____

_____

6. Chemical carcinogens act in two distinct ways. What are they?

_____

_____

_____

7. Cachexia is marked by a hypermetabolic state. Give two reasons for this and explain the consequences.

_____

_____

_____

8. What is paraneoplastic syndrome?

_____

_____

_____

9. List some of the common methods used for diagnosing cancer.

_____

_____

_____

10. Cancers are graded and staged on their characteristics in order to determine a treatment regimen. Explain the grading and staging system and how it is met.

_____

_____

_____

SECTION III: APPLYING YOUR KNOWLEDGE

Activity F *Consider the scenario and answer the questions.*

Eight year old Joe Cheapson has been diagnosed with acute lymphocytic leukemia (ALL). His treatment plan includes placement of an implanted central venous catheter and multiple administrations of chemotherapy. Joe says, "NO! I don't want to be stuck with needles all the time."

1. What would you tell Joe to decrease his anxiety?

_____

_____

_____

2. How would you explain the way chemotherapy works to Joe's parents?

_____

_____

_____

SECTION IV: PRACTICING FOR NCLEX

Activity G *Answer the following questions.*

1. The nurse has provided an educational session with a 56-year-old man, newly diagnosed with a benign tumor of the colon. The nurse knows that the patient needs further teaching when he makes which remark?

   a. This tumor I have, will I die from it?

   b. Even though benign tumors can't stop growing, they aren't considered cancer.

   c. Benign tumors still produce normal cells different from other cells around them.

   d. This kind of tumor can't invade other organs or travel to other places in the body to start new tumors.

2. The nurse on an oncology floor has just admitted a patient with metastatic cancer. The patient asks how cancer moves from one place to another in the body. What would the nurse answer?

   a. The cancer cells are not able to float around the original tumor in body fluids.

   b. Cancer cells enter the body's lymph system and thereby spread to other parts of the body.

   c. Cancer cells are moved from one place in the body to another by transporter cells.

   d. Cancer cells replicate and form a chain that spreads from the original tumor site to the site of the metastatic lesion.

3. It is well known that cancer is not a single disease. It follows then that cancer does not have a single cause. It seems more likely that the occurrence of cancer is triggered by the interactions of multiple risk factors. What are identified risk factors for cancer?

   a. Body type, age, and hereditary

   b. Radiation, cancer-causing viruses, and color of skin

   c. Hormonal factors, chemicals, and immunologic mechanisms

   d. Immunologic mechanisms, cancer-causing viruses, and color of skin

4. Several cancers have been identified as inheritable through an autosomal dominant gene. People who inherit these genes are generally only at increased risk for developing the cancer. There is one type of cancer, however, that is almost certain to develop in someone who inherits the dominant gene. Which cancer carries the highest risk of developing in someone who carries the gene?

   a. Retinoblastoma

   b. Osteosarcoma

   c. Acute lymphocytic leukemia

   d. Colon cancer

5. One group of chemical carcinogens is called indirect-reacting agents. Another term for these agents is *procarcinogens*, which become active only after metabolic conversion. One of the most potent procarcinogens is a group of dietary carcinogens called:

   a. Polycyclic aromatic hydrocarbons

   b. Aflatoxins

   c. Initiators

   d. Diethylstilbestrol

6. In some cancers, the presenting factor is an effusion, or fluid, in the pleural, pericardial, or peritoneal spaces. Research has found that almost 50% of undiagnosed effusions in people not known to have cancer turn out to be malignant. Which cancers are often found because of effusions?

   a. Colon and rectal cancers
   b. Lung and ovarian cancers
   c. Breast and colon cancers
   d. Ovarian and rectal cancers

7. Tumor markers are used for screening, establishing prognosis, monitoring treatment, and detecting recurrent disease. Which serum tumor markers have been proven to be among the most useful in clinical practice?

   a. Prostate-specific antigen and deoxyribonucleic acid
   b. Deoxyribonucleic acid and carcinoembryonic antigen
   c. Alpha-fetoprotein and human chorionic gonadotropin
   d. Chorionic gonadotropin and cyclin-dependent kinases

8. Cranial radiation therapy (CRT) has been used to treat brain tumors, ALL, head and neck soft tissue tumors, and retinoblastoma in children. Childhood cancer survivors who had CRT as therapy for their cancers are prone to growth hormone deficiency. In adults, what is growth hormone deficiency associated with?

   a. Hypocalcemia
   b. Cardiovascular longevity
   c. Hyperinsulinemia
   d. Dyslipidemia

9. A big difference in the treatment of childhood cancer as opposed to adult cancer is that chemotherapy is the most widely used treatment therapy for childhood cancer. What is the reason for this?

   a. Pediatric tumors are more responsive to chemotherapy than adult cancers.
   b. Children do not tolerate other forms of therapy as well as adults do.
   c. Children do not complain about the nausea and vomiting caused by chemotherapy like adults do.
   d. Children think losing their hair is "cool."

10. The inherent properties of a tumor that determine how the tumor responds to radiation is called radiosensitivity. When radiation is combined with cytotoxic drugs it has been noted that there is a radiosensitizing effect on tumor cells. Which drug is considered a radiosensitizer?

    a. Doxorubicin
    b. Cisplatin
    c. Vincristine
    d. Docetaxel

11. Cancer is a disorder of altered cell differentiation and growth. The term _____ refers to an abnormal mass of tissue in which the growth exceeds and is uncoordinated with that of the normal tissues.

12. A woman diagnosed with breast cancer asks the nurse how a malignant tumor in her breast could spread to other parts of her body. The nurse answers that a malignant neoplasm is made of up less well-differentiated cells that have which of the following abilities? Select all that apply.

    a. Break loose
    b. Reinvade their original site
    c. Enter the circulatory or lymphatic systems
    d. Be excreted through the alimentary canal
    e. Form secondary malignant tumors at other sites

13. Cancer cells differ from normal cells in many ways. They have lost the ability to accurately communicate with other cells, and they do not have to be anchored to other cells to survive. How else are they different from other cells? Select all that apply.

    a. Cancer cells have an increased tendency to stick together.
    b. Cancer cells have an unlimited life span.
    c. Cancer cells have lost contact inhibition.
    d. Cancer cells need increased amounts of growth factor to proliferate.
    e. Cancer cells are termed *genetically unstable*.

14. Match the following types of cancer with their screening tests.

Type of Cancer	Screening Test
1. Malignant melanoma	**a.** Mammography
2. Prostatic	**b.** Self-examination
3. Cervical	**c.** Pap smear
4. Breast	**d.** PSA

15. Childhood cancers are often diagnosed late in the disease process because the signs and symptoms mimic other childhood diseases. However, with the huge strides in treatment methods more and more children survive childhood cancer. These survivors face the uncertainty of what the life-saving treatment they received during their childhood may produce what late effects? Select all that apply.

a. Cardiomyopathy and pulmonary fibrosis

b. Cognitive dysfunction and hormonal dysfunction

c. Second malignancies and liver failure

d. Impaired growth and second malignancies

Disorders of Fluid, Electrolyte, and Acid-Base Balance

SECTION I: LEARNING OBJECTIVES

1. Define the terms *electrolyte*, *ion*, and *nonelectrolytes*.

2. Differentiate the intracellular from the extracellular fluid compartments in terms of distribution and composition of water, electrolytes, and other osmotically active solutes.

3. Relate the concept of a concentration gradient to the processes of diffusion and osmosis.

4. Describe the control of cell volume and the effect of isotonic, hypotonic, and hypertonic solutions on cell size.

5. Describe factors that control fluid exchange between the vascular and interstitial fluid compartments and relate them to the development of edema and third spacing of extracellular fluids.

6. Describe the manifestations and treatment of edema.

7. State the functions and physiologic mechanisms controlling body water levels and sodium concentration, including the effective circulating volume, sympathetic nervous system, renin-angiotensin-aldosterone system, and antidiuretic hormone.

8. Describe measures that can be used in assessing body fluid levels and sodium concentration.

9. Describe the causes, manifestations, and treatment of psychogenic polydipsia.

10. Describe the relationship between antidiuretic hormone and aquaporin channels in reabsorption of water by the kidney.

11. Compare the pathology, manifestations, and treatment of diabetes insipidus and the syndrome of inappropriate antidiuretic hormone.

12. Compare and contrast the causes, manifestations, and treatment of isotonic fluid volume deficit, isotonic fluid volume excess, hypotonic hyponatremia, and hypertonic hyponatremia.

13. Characterize the distribution of potassium in the body and explain how extracellular potassium levels are regulated in relation to body gains and losses.

14. State the causes of hypokalemia and hyperkalemia in terms of altered intake, output, and transcellular shifts.

15. Relate the functions of potassium to the manifestations of hypokalemia and hyperkalemia.

16. Describe methods used in diagnosis and treatment of hypokalemia and hyperkalemia.

17. Describe the associations among intestinal absorption, renal elimination, bone stores, and the functions of vitamin D and parathyroid hormone in regulating calcium, phosphate, and magnesium levels.

18. State the difference between ionized and bound forms of calcium in terms of physiologic function.

19. Describe the mechanisms of calcium gain and loss and relate them to the causes of hypocalcemia and hypercalcemia.

20. Relate the functions of calcium to the manifestations of hypocalcemia and hypercalcemia.

21. Describe the mechanisms of phosphate gain and loss and relate them to causes of hypophosphatemia and hyperphosphatemia.

22. State the definition of an acid and a base.

23. Describe the three forms of carbon dioxide transport and their contribution to acid-base balance.

24. Define pH and use the Henderson-Hasselbalch equation to calculate the pH and to compare compensatory mechanisms for regulating pH.

25. Describe the intracellular and extracellular mechanisms for buffering changes in body pH.

26. Compare the role of the kidneys and respiratory system in regulation of acid-base balance.

27. Explain how the transcellular hydrogen-potassium exchange system contributes to the regulation of pH.

28. Differentiate the terms *acidemia, alkalemia, acidosis,* and *alkalosis.*

29. Describe a clinical situation involving an acid-base disorder in which both primary and compensatory mechanisms are present.

30. Define metabolic acidosis, metabolic alkalosis, respiratory acidosis, and respiratory alkalosis.

31. Explain the use of the plasma anion gap in differentiating types of metabolic acidosis.

32. List common causes of metabolic and respiratory acidosis and metabolic and respiratory alkalosis.

33. Contrast and compare the clinical manifestations and treatment of metabolic and respiratory acidosis and of metabolic and respiratory alkalosis.

SECTION II: ASSESSING YOUR UNDERSTANDING

Activity A *Fill in the blanks.*

1. The _____ consists of fluid contained within all of the billions of cells in the body.

2. The _____ contains all the fluids outside the cells, including those in the interstitial or tissue spaces and blood vessels.

3. _____ are substances that dissociate in solution to form ions.

4. Particles that do not dissociate into ions such as glucose and urea are called _____.

5. _____ is the movement of charged or uncharged particles along a concentration gradient.

6. _____ is the movement of water across a semipermeable membrane.

7. _____ refers to the osmolar concentration in 1 L of solution and _____ to the osmolar concentration in 1 kg of water.

8. The predominant osmotically active particles in the extracellular fluid are _____ and its associated anions (Cl^- and HCO_3^-).

9. The difference between the calculated and measured osmolality is called the _____.

10. _____ proteins and other organic compounds cannot pass through the membrane.

11. The _____ membrane pump continuously removes three Na^+ ions from the cell for every two K^+ ions that are moved back into the cell.

12. _____ refers to the movement of water through capillary pores because of a mechanical, rather than an osmotic, force.

13. The _____ represents an accessory route whereby fluid from the interstitial spaces can return to the circulation.

14. _____ is a palpable swelling produced by expansion of the interstitial fluid volume.

15. Edema due to decreased capillary colloidal osmotic pressure usually is the result of inadequate production or abnormal loss of _____.

16. _____ edema occurs at times when the accumulation of interstitial fluid exceeds the absorptive capacity of the tissue gel.

17. _____ represent an accumulation or trapping of body fluids that contribute to body weight but not to fluid reserve or function.

18. Water losses that occur through the skin and lungs are referred to as _____ because they occur without a person's awareness.

19. Most sodium losses occur through the _____.

20. The major regulator of sodium and water balance is the maintenance of the _____

21. RAAS exerts its action through _____ and _____.

22. _____ is primarily a regulator of water intake and _____ is a regulator of water output.

23. _____ involves compulsive water drinking and is usually seen in persons with psychiatric disorders, most commonly schizophrenia.

24. _____ (DI) is caused by a deficiency of or a decreased response to antidiuretic hormone (ADH).

25. Disorders of sodium concentration produce a change in the osmolality of the extracellular fluid (ECF) with movement water from the ECF compartment into the intracellular fluid (ICF) compartment, known as _____, or from ICF compartment into the ECF fluid compartment known as _____.

26. When the effective circulating blood volume is compromised, the condition is often referred to as _____.

27. _____ cause sequestering of ECF in the serous cavities, extracellular spaces in injured tissues, or lumen of the gut.

28. Fluid volume excess represents an _____ expansion of the ECF compartment with increases in both interstitial and vascular volumes.

29. _____ represents a plasma sodium concentration below 135 mEq/L.

30. _____ hyponatremia represents retention of water with dilution of sodium while maintaining the ECF volume within a normal range.

31. MDMA (Ecstasy) and its metabolites have been shown to produce enhanced release of _____ from the hypothalamus.

32. _____ implies a plasma sodium level above 145 mEq/L.

33. Hypernatremia represents a deficit of _____ in relation to the body's sodium stores.

34. The effects of aldosterone on potassium elimination are mediated through a _____ located in the late distal and cortical collecting tubules of the kidney.

35. The _____ is determined by the ratio of ICF to ECF potassium concentration.

36. With severe _____, the resting membrane approaches the threshold potential causing sustained subthreshold depolarization with a resultant inactivation of the sodium channels and a net decrease in excitability.

37. The renal processes that conserve potassium during _____ interfere with the kidney's ability to concentrate urine.

38. Chronic hyperkalemia is usually associated with _____.

39. The signs and symptoms of potassium _____ are closely related to a decrease in neuromuscular excitability.

40. _____ acts to sustain normal plasma levels of calcium and phosphate by increasing their absorption from the intestine. It also is necessary for normal bone formation.

41. _____ serves as a cofactor in the generation of cellular energy and is important in the function of second messenger systems.

42. The manifestations of acute _____ reflect the increased neuromuscular excitability.

43. The manifestations of _____ result from a decrease in cellular energy stores due to deficiency in ATP.

44. Many of the signs and symptoms of a phosphate excess are related to a _____ deficit.

45. _____ acts as a cofactor in many intracellular enzyme reactions, including the transfer of high-energy phosphate groups in the generation of ATP from adenosine diphosphate.

46. Normally, the concentration of body acids and bases is regulated so that the pH of extracellular body fluids is maintained within a very narrow range of _____ to _____.

47. The H^+ concentration is commonly expressed in terms of the _____

48. Acids are continuously generated as by-products of _____ processes.

49. Physiologically, these acids fall into two groups: the _____ acid H_2CO_3 and all other _____ acids.

50. The _____ content of the blood can be calculated by multiplying the partial pressure of CO_2 (P_{CO_2}) by its solubility coefficient.

51. The metabolism of _____ and other substances results in the generation of fixed or nonvolatile acids and bases.

52. The plasma pH can be calculated using an equation called the _____.

53. The _____ buffer system is the principle ECF buffer.

54. _____ is a systemic disorder caused by an increase in plasma pH due to a primary excess in HCO_3^-.

55. Metabolic alkalosis also leads to a compensatory _____ with development of various degrees of _____ and respiratory acidosis.

56. Respiratory _____ occurs in acute or chronic conditions that impair effective alveolar ventilation and cause an accumulation of P_{CO_2}.

57. Respiratory _____ is caused by hyperventilation or a respiratory rate in excess of that needed to maintain normal plasma

Activity B   *Consider the following figure.*

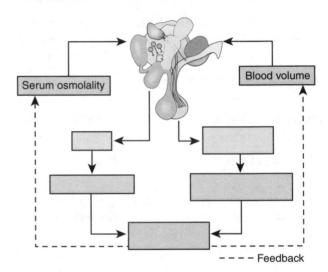

Serum osmolality

Blood volume

- - - - Feedback

Complete the above flow chart using the following terms:

- Extracellular water volume
- Thirst
- Secretion of ADH
- Reabsorption of water by the kidney
- Water ingestion

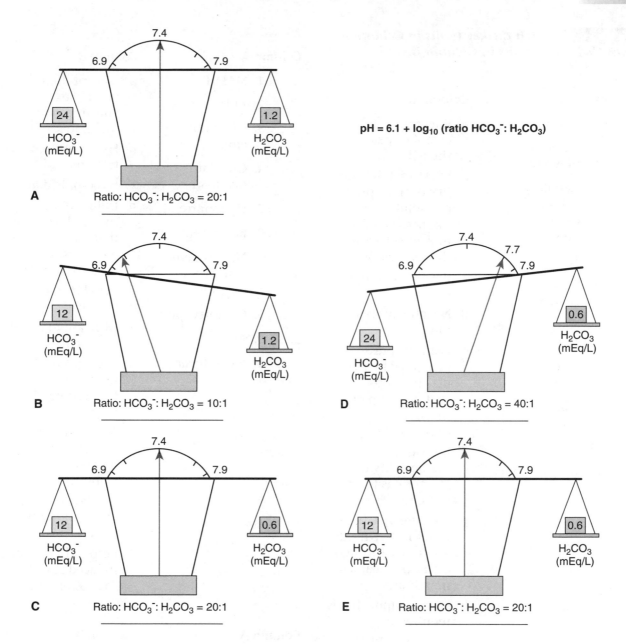

$$pH = 6.1 + \log_{10} (\text{ratio } HCO_3^- : H_2CO_3)$$

In the diagram above, label each scale to reflect the acid-base state and if there is any compensation present.

- Normal, pH 7.4
- Metabolic acidosis
- Metabolic acidosis with respiratory compensation
- Respiratory alkalosis
- Respiratory alkalosis with renal compensation

Activity C *Match the key terms in Column A with their definitions in Column B.*

1.

Column A

____ **1.** Cations

____ **2.** Osmotic pressure

____ **3.** Capillary colloidal osmotic pressure

____ **4.** Tonicity

____ **5.** Generalized edema

____ **6.** Glomerulone-phritis

____ **7.** Isotonic solution

____ **8.** Obligatory urine output

____ **9.** Anions

____ **10.** Lymphedema

Column B

a. Effective osmolality same as the ICF

b. Effect that the effective osmotic pressure of a solution on cell size because of water movement across the cell membrane

c. Positively charged ions

d. Negatively charged ions

e. Osmotic pressure generated by the plasma proteins that do not pass through the pores of the capillary wall

f. Increased permeability of glomerulus to proteins

g. Pressure by which water is drawn into a solution through a semipermeable membrane

h. Urine output that is required to eliminate wastes

i. Edema due to impaired lymph drainage

j. The result of increased vascular volume

2.

Column A

____ **1.** SIADH

____ **2.** Aldosterone

____ **3.** Hypernatr-emia

____ **4.** Circulatory overload

____ **5.** Hyponatremia

____ **6.** Baroreceptors

____ **7.** Nephrogenic diabetes insipidus

____ **8.** Osmoreceptors

____ **9.** ANP

____ **10.** Hypodipsia

Column B

a. State of fluid volume excess affecting cardiac function

b. Hypertonic concentration

c. Hypotonic dilution

d. Failure of the negative feedback system that regulates the release and inhibition of ADH

e. Renal insensitivity to ADH

f. Decrease in the ability to sense thirst

g. Respond to changes in ECF osmolality by swelling or shrinking

h. Acts at the cortical collecting tubules to increase sodium reabsorption

i. Increases sodium excretion by the kidney

j. Respond to pressure-induced stretch of the vessel walls

3.

Column A

____ **1.** Amphoteric

____ **2.** Acid

____ **3.** Whole blood buffer base

____ **4.** Delta gap

____ **5.** MELAS

____ **6.** Excess base loading

____ **7.** Base

____ **8.** Carbonic anhydrase

Column B

a. Molecule that can release an H^+

b. Acute increases in HCO_3^-

c. Genetic mitochondrial disorder

d. Ion or molecule that can accept an H^+

e. Can function as acid or base

f. Increase in plasma P_{CO_2}

____ 9. Hypercapnia

____ 10. Dissociation constant

g. The degree to which an acid or base in a buffer system dissociates

h. Anion gap of urine

i. Measures the level of all the buffer systems of the blood

j. Catalyzes bicarbonate reaction

Activity D *Draw a flow chart that puts the following steps of calcium concentration by parathyroid hormone in order. Include the involved organs: parathyroid glands, bone, kidney, and intestine.*

- Increased serum calcium
- Increased intestinal calcium absorption
- Activated vitamin D
- Decreased calcium elimination
- Release of calcium from bone
- Decreased serum calcium
- Release of parathyroid hormone

Activity E *Briefly answer the following.*

1. Compare and contrast the ICF from the ECF.

_____

_____

_____

2. What are the forces that control the movement of water between the capillary and interstitial spaces?

_____

_____

3. What are the physiological mechanisms that produce edema?

_____

_____

4. How are sodium and water levels maintained in the body?

_____

_____

_____

5. What are the three types of polydipsia?

_____

_____

_____

6. What are the physical manifestations of an isotonic volume expansion?

_____

_____

_____

7. What are the changes seen in an electrocardiogram during hypokalemia and why are they present?

_____

_____

_____

8. What are the systemic effects of hypercalcemia?

_____

_____

_____

9. Why does someone with kidney disease need to worry about the integrity of the skeletal system?

_____

_____

_____

10. How are pH and K^+ related? How do they serve as a buffer?

_____

_____

_____

11. How do the kidneys regulate acid-base balance?

_____

_____

_____

12. What are the two types of acid-base disorders?

_____

_____

_____

SECTION III: APPLYING YOUR KNOWLEDGE

Activity F *Consider the scenario and answer the questions.*

Case study: The parents of a 10-year-old child arrive at the burn unit to see their child for the first time since her admission. The client was admitted 8 hours ago with second- and third-degree burns over 60% of her body. She is edematous and in pain.

a. The parents state, "When we left here, just a few hours ago, she wasn't all swollen like that. What causes all that swelling?" What answer would you give?

_____

_____

_____

b. The doctor explains to the parents that because their daughter has a large burned area she has lost a large amount of fluid. The concern for the client is now not only the burn, but a disorder called fluid volume deficit. After the doctor leaves, the parents ask the nurse if the doctor is sure their daughter has fluid volume deficit. What should the nurse know about fluid volume deficit?

_____

_____

_____

Activity G *Consider the scenario and answer the questions.*

A college student is brought to the emergency department by her friend. It is reported by the young woman's friend that they found her wandering around outside the dorm and she did not know where she was or why she was there. The friend stated that the young woman had complained of being "very tired" lately and she had lost weight because she was not eating or drinking. Vital signs are: blood pressure, 118/78; respiration, 30; pulse, 66. An ABG is ordered and results are: PO_2 of 95; Pco_2 35; HCO_3^- of 20, and a pH of 7.1.

1. What are this patient's laboratory values indicative of?

_____

_____

_____

2. The physician orders a blood glucose level to be drawn. Why would a blood glucose level be important for this patient?

_____

_____

_____

SECTION IV: PRACTICING FOR NCLEX

Activity H *Answer the following questions.*

1. Edema is an excess in the interstitial fluid volume. What mechanisms play a part in the formation of edema? (Mark all that apply.)

   a. Mechanisms that increase capillary permeability

   b. Mechanisms that increase capillary filtration pressure

   c. Mechanisms that increase capillary colloidal osmotic pressure

   d. Mechanisms that produce obstruction to the flow of lymph

   e. Mechanisms that decrease capillary colloidal osmotic pressure

2. Match the following elements with their actions in the body.

Element	Action in the Body
1. Sodium	**a.** Increases the absorption of calcium from the intestine
2. Potassium	**b.** Required for cellular energy metabolism
3. Calcitriol	**c.** Needed for metabolism of glucose, fat, and protein
4. Phosphate	**d.** Regulates the ECF volume
5. Magnesium	**e.** Maintenance of the osmotic integrity of cells

3. The effective circulating volume is the major regulator of water balance in the body. What else does it regulate?

a. Sodium

b. Magnesium

c. Calcium

d. Potassium

4. Psychogenic polydipsia is most commonly seen in people with schizophrenia. It is a disease that involves compulsive water drinking without thirst and excessive urine output. It may be worsened by things that cause by excessive ADH secretion. What may be reasons that there is excessive ADH secretion in the body?

a. Excessive sleeping combined with irregular eating

b. Antipsychotic medications and smoking

c. An increased need in the aquaporin channel and coffee drinking

d. Antipsychotic medications and coffee drinking

5. There are two types of diabetes insipidus (DI), neurogenic and nephrogenic. In nephrogenic DI there is an inability of the kidney to concentrate urine and to conserve free water. Nephrogenic DI can be either genetic or acquired. What are the causes of nephrogenic DI?

a. Head injury and cranial surgery

b. Oral antidiabetic drugs and smoking

c. Lithium and hypokalemia

d. Hypocalcemia and hypernatremia

6. In a person with fluid volume deficit, there is a dehydration of brain and nerve cells. What can occur if fluid volume deficit is corrected to rapidly?

a. Nerve cells absorb too much sodium and cease to function

b. Brain cells shut down to prevent cerebral edema

c. Fluid volume increases at a rate the body cannot tolerate

d. Cerebral edema occurs with potentially severe neurologic impairment

7. Potassium is the major cation in the body. It plays many important roles, including the excitability of nerves and muscles. Where is this action particularly important?

a. The heart

b. The brain

c. The lungs

d. The liver

8. Vitamin D, officially classified as a vitamin, functions as a hormone in the body. What other hormone is necessary in the body for vitamin D to work?

a. Thyroid hormone

b. Parathyroid hormone

c. Antidiuretic hormone

d. Angiotensin-II

9. The sodium-phosphate cotransporter (NPT2) creates the action by which phosphate is reabsorbed from the filtrate in the proximal tubule. NPT2 is inhibited by phosphatonin. What condition can cause an overproduction of phosphatonin resulting in hypophosphatemia?

a. Tumor-induced osteomyelitis

b. Tumor-induced hypopituitarism

c. Tumor-induced syndrome of antidiuretic hormone

d. Tumor-induced osteomalacia

10. Magnesium levels are important indicators to a variety of bodily functions. What is severe hypermagnesemia associated with?

a. Muscle and respiratory paralysis

b. Cardiac arrest and 2° pulmonary paralysis

c. Complete heart block and cardiac arrythmias

d. Cardiac arrythmias and respiratory paralysis

11. To calculate the H_2CO_3 content of the blood, you need to measure the P_{CO_2} (partial pressure of CO_2) by its solubility coefficient. What is the solubility coefficient of CO_2?

a. 0.03

b. 0.3

c. 0.04

d. 0.4

12. The body regulates the pH of its fluids by what mechanism? (Mark all that apply.)
    a. Chemical buffer systems of the body fluids
    b. The liver
    c. The lungs
    d. The cardiovascular system
    e. The kidneys

13. By reabsorbing HCO_3 from the glomerular filtrate and excreting H^+ from the fixed acids that result from lipid and protein metabolism, the kidneys work to return or maintain the pH of the blood to normal or near-normal values. How long can this mechanism function when there is a change in the pH of body fluids?
    a. Minutes
    b. Hours
    c. Days
    d. Weeks

14. Laboratory tests give us very valuable information about what is happening in the body. What laboratory test is a good indicator of the how the buffer systems in the body are working?
    a. Acid-base test
    b. Urine acidity test
    c. H^+ level test
    d. Base excess or deficit test

15. There are both metabolic and respiratory effects on the acid-base balance in the body. How do metabolic disorders change the pH of the body?
    a. Alter the plasma H_{CO_3}
    b. Alter urine H^+ content
    c. Alter CO_2 levels in the lungs
    d. Alter O_2 levels in the major organ systems

16. The body has built-in compensatory mechanisms that take over when correction of pH is not possible or cannot be immediately achieved. What are these compensatory mechanisms considered?
    a. Long-term measures that back up first-line correction mechanisms
    b. Interim measures that permit survival
    c. Short-term measures that depend on first-line correction mechanisms
    d. Ways to correct the primary disorder

17. Metabolic acidosis has four main causes. Which laboratory test is used to determine the cause of metabolic acidosis?
    a. Acid-base deficit
    b. Arterial blood gas
    c. Anion gap
    d. Serum bicarbonate

18. A change in the pH of the body affects all organ systems. When the pH falls to less than 7. 0, what can occur in the cardiovascular system? (Mark all that apply?)
    a. Vasodilate the vascular bed, causing the client to go into shock
    b. Vasoconstrict the vascular bed to preserve the primary organs
    c. Increase cardiac contractility, causing cardiac dysrhythmias
    d. Reduce cardiac contractility, causing cardiac dysrhythmias

19. Respiratory acidosis occurs at a time when the plasma pH falls below 7.35, and arterial P_{CO_2} rises above 50 mm Hg. Because CO_2 easily crosses the blood-brain barrier, what signs and symptoms of respiratory acidosis might you see? (Mark all that apply.)
    a. Irritability
    b. Muscle twitching
    c. Psychological disturbances
    d. Seizures
    e. Psychotic breaks

20. Respiratory alkalosis is caused by hyperventilation, which is recognized as a respiratory rate in excess of that which maintains normal plasma P_{CO_2} levels. What is a common cause of respiratory alkalosis?
    a. Hyperventilation syndrome
    b. Hypoventilation syndrome
    c. Cluster breathing
    d. Kussmaul breathing

Stress and Adaptation

SECTION I: LEARNING OBJECTIVES

1. Cite Cannon's four features of homeostasis.

2. Describe the components of a control system, including the function of a negative feedback system.

3. State Selye's definition of stress.

4. Define *stressor.*

5. Explain the interactions among components of the nervous system in mediating the stress response.

6. Describe the stress responses of the neuroendocrine and immune, and the musculoskeletal system.

7. Explain the purpose of adaptation.

8. List factors that influence a person's adaptive capacity.

9. Contrast anatomic and physiologic reserve.

10. Propose a way by which social support may serve to buffer challenges to adaptation.

11. Describe the physiologic and psychological effects of a chronic stress response.

12. Describe the three states characteristic of posttraumatic stress disorder.

13. List five nonpharmacologic methods of treating stress.

SECTION II: ASSESSING YOUR UNDERSTANDING

Activity A *Fill in the blanks.*

1. The ability of the body to function and maintain _____ under conditions of change in the internal and external environment depends on the thousands of _____ control systems that regulate body function.

2. _____ is achieved only through a system of carefully coordinated physiologic processes that oppose change.

3. Most control systems in the body operate by _____ feedback mechanisms.

4. Selye described _____ as a state manifested by a specific syndrome of the body developed in response to any stimuli that made an intense systemic demand on it.

5. Stress may contribute directly to the production or exacerbation of a _____ .

6. There is evidence that the _____ axis, the _____ hormonal, and the _____ nervous systems are differentially activated depending on the type and intensity of the stressor.

7. Human beings, because of their highly developed nervous system and intellect, usually have alternative mechanisms for _____ and have the ability to control many aspects of their environment.

8. The means used to attain this balance are called _____.

9. _____ is considered a restorative function in which energy is restored and tissues are regenerated.

10. _____ is commonly used in excess and can suppress the immune system.

Activity B *Consider the following figure.*

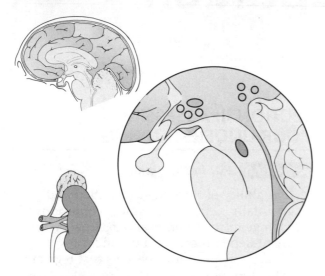

1. In the above figure, trace the activation of the hypothalamus to the release of corticotrophin to the effect on the adrenal gland and to the final release of cortisol. Also, label the locus ceruleus.

Activity C *Match the key terms in Column A with their definitions in Column B.*

Column A

____ **1.** Conditioning factors

____ **2.** Antidiuretic hormone

____ **3.** Baroreflex

____ **4.** Allostasis

____ **5.** Physiologic reserve

____ **6.** Angiotensin II

____ **7.** Hardiness

____ **8.** Cortisol

____ **9.** ACTH

____ **10.** Coping mechanisms

Column B

a. A personality characteristic that includes a sense of having control over the environment

b. Factors used to create a new balance between a stressor and the ability to deal with it

c. Physiologic changes in the neuro-endocrine, autonomic, and immune systems in response to real or perceived challenges to homeostasis

d. Stressor that produces a response

e. Enhances stress-induced release of vasopressin from the posterior pituitary

f. Ability of body systems to increase their function given the need to adapt

g. Regulation of heart rate and vasomotor tone

h. Suppresses osteoblast activity, hematopoiesis, and protein synthesis

i. Stimulates the adrenal gland to synthesize and secrete the glucocorticoid hormones

j. Increases water retention by the kidneys and produces vasoconstriction of blood vessels

Activity D *Briefly answer the following.*

1. How does the body regulate and maintain homeostasis? Give one example.

_____

_____

_____

2. Describe the stages of general adaptation syndrome.

_____

_____

_____

3. Stress will activate numerous body systems. Many are based in neuroendocrine activity. List the effects of neuroendocrine activation in response to stress.

_____

_____

_____

4. Trained athletes use physiological and anatomic reserve to achieve top-level performance. Explain and give examples of how this is accomplished.

_____

_____

_____

5. What are the physiologic and anatomic causes of posttraumatic stress disorder?

_____

_____

_____

SECTION III: PRACTICING FOR NCLEX

Activity E *Answer the following questions.*

1. The control systems of the body act in many ways to maintain homeostasis. These control systems regulate the functions of the cell and integrate the functions of different organ systems. What else do they do?
   a. Control life processes
   b. Feed cells under stress
   c. Act on invading organisms
   d. Shut down the body at death

2. It has long been known that our bodies need a stable internal environment to function optimally. What serves to fulfill this need?
   a. Organ systems
   b. Control systems
   c. Biochemical messenger systems
   d. Neurovascular systems

3. The general adaptation syndrome is what occurs in the body in response to stressors. When the body's defenses are depleted, signs of "wear and tear" or systemic damage appear. Which of the following diseases have been linked to stress and are thought to be encouraged by the body itself when it can no longer adapt to the stress in a healthy manner?
   a. Psychotic disorders
   b. Osteogenesis sarcomas
   c. Rheumatic disorders
   d. Infections of the head and neck

4. A number of responses occur in the body to the release of neurohormones when the body encounters stress, including which of the following?
   a. Increase in appetite
   b. Decreased cerebral blood flow
   c. Decrease in awareness
   d. Inhibition of reproductive function

5. Chronic and excessive activation of the stress response has been shown to play a part in the development of long-term health problems. The stress response can also result from chronic illness. Which health problems have been linked to a stress response that is chronic and excessive?
   a. Suicide and immune disorders
   b. Depression and renal disease
   c. Immune disorders and brain tumors
   d. Suicide and thrombosis in the extremities

6. Our body's response to psychological perceived threats is not regulated to the same degree as our body's response to physiologic perceived threats. The psychological responses may be:
   a. Appropriate and limited.
   b. Inappropriate and sustained.
   c. Regulated by a positive feedback system
   d. The result of a baroreflex-mediated response

7. Adaptation implies that an individual has successfully created a new balance between the stressor and the ability to deal with it. The safety margin for adaptation of most body systems is considerably greater than that needed for normal activities. The method of adaptation that allows the body to live with only one of a pair of organs (i.e., one lung or one kidney) is called?
   a. Genetic endowment
   b. Physiologic reserve
   c. Anatomic reserve
   d. Health status

8. Psychosocial factors can impact the body's response to stress either positively or negatively. It has been shown that social networks play a part in the psychosocial and physical integrity of a person. How do social networks affect how a body deals with stress?

   a. By stepping in and making decisions for the person
   b. By reapportioning the finances of the person
   c. By mobilizing the resources of the person
   d. By protecting the person from other internal stressors

9. The acute stress response can be detrimental in people with pre-existing physical or mental health problems. In which of these clients could the acute stress response cause further problems?

   a. Client who is post resection of a brain tumor
   b. Client who is schizophrenic and off his or her medications
   c. Client with a broken femur
   d. Client with heart disease

10. Some clients experience chronic activation of the stress response as a result of experiencing a severe trauma. Which of the following is the disorder that can occur when the stress response is chronically activated?

    a. Posttraumatic stress disorder
    b. Chronic renal insufficiency
    c. Schizophrenia
    d. Postdelivery depression

11. In a _____ organism it is necessary for the composition of the internal environment to be compatible with the survival needs of the individual cells.

12. Selye suggested that stress could have positive influences on the body, and these periods of positive stress are called _____.

13. The first goal of treatment of stress disorders is to aid clients in avoiding those coping mechanisms that cause their health to be at risk. Secondly, the treatment of stress disorders should engage them in alternative strategies that reduce stress. Which are non-pharmacologic treatments of stress disorders? Select all that apply.

    a. Lithium therapy
    b. Music therapy
    c. Education therapy
    d. Massage therapy

14. Match the following terms with their definitions.

Term	Definition
1. Corticotropin-releasing factor	a. Increased corticosteroid production and atrophy of the thymus
2. Fight-or-flight response	b. Endocrine regulator of pituitary and adrenal activity and neurotransmitter involved in autonomic nervous system activity, metabolism, and behavior
3. Allostatic load	c. Physiologic changes in the neuroendocrine, autonomic, and immune systems occurring in response to real or perceived challenges to homeostasis
4. Endocrine-immune interactions	d. Most rapid of the stress responses, representing the basic survival response

15. It is thought that there is an interaction between the neuroendocrine system and the immune system. It has been postulated that these interactions play a significant role in autoimmune diseases. These systems have what in common? Select all that apply.

    a. They share common signal pathways.
    b. Hormones and neuropeptides can change what immune cells do.
    c. Mediators of the immune system can modify neuroendocrine function.
    d. They are symbiotic systems and cannot work without each other.

CHAPTER 10

Disorders of Nutritional Status

SECTION I: LEARNING OBJECTIVES

1. Define *nutritional status*.

2. Define *calorie* and state the number of calories derived from the oxidation of 1 g of protein, fat, or carbohydrate.

3. Describe the function of adipose tissue in terms of energy storage.

4. State the purpose of the Recommended Dietary Allowance of calories, proteins, fats, carbohydrates, vitamins, and minerals.

5. Describe methods used for a nutritional assessment.

6. State the factors used in determining body mass index and explain its use in evaluating body weight in terms of undernutrition and overnutrition.

7. Define and discuss the causes of obesity and health risks associated with obesity.

8. Differentiate upper and lower body obesity and their implications in terms of health risk.

9. Discuss the treatment of obesity in terms of diet, behavior modification, exercise, social support, pharmacotherapy, and surgical methods.

10. Explain the use of body mass index in evaluating body weight in terms of overnutrition.

11. List the major causes of malnutrition and starvation.

12. State the difference between protein-calorie starvation (i.e., marasmus) and protein malnutrition (i.e., kwashiorkor).

13. Compare the eating disorders and complications associated with anorexia nervosa and the binge-purge syndrome.

SECTION II: ASSESSING YOUR UNDERSTANDING

Activity A *Fill in the blanks.*

1. _____ describes the condition of the body related to the availability and use of nutrients.

2. _____ is the organized process through which nutrients such as carbohydrates, fats, and proteins are broken down, transformed, or otherwise converted into cellular energy.

3. Energy expenditure can be increased by increasing _____ and/or nonexercise activity thermogenesis.

4. More than 90% of body energy is stored in the _____ tissues of the body.

5. _____ acts at the level of the hypothalamus to decrease food intake and increase energy expenditure through an increase in thermogenesis and sympathetic nervous system activity.

6. The _____ defines the intakes that meet the nutrient needs of almost all healthy persons in a specific age and sex group.

7. _____ (% DV) tells the consumer what percent of the DV one serving of a food or supplement supplies.

8. _____ are required for growth and maintenance of body tissues, enzymes and antibody formation, fluid and electrolyte balance, and nutrient transport.

9. The rate of protein breakdown can be estimated by measuring the amount of _____ in the urine.

10. The saturated fatty acids _____ blood cholesterol, whereas the monounsaturated and polyunsaturated fats _____ blood cholesterol.

11. Trans fatty acids _____ LDL cholesterol and _____ HDL cholesterol.

12. There is no specific dietary requirement for _____.

13. _____ are a group of organic compounds that act as catalysts in various chemical reactions.

14. _____ increases stool bulk and facilitates bowel movements.

15. The _____ contains the feeding center for hunger and satiety.

16. A decrease in blood _____ causes hunger.

17. _____ measurements provide a means for assessing body composition, particularly fat stores and skeletal muscle mass.

18. The _____ uses height and weight to determine healthy weight.

19. Studies have indicated that waist _____ at the abdomen is highly correlated with insulin resistance.

20. _____ is defined as having excess body fat, enlarged fat cells, and even an increased number of fat cells.

21. Research suggests that _____ may be a more important factor for morbidity and mortality than overweight or obesity.

22. _____ has been found to have little or no effect on metabolic variables, central obesity, or cardiovascular risk factors or future amount of weight loss.

23. There is convincing evidence that _____ physical activity decreases the risk of overweight and obesity.

24. _____ does afford significant weight loss, long-term weight loss maintenance, improved quality of life, decreased incidence of associated diseases, and decreased all-cause mortality.

25. Obesity is the most prevalent nutritional disorder affecting the _____ population in the United States.

26. _____ and _____ are conditions in which a person does not receive or is unable to use an adequate amount of nutrients for body function.

27. Protein and energy malnutrition represents a depletion of the body's lean tissues caused by _____ and/or catabolic stress.

28. The child with _____ has a wasted appearance, with loss of muscle mass, stunted growth, and loss of subcutaneous fat.

29. Bulimia nervosa is defined by _____ binge eating and activities including vomiting, fasting, excessive exercise, and use of diuretics, laxatives, or enemas to compensate for that behavior.

Activity B *Match the key terms in Column A with their definitions in Column B.*

1.

Column A	Column B
___ 1. Adipocytes	a. The amount of nitrogen taken in by way of protein is equivalent to the nitrogen excreted
___ 2. Skinfold thickness	
___ 3. Kwashiorkor	b. Malnutrition caused by inadequate protein intake in the presence of fair to good energy
___ 4. Calorie	
___ 5. Diet-induced thermogenesis	
___ 6. Metabolites	c. Chemical intermediates of metabolism
___ 7. Nitrogen balance	d. A reasonable assessment of body fat, particularly if taken at multiple sites
___ 8. Catabolism	

___ **9.** Resting energy equivalent

___ **10.** Kilocalorie

e. The amount of energy needed to raise the temperature of 1 kg of water by 1°C

f. Fat cells

g. Breakdown of complex molecules

h. Amount of heat or energy required to raise the temperature of 1 g of water by 1°C

i. Energy used by the body for the digestion, absorption, and assimilation

j. Used for predicting energy expenditure

2.

Column A

___ **1.** Anorexia nervosa

___ **2.** Ghrelin

___ **3.** Dermatitis

___ **4.** Triglycerides

___ **5.** Marasmus

___ **6.** Trans fatty acids

___ **7.** Macrominerals

Column B

a. Mixture of fatty acids and glycerol

b. Result of a deficiency of linoleic acid

c. Hormone that may stimulate hunger

d. Unsaturated oils are partially hydrogenated

e. Minerals present in large amounts in the body

f. Characterized by determined dieting, often accompanied by compulsive exercise

g. Protein and calorie deficiency

Activity C *Briefly answer the following.*

1. What are the two types of adipose tissue? How do they differ?

_____

_____

_____

2. How is bioimpedance preformed and what does it do?

_____

_____

_____

3. What are the nongenetic causes of obesity?

_____

_____

_____

4. What are the causes of anorexia?

_____

_____

_____

5. What are the criteria for the diagnosis of bulimia nervosa?

_____

_____

_____

6. Describe the criteria for binge eating.

_____

_____

_____

SECTION III: APPLYING YOUR KNOWLEDGE

Activity D *Consider the scenario and answer the questions.*

A 14-year-old girl is brought to the clinic by her mother for a sports physical. The young lady is 5 feet, 4 inches tall, weighs 95 pounds, and is considered to have a small frame. The nurse notes the client's weight and suspects an eating disorder.

1. What questions would be appropriate in the nursing history to assess for an eating disorder?

_____

_____

_____

2. The nurse knows that the DSM-IV-TR diagnostic criteria for anorexia nervosa include what?

_____

_____

_____

SECTION IV: PRACTICING FOR NCLEX

Activity E *Answer the following questions.*

1. Adipose tissue is now known to be both an endocrine and a paracrine organ because of the factors it secretes. What are these factors? (Mark all that apply.)
   a. Leptin
   b. Growth hormone
   c. Adipokines
   d. Insulin resistance factor
   e. Adiponectin

2. When nutritional requirements are needed for a specific group, what dietary requirements are used?
   a. Estimated average requirement
   b. Adequate intake
   c. Recommended Dietary Allowance
   d. Dietary Reference Intake

3. Fat is a necessary part of the diet. The Food and Nutrition Board has set what percent of fat as necessary in our diet?
   a. 10%
   b. 20%
   c. 30%
   d. 40%

4. It is the hypothalamus that tells us when we are hungry or full. Its message is mediated by input from the gastrointestinal tract. There are also centers in the hypothalamus that regulate energy balance and metabolism based on the secretion of what hormones?
   a. Cholecystokinin (CCK) and glucagon-like peptide-1 (GLP-1)
   b. Ghrelin and thyroid
   c. Thyroid and adrenocortical hormones
   d. Adrenocortical hormones and cholecystokinin (CCK)

5. The body mass index (BMI) is the measurement used to determine a person's healthy weight. A BMI between 18.5 and 24.9 is considered the lowest health risk in relation to the weight of a person. How is the BMI calculated?
   a. BMI = weight [pounds]/height [feet^2]
   b. BMI = weight [kg]/height [feet^2]
   c. BMI = weight [pounds]/height [meter^2]
   d. BMI = weight [kg]/height [meter^2]

6. Two types of obesity are recognized: upper body obesity and lower body obesity. How is the type of obesity determined?
   a. Waist/hip circumference
   b. Chest circumference/weight
   c. Chest/hip circumference
   d. Waist circumference/weight

7. Anorexia nervosa, bulimia nervosa, and binge-eating disorder are becoming more and more common, with assessments for these disorders being made as young 9 years of age. In the adult population, what means of controlling binge eating is most prevalent in men?
   a. Self-induced vomiting
   b. Compulsive exercise
   c. Laxative use
   d. Compulsive working

8. Childhood obesity has now been recognized as a major problem in the pediatric population. What diseases are pediatricians now seeing in their clients as a direct result of childhood obesity?
   a. Type I diabetes
   b. Dyslipidemia
   c. Hypotension
   d. Psychosocial acceptance

9. Malnutrition is not something that is considered common in the general population in the United States. However, certain populations are more prone to malnutrition than others. One of these populations is hospitalized patients. Why is this true?
   a. Appetites are increased by fever and pain
   b. Special diets can increase appetite
   c. Pain and medications can decrease appetite
   d. Only healthy diets are served in hospitals.

Disorders of White Blood Cells and Lymphoid Tissues

SECTION I: LEARNING OBJECTIVES

1. List the cells and tissues of the hematopoietic system.

2. Trace the development of the different blood cells from their origin in the pluripotent bone marrow stem cell to their circulation in the bloodstream.

3. Define the terms *leukopenia, neutropenia,* and *aplastic anemia.*

4. Cite two general causes of neutropenia.

5. Describe the mechanism of symptom production in neutropenia.

6. Use the concepts regarding the central and peripheral lymphoid tissues to describe the site of origin of the malignant lymphomas, leukemias, and plasma cell dyscrasias.

7. Explain how changes in chromosomal structure and gene function can contribute to the development of malignant lymphomas, leukemias, and plasma cell dyscrasias.

8. Contrast and compare the signs and symptoms of non-Hodgkin and Hodgkin lymphomas.

9. Describe the measures used in treatment of non-Hodgkin and Hodgkin lymphomas.

10. Use the predominant white blood cell type and classification of acute or chronic to describe the four general types of leukemia.

11. Explain the manifestations of leukemia in terms of altered cell differentiation.

12. Describe the following complications of acute leukemia and its treatment: leukostasis, tumor lysis syndrome, hyperuricemia, and blast crisis.

13. Relate the clonal expansion of immunoglobulin-producing plasma cells and accompanying destructive skeletal changes that occur with multiple myeloma in terms of manifestations and clinical course of the disorder.

SECTION II: ASSESSING YOUR UNDERSTANDING

Activity A *Fill in the blanks.*

1. The white blood cells include the _____, monocyte/macrophages, and lymphocytes.

2. T lymphocytes mature in the _____.

3. The B lymphocytes differentiate to form immunoglobulin-producing _____ cells.

4. Another population of lymphocytes includes the _____ cells, which do not share the specificity or characteristics of the T or the B lymphocytes, but have the ability to lyse target cells.

5. The granulocyte and monocyte cell lines derive from the _____ stem cells and the lymphocytes from the _____ stem cells.

6. The body's lymphatic system consists of the lymphatic vessels, lymphoid tissue and lymph nodes, _____, and _____.

7. T lymphocytes travel to the thymus where they differentiate into _____ helper T cells and _____ cytotoxic T cells.

8. In _____ anemia, all of the myeloid stem cells are affected, resulting in anemia, thrombocytopenia, and agranulocytosis.

9. _____ denotes a virtual absence of neutrophils.

10. Early signs of infection of _____ include mild skin lesions, stomatitis, pharyngitis, and diarrhea.

11. _____ is a self-limiting lymphoproliferative disorder caused by the Epstein-Barr virus.

12. _____ can involve lymphocytes, granulocytes, and other blood cells.

13. _____ originate in peripheral lymphoid structures such as the lymph nodes where B and T lymphocytes undergo differentiation and proliferation.

14. _____-cell lymphomas are the most common type of lymphoma in the Western world.

15. Four variants of classical Hodgkin lymphoma have been described: _____ sclerosis, mixed cellularity, _____-rich, and lymphocyte depleted.

16. Persons with _____ are staged according to the number of lymph nodes that are involved, whether the lymph nodes are on one or both sides of the diaphragm, and whether there is disseminated disease involving the bone marrow, liver, lung, or skin.

17. The _____ are malignant neoplasms of cells originally derived from hematopoietic precursor cells.

18. The _____ leukemias involve immature lymphocytes and their progenitors that originate in the bone marrow but infiltrate the spleen, lymph nodes, CNS, and other tissues.

19. Cytogenetic studies have shown that recurrent chromosomal changes occur in over half of all cases of _____.

20. _____ usually have a sudden and stormy onset with signs and symptoms related to depressed bone marrow function.

21. There are two types of acute leukemia: acute _____ and acute _____.

22. _____ are malignancies involving proliferation of more fully differentiated myeloid and lymphoid cells.

23. Chronic lymphocytic leukemia, a clonal malignancy of _____, is the most common form of leukemia in adults in the Western world.

24. Severe congenital neutropenia is known as _____ syndrome.

25. It is generally believed that chronic myelogenous leukemia (CML) develops when a single, pluripotential, hematopoietic stem cell acquires a _____ chromosome.

26. _____ are characterized by expansion of a single clone of immunoglobulin-producing plasma cells and a resultant increase in serum levels of a single monoclonal immunoglobulin or its fragments.

27. The development of _____ lesions in multiple myeloma is thought to be related to an increase in expression by osteoblasts of the receptor activator of the nuclear factor-κB.

28. One of the characteristics resulting from the proliferating osteoclasts in multiple myeloma is the unregulated production of a monoclonal antibody referred to as the _____.

Activity B *Match the key terms in Column A with their definitions in Column B.*

Column A

____ **1.** Heterophil

____ **2.** Leukopoiesis

____ **3.** Burkitt lymphoma

____ **4.** Non-Hodgkin lymphomas

____ **5.** Neutropenia

____ **6.** Reed-Sternberg cells

____ **7.** Kostmann syndrome

____ **8.** Philadelphia chromosome

____ **9.** Blast cells

____ **10.** ZAP-70

Column B

a. Neoplasm involving B or T cells

b. Translocation on chromosome 8

c. Found in more than 90% of persons with CML

d. Production of white blood cells

e. Used for the diagnosis of infectious mononucleosis

f. An abnormally low number of neutrophils

g. Immature precursor cells

h. Definitive marker for Hodgkin lymphoma

i. An arrest in myeloid maturation

j. Normal T-cell protein, abnormal in chronic lymphocytic leukemia (CLL)

Activity C *Briefly answer the following.*

1. Neutrophils are very important as a first line of defense against viral/bacterial infection. Explain what a neutrophil does and the condition that results from a deficiency of neutrophils.

_____

_____

_____

2. Describe the pathogenesis of infectious mononucleosis.

_____

_____

_____

3. Describe the clinical manifestations of non-Hodgkin lymphoma (NHL) and relate the symptoms to the pathologic cause.

_____

_____

_____

4. There are two major differences between Hodgkin lymphoma and NHL. Differentiate Hodgkin lymphoma from NHL.

_____

_____

_____

5. What are the potential causes of leukemia?

_____

_____

_____

6. Compare and contrast acute lymphocytic leukemia (ALL) and acute myelocytic leukemia (AML).

_____

_____

_____

7. Describe the progression of CML through its three stages.

_____

_____

_____

8. What are the potential causes of multiple myeloma?

_____

_____

_____

SECTION III: APPLYING YOUR KNOWLEDGE

Activity D *Consider the scenario and answer the questions.*

Lucy, a 2 year old, has been diagnosed with ALL and has been admitted to your unit for treatment. How would you answer when the parents ask,

1. "What caused Lucy's leukemia?"

_____

_____

_____

2. "What kind of treatment will Lucy have?"

_____

_____

_____

SECTION IV: PRACTICING FOR NCLEX

Activity E *Answer the following questions.*

1. Progenitor cells, or parent cells, for myelopoiesis and lymphopoiesis are derived from which of the following?
   a. Pluripotent stem cells
   b. Unipotent cells
   c. Multipotential progenitor cells
   d. Myeloproliferative cells

2. What is the name of the region of the lymph nodes that contain most of the T cells?
   a. The primary follicles
   b. The paracortex
   c. The secondary follicles
   d. The primary cortex

3. Kostmann syndrome is a severe congenital neutropenia. Which of the following is characteristic of this condition?
   a. Bone marrow disorders
   b. Severe viral infections
   c. Autoimmune disorders
   d. Severe bacterial infections

4. Drug-induced neutropenia is a disease that has significantly increased in incidence over the last several decades. What is the attributing factor in the increased incidence of drug-induced neutropenia?
   a. Treatment of cancer by chemotherapeutic drugs
   b. The decrease in the use of street drugs
   c. The destruction of tissue cells by cocaine
   d. The new drugs developed to treat autoimmune diseases

5. Infectious mononucleosis is a lymphoproliferative disorder caused by the EBV that is usually self-limiting and nonlethal. Which of the following complications can arise during this mostly benign disease?
   a. Peripheral nerve palsies
   b. Rupture of the spleen
   c. Rupture of the lymph nodes
   d. Severe bacterial infections

6. You are presenting an educational event to a group of cancer patients. What would you cite as the most commonly occurring hematologic cancer?
   a. Acute lymphocytic leukemia
   b. Hodgkin lymphomas
   c. Non-Hodgkin lymphomas
   d. Mantle cell lymphoma

7. Endemic Burkitt lymphoma occurs in regions of Africa where what other infections are common?
   a. Herpes zoster and Epstein Barr
   b. Herpes zoster and streptococcal
   c. Malaria and streptococcal
   d. Epstein Barr and malaria

8. ALL and AML are two distinct disorders with similar presenting clinical features. What clinical feature do ALL and AML share?
   a. Night sweats
   b. Weight gain
   c. High fever
   d. Polycythemia

9. Definitive diagnosis of multiple myeloma includes the triad of bone marrow plasmacytosis, lytic bone lesions, and what?
   a. Oligoclonal bands in the CSF
   b. Bence-Jones proteins in the urine
   c. Serum M-protein depression
   d. BCR-ABL fusion protein in serum

10. CLL commonly causes hypogammaglobulinemia. This makes clients with CLL more susceptible to infection. What are the most common infectious organisms that attack clients with CLL?
    a. Acne rosacea
    b. *Pseudomonas aeruginosa*
    c. *Staphylococcus aureus*
    d. *Escherichia coli*

11. Large granular lymphocytes, or natural killer cells, have the ability to _____ target cells.

12 Which lymphatic tissue is associated with mucous membranes and called mucus-associated lymphatic tissue, or MALT? (Mark all that apply.)
    a. Genitourinary systems and central nervous system
    b. Respiratory passages and cardiovascular system
    c. Alimentary canal and genitourinary systems
    d. Cardiovascular system central nervous system

13. You are speaking to a group of genetic students touring your hospital's laboratory. You talk about the possibility of a genetic predisposition for the leukemias being suggested because of the increased incidence of the disease among a number of congenital disorders. Which congenital disorders are these? (Mark all that apply.)
    a. Cushing syndrome
    b. Neurofibromatosis
    c. Fanconi anemia
    d. Down syndrome
    e. Prader-Willi syndrome

14. Tumor lysis syndrome, the massive necrosis of malignant cells that can occur during the initial phase of treatment of ALL, can lead to metabolic disorders that are life-threatening. Which metabolic disorders can occur because of tumor lysis syndrome? (Mark all that apply.)
    a. Hyperuricemia
    b. Hypokalemia
    c. Acidosis
    d. Alkalosis
    e. Hypocalcemia

15. Secondary malignancies in survivors of Hodgkin lymphoma have been attributed mainly to _____ therapy.

CHAPTER 12

Disorders of Hemostasis

SECTION I: LEARNING OBJECTIVES

1. Describe the five stages of hemostasis.

2. Explain the formation of the platelet plug.

3. State the purpose of blood coagulation.

4. State the function of clot retraction.

5. Trace the process of fibrinolysis.

6. Compare normal and abnormal clotting.

7. Describe the causes and effects of increased platelet function.

8. State two conditions that contribute to increased clotting activity.

9. State the mechanisms of drug-induced thrombocytopenia and idiopathic thrombocytopenia and the differing features of the disorders in terms of onset and resolution.

10. Describe the manifestations of thrombocytopenia.

11. Characterize the role of vitamin K in coagulation.

12. State three common defects of coagulation factors and the causes of each.

13. Differentiate between the mechanisms of bleeding in hemophilia A and von Willebrand disease.

14. Describe the effect of vascular disorders on hemostasis.

15. Explain the physiologic basis of acute disseminated intravascular coagulation.

SECTION II: ASSESSING YOUR UNDERSTANDING

Activity A *Fill in the blanks.*

1. The term _____ refers to the stoppage of blood flow.

2. Platelets have a cell membrane, but have no _____ and cannot reproduce.

3. The platelet shape is maintained by microtubules and _____ and _____ filaments that support the cell membrane.

4. The release of _____ from platelets results in the proliferation and growth of vascular endothelial cells, smooth muscle cells, and fibroblasts, and is important in vessel repair.

5. The combined actions of _____ and _____ lead to the expansion of the enlarging platelet aggregate, which becomes the primary hemostatic plug.

6. The _____ is a step-wise process resulting in the conversion of the soluble plasma protein, fibrinogen, into fibrin.

7. Most of the coagulation factors are proteins synthesized in the _____.

8. It has been suggested that some of these natural anticoagulants may play a role in the bleeding that occurs with _____.

9. _____ represents an exaggerated form of hemostasis that predisposes to thrombosis and blood vessel occlusion.

10. _____, elevated levels of blood lipids and cholesterol, hemodynamic stress, diabetes mellitus, and immune mechanisms may cause vessel damage, platelet adherence, and, eventually, thrombosis.

11. The common clinical manifestations of essential _____ are thrombosis and hemorrhage.

12. In persons with inherited defects in factor V, the mutant factor Va cannot be inactivated by _____.

13. Secondary factors that lead to increased _____ and thrombosis are venous stasis due to prolonged bed rest and immobility, myocardial infarction, cancer, hyperestrogenic states, and oral contraceptives.

14. _____ from mucous membranes of the nose, mouth, gastrointestinal tract, and uterine cavity is characteristic of platelet bleeding disorders.

15. A reduction in platelet number is referred to as _____.

16. _____ destruction may be caused by antiplatelet antibodies, resulting in thrombocytopenia.

17. _____ thrombocytopenic purpura results in platelet antibody formation and excess destruction of platelets.

18. _____ may result from inherited disorders of adhesion or acquired defects caused by drugs, disease, or extracorporeal circulation.

19. Hemophilia A is an _____ recessive disorder that primarily affects males.

20. In liver disease, synthesis of these _____ is reduced, and bleeding may result.

21. Vitamin C deficiency results in _____, where poor collagen synthesis and failure of the endothelial cells to be cemented together properly causes a fragile wall and bleeding.

22. Common clinical conditions that may cause _____ include obstetrical disorders, massive trauma, shock, sepsis and malignant disease.

Activity B *Consider the following figure.*

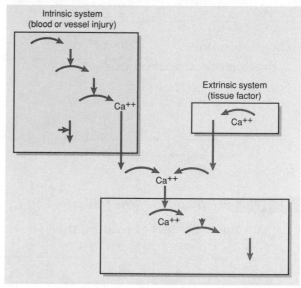

1. In the above figure, place the activated factors and proteins in their respective places: XIIa, XIa, IXa, Xa, VIIa, thrombin, prothrombin, fibrinogen, and fibrin.

Activity C *Match the key terms in Column A with their definitions in Column B.*

Column A

____ 1. Thrombin

____ 2. Fibrinolysis

____ 3. Thrombo-cytosis

____ 4. Thromboxane A2

____ 5. Plasmin

____ 6. Antiphospho-lipid syndrome

____ 7. Megakaryocytes

____ 8. Factor x

____ 9. Hemophilia a

____ 10. Thrombocy-topenia

Column B

a. Breaks down fibrin

b. May be caused by aplastic anemia

c. Enzyme that converts fibrinogen to fibrin

d. Factor VIII deficiency

e. Stimulates vasoconstriction

f. Autoantibodies that result in increased coagulation activity

g. Process of blood clot dissolution

h. Converts prothrombin to thrombin

i. Describes elevations in the platelet count above 1,000,000/μL.

j. Thrombocyte precursor

Activity D *Write the correct sequence of the terms listed in the boxes provided below.*

a. Clot retraction

b. Clot dissolution

c. Activation of coagulation cascade

d. Formation of platelet plug

e. Vessel spasm

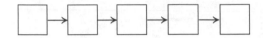

Activity E *Briefly answer the following.*

1. Explain the five stages of hemostasis.

   _____

   _____

   _____

2. Describe the process of platelet activation and plug formation.

   _____

   _____

   _____

3. The coagulation cascade is activated in multiple ways and is integral in maintaining hemostasis. Explain the general stimulation and end results.

   _____

   _____

   _____

4. There are many causes of bleeding disorders. One of the more clinically relevant is drug-induced thrombocytopenia. Explain how drugs such as quinine, quinidine, and certain sulfa-containing antibiotics may induce thrombocytopenia.

   _____

   _____

   _____

5. Disseminated intravascular coagulation is a severe condition that is characterized by widespread coagulation and bleeding. Explain how the disease is initiated and describe its progression.

   _____

   _____

   _____

SECTION III: PRACTICING FOR NCLEX

Activity F *Answer the following questions.*

1. Many different proteins, enzymes, and hormones are involved in maintaining hemostasis. Which protein is required for platelet adhesion?

   a. von Willebrand factor

   b. Growth factors

   c. Ionized calcium

   d. Platelet factor 4

2. There are two pathways that can be activated by the coagulation process. One pathway begins when factor XII is activated. The other pathway begins when there is trauma to a blood vessel. What are these pathways?

   a. Clotting and bleeding pathways

   b. Extrinsic and intrinsic pathways

   c. Inner and outer pathways

   d. Factor and trauma pathways

3. Anticoagulant drugs prevent thromboembolic disorders. How does warfarin, one of the anticoagulant drugs, act on the body?

   a. Alters vitamin K, reducing its ability to participate in the coagulation of the blood

   b. Increases prothrombin

   c. Increases vitamin K–dependent factors in the liver

   d. Increases procoagulation factors

4. Heparin is an anticoagulant given by injection to prevent the formation of blood clots. How does heparin work?
   a. Binds to factor X
   b. Promotes the inactivation of clotting factors
   c. Binds to factor Xa
   d. Promotes the inactivation of factor VIII

5. The process of clot retraction squeezes serum from the clot, thereby joining the edges of the broken vessel. Through the action of actin and myosin, filaments in platelets contribute to clot retraction. Failure of clot retraction is indicative of what?
   a. Absence of factor Xa
   b. A low platelet count
   c. An overabundance of factor Xa
   d. A high platelet count

6. Thrombocytosis is used to describe elevations in the platelet count above $1,000,000/\mu L$. It is either a primary or a secondary thrombocytosis. Secondary thrombocytosis can occur as a reactive process due to what?
   a. Crohn disease
   b. Lyme disease
   c. Hirschsprung disease
   d. Megacolon

7. A 57-year-old man is diagnosed with thrombocytopenia. The nurse knows that thrombocytopenia refers to a decrease in the number of circulating platelets. The nurse also knows that thrombocytopenia can result from what?
   a. Decreased platelet production
   b. Increased platelet survival
   c. Decreased sequestration of platelets
   d. Increased platelet production

8. A young man has been diagnosed with hemophilia and the nurse is planning his discharge teaching. She knows to include what in her discharge teaching?
   a. Only use nonsteroidal anti-inflammatory drugs for mild pain
   b. Prevent trauma to the body
   c. The client will be on IV factor VIII therapy at home
   d. It is an X-linked recessive disorder

9. A teenage girl, seen in the clinic, is diagnosed with nonthrombocytopenic purpura. The girl states, "You have taken a lot of blood from me. Which of my tests came back abnormal?" How should the nurse respond?
   a. Your complete blood count (CBC) with differential showed a shift to the left.
   b. Your CBC with differential showed you do not have enough iron
   c. Your CBC with differential showed a normal platelet count
   d. Your CBC with differential showed a normal hematocrit

10. Disseminated intravascular coagulation is a grave coagulopathy resulting from the overstimulation of clotting and anticlotting processes in response to what?
    a. Disease or injury
    b. Septicemia and acute hypertension
    c. Neoplasms and nonpoisonous snakebites
    d. Severe trauma and acute hypertension

11. The five stages of hemostasis are given below in random order. Put them into their correct order.
    A. Clot dissolution
    B. Blood coagulation
    C. Vessel spasm
    D. Clot retraction
    E. Formation of platelet plug
    a. CABED
    b. ACBDE
    c. CEBDA
    d. ECDBA

12. The coagulation cascade is the third component of the hemostatic process. It is a stepwise process resulting in the conversion of the soluble plasma protein, fibrinogen, into fibrin. This multistep process ensures that a massive episode of _____ clotting does not occur by chance.

13. _____ is a natural mucopolysaccharide anticoagulant that occurs in the lungs and intestinal mucosa.

14. When platelets adhere to the vessel wall, they release growth factors that cause smooth muscle to grow. This is a major factor in causing atherosclerosis. What are the factors that influence platelets to adhere to the vessel wall? (Mark all that apply.)

    a. Hemodynamic stress
    b. High cholesterol
    c. Diabetes
    d. Low blood lipids
    e. Smoking

15. In a client with DIC, microemboli form, causing obstruction of blood vessels and tissue hypoxia. Common clinical signs may be due to what? (Mark all that apply.)

    a. Circulatory failure
    b. Immunologic failure
    c. Renal failure
    d. Right ventricular failure
    e. Respiratory failure

CHAPTER 13

Disorders of Red Blood Cells

SECTION I: LEARNING OBJECTIVES

1. Trace the development of a red blood cell (RBC) from erythroblast to erythrocyte.

2. Discuss the function of iron in the formation of hemoglobin.

3. Describe the formation, transport, and elimination of bilirubin.

4. State the meaning of the RBC count, percentage of reticulocytes, hemoglobin, hematocrit, mean corpuscular volume, and mean corpuscular hemoglobin concentration as it relates to the diagnosis of anemia.

5. Describe the manifestations of anemia and their mechanisms.

6. Explain the difference between intravascular and extravascular hemolysis.

7. Compare the hemoglobinopathies associated with sickle cell disease and thalassemia.

8. Explain the cause of sickling in sickle cell disease.

9. Cite common causes of iron-deficiency anemia in infancy, adolescence, and adulthood.

10. Describe the relation between vitamin B_{12} deficiency and megaloblastic anemia.

11. List three causes of aplastic anemia.

12. Compare characteristics of the RBCs in acute blood loss, hereditary spherocytosis, sickle cell disease, iron-deficiency anemia, and aplastic anemia.

13. Differentiate red cell antigens from antibodies in persons with type A, B, AB, or O blood.

14. Explain the determination of the Rh factor.

15. List the signs and symptoms of a blood transfusion reaction.

16. Define the term *polycythemia*.

17. Compare causes of polycythemia vera and secondary polycythemia.

18. Describe the manifestations of polycythemia.

19. Cite the factors that predispose to hyperbilirubinemia in the infant.

20. Describe the pathogenesis of hemolytic disease of the newborn.

21. Compare conjugated and unconjugated bilirubin in terms of production of encephalopathy in the neonate.

22. Explain the action of phototherapy in the treatment of hyperbilirubinemia in the neonate.

SECTION II: ASSESSING YOUR UNDERSTANDING

Activity A *Fill in the blanks.*

1. The _____ shape of an erythrocyte provides a larger surface area for oxygen diffusion than would a spherical cell of the same volume, and the thinness of the _____ enables oxygen to diffuse rapidly between the exterior and the innermost regions of the cell.

2. The rate at which hemoglobin is synthesized depends on the availability of _____ for heme synthesis.

3. During its transformation from normoblast to reticulocyte, the RBC accumulates hemoglobin as the _____ condenses and is finally lost.

4. Mature RBCs have a life span of approximately _____ months.

5. The RBC relies on the _____ pathway for its metabolic needs.

6. Large doses of nitrites can result in high levels of _____, causing pseudo-cyanosis and tissue hypoxia.

7. The _____ measures the total number of RBCs in a microliter of blood.

8. The _____ measures the volume of red cell mass in 100 mL of plasma volume.

9. The _____ is the concentration of hemoglobin in each cell.

10. _____ is defined as an abnormally low number of circulating RBCs or level of hemoglobin.

11. Tissue _____ can give rise to fatigue, weakness, dyspnea, and sometimes angina.

12. _____ anemia is characterized by the premature destruction of red cells, the retention in the body of iron and the other products of hemoglobin destruction, and an increase in erythropoiesis.

13. Two main types of hemoglobinopathies can cause red cell hemolysis: the abnormal substitution of an amino acid in the hemoglobin molecule, as in _____ anemia, and the defective synthesis of one of the polypeptide chains that form the globin portion of hemoglobin, as in the _____.

14. Hereditary _____ is caused by abnormalities of the spectrin and ankyrin membrane proteins that lead to a gradual loss of the membrane surface.

15. _____ are caused by deficient synthesis of the β chain and _____ by deficient synthesis of the α chain.

16. The most common inherited enzyme defect that results in hemolytic anemia is a deficiency of _____.

17. _____ anemia results from dietary deficiency, loss of iron through bleeding, or increased demands.

18. Iron deficiency in adults in the Western world is usually the result of _____.

19. _____ anemias are caused by impaired DNA synthesis that results in enlarged red cells as a result of impaired maturation and division.

20. _____ anemia is a specific form of megaloblastic anemia caused by atrophic gastritis.

21. _____ describes a disorder of pluripotential bone marrow stem cells that results in a reduction of all three hematopoietic cell lines.

22. _____ is an abnormally high total RBC mass with a hematocrit greater than 50%.

23. At birth, changes in the RBC indices reflect the transition to extrauterine life and the need to transport _____ from the lungs.

24. Jaundice in infants is the result of increased red cell breakdown and the inability of the immature liver to _____ bilirubin.

25. The diagnosis of _____ in the elderly requires a complete physical examination, a complete blood count, and studies to rule out comorbid conditions such as malignancy, gastrointestinal conditions that cause bleeding, and pernicious anemia.

Activity B *Consider the following figure.*

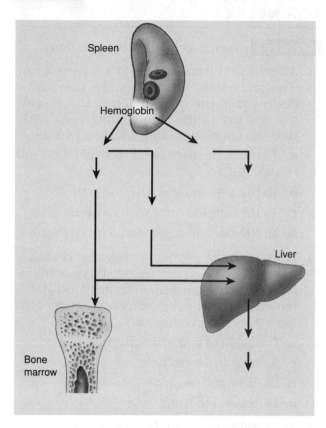

In the above figure, fill in the steps associated with RBC breakdown and secretion from the body.

- Begin by labeling where heme and the globin proteins separate. Trace the iron as it is recycled or as it is conjugated by the liver.

Activity C *Match the key terms in Column A with their definitions in Column B.*

Column A

____ **1.** Thalassemia

____ **2.** Severe G6PD deficiency

____ **3.** Erythropoietin

____ **4.** Mean corpuscular volume

____ **5.** Transferrin

____ **6.** Glucuronide

____ **7.** B$_{12}$ deficiency

____ **8.** Erythropoiesis

Column B

a. Chronic hemolytic anemia

b. Common cause of megaloblastic anemias

c. Measure of size of RBC

d. Red blood cell production

e. Caused by deficient goblin production

____ **9.** Jaundice

____ **10.** Normochromic cell

f. Regulator of RBC production

g. Normal hemoglobin concentration in RBC

h. Yellow discoloration of skin due to high levels of bilirubin

i. Transports iron to plasma

j. Conjugated with bilirubin to render it water

Activity D *Briefly answer the following.*

1. Hemoglobin is the oxygen-carrying protein found in RBCs. Describe the molecular structure of hemoglobin. Also, explain how oxygen interacts with hemoglobin.

_____

_____

_____

2. Red blood cells have a finite life span. How long is the life span, and what is the fate of RBCs?

_____

_____

_____

3. What are the three categories of anemic effects?

_____

_____

_____

4. Describe and explain the two consequences of sickle cell anemia.

_____

_____

_____

5. Anemia is a common side effect of cancer treatments. Which type of anemia usually develops and why?

_____

_____

_____

6. Polycythemia vera is a neoplastic disorder of RBCs. Describe the complications that arise from the rapid increase in hematocrit.

_____

_____

_____

7. Infantile jaundice is caused by the under-developed liver being unable conjugate bilirubin. What are the treatment methods for infantile jaundice and how do they work?

_____

_____

_____

SECTION III: APPLYING YOUR KNOWLEDGE

Activity E *Consider the scenario and answer the questions.*

Mrs. McFee, a 62-year-old woman, is in the outpatient procedure area of the hospital. She has a long history of rheumatoid arthritis and is to receive a blood transfusion to treat a chronic disease anemia. She appears very nervous as the nurse begins the transfusion. She states, "My friends have told me that there are serious things that can happen to you because of a transfusion."

1. The nurse would respond that there are several side effects that need to be watched for during a blood transfusion. Together, the nurse and Mrs. McFee will watch for what types of symptoms of a transfusion reaction?

_____

_____

_____

2. The nurse would also explain to Mrs. McFee that two people always check the donor blood against the recipient information at least two times before it is transfused. Once, when it leaves the laboratory, and, again, before it is infused into the patient. Why is this attention given to checking the blood?

_____

_____

_____

SECTION IV: PRACTICING FOR NCLEX

Activity F *Answer the following questions.*

1. All cells of the body age and are replaced in a natural order. When RBCs age, they are destroyed in the spleen. During this process the iron from their hemoglobin is released into the circulation and returned where?
a. To the bone marrow for incorporation into new RBCs.
b. To the liver to bind with oxygen.
c. To the lungs to bind with oxygen.
d. To the muscles to be stored for strength.

2. Bilirubin is the pigment of bile and is made when RBCs die. There are two types of bilirubin that can be measured in the blood and reported on by the laboratory. What does the laboratory reports them as?
a. Conjugated and unconjugated
b. Soluble and unsoluble
c. Positive and negative
d. Direct and indirect

3. Neonatal hyperbilirubinemia is an increased level of bilirubin in the infant's blood. It is usually a benign condition characterized by what?
a. A yellow, jaundiced color
b. Failure to thrive
c. Brain damage
d. A reddish, ruddy complexion

4. Anemia resulting from blood loss can be reversed if the blood loss is not so severe that it results in death. How long does it take for the red cell concentration to return to normal?
a. 8 to 10 days
b. 3 to 4 weeks
c. 10 to 14 days
d. 5 to 6 weeks

5. During chronic blood loss, iron-deficiency anemia occurs. Most patients are asymptomatic until their hemoglobin falls below 8 g/dL. The red cells that the body does produce have too little hemoglobin. What is the term for the resulting anemia?

   a. Macrocytic hyperchromic

   b. Macrocytic hypochromic

   c. Microcytic hypochromic

   d. Microcytic hyperchromic

6. In hemolytic anemia the RBCs are destroyed prematurely. What distinguishes almost all types of hemolytic anemia?

   a. Normocytic hypochromic cells

   b. Microcytic normochromic cells

   c. Macrocytic hyperchromic cells

   d. Normocytic normochromic cells

7. When hemolytic anemia has intravascular hemolysis, it can be characterized in different ways. Which of the following is not a characterization of hemolytic anemia with intravascular hemolysis?

   a. Hemoglobinemia

   b. Jaundice

   c. Hemosiderinuria

   d. Spherocytosis

8. Aplastic anemia is a serious anemia that is a disorder of the pluripotential bone marrow stem cells and causes all three hematopoietic cell lines to be reduced. What is the treatment for aplastic anemia in the young and severely affected client?

   a. There is no treatment for aplastic anemia.

   b. Bone marrow transplant

   c. Spleen transplant

   d. Liver transplant

9. When a client is in chronic renal failure, he or she almost always has anemia because of a deficiency of erythropoietin. What else contributes to the anemia experienced by clients in chronic renal failure?

   a. Uremic toxins and retained nitrogen

   b. Bleeding tendencies and lack of fibrinogen in blood

   c. Hemodialysis and decreased nitrogen

   d. Hemolysis of RBCs and lack of fibrinogen in blood

10. When an Rh-negative mother gives birth to an Rh-positive infant, the mother usually produces antibodies that will attack any subsequent pregnancies in which the fetus is Rh-positive. When subsequent babies are Rh-positive, erythroblastosis fetalis occurs. What is another name for erythroblastosis fetalis?

    a. Microcytic disease of the newborn

    b. Hemolytic iron-deficiency anemia

    c. Hemolytic disease of the newborn

    d. Macrocytic disease of the newborn

11. Pernicious anemia is thought to be an autoimmune disease that destroys the gastric mucosa. This results in chronic atrophic gastritis and the production of antibodies that interfere with _____ binding to intrinsic factor.

12. Sickle cell anemia is an inherited disorder seen in African American people. It is marked by the characteristic sickling of red blood cells. This causes both chronic hemolytic anemia and occlusion of blood vessels. Which are considered to be triggers of an episode of sickling? (Mark all that apply.)

    a. Infection

    b. Stress

    c. Heat

    d. Dehydration

    e. Alkalosis

13. The indices of the RBC are used to differentiate the anemias by size and color of cell. Match the term for a red blood cell with its definition:

Term	Definition
1. Mean corpuscular hemoglobin concentration (MCHC)	a. The concentration of hemoglobin in each cell
2. Mean cell hemoglobin (MCH)	b. The mass of the red cell
3. Mean corpuscular volume (MCV)	c. The volume or size of the red cells

14. A pregnant woman at her first prenatal visit complains to the nurse that she is always tired. The nurse knows that fatigue is one symptom of anemia. What are other symptoms of anemia? (Mark all that apply.)

   a. Faintness

   b. Dim vision

   c. Ruddy skin

   d. Bradycardia

15. Polycythemia vera most often occurs in men with a median age of 62. It is a neoplastic disease of the bone marrow that is characterized by which of the following signs and symptoms? (Mark all that apply.)

   a. Headache

   b. Dusky red appearance

   c. Ability to concentrate better

   d. Cyanosis of trunk

   e. Hearing difficulty

16. Thalassemia can be classed as major or minor. In thalassemia major it is necessary to start _____ therapy as early as 6 months of age. If therapy is not started in infants who present with this disease, severe growth retardation will occur.

CHAPTER 14

Mechanisms of Infectious Disease

SECTION I: LEARNING OBJECTIVES

1. Define the terms *host, infectious disease, colonization, microflora, virulence, pathogen,* and *saprophyte.*

2. Describe the concept of host-microorganism interaction using the concepts of commensalism, mutualism, and parasitic relationships.

3. Describe the structural characteristics and mechanisms of reproduction for prions, viruses, bacteria, fungi, and parasites.

4. Use the concepts of incidence, portal of entry, source of infection, symptomatology, disease course, site of infection, agent, and host characteristics to explain the mechanisms of infectious diseases.

5. Differentiate between incidence and prevalence and among endemic, epidemic, and pandemic.

6. Describe the stages of an infectious disease after the potential pathogen has entered the body.

7. List the systemic manifestations of infectious disease.

8. Describe mechanisms and significance of antimicrobial and antiviral drug resistance.

9. Explain the actions of intravenous immunoglobulin and cytokines in the treatment of infectious illnesses.

10. State the two criteria used in the diagnosis of an infectious disease.

11. Explain the differences among culture, serology, and antigen, metabolite, or molecular detection methods for diagnosis of infectious disease.

12. Cite three general intervention methods that can be used in treatment of infectious illnesses.

13. State four basic mechanisms by which antibiotics exert their action.

14. Differentiate bactericidal from bacteriostatic.

15. List the infectious agents considered to pose the highest level of bioterrorism threat.

SECTION II: ASSESSING YOUR UNDERSTANDING

Activity A *Fill in the blanks.*

1. The colonizing bacteria acquire nutritional needs and shelter, the host is not adversely affected by the relationship; an interaction such as this is called _____.

2. The term _____ describes the presence, multiplication, and subsequent injury within a host by another living organism.

3. A _____ relationship is one in which only the infecting organism benefits from the relationship and the host either gains nothing from the relationship or sustains injury from the interaction.

4. All microorganisms can be _____ pathogens capable of producing an infectious disease when the health and immunity of the host have been severely weakened.

5. The various prion-associated diseases produce very similar symptoms and pathology in the host and are collectively called _____ diseases.

6. _____ are the smallest obligate intracellular pathogens.

7. Bacteria are autonomously replicating unicellular organisms known as _____ because they lack an organized nucleus.

8. _____ characteristics and microscopic morphology are used in combination to describe bacteria.

9. The _____ are an eccentric category of bacteria that are mentioned separately because of their unusual cellular morphology and distinctive mechanism of motility.

10. The _____ are unicellular prokaryotes capable of independent replication.

11. Serious _____ infections are rare and usually initiated through puncture wounds or inhalation.

12. The fungi can be separated into two groups, _____ and _____, based on rudimentary differences in their morphology.

13. Parasitic infection results from the ingestion of highly resistant cysts or spores that are shed in the _____ of an infected host.

14. The _____ is the initial appearance of symptoms in the host.

15. The period during which the host experiences the maximum impact of the infectious process corresponding to rapid proliferation and dissemination of the pathogen is known as the _____.

16. The _____ is characterized by the containment of infection, progressive elimination of the pathogen, repair of damaged tissue, and resolution of associated symptoms.

17. Inflammation of an anatomic location is usually designated by adding the suffix -_____ to the name of the involved tissue in an infection.

18. The suffix -_____ is used to designate the presence of a substance in the blood.

19. _____ factors are substances or products generated by infectious agents that enhance their ability to cause disease.

20. In contrast to _____, endotoxins do not contain protein, are not actively released from the bacterium during growth, and have no enzymatic activity.

Activity B *Consider the following figure.*

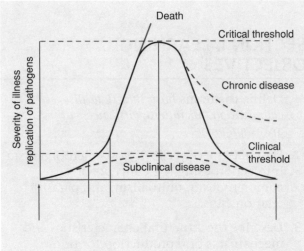

In the above figure, label the areas that represent the course through which a disease progresses: resolution, acute phase, convalescent phase, incubation phase, infection, and prodromal phase.

Activity C *Match the key terms in Column A with their definitions in Column B.*

1.

Column A	Column B
___ 1. Microflora	a. Describes the act of establishing an infection
___ 2. Host	
___ 3. Infection	b. Microorganisms that live with a host
___ 4. Disease	
___ 5. Colonization	c. Microorganisms so virulent that they are rarely found in the absence of disease
___ 6. Virulence	

_____ **7.** Pathogens

_____ **8.** Saprophytes

_____ **9.** Prions

_____ **10.** Rickettsiae

d. The presence, multiplication, and subsequent injury within a host by another living organism

e. Disease-producing potential of a the microorganism

f. Any organism capable of supporting the nutritional and physical growth requirements of another

g. Condition of an organism that impairs normal physiological function.

h. Harmless, free-living organisms

i. Disease-causing protein particles that lack any kind of a demonstrable genome

j. Organisms combining characteristics of viral and bacterial agents to produce disease in humans

2.

Column A

_____ **1.** Plasmids

_____ **2.** Mycoplasmas

_____ **3.** Fastidious bacteria

_____ **4.** Ectoparasites

_____ **5.** *Orthomyxoviridae*

_____ **6.** Enveloped viruses

_____ **7.** Rickettsiae

_____ **8.** Oncogenic viruses

Column B

a. Organisms are less than one-third the size of bacteria

b. Cause Rocky Mountain fever

c. Flu viruses

d. Herpesvirus and paramyxoviruses

e. Infest external body surfaces

f. Bacterial DNA that may increase virulence

g. Bacteria that can adapt metabolism

_____ **9.** Facultatively anaerobic bacteria

_____ **10.** *Chlamydia trachomatis*

h. Virus capable of transforming a cell

i. Sexually transmitted genital infections

j. Cannot live long outside strict growth requirements

Activity D

1. Write the correct sequence of the following in the boxes provided below.

a. Viral DNA copy is integrated into the host chromosome

b. Host cell lysis

c. Reactivation of virus

d. Entry into the host cell

e. Viral RNA genome is first translated into DNA

f. Replication of virus

□→□→□→□→□→□

Activity E *Briefly answer the following.*

1. Explain the general mechanism of cellular viral infection and replication. Differentiate between those that cause lysis and those that do not. Also, explain the concept of a latent virus.

_____

_____

_____

2. Describe the various methods of infiltration taken by organisms that will cause infection, from the organism entering the host to the manifestation of the disease state.

_____

_____

_____

3. Explain the concept of "disease course" and list all the stages that the disease course takes.

_____

_____

_____

4. What is the goal of treatment in regard to infective organisms? Provide the common methods of treatment.

_____

_____

_____

5. Explain the categorization of organisms that carry the potential for bioterrorism.

_____

_____

_____

SECTION III: APPLYING YOUR KNOWLEDGE

Activity F *Consider the scenario and answer the questions.*

You are a nurse working for a public health agency. You have been asked to give a talk to the local Rotary Club about infectious diseases. In your presentation you are going to include information about treatment of these diseases.

1. In discussing the role of antibiotics in the treatment of infectious diseases, you would include definitions of the terms *bactericidal* and *bacteriostatic.* What are these definitions?

_____

_____

_____

2. What drugs are used for HIV infections? How are these drugs classified?

_____

_____

_____

SECTION IV: PRACTICING FOR NCLEX

Activity G *Answer the following questions.*

1. What is the term for parasitic relationships between microorganisms and the human body in which the human body is harmed?

a. Infectious disease

b. Mutual disease

c. Communicable disease

d. Commensal disease

2. The infectious agents that cause Rocky Mountain spotted fever and epidemic typhus are transmitted to the human body via vector such as a tick. What are these infectious agents?

a. Viruses

b. Rickettsiae

c. Chlamydiae

d. Ehrlichiae

3. Severe acute respiratory syndrome (SARS), a highly transmissible respiratory infection, crossed international borders in the winter of 2002. What terms are used to describe the outbreak of SARS?

a. Pandemic and nosocomial

b. Regional and endemic

c. Epidemic and pandemic

d. Nosocomial and endemic

4. The clinical picture, or presentation of a disease in the body, is called what?

a. Virulence of the disease

b. Source of the disease

c. Diagnosis of the disease

d. Symptomatology of the disease

5. There are two criteria that have to be met in order for a diagnosis of an infectious disease to occur. What are these two criteria?

a. Recovery of probable pathogen and documentation of signs and symptoms compatible with an infectious process.

b. Propagation of a microorganism outside the body and testing to see what destroys it.

c. Identification by microscopic appearance and Gram stain reaction

d. Serology and an antibody titer specific to the serology

6. Levels A, B, and C are levels assigned to potential agents of bioterrorism. What are these categorical assignments based on?
   a. Safety to terrorist
   b. Transmissibility
   c. Environmental impact
   d. Ease of use to terrorist

7. Global infectious diseases are now being recognized. These diseases, known as endemic to one part of the world, are now being found in other parts of the world because of international travel and a global marketplace. Which of the following is considered a global infectious disease?
   a. Coxsackie disease
   b. Respiratory syncytial disease
   c. West Nile virus
   d. Hand, foot, and mouth disease

8. Which of the following sequences accurately describes the stages of a disease?
   a. Incubation, prodromal, current, recovery, and resolution
   b. Subacute, prodromal, acute, postacute, and convalescent
   c. Prodromal, subacute, acute, postdromal, and resolution
   d. Incubation, prodromal, acute, convalescent, and resolution.

9. Sometimes the host's white blood cells are unable to eliminate the microorganism, but the body is able to contain the dissemination of the pathogen. What is this called?
   a. Abscess
   b. Pimple
   c. Lesion
   d. Acne

10. *Escherichia coli* (*E. coli*) produces an exotoxin called Shiga toxin that enters the body when you eat undercooked hamburger meat and fruit juices that are not pasteurized. What can *E. coli* infection cause?
    a. Nephritic syndrome
    b. Hemorrhagic colitis
    c. Hemolytic thrombocytopenia
    d. Neuroleptic malignant syndrome

11. Transmissible neurodegenerative diseases such as Creutzfeldt-Jakob disease are associated with _____.

12. _____ infections refer to vertically transmitted infections, infections that are transmitted from mother to infant.

13. Match the category of infectious diseases with its source.

Category	Source
1. Zoonoses	a. Passed from mother to child at birth
2. Perinatal infections	b. Health care facility
3. Opportunistic	c. Passed from animals to humans
4. Nosocomial	d. Acquired from client's own body

14. Infectious agents produce products or substances called virulence factors that make it easier for them to cause disease. Which of these are virulence factors? (Mark all that apply.)
    a. Invasive factors
    b. Prodromal factors
    c. Adhesion factors
    d. Toxins
    e. Evasive factors

15. Evasive factors, one type of virulence factor, are factors produced by infectious microorganisms to keep the host's immune system from destroying the microorganism. Which of these are evasive factors? (Mark all that apply.)
    a. Capsules
    b. Phospholipases
    c. Collagenases
    d. Slime
    e. Mucous layers

CHAPTER 15

Innate and Adaptive Immunity

SECTION I: LEARNING OBJECTIVES

1. Discuss the function of the immune system.

2. Contrast and compare the general properties of innate and adaptive immunity.

3. Describe the cells of the immune system.

4. Characterize the chemical mediators that orchestrate the immune response.

5. Characterize the function of the innate immune system.

6. Describe components of the innate immune system including epithelial barriers, soluble chemical agents, and cellular components.

7. Describe the recognition systems for pathogens in innate immunity.

8. State the types and functions of leukocytes that participate in innate immunity.

9. Describe the functions of the various cytokines involved in innate immunity.

10. Define the role of the complement system in immunity and inflammation.

11. State the properties associated with adaptive immunity.

12. Define and describe the characteristics of an antigen.

13. Characterize the significance and function of major histocompatibility complex (MHC) molecules.

14. Describe the antigen-presenting functions of macrophages and dendritic cells.

15. Contrast and compare the development and function of the T and B lymphocytes.

16. State the function of the five classes of immunoglobulins.

17. Differentiate between the central and peripheral lymphoid structures.

18. Describe the function of cytokines involved in the adaptive immune response.

19. Compare passive and active immunity.

20. Explain the transfer of passive immunity from mother to fetus and from mother to infant during breast-feeding.

21. Characterize the development of active immunity in the infant and small child.

22. Describe changes in the immune response that occur with aging.

SECTION II: ASSESSING YOUR UNDERSTANDING

Activity A *Fill in the blanks.*

1. The _____ has evolved in multicellular organisms to defend against bacteria, viruses, and other foreign substances.

2. Although the immune response normally is protective, it also can produce undesirable effects such as when the response is excessive, as in _____, or when it recognizes self-tissue as foreign, as in _____ disease.

3. As the first line of defense, _____ immunity consists of the physical, chemical, molecular, and cellular defenses.

4. _____ immunity is the second major immune defense.

5. Substances that elicit adaptive immune responses are called _____.

6. _____ immunity, generated by B lymphocytes, is mediated by molecules called antibodies and is the principal defense against extracellular microbes and toxins.

7. _____ immunity is mediated by specific T lymphocytes and defends against intracellular microbes such as viruses.

8. Dendritic cells and _____ function as antigen-presenting cells for adaptive immunity.

9. The key cells of innate immunity are _____, _____, and natural killer cells.

10. _____ are the early responding cells of innate immunity.

11. During an inflammation response, the monocyte leaves the blood vessel, transforms into a tissue _____, and phagocytoses bacteria, damaged cells, and tissue debris.

12. _____ cells and _____ cells are the only cells in the body capable of specifically recognizing different antigenic determinants of microbial agents and other pathogens.

13. _____ are part of the innate immune system, and may be the first line of defense against viral infections.

14. _____ cells are specialized, bone marrow-derived leukocytes found in lymphoid tissue that are important intermediaries between the innate and adaptive immune systems.

15. _____ are cytokines that stimulate the migration and activation of immune and inflammatory cells.

16. Cytokines that stimulate bone marrow pluripotent stem and progenitor or precursor cells to produce large numbers of platelets, erythrocytes, lymphocytes, neutrophils, monocytes, eosinophils, basophils, and dendritic cells are known as _____.

17. The mucous membrane linings of the gastrointestinal, respiratory, and urogenital tracts are protected by sheets of tightly packed _____ cells that block the entry of microbes.

18. The binding of _____ to the pattern recognition receptors on leukocytes initiates the signaling events that lead to innate immunity and tissue changes associated with acute inflammation.

19. _____ is the coating of a microorganism with soluble molecules that tag the microorganism for more efficient recognition by phagocytes.

20. _____ are substances foreign to the host that can stimulate an immune response.

21. Antibodies comprise a class of proteins called _____.

22. _____ immunity depends on maturation of B lymphocytes into plasma cells, which produce and secrete antibodies.

23. The _____ serves as a master regulator for the immune system.

24. _____ T cells suppress immune responses by inhibiting the proliferation of other potentially harmful self-reactive lymphocytes.

25. The central lymphoid organs, the _____ and the _____, provide the environment for immune cell production and maturation.

26. The white pulp layer of the _____ contains concentrated areas of B and T lymphocytes permeated by macrophages and dendritic cells.

Activity B *Consider the following figure.*

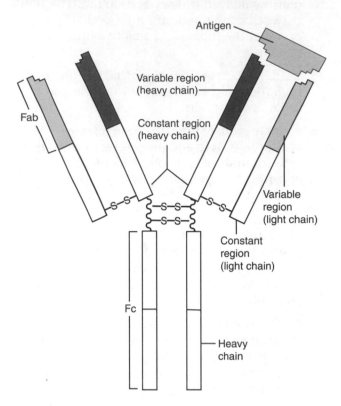

f. The physical barrier of skin to infection

g. Disrupts virus infections

h. Small cationic peptides found in the stomach

i. Regulates the production of cytokines and adhesion molecules

j. Hydrolytic enzyme capable of cleaving the walls of bacterial cell

1. What does this figure depict? Discuss the significance of the different parts depicted in this model.

Activity C *Match the key terms in Column A with their definitions in Column B*

1.

Column A

____ **1.** Mucins

____ **2.** Lysozyme

____ **3.** Epithelial barrier

____ **4.** Defensins

____ **5.** Collectins

____ **6.** Cilia

____ **7.** Toll-like receptors

____ **8.** Opsonins

____ **9.** NF-κβ

____ **10.** Interferons

Column B

a. Pathogen-associated molecular pattern receptors

b. Renders bacteria and other cells susceptible to phagocytosis

c. Traps and washes away potential invaders

d. Epithelial protrusion that moves mucus to throat

e. Surfactant proteins in respiratory track

2.

Column A

____ **1.** Epitopes

____ **2.** CD4⁺

____ **3.** Perforins

____ **4.** Cell-mediated immunity

____ **5.** Antigen presentation

____ **6.** Antibody-mediated immunity

____ **7.** Major histocompatibility complex

____ **8.** Haptens

____ **9.** CD8⁺

____ **10.** Tolerance

Column B

a. Processing a complex antigen into epitopes and then displaying the foreign and self peptides on their membranes

b. Dependent on B cells

c. Self-recognition proteins

d. Type of T helper cell

e. Dependent on T cells

f. Pore-forming molecules

g. Immunologically active sites on antigens

h. Combine with larger protein molecules and serve as antigens

i. Ability of the immune system to be nonreactive to self-antigens

j. Cytotoxic T cells

Activity D *Briefly answer the following.*

1. How do the cells of the immune system communicate with each other?

_____

_____

_____

2. What is the innate immune system and what is its function?

_____

_____

_____

3. What is the general function of neutrophils and macrophages in the inflammatory response?

_____

_____

_____

4. What are the methods of initiating the complement system and what are the results of activation?

_____

_____

_____

5. What is the function of MHC proteins, and how are they classified?

_____

_____

_____

6. Explain how a macrophage participates in antigen presentation.

_____

_____

_____

7. How many classes of antibody are there? Give a brief definition of function for each one.

_____

_____

_____

8. Compare and contrast active versus passive immunity.

_____

_____

_____

SECTION III: APPLYING YOUR KNOWLEDGE

Activity E *Consider the scenario and answer the question.*

A young new mother has her 2-week old infant at the clinic for a well-baby check-up. She is concerned because her baby has been exposed to chickenpox. She states, "What am I going to do? I didn't know my friend's son had just gotten over the chickenpox. Will my baby get chickenpox?"

1. In talking with this mother, the nurse explains passive immunity. What key points will the nurse be sure to mention?

_____

_____

_____

SECTION IV: PRACTICING FOR NCLEX

Activity F *Answer the following questions.*

1. Natural killer cells are specialized lymphocytes that are one of the major parts of which immunity?
   a. Innate
   b. Adaptive
   c. Humoral
   d. Cell-mediated

2. Both innate and adaptive immunity have cells that produce cytokines. Cytokines mediate the actions of many cells in both innate and adaptive immunity. How are the actions of cytokines described?
   a. Rapid and self-limiting
   b. Pleiotropic and redundant
   c. Cell-specific and targeted
   d. Dendritic and morphologic

3. Stem cells in the bone marrow produce T lymphocytes or T cells, and release them into the vascular system. The T cells then migrate where to mature?

   a. Spleen

   b. Liver

   c. Thymus

   d. Pancreas

4. Cell-mediated immunity is involved in resistance to infectious diseases caused by bacteria and some viruses. It is also involved in cell-mediated hypersensitivity reactions. Which of these does not cause a cell-mediated hypersensitivity reaction?

   a. Latex

   b. Poison ivy

   c. X-ray dye

   d. Blood transfusion

5. Passive immunity is immunity that is transferred from another source and lasts only weeks to months. What is an example of passive immunity?

   a. An injection of γ-globulin

   b. An immunization

   c. Exposure to poison ivy

   d. Allergy shots

6. An essential property of the immune system is self-regulation. An immune response that is not adequate can lead to immuno-deficiency, while an immune response that is excessive can lead to conditions from allergic responses all the way to autoimmune diseases. Which of these is not an example of a breakdown of the self-regulation of the immune system?

   a. Multiple sclerosis

   b. Huntington disease

   c. Systemic lupus

   d. Fibromyalgia

7. One of the self-regulatory actions of the immune system is to identify self-antigens and be nonreactive to them. What is this ability of the immune system defined as?

   a. Antigen specificity

   b. Nonre activity

   c. Tolerance

   d. Antigen diversity

8. The laboratory finds IgA in a sample of cord blood from a newborn infant. This finding is important because it signifies what?

   a. Fetal reaction to an infection acquired at birth

   b. Maternal reaction to an infection in the fetus

   c. Maternal exposure to an infection in a sexual partner

   d. Fetal reaction to exposure to an intrauterine infection

9. The daughter of a 79-year-old woman asks the nurse why her mother gets so many infections. The daughter states, "My mother has always been healthy, but now she has pneumonia. Last month she got cellulitis from a bug bite she scratched. The month before that was some other infection. How come she seems to get sick so often now?" What is the nurse's best response?

   a. As people get older their immune system does not respond as well as it did when they were younger.

   b. About the time we are 75 or 76 years old our immune system quits working.

   c. Your mother just seems to be prone to getting infections.

   d. Your mother gets infections frequently because she wants attention from you.

10. The results of recent research suggest that a key role in the origin of some diseases is played by inflammation. Which of these diseases is it thought that inflammation has a role in its beginnings?

    a. Osteoporosis

    b. Rheumatoid arthritis

    c. Osteogenesis imperfecta

    d. Hydronephrosis

11. _____, or immunogens, are substances foreign to the host that can stimulate an immune response.

12. Each immunoglobulin has a different role in the immune response. Match each immunoglobulin with its role.

Immunoglobulin

1. IgG
2. IgA
3. IgM
4. IgD
5. IgE

Role

a. Is the first circulating immunoglobulin to appear in response to an antigen and is the first antibody type made by a newborn

b. Involved in inflammation, allergic responses, and combating parasitic infections

c. Serves as an antigen receptor for initiating the differentiation of B cells

d. Protects against bacteria, toxins, and viruses in body fluids and activates the complement system

e. A primary defense against local infections in mucosal tissues

13. The mucous membrane linings of the gastrointestinal, respiratory, and urogenital tracts are protected by sheets of tightly packed _____ cells that block the entry of microbes and destroy them by secreting antimicrobial enzymes, proteins, and peptides.

14. In both the innate and the adaptive immune systems, cells communicate information about invading organisms by the secretion of chemical mediators. Which are these mediators? (Mark all that apply.)

a. Virulence factors
b. Chemokines
c. Colony-stimulating factors
d. Coxiellas

15. There are many cells that make up the passive and adaptive immune systems. Which cells are responsible for the specificity and memory of adaptive immunity? (Mark all that apply.)

a. Phagocytes
b. T lymphocytes
c. Dendritic cells
d. Natural killer cells
e. B lymphocytes

Disorders of the Immune Response

SECTION I: LEARNING OBJECTIVES

1. State the difference in causes of primary and secondary immunodeficiency disorders.

2. Compare and contrast pathology and manifestations of humoral (B-cell), cellular (T-cell), and combined T- and B-cell immunodeficiency disorders.

3. Differentiate between adaptive immune responses that protect against microbial agents and hypersensitivity responses.

4. Describe the immune mechanisms involved in a type I, type II, type III, and type IV hypersensitivity reaction.

5. Describe the pathogenesis of allergic rhinitis, food allergy, serum sickness, Arthus reaction, contact dermatitis, and hypersensitivity pneumonitis.

6. Characterize the differences in a type I, immunoglobulin E (IgE)-mediated hypersensitivity response and that caused by a type IV, cell-mediated response.

7. Relate the mechanisms of self-tolerance to the possible explanations for development of autoimmune disease.

8. Discuss the rationale for matching of human leukocyte antigen or major histocompatibility complex types in organ transplantation.

9. Compare the immune mechanisms involved in allogeneic transplant rejection.

10. Describe the mechanisms and manifestations of graft-versus-host disease.

11. Name four or more diseases attributed to autoimmunity.

12. Describe three or more postulated mechanisms underlying autoimmune disease.

13. State the criteria for establishing an autoimmune basis for a disease.

SECTION II: ASSESSING YOUR UNDERSTANDING

Activity A *Fill in the blanks.*

1. Under normal conditions, the _____ response deters or prevents disease.

2. _____ can be defined as an abnormality in the immune system that renders a person susceptible to diseases normally prevented by an intact immune system.

3. The _____ immune system is composed of the phagocytic leukocytes, natural killer (NK) cells, and complement proteins.

4. The _____ immune response is composed mainly of T and B cells and responds to infections more slowly, but more specifically, than the innate immune system.

5. The adaptive immune system is further divided into the _____ and _____ immune systems.

6. A large number of primary immunodeficiency diseases have been mapped to the _____ chromosome.

7. Defects in humoral immunity increase the risk of recurrent _____ infections.

8. During the first few months of life, infants are protected from infection by IgG antibodies that originate in _____ circulation during fetal life.

9. Of all the primary immunodeficiency diseases, those affecting _____ production are the most frequent.

10. Abnormal immunoglobulin loss can occur with chronic _____ disease; because of abnormal glomerular filtration, patients lose serum IgA and IgG in their urine.

11. Secondary humoral immunodeficiencies can also result from a number of _____, including chronic lymphocytic leukemia, lymphoma, and multiple myeloma that interfere with normal immunoglobulin production.

12. T cells can be functionally divided into two subtypes: _____ and _____ T cells.

13. Collectively, _____ protect against fungal, protozoan, viral, and intracellular bacterial infections; control malignant cell proliferation; and are responsible for coordinating the overall immune response.

14. Disorders that affect both B and T lymphocytes, with resultant defects in both humoral and cell-mediated immunity, fall under the broad classification of _____ syndrome.

15. In _____, genetic mutations lead to absence of all T and B cell function and, in some cases, a lack of NK cells.

16. SCID is more commonly found in _____, as it is X linked.

17. Hereditary angioneurotic edema is a form of _____ deficiency.

18. Chronic cirrhosis of the liver would reduce the production of complement proteins; this type of deficiency would be classified as _____.

19. Chédiak-Higashi syndrome is an abnormality of _____ of phagocytes.

20. Chronic granulomatous disease is a group of inherited disorders that greatly reduce or inactivate the ability of phagocytic cells to produce the _____.

21. _____ disorders refer to excessive or inappropriate activation of the immune system.

22. Type I hypersensitivity reactions to antigens are referred to as _____.

23. _____ is a systemic life-threatening hypersensitivity reaction characterized by widespread edema, vascular shock secondary to vasodilation, and difficulty breathing.

24. Persons with _____ allergic conditions tend to have high serum levels of IgE and increased numbers of basophils and mast cells.

25. Allergic _____ is characterized by symptoms of sneezing, itching, and watery discharge from the nose and eyes.

26. There are three different types of antibody-mediated mechanisms involved in _____ reactions: opsonization and complement- and antibody receptor-mediated phagocytosis, complement- and antibody receptor-mediated inflammation, and antibody-mediated cellular dysfunction.

27. _____ mediated destruction of cells that are coated with low levels of IgG antibody and are killed by a variety of effector cells, which bind to their target by their receptors for IgG, and cell lysis occurs without phagocytosis.

28. _____ hypersensitivity reactions are responsible for the vasculitis seen in certain autoimmune diseases such as systemic lupus erythematosus (SLE), or the kidney damage seen with acute glomerulonephritis.

29. _____ sickness is a systemic immune complex disorder that is triggered by the deposition of insoluble antigen-antibody complexes in blood vessels, joints, heart, and kidney tissue.

30. A term used by pathologists and immunologists to describe localized tissue necrosis caused by immune complexes is the _____.

31. Hypersensitivity reactions that are mediated by specifically sensitized T lymphocytes are divided into two basic types: direct cell-mediated cytotoxicity and delayed-type hypersensitivity, and generally classified as _____.

32. Allergic _____ denotes an inflammatory response confined to the skin that is initiated by re-exposure to an allergen to which a person had previously become sensitized.

33. A major barrier to _____ is the process of rejection in which the recipient's immune system recognizes the graft as foreign and attacks it.

34. Transplanted tissue can be categorized as an _____ graft if donor and recipient are the same person, _____ graft if the donor and recipient are identical twins, and _____ if the donor and recipient are related or unrelated but share similar HLA types.

35. _____ occurs when immunologically competent cells or precursors are transplanted into recipients who are immunologically compromised.

36. _____ diseases represent a group of disorders that are caused by a breakdown in the ability of the immune system to differentiate between self- and non–self-antigens.

37. The ability of the immune system to differentiate self from nonself is called _____.

38. Loss of self-tolerance with development of _____ is characteristic of a number of autoimmune disorders.

Activity B *Consider the following figure.*

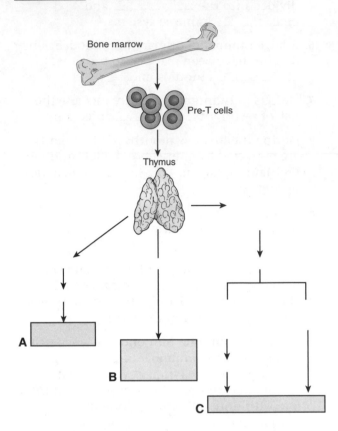

In the above figure, label and diagram the process of T-cell selection. Be sure to include the end result of each pathway.

Activity C *Match the key terms in Column A with their definitions in Column B.*

Column A	Column B
____ **1.** DiGeorge syndrome	**a.** Essentially undetectable levels of all serum immunoglobulins
____ **2.** Secondary immunodeficiency	
____ **3.** Hyper-IgM syndrome	**b.** Complement-mediated immune disorders
____ **4.** X-linked agammaglobulinemia	**c.** Decreases in one or more of IgG subgroups

_____ 5. Selective
IgA deficiency

_____ 6. Adenosine
deaminase
deficiencies
and T-cell
cytokine
receptor
mutations

_____ 7. Transient
hypogam
maglobuli-
nemia
of infancy

_____ 8. Ataxia-
telangiectasia

_____ 9. Common
variable
immunode-
ficiency

_____ 10. Immunoglo-
bulin
G subclass
deficiency

_____ 11. Wiskott-
Aldrich
syndrome

_____ 12. Type I
hypersensitivity
reaction

_____ 13. Type II
hypersensitivity
reaction

_____ 14. Type III
hypersensitivity
reaction

_____ 15. Type IV
hypersensi-
tivity
reaction

d. Repeated bouts of
upper respiratory
and middle ear
infections

e. Partial or complete
failure of develop-
ment of the
thymus and
parathyroid glands

f. In levels of serum
and secretory IgA

g. Antibody-mediated
disorders

h. Acquired later in
life

i. The terminal
differentiation of
mature B cells to
plasma cells is
blocked

j. Ig-E mediated
disorders

k. Lymphopenia and
a decrease in the
ratio of CD4$^+$
helper T cells to
CD8$^+$ suppressor T
cells

l. Low IgG and IgA
levels, high IgM
concentrations

m. Cause of SCID

n. Susceptible to
infections caused
by encapsulated
microorganisms

o. T-cell-mediated
disorders

Activity D

Put the normal sequence of actions of a polymorphonuclear phagocyte in order in the boxes below.

a. Phagocytosis

b. Kill the ingested pathogens

c. Chemotaxis

d. Generate microbicidal substances

e. Adherence

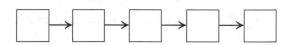

Activity E *Briefly answer the following.*

1. What is the difference between a primary and
a secondary immunodeficiency?

_____

_____

_____

2. Why does it take up to 6 months for the
symptoms of a primary immunodeficiency to
show up?

_____

_____

_____

3. Explain how a patient can become sensitized
to an allergen (antigen) in a type I hypersensitivity reaction.

_____

_____

_____

4. Compare the direct cell-mediated cytotoxicity
of type IV hypersensitivity reactions with the
delayed-type hypersensitivity reactions.

_____

_____

_____

5. What is SCID?

_____

_____

_____

SECTION III: APPLYING YOUR KNOWLEDGE

Activity F *Consider the scenario and answer the questions.*

A 30-year-old woman has just been diagnosed with SLE. She presents with arthritis, a "butterfly rash," weight loss, weakness, and fatigue. She is distraught and she states, "How can the doctor be sure that I have this disease?"

1. The correct response to this patient about the diagnosis would include information about which test?

_____

_____

_____

2. When planning patient education for this woman, what medications would the nurse tell the patient about?

_____

_____

_____

SECTION IV: PRACTICING FOR NCLEX

Activity G *Answer the following questions.*

1. Infants are born with a passive immunity that occurs when immunoglobulin antibodies cross the placenta from the maternal circulation prior to birth. Which immunoglobulin is capable of crossing the placenta?

   a. IgM

   b. IgD

   c. IgG

   d. IgE

2. Drug-induced secondary hypogammaglobulinemia is considered reversible. Which drugs produce hypogammaglobulinemia? (Mark all that apply.)

   a. Phenytoin

   b. Corticosteroids

   c. Carbamazepine

   d. Disease-modifying antirheumatic drugs

   e. Interferon beta-1a drugs

3. Primary cell-mediated disorders of the immune system cause severe problems with infections. Children with these disorders rarely survive beyond childhood without a bone marrow transplant. Which of the following is a disease that involves primary cell-mediated disorders of the immune system?

   a. DiGeorge syndrome

   b. Y-linked hyper-IgM syndrome

   c. X-linked agammaglobulinemia

   d. Y-linked agammaglobulinemia

4. Combined immunodeficiency syndrome is a disorder in which both B and T lymphocytes are affected. This results in defects in both humoral and cell-mediated immunity. What could be the cause of this disorder?

   a. Multiple misplaced genes that influence lymphocyte development and response

   b. A single mutation in any gene that influences major histocompatibility antigens

   c. A single misplaced gene that influences major histocompatibility

   d. Multiple mutations in genes that influence lymphocyte development and response

5. Combined immunodeficiency (CID) is distinguished by low, not absent, T-cell function. These diseases are usually associated with other disorders and arise from diverse genetic causes. Which of the following diseases is considered a CID?
   a. Pierre-Robin syndrome
   b. Angelman syndrome
   c. Ataxia-telangiectasia
   d. Adair-Dighton syndrome

6. The immune system typically responds to invaders of all types in our body. However, it can also cause tissue injury and disease. What is this effect called?
   a. Hypersensitivity action
   b. Antigen reaction
   c. Mediator response action
   d. Allergen stimulating reaction

7. Some people are so sensitive to certain antigens that they react within minutes by developing itching, hives, and skin erythema, followed shortly thereafter by bronchospasm and respiratory distress. What is this commonly known as?
   a. Antigen reaction
   b. Anaphylactic reaction
   c. Hyposensitive reaction
   d. Arthus reaction

8. A systemic immune complex disorder that is caused by insoluble antigen-antibody complexes being deposited in blood vessels, the joints, the heart, or kidney tissue is called what?
   a. Anti-immune disease
   b. Systemic lupus erythematosus
   c. Serum sickness
   d. Antigen-antibody sickness

9. The incidence of latex allergy is skyrocketing because of diseases such as HIV. It is known that the use of latex examining gloves has played a major role in the increasing incidence of latex allergy. What plays a significant role in the allergic response to latex gloves?
   a. Baking powder used inside the gloves
   b. Airborne pieces of latex
   c. Latex proteins that attach to clothing
   d. Cornstarch powder used inside the gloves

10. A transplant reaction that occurs immediately after transplantation is caused by _____ antibodies that are present.

11. It has been postulated that an autoimmune disease needs a "trigger event" for it to clinically manifest itself in a body. What are these "trigger events" thought to be? (Mark all that apply.)
    a. A. microorganism or virus
    b. A self-antigen from a previously sequestered body tissue
    c. A breakdown in the antigen-antibody response
    d. A chemical substance
    e. A systemic ability for self-tolerance

CHAPTER 17

Control of Cardiovascular Function

SECTION I: LEARNING OBJECTIVES

1. Compare the function and distribution of blood flow and blood pressure in the systemic and pulmonary circulations.

2. State the relation between blood volume and blood pressure in arteries, veins, and capillaries of the circulatory system.

3. Define the term *hemodynamics* and describe the effects of blood pressure, vessel radius, vessel length, vessel cross-sectional area, and blood viscosity on blood flow.

4. Use the law of Laplace to explain the effect of radius size on the pressure and wall tension in a vessel.

5. Use the term *compliance* to describe the characteristics of arterial and venous blood vessels.

6. Describe the structural components and function of the pericardium, myocardium, endocardium, and the heart valves and fibrous skeleton.

7. Draw a figure of the cardiac cycle, incorporating the volume, pressure, heart sounds, and electrocardiographic changes that occur during atrial and ventricular systole and diastole.

8. Define the terms *preload* and *afterload*.

9. Describe the cardiac reserve and relate it to the Frank-Starling mechanism.

10. Compare the structure and function of arteries and veins.

11. Describe the structure and function of vascular smooth muscle.

12. Define autoregulation and characterize mechanisms responsible for short-term and long-term regulation of blood flow.

13. Describe mechanisms involved in the humoral control of blood flow.

14. Define the term *microcirculation*.

15. Describe the structure and function of the capillaries.

16. Explain the forces that control the fluid exchange between the capillaries and the interstitial spaces.

17. Describe the structures of the lymphatic system and relate them to the role of the lymphatics in controlling interstitial fluid volume.

18. Describe the roles of the medullary vasomotor and cardioinhibitory centers in controlling the function of the heart and blood vessels.

19. Relate the performance of baroreceptors and chemoreceptors in the control of cardiovascular function.

20. Describe the distribution of sympathetic and parasympathetic nervous system in the innervation of the circulatory system and their effects on heart rate and cardiac contractility.

21. Relate the role of the central nervous system in terms of regulating circulatory function.

SECTION II: ASSESSING YOUR UNDERSTANDING

Activity A *Fill in the blanks.*

1. The circulatory system delivers _____ and nutrients needed for metabolic processes to the tissues, carries _____ products from the tissues to the kidneys and other excretory organs for elimination, and circulates electrolytes and _____ needed to regulate body function.

2. The circulatory system can be divided into two parts: the _____ circulation and the _____ circulation.

3. The _____ circulation consists of the right heart, the pulmonary artery, the pulmonary capillaries, and the pulmonary veins.

4. The _____ circulation consists of the left heart, the aorta and its branches, the capillaries that supply the brain and peripheral tissues, and the systemic venous system and the vena cava.

5. The _____ pressure of the pulmonary circulation allows blood to move through the lungs more slowly, which is important for gas exchange.

6. The _____ function as collection chambers for blood and the _____ are the main pumping chambers of the heart.

7. Because it is a closed system, the effective function of the circulatory system requires that the outputs of both sides of the heart pump the _____ amount of blood over time.

8. Blood flow in the circulatory system depends on a blood _____ that is sufficient to fill the blood vessels and a _____ difference across the system that provides the force to move blood forward.

9. The term _____ refers to the principles that govern blood flow in the circulatory system.

10. Because flow is directly related to the radius, small changes in vessel radius can produce _____ changes in flow to an organ or tissue.

11. _____ is the resistance to flow caused by the friction of molecules in a fluid.

12. _____ blood flow may predispose to clot formation as platelets and other coagulation factors are exposed to the endothelial lining of the vessel.

13. Wall tension is inversely related to wall thickness, such that the _____ the vessel wall, the lower the tension.

14. The total quantity of blood that can be stored in a given portion of the circulation for each millimeter rise in pressure is termed *compliance*, and reflects the _____ of the blood vessel.

15. The _____ and _____ valves control the movement of blood out of the ventricles.

16. The electrical activity, recorded on the electrocardiogram, _____ the mechanical events of the cardiac cycle.

17. The aorta is highly _____ and as such stretches during systole to accommodate the blood that is being ejected from the left heart during systole.

18. _____ is marked by ventricular relaxation and filling.

19. The difference between the end-diastolic and end-systolic volumes (approximately 70 mL) is called the _____.

20. The stroke volume divided by the end-diastolic volume is the _____ fraction.

21. The efficiency of the heart as a pump often is measured in terms of the _____ or the amount of blood the heart pumps each minute.

22. The _____ refers to the maximum percentage of increase in cardiac output that can be achieved above the normal resting level.

23. The _____ mechanism allows the heart to adjust its pumping ability to accommodate various levels of venous return.

24. The _____ determines the frequency with which blood is ejected from the heart.

25. The outermost layer of a vessel, the _____, is composed primarily of loosely woven collagen fibers. The middle layer, the _____, is largely a smooth muscle layer. The innermost layer, the _____ consists of a single layer of flattened endothelial cells.

26. The _____ represents the energy that is transmitted from molecule to molecule along the length of the vessel.

27. With peripheral arterial disease, there is a delay in the transmission of the reflected wave so that the pulse _____ in amplitude.

28. Pressure in the right atrium is called the _____.

29. _____ in the veins of extremities prevent retrograde flow with the help of skeletal muscles that surround and intermittently compress the leg veins to move blood forward to the heart.

30. _____ of blood flow is mediated by changes in blood vessel tone due to changes in flow through the vessel or by local tissue factors.

31. An increase in local blood flow is called _____.

32. In the heart and other vital structures, _____ channels exist between some of the smaller arteries.

33. The term _____ refers to the functions of the smallest blood vessels, the capillaries, and the neighboring lymphatic vessels.

34. Water-filled junctions, called the _____, join the capillary endothelial cells and provide a pathway for passage of substances through the capillary wall.

35. The key factor that restrains fluid loss from the capillaries is the _____ pressure generated by the plasma proteins.

36. The neural control centers for the integration and modulation of cardiac function and blood pressure are located bilaterally in the _____.

37. The neural control of the circulatory system occurs primarily through the _____ and _____ divisions of the autonomic nervous system.

38. When the intracranial pressure rises to levels that equal intra-arterial pressure, blood vessels to the vasomotor center become compressed, initiating the CNS ischemic response. This is known as the _____.

Activity B *Consider the following figures.*

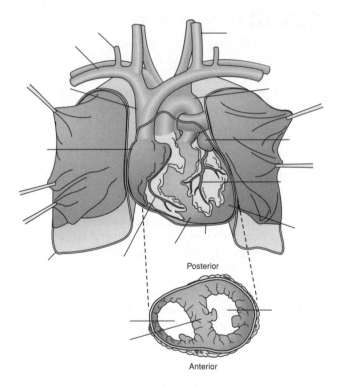

Posterior

Anterior

1. Label the following structures.
   - Pericardium
   - Pleura
   - Right ventricle
   - Right coronary artery
   - Right atrium
   - Subclavian vein
   - External jugular vein
   - Internal jugular vein
   - Intraventricular septum
   - Aortic arch

- Left atrium
- Left coronary artery
- Left ventricle
- Superior vena cava

2. Label the following structures.

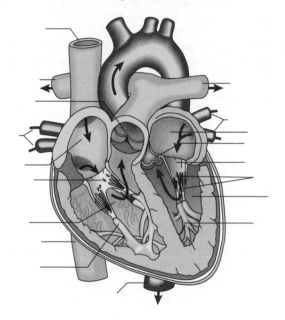

- Chordae tendineae
- Tricuspid valve
- Superior vena cava
- Inferior vena cava
- Pulmonic valve
- Papillary muscle
- Left pulmonary artery
- Right pulmonary artery
- Pulmonary veins
- Aortic valve
- Mitral valve
- Left atrium
- Right atrium
- Left ventricle
- Right ventricle
- Descending aorta
- Papillary muscles

Activity C *Match the key terms in Column A with their definitions in Column B.*

Column A

____ **1.** Diastole

____ **2.** Pericardium

____ **3.** End-diastolic volume

____ **4.** Preload

____ **5.** Myocardium

____ **6.** Cardiac output

____ **7.** Heart valves

____ **8.** End-systolic volume

____ **9.** Systole

____ **10.** Afterload

Column B

a. Contractile phase of cardiac cycle

b. Sac that covers the heart

c. Ventricular filling

d. Resting phase of cardiac cycle

e. Semilunar and atrioventricular

f. Residual blood volume following contraction

g. Resistance to ejection of blood from heart

h. Heart rate × stroke volume

i. Muscular wall of heart

j. Volume in heart following passive filling phase

Activity D *Briefly answer the following.*

1. What are the factors involved in regulating the flow of blood and how are they related?

_____

_____

_____

2. The velocity of blood in the circulatory system varies considerably between large vessels and capillaries. Normally, when fluid flows from a large vessel to a smaller vessel, the velocity increases, but this does not occur in the circulatory system. Why and for what purpose?

_____

_____

_____

3. What is the importance of the Frank-Starling mechanism?

_____

_____

_____

4. How is blood vessel diameter controlled?

_____

_____

_____

5. What are the factors that travel in the blood-stream that will regulate blood flow? Indicate if each factor is a dilator or a vasoconstrictor.

_____

_____

_____

SECTION III: PRACTICING FOR NCLEX

Activity E *Answer the following questions.*

1. Blood volume is dictated by age and body weight. Neonates have a higher blood volume per kilogram than do adults. What is the blood volume range per kilogram in an adult?
   a. 70 to 75 mL/kg
   b. 85 to 90 mL/kg
   c. 60 to 65 mL/kg
   d. 90 to 100 ml/kg

2. Resistance to flow is determined by the blood vessels and the blood vessel itself. An equation has been developed for understanding the relationship between the diameter of the blood vessel, the viscosity of the blood, and resistance. What is the equation called?
   a. LaPlace's law
   b. Poiseuille's law
   c. Laminar's law
   d. Pierre's law

3. The distensibility of the blood vessel is the major factor in which of the vessels characteristics?
   a. Wall tension
   b. Compliance
   c. Laminar blood flow
   d. Resistance

4. When intracranial pressure (ICP) equals intra-arterial pressure, the CNS ischemic response is initiated. This response is directed at raising arterial pressure above ICP, thereby re-establishing blood flow to the vasomotor center of the brain. What is this response called?
   a. Cushing's law
   b. Cushing response
   c. Cushing reflex
   d. Cushing syndrome

5. The troponin complex is one of a number of important proteins that regulate actin-myosin binding. Troponin works in striated muscle to help regulate calcium-mediated contraction of the muscle. Which of the troponin complexes are diagnostic of a myocardial infarction?
   a. Troponin C and troponin T
   b. Troponin A and troponin I
   c. Troponin T and troponin I
   d. Troponin A and troponin C

6. The stroke volume is the amount of blood ejected with every contraction of the ventri-cle. It is broken down into quarters. What is the approximate amount of the stroke volume per quarter?
   a. 25%, 25%, 25%, and 25%
   b. 50%, 30%, 20%, and little blood
   c. 40%, 40%, 10%, and 10%
   d. 60%, 20%, 20%, and little blood

7. Downstream peripheral pulses have a higher pulse pressure because the pressure wave travels faster than the blood itself. What occurs in peripheral arterial disease?

   a. The pulse decreases rather than increases in amplitude

   b. The reflected wave is transmitted more rapidly through the aorta

   c. Downstream peripheral pulses are increased even more than normal

   d. Downstream peripheral pulses are greater than upstream pulses.

8. Cardiac output (CO) is used to measure the efficiency of the heart as a pump. What is the equation used to express CO?

   a. $CO = HR \times AV$

   b. $CO = SV \times HR$

   c. $CO = AV \times SV$

   d. $CO = HR \times EF$

9. As the needs of the body change, the heart's ability to increase output necessarily needs to change to. This ability in the heart depends on what factors? (Mark all that apply.)

   a. Cardiac reserve

   b. Cardiac contractility

   c. Heart rate

   d. Preload

   e. Afterload

10. Nitroglycerin is the drug of choice in treating angina. What does nitroglycerin release into the vascular smooth muscle of the target tissues?

    a. Antithrombin factor

    b. Platelet aggregating factor

    c. Calcium channel blocker

    d. Nitric oxide

11. Colloidal osmotic pressure acts differently than the osmotic effects of the plasma proteins. What is its action?

    a. Pulls fluid back into the capillary

    b. Pushes fluid into the extracellular spaces

    c. Controls the direction of the fluid flow in the large arteries

    d. Pulls fluid into the interstitial spaces

12. The lymph system correlates with the vascular system without actually being a part of the vascular system. Among other things, the lymph system is the main route for the absorption of fats from the gastrointestinal system. The lymph system empties into the right and left thoracic ducts, which are the points of juncture with the vascular system. What are these points of juncture?

    a. The bifurcation of the common carotid arteries

    b. The internal and external jugular veins

    c. Junctions of the subclavian and internal jugular veins

    d. The junction of the subclavian and the pulmonary veins

13. The heart and blood vessels receive both sympathetic and parasympathetic innervation from neural control. What controls the parasympathetic-mediated slowing of the heart rate?

    a. The vasomotor center

    b. The cardioinhibitory center

    c. The medullary center

    d. The innervation center

Disorders of Blood Flow and Blood Pressure

SECTION I: LEARNING OBJECTIVES

1. Describe the functions of the endothelial cells and define the term *endothelial dysfunction*.

2. Describe the function of vascular smooth muscle and its role in vascular repair.

3. List the five types of lipoproteins and state their function in terms of lipid transport and development of atherosclerosis.

4. Describe the role of lipoprotein receptors in removal of cholesterol from the blood.

5. Cite the criteria for diagnosis of hypercholesterolemia.

6. Describe possible mechanisms involved in the development of atherosclerosis.

7. List risk factors in atherosclerosis.

8. List the vessels most commonly affected by atherosclerosis and describe the vessel changes that occur.

9. State the signs and symptoms of acute arterial occlusion.

10. Describe the pathology associated with the vasculitides and relate it to four disease conditions associated with vasculitis.

11. Compare the mechanisms and manifestations of ischemia associated with atherosclerotic peripheral vascular disease, Raynaud phenomenon, and thromboangiitis obliterans (i.e., Buerger disease).

12. Distinguish between the pathology and manifestations of aortic aneurysms and dissection of the aorta.

13. Describe venous return of blood from the lower extremities, including the function of the muscle pumps and the effects of gravity, and relate to the development of varicose veins.

14. Differentiate primary from secondary varicose veins.

15. Characterize the pathology of venous insufficiency and relate to the development of stasis dermatitis and venous ulcers.

16. List the four most common causes of lower leg ulcer.

17. Cite risk factors associated with venous thrombosis and describe the manifestation of the disorder and its treatment.

18. Define the terms *systolic blood pressure*, *diastolic blood pressure, pulse pressure,* and *mean arterial blood pressure.*

19. Explain how cardiac output and peripheral vascular resistance interact in determining systolic and diastolic blood pressure.

20. Describe the mechanisms for short-term and long-term regulation of blood pressure.

21. Describe the requirements for accurate and reliable blood pressure measurement in terms of cuff size, determining the maximum inflation pressure, and deflation rate.

22. Cite the definition of hypertension put forth by the seventh report of the Joint National Committee on Detection, Evaluation, and Treatment of Hypertension.

23. Differentiate essential, systolic, and secondary forms of hypertension.

24. Describe the possible influence of genetics, age, race, obesity, diet and sodium intake, and alcohol consumption on the development of essential hypertension.

25. Cite the risks of hypertension in terms of target organ damage.

26. Describe behavior modification strategies used in the prevention and treatment of hypertension.

27. List the different categories of drugs used to treat hypertension and state their mechanisms of action in the treatment of high blood pressure.

28. Explain the changes in blood pressure that accompany normal pregnancy and describe the four types of hypertension that can occur during pregnancy.

29. Define systolic hypertension and relate the circulatory changes that occur with aging that predispose to the development of systolic hypertension.

30. Define the term *orthostatic hypotension.*

31. Describe the cardiovascular, neurohumoral, and muscular responses that serve to maintain blood pressure when moving from the supine to standing position.

SECTION II: ASSESSING YOUR UNDERSTANDING

Activity A *Fill in the blanks.*

1. Although the heart is the center of the cardiovascular system, _____ transport blood throughout the body.

2. Endothelial cells form a continuous lining for the entire vascular system called the _____.

3. Vascular smooth muscle cells, which form the predominant cellular layer in the tunica media, produce _____ or _____ of blood vessels.

4. The term _____ denotes a reduction in arterial flow to a level that is insufficient to meet the oxygen demands of the tissues.

5. _____ refers to an area of ischemic necrosis in an organ produced by occlusion of its arterial blood supply or its venous drainage.

6. Elevated levels of blood _____ are implicated in the development of atherosclerosis with its attendant risk of heart attack and stroke.

7. Because _____ and _____ are insoluble in plasma, they are encapsulated by a stabilizing coat of water-soluble lipoproteins.

8. The _____ transport cholesterol and triglycerides to various tissues for energy utilization, lipid deposition, steroid hormone production, and bile acid formation.

9. Some of the apoproteins activate the _____ enzymes that facilitate the removal of lipids from the lipoproteins.

10. There are two sites of lipoprotein synthesis: the _____ and the _____

11. _____ transfer their triglycerides to the cells of adipose and skeletal muscle tissue.

12. LDL, sometimes called the _____, is the main carrier of cholesterol.

13. LDL is removed from the circulation either by _____ or by _____ cells.

14. The uptake of LDL by macrophages in the arterial wall can result in the accumulation of insoluble cholesterol esters, the formation of foam cells, and the development of _____.

15. HDL is synthesized in the liver and often is referred to as the _____.

16. Lipoprotein measurements are particularly important in persons at high risk for development of _____.

17. Many types of primary hypercholesterolemia have a _____ basis.

18. Causes of _____ hyperlipoproteinemia include obesity with high-calorie intake and diabetes mellitus.

19. Excess calories consistently _____ HDL and less consistently _____ LDL.

20. _____ is a type of arteriosclerosis or hardening of the arteries.

21. The major risk factor for atherosclerosis is _____.

22. _____ is closely linked with coronary heart disease and sudden death.

23. Considerable interest in the role of _____ in the etiology of atherosclerosis has emerged over the last few years.

24. _____ is a serum marker for systemic inflammation.

25. _____ inhibits elements of the anticoagulant cascade and is associated with endothelial damage, which is thought to be an important first step in the development of atherosclerosis.

26. Activated macrophages release _____ that oxidize LDL.

27. Small vessel _____ are sometimes associated with antineutrophil cytoplasmic antibodies.

28. An _____ is a freely moving particle such as a blood clot that breaks loose and travels in the larger vessels of the circulation until lodging in a smaller vessel and occluding blood flow.

29. _____ is an inflammatory arterial disorder that causes thrombus formation.

30. _____ is a functional disorder caused by intense vasospasm of the arteries and arterioles in the fingers and, less often, the toes.

31. An _____ is an abnormal localized dilatation of a blood vessel.

32. An aneurysm also may be _____, with the first evidence of its presence being associated with vessel _____.

33. Aortic dissection involves _____ into the vessel wall with longitudinal tearing of the vessel wall to form a blood-filled channel.

34. Venous _____ prevent the retrograde flow of blood.

35. The most common cause of secondary varicose veins is _____.

36. _____ leads to tissue congestion, edema, and eventual impairment of tissue nutrition.

37. Virchow described the triad that has come to be associated with venous thrombosis: _____, _____, and _____.

38. _____ blood pressure reflects the rhythmic ejection of blood from the left ventricle into the aorta.

39. The pressure at the height of the pressure pulse is _____ pressure, and the lowest pressure is the _____ pressure.

40. The difference between the systolic and diastolic pressure (approximately 40 mm Hg) is called the _____.

41. The _____ represents the average pressure in the arterial system during ventricular contraction and relaxation.

42. The mean arterial blood pressure is determined mainly by the _____ and the _____.

43. The *renin-angiotensin-aldosterone* system plays a central role in blood pressure by increasing _____ and _____.

44. The extracellular fluid volume and arterial blood pressure are regulated around an _____ point, which represents the normal pressure for a given individual.

45. The role that the _____ play in blood pressure regulation is emphasized by the fact that many hypertension medications produce their blood pressure-lowering effects by increasing _____ and _____ elimination.

46. _____ *hypertension* is the term applied to 95% of cases in which no cause for hypertension can be identified. In _____ hypertension, the elevation of blood pressure results from some other disorder.

47. A diagnosis of hypertension is made if the systolic blood pressure is _____ or higher and the diastolic blood pressure is _____ or higher.

48. The _____ risk factors include a family history of hypertension, race, and age-related increases in blood pressure.

49. An elevation in blood pressure increases the workload of the _____ by increasing the pressure against which the heart must pump as it ejects blood into the systemic circulation.

50. Chronic hypertension leads to _____, a common cause of chronic kidney disease.

51. Hypertension is a major risk factor for _____ stroke and intracerebral _____.

52. The main objective for treatment of essential hypertension is to achieve and maintain arterial blood pressure below _____.

53. _____ lower blood pressure initially by decreasing vascular volume and cardiac output.

54. The _____ blockers are effective in treating hypertension because they decrease heart rate and cardiac output, as they are cardioselective.

55. The _____ drugs inhibit the movement of calcium into cardiac and vascular smooth muscle.

56. Elevated pressures during _____ favor the development of left ventricular hypertrophy, increased myocardial oxygen demands, and eventual left heart failure.

57. Many of the conditions causing _____ hypertension can be corrected or cured by surgery or specific medical treatment.

58. The use of _____ pills is probably the most common cause of secondary hypertension in young women.

59. _____ is defined as an elevation in blood pressure and proteinuria developing after 20 weeks of gestation.

60. Any disease condition that reduces blood volume, impairs mobility, results in prolonged inactivity, or impairs autonomic nervous system function may also predispose to _____ .

Activity B *Consider the following figures.*

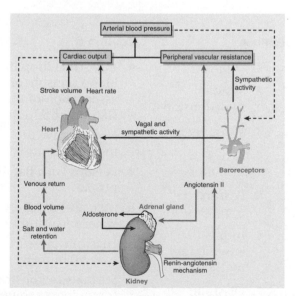

In the figure of a fibrofatty plaque above, label the following: media, lymphocytes, endothelial cells, smooth muscle cells, macrophages, CAP region, and necrotic core.

What does this figure depict? Describe what the solid lines represent and what the dashed lines represent.

Activity C *Match the key terms in Column A with their definitions in Column B.*

1.

Column A

____ **1.** Chylo-microns

____ **2.** CRP

____ **3.** Familial hyperchole-sterolemia

____ **4.** Xanthomas

____ **5.** Hyperchol-esterolemia

____ **6.** Vasculitis

____ **7.** VLDL

____ **8.** Homocysteine

____ **9.** Atherosclerosis

____ **10.** LDL

Column B

a. Necrosis of the blood vessel wall

b. Main carrier of cholesterol

c. Derived from the metabolism of dietary methionine

d. Elevated levels of blood cholesterol

e. LDL-related arteriosclerosis

f. Carries large amounts of triglycerides

g. Caused by LDL receptor deficiency, which prevents uptake of LDL

h. Transfer triglycerides to skeletal muscle, smaller than VLDLs

i. Elevated levels associated with arterial disease

j. Cholesterol deposits

2.

Column A

____ **1.** Dippers

____ **2.** Systolic hypertension

____ **3.** Vasopressin

____ **4.** ACE inhibitors

____ **5.** Postural hypotension

____ **6.** Indirect auscultatory method

____ **7.** Diastolic hypertension

Column B

a. Abnormal drop in blood pressure on assumption of the standing position

b. Noninvasive BP measurement

c. Persons with flat BP profile

d. Increases renal water retention

e. Diastolic pressure over 90 mm Hg

f. Strong vasoconstric-tor, reduces sodium excretion

____ **8.** Coarctation of the aorta

____ **9.** ANG II

____ **10.** Nondippers

g. Narrowing of the aorta

h. Systolic pressure over 140 mm Hg

i. Persons whose BP follows circadian rhythms

j. Block formation of ANG II

Activity D *Put the sequence and actions of the renin-angiotensin-aldosterone system into chronological order.*

a. Water retention

b. Stimulation of juxtaglomerular apparatus

c. Conversion of angiotensinogen to angiotensin I

d. Conversion of ANG I to ANG II by angiotensin-converting enzyme

e. Increased vascular resistance, release of aldos-terone

f. Stimulation of juxtaglomerular apparatus

g. Increased vascular resistance, release of aldos-terone

h. Na$^+$ retention, stimulation of ADH release

Activity E *Briefly answer the following.*

1. Describe the role of the endothelium.

_____

_____

_____

2. Describe the causation of secondary hyperlipoproteinemia.

_____

_____

_____

3. Describe the general mechanisms of drug therapy to lower serum LDL levels.

_____

_____

_____

4. What are the seven signs and symptoms of acute arterial occlusion?

_____

_____

_____

5. What are the physical effects of Raynaud phenomenon?

_____

_____

_____

6. How do skeletal muscles of the leg contribute to returning blood to the heart?

_____

_____

_____

7. Explain the short-term regulation of blood pressure.

_____

_____

_____

8. Why does the kidney play a major role in the development of secondary hypertension?

_____

_____

_____

SECTION III: PRACTICING FOR NCLEX

Activity F *Answer the following questions.*

1. A variety of etiologies are responsible for altering the blood flow in the systemic circulation. Match the disturbance of blood flow with the cause.

Disturbance in Blood Flow

1. Abnormal vessel dilation

2. Pathologic changes in vessel wall

3. Acute vessel obstruction

4. Pathologic changes in vessel wall

Cause

a. Atherosclerosis (arterial)

b. Raynaud phenomenon (vasospasm)

c. Venous thrombosis (venous)

d. Varicose veins (venous)

e. Vasculitis (arterial)

5. Abnormal vessel dilation

6. Acute vessel obstruction

f. Arterial aneurysms (arterial)

2. Where in the body is lipoprotein is synthesized? (Mark all that apply.)
   a. The small intestine
   b. The large intestine
   c. The pancreas
   d. The liver

3. A 35-year-old man presents to the emergency department complaining of chest pain for the last 2 hours. He describes the pain as crushing, like a huge weight is on his chest. He also states that the pain goes up into his neck and down his left arm. An acute myocardial infarction (MI) is diagnosed. When taking his history, the following things are noted:
   - Hyperlipoproteinemia for past 7 years
   - Family history of early MI
   - Cholesterol deposits along the tendons (diagnosed 1 year ago)
   - Atherosclerosis (diagnosed 6 months ago)
   - Diabetes mellitus (type 1) diagnosed at age 16

The nurse suspects which of the following diagnosis will be made?
   a. Familial hypercholesterolemia (type 2A)
   b. Homozygotic cutaneous xanthoma
   c. Adult-onset hypercholesterolemia (type 1A)
   d. Secondary hyperlipoproteinemia

4. Atherosclerosis begins in an insidious manner with symptoms becoming apparent as long as 20 to 40 years after the onset of the disease. Although an exact etiology of the disease has not been identified, epidemiologic studies have shown that there are predisposing risk factors to this disease. What is the major risk factor for developing atherosclerosis?
   a. Male sex
   b. Hypercholesterolemia
   c. Familial history of premature coronary heart disease
   d. Increasing age

5. A group of vascular disorders called vasculitides cause inflammatory injury and necrosis of the blood vessel wall (i.e., vasculitis). These disorders are common pathways for tissue and organ involvement in many different disease conditions. What is the most common of the vasculitides?
   a. Polyarteritis nodosa
   b. Raynaud disease
   c. Temporal arteritis
   d. Varicose veins

6. A 69-year-old man is admitted to the floor following a popliteal embolectomy. He asks the nurse why he had to have surgery on his leg. What is the best response by the nurse?
   a. The doctor wanted to look into your artery make sure everything was okay.
   b. Didn't the doctor explain everything to you before your surgery?
   c. The artery that runs behind your knee was blocked by a blood clot, and the doctor removed it.
   d. Your upper leg was not getting enough blood so the doctor had to fix it.

7. A 45-year-old woman with a diagnosis of multiple sclerosis comes to the clinic complaining of coldness and pain in her fingers. She says that her fingers turn blue, and then her fingers get red, and they throb and tingle. The nurse would expect what diagnosis and treatment for this patient? (Mark all that apply.)
   a. Raynaud disease; protecting the digits from cold
   b. Arterial thrombosis; streptokinase
   c. Peripheral artery disease; aspirin
   d. Raynaud phenomenon; stop smoking

8. Aortic aneurysms take varied forms and can occur anywhere along the aorta. What are the types of aneurysm termed *abdominal aortic aneurysms*? (Mark all that apply.)
   a. Berry aneurysms
   b. Dissecting aneurysms
   c. Saccular aneurysms
   d. Fusiform aneurysms
   e. Bifurcating aneurysms

9. A 56-year-old woman presents at the clinic complaining of the unsightliness of her varicose veins and wants to know what can be done about them. The nurse explains that the treatment for varicose veins includes which of the following interventions?
   a. Surgical or fibrotherapy
   b. Sclerotherapy or surgery
   c. Trendelenburg therapy or sclerotherapy
   d. Surgery or Trendelenburg therapy

10. Venous thrombosis most commonly occurs in the lower extremities. Risk factors for venous thrombosis include which of the following?
    a. Stasis of blood, hypercoagulability, inflammation
    b. Hypocoagulability, vessel wall injury, increased pressure on deep veins
    c. Vessel wall injury, hypocoagulability, decreased venous blood flow
    d. Stasis of blood, hypercoagulability, vessel wall injury

11. For people who suffer from hypertension and other diseases that affect blood pressure, important information about the status of their disease is gathered from measurements including systolic and diastolic pressures, pulse pressure, and mean arterial pressure. What is the mean arterial pressure estimated to be when the blood pressure is 130/85?
    a. 90
    b. 95
    c. 100
    d. 105

12. Although the etiology of essential hypertension is mainly unknown, several risk factors have been identified. These risk factors fall under the categories of constitutional risk factors and lifestyle factors. What are the primary risk factors for essential hypertension? (Mark all that apply.)
    a. Race and excessive sodium chloride intake
    b. Type 2 diabetes and obesity
    c. Age and high intake of potassium
    d. Race and smoking
    e. Family history and excessive alcohol consumption

13. A 37-year-old woman is admitted to your unit with a differential diagnosis of rule out pheo-chromocytoma. What are the most common symptoms you would expect this patient to exhibit?
    a. Nervousness and periodic severe headache
    b. Variability in blood pressure and weight loss
    c. Excessive sweating and pallor
    d. Periodic severe headache and marked vari-ability in blood pressure

14. The extended, severe exposure of the walls of the blood vessels to the exaggerated pressures that occur in malignant hypertension cause injuries to the walls of the arterioles. Blood vessels in the renal system are particularly vul-nerable to this type of damage. Because hyper-tension is a chronic disease and is associated with autoregulatory changes in the blood flow to major organs, what would be the initial treatment goal for malignant hypertension?
    a. Partial reduction in blood pressure to less critical values
    b. Reduction to normotensive levels of blood pressure
    c. Rapid decrease in blood pressure to less critical levels
    d. Slow, gradual decrease in blood pressure to normotensive blood pressures

15. A client with malignant hypertension is at risk for a hypertensive crisis, including the cerebral vascular system often causing cerebral edema. As the nurse caring for this patient, what are the signs and symptoms you would assess for?
    a. Papilledema and lethargy
    b. Headache and confusion
    c. Restlessness and nervousness
    d. Stupor and hyperreflexia

16. Pregnancy-induced hypertension is a serious condition affecting between 5% and 10% of pregnant women. The most serious classifica-tion of hypertension in pregnancy is preeclampsia-eclampsia. It is a pregnancy-specific syndrome that can have both mater-nal and fetal manifestations. What is a life-threatening manifestation of the preeclampsia-eclampsia classification of preg-nancy-induced hypertension?
    a. Hepatocellular necrosis
    b. Thrombocytopenia

    c. HELLP syndrome
    d. Decreased renal filtration rate

17. In infants and children, secondary hyperten-sion is the most common form of hypertension. What is the most common cause of hypertension in an infant?
    a. Cerebral vascular bleed
    b. Coarctation of the aorta
    c. Pheochromocytoma
    d. Renal artery thrombosis

18. Hypertension in the elderly is a common finding. This is because of the age-related rise in systolic blood pressure. Among the aging processes, what is a contributor to hyperten-sion?
    a. Baroreceptor sensitivity
    b. Aortic softening
    c. Decreased peripheral vascular resistance
    d. Increased renal blood flow

19. A 75-year-old man presents at the clinic for a routine physical check-up. He is found to be hypertensive. While taking his blood pressure in the sitting, standing, lying positions, the nurse notes that the brachial artery is pulseless at a high cuff pressure, but she can still feel it. What condition would the nurse suspect?
    a. Essential hypertension
    b. Pseudohypertension
    c. Orthostatic hypertension
    d. Secondary hypertension

20. The rennin-angiotensin-aldosterone system is a negative feedback system that plays a central role in blood pressure regulation. How does the end result of this feedback loop regulate blood pressure in the body?
    a. Vasodilates blood vessels to decrease blood pressure
    b. Vasoconstricts blood vessels to increase blood pressure
    c. Increases salt and water retention by the kidney
    d. Decreases salt and water retention by the kidney

CHAPTER **19**

Disorders of Cardiac Function

SECTION I: LEARNING OBJECTIVES

1. Characterize the function of the pericardium.

2. Compare the clinical manifestations of acute pericarditis and chronic pericarditis.

3. Describe the physiologic impact of pleural effusion on cardiac function and relate it to the life-threatening nature of cardiac tamponade.

4. Relate the pathophysiology of constrictive pericarditis to its clinical manifestations.

5. Describe blood flow in the coronary circulation and relate it to the determinants of myocardial oxygen supply and demand.

6. Define the term *acute coronary syndrome* (ACS) and distinguish among chronic stable angina, unstable angina, non–ST-segment elevation myocardial infarction (MI), and ST-segment elevation infarction in terms of pathology, symptomatology, electrocardiograph (ECG) changes, and serum cardiac markers.

7. Compare the treatment goals for stable angina and the acute coronary syndromes.

8. Define the term *cardiomyopathy* as it relates to both the mechanical and electrical function of the myocardium.

9. Describe the role of genetics in the etiology of the primary cardiomyopathies.

10. Differentiate among the pathophysiologic changes that occur with hypertrophic cardiomyopathy, arrhythmogenic right ventricular cardiomyopathy, dilated cardiomyopathies, and myocarditis.

11. List four causes of secondary cardiomyopathy.

12. Describe the treatment strategies of both primary and secondary cardiomyopathy.

13. Distinguish between the roles of infectious organisms and the immune system in infective endocarditis and rheumatic fever.

14. Describe the relation between the infective vegetations associated with infective endocarditis and the extracardiac manifestations of the disease.

15. Describe the long-term effects of rheumatic fever and primary and secondary prevention strategies for rheumatic fever and rheumatic heart disease.

16. State the function of the heart valves and relate alterations in hemodynamic function of the heart that occur with valvular disease.

17. Compare the effects of stenotic and regurgitant mitral and aortic valvular heart disease on cardiovascular function.

18. Compare the methods of and diagnostic information obtained from cardiac auscultation and echocardiography as they relate to valvular heart disease.

19. Trace the flow of blood in the fetal circulation, state the function of the foramen ovale and ductus arteriosus, and describe the changes in circulatory function that occur at birth.

20. Compare the effects of left-to-right and right-to-left shunts on the pulmonary circulation and production of cyanosis.

21. Describe the anatomic defects and altered patterns of blood flow in children with atrial septal defects, ventricular septal defects, endocardial cushion defects, pulmonary stenosis, tetralogy of Fallot, patent ductus arteriosus, transposition of the great vessels, coarctation of the aorta, and single-ventricle anatomy.

22. Describe the prevalence of the condition and issues of concern for adults with congenital heart disease.

23. Describe the manifestations related to the acute, subacute, and convalescent phases of Kawasaki disease.

SECTION II: ASSESSING YOUR UNDERSTANDING

Activity A *Fill in the blanks.*

1. The _____ is a double-layered serous membrane that isolates the heart from other thoracic structures, maintains its position in the thorax, prevents it from overfilling, and serves as a barrier to infection.

2. Pericardial fluid acts as a lubricant that prevents _____ forces from developing as the heart contracts and relaxes.

3. The manifestations of acute _____ include a triad of chest pain, pericardial friction rub, and ECG changes.

4. Pericardial _____ refers to the accumulation of fluid in the pericardial cavity, usually because of an inflammatory and or infectious process.

5. Pericardial effusion can lead to cardiac _____, in which there is compression of the heart due to the accumulation of fluid, pus, or blood in the pericardial sac.

6. In _____ pericarditis, fibrous, calcified scar tissue develops between the visceral and parietal layers of the serous pericardium.

7. In most cases, coronary artery disease (CAD) is caused by _____.

8. Myocardial blood flow, in turn, is largely regulated by the _____ of the myocardium and _____ mechanisms that control vessel dilation.

9. There is little oxygen reserve in the blood; therefore, coronary arteries must increase their flow to meet the metabolic needs of the myocardium during periods of _____.

10. The _____ is the most frequently used cardiovascular diagnostic procedure.

11. _____ uses ultrasound signals that inaudible to the human ear.

12. _____ is by far the most common cause of CAD.

13. There are two types of atherosclerotic lesions: the _____ plaque, which obstructs blood flow, and the _____ plaque, which can rupture and cause platelet adhesion and thrombus formation.

14. Coronary artery disease is commonly divided into two types of disorders: _____ and _____.

15. The classic ECG changes that occur with ACS involve _____, _____, and _____.

16. Acute severe ischemia reduces the _____ and shortens the duration of the action potential in the ischemic area.

17. The _____ have high specificity for myocardial tissue and have become the primary biomarker for the diagnosis of MI.

18. _____ myocardial infarction is characterized by the ischemic death of myocardial tissue associated with atherosclerotic disease of the coronary arteries.

19. Irreversible myocardial cell death occurs after _____ minutes of severe ischemia.

20. Infarcted and noninfarcted areas of the heart muscle in patients with ST-segment elevation myocardial infarction (STEMI) can change size, shape, and thickness, a term referred to as _____.

21. The gastrointestinal symptoms of STEMI are thought to be related to the severity of the pain and _____ stimulation.

22. The medication used to alleviate angina, _____, is given because of its vasodilating effect.

23. _____ is a mechanical technique to remove atherosclerotic tissue during angioplasty.

24. Partial or complete rupture of a _____ is a rare but often fatal complication of transmural myocardial infarction.

25. _____ is the initial manifestation of ischemic heart disease in approximately half of persons with CAD.

26. Typically, chronic stable angina is provoked by _____ or _____ stress and relieved within minutes by rest or the use of nitroglycerin.

27. The _____ cardiomyopathies include hypertrophic cardiomyopathy, arrhythmogenic right ventricular cardiomyopathy, left ventricular noncompaction cardiomyopathy, inherited conduction system disorders, and ion channelopathies.

28. The _____ cardiomyopathies, which include dilated cardiomyopathy, are of both genetic and nongenetic origin.

29. The physiologic abnormality in _____ is reduced left ventricular chamber size, poor compliance with reduced stroke volume that results from impaired diastolic filling, and dynamic obstruction of left ventricular outflow.

30. _____ cardiomyopathies are characterized by atrophic and hypertrophic myocardial fibers and interstitial fibrosis.

31. _____ is the most common, and frequently the first, manifestation of rheumatic fever.

32. The _____ manifestation of rheumatic fever is Sydenham chorea, in which the child often is fidgety, cries easily, begins to walk clumsily, and drops things.

33. The function of the heart _____ is to promote directional flow of blood through the chambers of the heart.

34. Mitral valve _____ represents the incomplete opening of the mitral valve during diastole with left atrial distention and impaired filling of the left ventricle.

35. Mitral valve _____ is characterized by incomplete closure of the mitral valve, with the left ventricular stroke volume being divided between the forward stroke volume that moves into the aorta and the regurgitant stroke volume that moves back into the left atrium during systole.

36. Most persons with mitral valve _____ are asymptomatic and the disorder is discovered during a routine physical examination.

37. Increased resistance to ejection of blood from the left ventricle into the aorta characterizes aortic valve _____.

38. Aortic _____ is the result of an incompetent aortic valve that allows blood to flow back to the left ventricle during diastole.

39. The major development of the _____ occurs between the fourth and seventh weeks of gestation, and most congenital heart defects arise during this time.

40. Congenital heart defects produce their effects mainly through abnormal shunting of _____, production of _____, and disruption of _____ blood flow.

41. Congenital heart defects that result in a left-to-right shunt are usually categorized as _____ disorders because they do not compromise oxygenation of blood in the pulmonary circulation.

42. A _____ defect is an opening in the ventricular septum that results from an incomplete separation of the ventricles during early fetal development.

43. _____ disease, also known as mucocutaneous lymph node syndrome, is an acute febrile disease of young children.

Activity B *Consider the following figure.*

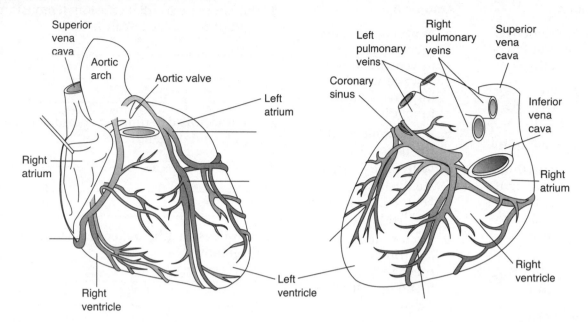

In the figure above, label the coronary arteries.

Activity C *Match the key terms in Column A with their definitions in Column B.*

1.

Column A

___ **1.** Unstable angina

___ **2.** Effusive-constrictive pericarditis

___ **3.** Ischemia

___ **4.** Pericardial effusion

___ **5.** Prinzmetal angina

___ **6.** Cardiac tamponade

___ **7.** Silent myocardial ischemia

___ **8.** Heart attack

___ **9.** Infective endocarditis

___ **10.** Pulsus paradoxus

Column B

a. Chest pain due to a coronary artery spasm

b. ST elevation myocardial infarction

c. Decreased blood flow to tissue

d. Accumulation of fluid in the pericardial cavity

e. Invasion of the heart valves and the mural endocardium by a microbial agent

f. Mechanical compression of the heart

g. Occurs in the absence of anginal pain

h. Combination of effusion-tamponade and constriction

i. Chest pain occurring while at rest

j. Exaggeration of the normal variation in the pulse during the inspiratory phase of respiration

2.

Column A

_____ **1.** Restrictive cardiomyo-pathy

_____ **2.** Ion channelo-pathies

_____ **3.** Myocarditis

_____ **4.** Arrhythmo-genic right ventricular cardiomyo-pathy

_____ **5.** Dilated cardiomyo-pathy

_____ **6.** Stress cardiomyo-pathy

_____ **7.** Hypertrophic cardiomyo-pathy

_____ **8.** Left ventricular noncomp-action

_____ **9.** Secondary cardiomyo-pathy

_____ **10.** Peripartum cardiomyo-pathy

Column B

a. Ventricular enlarge-ment, a reduction in ventricular wall thickness, and impaired systolic function

b. An inflammation of the heart

c. With disproportion-ate thickening of the ventricular septum and left ventricle

d. Occurs during the last trimester of pregnancy or the first 6 months after delivery

e. Conduction disorders in the heart resulting from abnormal membrane potentials (long QT/short QT syndromes)

f. Left ventricular dysfunction in response to profound psychological or emotional stress

g. Ventricular filling is restricted because of excessive rigidity of the ventricular walls

h. Heart muscle disease that affects primarily the right ventricle

i. Heart muscle disease in the presence of a multisystem disorder

j. Failure of trabecular compaction in the developing myocardium

Activity D _Briefly answer the following._

1. Why does pericardial effusion demonstrate signs of right-sided heart failure?

_____

_____

_____

2. What factors determine myocardial oxygen supply and demand?

_____

_____

_____

3. How does an atherosclerotic plaque stimulate thrombosis?

_____

_____

_____

4. What changes are seen in the blood (serum) during ACS?

_____

_____

_____

5. Describe the pathologic process that is seen in unstable angina/non–ST-segment elevation myocardial infarction.

_____

_____

_____

6. What is the damage that results from an acute myocardial infarction and what are the factors that determine severity?

_____

_____

_____

7. What is meant by "reperfusion therapy" and what is its goal?

_____

_____

_____

8. What is the definition of a cardiomyopathy, according to the American Heart Association?

_____

_____

_____

9. What is the relationship between strep throat and heart valve disorders?

_____

_____

_____

10. Describe the clinical manifestation of patent ductus arteriosus.

_____

_____

_____

11. Describe the tetralogy of Fallot.

_____

_____

_____

SECTION III: APPLYING YOUR KNOWLEDGE

Activity E *Consider the scenario and answer the questions.*

A 55-year-old woman is brought to the emergency department by ambulance and is complaining of severe, acute chest pain. The patient states that "It just came on all of a sudden. Like someone sitting on my chest crushing me." An ECG shows ST-segment elevation and the presumptive diagnosis is acute STEMI.

1. While obtaining a history on this patient, what symptoms would the nurse pay particular attention to as they are further indications of a STEMI?

_____

_____

_____

2. What are the emergency department goals of management for a patient with a STEMI?

_____

_____

_____

SECTION IV: PRACTICING FOR NCLEX

Activity F *Answer the following questions.*

1. Nearly everyone with pericarditis has chest pain. With acute pericarditis the pain is abrupt in onset, sharp, and radiates to the neck, back, abdomen, or sides. What can be done to ease the pain of acute pericarditis?
   a. Have patient sit up and lean forward
   b. Have patient change positions to unaffected side
   c. Have patient breathe deeply
   d. Have patient swallow slowly and frequently

2. Cardiac tamponade is a serious life-threatening condition that can arise from a number of other conditions. What is a key diagnostic finding in cardiac tamponade?
   a. Increase in stroke volume
   b. Pulsus paradoxus
   c. Narrowed pulse pressure
   d. Rise in systolic blood pressure

3. The scar tissue that occurs between the layers of the pericardium becomes rigid and constrictive from scar tissue in constrictive pericarditis. What is a physiologic sign of constrictive pericarditis?
   a. Kussmaul breathing
   b. Pulsus paradoxus
   c. Kussmaul sign
   d. Widening pulse pressure

4. Unstable plaque, a condition of atherosclerotic heart disease, occurs in unstable angina and myocardial infarction. Unstable plaque can rupture, causing platelet aggregation and thrombus formation. What are the major determinants of the vulnerability of plaque to rupture? (Mark all that apply.)

   a. Size of lipid-rich core

   b. Preponderance of smooth muscle cells

   c. Presence of inflammation

   d. Decrease in blood pressure and coronary blood flow

   e. Thickness of fibrous cap

5. A patient with a suspected MI is brought to the emergency department by ambulance. As the nurse caring for this patient, what laboratory work would you expect to receive an order for, to confirm a diagnosis of MI?

   a. Creatine kinase marker

   b. Complete blood components

   c. Calcium level

   d. Troponin level

6. Unstable angina (UA)/non–ST-segment elevation myocardial infarction (NSTEMI) is a clinical syndrome that ranges in severity between stable angina to MI. It is classified according to its risk of causing an acute MI and is diagnosed based on what? (Mark all that apply.)

   a. Severity of pain and abruptness of onset

   b. Serum biomarkers

   c. Coexisting chronic conditions

   d. ECG pattern

   e. Blood-flow angiography

7. When an acute MI occurs, many physiologic changes occur very rapidly. What causes the loss of contractile function of the heart within seconds of the onset of an MI?

   a. Conversion from aerobic to anaerobic metabolism

   b. Overproduction of energy capable of sustaining normal myocardial function

   c. Conversion from anaerobic to aerobic metabolism

   d. Inadequate production of glycogen with mitochondrial shrinkage

8. ST-elevated myocardial infarction is accompanied by severe, crushing pain. Morphine is the drug of choice used to treat the pain of STEMI when the pain cannot be relieved with oxygen and nitrates. Why is morphine considered the drug of choice in STEMI?

   a. Action increases autonomic nervous system activity

   b. Action decreases metabolic demands of the heart

   c. Action increases anxiety increasing metabolic demands of heart

   d. Action relieves pain and gives sense of depression

9. During an acute MI there is ischemic damage to the heart muscle. The location and extent of the ischemic damage is the major predictor of complications, ranging from cardiac insufficiency to death, following an MI. What is the "window of opportunity" in restoring blood flow to the affected area so as to diminish the ischemic damage to the heart and maintain the viability of the cells?

   a. 10 to 20 minutes

   b. 30 to 40 minutes

   c. 20 to 40 minutes

   d. 10 to 30 minutes

10. Angina pectoris is a chronic ischemic CAD that is characterized by a symptomatic paroxysmal chest pain or pressure sensation associated with transient myocardial ischemia. What precipitates an attack of angina pectoris?

    a. Exposure to heat

    b. Sedentary lifestyle

    c. Abrupt change in position

    d. Emotional stress

11. The diagnosis of chronic stable angina is based on a detailed pain history, the presence of risk factors, invasive and noninvasive studies, and laboratory studies. What test is not used in the diagnosis of angina?

    a. Serum biochemical markers

    b. Cardiac catheterization

    c. Echocardiogram

    d. Nuclear imaging studies

12. Cardiomyopathies are classified as either primary or secondary. The primary cardiomyopathies are further classified as genetic, mixed, or acquired. Identify whether the following conditions are classified as *genetic, acquired,* or *mixed.*

    a. Hypertrophic cardiomyopathy

    b. Left ventricular noncompaction

    c. Myocarditis

    d. Dilated cardiomyopathy

    e. Peripartum cardiomyopathy

13. It is known that over 100 distinct myocardial diseases can demonstrate clinical features associated with dilated cardiomyopathy (DCM). What is the most common identifiable cause of DCM in the United States?

    a. Hepatic cardiomyopathy

    b. Alcoholic cardiomyopathy

    c. Cardiotoxic cardiomyopathy

    d. Exercise induced cardiomyopathy

14. In infective endocarditis vegetative lesions grow on the valves of the heart. These vegetative lesions consist of a collection of infectious organisms and cellular debris enmeshed in the fibrin strands of clotted blood. What are the possible systemic effects of these vegetative lesions?

    a. They can block the heart valves from closing completely

    b. They can keep the heart valves from opening

    c. They can fragment and cause cerebral emboli

    d. They can fragment and make the lesions larger

15. Antibodies directed against the M protein of certain strains of streptococcal bacteria seem to cross-react with glycoprotein antigens in the heart, joint, and other tissues to produce an autoimmune response resulting in rheumatic fever and rheumatic heart disease. This occurs through what phenomenon?

    a. The Aschoff reaction

    b. The Sydenham reaction

    c. C-reactive mimicry

    d. Molecular mimicry

16. Mitral valve prolapse occurs frequently in the population at large. Its treatment is aimed at relieving the symptoms and preventing complications of the disorder. Which drug is used in the treatment of mitral valve prolapse to relieve symptoms and aid in preventing complications?

    a. β-Adrenergic–blocking drugs

    b. Calcium channel blocking drugs

    c. Antianxiety drugs

    d. Broad-spectrum antibiotic drugs

17. Heart failure in an infant usually manifests itself as tachypnea or dyspnea, both at rest and on exertion. When does this most commonly occur with an infant?

    a. During bathing

    b. During feeding

    c. During burping

    d. During sleep

18. Tetralogy of Fallot is a congenital condition of the heart that manifests in four distinct anomalies of the infant heart. It is considered a cyanotic heart defect because of the right-to-left shunting of the blood through the ventricular septal defect. A hallmark of this condition is the "tet spells" that occur in these children. What is a tet spell?

    a. A stressful period right after birth that occurs without evidence of cyanosis.

    b. A hyperoxygenated period when the infant is at rest

    c. A hypercyanotic attack brought on by periods of stress

    d. A hyperpneic attack in which the infant loses consciousness

CHAPTER 20

Heart Failure and Circulatory Shock

SECTION I: LEARNING OBJECTIVES

1. Define heart failure.

2. Describe the contractile properties of the myocardium.

3. Explain how the Frank-Starling mechanism, sympathetic nervous system, renin-angiotensin-aldosterone mechanism, natriuretic peptides, endothelins, and myocardial hypertrophy and remodeling function as adaptive and maladaptive mechanisms in heart failure.

4. Differentiate high-output versus low-output heart failure, systolic versus diastolic heart dysfunction, and right-sided versus left-sided heart failure in terms of causes, impact on cardiac function, and major manifestations.

5. Differentiate chronic heart failure from acute heart failure syndromes.

6. Describe the manifestations of heart failure and relate to the function of the heart.

7. Describe the methods used in diagnosis and assessment of cardiac function in persons with heart failure.

8. Relate the pharmacologic actions of angiotensin-converting enzyme inhibitors and receptor blockers, β-adrenergic blockers, diuretics, digoxin, and vasodilatory agents to the treatment of heart failure.

9. Relate the use of cardiac resynchronization, implantable cardioverter-defibrillators, left ventricular assist devices, heart transplantation, and other surgical alternatives to the treatment of selected types of heart failure.

10. State a clinical definition of shock.

11. Compare the causes, pathophysiology, and chief characteristics of cardiogenic, hypovolemic, obstructive, and distributive shock.

12. Describe the complications of shock as they relate to the lungs, kidneys, gastrointestinal tract, and blood clotting.

13. State the rationale for treatment measures to correct and reverse shock.

14. Define multiple organ dysfunction syndrome and cite its significance in shock.

15. Describe the causes of heart failure in infants and children.

16. Cite how the aging process affects cardiac function and predisposes to ventricular dysfunction.

17. State how the signs and symptoms of heart failure may differ between younger and older adults.

SECTION II: ASSESSING YOUR UNDERSTANDING

Activity A *Fill in the blanks.*

1. _____ has been defined as a complex syndrome that results from any functional or structural disorder of the heart that results in decreased pumping.

2. Among the most common causes of heart failure are _____, _____, dilated cardiomyopathy, and _____ heart disease.

3. Endurance athletes have _____ cardiac reserves.

4. _____ can be expressed as the product of the heart rate and stroke volume.

5. The heart rate is regulated by a balance between the activity of the _____ nervous system, which produces an increase in heart rate, and the _____ nervous system, which slows it down.

6. The _____ is a function of preload, afterload, and myocardial contractility.

7. _____ is the percentage of blood pumped out of the ventricles with each contraction.

8. In systolic ventricular dysfunction, myocardial contractility is impaired, leading to a _____ in the ejection fraction and cardiac output.

9. Diastolic ventricular dysfunction is characterized by a _____ ejection fraction but impaired diastolic ventricular relaxation leading to a decrease in ventricular filling, which ultimately causes a decrease in preload, stroke volume, and cardiac output.

10. With both systolic and diastolic ventricular dysfunction, _____ are usually able to maintain adequate resting cardiac function until the later stages of heart failure.

11. The rise in preload seen in systolic dysfunction is thought to be a compensatory mechanism to help maintain stroke volume via the _____ mechanism despite a drop in ejection fraction.

12. Systolic dysfunction commonly results from conditions that impair the _____ performance of the heart (e.g., ischemic heart disease and cardiomyopathy), produce a _____ (e.g., valvular insufficiency and anemia), or generate a _____ (e.g., hypertension and valvular stenosis) on the heart.

13. In _____ dysfunction, cardiac output is compromised by the abnormal filling of the ventricle.

14. Among the conditions that cause diastolic dysfunction are those that _____ the ventricle (e.g., pericardial effusion, constrictive pericarditis), those that _____ wall thickness and reduce chamber size (e.g., myocardial hypertrophy, hypertrophic cardiomyopathy), and those that _____ diastolic relaxation (e.g., aging, ischemic heart disease).

15. Diastolic dysfunction can be aggravated by _____ and can be improved by a reduction in heart rate.

16. Heart failure can be classified according to the _____ of the heart that is primarily affected.

17. A major effect of right-sided heart failure is the development of _____.

18. As venous distention progresses in right-sided heart failure, blood backs up in the _____ veins that drain into the inferior vena cava, and the liver becomes engorged.

19. _____ is the most common cause of right ventricular failure.

20. The most common causes of _____ ventricular dysfunction are acute myocardial infarction and cardiomyopathy.

21. _____ is an uncommon type of heart failure that is caused by an excessive need for cardiac output.

22. _____ is caused by disorders that impair the pumping ability of the heart, such as ischemic heart disease and cardiomyopathy.

23. The development of _____ constitutes one of the principle mechanisms by which the heart compensates for an increase in workload.

24. A gradual or rapid change in heart failure signs and symptoms resulting in a need for urgent therapy is defined as _____ syndrome.

25. _____ dyspnea is a sudden attack of dyspnea that occurs during sleep.

26. _____ is the most dramatic symptom of acute heart failure syndromes.

27. In acute or severe left-sided failure, cardiac output may fall to levels that are insufficient for providing the _____ with adequate oxygen.

28. Ascites is a common manifestation associated with _____ ventricular failure and long-standing elevation of systemic venous pressures.

29. Central cyanosis is caused by conditions that impair _____ of the arterial blood.

30. In persons with ventricular dysfunction, sudden death is caused most commonly by _____ tachycardia or fibrillation.

31. Measurements of _____ are recommended to confirm the diagnosis of heart failure to evaluate the severity of left ventricular compromise and estimate the prognosis, and predict future cardiac events such as sudden death, and to evaluate the effectiveness of treatment.

32. β-Adrenergic receptor blocking drugs are used to decrease _____ dysfunction associated with activation of the sympathetic nervous system.

33. _____ can be described as an acute failure of the circulatory system to supply the peripheral tissues and organs of the body with an adequate blood supply, resulting in cellular hypoxia.

34. The most common cause of cardiogenic shock is _____.

35. _____ shock is characterized by diminished blood volume such that there is inadequate filling of the vascular compartment.

36. _____ shock is characterized by loss of blood vessel tone, enlargement of the vascular compartment, and displacement of the vascular volume away from the heart and central circulation.

37. A defect in the vasomotor center in the brain stem or the sympathetic outflow to the blood vessels is known as _____.

38. Anaphylactic shock results from an _____ mediated reaction in which vasodilator substances such as histamine are released into the blood.

39. _____ heart defects are the most common cause of heart failure in children.

40. _____ is associated with impaired left ventricular filling that is due to changes in myocardial relaxation and compliance.

Activity B *Match the key terms in Column A with their definitions in Column B.*

1.

Column A	Column B
___ 1. Inotropy	a. Volume or loading conditions of the ventricle at the end of diastole
___ 2. Cardiac output	b. Right heart failure occurs in response to chronic pulmonary disease
___ 3. Afterload	c. Ability to increase cardiac output during increased activity
___ 4. Pulmonary congestion	
___ 5. Cardiac reserve	d. The force that the contracting heart muscle must generate to eject blood from the filled heart
___ 6. Cor pulmonale	
___ 7. High-output failure	e. Failure that is caused by an excessive need for cardiac output
___ 8. Preload	f. Amount of blood the ventricles eject each minute
___ 9. Systolic dysfunction	g. Ejection fraction less than 40%
___ 10. Endothelins	h. Potent vasoconstrictors
	i. Common sign of left ventricular failure
	j. Contractile performance of the heart

2.

Column A	Column B
____ **1.** Hydrothorax	**a.** Periodic breathing characterized by gradual increase in depth followed by a decrease resulting in apnea
____ **2.** Cyanosis	
____ **3.** Cheyne-Stokes respiration	
____ **4.** Dyspnea	**b.** Bronchospasm due to congestion of the bronchial mucosa
____ **5.** *Cardiac asthma*	
____ **6.** Circulatory failure	**c.** Bluish discoloration of the skin
____ **7.** *Orthopnea*	**d.** Labored breathing
____ **8.** Ascites	**e.** Transudation of fluid into the peritoneal cavity
	f. Hypoperfusion of organs and tissues
	g. Transudation of fluid into the pleural cavity
	h. Shortness of breath when supine

3.

Column A	Column B
____ **1.** Cardiogenic shock	**a.** An acute failure of the circulatory system to supply the peripheral tissues and organs of the body with an adequate blood supply
____ **2.** Obstructive shock	
____ **3.** Distributive shock	
____ **4.** Hypovolemic shock	**b.** Caused by excessive vasodilation with mal distribution of blood flow
____ **5.** Circulatory shock	
	c. Caused by alteration in cardiac function
	d. Caused by a decrease in blood volume
	e. Caused by obstruction of blood flow through the circulatory system

Activity C

1. The pathophysiology of right- and left-sided heart failure has distinct features. Construct a flow chart of the following symptoms and their causes:

- Right heart failure
- Left heart failure
- Orthopnea
- Cyanosis
- Activity intolerance
- Anorexia
- Weight loss
- Impaired liver function
- Gastrointestinal (GI) tract congestion
- Impaired gas exchange
- Pulmonary edema
- Dependent edema and ascites
- Congestion of peripheral tissues
- Decreased cardiac output
- Pulmonary congestion

Activity D *Briefly answer the following.*

1. How is cardiac contractility regulated?

_____

_____

_____

2. Why is it advisable to test cardiac function during exercise (stress) rather than at rest?

_____

_____

_____

3. How does diastolic dysfunction produce the typical signs and symptoms that characterize the condition?

_____

_____

_____

4. Often, the early signs of heart failure are silent. This is because of the many compensatory mechanisms of the cardiovascular system. Explain, briefly, how these mechanisms work and why in the end they only serve to make the heart failure worse.

_____

_____

_____

5. What are the common manifestations of heart failure? Why?

_____

_____

_____

6. What effect does diuretic therapy have on heart failure?

_____

_____

_____

7. What are the cellular consequences of shock?

_____

_____

_____

8. What are the five major complications of severe shock?

_____

_____

_____

SECTION III: PRACTICING FOR NCLEX

Activity E *Answer the following questions.*

1. Match the following conditions with the type of heart failure they cause.

Condition	Type of Heart Failure
1. Valvular insufficiency	a. Diastolic dysfunction
2. Ischemic heart disease	b. Left ventricular dysfunction
3. Aortic or mitral stenosis	c. Right ventricular dysfunction
4. Acute myocardial infarction	d. Low-output failure
5. Paget disease	e. High-output failure
6. Cardiomyopathy	f. Systolic dysfunction

2. What are the signs and symptoms of heart failure? (Mark all that apply.)
   a. Fluid retention
   b. Ruddy complexion
   c. Fatigue
   d. Bradycardia
   e. Chronic productive cough

3. When an acute event occurs and the circulatory system can no longer provide the body with adequate perfusion of its tissues and organs, cellular hypoxia occurs and the body goes into shock. What are the causes of shock in the human body?
   a. Maldistribution of blood flow
   b. Hypovolemia
   c. Excessive vasoconstriction
   d. Obstruction of blood flow
   e. Hypervolemia

4. What are the physiologic signs and symptoms of cardiogenic shock? (Mark all that apply.)
   a. Decrease in mean arterial blood pressures
   b. Increased urine output related to increased renal perfusion
   c. Rise in central venous pressure (CVP)
   d. Hypercapnic lips and nail beds
   e. Increased extraction of O_2 from hemoglobin

5. In hypovolemic shock the main purpose of treatment is correcting or controlling the underlying cause of the hypovolemia and improving the perfusion of the tissues and organs of the body. Which of the following treatments is *not* a primary form of therapy for hypovolemic shock?
   a. Surgery
   b. Administration of intravenous fluids and blood
   c. Vasoconstrictive drugs
   d. Infusion of blood and blood products

6. Neurogenic shock, or spinal shock, is a phenomenon caused by the inability of the vasomotor center in the brain stem to control blood vessel tone through the sympathetic outflow to the blood vessels. In neurogenic shock, what happens to the heart rate and the skin?
   a. Heart rate slower than normal; skin warm and dry
   b. Heart rate faster than normal; skin cool and moist
   c. Heart rate slower than normal; skin cool and moist
   d. Heart rate slower than normal; skin warm and dry

7. Anaphylactic shock is the most severe form of systemic allergic reaction. Immunologically medicated substances are released into the blood, causing vasodilation and an increase in capillary permeability. What physiologic response often accompany the vascular response in anaphylaxis?
   a. Uterine smooth muscle relaxation
   b. Laryngeal edema
   c. Bronchodilation
   d. Gastrointestinal relaxation

8. Sepsis is growing in incidence in the United States. Its pathogenesis includes neutrophil activation, which kills microorganisms. Neutrophils also injure the endothelium, releasing mediators that increase vascular permeability. What else do neutrophils do in sepsis?
   a. Releases nitric oxide
   b. Vasoconstricts the capillary bed
   c. Causes bradycardia
   d. Activates erythropoiesis

9. What is the primary physiologic result of obstructive shock?
   a. Left ventricular hypertrophy
   b. Elevated right heart pressure
   c. Right atrial hypertrophy
   d. Decreased right heart pressure

10. An important factor in the mortality of severe shock is acute renal failure. What is the degree of renal damage related to in shock?
    a. Loss of perfusion and duration of shock
    b. Loss of perfusion and degree of immune-mediated response
    c. Severity and duration of shock
    d. Severity of shock and degree of immune-mediated response

11. The pathogenesis of multiorgan dysfunction syndrome (MODS) is not clearly understood at this time. Supportive management is currently the focus of treatment in this disorder. What is not a major risk factor in MODS?
    a. Advanced age
    b. Alcohol abuse
    c. Respiratory dysfunction
    d. Infarcted bowel

12. What is the primary cause of heart failure in infants and children?
    a. Idiopathic heart disease
    b. Structural heart defects
    c. Hyperkalemia
    d. Reactions to medications

CHAPTER 21

Control of Respiratory System

SECTION I: LEARNING OBJECTIVES

1. State the difference between the conducting and the respiratory airways.

2. Trace the movement of air through the airways, beginning in the nose and oropharynx and moving into the respiratory tissues of the lung.

3. Describe the function of the mucociliary blanket.

4. Compare the supporting structures of the large and small airways in terms of cartilaginous and smooth muscle support.

5. State the function of the two types of alveolar cells.

6. Differentiate the function of the bronchial and pulmonary circulations that supply the lungs.

7. Describe the basic properties of gases in relation to their partial pressures and their pressures in relation to volume and temperature.

8. State the definition of intrathoracic, intrapleural, and intra-alveolar pressures, and state how each of these pressures changes in relation to atmospheric pressure during inspiration and expiration.

9. Use the law of Laplace to explain the need for surfactant in maintaining the inflation of small alveoli.

10. Differentiate between the determinants of airway resistance and lung compliance and their effect on the work of breathing.

11. Define inspiratory reserve, expiratory reserve, vital capacity, residual lung volume, and $FEV_{1.0}$.

12. Trace the exchange of gases between the air in the alveoli and the blood in the pulmonary capillaries.

13. Differentiate between pulmonary and alveolar ventilation.

14. Explain why ventilation and perfusion must be matched.

15. Cite the difference between dead air space and shunt.

16. List four factors that affect the diffusion of gases in the alveoli.

17. Explain the difference between PO_2 and hemoglobin-bound oxygen and O_2 saturation, and oxygen content.

18. Explain the significance of a shift to the right and a shift to the left in the oxygen-hemoglobin dissociation curve.

19. Compare the neural control of the respiratory muscles, which control breathing, with that of cardiac muscle, which controls the pumping action of the heart.

20. Describe the function of the chemoreceptors and lung receptors in the regulation of ventilation.

21. Trace the integration of the cough reflex from stimulus to explosive expulsion of air that constitutes the cough.

22. Define dyspnea and list three types of conditions in which dyspnea occurs.

SECTION II: ASSESSING YOUR UNDERSTANDING

Activity A *Fill in the blanks.*

1. The primary function of the respiratory system is _____.

2. Functionally, the respiratory system can be divided into two parts: the _____ airways, through which air moves as it passes between the atmosphere and the lungs, and the _____ tissues of the lungs, where gas exchange takes place.

3. The _____ airways consist of the nasal passages, mouth and pharynx, larynx, trachea, bronchi, and bronchioles.

4. The air we breathe is _____, _____, and _____ as it moves through the conducting airways.

5. The _____ produced by the epithelial cells in the conducting airways forms a layer that protects the respiratory system by entrapping dust, bacteria, and other foreign particles that enter the airways.

6. The vocal folds and the elongated opening between them are called the _____.

7. The walls of the trachea are supported by horseshoe- or C-shaped rings of _____ cartilage, which prevent it from collapsing when the pressure in the thorax becomes negative.

8. Each primary bronchus, accompanied by the pulmonary arteries, veins, and lymph vessels, enters the lung through a slit called the _____.

9. Each _____ is supplied by a branch of a terminal bronchiole, an arteriole, the pulmonary capillaries, and a venule.

10. The _____ are the terminal air spaces of the respiratory tract and the actual sites of gas exchange between the air and the blood.

11. The pulmonary circulation arises from the _____ artery and provides for the gas exchange function of the lungs.

12. Particulate matter entering the lung is partly removed by _____ vessels, as are the plasma proteins that have escaped from the pulmonary capillaries.

13. It is _____ stimulation, through the vagus nerve, that is responsible for the slightly constricted smooth muscle tone in the normal resting lung.

14. Stimulation of the _____ nervous system causes airway relaxation, blood vessel constriction, and inhibition of glandular secretion.

15. The pressure exerted by a single gas in a mixture is called the _____.

16. Air moves between the atmosphere and the lungs because of a _____.

17. The pressure in the pleural cavity is called the _____ pressure.

18. The _____ maneuver is used to study the cardiovascular effects of increased intrathoracic pressure on peripheral venous pressures, cardiac filling and cardiac output, as well as poststrain heart rate and blood pressure responses.

19. Lung _____ refers to the ease with which the lungs can be inflated.

20. The _____ is the volume of air inspired (or exhaled) with each breath.

21. The maximum amount of air that can be inspired in excess of the normal tidal volume (TV) is called the _____, and the maximum amount that can be exhaled in excess of the normal TV is the _____.

22. The _____ is the amount of air a person can breathe in beginning at the normal expiratory level and distending the lungs to the maximal amount.

23. The _____ equals the IRV plus the TV plus the ERV and is the amount of air that can be exhaled from the point of maximal inspiration.

24. The _____ is the amount of air that is exchanged in 1 minute.

25. _____ ventilation refers to the total exchange of gases between the atmosphere and the lungs; _____ ventilation is the exchange of gases within the gas exchange portion of the lungs.

26. Even at low lung volumes, some air remains in the alveoli of the lower portion of the lungs, preventing their _____ .

27. _____ refers to the air that is moved with each breath but does not participate in gas exchange.

28. Both dead air space and shunt produce a _____ of ventilation and perfusion.

29. Although the lungs are responsible for the exchange of gases with the external environment, the _____ transports gases between the lungs and body tissues.

30. _____ carries about 98% to 99% of oxygen in the blood and is the main transporter of oxygen.

31. Oxygen binds _____ with the heme groups on the hemoglobin molecule.

32. Hemoglobin's affinity for oxygen is influenced by _____ , _____ concentration, and body _____ .

33. Carbon dioxide is transported in the blood in three forms: as _____ (10%), attached to _____ (30%), and as _____ (60%).

34. The pacemaker properties of the respiratory center result from the cycling of the two groups of respiratory neurons: the _____ center in the upper pons and the _____ center in the lower pons.

35. The automatic regulation of ventilation is controlled by input from two types of sensors or receptors: _____ and _____ receptors.

36. The _____ content in the blood regulates ventilation through its effect on the pH of the extracellular fluid of the brain.

37. _____ is a subjective sensation or a person's perception of difficulty in breathing that includes the perception of labored breathing and the reaction to that sensation.

Activity B *Consider the following figure.*

In the figure of the respiratory system, label the following structures:

• Secondary bronchi
• Tracheal cartilage
• Left primary bronchus
• Terminal bronchioles
• Segmental bronchi

Activity C *Match the key terms in Column A with their definitions in Column B.*

Column A	Column B
____ 1. Mediastinum	a. Mucus lining of the conducting airways
____ 2. Elastic recoil	b. Form part of respiratory membrane
____ 3. Epiglottis	c. Pressure inside the airways and alveoli
____ 4. Type I pneumocytes	d. The trachea, bronchi, and bronchioles
____ 5. Angiogenesis	e. Synthesize pulmonary surfactant
____ 6. Mucociliary blanket	
____ 7. Alveolar pressure	

_____ 8. Brush cells

_____ 9. Tracheobron-
chial

_____ 10. Type II
pneumocytes

f. Space between
lungs that contains
heart, blood vessels,
lymph nodes,
nerves and the
esophagus

g. The ability of the
elastic components
of the lung to recoil
to their original
position

h. Routes liquids and
foods into the
esophagus

i. Formation of new
blood vessels

j. Act as receptors that
monitor the air
quality of the lungs

Activity D *Put these respiratory structures in
anatomic order.*

   a. Nasopharynx

   b. Trachea

   c. Epiglottis

   d. Alveoli

   e. Respiratory bronchiole

   f. Intrapulmonary bronchus

   g. Extrapulmonary bronchus

Activity E *Briefly answer the following.*

1. Describe the pleura and explain its function.

   _____

   _____

   _____

2. Describe the events of the respiratory cycle.

   _____

   _____

   _____

3. What is the function of pulmonary
surfactant?

   _____

   _____

   _____

4. What is the mathematical formula used to
describe the diffusion of gas across the respiratory membrane?

   _____

   _____

   _____

5. In the clinic, what type of blood is used for
blood gas measurements and why?

   _____

   _____

   _____

6. What causes us to cough?

   _____

   _____

   _____

SECTION III: APPLYING YOUR KNOWLEDGE

Activity F *Consider the scenario and answer
the questions.*

Seventy-nine-year old Mr. Borden is brought to
the clinic by his daughter who says, "I am
worried about him. He is so stubborn, he just
won't complain. When he walks, he gets so short
of breath. I don't think he is getting enough oxygen!" Mr. Borden's O_2 level is 87% and his nail
beds are dusky with a delayed capillary refill
time. There is no clubbing to Mr. Borden's
fingertips.

1. How would the nurse explain generalized
hypoxia to Mr. Borden's daughter?

   _____

   _____

   _____

2. What diagnostic tests would the doctor order
to confirm a diagnosis of generalized hypoxia?

   _____

   _____

   _____

SECTION IV: PRACTICING FOR NCLEX

Activity G *Answer the following questions.*

1. The lungs are the working structures of the respiratory system and they have several functions. What are the functions of the lungs? (Mark all that apply.)
   a. Produce heparin
   b. Activate vasoactive substances
   c. Convert angiotensin I to angiotensin II
   d. Activate bradykinin
   e. Convert glucose to glycogen

2. Bronchial blood vessels have several functions. They warm and humidify incoming air as well as distribute blood to the conducting airways and the supporting structures of the lung. What is it that makes bronchial blood vessels unique in the body?
   a. They can undergo angiogenesis
   b. They drain blood into the bronchiole arteries
   c. They participate in gas exchange
   d. They carry oxygenated blood to the lung tissues

3. Match the respiratory pressures with their definitions.

Pressure	Definition
1. Alveolar pressure	a. The pressure in the thoracic cavity
2. Intrapleural pressure	b. Pressure inside the airways and alveoli of the lungs
3. Transpulmonary pressure	c. The difference between the intra-alveoli and intrapleural pressures.
4. Intrathoracic pressure	d. Pressure in the pleural cavity

4. What does the equation $C = \Delta V / \Delta P$ stand for?
   a. Surface tension inside the lungs
   b. Lung compliance
   c. Airway resistance
   d. Change in peak expiratory flow

5. An 82-year-old man with chronic obstructive pulmonary disease (COPD) is at the clinic for a regular check-up. Because of his diagnosis, the nurse would expect his respiratory rate under normal circumstances to be what?
   a. Tachypneic
   b. ≥ 18 to 20 bpm
   c. ≤ 18 to 20 bpm
   d. Hyperpneic

6. Our ability to oxygenate the tissues and organs of our bodies depends on our ability to ventilate, or exchange, gases in our respiratory system. The resultant distribution of ventilation or the areas of the body open to the exchange of gases in our respiratory system depends on what?
   a. Effects of gravity intrathoracic pressure
   b. Body position and alveolar pressure
   c. Effects of gravity and body position
   d. Intrathoracic pressure and alveolar pressure

7. Alveolar oxygen levels directly impact the blood vessels in the pulmonary circulation. In a person with lung disease, there is vasoconstriction throughout the lung, causing a generalized hypoxia. What can prolonged hypoxia lead to?
   a. Hypertension and increased workload on the left heart
   b. Pulmonary hypertension and left ventricular hypertrophy
   c. Hypertension and increased workload on the right heart
   d. Pulmonary hypertension and increased workload on the right heart.

8. When there is a mismatching of ventilation and perfusion within the lung itself, insufficient ventilation occurs. There is a lack of enough oxygen to adequately oxygenate the blood flowing through the alveolar capillaries, creating a physiologic shunt. What causes a physiologic right-to-left shunting of blood in the respiratory system?
   a. Destructive lung disease or heart failure
   b. Obstructive lung disease or heart failure
   c. Heart failure or pulmonary hypertension
   d. Heart failure or regional hypoxia

9. Blood transports both oxygen and carbon dioxide in a physically dissolved form to the tissues and organs of the body. It is the measurements of the components of the gases in the blood that are used as indicators of the body's status by health care workers. Why is it commonly the blood in the arteries that is measured for its components rather than the blood in the veins?

   a. Arterial blood most adequately measures the metabolic demands of the tissues along with the gas exchange function of the lungs.

   b. Venous blood measures the metabolic demands of the tissues rather than the gas exchange function of the lungs.

   c. Arterial blood only measures the gas exchange function of the lung after it has met the metabolic demands of the tissues.

   d. Venous blood only measures the hypoxic reflex of the body, not the gas exchange function of the lungs.

10. Respiration has both automatic and voluntary components that are sent to the respiratory center of the brain from a number of sources. What physiologic forces can exert their influence on respiration through the lower brain centers? (Mark all that apply.)

    a. Fever
    b. Cold
    c. Pain
    d. Endorphins
    e. Emotion

11. There are several actions the body makes to initiate a cough. Put these actions into the correct order.

    a. Elevation of intrathoracic pressures
    b. Rapid opening of glottis
    c. Closure of glottis
    d. Rapid inspiration of large volume of air
    e. Forceful contraction of abdominal and expiratory muscles

12. Dyspnea is defined as an uncomfortable sensation or difficulty in breathing that is subjectively defined by the client. Which of the following disease states is *not* characterized by dyspnea?

    a. Pneumonia
    b. Emphysema
    c. Myasthenia gravis
    d. Multiple sclerosis

CHAPTER 22

Respiratory Tract Infections, Neoplasms, and Childhood Disorders

SECTION I: LEARNING OBJECTIVES

1. Describe the transmission of the common cold from one person to another.

2. Describe the causes, manifestations, and treatment of acute and chronic sinusitis.

3. Relate the characteristics of the influenza virus to its contagious properties and the need for a yearly "flu shot."

4. Characterize community-acquired pneumonia, hospital-acquired pneumonia, and pneumonia in immunocompromised persons in terms of pathogens, manifestations, and prognosis.

5. Describe the immunologic properties of the tubercle bacillus, and differentiate between primary tuberculosis and reactivated tuberculosis on the basis of their pathophysiology.

6. State the mechanism for the transmission of fungal infections of the lung.

7. Cite risk factors associated with lung cancer.

8. Compare small cell lung cancer and non–small cell lung cancer in terms of histopathology, prognosis, and treatment methods.

9. Describe the manifestations of lung cancer and list two symptoms of lung cancer that are related to the invasion of the mediastinum.

10. Define the term *paraneoplastic* and cite three paraneoplastic manifestations of lung cancer.

11. Characterize the effect of age on treatment of lung cancer.

12. Trace the development of the respiratory tract through the five stages of embryonic and fetal development.

13. Cite the function of surfactant in lung function in the neonate.

14. Cite the possible cause and manifestations of respiratory distress syndrome and bronchopulmonary dysplasia.

15. Describe the physiologic basis for sternal and chest wall retractions and grunting, stridor, and wheezing as signs of respiratory distress in infants and small children.

16. Compare croup, epiglottitis, and bronchiolitis in terms of incidence by age, site of infection, and signs and symptoms.

17. List the signs of impending respiratory failure in small children.

SECTION II: ASSESSING YOUR UNDERSTANDING

Activity A *Fill in the blanks.*

1. _____ are the most frequent cause of respiratory tract infections.

2. Viral infections can damage _____ epithelium, _____ airways, and lead to secondary _____ infections.

3. The common cold is a viral infection of the _____ respiratory tract.

4. Outbreaks of colds due to _____ are most common in early fall and late spring.

5. _____ are popular over-the-counter treatments for colds because of their action in drying nasal secretions.

6. _____ refers to inflammation of the nasal passages, and sinusitis as inflammation of the _____ sinuses.

7. The lower _____ content in the sinuses facilitates the growth of organisms, impairs local defenses, and alters the function of immune cells.

8. Host antibodies to _____ and _____ prevent or ameliorate infection by the influenza virus.

9. The influenza viruses can cause three types of infections: an uncomplicated _____ respiratory infection, _____ pneumonia, and a respiratory viral infection followed by a _____ infection.

10. Because influenza is so highly contagious, prevention relies primarily on _____.

11. Avian strains of the influenza virus do not usually cause outbreaks of disease in humans unless a _____ of the virus genome has occurred within an intermediate mammalian host such as a pig.

12. The term _____ describes inflammation of parenchymal structures of the lung, such as the alveoli and the bronchioles.

13. _____ refers to consolidation of a part or all of a lung lobe; and _____ signifies a patchy consolidation involving more than one lobe.

14. Hospital-acquired, or _____, pneumonia is defined as a lower respiratory tract infection that was not present or incubating on admission to the hospital.

15. The term _____ host usually is applied to persons with a variety of underlying defects in host defenses.

16. _____ disease is a form of bronchopneumonia; infection normally occurs by acquiring the organism from the environment.

17. The primary atypical pneumonias are caused by a variety agents, the most common being _____ pneumonia.

18. _____ is the world's foremost cause of death from a single infectious agent.

19. Mycobacteria are similar to other bacterial organisms except for an outer _____ that makes them more resistant to destruction.

20. _____ tuberculosis is a form of the disease that develops in previously unexposed, and therefore unsensitized, persons.

21. The most frequently used screening methods for pulmonary tuberculosis are the _____ tests and chest _____.

22. _____ is caused by the dimorphic fungus *Histoplasma capsulatum* and is one of the most common fungal infections in the United States.

23. _____ respiratory infections produce pulmonary manifestations that resemble tuberculosis.

24. The number of Americans who develop lung cancer is decreasing, primarily because of a decrease in _____.

25. Cigarette smoking causes more than _____ of cases of lung cancer.

26. _____ are aggressive, locally invasive, and widely metastatic tumors that arise from the epithelial lining of major bronchi.

27. The _____ are small, round to oval cells that are approximately the size of a lymphocyte and grow in clusters that exhibit neither glandular nor squamous organization.

28. The _____ include squamous cell carcinomas, adenocarcinomas, and large cell carcinomas.

29. _____ is characterized by inspiratory stridor, hoarseness, and a barking cough.

30. By the _____ weeks of gestation, sufficient terminal air sacs are present to permit survival of the premature infant.

Activity B *Consider the following figures.*

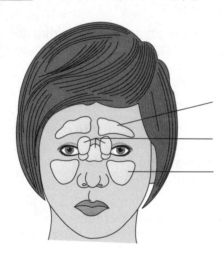

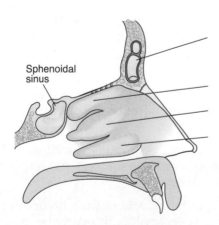

In the figures above, label the following structures:

• Frontal sinus
• Ethmoid sinuses
• Maxillary sinus
• Superior turbinate
• Middle turbinate
• Inferior turbinate

Activity C *Match the key terms in Column A with their definitions in Column B.*

Column A

_____ 1. SCLCs

_____ 2. Typical pneumonias

_____ 3. Stridor

_____ 4. Anergy

_____ 5. Hemagglutinin

_____ 6. Squamous cell

_____ 7. Paraneoplastic syndrome

_____ 8. Atypical pneumonias

_____ 9. Neuraminidase

_____ 10. Reye syndrome

Column B

a. Audible crowing sound during inspiration

b. False-negative tuberculin skin tests

c. Result from infection by bacteria

d. Attachment protein that allows the influenza virus to enter epithelial cells in the respiratory tract

e. Symptoms that develop when substances released by some cancer cells disrupt the normal function

f. Viral and mycoplasma infection

g. Facilitates influenza viral replication and release from the cell

h. Fatty liver with encephalitis

i. Highly aggressive lung cancer

j. Carcinoma is associated with the paraneoplastic syndromes that produce hypercalcemia

Activity D

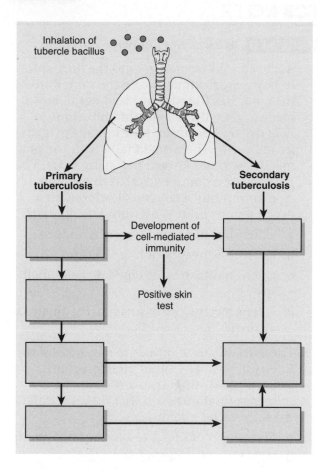

Use the following terms to complete the flowchart above:

- Reinfection
- Ghon complex
- Granulomatous inflammatory response
- Healed dormant lesion
- Cell-mediated hypersensitivity response
- Reactivated tuberculosis
- Progressive or disseminated tuberculosis

Activity E *Briefly answer the following.*

1. How is the cold virus spread?

_____

_____

_____

2. How does the influenza virus reinfect someone? How is it so contagious?

_____

_____

_____

3. What is a common complication of influenza (usually of the elderly or those with cardiopulmonary disease)?

_____

_____

_____

4. What type of pneumonia results from inhalation or aspiration of nasopharyngeal secretions during sleep?

_____

_____

_____

5. What are the pathophysiologic stages of pneumococcal pneumonia infection?

_____

_____

_____

6. How is *Mycobacterium tuberculosis hominis* spread?

_____

_____

_____

7. Describe the pathogenic mechanisms of *M. tuberculosis hominis.*

_____

_____

_____

8. How is lung cancer categorized?

_____

_____

_____

9. What causes the varied manifestations of lung cancer?

_____

_____

_____

10. What is the result of the absence of surfactant in premature infants?

_____

_____

_____

SECTION III: APPLYING YOUR KNOWLEDGE

Activity F *Consider the scenario and answer the questions.*

Mr. Jones, who is 68 years old, presents to the clinic with lack of appetite and weight loss of 30 pounds over the past 6 months. He has a history of a chronic, nonproductive cough; shortness of breath, which is worse on exertion; and wheezing. He tells the nurse that he is now coughing up "bloody stuff," and he wants to know what is wrong with him. When asked about pain he says, "I get heartburn once in awhile, but the pain is dull instead of burning." Routine laboratory work is ordered and the only abnormal finding is hypercalcemia. The suspected diagnosis is squamous cell cancer of the lung.

1. What diagnostic tests would the nurse expect to be ordered?

_____

_____

_____

2. Mr. Jones wants to know how his cancer will be treated. The nurse knows that treatments are available. Which treatments are used for squamous cell (NSCLC) cancer of the lung?

_____

_____

_____

SECTION IV: PRACTICING FOR NCLEX

Activity G *Answer the following questions.*

1. A 23-year-old woman goes to the drug store to buy a medication to ease the symptoms of her cold. Her friends have told her to buy a medication with an antihistamine in it to help dry up her runny nose and make it easier to breath. The woman talks with the pharmacist, who has known her many years. The pharmacist recommends that this young woman not buy a cold medication with a decongestant in it. Why would he do that?
   a. Client has history of hyperthyroidism
   b. Client has history of hypotension
   c. Client has history of type I diabetes mellitus
   d. Client has history of juvenile rheumatoid arthritis

2. The early stages of influenza pass by as if the infection were any other viral infection. What is the distinguishing feature of an influenza viral infection that makes it different from other viral infections?
   a. Slow onset of upper respiratory symptoms
   b. Rapid onset of profound malaise
   c. Slow onset of fever and chills
   d. Rapid onset of productive cough

3. Influenza A subtype H5N1 has been documented in poultry in both East and Southeast Asian Countries. This form of Avian flu (bird flu) is highly contagious from bird to bird, but rarely is passed from human to human. There is a large amount of concern that the H5N1 strain might mutate, making it easier to be passed from human to human, carrying with it a high mortality rate. What is the main concern if the H5N1 strain does mutate?
   a. An epidemic in Southeast Asia.
   b. Inability to develop a vaccine for the newly infected poultry
   c. Initiation of a pandemic
   d. Several small pockets of infection so widespread it will be difficult to control them

4. Community-acquired pneumonia can be categorized according to several indexes. What are these indexes? (Mark all that apply.)
   a. Radiologic findings
   b. Serologic findings
   c. Age
   d. Presence of coexisting disease
   e. Need for hospitalization in long-term care facility

5. An immunocompromised host is open to pneumonia from all types of organisms. There is, however, a correlation between specific types of immunologic deficits and specific invading organisms. What organism is most likely to cause pneumonia in an immunocompromised host with neutropenia and impaired granulocyte function?
   a. β-Hemolytic streptococcus
   b. Gram-positive bacilli
   c. *Eosinophilic bacillus subtilis*
   d. *Haemophilus influenza*
   e. *Staphylococcus aureus*

6. Elderly people are very susceptible to pneumonia in all its varieties. The symptoms the elderly exhibit can be very different than those of other age groups who have pneumonia. What signs and symptoms are elderly people with pneumonia less likely to experience than people with pneumonia in other age groups?
   a. Marked elevation in temperature
   b. Loss of appetite
   c. Deterioration in mental status
   d. Pleuritic pain

7. Tuberculosis is a highly destructive disease because the tubercle bacillus activates a tissue hypersensitivity to the tubercular antigens. What does the destructive nature of tuberculosis cause in a previously unexposed immunocompetent person?
   a. Cavitation and rapidly progressing pulmonary lesions
   b. Caseating necrosis and cavitation
   c. Rapidly progressing lesions and purulent necrosis
   d. Caseating necrosis and purulent pulmonary lesions

8. Coccidioidomycosis is a pulmonary fungal infection resembling tuberculosis. Less severe forms of the infection are treated with oral antifungal medications. For persons with progressive disease, what is the drug of choice?
   a. IV fluconazole
   b. IV BCG
   c. IV amphotericin B
   d. IV rifampin

9. Non–small cell lung cancers (NSCLCs) mimic Small cell lung cancers (SCLCs) through their abilities to do what?
   a. Synthesize bioactive products and produce pan-neoplastic syndromes
   b. Neutralize bioactive products, which produce paraneoplastic syndromes
   c. Produce paraneoplastic syndromes and synthesize adrenocorticotropic hormone (ACTH)
   d. Synthesize bioactive products and produce paraneoplastic syndromes

10. Premature infants who are treated with mechanical ventilation, mostly for respiratory distress syndrome, are at risk for developing bronchopulmonary dysplasia (BPD), a chronic lung disease. What are the signs and symptoms of BPD?
    a. Rapid and shallow breathing and chest retractions
    b. Weight loss and a barrel chest
    c. Tachycardia and slow shallow breathing
    d. A barrel chest and rapid weight gain

11. For each of the following conditions, identify where it occurs in the respiratory tract of children: upper airway or lower airway.
    Epiglottitis
    Acute bronchiolitis
    Asthma
    Spasmodic croup
    Laryngotracheobronchitis

12. What is the underlying cause of respiratory failure in a child with bronchiolitis?
    a. Obstructive process
    b. Impaired gas exchange
    c. Hypoxemia and hypercapnia
    d. Metabolic acidosis

Disorders of Ventilation and Gas Exchange

CHAPTER 23

SECTION I: LEARNING OBJECTIVES

1. Define the terms *hypoxemia* and *hypercapnia*.

2. Characterize the mechanisms whereby disorders of ventilation and diffusion cause hypoxemia and hypercapnia.

3. Compare the manifestations of hypoxemia and hypercapnia.

4. Characterize the pathogenesis and manifestations of transudative and exudative pleural effusion, chylothorax, and hemothorax.

5. Differentiate among the causes and manifestations of spontaneous pneumothorax, secondary pneumothorax, and tension pneumothorax.

6. Describe the causes of pleuritis and differentiate the characteristics of pleural pain from other types of chest pain.

7. Describe the causes and manifestations of atelectasis.

8. Describe the physiology of bronchial smooth muscle as it relates to airway disease.

9. Describe the interaction between heredity, alterations in the immune response, and environmental agents in the pathogenesis of bronchial asthma.

10. Characterize the acute- or early-phase and late-phase responses in the pathogenesis of bronchial asthma and relate them to current methods for treatment of the disorder.

11. Explain the distinction between chronic bronchitis and emphysema in terms of pathology and clinical manifestations.

12. State the chief manifestations of bronchiectasis.

13. Describe the genetic abnormality responsible for cystic fibrosis and relate it to the manifestations of the disorder.

14. State the difference between chronic obstructive pulmonary diseases and chronic restrictive lung diseases in terms of their pathology and manifestations.

15. Describe the causes of hypersensitivity pneumonitis.

16. Characterize the organ involvement in sarcoidosis.

17. State the most common cause of pulmonary embolism and the clinical manifestations of the disorder.

18. Describe the pathophysiology of pulmonary arterial hypertension and state three causes of secondary pulmonary hypertension.

19. Describe the alterations in cardiovascular function that are characteristic of cor pulmonale.

20. Describe the pathologic lung changes that occur in acute respiratory distress syndrome and relate them to the clinical manifestations of a general definition of respiratory failure.

21. Differentiate between the causes and manifestations of hypoxemic and hypercapnic/hypoxemic respiratory failure.

22. Describe the treatment of respiratory failure.

SECTION II: ASSESSING YOUR UNDERSTANDING

Activity A *Fill in the blanks.*

1. The primary function of the respiratory system is to remove appropriate amounts of _____ from the blood entering the pulmonary circulation and to add adequate amounts of _____ to the blood leaving the pulmonary circulation.

2. _____ involves the movement of fresh atmospheric air to the alveoli for delivery provision of O_2 and removal of CO_2.

3. As a general rule, _____ of the blood primarily depends on factors that promote diffusion of O_2 from the alveoli into the pulmonary capillaries; whereas, _____ primarily depends on the minute ventilation and elimination of CO_2 from the alveoli.

4. _____ refers to a reduction in blood O_2 levels.

5. Hypoxemia produces its effects through tissue _____ and the compensatory mechanisms that the body uses to adapt to the lowered oxygen level.

6. The body compensates for chronic hypoxemia by increased _____, pulmonary _____, and increased production of _____ cells.

7. _____ can occur in a number of disorders that cause hypoventilation or mismatching of ventilation and perfusion resulting in increased arterial CO_2.

8. Elevated levels of P_{CO_2} produce a decrease in _____ and respiratory _____.

9. _____ refers to an abnormal collection of fluid in the pleural cavity.

10. _____ is a specific type of pleural effusion in which there is blood in the pleural cavity.

11. Primary atelectasis of the newborn implies that the lung has never been _____.

12. Obstructive airway disorders are caused by disorders that limit _____ airflow.

13. Bronchial _____ is a chronic disorder of the airways that causes episodes of airway obstruction, bronchial hyperresponsiveness, and airway inflammation that are usually reversible.

14. Recent research has focused on the role of _____ in the pathogenesis of bronchial asthma.

15. _____ pulmonary disease (COPD) is characterized by chronic and recurrent obstruction of airflow in the pulmonary airways.

16. In COPD, _____ and _____ of the bronchial wall, along with excess mucus secretion, obstruct airflow and cause mismatching of ventilation and perfusion.

17. _____ is thought to result from the breakdown of elastin and other alveolar wall components by enzymes, called _____, that digest proteins.

18. A hereditary deficiency in _____ accounts for approximately 1% of all cases of COPD and is more common in young persons with emphysema.

19. The earliest feature of chronic bronchitis is _____ in the large airways, associated with hypertrophy of the submucosal glands in the trachea and bronchi.

20. Persons with predominant emphysema are classically referred to as _____, a reference to the lack of cyanosis, the use of accessory muscles, and pursed-lip breathing.

21. Persons with a clinical syndrome of chronic bronchitis are classically labeled _____, a reference to cyanosis and fluid retention associated with right-sided heart failure.

22. _____ is a permanent dilation of the bronchi and bronchioles caused by destruction of the muscle and elastic supporting tissue resulting from a vicious cycle of infection and inflammation.

23. _____ is an autosomal recessive disorder involving fluid secretion in the exocrine glands in the epithelial lining of the respiratory, gastrointestinal, and reproductive tracts.

24. The diffuse _____ diseases are a diverse group of lung disorders that produce similar inflammatory and fibrotic changes in the interalveolar septa of the lung.

25. The interstitial lung disorders exert their effects on the _____ and _____ connective tissue found between the delicate interstitium of the alveolar walls.

26. Pulmonary _____ develops when a blood-borne substance lodges in a branch of the pulmonary artery and obstructs the flow, almost all of which are thrombi that arise from deep vein thrombosis.

27. Chest pain, dyspnea, and increased respiratory rate are the most frequent signs and symptoms of _____.

28. _____ is a disorder characterized by an elevation of pressure within the pulmonary circulation, namely the pulmonary arterial system.

29. Continued exposure of the pulmonary vessels to _____ is a common cause of pulmonary hypertension.

30. _____ can be viewed as a failure in the gas exchange due either to pump or lung failure, or both.

Activity B *Consider the following figure.*

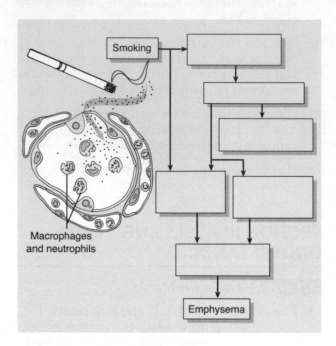

Complete the above flowchart using the items below:

- Destruction of elastic fibers in lung
- Decreased α_1-antitrypsin activity
- Action inhibited by α_1-antitrypsin
- Inherited α_1-antitrypsin deficiency
- Release of elastase
- Attraction of inflammatory cells

Activity C *Match the key terms in Column A with their definitions in Column B.*

1.

Column A	Column B
____ 1. Ventilation	a. Ratio of carbon dioxide production to oxygen consumption
____ 2. PF ratio	
____ 3. Cyanosis	
____ 4. Respiratory quotient	b. Difference between arterial PO_2 and the fraction of inspired oxygen
____ 5. Empyema	
____ 6. Hypercapnia	c. Infection of the pleura
____ 7. Venous oxygen saturation	d. Movement of gas into or out of lungs
____ 8. Pneumothorax	

_____ **9.** Hypoxemia

_____ **10.** Pleuritis

e. Increase in the carbon dioxide content of the arterial blood

f. Reflects the body's extraction and utilization of O_2 at the tissue levels

g. Air in pleural space

h. Decreased oxygenation

i. Results from an excessive concentration of reduced hemoglobin

j. Infection in the pleural cavity

i. Acute respiratory distress syndrome

j. Areas of the lung are ventilated but not perfused, or when areas are perfused but not ventilated

Activity D *Put the events of IgE-mediated asthma reaction in order in the boxes below:*

a. Infiltration of inflammatory cells

b. Mast cell activation

c. Bronchospasm

d. Increased airway responsiveness

e. Exposure to allergen

f. Airway inflammation

□→□→□→□→□→□

2.

Column A

_____ **1.** Cor pulmonale

_____ **2.** Pneumoconioses

_____ **3.** CFTR

_____ **4.** ARDS

_____ **5.** Atelectasis

_____ **6.** Mismatching of ventilation and perfusion

_____ **7.** Bronchiectasis

_____ **8.** Emphysema

_____ **9.** Sarcoidosis

_____ **10.** Chronic bronchitis

Column B

a. Lung tissue destruction resulting from a vicious cycle of infection and inflammation

b. Caused by the inhalation of inorganic dusts and particulate matter

c. With increased mucus production, obstruction of small airways, and a chronic productive cough

d. Incomplete expansion of a lung or portion of a lung

e. Right heart failure resulting from primary lung disease

f. Granulomas found in the lung and lymphatic system

g. Cystic fibrosis transmembrane regulator

h. Enlargement of air spaces and destruction of lung tissue

Activity E *Briefly answer the following.*

1. What are the mechanisms of hypoxemia?

_____

_____

_____

2. What are the clinical features of atelectasis?

_____

_____

_____

3. Explain what is meant by the acute-response and the late-phase reactions of asthma.

_____

_____

_____

4. What factors are causative to the development of bronchiectasis?

_____

_____

_____

5. Describe the pathogenic mechanism of cystic fibrosis.

_____

_____

_____

6. What are the effects of a pulmonary embolism on lung tissue?

_____

_____

_____

7. Describe the disease-producing changes of acute respiratory distress syndrome.

_____

_____

_____

SECTION III: APPLYING YOUR KNOWLEDGE

Activity F *Consider the scenario and answer the questions.*

The parents of a 14-year-old girl arrive in the emergency department after being notified by the school nurse that their daughter had a "spell" at school and was taken to the emergency department by ambulance. When they arrive their daughter is sitting up on the stretcher, has oxygen on at 1 L/min, and is answering questions asked by the nurse.

1. The doctor talks to the family and tells them he suspects their daughter has asthma. What diagnostic tests would the nurse expect to be ordered to confirm the diagnosis of asthma?

_____

_____

_____

2. The parents mention to the nurse that their daughter values her independence. They want to know how her treatment plan will impact her independence. How would the nurse correctly respond?

_____

_____

_____

SECTION IV: PRACTICING FOR NCLEX

Activity G *Answer the following questions.*

1. There can be many reasons for a patient to present with hypoxemia. For a client's PO_2 to fall, a respiratory disease is usually involved. Often, patients have involvement from more than one mechanism. Match the mechanism involved with the end result (hypoxemia or decreased levels of PO_2).

Mechanism	Outcome
Decreased oxygen in air	
Inadequate circulation through pulmonary capillaries	
Hypoventilation	
Disease in respiratory system	
Mismatched ventilation and perfusion	
Dysfunction of neurologic system	

2. When CO_2 levels in the blood rise, a state of hypercapnia occurs in the body. What factors contribute to hypercapnia? (Mark all that apply.)
   a. Alteration in carbon dioxide production
   b. Abnormalities in respiratory function
   c. Disturbance in gas exchange function
   d. Decrease in carbon dioxide production
   e. Changes in neural control of respiration

3. The complications of a hemothorax can impact the total body. Left untreated, what can a moderate or large hemothorax cause?
   a. Calcification of the lung tissue
   b. Fibrothorax
   c. Pleuritis
   d. Atelectasis

4. Talc lung can occur from injected or inhaled talc powder that has been mixed with heroin, methamphetamine, or codeine as a filler. What are people with talc lung very susceptible to?

   a. Hemothorax

   b. Chylothorax

   c. Fibrothorax

   d. Pneumothorax

5. Pleuritis, an inflammatory process of the pleura, is a common in infectious processes that spread to the pleura. Which are the drugs of choice for treating pleural pain?

   a. Indomethacin

   b. Aspirin

   c. Acetaminophen

   d. Inderal

6. *Atelectasis* is the term used to designate an incomplete expansion of a portion of the lung. Depending on the size of the collapsed area and the type of atelectasis occurring, you may see a shift of the mediastinum and trachea. Which way does the mediastinum and trachea shift in compression atelectasis?

   a. Toward the affected lung

   b. Toward the mediastinum

   c. Away from the affected lung

   d. Away from the trachea

7. Infants and small children have asthma and need to be medicated, just as adults do. There are special systems manufactured for the delivery of inhaled medications to children. At what age is it recommended that children may begin using an metered-dose inhaler (MDI) with a spacer?

   a. 3 to 5 years

   b. 4 to 6 years

   c. 2 to 4 years

   d. 5 to 7 years

8. Chronic obstructive pulmonary disease (COPD) is a combination of disease processes. What disease processes have been identified as being part of COPD?

   a. Emphysema and asthma

   b. Chronic obstructive bronchitis and emphysema

   c. Chronic obstructive bronchitis and asthma

   d. Chronic bronchitis and emphysema

9. Bronchiectasis is considered a secondary COPD and, with the advent of antibiotics, it is not a common disease entity. In the past, bronchiectasis often followed specific diseases. Which disease did it not follow?

   a. Necrotizing bacterial pneumonia

   b. Complicated measles

   c. Chickenpox

   d. Influenza

10. Cystic fibrosis (CF) is an autosomal recessive disorder involving the secretion of fluids in specific exocrine glands. The genetic defect in CF inclines a person to chronic respiratory infections from a small group of organisms. Which organisms create chronic infection in a child with cystic fibrosis?

   a. *Pseudomonas aeruginosa* and *Escherichia coli*

   b. *Staphylococcus aureus* and Hepatitis C

   c. *Haemophilus influenzae* and Influenza A

   d. *Pseudomonas aeruginosa* and *S. aureus*

11. What etiologic determinants are important in the development of the pneumoconioses? (Mark all that apply.)

   a. Chemical nature of the dust particle

   b. Size of dust particle

   c. Density of dust particle

   d. Biologic nature of the dust particle

   e. Ability of particle to incite lung destruction

12. There are cytotoxic drugs used in the treatment of cancer that cause pulmonary damage because of their direct toxicity and because they stimulate an influx of inflammatory cells into the alveoli. Which cardiac drug is known for its toxic effect in the lungs?

   a. Amiodarone

   b. Inderal

   c. Methotrexate

   d. Busulfan

13. A pulmonary embolism occurs when there is an obstruction in the pulmonary artery blood flow. Classic signs and symptoms of a pulmonary embolism include dyspnea, chest pain, and increased respiratory rate. What is a classic sign of pulmonary infarction?
    a. Mediastinal shift to the left
    b. Pleuritic pain
    c. Tracheal shift to the right
    d. Pericardial pain

14. Pulmonary hypertension is usually caused by long-term exposure to hypoxemia. When pulmonary vessels are exposed to hypoxemia, what is their response?
    a. Pulmonary vessels dilate
    b. Pulmonary vessels constrict
    c. Pulmonary vessels spasm
    d. Pulmonary vessels infarct

15. The management of cor pulmonale is directed at the underlying lung disease and heart failure. Why is low-flow oxygen therapy a part of the management of cor pulmonale?
    a. Stimulates body to breathe on its own
    b. Inhibits the respiratory center of the brain from initiating tachypnea
    c. Reduces pulmonary hypertension and polycythemia associated with chronic lung disease
    d. Reduces pulmonary hypertension and formation of pulmonary embolism

16. Acute lung injury/acute respiratory distress syndrome (ALI/ARDS) are distinguishable between the two by the extent of hypoxemia involved. What is the clinical presentation of ARDS? (Mark all that apply.)
    a. Diffuse bilateral infiltrates of lung tissue without cardiac dysfunction
    b. Rapid onset
    c. Signs of respiratory distress
    d. Increase in respiratory rate
    e. Hypoxemia refractory to treatment

17. Acute respiratory failure is commonly signaled by varying degrees of hypoxemia and hypercapnia. Respiratory acidosis develops manifested by what?
    a. Decrease in cerebral blood flow
    b. Arterial vasoconstriction
    c. Increase in cardiac contractility
    d. Increased cerebral spinal fluid pressure

CHAPTER 24

Structure and Function of the Kidney

SECTION I: LEARNING OBJECTIVES

1. Describe the location and gross structure of the kidney.

2. Explain why the kidney receives such a large percentage of the cardiac output and describe the mechanisms for regulating renal blood flow.

3. Describe the structure and function of the glomerulus and tubular components of the nephron in terms of regulating the composition of the extracellular fluid compartment.

4. Explain the concept of tubular transport mechanisms.

5. Describe how the kidney produces concentrated or diluted urine.

6. Characterize the function of the juxtaglomerular complex.

7. Relate the function of the kidney to drug elimination.

8. Explain the endocrine functions of the kidney.

9. Relate the sodium reabsorption function of the kidney to action of diuretics.

10. Describe the characteristics of normal urine.

11. Explain the significance of casts in the urine.

12. Explain the value of urine specific gravity in evaluating renal function.

13. Explain the concept of the glomerular filtration rate.

14. Explain the value of serum creatinine levels in evaluating renal function.

SECTION II: ASSESSING YOUR UNDERSTANDING

Activity A *Fill in the blanks.*

1. The _____ are paired, bean-shaped organs that lie outside the peritoneal cavity in the back of the upper abdomen.

2. The _____ is the place where blood vessels and nerves enter and leave the kidney.

3. _____ are the functional units of the kidney.

4. The _____ contains the glomeruli and convoluted tubules of the nephron and blood vessels.

5. The medulla consists of the _____ that extend into the medulla.

6. Each kidney is supplied by a single renal artery that arises on either side of the _____.

7. The afferent arterioles that supply the _____ arise from the intralobular arteries.

8. The _____ is a unique, high-pressure capillary filtration system.

9. _____ are low-pressure vessels that are adapted for reabsorption rather than filtration.

10. The _____ passes through each of these segments before reaching the pelvis of the kidney.

11. The _____ is regulated by the constriction and relaxation of the afferent and efferent arterioles.

12. Substances move from the tubular filtrate into the tubular cell along a _____ gradient, but they require facilitated transport or carrier systems to move across the _____ membrane into the interstitial fluid, where they are absorbed into the peritubular capillaries.

13. _____ uses a carrier system in which the downhill movement of one substance such as sodium is coupled to the uphill movement of another substance such as glucose or an amino acid.

14. In the _____ tubule, there is almost complete reabsorption of nutritionally important substances from the filtrate.

15. The plasma level at which the substance appears in the urine is called the _____.

16. The _____ establishes a high concentration of osmotically active particles in the interstitium surrounding the medullary collecting tubules where the antidiuretic hormone (ADH) exerts its effects.

17. The thick portion of the loop of Henle contains a _____ cotransport system.

18. The _____ tubule is relatively impermeable to water, and reabsorption of sodium chloride from this segment further dilutes the tubular fluid.

19. The _____ assists in maintenance of the extracellular fluid volume by controlling the permeability of the medullary collecting tubules.

20. Increased _____ activity causes constriction of the afferent and efferent arterioles and thus a decrease in renal blood flow.

21. Renal _____ is the volume of plasma that is completely cleared each minute of any substance that finds its way into the urine.

22. _____ functions in the regulation of sodium and potassium elimination.

23. Atrial natriuretic peptide contributes to the regulation of _____ elimination.

24. The kidneys regulate body pH by conserving base _____ and eliminating _____ ions.

25. _____ is an end product of protein metabolism.

26. The synthesis of _____ is stimulated by tissue hypoxia, which may be brought about by anemia, residence at high altitudes, or impaired oxygenation of tissues due to cardiac or pulmonary disease.

27. _____ represents excessive protein excretion in the urine.

28. Urine _____ provides a valuable index of the hydration status and functional ability of the kidneys.

29. _____ levels in the blood and urine can be used to measure glomerular filtration rate (GFR).

30. _____, therefore, is related to the GFR but, unlike creatinine, also is influenced by protein intake, gastrointestinal bleeding, and hydration status.

Activity B *Match the key terms in Column A with their definitions in Column B.*

Column A

____ **1.** Counter-transport

____ **2.** Glomerular filtration rate

____ **3.** Vasopressin

____ **4.** Cortical nephrons

____ **5.** Vitamin D

____ **6.** Principal cells

____ **7.** Juxtamedullary nephrons

____ **8.** Countercurrent

____ **9.** Transport maximum

____ **10.** Mesangial cells

Column B

a. Originate in the superficial part of the cortex

b. Originate deeper in the cortex

c. Contribute to regulation of glomerular blood flow

d. Milliliter of filtrate formed per minute

e. The movement of one substance enables the movement of a second substance in the opposite direction

f. Maximum amount of substance that can be reabsorbed per unit of time

g. Site of aldosterone action

h. Flow of fluids in opposite directions

i. Stimulate expression of aquaporin-2 channels

j. Converted to active form in kidney

Activity C

1. Put the components of the renin-angiotensin-aldosterone system in order from stimulation to end hormone action:

• Conversion of angiotensin I to angiotensin II by angiotensin converting enzyme
• Decreased GFR
• Sodium and Water retention
• Angiotensin II stimulates release of ADH and aldosterone
• Juxtaglomerular release of renin
• Conversion of angiotensinogen to angiotensin I by renin

Activity D *Briefly answer the following.*

1. Describe the three layers of the glomerular membrane.

_____

2. Describe the various methods of transport across the epithelial layer of the renal tubule.

_____

3. How does the juxtaglomerular apparatus regulate GFR?

_____

4. What are the actions of atrial natriuretic peptide (ANP)?

_____

5. What are the endocrine functions of the kidney?

_____

6. How do Na^+ blockers function as a diuretic?

_____

SECTION III: APPLYING YOUR KNOWLEDGE

Activity E *Consider the scenario and answer the questions.*

An 18-year-old girl is brought to the emergency department by her friends. Her blood pressure is 115/85; pulse is 99; respiratory rate in 35 bpm. The girl is doubled over and she is holding her abdomen saying, "I hurt so bad; I hurt so bad." Her friends deny the girl has been using recreational drugs. They tell the triage nurse that the girl started complaining that her side hurt about 3 hours prior to the trip to the emergency department. Asked if the girl's parents had been notified, the friends tell the triage nurse that they have been unable to reach the girl's parents. On examination, a suspected diagnosis of kidney impairment is arrived at.

1. What tests would the nurse expect to be ordered to either confirm or deny the diagnosis?

   _____

   _____

   _____

2. The girl says, "My father just had a kidney stone removed. Is that what I have?" What noninvasive test would the nurse expect to be ordered to rule out a kidney stone?

   _____

   _____

   _____

SECTION IV: PRACTICING FOR NCLEX

Activity F *Answer the following questions.*

1. Many substances are both filtered out of the blood and reabsorbed into the blood in the kidneys. What is the plasma level at which a specific substance can be found in the urine?
   a. Renal threshold
   b. Renal clearance
   c. Renal filtration rate
   d. Renal transport level

2. You are admitting to the floor a 45-year-old woman with a presumptive diagnosis of diabetes mellitus. While taking her history, she mentions that she has been eating a lot of sweets lately. How would you expect this diet to impact her renal system?
   a. Decrease tubular reabsorption
   b. Increase renal blood flow
   c. Decrease renal blood flow
   d. Increase sodium excretion

3. The renal clearance of a substance is measured independently. What are the factors that determine renal clearance of a substance? (Mark all that apply.)
   a. The ability of the substance to be filtered in the glomeruli
   b. The capacity of the renal tubules to reabsorb or secrete the substance
   c. The normal electrolyte and pH composition of the blood
   d. The rate of renal blood flow
   e. The rate sodium is excreted from the body

4. It is known that high levels of uric acid in the blood can cause gout, while high levels in the urine can cause kidney stones. What medication competes with uric acid for secretion in to the tubular fluid, thereby reducing uric acid secretion?
   a. Ibuprofen
   b. Acetaminophen
   c. Aspirin
   d. Advil

5. Many drugs are eliminated in the urine. These drugs cannot be bound to plasma proteins if the glomerulus is going to filter them out of the blood. In what situation would it be necessary to create either an alkaline or acid diuresis in a client?
   a. Nontherapeutic drug levels in blood
   b. Noncompliance with medication regimen
   c. The need to use a loading dose of a specific drug and keep it in the system for a long time.
   d. In the case of a drug overdose

6. The anemia that occurs with end-stage kidney disease is often caused by the kidneys themselves. What inability of the kidney disease causes anemia in end-stage kidney disease?

    a. Produce erythropoietin

    b. Produce rennin

    c. Produce angiotensin

    d. Inactivate vitamin D

7. Diuretics can either block the reabsorption of components of the urine, or they can block the reabsorption of water back into the body. What does the increase in urine flow from the body depend on with a patient taking diuretics?

    a. The amount of water reabsorption back into the body

    b. The amount of sodium and chloride reabsorption that it blocks

    c. The amount of sodium and chloride that it excretes through the kidney

    d. The amount of water excreted by the body

8. Urine specific gravity is normally 1.010 to 1.025 with adequate hydration. When there is loss of renal concentrating ability due to impaired renal function, low concentration levels are exhibited. When would the nurse consider the low levels of concentration to be significant?

    a. At noon

    b. First void in morning

    c. Last void at night

    d. After a nap

9. An elderly man is brought into the clinic by his daughter who states, "My father hasn't been himself lately. Now I think he looks a little yellow." What test would the nurse expect to have ordered to check this man's creatinine level?

    a. BUN level

    b. 24 hour urine test

    c. Urine test, first void in morning

    d. Serum creatinine

10. A patient suffering from a previous myocardial infarction is displaying an inability to dilate the blood vessels and increased sodium retention. Which hormone level may have been affected by the MI?

    a. ANP

    b. ADH

    c. BNP

    d. ACTH

CHAPTER 25

Disorders of Renal Function

SECTION I: LEARNING OBJECTIVES

1. Describe the two types of immune mechanisms involved in glomerular disorders.

2. Use the terms *proliferation, sclerosis, membranous, diffuse, focal, segmental,* and *mesangial* to explain changes in glomerular structure that occur with glomerulonephritis.

3. Relate the proteinuria, hematuria, pyuria, oliguria, edema, hypertension, and azotemia that occur with glomerulonephritis to changes in glomerular structure.

4. Briefly describe the difference among the nephritic syndromes, rapidly progressive glomerulonephritis, nephrotic syndrome, asymptomatic glomerular disorders, and chronic glomerulonephritis.

5. Cite a definition of tubulointerstitial kidney disease.

6. Differentiate between the defects in tubular function that occur in proximal and distal tubular acidosis.

7. Explain the pathogenesis of kidney damage in acute and chronic pyelonephritis.

8. Describe the inheritance, pathology, and manifestations of the different types of polycystic kidney disease.

9. List four common causes of urinary tract obstruction.

10. Define the term *hydronephrosis* and relate it to the destructive effects of urinary tract obstructions.

11. Describe the role of urine supersaturation, nucleation, and inhibitors of stone formation in the development of kidney stones.

12. Explain the mechanisms of pain and infection that occur with kidney stones.

13. Describe methods used in the diagnosis and treatment of kidney stones.

14. Cite the organisms most responsible for urinary tract infections (UTIs) and state why urinary catheters, obstruction, and reflux predispose to infections.

15. List three physiologic mechanisms that protect against UTIs.

16. Describe the signs and symptoms of UTIs.

17. Describe factors that predispose to UTIs in children, sexually active women, pregnant women, and older adults.

18. Compare the manifestations of UTIs in different age groups, including infants, toddlers, adolescents, adults, and older adults.

19. Cite measures used in the diagnosis and treatment of UTIs.

20. Explain the vulnerability of the kidneys to injury caused by drugs and toxins.

21. Characterize Wilms tumor in terms of age of onset, possible oncogenic origin, manifestations, and treatment.

22. Cite the risk factors for renal cell carcinoma, describe its manifestations, and explain why the 5-year survival rate has been so low.

SECTION II: ASSESSING YOUR UNDERSTANDING

Activity A *Fill in the blanks.*

1. Anomalies in _____ and _____ of the kidneys are the most common form of congenital renal disorder.

2. The term *dysgenesis* refers to a failure of an organ to develop normally and _____ refers to complete failure of an organ to develop.

3. Newborns with renal agenesis often have characteristic facial features, termed _____, resulting from the effects of oligohydramnios.

4. In renal _____, the kidneys do not develop to normal size.

5. Renal _____ is due to an abnormality in the differentiation of kidney structures during embryonic development.

6. Unilateral _____ renal dysplasia is the most common cause of an abdominal mass in newborns.

7. _____ kidney diseases are a group of kidney disorders characterized by fluid-filled sacs or segments that have their origin in the tubular structures of kidney.

8. In the _____ form of polycystic kidney disease, thousands of large cysts are derived from every segment of the nephron.

9. The _____ effects of urinary obstruction on kidney structures are determined by the degree and the duration of the obstruction.

10. _____ of urine predisposes to infection, which may spread throughout the urinary tract.

11. _____ refers to urine-filled dilatation of the renal pelvis and calyces associated with progressive atrophy of the kidney due to obstruction of urine outflow.

12. Obstruction of the urinary track may provoke pain due to _____ of the collecting system and renal capsule.

13. The most common cause of upper urinary tract obstruction is urinary _____.

14. In addition to a supersaturated urine, kidney stone formation requires a _____ that facilitates crystal aggregation.

15. Most kidney stones are _____ stones.

16. The major manifestation of kidney stones is _____.

17. Urinary tract infections are the _____ most common type of bacterial infection seen by health care providers.

18. Most uncomplicated lower UTIs are caused by _____.

19. Most UTIs are caused by bacteria that enter through the _____.

20. Urinary tract infections are _____ common in women than men.

21. In UTIs associated with stasis of urine flow, the obstruction may be _____ or _____.

22. _____-associated bacteriuria remains the most frequent cause of Gram-negative septicemia in hospitalized patients.

23. An acute episode of _____ is characterized by frequency of urination, lower abdominal or back discomfort, and burning and pain on urination.

24. _____ is second leading cause of kidney failure worldwide and it ranks third, after diabetes and hypertension, as a cause of chronic kidney disease in the United States.

25. The _____ syndromes produce a proliferative inflammatory response, whereas the _____ syndrome produces increased permeability of the glomerulus.

26. _____ syndrome is characterized by sudden onset of hematuria, variable degrees of proteinuria, diminished glomerular filtration rate, oliguria, and signs impaired renal function.

27. Acute postinfectious glomerulonephritis usually occurs after infection with certain strains of group A β-hemolytic streptococci and is caused by _____ of immune complexes.

28. The _____ of postinfectious glomerulonephritis is caused by infiltration of leukocytes, both neutrophils and monocytes; proliferation of endothelial and mesangial cells; and, in severe cases, formation of crescents.

29. _____ syndrome is an uncommon and aggressive form of glomerulonephritis that is caused by antibodies to the glomerular basement membrane.

30. _____ syndrome is characterized by massive proteinuria and lipiduria, along with an associated hypoalbuminemia, generalized edema, and hyperlipidemia.

31. _____ glomerulonephritis is caused by diffuse thickening of the glomerular basement membrane due to deposition of immune complexes.

32. _____ is a primary glomerulonephritis characterized by the presence of glomerular IgA immune complex deposits.

33. Alport syndrome represents a hereditary defect of the glomerular _____ that results in hematuria and may progress to chronic renal failure.

34. _____ refers to a group of tubular defects in reabsorption of bicarbonate ions or excretion of hydrogen ions (H^+) that result in metabolic acidosis and its subsequent complications, including metabolic bone disease, kidney stones, and growth failure in children.

35. Proximal renal tubular acidosis involves a defect in proximal tubular reabsorption of _____.

36. _____ represents an infection of the upper urinary tract, specifically the renal parenchyma and renal pelvis.

37. _____ is one of the most common primary neoplasms of young children.

38. Kidney cancer is suspected when there are findings of _____ and a renal _____.

Activity B *Consider the following figure.*

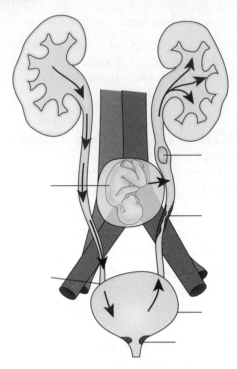

In the figure above, identify the common locations and causes of urinary track obstructions:

- Pregnancy or tumor
- Ureterovesical junction stricture
- Kidney stone
- Scar tissue
- Neurogenic bladder
- Bladder outflow obstruction

Activity C *Match the key terms in Column A with their definitions in Column B.*

Column A	Column B
____ 1. Urease	a. Low renal mass in infant
____ 2. Hypogenesis	
____ 3. Oliguria	b. Blood cells in urine
____ 4. PKD 1 and 2	c. Urea splitting bacterial enzyme
____ 5. Hydronephrosis	
____ 6. Proteinuria	d. Change in renal structure
____ 7. Renal dysplasia	e. Dilatation of the renal pelvis and calyces associated with progressive atrophy
____ 8. Nephrolithiasis	
____ 9. Hematuria	
____ 10. Oligohydramnios	

f. Very low urine
   production

g. Genes responsible
   for autosomal
   dominant polycys-
   tic kidney disease
   (ADPKD)

h. Kidney stone
   formation

i. Protein loss in
   urine

j. Low amniotic fluid
   levels

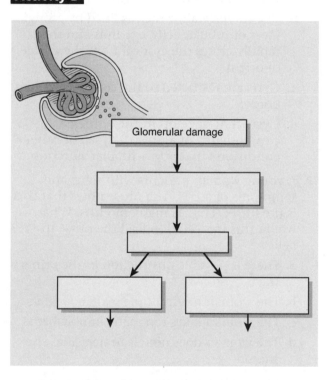

Glomerular damage

Complete the above flowchart using the bullet
points below.
- Edema
- Hyperlipidemia
- Increased permeability to proteins
- Decreased plasma oncotic pressure
- Hypoproteinemia
- Compensatory synthesis of proteins by liver

Activity E *Briefly answer the following.*

1. What is the mechanism of tissue damage in
   urinary track obstructions?

   _____

   _____

   _____

2. What are the factors involved in kidney stone
   formation?

   _____

   _____

   _____

3. For whom are the risk factors for UTIs higher?

   _____

   _____

   _____

4. What are the host defense mechanisms
   against the development of a UTI?

   _____

   _____

   _____

5. What are the cellular changes associated with
   glomerular disease?

   _____

   _____

   _____

6. Describe the disease progress and the production of symptoms in poststreptococcal
   glomerulonephritis.

   _____

   _____

   _____

7. Describe the mechanisms of a diabetic
   nephropathy.

   _____

   _____

   _____

8. How do medications and toxins from the environment damage renal structures?

_____

_____

_____

SECTION III: APPLYING YOUR KNOWLEDGE

Activity F *Consider the scenario and answer the question.*

An elderly woman, hospitalized with a broken hip, has an indwelling catheter in place. On the third day of hospitalization the woman's urine becomes cloudy and foul smelling. The nurse knows that catheters have a high incidence of causing UTIs in hospitalized patients.

1. What orders would the nurse expect to receive for this patient to determine if there is an infection?

_____

_____

_____

SECTION IV: PRACTICING FOR NCLEX

Activity G *Answer the following questions.*

1. Congenital disorders of the kidneys are fairly common, occurring in approximately 1:1000 live births. What is the result to the newborn when bilateral renal dysplasia occurs? (Mark all that apply.)
   a. Potter facies
   b. Oligohydramnios
   c. Pulmonary hypoplasia
   d. Multicystic kidneys
   e. Renal failure

2. Match the type of polycystic kidney disorder with the characteristic cysts.

Type of Polycystic Kidney Disorder
1. Autosomal dominant polycystic kidney disease (ADPKD)
2. Autosomal recessive polycystic kidney disease (ARPKD)
3. Acquired cysts
4. Nephronophthisis-medullary cystic kidney disease

Characteristic Cysts
a. Small elongated cysts form in the collecting ducts and maintain contact with the nephron of origin
b. The tubule wall, which is lined by a single layer of tubular cells, expands and then rapidly closes the cyst off from the tubule of origin.
c. Cysts are restricted to the corticomedullary border.
d. Cysts that develop in the kidney as a consequence of aging, dialysis, or other conditions that affect tubular function

3. A young woman presents with signs and symptoms of a UTI. The nurse notes that this is the fifth UTI in as many months. What would this information lead the nurse to believe?
   a. There is possible obstruction in the urinary tract
   b. The woman has multiple sexual partners
   c. The woman takes too many bubble baths
   d. The woman does not clean herself as she should

4. Staghorn kidney stones, or struvite stones, are usually located in the renal pelvis. These stones are made from what?
   a. Calcium oxalate
   b. Magnesium ammonium phosphate
   c. Cystine
   d. Uric acid

5. What is the most common cause of a lower UTI?
   a. *Staphylococcus saprophyticus*
   b. *Pseudomonas aeruginosa*
   c. *Escherichia coli*
   d. *Staphylococcus aureus*

6. Urinary tract infections in children do not generally present as UTIs as they do in adults. What are the signs and symptoms of a UTI in a toddler? (Mark all that apply.)
   a. Frequency
   b. Diarrhea
   c. Abdominal pain
   d. Poor growth
   e. Burning

7. Acute postinfectious glomerulonephritis, as its name implies, follows an acute infection somewhere else in the body. What is the most common cause of acute postinfectious glomerulonephritis?
   a. *E. coli*
   b. *S. aureus*
   c. *P. aeruginosa*
   d. Group A β-hemolytic streptococci

8. Both type I and type II diabetes mellitus can cause damage to the glomeruli of the kidneys. What renal disease is diabetic nephropathy associated with?
   a. Nephrotic syndrome
   b. Acute glomerulonephritis
   c. Nephritic syndrome
   d. Acute glomerulonephritis

9. Acute pyelonephritis is an infection of the renal parenchyma and renal pelvis. What is the most common cause of acute pyelonephritis?
   a. Group A β-hemolytic streptococci
   b. *P. aeruginosa*
   c. *Haemophilus influenza*
   d. *Candida albicans*

10. Drug-related nephropathies occur all too often. They involve functional and/or structural changes to the kidney after exposure to a drug. What does the tolerance to drugs depend on?
    a. Vesicoureteral reflux
    b. Glomerular filtration rate
    c. State of hydration
    d. Proteinuria

11. Wilms tumor is a tumor of childhood. It is usually an encapsulated mass occurring in any part of the kidney. What are the common presenting signs of a Wilms tumor?
    a. Hypotension and a large abdominal mass
    b. Vomiting and oliguria
    c. Abdominal pain and diarrhea
    d. Large asymptomatic abdominal mass and hypertension

CHAPTER 26

Acute Renal Failure and Chronic Kidney Disease

SECTION I: LEARNING OBJECTIVES

1. Describe acute renal failure in terms of its causes, treatment, and outcome.

2. Differentiate the prerenal, intrinsic, and postrenal forms of acute renal failure in terms of the mechanisms of development and manifestations.

3. Cite the two most common causes of acute tubular necrosis and describe the course of the disease in terms of the initiation, maintenance, and recovery phases.

4. State the most common causes of chronic kidney disease.

5. Describe the five stages of chronic kidney disease.

6. Describe the methods used to arrive at an accurate estimation of the glomerular filtration rate (GFR) and explain the rationale for its use in defining the stages of chronic kidney disease.

7. Explain the physiologic mechanisms underlying the common problems associated with chronic kidney disease, including alterations in fluid and electrolyte balance and disorders of skeletal, hematologic, cardiovascular, immune system, neurologic, skin, and sexual function.

8. State the basis for adverse drug reactions in patients with chronic kidney disease.

9. Describe the scientific principles underlying dialysis treatment, and compare hemodialysis with peritoneal dialysis.

10. Cite the possible complications of kidney transplantation.

11. State the goals for dietary management of persons with chronic kidney disease.

12. List the causes of chronic kidney disease (CKD) in children and describe the special problems of children with kidney failure.

13. State why CKD is more common in the elderly and describe measures to prevent or delay the onset of kidney failure in this population.

14. Describe the treatment of CKD in children and the elderly.

SECTION II: ASSESSING YOUR UNDERSTANDING

Activity A *Fill in the blanks.*

1. _____ represents a rapid decline in kidney function sufficient to increase blood levels of nitrogenous wastes and impair fluid and electrolyte balance.

2. The causes of acute renal failure commonly are categorized as _____, _____, or _____.

3. _____ failure, the most common form of acute renal failure, is characterized by a marked decrease in renal blood flow.

4. Because of their high metabolic rate, the _____ cells are most vulnerable to ischemic injury.

5. Prerenal failure is manifested by a sharp decrease in urine output and a disproportionate elevation of _____ in relation to serum creatinine levels.

6. _____ failure results from obstruction of urine outflow from the kidneys.

7. A major concern in the treatment of acute renal failure is identifying and correcting the _____.

8. Regardless of cause, _____ represents a loss of functioning kidney nephrons with progressive deterioration of glomerular filtration, tubular reabsorptive capacity, and endocrine functions of the kidneys.

9. The normal GFR, which varies with age, gender, and body size, is approximately _____ mL/minute (1.73 mL/minute per square millimeter) for normal young healthy adults.

10. In clinical practice, GFR is usually estimated using the serum _____ concentration.

11. Increased excretion of low-molecular-weight globulins is a marker of _____ disease, and excretion of _____ a marker of CKD.

12. The _____ state includes signs and symptoms of altered fluid, electrolyte, and acid-base balance; and alterations in regulatory functions.

13. Chronic renal failure can produce _____ or fluid _____, depending on the pathology of the kidney disease.

14. In chronic renal failure, the kidneys lose the ability to regulate _____ excretion.

15. The acidosis that occurs in persons with kidney failure seems to stabilize as the disease progresses, probably as a result of the tremendous buffering capacity of _____.

16. The term *renal* _____ is used to describe the skeletal complications of CKD.

17. _____ commonly is an early manifestation of chronic renal failure.

18. Anorexia, nausea, and vomiting are common in patients with _____, along with a metallic taste in the mouth that further depresses the appetite.

19. Neuropathy is caused by _____ and _____ of nerve fibers, possibly caused by uremic toxins.

20. Normal aging is associated with a decline in the _____ and subsequently with reduced homeostatic regulation under stressful conditions.

Activity B *Consider the following figure.*

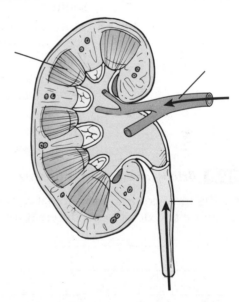

In the figure above, label the sites of prerenal, intrinsic, and postrenal causes of renal failure.

Activity C *Match the key terms in Column A with their definitions in Column B.*

Column A

___ 1. Isosthenuria
___ 2. Azotemia
___ 3. Creatinine
___ 4. Salt wasting
___ 5. Oliguria
___ 6. Uremic encephalopathy
___ 7. Prostatic hyperplasia
___ 8. Hemodialysis
___ 9. Uremia
___ 10. Osteitis fibrosa

Column B

a. Decreased urine production

b. Polyuria with urine that is almost isotonic with plasma

c. Increased bone resorption and formation

d. By-product of muscle metabolism

e. Decreased CNS activity

f. Presence of excessive amounts of urea in the blood

g. Impaired tubular reabsorption of sodium

h. Most common cause of postrenal failure

i. Use of artificial kidney to filter blood

j. Accumulation of nitrogenous wastes in the blood

Activity D *Briefly answer the following.*

1. Name the most common intrarenal cause of renal failure and describe its different forms.

_____

_____

_____

2. Describe the progression of acute tubular necrosis (ATN).

_____

_____

_____

3. How is chronic kidney disease classified?

_____

_____

_____

4. Why is chronic kidney disease considered to have an insidious progression?

_____

_____

_____

5. What are the clinical manifestations of chronic kidney disease?

_____

_____

_____

6. How is anemia related to chronic kidney disease?

_____

_____

_____

7. How does renal disease cause cardiovascular disease?

_____

_____

_____

SECTION III: APPLYING YOUR KNOWLEDGE

Activity E *Consider the scenario and answer the questions.*

The parents of a hospitalized 4-year-old boy have just been told that their son has a chronic renal disease. The nurse is planning discharge teaching for this family.

1. What would the nurse know to include in the discharge teaching for this child and his family?

_____

_____

_____

2. The parents inquire about treatment for their son and if kidney transplantation could occur. What would be the nurse's best response?

_____

_____

_____

SECTION IV: PRACTICING FOR NCLEX

Activity F *Answer the following questions.*

1. Acute renal failure occurs at a high rate in seriously ill people who are in intensive care units. What is the most common indicator of acute renal failure?
   a. Azotemia and a decrease in the GFR
   b. Proteinuria and a decrease in the GFR
   c. Azotemia and an increase in the GFR
   d. Proteinuria and an increase in the GFR

2. Acute tubular necrosis is the most common cause of intrinsic renal failure. One of the causes of ATN is ischemia. What are the most common causes of ischemic ATN? (Mark all that apply.)
   a. Severe hypovolemia
   b. Severe hypertension
   c. Burns
   d. Overwhelming sepsis
   e. Severe hypervolemia

3. The GFR is considered to be the best measure of renal function. What is used to estimate the GFR?
   a. BUN
   b. Serum creatinine
   c. Albumin level
   d. Serum protein

4. Chronic kidney disease impacts many systems in the body. What is the number one hematologic disorder caused by CKD?
   a. Polycythemia
   b. Erythrocythemia
   c. Anemia
   d. Leukocytosis

5. Uremic pericarditis is a disorder that accompanies CKD. What are its presenting signs and symptoms? (Mark all that apply.)
   a. Pericardial friction rub
   b. Chest pain with respiratory accentuation
   c. Fever without infection
   d. Shortness of breath
   e. Thromboangiitis

6. Neuromuscular disorders can be triggered by CKD. For those clients on dialysis, approximately two-thirds suffer from what peripheral neuropathy?
   a. Reynaud syndrome
   b. Burning hands and feet
   c. Tingling and loss of sensation in lower limbs
   d. Restless leg syndrome

7. People with CKD have impaired immune responses to infection because of high levels of urea and metabolic wastes in the blood. What is one thing that is missing in an immune response in people with CKD?
   a. Failure to mount a fever with infection
   b. Failure of a phagocytic response with infection
   c. Decrease in granulocyte count
   d. Impaired humoral immunity response with infection

8. Sexual dysfunction in people with CKD is thought to be multifactorial. What are thought to be causes of sexual dysfunction in people with CKD? (Mark all that apply.)
   a. Antihypertensive drugs
   b. Psychological factors
   c. Uremic toxins
   d. Inability to vasodilate veins
   e. High incidence of sexually transmitted diseases

9. In hemodialysis, access to the vascular system is most commonly through what?
   a. External arteriovenous shunt
   b. Internal arteriovenous fistula
   c. Internal arteriovenous shunt
   d. External arteriovenous fistula

10. Dietary restrictions placed on people with CKD include limiting protein in their diet. The recommended sources of protein for people with CKD include what source of protein?
    a. Red meat
    b. Fowl
    c. Milk
    d. Fish

CHAPTER 27

Disorders of the Bladder and Lower Urinary Tract

SECTION I: LEARNING OBJECTIVES

1. Trace the ascending sensory and descending motor impulses between the detrusor muscle and external urinary sphincter and the spinal cord, pontine micturition center, and cerebral cortex.

2. Explain the mechanism of low-pressure urine storage in the bladder.

3. Describe at least three urodynamic studies that can be used to assess bladder function.

4. Describe the causes of and compensatory changes that occur with urinary tract obstruction.

5. Differentiate lesions that produce storage dysfunction associated with spastic bladder from those that produce emptying dysfunction associated with flaccid bladder in terms of the level of the lesions and their effects on bladder function.

6. Describe methods used in treatment of neurogenic bladder.

7. Define *incontinence* and differentiate between stress incontinence, overactive bladder/urge incontinence, and overflow incontinence.

8. Describe behavioral, pharmacologic, and surgical methods used in treatment of the different types of incontinence.

9. List the treatable causes of incontinence in the elderly.

10. Discuss the difference between superficial and invasive bladder cancer in terms of bladder involvement, extension of the disease, and prognosis.

11. State the most common sign of bladder cancer.

SECTION II: ASSESSING YOUR UNDERSTANDING

Activity A *Fill in the blanks.*

1. The _____ stores urine and controls its elimination from the body.

2. The bladder is a freely movable organ located _____ on the pelvic floor, just posterior to the pubic _____.

3. In the male, the _____ gland surrounds the neck of the bladder where it empties into the urethra.

4. Urine passes from the kidneys to the bladder through the _____.

5. The tonicity and composition of the urine often is quite different from that of the blood, and the _____ of the bladder acts as an effective barrier to prevent the passage of water and other urine elements between the bladder and the blood.

6. The _____ operates as a reserve mechanism to stop micturition when it is occurring and to maintain continence in the face of unusually high bladder pressure.

7. The motor component of the neural reflex that causes bladder emptying is controlled by the _____ nervous system, while the relaxation and storage function of the bladder is controlled by the _____ nervous system.

8. The parasympathetic lower motor neurons for the detrusor muscle of the bladder are located in the _____ segments of the spinal cord; their axons travel to the bladder by way of the _____.

9. The immediate coordination of the normal micturition reflex occurs in the micturition center in the _____, facilitated by descending input from the forebrain and ascending input from the reflex centers in the spinal cord.

10. _____ brain centers enable inhibition of the micturition center in the pons and conscious control of urination.

11. The _____ receptors are found in the detrusor muscle; they produce relaxation of the detrusor muscle, increasing the bladder volume at which the micturition reflex is triggered.

12. The activation of _____ produces contraction of the intramural ureteral musculature, bladder neck, and internal sphincter.

13. Alterations in bladder function include urinary _____ with retention or stasis of urine and urinary _____ with involuntary loss of urine.

14. The most important cause of urinary obstruction in males is external compression of the urethra caused by the enlargement of the _____.

15. Neurogenic disorders of bladder function commonly are manifested in one of two ways: failure to _____ urine or failure to _____.

16. Spastic bladder is caused by conditions that produce partial or extensive neural damage above the _____ center in the sacral cord.

17. A mild form of reflex neurogenic bladder can develop after a _____.

18. _____ of the detrusor muscle and loss of the perception of bladder fullness permit the overstretching of the detrusor muscle that contributes to weak and ineffective bladder contractions seen in detrusor muscle areflexia.

19. _____ is the involuntary loss of urine during coughing, laughing, sneezing, or lifting that increases intra-abdominal pressure.

20. Two mechanisms are thought to contribute to its symptomatology of overactive bladder: CNS and neural control of bladder sensation and emptying, _____ and those involving the smooth muscle of the bladder itself, _____.

21. Approximately 90% of bladder cancers are derived from the _____ epithelial cells that line the bladder.

22. The most common sign of bladder cancer is painless _____.

Activity B *Consider the following figure.*

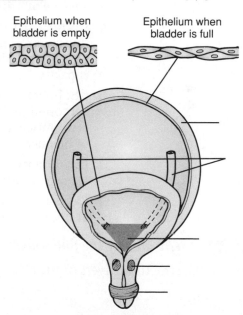

Epithelium when bladder is empty

Epithelium when bladder is full

1. In the diagram of the bladder above, please locate and label the following:

   • Detrusor muscle
   • Ureters
   • Trigone
   • Internal sphincter
   • External sphincter

Activity C *Match the key terms in Column A with their definitions in Column B.*

Column A

_____ **1.** Incontinence

_____ **2.** Micturition

_____ **3.** Kegel exercises

_____ **4.** Muscarinic

_____ **5.** Nocturia

_____ **6.** Antimuscarinic drugs

_____ **7.** Detrusor-sphincter dyssynergia

_____ **8.** May cause urinary retention

_____ **9.** Nicotinic

_____ **10.** β_2-adrenergic receptors

Column B

a. Muscle-tensing exercises of the pelvic muscles

b. Uninhibited spinal reflex-controlled contraction of the bladder without relaxation of the external sphincter

c. Produce relaxation of the detrusor muscle, increasing the bladder volume at which the micturition reflex is triggered

d. Cholinergic receptor found on external sphincter muscle

e. Antihistamine

f. Passage of urine

g. Decrease detrusor muscle tone and increase bladder capacity

h. Cholinergic receptor found on striated muscle fibers of bladder

i. Involuntary loss or leakage of urine

j. Excessive urination at night

Activity D *Briefly answer the following.*

1. Describe the structural layers of the bladder.

2. List the name and function of the major nerves that regulate bladder function.

3. Describe the activities of the pontine micturition center and cortical brain centers.

4. Describe the actions that take place in the bladder during micturition.

5. What are the necessary factors that every child must possess in order to attain conscious control of bladder function?

6. Describe the effects of prolonged urinary tract obstruction disorders on the bladder.

7. Why do many women develop incontinence following childbirth?

8. Describe how chronic neurologic disorders can contribute to overactive bladder.

9. What are the factors associated with age that contribute to incontinence in the elderly?

SECTION III: APPLYING YOUR KNOWLEDGE

Activity E *Consider the scenario and answer the questions.*

A 53-year-old woman with multiple sclerosis presents at the clinic with urinary frequency and bladder spasms. A urinalysis is negative for infection. A complete history is taken and a physical examination is performed by the primary care physician. The woman asks the nurse why she is having bladder spasms and urinary frequency if she does not have a bladder infection.

1. What would the nurse respond?

_____

_____

_____

2. What would the nurse expect the doctor to do for this woman to treat her bladder spasms?

_____

_____

_____

SECTION IV: PRACTICING FOR NCLEX

Activity F *Answer the following questions.*

1. You are caring for a 16-year-old male patient, newly diagnosed with a spinal cord injury. He asks you why he can no longer control his bladder. What would you explain to him? (Mark all that apply.)

   a. Your spinal cord injury has disrupted the control your brain has over your bladder.

   b. You will always have to wear an internal catheter.

   c. You will have to learn how to in-and-out catheterize yourself.

   d. You have a condition known as a *relaxed bladder.*

   e. You have a condition known as *detrusor-sphincter dyssynergia.*

2. Children usually achieve bladder control by age 5. Girls generally achieve bladder control before boys do. What is the general rule for bladder capacity in a child?

   a. Up to the age of 12 to 14, the capacity of the bladder is the child's age in years plus 2.

   b. Up to the age of 5, the capacity of the bladder is the child's age in years plus 3.

   c. The capacity of the bladder is equal to the child's age in years.

   d. Age has nothing to do with bladder capacity; it has adult capacity from toddlerhood.

3. One of the many tests done during urodynamic studies is the sphincter electromyograph (EMG). What does this test study?

   a. Ability of the bladder to store urine

   b. Activity of the voluntary muscles of the perineal area

   c. The pressure of the bladder during filling and emptying

   d. The flow rate during urination

4. Urinary obstruction in the lower urinary tract triggers changes to the urinary system to compensate for the obstruction. What is an early change the system makes in its effort to cope with an obstruction?

   a. Ability to suppress urination is increased

   b. The stretch receptors in the bladder wall become hypersensitive

   c. The bladder begins to shrink

   d. Bladder contraction weakens

5. What is a common cause of spastic bladder dysfunction?

   a. Central nervous system lesions

   b. Constriction of the internal sphincter muscles

   c. External sphincter spasticity

   d. Vesicoureteral reflux

6. Acute overdistention of the bladder can occur in anyone with a neurogenic bladder that does not empty. How much urine would the nurse empty out of the bladder at one time?

   a. Everything in the bladder, no matter how full it is

   b. No more than 600 mL of urine at one time

   c. No more than 500 mL of urine at one time

   d. No more than 1000 mL of urine at one time

7. In women, stress incontinence is a common problem. The loss of the angle between the urethrovesical junction and the bladder contributes to stress incontinence. What is the normal angle between the bladder and the urethrovesical junction?

   a. 90 to 100 degrees
   b. 100 to 1110 degrees
   c. 80 to 90 degrees
   d. 95 to 105 degrees

8. Incontinence can be transient. What are the causes of transient urinary incontinence? (Mark all that apply.)

   a. Spinal cord injury
   b. Confusional states
   c. Stool impaction
   d. Diarrhea
   e. Recurrent urinary tract infections

9. Urinary incontinence can be a problem with the elderly. One method of treatment is habit training, or bladder training. When using this treatment with an elderly person how frequently should they be voiding?

   a. Every 1 to 3 hours
   b. Every 2 to 4 hours
   c. Every 3 to 5 hours
   d. Every 4 to 6 hours

10. One of the treatments for bladder cancer in situ is the intervesicular administration of what drug?

   a. Adriamycin
   b. Mitomycin C
   c. Bacillus Calmette-Guérin vaccine
   d. Thiotepa

CHAPTER 28

Structure and Function of the Gastrointestinal System

SECTION I: LEARNING OBJECTIVES

1. Describe the anatomic structures of the upper, middle, and lower gastrointestinal (GI) tract.

2. List the five layers of the GI tract wall and describe their function.

3. Characterize the structure and function of the peritoneum and describe its attachment to the abdominal wall.

4. Characterize the properties of the interstitial smooth muscle cells that act as pacemakers for the GI tract.

5. Compare the actions of the enteric and autonomic nervous systems as they relate to motility of the GI tract.

6. Trace a bolus of food through the stages of swallowing.

7. Differentiate tonic and peristaltic movements in the GI tract.

8. Describe the action of the internal and external sphincters in the control of defecation.

9. State the source and function of water and electrolytes that are secreted in digestive secretions.

10. Explain the protective function of saliva.

11. Describe the function of the gastric secretions in the process of digestion.

12. List three major GI hormones and cite their function.

13. Describe the site of gastric acid and pepsin production and secretion in the stomach.

14. Describe the function of the gastric mucosal barrier.

15. Describe the functions of the secretions of the small and the large intestine.

16. Describe and differentiate between anorexia, nausea, and vomiting.

SECTION II: ASSESSING YOUR UNDERSTANDING

Activity A *Fill in the blanks.*

1. The major physiologic function of the _____ is to digest food and absorb nutrients into the bloodstream

2. The upper esophageal sphincter, the _____ sphincter, consists of a circular layer of striated muscle.

3. The lower esophageal sphincter, the _____ sphincter, lies just above the area where the esophagus joins the stomach.

4. The _____ lies in the left side of the abdomen and serves as a food storage reservoir during the early stages of digestion.

5. The small intestine, which forms the middle portion of the digestive tract, consists of three subdivisions: the _____, _____, and _____.

6. Bile and pancreatic juices enter the intestine through openings for the common bile duct and the main pancreatic duct in the _____.

7. The _____ cells carry out the secretory and absorptive functions of the GI tract and they produce the _____ that lubricates and protects the inner surface of the alimentary canal.

8. _____ fluid forms a moist and slippery surface that prevents friction between the continuously moving abdominal structures.

9. The _____ contains the blood vessels, nerves, and lymphatic vessels that supply the intestinal wall.

10. Like the self-excitable cardiac muscle cells in the heart, some smooth muscle cells of the GI tract function as _____ cells.

11. The _____ nervous system consists of the myenteric and submucosal plexuses in the wall of the GI tract.

12. _____ monitor the stretch and distention of the GI tract wall, and _____ monitor the chemical composition of its contents.

13. Numerous _____ reflexes influence motility and secretions of the digestive tract.

14. Swallowing consists of three phases: an _____ phase, a _____ phase, and an _____ phase.

15. The _____ is the major site for the digestion and absorption of food.

16. _____ normally is initiated by the mass movements of the large intestine.

17. The GI tract produces _____ that act locally, pass into the general circulation for distribution to more distant sites, and interact with the central nervous system by way of the enteric and autonomic nervous systems.

18. The primary function of _____ is the stimulation of gastric acid secretion.

19. _____ has potent growth hormone-releasing activity and has a stimulatory effect on food intake and digestive function, while reducing energy expenditure.

20. _____ potentiates the action of secretin, increasing the pancreatic bicarbonate response to low circulating levels of secretin, stimulates biliary secretion of fluid and bicarbonate, and regulates gallbladder contraction and gastric emptying.

21. The _____ cells secrete hydrochloric acid and intrinsic factor, which is necessary for the absorption of _____.

22. The chief cells secrete _____, an enzyme that initiates proteolysis or breakdown of proteins.

23. G cells secrete _____.

24. _____ secrete large amounts of alkaline mucus that protect the duodenum from the acid content in the gastric chyme and from the action of the digestive enzymes.

25. The stomach and small intestine contain only a few species of _____, probably because of the composition of luminal contents.

26. The major metabolic function of colonic microflora is the fermentation of _____ and endogenous mucus produced by the epithelial cells.

27. _____ is the process of dismantling foods into their constituent parts.

28. _____ is the process of moving nutrients and other materials from the external environment of the GI tract into the internal environment.

29. Each villus is covered with cells called _____ that contribute to the absorptive and digestive functions of the small bowel, and goblet cells that provide mucus.

30. The enterocytes secrete _____ that adhere to the border of the villus structures.

31. Triglycerides are broken down by pancreatic _____.

32. _____ represents a loss of appetite.

33. _____ is the conscious sensation resulting from stimulation of the medullary vomiting center that often precedes or accompanies vomiting.

34. _____ is the sudden and forceful oral expulsion of the contents of the stomach.

Activity B *Consider the following figures.*

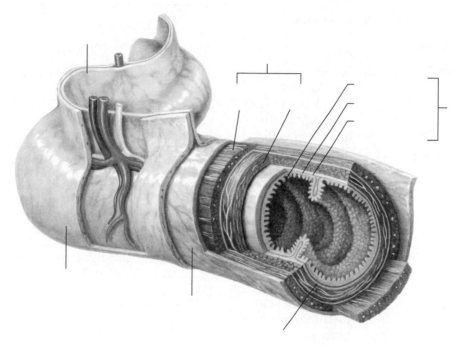

1. In the transfers section of the digestive tract above, locate and label the following layers/structures:

   • Mesentery
   • Muscularis mucosae
   • Serosa (mesothelium)

   • Longitudinal muscle
   • Circular muscle
   • Submucosa
   • Mucosa
   • Serosa (connective tissue)
   • Muscularis externa

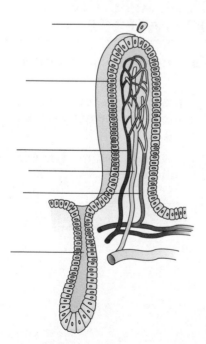

2. In the transfers section of the digestive tract above, locate and label the following layers/structures:

   • Extruded enterocyte
   • Enterocyte
   • Vein
   • Lacteal
   • Artery
   • Crypt of Lieberkühn

Activity C *Match the key terms in Column A with their definitions in Column B.*

Column A

____ **1.** Amylase

____ **2.** Mastication

____ **3.** Mesentery

____ **4.** Interstitial cells of Cajal

____ **5.** Peritoneum

____ **6.** Submucosal plexus

____ **7.** Haustrations

____ **8.** Chyme

____ **9.** Myenteric plexus

____ **10.** Secretin

Column B

a. Responsible for motility along the length of the gut

b. Blood vessels, nerves, and lymphatic vessels that supply the intestinal wall

c. Breaks down starch

d. Result of chemical breakdown of proteins in stomach

e. Chewing of food

f. Generate slow waves of electrical activity

g. The largest serous membrane in the body

h. Segmental mixing movements of the large intestine

i. Controls function of each segment of intestinal tract

j. Inhibits gastric acid secretion

Activity D

1. Describe the functional divisions of the GI tract.

_____

_____

_____

2. What factors are involved in stimulating the emptying of the stomach?

_____

_____

_____

3. Describe the two types of contractions seen in the small intestine.

_____

_____

_____

4. Describe the incretin effect.

_____

_____

_____

5. What are the three functions of saliva?

_____

_____

_____

6. What is the mechanism of acid secretion by the parietal cells of the stomach?

_____

_____

_____

7. How are carbohydrates broken down to absorbable units?

_____

_____

_____

8. Describe protein digestion and absorption.

_____

_____

_____

SECTION III: APPLYING YOUR KNOWLEDGE

Activity E *Consider the scenario and answer the question.*

The nurse is preparing an educational event for a group of children in elementary school who are studying the GI tract.

1. What facts would the nurse know to include for these children?

_____

_____

_____

SECTION IV: PRACTICING FOR NCLEX

Activity F *Answer the following questions.*

1. The circular layer of smooth muscle that lies between the stomach and the small intestine is called what?
   a. Pyloric sphincter
   b. Cardiac sphincter
   c. The antrum
   d. The cardiac orifice

2. Where in the GI tract is food digested and absorbed?
   a. The colon and the ileum
   b. The jejunum and ileum
   c. The stomach and the jejunum
   d. The jejunum and the colon

3. Some smooth muscle cells in the GI tract serve as pacemakers. They display rhythmic spontaneous oscillations in membrane potentials. What are these called?
   a. Peristalsis
   b. Intestinal spasms
   c. Slow waves
   d. Rapid contractility

4. Defecation is controlled by both an internal and an external sphincter. What nerve controls the external sphincter?
   a. Vagus nerve
   b. Femoral nerve
   c. Phrenic nerve
   d. Pudendal nerve

5. The stomach secretes two important hormones in the GI tract. One is gastrin. What is the second hormone secreted by the stomach?
   a. Ghrelin
   b. Secretin
   c. Incretin
   d. Cholecystokinin

6. Saliva has more than one function. What are the functions of saliva? (Mark all that apply.)
   a. Protection
   b. Lubrication
   c. Antibacterial
   d. Initiate digestion of starches
   e. Initiate digestion of protein

7. The colon is home to between 300 and 500 different species of bacteria. What is their main metabolic function?
   a. Digestion of insoluble fiber
   b. Fermentation of undigestible dietary residue
   c. Compaction of metabolic waste prior to leaving the body
   d. Absorption of calcium

8. Absorption is a major function of the GI tract. How is absorption accomplished in the GI tract?
   a. Osmosis and diffusion
   b. Active transport and osmosis
   c. Active transport and diffusion
   d. Diffusion and inactive transport

9. Nausea and vomiting can be side effects of many drugs as well as physiologic disturbances within the body. What is a common cause of nausea?
   a. Distention of the stomach
   b. Distention of the cecum
   c. Distention of the jejunum
   d. Distention of the duodenum

10. Several neurotransmitters have been identified with nausea and vomiting. In this capacity they act as neuromediators. What neuromediator is thought to be involved in the nausea and vomiting that accompanies chemotherapy?
    a. Serotonin
    b. Dopamine
    c. Acetylcholine receptors
    d. Opioid receptors

CHAPTER 29

Disorders of Gastrointestinal Function

SECTION I: LEARNING OBJECTIVES

1. Define and cite the causes of dysphagia, odynophagia, and achalasia.

2. Relate the pathophysiology of gastroesophageal reflux to measures used in the diagnosis and treatment of the disorder in adults and children.

3. State the reason for the poor prognosis associated with esophageal cancer.

4. Describe the anatomic and physiologic factors that contribute to the gastric mucosal barrier.

5. Differentiate between the causes and manifestations of acute and chronic gastritis.

6. Characterize the proposed role of *Helicobacter pylori* in the development of chronic gastritis and peptic ulcer and cite methods for diagnosis and treatment of the infection.

7. Describe the predisposing factors in development of peptic ulcer and cite the three complications of peptic ulcer.

8. Describe the goals for pharmacologic treatment of peptic ulcer disease.

9. Cite the etiologic factors in ulcer formation related to Zollinger-Ellison syndrome and stress ulcer.

10. List risk factors associated with gastric cancer.

11. State the diagnostic criteria for irritable bowel syndrome.

12. Compare the characteristics of Crohn disease and ulcerative colitis.

13. Relate an increase in dietary fiber to the treatment of diverticular disease.

14. Describe the pathogenesis of the symptoms associated with appendicitis.

15. Compare the causes and manifestations of small-volume diarrhea and large-volume diarrhea.

16. Explain why a failure to respond to the defecation urge may result in constipation.

17. Differentiate between mechanical and paralytic intestinal obstruction in terms of cause and manifestations.

18. Describe the characteristics of the peritoneum that increase its vulnerability to and protect it against the effects of peritonitis.

19. List three causes of intestinal malabsorption and describe their manifestations.

20. Describe the pathophysiology of celiac disease.

21. List the risk factors associated with colorectal cancer and cite the screening methods for detection.

SECTION II: ASSESSING YOUR UNDERSTANDING

Activity A *Fill in the blanks.*

1. The _____ functions primarily as a conduit for passage of food and liquid from the pharynx to the stomach.

2. _____ anomalies of the esophagus require early detection and correction because they are incompatible with life.

3. _____ can result from disorders that produce narrowing of the esophagus, lack of salivary secretion, weakness of the muscular structures that propel the food bolus, or neural networks coordinating the swallowing mechanism.

4. _____ is characterized by a protrusion of the stomach through the esophageal hiatus of the diaphragm.

5. The most frequent symptom of _____ is heartburn.

6. There is considerable evidence linking gastroesophageal reflux with _____.

7. _____ involves mucosal injury to the esophagus, hyperemia, and inflammation.

8. Symptoms of reflux esophagitis in an _____ include evidence of pain when swallowing, hematemesis, and anemia due to esophageal bleeding, heartburn, irritability, and sudden or inconsolable crying.

9. Most squamous cell esophageal carcinomas are attributable to _____ and _____ use.

10. The stomach lining usually is _____ to the acid it secretes, a property that allows the stomach to contain acid and pepsin without having its wall digested.

11. The _____ are thought to exert their effect through improved mucosal blood flow, decreased acid secretion, increased bicarbonate ion secretion, and enhanced mucus production.

12. _____ refers to inflammation of the gastric mucosa.

13. _____ is most commonly associated with local irritants such as aspirin or other nonsteroidal anti-inflammatory agents, alcohol, or bacterial toxins.

14. _____ is denoted by the absence of grossly visible erosions and the presence of chronic inflammatory changes leading eventually to atrophy of the glandular epithelium of the stomach.

15. Autoimmune gastritis results from the presence of _____ to components of gastric gland parietal cells and intrinsic factor.

16. _____ is a term used to describe a group of ulcerative disorders that occur in areas of the upper gastrointestinal tract that are exposed to acid-pepsin secretions.

17. The most common complications of peptic ulcer are _____, perforation and penetration, and gastric outlet _____.

18. Laboratory findings of hypochromic anemia and occult blood in the stools indicate _____.

19. _____ is the major physiologic mediator for hydrochloric acid secretion.

20. Persons at high risk for development of _____ include those with large–surface area burns, trauma, sepsis, acute respiratory distress syndrome, severe liver failure, and major surgical procedures.

21. Gastric _____ is the second most common tumor in the world.

22. _____ is a functional gastrointestinal disorder characterized by a variable combination of chronic and recurrent intestinal symptoms not explained by structural or biochemical abnormalities.

23. The term *inflammatory bowel disease* is used to designate two related inflammatory intestinal disorders: _____ disease and _____.

24. _____ disease is a recurrent, granulomatous type of inflammatory response that can affect any area of the gastrointestinal tract.

25. Ulcerative colitis is confined to _____ and _____.

26. _____ deficiencies are common in Crohn disease because of diarrhea, steatorrhea, and other malabsorption problems.

27. Characteristic of ulcerative colitis are the lesions that form in the crypts of _____ in the base of the mucosal layer.

28. _____ of the colon is one of the feared complications of ulcerative colitis.

29. The complications of _____ result from massive fluid loss or destruction of intestinal mucosa.

30. _____ is a condition in which the mucosal layer of the colon herniated through the muscularis layer.

31. _____ is a complication of diverticulosis in which there is inflammation and gross or microscopic perforation of the diverticulum.

32. The pain associated with _____ is caused by stretching of the appendix during the early inflammatory process.

33. The usual definition of _____ is excessively frequent passage of stools.

34. Toxin-producing bacteria or other agents that disrupt the normal absorption or secretory process in the small bowel commonly cause _____.

35. _____ diarrhea is often associated with conditions such as inflammatory bowel disease, irritable bowel syndrome, malabsorption syndrome, endocrine disorders, or radiation colitis.

36. _____ commonly is associated with acute or chronic inflammation or intrinsic disease of the colon, such as ulcerative colitis or Crohn disease.

37. _____ can be defined as the infrequent and/or difficult passage of stools.

38. _____ is the retention of hardened or puttylike stool in the rectum and colon, which interferes with normal passage of feces.

39. Intestinal obstruction designates an impairment of movement of intestinal contents in a _____ direction.

40. _____ obstruction results from neurogenic or muscular impairment of peristalsis.

41. Peritonitis is an inflammatory response of the _____ that lines the abdominal cavity and covers the visceral organs.

42. Celiac disease is an immune-mediated disorder triggered by ingestion of _____ containing grains.

43. _____ provides a means for direct visualization of the rectum and colon.

Activity B *Match the key terms in Column A with their definitions in Column B.*

1.

Column A

____ 1. Achalasia
____ 2. Esophageal atresia
____ 3. *Odynophagia*
____ 4. Gastroesophageal reflux
____ 5. *Dysphagia*
____ 6. Barrett esophagus
____ 7. Tracheoesophageal fistulae
____ 8. Mallory-Weiss syndrome
____ 9. Perforation
____ 10. *Helicobacter pylori*

Column B

a. Swallowing is painful
b. Most common cause of chronic gastritis in the United States
c. An ulcer erodes through all the layers of the stomach
d. Esophagus is connected to the trachea
e. Backward movement of gastric contents into the esophagus
f. The upper esophagus ends in a blind pouch
g. Difficulty passing food into the stomach
h. Squamous mucosa that lines the esophagus gradually is replaced by columnar epithelium
i. Tears in the esophagus at the esophagogastric junction
j. Difficulty in swallowing

2.

Column A	Column B
____ **1.** Fistulas	**a.** Immune-mediated disorder triggered by ingestion of gluten-containing grains
____ **2.** Zollinger-Ellison syndrome	
____ **3.** Celiac disease	
____ **4.** Osmotic diarrhea	**b.** Water is pulled into the bowel by the hyperosmotic nature of its contents
____ **5.** Hypergastrinemia	
____ **6.** Steatorrheic	
____ **7.** Cobblestone appearance	**c.** Tubelike passages that form connections between different sites in the gastrointestinal tract
____ **8.** Penetration	
____ **9.** Adenomatous polyps	
____ **10.** Rotavirus	**d.** Hallmark symptom of Crohn disease

e. Presence of an excess of gastrin in the blood

f. Ulcer crater erodes into adjacent organs

g. Gastrin-secreting tumor

h. Causes diarrhea in children

i. Benign neoplasms that arise from the mucosal epithelium of the intestine

j. Stools contain excess fat

Activity C *Briefly answer the following.*

1. What is GERD? What is the mechanism of damage?

_____

_____

_____

2. Describe how the gastric mucosal barrier functions to protect the stomach from it own secretions.

_____

_____

_____

3. Describe the progression and remission of peptic ulcers.

_____

_____

_____

4. What is the relationship between *H. pylori* infection and the development of stomach cancer?

_____

_____

_____

5. What are the typical characteristics of irritable bowel syndrome?

_____

_____

_____

6. What is hypothesized to be a cause of inflammatory bowel disease (ulcerative colitis and Crohn disease)?

_____

_____

_____

7. What is the mechanism of diverticulosis formation?

_____

_____

_____

8. What is the pathophysiology of constipation?

_____

_____

_____

9. How does diet expose a patient to colon cancer?

_____

_____

_____

SECTION III: APPLYING YOUR KNOWLEDGE

Activity D *Consider the scenario and answer the questions.*

A 67-year-old black man presents at the clinic with complaints of difficulty swallowing foods of any kind. He states, "It always feels like I have something caught in my throat." His medical history is significant for Barrett esophagus, unintentional weight loss of 15 pounds over past 4 months, and some pain when swallowing. The gentleman is scheduled for an esophagoscopy, and a diagnosis of esophageal cancer is subsequently confirmed. The physician explains that, depending on the stage of the tumor, there are options for treatment. The physician recommends chemotherapy followed by surgical resection of the tumor.

1. The man arrives for his first treatment of chemotherapy and asks the nurse why he has to have chemotherapy before having the surgery to remove the tumor. The nurse correctly responds by stating:

_____

_____

_____

2. Subsequent studies show that this client's tumor has already metastasized. The physician recommends that surgery be done right away, but emphasizes to the client that there is no cure for his cancer. The client arrives for surgery and asks the preoperative nurse why he needs the surgery if it will not cure his cancer. What would be the correct response by the nurse?

_____

_____

_____

SECTION IV: PRACTICING FOR NCLEX

Activity E *Answer the following questions.*

1. Hiatal hernias can cause severe pain if the hernia is large. Gastroesophageal reflux is a common comorbidity of hiatal hernia, and, when this occurs, what might the hernia do?
   a. Increase esophageal acid clearance
   b. Retard esophageal acid clearance
   c. Decrease esophageal acid clearance
   d. Accelerate esophageal acid clearance

2. Infants and children commonly have gastroesophageal reflux. Many times it is asymptomatic and resolves on its own. What are the signs and symptoms of gastroesophageal reflux in infants with severe disease?
   a. Consolable crying and early satiety
   b. Delayed satiety and sleeping after feeding
   c. Tilting of the head to one side and arching of the back
   d. Inconsolable crying and delayed satiety

3. The stomach secretes acid to begin the digestive process on the food that we eat. The gastric mucosal barrier works to prevent acids secreted by the stomach from actually damaging the wall of the stomach. What are the factors that make up the gastric mucosal barrier? (Mark all that apply.)
   a. An impermeable epithelial cell surface covering
   b. Mechanisms for selective transport of bicarbonate and potassium ions
   c. Characteristics of gastric mucus
   d. Cell coverings that act as antacids
   e. Mechanisms for selective transport of hydrogen and bicarbonate ions

4. *Helicobacter pylori* gastritis has a prevalence of over 50% of American adults over the age of 50, which is thought to be caused by a previous infection when the client was younger. What can chronic gastritis caused by *H. pylori* cause?
   a. Decreased risk of gastric adenocarcinoma
   b. Decreased risk of low-grade B-cell gastric lymphoma
   c. Duodenal ulcer
   d. Gastric atrophy

5. A 39-year-old white woman presents at the clinic with complaints of epigastric pain that is cramplike, rhythmic, and just below the xiphoid. She states that it wakes her up around 1 AM, and she is not sleeping well because of it. She further states that this is the third episode of having this pain in the past year. The nurse suspects the client has a peptic ulcer and expects to receive what orders from the physician?

   a. Schedule client for a complete metabolic panel and a complete blood count
   b. Schedule client for laparoscopic examination
   c. Schedule client for a swallow study
   d. Schedule client for a lower gastrointestinal study

6. A client in a nursing home complains to her nurse that she is not feeling well. When asked to describe how she feels, the client states that she really is not hungry anymore and seems to have indigestion a lot. The nurse checks the client's chart and finds that her vital signs are normal, but that she has lost weight over the past 2 months. She also notes that there is a history of gastric cancer in the client's family. The nurse notifies the physician and expects to receive what orders? (Mark all that apply.)

   a. Schedule a barium radiograph and an endoscopy
   b. Perform a Papanicolaou smear on the client's gastric secretions
   c. Order cytologic studies to be done during the endoscopy
   d. Schedule a lower gastrointestinal study
   e. Have the technician do an endoscopic ultrasound.

7. Irritable bowel syndrome is thought to be present in 10% to 15% of the population in the United States. What is its hallmark symptom?

   a. Nausea and abdominal pain unrelieved by defecation.
   b. Abdominal pain relieved by defecation with a change in consistency or frequency of stools.
   c. Diarrhea and abdominal pain unrelieved by defection.
   d. Abdominal pain relieved by defecation and bowel impaction.

8. Crohn disease is a recurrent inflammatory disease that can affect any area of the bowel. Characteristic of Crohn disease is granulomatous lesions that are sharply demarcated from the surrounding tissue. As the nurse caring for a client with newly diagnosed Crohn disease, you would know to include what in your teaching?

   a. Definition of Crohn disease that includes that it is a recurrent disease that affects only the large intestine.
   b. Information on which nonsteroidal anti-inflammatory drugs to take and how often to take them.
   c. Information on sulfasalazine including dosage, route, frequency, and side effects of the drug.
   d. Information on the chemotherapy that will be ordered to cure the disease.

9. Rotavirus is a common infection in children younger than 5 years of age. Like other diseases, rotavirus is most severe in children under 24 months of age. What is a symptom of rotavirus infection?

   a. Mild to moderate fever that gets higher after the second day
   b. Vomiting that lasts for the course of the disease
   c. Fever that disappears after 7 days
   d. Vomiting that disappears around the second day

10. Diverticulitis is the herniation of tissue of the large intestine through the muscularis layer of the colon. It is often asymptomatic and is found in approximately 80% of people over the age of 85. Diverticulitis is often asymptomatic, but when symptoms do occur what is the most common complaint of the client?

   a. Lower left quadrant pain with nausea and vomiting
   b. Right lower quadrant pain with nausea and vomiting
   c. Midepigastric pain with nausea and vomiting
   d. Right lower quadrant pain with rebound tenderness on the left

11. Diarrhea is described as a change in frequency of stool passage to a point where it is excessively frequent. Diarrhea can be acute or chronic, inflammatory, or noninflammatory. What are the symptoms of noninflammatory diarrhea? (Mark all that apply.)

   a. Small volume watery stools

   b. Nonbloody stools

   c. Periumbilical cramps

   d. Nausea and/or vomiting

   e. Large-volume blood stools

12. Peritonitis is an inflammatory condition of the lining of the abdominal cavity. What is one of the most important signs of peritonitis?

   a. Vomiting of coffee ground-appearing emesis

   b. The translocation of extracellular fluid into the peritoneal cavity

   c. The translocation of intracellular fluid into the peritoneal cavity

   d. Vomiting of bloody emesis

13. Celiac disease commonly presents in infancy as failure to thrive. It is an inappropriate T-cell−mediated immune response and there is no cure for it. What is the treatment of choice for celiac disease?

   a. Removal of protein from the diet

   b. Removal of fat from the diet

   c. Removal of gluten from the diet

   d. Removal of sugar from the diet

14. One of the accepted methods of screening for colorectal cancer is testing for occult blood in the stool. Because it is possible to get a false-positive result on these tests, you would instruct the client to do what?

   a. Eat lots of red meat for 3 or 4 days before the test is done.

   b. Take 1000 mg of vitamin C in supplement form for 1 week prior to testing.

   c. Eat citrus fruits at least 5 times a day for 2 days prior to testing.

   d. Avoid nonsteroidal anti-inflammatory drugs for 1 week prior to testing.

30

Disorders of Hepatobiliary and Exocrine Pancreas Function

SECTION I: LEARNING OBJECTIVES

1. Describe the function of the liver in terms of carbohydrate, protein, and fat metabolism.

2. Characterize the function of the liver in terms of bilirubin elimination and describe the pathogenesis of unconjugated and conjugated hyperbilirubinemia.

3. Relate the mechanism of bile formation and elimination to the development of cholestasis.

4. List four laboratory tests used to assess liver function and relate them to impaired liver function.

5. State the three ways by which drugs and other substances are metabolized or inactivated in the liver and provide examples of liver disease related to the toxic effects of drugs and chemical agents.

6. Compare hepatitis A, B, C, D, and E in terms of source of infection, incubation period, acute disease manifestations, development of chronic disease, and the carrier state.

7. Define chronic hepatitis and compare the pathogenesis of chronic autoimmune and chronic viral hepatitis.

8. Characterize the metabolism of alcohol by the liver and state metabolic mechanisms that can be used to explain liver injury.

9. Summarize the three patterns of injury that occur with alcohol-induced liver disease.

10. Describe the pathogenesis of intrahepatic biliary disorders.

11. Characterize the liver changes that occur with cirrhosis.

12. Describe the physiologic basis for portal hypertension and relate it to the development of ascites, esophageal varices, and splenomegaly.

13. Relate the functions of the liver to the manifestations of liver failure.

14. Characterize etiologies of hepatocellular cancer and state the reason for the poor prognosis in persons with this type of cancer.

15. Explain the function of the gallbladder in regulating the flow of bile into the duodenum and relate to the formation of cholelithiasis (gallstones).

16. Describe the clinical manifestations of acute and chronic cholecystitis.

17. Characterize the effects of choledocholithiasis and cholangitis on bile flow and the potential for hepatic and pancreatic complications.

18. Cite the possible causes and describe the manifestations and treatment of acute pancreatitis.

19. Describe the manifestations of chronic pancreatitis.

20. State the reason for the poor prognosis in pancreatic cancer.

SECTION II: ASSESSING YOUR UNDERSTANDING

Activity A *Fill in the blanks.*

1. The liver, the gallbladder, and the exocrine pancreas are classified as _____ organs of the gastrointestinal tract.

2. Approximately 300 mL of blood per minute enters the liver through the hepatic _____; another 1050 mL/minute enters by way of the _____.

3. The venous blood delivered by the _____ comes from the digestive tract and major abdominal organs, including the pancreas and spleen.

4. A major exocrine function of the liver is _____ secretion.

5. The most important of the secretory proteins of the liver is _____.

6. Acetyl-CoA units from fat metabolism also are used to synthesize _____ and _____ acids in the liver.

7. Almost all the _____ synthesis in the body from carbohydrates and proteins occurs in the liver.

8. Whenever a greater quantity of carbohydrates enters the body than can be immediately used, the excess is converted to _____ in the liver.

9. Bile salts serve an important function in digestion; they aid in _____ dietary fats, and they are necessary for the formation of the _____ that transport fatty acids and fat-soluble vitamins to the surface of the intestinal mucosa for absorption.

10. _____ represents a decrease in bile flow through the intrahepatic canaliculi and a reduction in secretion of water, bilirubin, and bile acids by the hepatocytes.

11. Common to all types of obstructive and hepatocellular cholestasis is the accumulation of _____ pigment in the liver.

12. _____ jaundice occurs when red blood cells are destroyed at a rate in excess of the liver's ability to remove the bilirubin from the blood.

13. _____ of bilirubin is impaired whenever liver cells are damaged, when transport of bilirubin into liver cells becomes deficient, or when the enzymes needed to conjugate the bile are lacking.

14. _____ result in chemical modification of reactive drug groups by oxidation, reduction, hydroxylation, or other chemical reactions carried out in hepatocytes.

15. Drugs such as alcohol and barbiturates can induce certain members of the _____ family to increase enzyme production, accelerating drug metabolism and decreasing the pharmacologic action of the drug.

16. _____, which involve the conversion of lipid-soluble derivatives to water-soluble substances, may follow phase 1 reactions or proceed independently.

17. Direct hepatotoxic reactions result from drug metabolism and the generation of _____.

18. _____ drug reactions result in decreased secretion of bile or obstruction of the biliary tree.

19. _____ refers to inflammation of the liver.

20. Currently, recreational _____ use is the most common mode of hepatitis C virus transmission in the United States and Canada. The main route of transmission of hepatitis C virus in the past was through contaminated _____ or blood products and _____

21. _____ hepatitis is a severe type of chronic hepatitis of unknown origin that is associated with high levels of serum immunoglobulins, including autoantibodies.

22. _____ biliary diseases disrupt the flow of bile through the liver, causing cholestasis and biliary cirrhosis.

23. _____ biliary cirrhosis results from prolonged obstruction of the extrabiliary tree.

24. Obesity, type 2 diabetes, the metabolic syndrome, and hyperlipidemia are coexisting conditions frequently associated with _____ liver disease.

25. _____ represents the end stage of chronic liver disease in which much of the functional liver tissue has been replaced by fibrous tissue.

26. _____ is characterized by increased resistance to flow in the portal venous system and sustained portal vein pressure above 12 mm Hg.

27. Complications of portal hypertension arise from the _____ pressure and _____ of the venous channels behind the obstruction.

28. _____ occurs when the amount of fluid in the peritoneal cavity is increased.

29. _____ is a complication in persons with both cirrhosis and ascites.

30. The _____ syndrome refers to a functional renal failure sometimes seen during the terminal stages of liver failure with ascites.

31. Hepatic _____ refers to the totality of central nervous system manifestations of liver failure.

32. Among the factors identified as etiologic agents in _____ are chronic viral hepatitis, cirrhosis, long-term exposure to environmental agents such as aflatoxin, and drinking water contaminated with arsenic.

33. The _____ is a distensible, pear-shaped, muscular sac located on the ventral surface of the liver.

34. _____ provides a strong stimulus for gallbladder contraction and is released when food enters the intestines.

35. Gallstones are caused by precipitation of substances contained in bile, mainly _____ and _____.

36. Acute _____ is a diffuse inflammation of the gallbladder, usually secondary to obstruction of the gallbladder outlet.

37. The _____ pancreas is made up of lobules that consist of acinar cells, which secrete digestive enzymes into a system of microscopic ducts.

38. Acute _____ represents a reversible inflammatory process of the pancreatic acini brought about by premature activation of pancreatic enzymes.

39. _____ is characterized by progressive destruction of the exocrine pancreas, fibrosis, and in the later stages, by destruction of the endocrine pancreas.

40. The most significant and reproducible environmental risk factor of pancreatic cancer is _____

Activity B *Consider the following figure.*

In the figure above, label the following structures:

- Liver
- Gallbladder
- Cystic duct
- Common bile duct
- Duodenum
- Tail of pancreas
- Head of pancreas
- Pancreatic duct
- Hepatic duct
- Spleen
- Diaphragm
- Ampulla of Vater
- Sphincter of Oddi

Activity C *Match the key terms in Column A with their definitions in Column B.*

1.

Column A

_____ 1. Kupffer cells

_____ 2. Albumin

_____ 3. Gluconeogenesis

_____ 4. Oxidative deamination

_____ 5. Beta oxidation

_____ 6. Extrahepatic cholestasis

_____ 7. Bilirubin

_____ 8. Jaundice

_____ 9. Steatosis

_____ 10. Cholestatic jaundice

Column B

a. formed from senescent red blood cells

b. conversion of amino acids to ketoacids and ammonia

c. capable of removing and phagocytosing old and defective blood cells

d. abnormally high accumulation of bilirubin in the blood

e. the splitting of fatty acids into two-carbon acetyl-coenzyme A

f. transport protein/plasma colloidal osmotic pressure

g. obstruction of the large bile ducts that reduces bile secretion

h. amino acids are used for producing glucose

i. fatty infiltration of the liver

j. occurs when bile flow is obstructed between the liver and the intestine

2.

Column A

_____ 1. Hepatitis A

_____ 2. Hepatitis B

_____ 3. Hepatitis C

_____ 4. Hepatitis D

_____ 5. Hepatitis E

Column B

a. Infection is linked to hepatitis B

b. Does not cause chronic hepatitis or the carrier state

c. Inoculation with infected blood and/or spread by oral or sexual contact

d. Occurs primarily by the fecal-oral route

e. The most common cause of chronic hepatitis, cirrhosis, and hepatocellular cancer in the world

Activity D

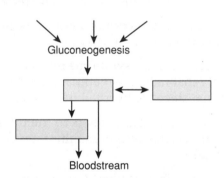

1. Complete the flowchart above for the hepatic pathways for the storage and synthesis of glucose

- Triglycerides
- Glucose
- Amino acids
- Glycogen
- Glycerol
- Lactic acid

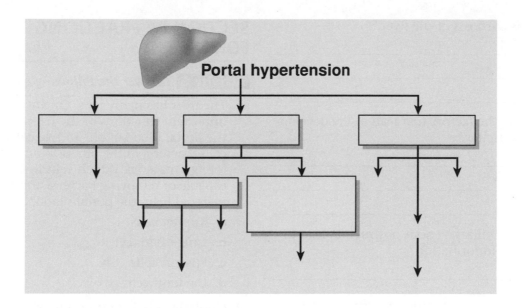

2. Complete the flowchart above using the following terms.

   - Increased pressure in peritoneal capillaries
   - Portosystemic shunting of blood
   - Splenomegaly
   - Ascites
   - Development of collateral channels
   - Shunting of ammonia and toxins into general circulation
   - Anemia
   - Leukopenia
   - Thrombocytopenia
   - Hepatic encephalopathy
   - Hemorrhoids
   - Esophageal varices
   - Caput medusae
   - Bleeding

Activity E *Briefly answer the following.*

1. What are the basic functions of the liver?

   _____

   _____

   _____

2. Describe the pathogenesis of cholestasis.

   _____

   _____

   _____

3. List the major causes and categories of jaundice.

   _____

   _____

   _____

4. What is measured in the serum to asses liver dysfunction?

   _____

   _____

   _____

5. Describe the clinical course of viral hepatitis.

   _____

   _____

   _____

6. How does ethanol cause tissue damage?

   _____

   _____

   _____

7. What changes take place in the liver resulting from the toxic affects of alcohol?

   _____

   _____

   _____

8. What is cirrhosis of the liver?

_____

_____

_____

9. What are the factors that lead to the development of ascites?

_____

_____

_____

10. How does biliary venous obstruction lead to hemorrhoid formation?

_____

_____

_____

SECTION III: APPLYING YOUR KNOWLEDGE

Activity F _Consider the scenario and answer the questions._

A 16-year-old female patient is brought to the clinic by her mother. She complains of recurrent fatigue and loss of appetite. Her mother states, "I am concerned because she has a yellow look in her eyes. It sort of comes and goes." While taking the client's history, the nurse finds that the client became sexually active 1 year ago and has had multiple partners during the past 12 months. On physical examination the physician notes an enlarged liver. The presumptive diagnosis is hepatitis C.

1. What confirmatory tests would the nurse expect to be ordered?

_____

_____

_____

2. The client's tests come back positive for hepatitis C. What medications might be ordered for this client?

_____

_____

_____

SECTION IV: PRACTICING FOR NCLEX

Activity G _Answer the following questions._

1. The liver has many jobs. One of the most important functions of the liver is to cleanse the portal blood of old and defective blood cells, bacteria in the bloodstream, and any foreign material. Which cells in the liver are capable of removing bacteria and foreign material from the portal blood?

a. Kupffer cells
b. Langerhans cells
c. Epstein cells
d. Davidoff cells

2. Cholestasis is a condition in which there is a decrease in bile flow through the intrahepatic canaliculi and a reduction in secretion of water, bilirubin, and bile acids by the hepatocytes. Cholestasis can have more than one cause, but, in all types of cholestasis, there is what?

a. Accumulation of bile pigment in the gallbladder
b. Accumulation of bile pigment in the liver
c. Accumulation of bile pigment in the blood
d. Accumulation of bile pigment in the portal vein

3. What is considered the normal amount of serum bilirubin found in the blood?

a. 1 to 2 mg/dL
b. 0.01to 0.02 mg/dL
c. 0.1 to 0.2 mg/dL
d. 0.001to 0.002 mg/dL

4. Many drugs are metabolized and detoxified in the liver. Most drug metabolizing occurs in the central zones of the liver. What condition is caused by these drug-metabolizing actions?

a. Central cirrhosis
b. Lobular cirrhosis
c. Lobular necrosis
d. Centrilobular necrosis

5. Primary biliary cirrhosis is an autoimmune disease that destroys the small intrahepatic bile ducts causing cholestasis. It is insidious in onset and is a progressive disease. What are the earliest symptoms of the disease?
   a. Unexplained pruritus
   b. Weight gain
   c. Pale urine
   d. Dark stools

6. One of the jobs the liver performs is to export triglyceride. When the liver's capacity to export triglyceride is maximized, excess fatty acids accumulate in the liver. What is the disease these excess fatty acids contribute to?
   a. Biliary cirrhosis
   b. Nonalcoholic fatty liver disease
   c. Cholelithiasis
   d. Alcoholic fatty liver disease

7. Ascites is an accumulation of fluid in the peritoneal cavity and usually occurs in advanced cirrhosis. What is the treatment of choice for ascites?
   a. Paracentesis
   b. Thoracentesis
   c. Diuretics
   d. DDAVP

8. A client is suspected of having liver cancer. What diagnostic tests would be ordered to confirm the diagnosis?
   a. Serum α-fetoprotein
   b. Endoscopy
   c. Ultrasound of liver
   d. MRI of liver

9. Gall stones are made up mostly of cholesterol. What is thought to be a precursor of gallstones?
   a. Gallbladder sludge
   b. Thinned mucoprotein
   c. Pieces of hard food trapped in the gallbladder
   d. Thickened bile

10. What laboratory markers are most commonly used to diagnose acute pancreatitis?
    a. Amylase and cholesterol
    b. Lipase and amylase
    c. Lipase and triglycerides
    d. Cholesterol and triglycerides

11. All diseases have risk factors. What is the most significant environmental risk factor for pancreatic cancer?
    a. Air pollution
    b. Water pollution
    c. Cigarette smoking
    d. Heavy metal toxicity

CHAPTER 31

Mechanisms of Endocrine Control

SECTION I: LEARNING OBJECTIVES

1. Characterize a hormone.

2. Differentiate vesicle-mediated and non–vesicle-mediated mechanisms of hormone synthesis in terms of their stimuli for hormone synthesis and release.

3. Describe mechanisms of hormone transport and inactivation.

4. State the function of a hormone receptor and the difference between cell surface hormone receptors and nuclear hormone receptors.

5. Describe the role of the hypothalamus in regulating pituitary control of endocrine function.

6. State the major difference between positive and negative feedback control mechanisms.

7. Describe methods used in diagnosis of endocrine disorders.

SECTION II: ASSESSING YOUR UNDERSTANDING

Activity A *Fill in the blanks.*

1. The endocrine system uses chemical substances called _____ as a means of regulating and integrating body functions.

2. The functions of the endocrine system are closely linked with those of the _____ system and the _____ system.

3. When hormones act locally on cells other than those that produced the hormone, the action is called _____.

4. Hormones also can exert an _____ action on the cells from which they were produced.

5. Hormones that are released into the bloodstream circulate either as _____ molecules, or as hormones _____ to transport carriers.

6. Hormones produce their effects through interaction with _____, which in turn are linked to one or more effector systems within the cell.

7. The structure of hormone _____ varies in a manner that allows target cells to respond to one hormone and not to others.

8. _____ hormones attach to intracellular receptors and form a hormone-receptor complex that travels to the cell nucleus.

9. The synthesis and release of anterior pituitary hormones is regulated by the action of releasing or inhibiting hormones from the _____, which is the coordinating center of the brain for endocrine, behavioral, and autonomic nervous system function.

10. The pituitary gland has been called the _____ because its hormones control the functions of many target glands and cells.

11. The easiest way to measure hormone levels during a specific period are by either blood samples or urine tests to measure _____ or _____.

Activity B *Match the key terms in Column A with their definitions in Column B.*

Column A

_____ 1. Autocrine

_____ 2. Half-life of a hormone

_____ 3. Hormones

_____ 4. Hypophysis

_____ 5. Paracrine

_____ 6. Second messenger

_____ 7. Hormone response element

Column B

a. Time it takes for the body to reduce the concentration of the hormone by one-half

b. Hormone acts on cell that produced it

c. Hormone affecting neighboring cells

d. The hypothalamus and the pituitary

e. Highly specialized organic molecules produced by endocrine organs that exert their action on specific target cells

f. Intracellular signal

g. Activate or suppress intracellular mechanisms such as gene activity

Activity C *Briefly answer the following.*

1. What is a hormone?

_____

_____

_____

2. What is the structure of a hormone?

_____

_____

_____

3. How do tissues regulate a hormones affect?

_____

_____

_____

4. What are the main types of cell membrane receptors and how do they exert their effects?

_____

_____

_____

5. Describe the global role of the anterior pituitary hormones.

_____

_____

_____

6. How does negative feedback regulate hormone levels?

_____

_____

_____

SECTION III: APPLYING YOUR KNOWLEDGE

Activity D *Consider the scenario and answer the questions.*

An 87-year-old woman has come to the clinic for a routine physical examination. She says she has no complaints and is concerned only about a 20-pound weight gain in the past 2 years. She says that she is not as active as she used to be. She also mentions that she has fallen several times and now has a large bruise on her right hip.

1. The nurse knows that this client is at risk for osteoporosis because of her decrease in activity. What test would the nurse expect to be ordered to either confirm or rule out osteoporosis in this patient?

_____

_____

_____

2. With the client's weight gain over the past 2 years and her decrease in activity level, the nurse would expect what test to be ordered to either rule out or confirm type II diabetes in this client?

_____

_____

_____

SECTION IV: PRACTICING FOR NCLEX

Activity E *Answer the following questions.*

1. The endocrine system is closely linked with both the immune system and the nervous system. What neurotransmitter can also act as a hormone?
   a. Epinephrine
   b. Norepinephrine
   c. Dopamine
   d. Succinylcholine

2. When hormones act locally rather than being secreted into the bloodstream, their actions are termed what?
   a. Autocratic and paracratic
   b. Autocrine and paracrine
   c. Localized and influential
   d. Preventers and inhibitors

3. Hormones can be synthesized by both vesicle-mediated pathways and non−vesicle-mediated pathways. What hormones are synthesized by non−vesicle-mediated pathways?
   a. Neurotransmitters that are also hormones
   b. Renin and angiotensin
   c. Androgens and estrogens
   d. Pepcin and ghrelin

4. To prevent the accumulation of hormones in our bodies, the hormones are constantly being metabolized and excreted. Where are adrenal and gonadal steroid hormones excreted?
   a. Feces and urine
   b. Bile and lungs
   c. Cell metabolites and lungs
   d. Bile and urine

5. The hypophysis is a unit formed by the pituitary and the hypothalamus. These two glands are connected by the blood flow in what system?
   a. Hypophyseal portal system
   b. Supraoptic portal system
   c. Paraventricular portal system
   d. Hypothalamic portal system

6. The hormone levels in the body need to be kept within an appropriate range. How is this accomplished for many of the hormones in the body?
   a. Positive feedback loop
   b. Negative feedback loop
   c. Regulated feedback loop
   d. Sensory feedback loop

7. Many hormones are measured for diagnostic reasons by using the plasma levels of the hormones. What is used today to measure plasma hormone levels?
   a. Nucleotide assay methods
   b. Selective binding methods
   c. Radioimmunoassay methods
   d. Radiolabeled hormone-antibody methods

8. Sometimes the measurement of hormones is done through a urine sample. What is an advantage of measuring hormone levels through a urine sample rather than a blood sample?
   a. Urine has more accurate measurements of hormones
   b. There are more hormone metabolites in urine than in blood
   c. Blood sampling has more pure hormone than urine does
   d. Urine samples are easily obtained

9. In an adult with acromegaly, a growth hormone (GH)-secreting tumor is suspected. What diagnostic test would be used for this client?

   a. A GH suppression test
   b. A GH stimulation test
   c. A GH serum assay test
   d. A GH urine assay test

10. Imaging has proven useful in both the diagnosis and follow-up of endocrine disorders. Two types of imaging studies are useful when dealing with endocrine disorders, isotopic imaging and nonisotopic imaging. What is an example of isotopic imaging?

    a. MRI
    b. Thyroid scan
    c. Renal angiography
    d. PET scan

Disorders of Endocrine Control of Growth and Metabolism

SECTION I: LEARNING OBJECTIVES

1. Describe the mechanisms of endocrine hypo-function and hyperfunction.

2. Differentiate primary, secondary, and tertiary endocrine disorders.

3. Discuss the classification of pituitary tumors.

4. Describe the clinical features and causes of hypopituitarism.

5. State the effects of a deficiency in growth hormone (GH).

6. Differentiate genetic short stature from constitutional short stature.

7. State the mechanisms of short stature in hypothyroidism, poorly controlled diabetes mellitus, chronic treatment with excessive glucocorticoid hormones, malnutrition, and psychosocial dwarfism.

8. List three causes of tall stature.

9. Relate the functions of GH to the manifestations of acromegaly and adult-onset GH deficiency.

10. Explain why children with precocious puberty are tall-statured children but short-statured adults.

11. Characterize the synthesis, transport, and regulation of thyroid hormone.

12. Diagram the hypothalamic-pituitary-thyroid feedback system.

13. Describe tests in the diagnosis and management of thyroid disorders.

14. Relate the functions of thyroid hormone to hypothyroidism and hyperthyroidism.

15. Describe the effects of congenital hypothyroidism.

16. Characterize the manifestations and treatment of myxedematous coma and thyroid storm.

17. Describe the function of the adrenal cortical hormones and their feedback regulation.

18. State the underlying cause of congenital adrenal hyperplasia.

19. Relate the functions of the adrenal cortical hormones to Addison disease (i.e., adrenal insufficiency) and Cushing syndrome (i.e., glucocorticoid excess).

SECTION II: ASSESSING YOUR UNDERSTANDING

Activity A *Fill in the blanks.*

1. Disturbances of endocrine function usually can be divided into two categories: _____ and _____.

2. _____ defects result in endocrine hypofunction due to the absence or impaired development of the gland or the absence of an enzyme needed for hormone synthesis.

3. Several hormones are essential for normal body _____ and maturation, including growth hormone (GH), insulin, thyroid hormone, and androgens.

4. Growth hormone cannot directly produce bone growth; instead, it acts indirectly by causing the liver to produce _____.

5. _____ secretion is stimulated by hypoglycemia, fasting, starvation, increased blood levels of amino acids, and stress conditions such as trauma, excitement, emotional stress, and heavy exercise.

6. _____ is a term used to describe children (particularly boys) who have moderately short stature, thin build, delayed skeletal and sexual maturation, and absence of other causes of decreased growth.

7. The term _____ is used to describe a child who is taller than his or her peers and is growing at a velocity that is within the normal range for bone age.

8. Growth hormone excess occurring before puberty and the fusion of the epiphyses of the long bones results in _____.

9. When GH excess occurs in adulthood or after the epiphyses of the long bones have fused, the condition is referred to as _____.

10. Long-term elevation of GH results in _____ of the beta cells, causing them literally to "burn out."

11. _____ sexual development may be idiopathic or may be caused by gonadal, adrenal, or hypothalamic disease.

12. _____ hormones are bound to thyroxine-binding globulin and other plasma proteins for transport in the blood.

13. Thyroid hormone has two major functions: it increases _____ and _____ synthesis, and it is necessary for growth and development in children.

14. Thyroid hormone increases the _____ of all body tissues except the retina, spleen, testes, and lungs.

15. Measures of T3, T4, and TSH have been made available through _____ methods.

16. Congenital hypothyroidism is a common cause of _____.

17. The term _____ implies the presence of a nonpitting mucus-type edema caused by the accumulation of hydrophobic extracellular matrix substances in the connective tissues of a number of body tissues.

18. _____ is the clinical syndrome that results when tissues are exposed to high levels of circulating thyroid hormone.

19. The most common cause of hyperthyroidism is _____ disease, which is accompanied by ophthalmopathy (or dermopathy) and diffuse goiter.

20. Many of the manifestations of hyperthyroidism are related to the increase in _____ consumption and use of _____ fuels associated with the hypermetabolic state, as well as to the increase in sympathetic nervous system activity that occurs.

21. _____ is manifested by a very high fever, extreme cardiovascular effects, and severe CNS effects.

22. The _____ forms the bulk of the gland and is responsible for secreting three types of hormones: the glucocorticoids, the mineralocorticoids, and the adrenal androgens.

23. _____ secretion is regulated by the renin-angiotensin mechanism and by blood levels of potassium.

24. When produced as part of the stress response, _____ hormones aid in regulating the metabolic functions of the body and in controlling the inflammatory response.

25. _____ stimulates glucose production by the liver, promotes protein breakdown, and causes mobilization of fatty acids.

26. Primary adrenal insufficiency, or _____ disease, is caused by destruction of the adrenal gland.

27. The term _____ refers to the manifestations of hypercortisolism from any cause.

Activity B *Consider the following figure.*

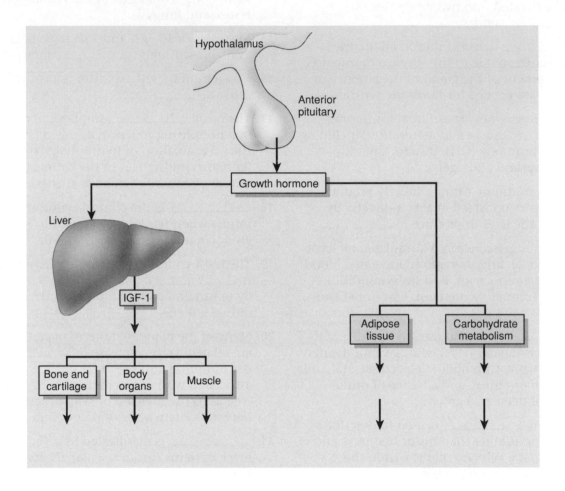

Complete the flowchart above with the following terms

- Anti-insulin effects
- Decreased glucose use
- Decrease in adiposity
- Growth-promoting actions
- Increased blood glucose

- Increased lean muscle mass
- Increased linear growth
- Increased lipolysis
- Increased protein synthesis
- Increased size and function

Activity C *Match the key terms in Column A with their definitions in Column B.*

Column A

___ **1.** Laron-type dwarfism

___ **2.** Hypopituitarism

___ **3.** Cretinism

___ **4.** Hashimoto thyroiditis

___ **5.** Panhypo-pituitarism

___ **6.** Ophthalmopathy

___ **7.** Goiter

___ **8.** Myxedema

___ **9.** Somatotropes

___ **10.** Pendred syndrome

Column B

a. Growth hormone-secreting cells

b. Deficiency of all pituitary-derived hormones

c. Dry skin and swellings around lips and nose as well as mental deterioration

d. Manifestations of untreated congenital hypothyroidism

e. An autoimmune disorder in which the thyroid gland may be totally destroyed

f. Increase in the size of the thyroid gland

g. Eyelid retraction, bulging eyes, light sensitivity, discomfort, double vision, and vision loss

h. Patients with goiter and congenital deafness

i. Growth hormone levels are normal or elevated, but there is a hereditary defect in insulinlike growth factor production

j. Decreased secretion of pituitary hormones

Activity D *Briefly answer the following.*

1. Explain the grouping of the root causes of endocrine disorders.

_____

_____

_____

2. What hormones are directly affected by hypopituitarism? What affect does it have on the rest of the endocrine system?

_____

_____

_____

3. What are the normal actions of GH?

_____

_____

_____

4. How is GH release stimulated? How is it inhibited?

_____

_____

_____

5. Describe the stimulation of the thyroid gland and explain the mechanism of negative feedback to inhibit thyroid activity.

_____

_____

_____

6. Describe the manifestations of hypothyroidism.

_____

_____

_____

7. What is the result of adrenal insufficiency?

_____

_____

_____

8. What are the manifestations of Cushing syndrome?

_____

_____

_____

SECTION III: APPLYING YOUR KNOWLEDGE

Activity E *Consider the scenario and answer the questions.*

The parents of a newborn have been notified by the hospital that they need to bring their newborn back to the hospital for further testing. The parents are informed that one of the tests done on the baby when it was first born needs to be repeated. When the parents arrive at the hospital, they meet with a pediatrician who explains that their infant's thyroid tests have come back abnormal and need to be repeated. He goes on to say that it might be a false-negative result on the original test and not to worry.

1. As the nurse prepares to take the infant's blood, the parents ask what it means if the first test result is not a mistake. The nurse knows the best information to give the parents is what?

_____

_____

_____

2. The parents want to know what will happen to their baby if the thyroid gland is not working correctly. The nurse correctly answers what?

_____

_____

_____

SECTION IV: PRACTICING FOR NCLEX

Activity F *Answer the following questions.*

1. Advances in technology have made it possible to assess hypothalamic-pituitary function by newly developed imaging and radioimmunoassay methods. When baseline tests are not sufficient, what suppression test gives information about combined hypothalamic-pituitary function?
   a. GH suppression test
   b. ACTH suppression test
   c. Cortisol suppression test
   d. Prolactin suppression test

2. Growth hormone is secreted by adults as well as by children. Growth hormone deficiency in children is treated by injections of GH on a daily basis. When teaching a family or child to give injections of GH, what is it important to teach them?
   a. Give the injections in the morning so the peak effect is before noon, like the body does.
   b. Give the injections at bedtime to produce the greatest effect at night, like the body does.
   c. Give the injections about 3 in the afternoon to produce the greatest effect in the evening, like the body does.
   d. Give the injections in the early afternoon to produce the greatest effect at dinner time, like the body does.

3. Growth hormone exerts its effects on the body in many ways. Which of these are effects of GH? (Mark all that apply.)
   a. Enhances fatty acid mobilization
   b. Increases insulin levels
   c. Facilitates the rate of protein synthesis
   d. Decreases ACTH production
   e. Decreases use of fatty acids for fuel

4. Acromegaly is a disorder that is caused by the production of excessive GH in the adult. Because the person cannot grow taller, the soft tissues continue to grow, presenting a very distinctive appearance. What is it that is distinctive in a person with acromegaly?
   a. Small hands and feet compared to length of arms and legs
   b. Broad, bulbous nose and a protruding lower jaw
   c. Slanting forehead and a receding lower jaw
   d. Protruding lower jaw and forehead

5. Precocious puberty is a disorder that occurs in both boys and girls. What does precocious puberty cause in adults?
   a. Early menopause in females
   b. Early erectile dysfunction problems in males
   c. Short stature in adults
   d. Gigantism in adults

6. When the assessment of thyroid autoantibodies is performed, what is the suspected diagnosis?
   a. Goiter
   b. Thyroid tumor
   c. Congenital hypothyroidism
   d. Hashimoto thyroiditis

7. An elderly woman is brought to the emergency department by her family. They relate to the nurse that the client has had mental status changes and cannot remember her grandchildren's names. They go on to say that she is intolerant of cold and is lethargic. On physical examination the nurse notes that the client has a husky voice, her face is puffy around the eyes, and her tongue appears to be enlarged. What diagnosis would the nurse suspect?
   a. Myxedema
   b. Hashimoto thyroiditis
   c. Hyperthyroidism
   d. Congenital hypothyroidism

8. Hyperthyroidism that is inadequately treated can cause a life-threatening condition known as a *thyroid storm*. What are the manifestations of a thyroid storm? (Mark all that apply.)
   a. Tachycardia
   b. Very low fever
   c. Delirium
   d. Bradycardia
   e. Very high fever

9. At times, it is necessary to give medications that suppress the adrenal glands on a long-term basis. When the suppression of the adrenals becomes chronic, the adrenal glands atrophy. What does the abrupt withdrawal of these suppressive drugs cause?
   a. Acute adrenal hyperplasia
   b. Acute adrenal insufficiency
   c. Acute adrenal hypoplasia
   d. Acute adrenal cortical hyperplasia

10. Congenital adrenal hyperplasia is a congenital disorder in which a deficiency exists in any of the enzymes necessary for the synthesis of cortisol. Infants of both sexes are affected, although boys are not diagnosed at birth unless of enlarged genitalia. Female infants often have ambiguous genitalia because of the oversecretion of adrenal androgens. What are the manifestations of the ambiguous genitalia caused by congenital adrenal hyperplasia?
    a. Small clitoris, fused labia, and urogenital sinus
    b. Small clitoris, open labia, and urogenital sinus
    c. Enlarged clitoris, fused labia, and urogenital sinus
    d. Enlarged clitoris, open labia, and urogenital sinus

11. In Addison disease the majority of the adrenal cortex has been destroyed. This causes a lack of mineralocorticoids and glucocorticoids. Therapy consists of oral replacement with what drug?
    a. Cortisol
    b. Aldosterone
    c. Glucocorticoid
    d. Hydrocortisone

12. In an acute adrenal crisis, the onset of symptoms is sudden, and in the case of Addison disease, can be precipitated by exposure to a minor illness or stress. What are the manifestations of acute adrenal crisis? (Mark all that apply.)

a. Hypertension

b. Muscle weakness

c. Dehydration

d. Altered mental status

e. Vascular collapse

13. The hallmark manifestations of Cushing syndrome are a moon face, a "buffalo hump" between the shoulder blades, and a protruding abdomen. What other manifestations of Cushing syndrome occur?

a. Thin extremities and muscle weakness

b. Muscle wasting and thickened extremities

c. Muscle weakness and thickened extremities

d. Thin extremities and increased strength

Diabetes Mellitus and the Metabolic Syndrome

SECTION I: LEARNING OBJECTIVES

1. State the functions of glucose, fats, and proteins in meeting the energy needs of the body.

2. Characterize the actions of insulin with reference to glucose, fat, and protein metabolism.

3. Explain what is meant by *counter-regulatory hormones*, and describe the actions of glucagon, epinephrine, growth hormone, and the glucocorticoid hormones in regulation of blood glucose levels.

4. Compare the distinguishing features of type 1 and type 2 diabetes mellitus, list causes of other specific types of diabetes, and cite the criteria for gestational diabetes.

5. Describe what is meant by the term *prediabetes*.

6. Relate the physiologic functions of insulin to the manifestations of diabetes mellitus.

7. Define the metabolic syndrome and describe its associations with the development of type 2 diabetes.

8. Discuss the role of diet and exercise in the management of diabetes mellitus.

9. Characterize the blood glucose-lowering actions of the hypoglycemic agents used in treatment of type 2 diabetes.

10. Name and describe the types (according to duration of action) of insulin.

11. Differentiate between the causes and clinical manifestations of diabetic ketoacidosis and the hyperosmolar hyperglycemic state.

12. Describe alterations in physiologic function that accompany diabetic peripheral neuropathy, retinopathy, and nephropathy.

13. Describe the causes of foot ulcers in people with diabetes mellitus.

14. Explain the relation between diabetes mellitus and infection.

SECTION II: ASSESSING YOUR UNDERSTANDING

Activity A *Fill in the blanks.*

1. The primary source of energy for the body is _____.

2. Because the _____ can neither synthesize nor store more than a few minutes' supply of glucose, normal cerebral function requires a continuous supply from the circulation.

3. Severe and prolonged _____ can cause brain death.

4. Glucose that is not needed for energy is removed from the blood and stored as _____ or converted to fat.

5. When blood glucose levels fall below normal, as they do between meals, a process called _____ breaks down glycogen, and glucose is released.

6. In addition to mobilizing its glycogen stores, the liver synthesizes glucose from amino acids, glycerol, and lactic acid in a process called _____.

7. Fat is the most efficient form of fuel storage, providing _____ kcal/g of stored energy, compared with the _____ kcal/g provided by carbohydrates and proteins.

8. _____ are essential for the formation of all body structures, including genes, enzymes, contractile structures in muscle, matrix of bone, and hemoglobin of red blood cells.

9. Because _____ cannot be converted to glucose, the body must break down _____ and use the amino acids as a major substrate for gluconeogenesis during periods when metabolic needs exceed food intake.

10. Because cell membranes are impermeable to glucose, they require a special carrier, called a _____, to move glucose from the blood into the cell.

11. _____ is the insulin-dependent glucose transporter for skeletal muscle and adipose tissue.

12. _____ maintains blood glucose between meals and during periods of fasting.

13. The most dramatic effect of glucagon is its ability to initiate _____ and _____.

14. The secretion of growth hormone normally is inhibited by _____ and increased levels of blood glucose.

15. _____ is a disorder of carbohydrate, protein, and fat metabolism resulting from an imbalance between insulin availability and insulin need.

16. A fasting plasma glucose of _____ or a 2-hour oral glucose tolerance test result _____ is considered normal.

17. _____ diabetes mellitus is characterized by destruction of the pancreatic beta cells.

18. The term _____ type 1B diabetes is used to describe those cases of beta cell destruction in which no evidence of autoimmunity is present.

19. _____ diabetes mellitus is a heterogeneous condition that describes the presence of hyperglycemia in association with relative insulin deficiency.

20. Insulin _____ initially stimulates an increase in insulin secretion, often to a level of modest hyperinsulinemia, as the beta cells attempt to maintain a normal blood glucose level.

21. While the insulin resistance seen in persons with type 2 diabetes can be caused by a number of factors, it is strongly associated with _____ and _____.

22. A major factor in persons with the metabolic syndrome that leads to type 2 diabetes is _____.

23. _____ diabetes mellitus refers to any degree of glucose intolerance that is first detected during pregnancy.

24. The _____ plasma glucose has been suggested as the preferred diagnostic test because of ease of administration, convenience, patient acceptability, and cost.

25. A _____ plasma glucose concentration that is unequivocally elevated (_____ 200 mg/dL) in the presence of classic symptoms of diabetes such as polydipsia, polyphagia, polyuria, and blurred vision is diagnostic of diabetes mellitus at any age.

26. In uncontrolled diabetes or diabetes with hyperglycemia, there is an increase in the level _____ in circulation.

27. Type 1 diabetes mellitus always requires treatment with _____, and many people with type 2 diabetes eventually require similar therapy.

28. Diabetic _____ most commonly occurs in a person with type 1 diabetes, in whom the lack of insulin leads to mobilization of fatty acids from adipose tissue because of the unsuppressed adipose cell lipase activity that breaks down triglycerides into fatty acids and glycerol.

29. The _____ is characterized by hyperglycemia (blood glucose >600 mg/dL), hyperosmolarity (plasma osmolarity >310 mOsm/L) and dehydration, the absence of ketoacidosis, and depression of the sensorium.

30. _____ are thought to produce structural defects in the basement membrane of the microcirculation and to contribute to eye, kidney, and vascular complications.

31. The term _____ is used to describe the combination of lesions that often occur concurrently in the diabetic kidney.

32. _____ is characterized by abnormal retinal vascular permeability, microaneurysm formation, neovascularization and associated hemorrhage, scarring, and retinal detachment.

33. Multiple risk factors for _____, including obesity, hypertension, hyperglycemia, hyperinsulinemia, hyperlipidemia, altered platelet function, endothelial dysfunction, systemic inflammation, and elevated fibrinogen levels, frequently are found in people with diabetes.

Activity B *Match the key terms in Column A with their definitions in Column B.*

Column A

____ 1. Incretin effect

____ 2. Somatostatin

____ 3. Epinephrine

____ 4. Secretagogues

____ 5. Adiponectin

____ 6. Triglyceride

____ 7. Somogyi effect

____ 8. PPAR-γ

____ 9. Amylin

____ 10. Glucocorticoid

____ 11. Dawn phenomenon

Column B

a. Three fatty acids linked by a glycerol molecule

b. Produce inhibition of gastric emptying and glucagon secretion

c. Inhibit the release of insulin and glucagon

d. Increase insulin release after an oral nutrient load

e. Agents that cause or stimulate secretion

f. Inhibits insulin release and promotes glycogenolysis

g. Stimulate gluconeogenesis by the liver

h. Increases tissue sensitivity to insulin

i. Nuclear receptor that leads to the regulation of genes controlling free fatty acid levels and glucose metabolism

j. Cycle of insulin-induced posthypoglycemic episodes

k. Increased levels of fasting blood glucose without precursor hypoglycemia

Activity C

1. Construct a flowchart, using the terms below, that reflects hormonal and hepatic regulation of blood glucose.

• Decreased blood glucose
• Removal of glucose from blood
• Decreased glucagon
• Increased insulin release from beta cells
• Deceased hepatic glucose production
• Increased blood glucose
• Decreased insulin and increased glucagon and gluconeogenesis

Activity D *Briefly answer the following.*

1. What are the results/actions of insulin release?

_____

_____

_____

2. How is insulin secretion from beta cells stimulated?

_____

_____

_____

3. Why are patients with type 1 diabetes mellitus especially prone to develop ketoacidosis?

_____

_____

_____

4. What is thought to cause type 1 diabetes mellitus?

_____

_____

_____

5. What are the metabolic changes that precede the development of type 2 diabetes?

_____

_____

_____

6. How does beta cell dysfunction develop in type 2 diabetics?

_____

_____

_____

7. What are the systemic manifestations of metabolic syndrome?

_____

_____

_____

8. What are the effects of insulin resistance and increased glucose production in obese patients with type 2 diabetes?

_____

_____

_____

9. What are the three "polys" and why are they significant?

_____

_____

_____

10. Why do patients with type 1 diabetes lose weight?

_____

_____

_____

11. How does continuous subcutaneous insulin infusion work?

_____

_____

_____

12. What are the three major challenges to normal physiology from diabetic ketoacidosis (DKA)?

_____

_____

_____

13. What are the common complications of chronic diabetes mellitus? How do they develop?

_____

_____

_____

14. What are the pathologic changes observed in peripheral neuropathies that are associated with chronic diabetes mellitus?

_____

_____

_____

15. What are the effects of diabetes mellitus on renal tissue?

_____

_____

_____

SECTION III: APPLYING YOUR KNOWLEDGE

Activity E *Consider the scenario and answer the questions.*

A 16-year-old boy is admitted to your unit with a new diagnosis of type 1A diabetes mellitus. His blood sugar on admission is 735; he is lethargic; his parents state that he has started eating continuously; and he is urinating much more than he usually does. They say he has lost 10 pounds over the past few months without trying. The client and his family state that they know nothing about diabetes and ask the nurse for an explanation of what the disease is.

1. The nurse would know to include what information in educating the client and his family about type 1A diabetes mellitus?

   _____

   _____

   _____

2. The client asks if there is any cure for type 1A diabetes. The nurse would know to respond:

   _____

   _____

   _____

SECTION IV: PRACTICING FOR NCLEX

Activity F *Answer the following questions.*

1. The pancreas is an endocrine organ that is composed of the acini and the islets of Langerhans. The islets of Langerhans have alpha, beta, and delta cells as well as the PP cell. Which cells secrete insulin?
   a. Alpha cells
   b. Beta cells
   c. Delta cells
   d. PP cells

2. Hormones that counteract insulin's storage function when regulating blood glucose during times when glucose intake is limited or glucose stores are depleted are called counter-regulatory hormones. What are the counter regulatory hormones? (Mark all that apply.)
   a. Glucocorticoids
   b. Growth hormone
   c. Catecholamines
   d. Mineralocorticoids
   e. Glucagon

3. During periods of fasting and starvation, the glucocorticoid and other corticosteroid hormones are critical for survival because of their stimulation of gluconeogenesis by the liver. When the glucocorticoid hormones remain elevated for extended periods of time what can occur?
   a. Hepatomegaly
   b. Portal hypertension
   c. Hyperglycemia
   d. Adrenal hyperplasia

4. Type 1A diabetes is now considered an autoimmune disorder. What factors are considered necessary for type 1A diabetes to occur?
   a. Genetic predisposition, environmental triggering event, and a T-lymphocyte−mediated hypersensitivity reaction against some beta cell antigen
   b. Genetic predisposition, physiologic triggering event, allergic reaction to pancreatic alpha cells
   c. Diabetogenic gene from both parents, physiologic triggering event, and an allergic reaction to pancreatic delta cells
   d. Diabetogenic gene from both parents, environmental triggering event, and a B-lymphocyte reaction to alpha cell antigens

5. Type 2 diabetes is caused by metabolic abnormalities in the presence of insulin. What are these metabolic abnormalities? (Mark all that apply.)
   a. Deranged secretion of insulin
   b. Decreased glucose production by the liver
   c. Insulin resistance
   d. Increased glucose production by the liver
   e. Hypersensitivity to insulin

6. Secondary diabetes occurs because of disorders that produce hyperglycemia by stimulating the hepatic production of glucose or decrease the cellular use of glucose. Which disorders can be causes of secondary diabetes?

   a. Pheochromocytoma and Cushing syndrome

   b. Pancreatic disease and dwarfism

   c. Acromegaly and pancreatic hyperplasia

   d. Hepatomegaly and pheochromocytoma

7. Gestational diabetes mellitus is a disorder of glucose intolerance that occurs during pregnancy. It is associated with increased risk for developing type 2 diabetes and with fetal abnormalities. What fetal abnormalities are associated with gestational diabetes mellitus?

   a. Microsomia and polycythemia

   b. Macrosomia and hypocalcemia

   c. Hypercalcemia and hyperbilirubinemia

   d. Hypoglycemia and hypercalcemia

8. What are the hallmark signs of diabetes mellitus?

   a. Polyuria, polydipsia, and pheochromocytoma

   b. Polyuria, polyphagia, and polycythemia

   c. Polyuria, polydipsia, and polyphagia

   d. Polycythemia, polydipsia, and pheochromocytoma

9. Match the type of oral antidiabetic agents with the name of a drug in its class.

   Type of Antidiabetic Agent

   1. Insulin secretagogues

   2. Biguanides

   3. α-Glucosidase inhibitors

   4. Thiazolidinediones

   5. Dipeptidyl peptidase 4 (DPP-4) enzyme inhibitors

   6. Glucagonlike polypeptide 1 agonists

   Drug

   a. Exenatide

   b. Rosiglitazone

   c. Metformin

   d. Repaglinide

   e. Acarbose

   f. Alogliptin

10. Diabetic ketoacidosis is a condition that mostly occurs in type 1 diabetics. What are the definitive diagnostic criteria for DKA?

    a. Blood glucose level >350 mg/dL; bicarbonate <05 mEq/L and pH <7.4

    b. Blood glucose level >250 mg/dL; bicarbonate <25 mEq/L and pH <7.3

    c. Blood glucose level >350 mg/dL; bicarbonate <05 mEq/L and pH <7.4

    d. Blood glucose level >250 mg/dL; bicarbonate <15 mEq/L and pH <7.3

11. A man is brought into the emergency department by paramedics who state that the client passed out on the street. The man smells of alcohol, and when roused says he has not eaten since yesterday. He is wearing a medic alert bracelet that says he is a diabetic. What would the nurse suspect as a diagnosis?

    a. Hypoglycemia

    b. Hyperglycemia

    c. Hyponatremia

    d. Hypernatremia

12. Hypoglycemia has a sudden onset with a progression of symptoms. What are the signs and symptoms of hypoglycemia?

    a. Difficulty problem solving and muscle spasms

    b. Altered cerebral function and headache

    c. Muscle spasms and headache

    d. Altered cerebral function and muscle spasms

13. Research has identified a cycle of insulin-induced posthypoglycemic episodes. What is this phenomenon called?

    a. Dawn phenomenon

    b. Joslin phenomenon

    c. Somogyi effect

    d. Sunset effect

14. Peripheral neuropathies occur in people with diabetes mellitus. With the loss of sensation in the lower extremities diabetics become predisposed to what?

   a. Denervation of the large muscles of the foot and bunions

   b. Displacement of the submetatarsal fat pad posteriorly and hammer toes

   c. Impairment of temperature and touch sensations

   d. Clawing of toes and denervation of the small muscles of the foot

15. Diabetics are at higher risk than the majority of the population for injury to organ systems in the body. Which organs are most at risk?

   a. Kidneys and eyes

   b. Kidneys and liver

   c. Liver and eyes

   d. Pancreas and eyes

16. Macrovascular disease includes coronary artery disease, cerebrovascular disease, and peripheral vascular disease. People with both type 1 and type 2 diabetes are at high risk for developing macrovascular disease. What are the risk factors for macrovascular disease in diabetics? (Mark all that apply.)

   a. Elevated fibrinogen levels and hyperinsulinemia

   b. Hyperlipidemia and hypotension

   c. Hyperglycemia and hypoinsulinemia

   d. Decreased fibrinogen levels and systemic inflammation

17. Diabetics are hospitalized for a number of reasons. What is the most common complication of diabetes requiring hospitalization?

   a. Diabetic ketoacidosis

   b. Foot problems

   c. Hypertensive crisis

   d. Macrovascular disease

18. Infections are common in people with diabetes. Which infection is thought to be related to a neurogenic bladder?

   a. Nephrotic syndrome

   b. Urinary retention

   c. Pyelonephritis

   d. Urinary incontinence

CHAPTER 34

Organization and Control of Neural Function

SECTION I: LEARNING OBJECTIVES

1. Distinguish between the functions of the neurons and supporting cells of the nervous system.

2. List the three parts of a neuron and describe their structure and function.

3. Name the supporting cells in the central nervous system (CNS) and peripheral nervous system and state their functions.

4. Describe the metabolic requirements of nervous tissue.

5. Describe the three phases of an action potential and relate the functional importance of ion channels to the different phases.

6. State the difference between electrical and chemical synapses.

7. Describe the interaction of the presynaptic and postsynaptic terminals.

8. Characterize the role of excitatory and inhibitory postsynaptic potentials as they relate to spatial and temporal summation of membrane potentials.

9. Briefly describe how neurotransmitters are synthesized, stored, released, and inactivated.

10. Use the segmental approach to explain the development of the nervous system and the organization of the postembryonic nervous system.

11. Define the terms *afferent, efferent, ganglia, association neuron, cell column,* and *tract.*

12. State the origin and destination of nerve fibers contained in the dorsal and ventral roots.

13. State the structures innervated by general somatic afferent, special visceral afferent, general visceral afferent, special somatic afferent, general visceral efferent, pharyngeal efferent, and general somatic efferent neurons.

14. Describe the longitudinal and transverse structures of the spinal cord.

15. Trace an afferent and efferent neuron from its site in the periphery through its entrance into or exit from the spinal cord.

16. Explain the innervation and function of spinal cord reflexes.

17. List the structures of the hindbrain, midbrain, and forebrain and describe their functions.

18. Name the cranial nerves and cite their location and function.

19. Describe the characteristics of the cerebrospinal fluid and trace its passage through the ventricular system.

20. Contrast and compare the blood-brain and cerebrospinal fluid-brain barriers.

21. Compare the sensory and motor components of the autonomic nervous system with those of the CNS.

22. Compare the anatomic location and functions of the sympathetic and parasympathetic nervous systems.

23. Describe neurotransmitter synthesis, release, and degradation, and receptor function in the sympathetic and parasympathetic nervous systems.

SECTION II: ASSESSING YOUR UNDERSTANDING

Activity A *Fill in the blanks.*

1. The _____ are the functional cells of the nervous system.

2. The supporting cells, such as _____ in the peripheral nervous system (PNS) and the _____ cells in the CNS, protect the nervous system and provide metabolic support for the neurons.

3. Neurons have three distinct parts: the cell _____, and its cytoplasm-filled processes, the _____ and _____ which form the functional connections, or _____, with other nerve cells, with receptor cells, or with effector cells.

4. _____ are multiple, short-branched extensions of the nerve cell body; they conduct information toward the cell body and are the main source of information for the neuron.

5. Supporting cells of the nervous system, the _____ and _____ cells of the PNS and the several types of neuroglial cells of the CNS, give the neurons protection and metabolic support.

6. _____ cells secrete a basement membrane that protects the cell body from the diffusion of large molecules.

7. In some pathologic conditions, such as multiple sclerosis in the CNS and Guillain-Barré syndrome in the PNS, the _____ may degenerate or be destroyed.

8. The _____ increase nerve conduction by allowing the impulse to jump from node to node through the extracellular fluid in a process called _____.

9. The _____ form the myelin in the CNS.

10. _____ is the major fuel source for the nervous system.

11. Nerve signals are transmitted by _____, which are abrupt, pulsatile changes in the membrane potential.

12. The excitability of neurons can be affected by conditions that alter the _____ moving it either closer to or further from the threshold potential.

13. Neurons communicate with each other through structures known as _____.

14. _____ synapses involve special presynaptic and postsynaptic membrane structures, separated by a synaptic cleft.

15. The secreted neurotransmitters diffuse into the _____ and unite with receptors on the postsynaptic membrane.

16. In excitatory synapses, binding of the neurotransmitter to the receptor produces _____ of the postsynaptic membrane, where as the binding of the neurotransmitter to the receptor in an inhibitory synapse induces _____ of the postsynaptic membrane by making the membrane more permeable to potassium or chloride.

17. When the combination of a neurotransmitter with a receptor site causes partial depolarization of the postsynaptic membrane, it is called an _____ potential.

18. The process of _____ involves the synthesis, storage, and release of a neurotransmitter; the reaction of the neurotransmitter with a receptor; and termination of the receptor action.

19. _____ molecules react with presynaptic or postsynaptic receptors to alter the release of or response to neurotransmitters.

20. _____ factors are required to maintain the long-term survival of the postsynaptic cell and are secreted by axon terminals independent of action potentials.

21. A functional system called the _____ operates in the lateral portions of the reticular formation of the medulla, pons, and especially the midbrain.

22. The spinal cord and the dorsal and ventral roots are covered by a connective tissue sheath, the _____, which also contains the blood vessels that supply the white and gray matter of the cord.

23. The peripheral nerves that carry information to and from the spinal cord are called _____.

24. Each spinal cord segment communicates with its corresponding body segment through the _____.

25. Spinal nerves do not go directly to skin and muscle fibers; instead, they form complicated nerve networks called _____.

26. A _____ is a highly predictable relationship between a stimulus and an elicited motor response.

27. The _____ reflex is stimulated by a damaging stimulus and quickly moves the body part away from the offending stimulus, usually by flexing a limb part.

28. Based on its embryonic development, the brain is divided into three regions, the _____, the _____, and the _____.

29. Damage to the _____ nerve results in weakness or paralysis of tongue muscles.

30. Sensory and motor components of the _____ nerve innervate the pharynx, the gastrointestinal tract, the heart, the spleen, and the lungs.

31. The sternocleidomastoid, a powerful head-turning muscle, and the trapezius muscle, which elevates the shoulders, are innervated by the _____.

32. The dorsolateral _____ contains the same components as the vagus nerve but for a more rostral segment of the gastrointestinal tract and the pharynx.

33. The special sensory afferent _____ is attached laterally at the junction of the medulla oblongata and the pons, often called the *caudal pons*.

34. The _____ innervates the nasopharynx and taste buds of the palate.

35. The _____ nerve abducts the eye.

36. The _____ is the main sensory nerve conveying the modalities of pain, temperature, touch, and proprioception to the superficial and deep regions of the face.

37. The _____ makes continuous adjustments, resulting in smoothness of movement, particularly during the delicate maneuvers.

38. The _____ plays a role in relaying critical information regarding motor activities to and from selected areas of the motor cortex.

39. A _____ is the ridge between two grooves, and the groove is called a _____.

40. The _____ supply axial and proximal unlearned and learned postures and movements, which enhance and add gracefulness to upper motor neuron-controlled manipulative movements.

41. The _____ is necessary for somesthetic perception, especially concerning perception of "where" the stimulus is in space and in relation to body parts.

42. Inside the skull and vertebral column, the brain and spinal cord are loosely suspended and protected by several connective tissue sheaths called the _____.

43. The _____ provides a supporting and protective fluid in which the brain and spinal cord float.

44. The ability to maintain homeostasis and perform the activities of daily living in an ever-changing physical environment is largely vested in the _____.

45. The functions of the _____ are concerned with conservation of energy, resource replenishment and storage, and maintenance of organ function during periods of minimal activity—the *rest and digest* response.

Activity B *Consider the following figure.*

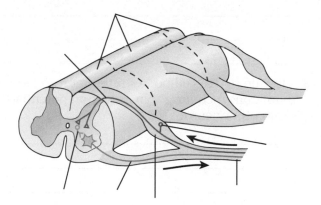

1. In the figure above of the segments of the spinal cord, please label the following structures:

   - IA neuron
   - Segments
   - Ventral root
   - Dorsal root ganglion
   - Spinal nerve
   - Dorsal root

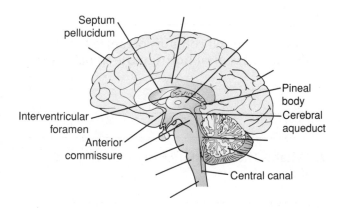

2. In the above figure of the brain, please label the following structures:

   - Spinal cord
   - Medulla oblongata
   - Pons
   - Midbrain
   - Frontal lobe
   - Corpus callosum
   - Occipital lobe
   - Third ventricle
   - Fourth ventricle
   - Cerebellum

Activity C *Match the key terms in Column A with their definitions in Column B.*

1.

Column A	Column B
____ 1. Microglia	a. Forms the lining of the neural tube cavity
____ 2. Depolarization	
____ 3. Neurotransmitters	b. Phase during which the polarity of the resting membrane potential is re-established
____ 4. Repolarization	
____ 5. Astrocytes	c. Membrane-bound sacs that store neurotransmitters
____ 6. Synaptic vesicles	
____ 7. Ependymal	d. Form the blood-brain barrier
____ 8. Plexus	e. Chemical transmitter molecules
____ 9. *Threshold potential*	f. Small phagocytic cell that is available for cleaning up debris after cellular damage, infection, or cell death
____ 10. Oligodendrocytes	
	g. Membrane potential at which neurons or other excitable tissues are stimulated
	h. Flow of electrically charged ions toward an equilibrium
	i. Production of CNS myelin
	j. Site of intermixing nerve branches

2.

Column A

____ **1.** Afferent

____ **2.** Bell's palsy

____ **3.** Efferent

____ **4.** *Proprioception*

____ **5.** Ganglia

____ **6.** Association neuron

____ **7.** Limbic system

____ **8.** Cell column

____ **9.** Tract

Column B

a. Neurons that communicate with CNS and peripheral neural cells

b. Nerves that conduct impulses from the periphery of the body to the brain or spinal cord.

c. Longitudinal columns of neurons

d. Communication over distances between neighboring and distal segment of neural tube

e. Carrying impulses from the CNS to an effector

f. Group of neural cell bodies

g. Sense of body movement and position

h. Involved in emotional experience and release of emotional behaviors, is located in the medial aspect of the cerebrum

i. Unilateral loss of facial nerve function

Activity D *Briefly answer the following.*

1. Describe the formation and attachment of myelin to the axonal membrane.

_____

_____

_____

2. Explain the fragileness of neural cells in regard to metabolic requirements.

_____

_____

_____

3. How do neural cell bodies interpret the numerous incoming signals (action potentials) from other neurons?

_____

_____

_____

4. How are neurotransmitters inactivated in the synaptic space following release?

_____

_____

_____

5. Describe the basic embryologic development of the nervous system.

_____

_____

_____

6. How are the cell columns organized in the dorsal and ventral horns of the spinal cord?

_____

_____

_____

7. What is the importance of cerebral spinal fluid?

_____

_____

_____

8. How does the blood-brain barrier affect drug/toxin actions on the brain?

_____

_____

_____

SECTION III: APPLYING YOUR KNOWLEDGE

Activity E *Consider the scenario and answer the questions.*

A woman in her fourth month of pregnancy comes to the clinic to have an ultrasound done. When the ultrasound is read, the physician tells the woman that her fetus has a neural tube defect and, when the infant is born, it will have a cystlike pouch on its lower back that contains cerebrospinal fluid, meninges, and spinal nerves.

1. The client asks if there is a name for the defect her child has. What is the correct response to the client's question?

   _____

   _____

   _____

2. The client asks what this defect will mean for her baby. What would be the correct response from the health care professional?

   _____

   _____

   _____

SECTION IV: PRACTICING FOR NCLEX

Activity F *Answer the following questions.*

1. There are two types of nervous tissue cells. One type is neurons, and the other type is the supporting cells. What is the function of the supporting cells?
   a. Protect nervous system and provide metabolic support for the neurons
   b. Transmit messages between parts of the PNS
   c. Transmit messages between the CNS and the PNS
   d. Provide metabolic support for the neurons and the PNS

2. Ion channels in nervous system cells generate action potentials in the cells. What are the ion channels guarded by?
   a. Schwann cells
   b. Voltage-dependent gates
   c. Ligand-gates
   d. Leyte cells

3. Neurons communicate through the use of synapses. These synapses may link neurons into functional circuits. What is the most common type of synapse?
   a. Electrical synapse
   b. Excitatory synapse
   c. Chemical synapse
   d. Inhibitory synapse

4. Neurotransmitters are small molecules that exert their actions through specific proteins, called *receptors*, embedded in the postsynaptic membrane. Where are neurotransmitters synthesized?
   a. In the dendrite terminal
   b. In the presynaptic junction
   c. In the postsynaptic junction
   d. In the axon terminal

5. Neuromodulators can produce slower and longer-lasting changes in membrane excitability by acting on postsynaptic receptors. What do neuromodulators do?
   a. Alter the release or response to neurotransmitters
   b. Alter the inhibitory response of postsynaptic electrical receptors
   c. Alter the metabolic function of Schwann cells
   d. Alter the Ligand-gate response to electrical activity

6. The basis for assessing the function of any peripheral nerve lies in what?
   a. Peripheral nerves contain only afferent processes from the cell columns
   b. Peripheral nerves contain processes of more than one of the four afferent and three efferent cell columns.
   c. Peripheral nerves contain only efferent processes from the cell columns
   d. Peripheral nerves contain no processes from the seven cell columns

7. The spinal cord does not hang freely within the spinal column. What is it supported by?
   a. The pia mater and the posterior vertebra
   b. The denticulate ligaments and the vertebral blood vessels
   c. The pia mater and the denticulate ligaments
   d. The vertebral blood vessels and the posterior vertebra

8. One of the spinal motor reflexes is the myotatic reflex. What does this reflex do for the body?
   a. Provides information to withdraw the body from noxious stimuli
   b. Provides information about nociceptive stimuli
   c. Provides information about equilibrium
   d. Provides information about proprioception

9. The cerebellum, separated from the cerebral hemispheres by the tentorium cerebelli, lies in the posterior fossa of the cranium. What is one of the functions of the cerebellum?
   a. Coordinates smooth and accurate movements of the body
   b. Conveys the senses of pain, temperature, touch, and proprioception to the superficial and deep regions of the face
   c. Contains the pontine nuclei
   d. Contains the main motor pathways between the forebrain and the pons

10. The basal ganglia, part of the cerebral hemispheres, are damaged by diseases such as Parkinson disease and Huntington chorea. What does this result in?
    a. Uncontrollable tremors on movement
    b. Abnormal movement patterns
    c. Explosive, inappropriate speech
    d. Inappropriate emotions

11. The sympathetic and the parasympathetic nervous systems are continuously at work in our bodies. This continual action gives a basal activity to all parts of the body. What is this basal activity referred to as?
    a. Tension
    b. Relaxation
    c. Tone
    d. Strength

12. Dopamine is an intermediate compound made during the synthesis of norepinephrine. It is the principal inhibitory transmitter of the internuncial neurons in the sympathetic ganglia. What other action does it have?
    a. Vasoconstricts renal and coronary blood vessels when given intravenously
    b. Acts as a neuromodulator in the hindbrain
    c. Acts as a neuromodulator in the forebrain
    d. Vasodilates renal and coronary blood vessels when given intravenously

CHAPTER 35

Somatosensory Function, Pain, and Headache

SECTION I: LEARNING OBJECTIVES

1. Describe the four major classes of somatosensory modalities and define a sensory unit.

2. Describe the organization of the somatosensory system in terms of first-, second-, and third-order neurons.

3. Characterize the structure and function of the dorsal root ganglion neurons in terms of sensory receptors, conduction velocities, and spinal cord projections.

4. Compare the discriminative pathway with the anterolateral pathway, and explain the clinical usefulness of this distinction.

5. Compare the tactile, thermal, and position sense modalities in terms of receptors, adequate stimuli, ascending pathways, and central integrative mechanisms.

6. Describe the role of clinical examination in assessing somatosensory function.

7. Differentiate among the specificity, pattern, gate control, and neuromatrix theories of pain.

8. Characterize the response of nociceptors to stimuli that produce pain.

9. State the difference between the Aδ- and C-fiber neurons in the transmission of pain information.

10. Trace the transmission of pain signals with reference to the neospinothalamic and paleospinothalamic, and reticulospinal pathways, including the role of chemical mediators and factors that modulate pain transmission.

11. Describe the function of endogenous analgesic mechanisms as they relate to transmission of pain information.

12. Compare pain threshold and pain tolerance.

13. Differentiate acute pain from chronic pain in terms of mechanisms, manifestations, and treatment.

14. Describe the mechanisms of referred pain, and list the common sites of referral for cardiac and other types of visceral pain.

15. Describe three methods for assessing pain.

16. State the proposed mechanisms of pain relief associated with the use of heat, cold, transcutaneous electrical nerve stimulation, and acupuncture.

17. Cite the mechanisms whereby nonnarcotic and narcotic analgesics, tricyclic antidepressants, and antiseizure drugs relieve pain.

18. Define allodynia, hypoesthesia, hyperesthesia, paresthesias, hyperpathia, analgesia, and hypoalgesia and hyperalgesia.

19. Describe the cause and characteristics and treatment of neuropathic pain, trigeminal neuralgia, postherpetic neuralgia, and complex regional pain syndrome.

20. Cite possible mechanisms of phantom limb pain.

21. State the importance of distinguishing between primary and secondary types of headache.

22. Differentiate between the periodicity of occurrence and manifestations of migraine headache, cluster headache, tension-type headache, and headache due to temporomandibular joint syndrome.

23. Characterize the nonpharmacologic and pharmacologic methods used in treatment of headache.

24. Cite the most common cause of temporomandibular joint pain.

25. State how the pain response may differ in children and older adults.

26. Explain how pain assessment may differ in children and older adults.

27. Explain how pain treatment may differ in children and older adults.

SECTION II: ASSESSING YOUR UNDERSTANDING

Activity A *Fill in the blanks.*

1. The _____ system is designed to provide the central nervous system (CNS) with information related to deep and superficial body structures as contrasted to special senses such sight and hearing.

2. _____ somatic afferent neurons have branches with widespread distribution throughout the body and with many distinct types of receptors that result in sensations such as pain, touch, and temperature.

3. _____ somatic afferent neurons sense position and movement of the body.

4. General _____ afferent neurons have receptors on various visceral structures that sense fullness and discomfort.

5. Somatosensory information from the face and cranial structures is transmitted by the _____ sensory neurons, which function in the same manner as the dorsal root ganglion neurons.

6. The region of the body wall that is supplied by a single pair of dorsal root ganglia is called a _____.

7. The _____ pathway is used for the rapid transmission of sensory information such as discriminative touch.

8. The _____ pathways provide for transmission of sensory information such as pain, thermal sensations, crude touch, and pressure that does not require discrete localization of signal source or fine discrimination of intensity.

9. Somatosensory experience can be divided into _____, a term used for qualitative, subjective distinctions between sensations such as touch, heat, and pain.

10. The receptive endings of different afferent neurons can initiate _____ to many forms of energy at high energy levels, but they usually are highly tuned to be differentially sensitive to low levels of a particular energy type.

11. The ability to discriminate the location of a somesthetic stimulus is called _____ and is based on the sensory field in a dermatome innervated by an afferent neuron.

12. The _____ system, which relays sensory information regarding touch, pressure, and vibration, is considered the basic somatosensory system.

13. _____ sensation is discriminated by three types of receptors: cold receptors, warmth receptors, and pain receptors.

14. Attention, motivation, past experience, and the meaning of the situation can influence the individual's reaction to _____.

15. The experience of pain depends on both _____ stimulation and _____.

16. _____ pain arises from direct injury or dysfunction of the sensory axons of peripheral or central nerves.

17. The _____ theory proposes that the brain contains a widely distributed neural network that contains somatosensory, limbic, and thalamocortical components.

18. _____ stimuli are objectively defined as stimuli of such intensity that they cause or are close to causing tissue damage.

19. Nociceptive stimulation that activates _____ can cause a response known as *neurogenic inflammation* that produces vasodilation and an increased release of chemical mediators to which nociceptors respond.

20. The faster-conducting fibers in the _____ tract are associated mainly with the transmission of sharp-fast pain information to the thalamus.

21. The _____ tract is a slower-conducting, multisynaptic tract concerned with the diffuse, dull, aching, and unpleasant sensations that commonly are associated with chronic and visceral pain.

22. Through research, it was found that electrical stimulation of the midbrain _____ regions produced a state of analgesia that lasted for many hours.

23. Three families of endogenous opioid peptides have been identified—the _____, _____, and _____.

24. Pain _____ and tolerance affect an individual's response to a painful stimulus.

25. _____ pain arises from superficial structures, such as the skin and subcutaneous tissues.

26. _____ pain originates in deep body structures, such as the periosteum, muscles, tendons, joints, and blood vessels.

27. The purpose of acute pain is to serve as a _____ system.

28. An _____ drug is a medication that acts on the nervous system to decrease or eliminate pain without inducing loss of consciousness.

29. Primary _____ describes pain sensitivity that occurs directly in damaged tissues.

30. _____ is the absence of pain on noxious stimulation or the relief of pain without loss of consciousness.

31. _____ is characterized by severe, brief, often repetitive attacks of lightning-like or throbbing pain.

32. _____ headache is a type of primary neurovascular headache that typically includes severe, unrelenting, unilateral pain located, in order of decreasing frequency, in the orbital, retro-orbital, temporal, supraorbital, and infraorbital region.

33. The most common type of headache is _____ headache.

34. A common cause of head pain is _____ syndrome.

Activity B *Consider the following figures.*

1. In the figure above, label the flowing structures:

- Receptor
- Dorsal root ganglion
- First-order neuron
- Second-order neuron
- Thalamus
- Somatosensory cortex
- Third-order neuron

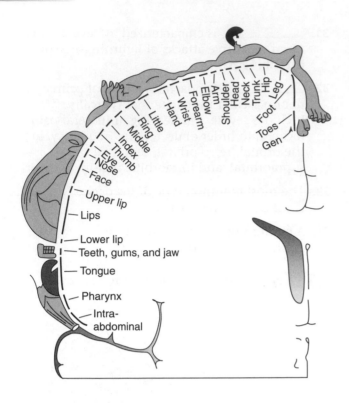

_____ **8.** Hyperpathia

_____ **9.** Type C fibers

_____ **10.** Type Aα fibers

2. Using the figure above, please answer the following questions:

• Which area has the smallest receptor field?
• Which area has the largest receptor field?
• Which area has the highest acuity?

Activity C *Match the key terms in Column A with their definitions in Column B.*

1.

Column A

_____ **1.** Perception

_____ **2.** Somesthesia

_____ **3.** Type A fibers

_____ **4.** *Polymodal receptors*

_____ **5.** Type B fibers

_____ **6.** *Hunting reflex*

_____ **7.** Primary somatosensory cortex

Column B

a. The perception of tactual, proprioceptive, or gut sensations

b. Transmit information about muscle length and tendon stretch

c. Sensory threshold is raised

d. Convey cutaneous pressure and touch sensation, cold sensation, mechanical pain, and heat pain.

e. Circulation to a cooled area undergoes alternating periods of pallor caused by ischemia and flushing caused by hyperemia

f. Awareness of the stimuli, localization and discrimination of their characteristics, and interpretation of their meaning.

g. Receives primary sensory information by way of direct projections from the thalamus

h. Convey warm-hot sensation and mechanical and chemical as well as heat- and cold-induced pain sensation

i. Respond to mechanical, thermal, and chemical stimuli

j. Transmit information from cutaneous and subcutaneous mechanoreceptors

2.

Column A

_____ **1.** Free nerve endings

_____ **2.** Meissner corpuscles

_____ **3.** Merkel disks

_____ **4.** Pacinian corpuscles

_____ **5.** Hair follicle end-organs

_____ **6.** Ruffini end-organs

Column B

a. Stimulated by rapid movements of the tissues and adapts within a few hundredths of a second

b. Unmyelinated fibers entwined around most of the length of the hair follicle that detect movement on the surface of the body

c. Are responsible for giving steady-state signals that allow for continuous determination of touch against the skin

d. Detect touch and pressure

e. Found in joint capsules

f. Elongated encapsulated nerve ending that is present in nonhairy parts of the skin

Activity D *Briefly answer the following.*

1. How are sensory systems organized?

_____

_____

_____

2. What are the types of sensory information that can be perceived by our sensory receptors?

_____

_____

_____

3. How much information can be obtained from a single pinprick to the bottom of your patient's foot?

_____

_____

_____

4. What is the gate control theory of pain?

_____

_____

_____

5. How can the phenomena of referred pain be explained?

_____

_____

_____

6. In many sports injuries the athlete may be instructed to place heat on the injured area. What is the effect on pain originating from the injury?

_____

_____

_____

7. What is phantom limb pain and what are some of the theories postulated to explain its presence?

_____

_____

_____

8. What are the differences and similarities between migraine headaches with aura and migraine headaches without aura?

_____

_____

_____

9. What is known about the pathology of pain during a migrainous headache?

_____

_____

_____

SECTION III: APPLYING YOUR KNOWLEDGE

Activity E *Consider the scenario and answer the questions.*

An 82-year-old woman is brought to the emergency department by ambulance from a local nursing home. The report from the accompanying staff member is that the client suffers from a physiologic dementia, and that 2 days ago she suffered a fall in the bathroom. The client denies pain, but has been restless and agitated since the fall, and today she will not use her right arm.

1. The caregiver asks the nurse how the health care team is going to assess this client's pain as the client cannot give them any accurate information. What is the nurse's best response?

_____

_____

_____

2. The client is diagnosed with a fractured right ulna. She is taken to the operating room, where the arm is aligned and cast. When the client is ready for release back to the nursing home, the caregiver asks what can be done for the client's discomfort. What teaching would the nurse include at discharge?

_____

_____

_____

SECTION IV: PRACTICING FOR NCLEX

Activity F *Answer the following questions.*

1. Match the type of neuron with the information they transmit and where they transmit it to.

Type of Neuron

1. Special somatic afferent neurons
2. General somatic afferent neurons
3. General visceral afferent neurons
4. First-order neurons
5. Second-order neurons
6. Third-order neurons
7. Dorsal root ganglion neurons
8. Trigeminal sensory neurons

Information Transmitted and Site

a. Sensations such as pain, touch, and temperature
b. Transmit sensory information from the periphery to the CNS
c. Communicate with various reflex networks and sensory pathways in the spinal cord and travel directly to the thalamus
d. Transmits all somatosensory information from the limbs and trunk
e. Sense position and movement of the body
f. Somatosensory information from the face and cranial structures
g. Sense fullness and discomfort
h. Relay information from the thalamus to the cerebral cortex

2. Match the term with the definition.

Term

1. Discriminative touch
2. Sensory unit
3. Type A fibers
4. Type Aα and Aδ fibers
5. Type B fibers
6. Dermatome
7. Discriminative pathway
8. Stereognosis
9. Anterolateral pathway

Definition

a. The region of the body wall that is supplied by a single pair of dorsal root ganglia
b. Stimulate autonomic nervous system responses, such as a rise in heart rate and blood pressure, dilation of the pupils, and the pale, moist skin that results from constriction of the cutaneous blood vessels and activation of the sweat glands

10. Free nerve endings

11. Nociceptors

c. Identifies the size and shape of objects and their movement across the skin; temperature sensation; sense of movement of the limbs and joints of the body; and nociception, or pain

d. Transmit information about muscle length and tendon stretch

e. Sensory receptors that are activated by noxious insults to peripheral tissues

f. Carry the information from the spinal cord to the thalamic level of sensation and relays precise information regarding spatial orientation

g. The cell body of the dorsal root ganglion neuron, its peripheral branch (which innervates a small area of periphery), and its central axon (which projects to the CNS)

h. Transmit information from cutaneous and subcutaneous mechanoreceptors

i. Convey cutaneous pressure and touch sensation, cold sensation, mechanical pain, and heat pain.

j. The sense of shape and size of an object in the absence of visualization

k. Detect touch and pressure

3. A neurologic assessment of the somatosensory function of the body is often necessary for diagnostic information. How is this assessment done?
  a. Testing the integrity of spinal segmental nerves
  b. Testing the integrity of cranial nerves
  c. Testing the integrity of peripheral nerves
  d. Testing the integrity of the CNS

4. When testing nociceptive stimuli to elicit a withdrawal reflex in the body, what stimuli are commonly used?
  a. Weak electrical current
  b. Pressure from a sharp object
  c. Skin temperature damp cotton ball
  d. Water heated to 5°C above skin temperature

5. One of the neurotransmitters between the nociceptive neurons and the dorsal horn neurons is a major excitatory neurotransmitter. What is this neurotransmitter?
  a. Norepinephrine
  b. Substance P
  c. Glutamate
  d. Dopamine

6. Which tract in the spinal cord conducts the diffuse, dull, aching sensations that are associated with chronic and visceral pain?
  a. Multisynaptic tract
  b. Neospinothalamic tract
  c. Anterolateral tract
  d. Paleospinothalamic tract

7. Match the type of pain with its description

Type of Pain	Description of Pain

Type of Pain

1. Deep somatic pain
2. Cutaneous pain
3. Visceral pain
4. Referred pain
5. Guarding
6. Acute pain
7. Chronic pain

Description of Pain

a. Extends for long periods of time and generally represents low levels of underlying pathology that does not explain the presence and/or extent of the pain.

b. The pain's location, radiation, intensity, and duration, as well as those factors that aggravate or relieve it, provide essential diagnostic clues.

c. Type of pain experienced from a sprained ankle.

d. A sharp pain with a burning quality and may be abrupt or slow in onset.

e. A protective reflex rigidity; its purpose is to protect the affected body parts.

f. Diffuse and poorly localized nature with a tendency to be referred to other locations

g. Perceived at a site different from its point of origin but innervated by the same spinal segment

8. It is often necessary to assess a client's pain. What factors would you assess when assessing pain? (Mark all that apply.)
   a. Nature and severity of pain
   b. Severity and spinal reflex involvement of pain
   c. Location and radiation of pain
   d. Spinal reflex involvement and nature of pain
   e. Spinal tract involvement and radiation of pain

9. When giving pain medicine for acute pain, health care workers are reluctant to provide much needed opioid pain medicine. What is the major concern of health care workers when providing opioid pain relief?
   a. Fear of addiction
   b. Fear of depressed respirations
   c. Fear of oversedation
   d. Fear of adverse reactions

10. Chronic pain is difficult to treat. Cancer, a common cause of chronic pain, has been especially addressed by the World Health Organization (WHO). What has WHO created to assist clinicians in choosing appropriate analgesics?
    a. An opioid ladder for pain control
    b. An analgesic ladder for pain control
    c. Stepping stones for pain control
    d. A list of nonpharmacologic ways to control pain

11. In describing the ideal analgesic, what factors would be included? (Mark all that apply.)
    a. Inexpensive
    b. Have minimal adverse effects
    c. Effective
    d. Addictive
    e. Decrease the level of consciousness

12. Using surgery to relieve severe, intractable pain has been successful to a degree. What can surgery be used for when a person is in pain?
    a. Relief of severe peripheral contractures
    b. Cure inoperable cancer
    c. Block transmission of phantom limb pain
    d. Cure severe myalgia

13. When a peripheral nerve is irritated enough, it becomes hypersensitive to the noxious stimuli, which results in increased painfulness or hyperalgesia. Health care professionals recognize both primary and secondary forms of hyperalgesia. What is primary hyperalgesia?
    a. Pain that occurs in the tissue surrounding an injury.
    b. Pain sensitivity that lasts longer than 1 week
    c. Pain sensitivity that occurs in the viscera
    d. Pain sensitivity that occurs directly in damaged tissues

14. Match the type of pain with its description.

Type of Pain

1. Neuropathic pain
2. Neuralgia
3. Tic douloureux
4. Postherpetic neuralgia

Description

a. Manifested by facial tics or spasms and characterized by paroxysmal attacks of stabbing pain that usually are limited to the unilateral sensory distribution of one or more branches of the trigeminal nerve, most often the maxillary or mandibular divisions.

b. Characterized by severe, brief, often repetitive attacks of lightning-like or throbbing pain.

c. Affected sensory ganglia and the peripheral nerve to the skin of the corresponding dermatomes cause a unilateral localized vesicular eruption and hyperpathia (i.e., abnormally exaggerated subjective response to pain).

d. Widespread pain that is not otherwise explainable, burning pain, and attacks of pain that occur without seeming provocation.

15. Phantom limb pain is a little understood pain that develops after an amputation. Because it is little understood, it is difficult to treat, even though the client is experiencing severe pain. What are the treatments for phantom limb pain?

a. Sympathetic blocks and hypnosis

b. Relaxation training and transcutaneous electrical nerve stimulation on the efferents in the area

c. Narcotic analgesics and relaxation training

d. Biofeedback and nonsteroidal anti-inflammatory drugs

16. Migraine headaches affect millions of people worldwide. What are first-line agents for the treatment of migraine headaches?

a. Ondansetron and morphine

b. Naproxen sodium and metoclopramide

c. Sumatriptan and tramadol

d. Caffeine and syrup of ipecac

17. A severe type of headache that occurs more frequently in men than women and is described as having unrelenting, unilateral pain located most frequently in the orbit is called what?

a. Migraine headache

b. Tension headache

c. Cluster headache

d. Chronic daily headache

18. When assessing pain in children, it is important to use the correct pain rating scale. What would be the appropriate pain rating scale with children from the 3- to 8-year-old range?

a. COMFORT pain scale

b. FLACC pain scale

c. CRIES pain scale

d. FACES pain scale

19. Children feel pain just as much as adults do. What is the major principle in pain management in the pediatric population?

a. Treat on individual basis and match analgesic agent with cause and level of pain.

b. Always use nonpharmacologic pain management before using pharmacologic pain management.

c. Base treatment of pain on gender and age group.

d. Treat pediatric pain the way the parents want you to.

CHAPTER 36

Disorders of Neuromuscular Function

SECTION I: LEARNING OBJECTIVES

1. Define the term *motor unit* and characterize its mechanism of controlling skeletal muscle movement.

2. Describe the distribution of upper and lower motor neurons in relation to the central nervous system (CNS).

3. Differentiate between the functions of the primary, premotor, and supplemental motor cortices.

4. Compare the effect of upper and lower motor neuron lesions on the spinal cord stretch reflex function and muscle tone.

5. Describe muscle atrophy and differentiate between disuse and denervation atrophy.

6. Relate the molecular changes in muscle structure that occur in Duchenne muscular dystrophy to the clinical manifestations of the disease.

7. Describe the actions of *Clostridium botulinum* neurotoxins in terms of their pathologic and therapeutic potential.

8. Relate the clinical manifestations of myasthenia gravis to its cause.

9. Define the term *peripheral nervous system* and describe the characteristics of peripheral nerves.

10. Trace the steps in regeneration of an injured peripheral nerve.

11. Compare the cause and manifestations of peripheral mononeuropathies with polyneuropathies.

12. Describe the manifestation of peripheral nerve root injury due to a ruptured intervertebral disk.

13. Relate the functions of the cerebellum to production of vestibulocerebellar dysfunction, decomposition of movement, and cerebellar tremor.

14. Describe the functional organization of the basal ganglia and communication pathways with the thalamus and cerebral cortex.

15. State the possible mechanisms responsible for the development of Parkinson disease and characterize the manifestations and treatment of the disorder.

16. Relate the pathologic upper motor neuron and lower motor neuron (LMN) changes that occur in amyotrophic lateral sclerosis to the manifestations of the disease.

17. Explain the significance of demyelination and plaque formation in multiple sclerosis.

17. Describe the manifestations of multiple sclerosis.

18. Relate the structures of the vertebral column to mechanisms of spinal cord injury.

19. Explain how loss of upper motor neuron function contributes to the muscle spasms that occur after recovery from spinal cord injury.

20. State the effects of spinal cord injury on ventilation and communication, the autonomic nervous system, cardiovascular function, sensorimotor function, and bowel, bladder, and sexual function.

SECTION II: ASSESSING YOUR UNDERSTANDING

Activity A *Fill in the blanks.*

1. _____, whether it involves walking, running, or precise finger movements, requires movement and maintenance of posture.

2. The _____ contains the neuronal circuits that mediate a variety of reflexes and automatic rhythmic movements.

3. Most reflexes are _____, meaning that they involve one or more interposed interneurons.

4. The medial descending systems of the brain stem contribute to the control of _____ by integrating visual, vestibular, and somatosensory information.

5. The _____ is the highest level of motor function.

6. The primary _____ cortex is located on the rostral surface and adjacent portions of the central sulcus.

7. The _____ and _____ provide feedback circuits that regulate cortical and brain stem motor areas.

8. Cerebellar _____ are involved with the timing and coordination of movements that are in progress and with learning of motor skills.

9. The _____, which are distributed throughout the belly of a muscle, relay information about muscle length and rate of stretch.

10. _____ are found in muscle tendons and transmit information about muscle tension or force of contraction at the junction of the muscle and the tendon that attaches to bone.

11. Stretch reflexes tend to be hypoactive or absent in cases of _____ nerve damage or ventral horn injury involving the test area.

12. Abnormalities in any part of the _____ pathway can produce muscle weakness.

13. Muscular _____ usually results from LMN lesions as well as diseases of the muscle themselves.

14. Any interruption of the myotatic or stretch reflex circuitry by peripheral nerve injury, pathology of the neuromuscular junction, injury to the spinal cord, or damage to the corticospinal system can results in disturbances of _____.

15. Hyperactive reflexes are suggestive of a _____ disorder.

16. _____ suggests the presence of a LMN lesion.

17. Disorders affecting the nerve cell body are often referred to _____, those affecting the nerve axon, as _____ neuropathies; and primary disorders affecting the muscle fibers as _____.

18. *Muscular* _____ is a term applied to a number of genetic disorders that produce progressive deterioration of skeletal muscles because of mixed muscle cell hypertrophy, atrophy, and necrosis.

19. If the LMN dies or its axon is destroyed, the skeletal muscle cell begins to have temporary spontaneous contractions, called _____.

20. _____ muscular dystrophy is inherited as a recessive single-gene defect on the X chromosome and is transmitted from the mother to her male offspring.

21. The _____ serves as a synapse between a motor neuron and a skeletal muscle fiber.

22. Neurotoxins from the botulism organism (*C. botulinum*) produce paralysis by blocking _____ release.

23. _____ is a disorder of transmission at the neuromuscular junction that affects communication between the motor neuron and the innervated muscle cell.

24. Lower motor neuron diseases are progressive neurologic illnesses that selectively affect the anterior horn cells of the _____ and _____ motor neurons.

25. There are two main types of _____ injury based on the target of the insult: segmental demyelination involving the Schwann cell and axonal degeneration involving the neuronal cell body and/or its axon.

26. _____ usually are caused by localized conditions such as trauma, compression, or infections that affect a single spinal nerve, plexus, or peripheral nerve trunk.

27. _____ involve demyelination or axonal degeneration of multiple peripheral nerves that leads to symmetric sensory, motor, or mixed sensorimotor deficits.

28. The signs and symptoms of a _____ are localized to the area of the body innervated by the nerve roots and include both motor and sensory manifestations.

29. Loss of _____ function can result in total incoordination of these functions even though its loss does not result in paralysis.

30. The _____ are a group of deep, interrelated subcortical nuclei that play an essential role in control of movement.

31. Disorders of the basal ganglia comprise a complex group of motor disturbances characterized by _____ and other involuntary movements, changes in posture and muscle tone, and poverty and slowness of movement.

32. _____ disease is a degenerative disorder of basal ganglia function that results in variable combinations of tremor, rigidity, and bradykinesia.

33. The cardinal manifestations of Parkinson disease are tremor, rigidity, and _____ or slowness of movement.

34. _____ affects motor neurons in three locations: the anterior horn cells of the spinal cord; the motor nuclei of the brain stem, particularly the hypoglossal nuclei; and the UMNs of the cerebral cortex.

35. _____ is characterized by inflammation and selective destruction of CNS myelin.

36. The pathophysiology of multiple sclerosis involves the _____ of nerve fibers in the white matter of the brain, spinal cord, and optic nerve.

37. The most common cause of _____ is motor vehicle accidents, followed by falls, violence (primarily gunshot wounds), and recreational sporting activities.

38. Sudden complete transection of the spinal cord results in complete _____ of motor, sensory, reflex, and autonomic function below the level of injury.

39. _____ is the impairment or loss of motor or sensory function (or both) after damage to neural structures in the cervical segments of the spinal cord.

40. _____ refers to impairment or loss of motor or sensory function (or both) in the thoracic, lumbar, or sacral segments of the spinal cord from damage of neural elements in the spinal canal.

41. Vagal stimulation that causes a marked bradycardia is called the _____ response.

42. _____ hypotension usually occurs in persons with injuries at T4 to T6 and above and is related to the interruption of descending control of sympathetic outflow to blood vessels in the extremities and abdomen.

43. The high risk for _____ in acute spinal cord injury patients is due to immobility, decreased vasomotor tone below the level of injury, and hypercoagulability and stasis of blood flow.

Activity B *Consider the following figure.*

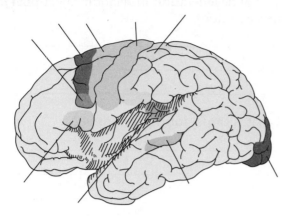

In the figure above, locate and label the following areas of the brain:

- Premotor cortex
- Motor cortex
- Broca area
- Vestibular cortex
- Primary auditory cortex
- Primary visual cortex
- Somatosensory cortex
- Frontal eye fields

Activity C *Match the key terms in Column A with their definitions in Column B.*

1.

Column A

___ 1. Clonus

___ 2. Paralysis

___ 3. Fasciculations

___ 4. Motor homunculus

___ 5. Spasticity

___ 6. Dysdiado-chokinesia

___ 7. Reflex

___ 8. Ataxia

___ 9. Proprioception

___ 10. Paresis

Column B

a. Increased muscle resistance that varies and commonly becomes worse at the extremities of the range of motion

b. Incomplete loss of strength

c. Loss of movement

d. Rhythmic contraction and alternate relaxation of a limb

e. Somatotopic array of the body representing motor areas

f. The failure to accurately perform rapid alternating movements

g. Sense of body movement and position

h. A wide-based unsteady gait

i. Visible squirming and twitching movements of muscle

j. Involuntary motor responses

2.

Column A

___ 1. Bradykinesia

___ 2. Dystonia

___ 3. Chorea

___ 4. Truncal ataxia

___ 5. Myoclonus

___ 6. Parkinsonism

___ 7. Dysmetria

___ 8. Denervation atrophy

___ 9. Constant conjugate readjustment of eye position

___ 10. Tremor

Column B

a. Muscle shrinkage due to loss of neural stimulus

b. Involuntary jerking movement

c. Slowness of movements

d. Rhythmic movements of a particular body part

e. Abnormal simultaneous contractions of agonist and antagonist muscles

f. Abnormal writhing movements

g. Inaccuracies of movements leading to a failure to reach a specified target

h. Nystagmus

i. Unsteadiness of the trunk

j. Syndrome arising from the degenerative changes in basal ganglia function

Activity D

1. In the boxes below, put the following events regarding synaptic transmission in order:

□→□→□→□→□→□

1. Inactivation by acetylcholinesterase
2. Action potential arrives at synaptic terminal
3. Depolarization of motor-end plate
4. Release of acetylcholine into synapse
5. Influx of Ca^{2+}

Activity E *Briefly answer the following.*

1. Describe the basic hierarchy of organization of motor movement.

_____

_____

_____

2. What is the basic unit of motor control? How does it vary between gross motor movement and fine motor movements?

_____

_____

_____

3. What is a muscle spindle and how does it work?

_____

_____

_____

4. What for areas must be integrated in order for muscle movement to be coordinated?

_____

_____

_____

5. Describe the molecular causation of Duchenne muscular dystrophy.

_____

_____

_____

6. Compare segmental demyelination with axonal degeneration in relation to peripheral nerve injuries.

_____

_____

_____

7. What is carpal tunnel syndrome?

_____

_____

_____

8. What are the clinical manifestations of Guillain-Barré syndrome?

_____

_____

_____

9. What is the current theory of the pathogenesis of Parkinson disease?

_____

_____

_____

10. What does amyotrophic lateral sclerosis imply?

_____

_____

_____

11. What are the two pathologic types of spinal chord injury?

_____

_____

_____

SECTION III: APPLYING YOUR KNOWLEDGE

Activity F *Consider the scenario and answer the questions.*

A 27-year-old man is brought into the emergency department after falling out of a tree stand while deer hunting. He is awake and alert and states that he cannot feel or move his legs. An MRI indicates a subluxation of the vertebrae with fractures above and below the subluxation.

1. The man's wife arrives at the emergency department. She asks the nurse what medicine is in the intravenous line and why her husband is receiving it. What would the nurse include in her answer to the wife?

_____

_____

_____

2. The client is transferred to a neurosurgical intensive care unit. As the nurse caring for this client, what orders would you expect to receive?

_____

_____

_____

SECTION IV: PRACTICING FOR NCLEX

Activity G *Answer the following questions.*

1. The spinal cord contains the basic factors necessary to coordinate function when a movement is planned. It is the lowest level of function. What is the highest level of function in planning movement?
   a. Frontal cortex
   b. Cerebral cortex
   c. Pons
   d. Cerebellum

2. Match the neurons with their function/description.

Neuron
1. Motor neurons
2. Motor unit
3. Lower motor neurons
4. Upper motor neurons

Function/Description
a. Motor neuron and the group of muscle fibers it innervates in a muscle
b. Control motor function
c. Project from the motor strip in the cerebral cortex to the ventral horn and are fully contained within the CNS
d. The motor neurons supplying a motor unit are located in the ventral horn of the spinal cord

3. Reflexes are basically "hard-wired" into the CNS. Anatomically, the basis of a reflex is an afferent neuron that synapses directly with an effector neuron that causes muscle movement. Sometimes the afferent neuron synapses with what intermediary between the afferent and effector neurons?
   a. Neurotransmitter
   b. Interneuron
   c. Intersegmental effectors
   d. Suprasegmental effectors

4. The signs and symptoms produced by disorders of the motor system are useful in finding the disorder. What signs and symptoms would you assess when looking for a disorder of the motor system? (Mark all that apply.)
   a. Spinal reflex activity
   b. Bulk
   c. Motor coordination
   d. Muscle innervation
   e. Tone

5. Duchenne muscular dystrophy usually does not produce any signs or symptoms until between the ages of 2 and 3. What muscles are usually first to be affected in Duchenne muscular dystrophy?
   a. Muscles of the upper arms
   b. Large muscles of the legs
   c. Postural muscles of hip and shoulder
   d. Spinal and neck muscles

6. Antibiotics such as gentamicin can produce a disturbance in the body that is similar to botulism by preventing the release of acetylcholine from nerve endings. In persons with pre-existing neuromuscular transmission disturbances these drugs can be dangerous. What disease falls into this category?
   a. Multiple sclerosis
   b. Duchenne muscular dystrophy
   c. Becker muscular dystrophy
   d. Myasthenia gravis

7. In myasthenia gravis, periods of stress can produce myasthenia crisis. When does myasthenia crisis occur?
   a. When muscle weakness becomes severe enough to compromise ventilation
   b. When the client is too weak to hold the head up
   c. When the client is so weak he or she cannot lift the arms
   d. When the client can no longer walk

8. Peripheral nerve disorders are not uncommon. What is an example of a fairly common mononeuropathy?
   a. Guillain-Barré syndrome
   b. Carpal tunnel syndrome
   c. Myasthenia gravis
   d. Phalen syndrome

9. Herniated disks occur when the nucleus pulposus is compressed enough that it protrudes through the annulus fibrosus, putting pressure on the nerve root. This type of injury occurs most often in the cervical and lumbar region of the spine. What is an important diagnostic test for a herniated disk in the lumbar region?
   a. Hip flexion test
   b. CT scan
   c. Straight-leg test
   d. Electromyelography

10. Match the cerebellar pathway with its function.

Cerebellar Pathway	Function
1. Vestibulocerebellar pathway	a. Maintains equilibrium and posture
2. Spinocerebellar pathway	b. Provides the circuitry for coordinating the movements of the distal portions of the limbs
3. Cerebrocerebellar pathway	c. Coordinates sequential body and limb movements.

11. The basal ganglia play a role in coordinated movements. Part of the basal ganglia system is the striatum, which involves local cholinergic interneurons. What disease is thought to be related to the destruction of the cholinergic interneurons?
    a. Parkinson syndrome
    b. Guillain-Barré syndrome
    c. Myasthenia gravis
    d. Huntington disease

12. What disease results from the degeneration of the dopamine nigrostriatal system of the basal ganglia?
    a. Parkinson disease
    b. Huntington disease
    c. Guillain-Barré syndrome
    d. Myasthenia gravis

13. Amyotrophic lateral sclerosis is considered a disease of the upper motor neurons. What is the most common clinical presentation of amyotrophic lateral sclerosis?
    a. Rapidly progressive weakness and atrophy in distal muscles of both upper extremities
    b. Slowly progressive weakness and atrophy in distal muscles of one upper extremity
    c. Rapidly progressive weakness and atrophy in distal muscles of both lower extremities
    d. Slowly progressive weakness and atrophy in distal muscles of one lower extremity

14. While there is no laboratory test that is diagnostic for multiple sclerosis, some patients have alterations in their cerebrospinal fluid (CSF) that can be seen when a portion of the CSF is removed during a spinal tap. What finding in CSF is suggestive of multiple sclerosis?

   a. Decreased immunoglobulin G levels

   b. Decreased total protein levels

   c. Oligoclonal patterns

   d. Decreased lymphocytes

15. At what level of the cervical spine would an injury allow finger flexion?

   a. C5

   b. C6

   c. C7

   d. C8

16. A 14-year-girl has been thrown from the back of a pick-up truck. MRI shows broken vertebrae at the C2 level. What is the main significance of an injury at this level of the spinal column?

   a. Cannot breathe on own, needs ventilator assistance

   b. Partial or full diaphragmatic function; ventilation is diminished because of the loss of intercostal muscle function, resulting in shallow breaths and a weak cough

   c. Intercostal and abdominal musculature is affected; the ability to take a deep breath and cough is less impaired

   d. Needs maintenance therapy to strengthen existing muscles for endurance and mobilization of secretions

17. Approximately 6 months after a spinal cord injury, a 29-year-old man has an episode of autonomic dysreflexia. What are the characteristics of autonomic dysreflexia? (Mark all that apply.)

   a. Hypertension

   b. Fever

   c. Skin pallor

   d. Vasoconstriction

   e. Piloerector response

18. Bowel dysfunction is one of the most difficult problems to deal with after a spinal cord injury. After a spinal cord injury, most people experience constipation. Why does this occur?

   a. Innervation of the bowel is absent

   b. Defecation reflex is lost

   c. Internal anal sphincter will not relax

   d. Peristaltic movements are not strong enough to move stool through the colon

Disorders of Brain Function

SECTION I: LEARNING OBJECTIVES

1. Differentiate cerebral hypoxia from cerebral ischemia and focal from global ischemia.

2. Characterize the role of excitatory amino acids as a common pathway for neurologic disorders.

3. State the determinants of intracranial pressure and describe compensatory mechanisms used to prevent large changes in intracranial pressure when there are changes in brain, blood, and cerebrospinal fluid (CSF) volumes.

4. Explain the causes of tentorial herniation of the brain and its consequences.

5. Compare the causes of communicating and noncommunicating hydrocephalus.

6. Compare cytotoxic, vasogenic, and interstitial cerebral edema.

7. Differentiate primary and secondary brain injuries due to head trauma.

8. Describe the mechanism of brain damage in coup–contrecoup injuries.

9. List the constellation of symptoms involved in the postconcussion syndrome.

10. Differentiate among the location, manifestations, and morbidity of epidural, subdural, and intracerebral hematoma.

11. Define consciousness and trace the rostral-to-caudal progression of consciousness in terms of pupillary changes, respiration, and motor function as the effects of brain dysfunction progress to involve structures in the diencephalon, midbrain, pons, and medulla.

12. List the major vessels in the cerebral circulation and state the contribution of the internal carotid arteries, the vertebral arteries, and the circle of Willis to the cerebral circulation.

13. Describe the autoregulation of cerebral blood flow.

14. Explain the substitution of "brain attack" for stroke in terms of making a case for early diagnosis and treatment.

15. Differentiate the pathologies of ischemic and hemorrhagic stroke.

16. Explain the significance of transient ischemic attacks, the ischemic penumbra, and watershed zones of infarction and how these conditions relate to ischemic stroke.

17. Cite the most common cause of subarachnoid hemorrhage and state the complications associated with subarachnoid hemorrhage.

18. Describe the alterations in cerebral vasculature that occur with arteriovenous malformations.

19. Describe the patterns of motor deficits and typical problems with speech and language that occur as a result of stroke.

20. List the sequence of events that occur with meningitis.

21. Describe the symptoms of encephalitis.

22. List the major categories of brain tumors and interpret the meaning of benign and malignant as related to brain tumors.

23. Describe the general manifestations of brain tumors.

24. List the methods used in diagnosis and treatment of brain tumors.

25. Explain the difference between a seizure and epilepsy.

26. State four or more causes of seizures other than epilepsy.

27. Differentiate between the origin of seizure activity in partial and generalized forms of epilepsy and compare the manifestations of simple partial seizures with those of complex partial seizures and major and minor motor seizures.

28. Characterize status epilepticus.

SECTION II: ASSESSING YOUR UNDERSTANDING

Activity A *Fill in the blanks.*

1. A number of regulatory mechanisms, including the blood-brain barrier and autoregulatory mechanisms that ensure its blood supply, maintains the _____ electrically active cells.

2. Although the brain makes up only 2% of the body weight, it receives 15% of the resting cardiac output and accounts for _____% of the oxygen consumption.

3. Because _____ indicates decreased oxygen levels in all brain tissue, it produces a generalized depressant effect on the brain.

4. Cerebral ischemia can be_____, as in stroke, or _____, as in cardiac arrest.

5. Excessive influx of _____ during neural ischemia results in neuronal and interstitial edema.

6. _____ refers to short serpiginous segments of necrosis that occur within and parallel to the cerebral cortex, in areas supplied by the penetrating arteries during an ischemic event.

7. In many neurologic disorders, various mediators including excitatory _____, catecholamines, nitric oxide, free radicals, inflammatory cells, apoptosis, and intracellular _____ may cause injury to neurons.

8. Increased _____ pressure is a common pathway for brain injury from different types of insults and agents.

9. Brain _____ represents a displacement of brain tissue under the falx cerebri or through the tentorial notch or incisura of the tentorium cerebelli.

10. Cerebral _____ is an increase in tissue volume secondary to abnormal fluid accumulation.

11. The functional manifestations of _____ edema include focal neurologic deficits, disturbances in consciousness, and severe intracranial hypertension.

12. _____ edema involves an increase in intracellular fluid.

13. The effects of traumatic head injuries can be divided into two categories: _____ injuries, in which damage is caused by impact; and secondary injuries, in which damage results from the subsequent brain swelling, infection, or _____.

14. _____ usually are caused by head injury in which the skull is fractured.

15. A subdural hematoma develops in the area between the dura and the arachnoid and usually is the result of a _____ in the small bridging veins that connect veins on the surface of the cortex to dural sinuses.

16. _____ is the state of awareness of self and the environment and of being able to become oriented to new stimuli.

17. Brain death is defined as the irreversible loss of function of the _____, including the brain stem.

18. The _____ state is characterized by loss of all cognitive functions and the unawareness of self and surroundings.

19. Cerebral _____ has been classically defined as the ability of the brain to maintain constant cerebral blood flow despite changes in systemic arterial pressure.

20. At least three metabolic factors affect cerebral blood flow: _____, _____, and _____ concentration.

21. _____ is the syndrome of acute focal neurologic deficit from a vascular disorder that injures brain tissue.

22. _____ strokes are caused by an interruption of blood flow in a cerebral vessel, and _____ strokes are caused by bleeding into brain tissue.

23. TIA or "_____" is equivalent to "brain angina" and reflects a temporary disturbance in focal cerebral blood flow, which reverses before infarction occurs, analogous to _____ in relation to heart attack.

24. _____ are the most common cause of ischemic strokes, usually occurring in atherosclerotic blood vessels.

25. _____ infarcts result from occlusion of the smaller penetrating branches of large cerebral arteries, commonly the middle cerebral and posterior cerebral arteries.

26. An _____ stroke is caused by a moving blood clot that travels from its origin to the brain.

27. The most frequently fatal stroke is a spontaneous _____ into the brain.

28. The specific manifestations of stroke or TIA are determined by the _____ that is affected, by the area of brain tissue that is supplied by that vessel, and by the adequacy of the collateral circulation.

29. Aneurysmal subarachnoid hemorrhage represents bleeding into the subarachnoid space caused by a ruptured _____.

30. _____ malformations are a complex tangle of abnormal arteries and veins linked by one or more fistulas.

31. _____ represents a generalized infection of the parenchyma of the brain or spinal cord.

32. _____ occurs with or without nausea, may be projectile, and is a common symptom of increased intracranial pressure (ICP) and brain stem compression.

33. The use of _____ for brain tumors is somewhat limited by the blood-brain barrier.

34. A _____ represents the abnormal behavior caused by an electrical discharge from neurons in the cerebral cortex.

35. _____ seizures usually involve only one hemisphere and are not accompanied by loss of consciousness or responsiveness.

36. _____ seizures involve impairment of consciousness and often arise from the temporal lobe.

37. Myoclonic seizures involve brief involuntary _____ induced by stimuli of cerebral origin.

38. _____ seizures usually present with a person having a vague warning and experience a sharp tonic contraction of the muscles with extension of the extremities and immediate loss of consciousness.

39. Seizures that do not stop spontaneously or occur in succession without recovery are called _____.

Activity B *Consider the following figure.*

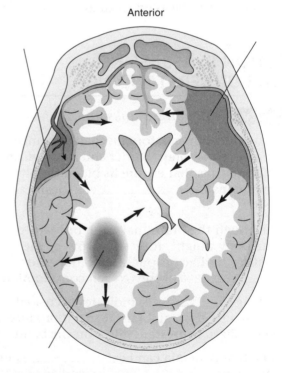

Anterior

Posterior

In the figure above, identify the subdural hematoma, the epidural hematoma, and the intracerebral hematoma.

Activity C *Match the key terms in Column A with their definitions in Column B.*

Column A

____ **1.** Vasogenic edema

____ **2.** Hypoxia

____ **3.** Tentorium cerebelli

____ **4.** Hydrocephalus

____ **5.** Aphasia

____ **6.** Microneurons

____ **7.** Ischemia

____ **8.** Decorticate posturing

____ **9.** Hemineglect

____ **10.** Macroneurons

Column B

a. To attend to and react to stimuli coming from the contralateral side

b. Inability to comprehend, integrate, and express language

c. Small cells intimately involved in local circuitry

d. Divides the cranial cavity into anterior and posterior fossae

e. Reduced or interrupted blood flow

f. Occurs when integrity of the blood-brain barrier is disrupted

g. Deprivation of oxygen with maintained blood flow

h. Results from lesions of the cerebral hemisphere

i. Large cells with long axons that leave the local network of intercommunicating neurons to send action potentials to other regions of the nervous system

j. Abnormal increase in CSF volume in any part or all of the ventricular system

Activity D

1. Write the correct sequence in the boxes provided below.

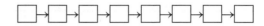

Put the pathologic process of bacterial meningitis in order:

1. Release endotoxins
2. Development of a cloudy, purulent exudate in CSF
3. Endotoxins initiate inflammatory response
4. Meninges thicken and adhesions form
5. Bacteria replicate and undergo lysis in CSF
6. Vascular congestion and infarction in the surrounding tissues
7. Pathogens, neutrophils, and albumin to move across the capillary wall into the CSF
8. Adhesions may impinge on the cranial nerves or may impair the outflow of CSF

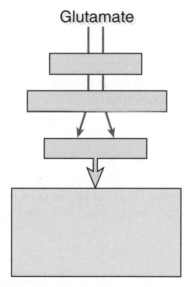

2. Complete the flowchart above using the following terms:

- Release of intracellular proteases, free radicals, and fragmentation of nuclei
- Calcium cascade
- Opening calcium channels
- NMDA receptor activation

Activity E *Briefly answer the following.*

1. What does "global ischemia" refer to and what is the result?

_____

_____

_____

2. Explain what watershed infarcts are and why they occur.

_____

_____

_____

3. What is the mechanism of toxicity of excito-toxic amino acids?

_____

_____

_____

4. What is postconcussion syndrome?

_____

_____

_____

5. Compare the general manifestations of global and focal brain injury.

_____

_____

_____

6. What are the two components of consciousness? What are the signs of altered consciousness?

_____

_____

_____

7. How are pupillary reflexes used to evaluate levels of brain function?

_____

_____

_____

8. What is the ischemic penumbra of an ischemic stroke and how does it affect the amount of irreversible damage?

_____

_____

_____

9. Why do arteriovenous malformations predispose a patient to stroke?

_____

_____

_____

10. What are some of the possible causes of a seizure?

_____

_____

_____

SECTION III: APPLYING YOUR KNOWLEDGE

Activity F *Consider the scenario and answer the questions.*

Case Study: A 78-year-old African American woman is brought to the emergency department by ambulance. She was found on the floor of her bedroom by her daughter in a confused state, and she could not move her left leg. A diagnosis of stroke is suspected.

a. When taking the nursing history, what risk factors would the nurse assess for?

_____

_____

_____

b. The diagnosis of ischemic stroke is confirmed. What orders would the nurse expect to receive from the physician for acute ischemic stroke?

_____

_____

_____

SECTION IV: PRACTICING FOR NCLEX

Activity G *Answer the following questions.*

1. Match the type of brain insult to its definition.

Type	Definition
1. Hypoxic	**a.** Excessive activity of the excitatory neurotransmitters and their receptor-mediated effects.
2. Ischemic	
3. Excitotoxic	
4. Increased intercranial volume and pressure	**b.** Displacement of brain tissue under the falx cerebri or through the tentorial notch or incisura of the tentorium cerebelli
5. Brain herniation	
6. Cerebral edema	**c.** Interferes with delivery of oxygen and glucose as well as the removal of metabolic wastes
7. Hydrocephalus	
	d. An abnormal increase in CSF volume in any part or all of the ventricular system
	e. Swelling of the brain
	f. Increase in intercranial tissue causing an increase in ICP
	g. Decreased oxygen levels in all brain tissue

2. Match the type of brain insult to its effect on the brain

Type	Effect on Brain
1. Brain herniation	**a.** Can be focal or global with only one part of the brain being under perfused or all of the brain being compromised
2. Hypoxic	
3. Ischemic	
4. Increased intercranial volume and pressure	**b.** Neuronal cell injury and death
5. Excitotoxic	**c.** Clouding of consciousness, bilaterally small pupils (approximately 2 mm in diameter) with a full range of constriction, and motor responses to pain that are purposeful or semipurposeful (localizing) and often asymmetric
6. Hydrocephalus	
7. Cerebral edema	
	d. Depends on the brain's compensatory mechanisms and the extent of the swelling
	e. Generalized depressant effect on the brain
	f. Cerebral hemispheres become enlarged, and the ventricular system beyond the point of obstruction is dilated. The sulci on the surface of the brain become effaced and shallowed, and the white matter is reduced in volume.
	g. Tissue perfusion becomes inadequate, cellular hypoxia results, and neuronal death may occur.

3. There are several types of brain injuries that can occur. What are the primary (or direct) brain injuries? (Mark all that apply.)

   a. Focal lesions of laceration

   b. Contusion

   c. Hypoxic

   d. Diffuse axonal

   e. Hemorrhage

4. Global and focal brain injuries manifest differently. What is almost always a manifestation of a global brain injury?
   a. Altered level of consciousness
   b. Change in behavior
   c. Respiratory instability
   d. Loss of eye movement reflexes

5. You are the nurse caring for a 31-year-old trauma victim is admitted to the neurologic intensive care unit. While doing your initial assessment you find that the client is flexing the arms, wrists and fingers. There is abduction of the upper extremities with internal rotation and plantar flexion of the lower extremities. How would you describe this in your nursing notes?
   a. Decerebrate posturing
   b. Decorticate posturing
   c. Extensor posturing
   d. Diencephalon posturing

6. *Brain death* is the term that is used when the loss of function of the entire brain is irreversible. A clinical examination must be done and repeated at least 6 hours later with the same findings for brain death to be declared. What is not assessed in the clinical examination for brain death?
   a. Blink reflex
   b. Responsiveness
   c. Electrocardiogram
   d. Respiratory effort

7. Much like brain death, there are criteria for the diagnosis of a persistent vegetative state, and the criteria have to have lasted for more than 1 month. What are criteria for the diagnosis of persistent vegetative state? (Mark all that apply.)
   a. Bowel and bladder incontinence
   b. Ability to open the eyes
   c. Lack of language comprehension
   d. Lack of enough hypothalamic function to maintain life
   e. Variable preserved cranial nerve reflexes

8. The regulation of cerebral blood flow is accomplished through both autoregulation and local regulation. This allows for the brain to meet its metabolic needs. What is the low parameter for blood pressure before cerebral blood flow becomes severely compromised?
   a. 30 mm Hg
   b. 40 mm Hg
   c. 50 mm Hg
   d. 60 mm Hg

9. Intracranial aneurysms that rupture cause subarachnoid hemorrhage in the client. How is the diagnosis of intracranial aneurysms and subarachnoid hemorrhage made?
   a. Lumbar puncture
   b. MRI
   c. Loss of cranial nerve reflexes
   d. Venography

10. When the suspected diagnosis is bacterial meningitis, what assessment techniques can assist in determining of meningeal irritation is present?
    a. Kernig sign and Chadwick sign
    b. Brudzinski sign and Kernig sign
    c. Brudzinski sign and Chadwick sign
    d. Chvostek's sign and Guedel sign

11. Manifestations of brain tumors are focal disturbances in brain function and increased ICP. What causes the focal disturbances manifested by brain tumors?
    a. Tumor infiltration and increased blood pressure
    b. Brain compression and decreased ICP
    c. Brain edema and disturbances in blood flow
    d. Tumor infiltration and decreased ICP

12. Match the type of seizure with its definition.

Type of Seizure

1. Unprovoked
2. Complex partial seizures
3. Generalized-onset
4. Absence seizures
5. Atonic
6. Tonic-clonic

Definition

a. Motion takes the form of automatisms such as lip smacking, mild clonic motion (usually in the eyelids), increased or decreased postural tone, and autonomic phenomena

b. These seizures also are known as *drop attacks*

c. Most common major motor seizure

d. Clinical signs, symptoms, and supporting electroencephalogram changes indicate involvement of both hemispheres at onset

e. Begins in a localized area of the brain but may progress rapidly to involve both hemispheres

f. No identifiable cause can be determined

13. For seizure disorders that do not respond to anticonvulsant medications, the option for surgical treatment exists. What is removed in the most common surgery for seizure disorders?

a. Temporal neocortex
b. Hippocampus
c. Entorhinal cortex
d. Amygdala

14. Generalized convulsive status epilepticus is a medical emergency caused by a tonic-clonic seizure that does not spontaneously end, or recurs in succession without recovery. What is the first-line drug of choice to treat status epilepticus?

a. Intravenous diazepam
b. Intramuscular lorazepam
c. Intravenous cyclobenzaprine
d. Intramuscular cyproheptadine

CHAPTER 38

Disorders of Special Sensory Function: Vision, Hearing, and Vestibular Function

SECTION I: LEARNING OBJECTIVES

1. Compare symptoms associated with red eye caused by conjunctivitis, corneal irritation, and acute glaucoma.

2. Describe the appearance of corneal edema.

3. Characterize the manifestations, treatment, and possible complications of bacterial, *Acanthamoeba*, and herpes keratitis.

4. Describe tests used in assessing the pupillary reflex and cite the possible causes of abnormal pupillary reflexes.

5. Describe the formation and outflow of aqueous humor from the eye and relate to the development of glaucoma.

6. Compare open-angle and angle-closure glaucoma in terms of pathology, symptomatology, and diagnosis and treatment.

7. Explain why glaucoma leads to blindness.

8. Describe changes in eye structure that occur with nearsighted and farsighted vision.

9. Describe the changes in lens structure that occur with cataract.

10. Cite risk factors and visual changes associated with cataract.

11. Describe the treatment of persons with cataracts.

12. Relate the phagocytic function of the retinal pigment epithelium to the development of retinitis pigmentosa.

13. Cite the manifestations and long-term visual effects of papilledema.

14. Describe the pathogenesis of background and proliferative diabetic retinopathies and their mechanisms of visual impairment.

15. Relate the role of posterior vitreous detachment to the development of retinal tears and detachment.

16. Explain the pathology and visual changes associated with macular degeneration.

17. Characterize what is meant by a *visual field defect*.

18. Explain the use of perimetry in the diagnosis of a visual field defect.

19. Define the terms *hemianopia, quadrantanopia, heteronymous hemianopia,* and *homonymous hemianopia* and relate them to disorders of the optic pathways.

20. Describe visual defects associated with disorders of the visual cortex and visual association areas.

21. Describe the function and innervation of the extraocular muscles.

22. Explain the difference between paralytic and nonparalytic strabismus.

23. Define *amblyopia* and explain its pathogenesis.

24. Explain the need for early diagnosis and treatment of eye movement disorders in children.

25. List the structures of the external, middle, and inner ear and cite their function.

26. Describe two common disorders of the outer ear.

27. Relate the functions of the eustachian tube to the development of middle ear problems, including acute otitis media and otitis media with effusion.

28. Describe anatomic variations as well as risk factors that make infants and young children more prone to develop acute otitis media.

29. List three common symptoms of acute otitis media.

30. Describe the disease process associated with otosclerosis and relate it to the progressive conductive hearing loss that occurs.

31. Characterize tinnitus.

32. Differentiate between conductive, sensorineural, and mixed hearing loss and cite the more common causes of each.

33. Describe methods used in the diagnosis and treatment of hearing loss.

34. Characterize the causes of hearing loss in infants and children and describe the need for early diagnosis and treatment.

35. Explain the function of the vestibular system with respect to postural reflexes and maintaining a stable visual field despite marked changes in head position.

36. Relate the function of the vestibular system to nystagmus and vertigo.

37. Differentiate the structures of peripheral and central vestibular function.

38. Characterize the physiologic cause of motion sickness.

39. Compare the manifestations and pathologic processes associated with benign positional vertigo and Ménière disease.

40. Differentiate the manifestations of peripheral and central vestibular disorders.

SECTION II: ASSESSING YOUR UNDERSTANDING

Activity A *Fill in the blanks.*

1. The optic globe, commonly called the _____, is a remarkably mobile, nearly spherical structure contained in a pyramid-shaped cavity of the skull called the orbit.

2. The outer layer of the eyeball consists of a tough, opaque, white, fibrous layer called the _____.

3. Two striated muscles, the _____ and the _____, provide for movement of the eyelids.

4. Symptoms of _____ are a foreign body sensation, a scratching or burning sensation, itching, and photophobia.

5. _____ conjunctivitis is a severe, sight-threatening ocular infection.

6. The _____ is avascular and obtains its nutrient and oxygen supply by diffusion from blood vessels of the adjacent sclera, from the aqueous humor at its deep surface, and from tears.

7. _____ refers to inflammation of the cornea caused by infections, misuse of contact lenses, hypersensitivity reactions, ischemia, trauma, defects in tearing, and interruption in sensory innervation, as occurs with local anesthesia.

8. Herpes simplex virus _____ with stromal scarring is the most common cause of corneal ulceration and blindness in the Western world.

9. Herpes zoster _____ usually presents with malaise, fever, headache, and burning and itching of the periorbital area.

10. The _____ is an adjustable diaphragm that permits changes in pupil size and in the light entering the eye.

11. Inflammation of the entire uveal tract, which supports the lens and neural components of the eye, is called _____.

12. With diffuse damage to the forebrain involving the thalamus and hypothalamus, the _____ are typically small but respond to light.

13. _____ includes a group of conditions that produce an elevation in intraocular pressure.

14. In persons with glaucoma, temporary or permanent impairment of vision results from _____ changes in the retina and optic nerve and from corneal edema and opacification.

15. _____ glaucoma is caused by a disorder in which the anterior chamber retains its fetal configuration, with aberrant trabecular meshwork extending to the root of the iris, or is covered by a membrane.

16. Nonuniform curvature of the refractive medium comparing the horizontal and vertical planes is called _____.

17. _____ is neurologically associated with convergence of the eyes, pupillary constriction, and results from thickening of the lens through contraction of the ciliary muscle.

18. A _____ is a lens opacity that interferes with the transmission of light to the retina.

19. The function of the _____ is to receive visual images, partially analyze them, and transmit this modified information to the brain.

20. The genetically _____ person has never experienced the full range of normal color vision and is unaware of what he or she is missing.

21. _____ represents a group of hereditary diseases that cause slow degenerative changes in the retinal photoreceptors.

22. _____ degeneration is characterized by degenerative changes in the central portion of the retina that results primarily in loss of central vision.

23. The _____ refers to the area that is visible during fixation of vision in one direction.

24. Three pairs of extraocular muscles—the superior and _____, the medial, and _____, and the superior and inferior _____ control the movement of each eye.

25. _____ movements are those in which the optical axes of the two eyes are kept parallel, sharing the same visual field.

26. _____ refers to any abnormality of eye coordination or alignment that results in loss of binocular vision.

27. _____ describes a decrease in visual acuity resulting from abnormal visual development in infancy or early childhood.

28. The external _____ consists of the auricle, which collects sound, and external acoustic meatus or ear canal, which conducts the sound to the tympanic membrane.

29. Impacted _____ usually produces no symptoms unless it hardens and touches the tympanic membrane, or the canal becomes irritated resulting in symptoms of pain, itching, and a sensation of fullness.

30. _____ is an inflammation of the external ear that can vary in severity from mild allergic dermatitis to severe cellulitis.

31. The tympanic cavity is a small, mucosa-lined cavity within the petrous portion of the _____ bone.

32. The _____ tube, which connects the nasopharynx with the middle ear, is located in a gap in the bone between the anterior and medial walls of the middle ear.

33. The _____ eustachian tube does not close or does not close completely.

34. _____ refers to inflammation of the middle ear without reference to etiology or pathogenesis.

35. _____ is characterized by acute onset of otalgia (or pulling of the ears in an infant), fever, and hearing loss.

36. _____ refers to the formation of new spongy bone around the stapes and oval window, which results in progressive deafness.

37. The spiral canal of the _____, which is shaped like a snail shell, begins at the vestibule and winds around a central core of spongy bone called the modiolus.

38. _____ hearing loss occurs with disorders that affect the inner ear, auditory nerve, or auditory pathways of the brain.

39. Deafness or some degree of hearing impairment is the most common serious complication of _____ in infants and children.

40. Acoustic neuromas are benign Schwann cell tumors affecting _____.

41. The most common infectious cause of congenital sensorineural hearing loss is _____.

42. The _____ system maintains and assists recovery of stable body and head position through control of postural reflexes, and it maintains a stable visual field despite marked changes in head position.

43. Disorders of vestibular function are characterized by a condition called _____, in which an illusion of motion occurs.

44. _____ is a form of normal physiologic vertigo, caused by repeated rhythmic stimulation of the vestibular system, and such as is encountered in car, air, or boat travel.

45. Benign _____ vertigo is the most common cause of pathologic vertigo.

46. Acute _____ is characterized by an acute onset (usually hours) of vertigo, nausea, and vomiting lasting several days and not associated with auditory or other neurologic manifestations.

47. _____ disease is a disorder of the inner ear due to distention of the endolymphatic compartment of the inner ear, causing a triad of hearing loss, vertigo, and tinnitus.

48. Abnormal nystagmus and vertigo can occur as a result of CNS lesions involving the _____ and lower brain stem.

Activity B *Consider the following figures.*

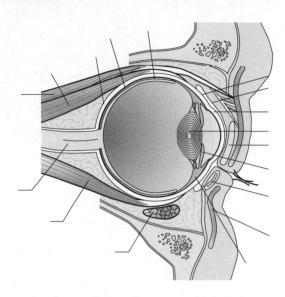

1. In the figure above, locate and label the following structures:
   - Conjunctiva
   - Cornea
   - Lens
   - Iris
   - Meibomian gland
   - Orbicularis oculi muscle
   - Inferior oblique muscle
   - Inferior rectus
   - Superior rectus
   - Levator palpebrae superioris
   - Choroid
   - Retina
   - Superior tarsal plate
   - Ciliary body
   - Sclera
   - Optic nerve

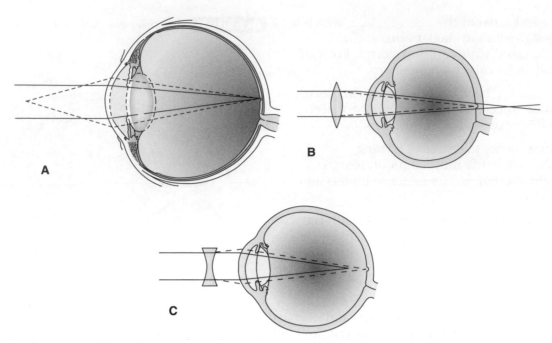

2. In the figure above, which eye represents myopia? Which eye represents hyperopia? Which eye represents normal focal length?

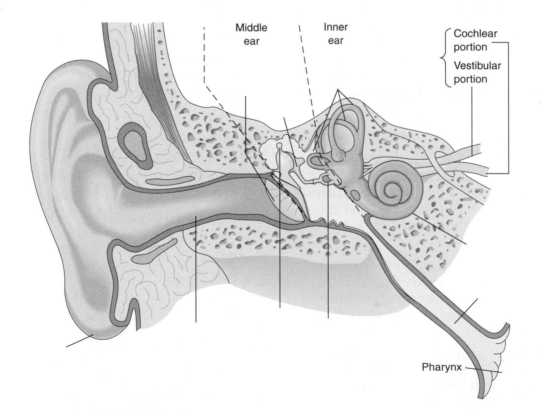

3. In the figure above, locate and label the following structures:

- Auricle
- External acoustic meatus
- Malleus
- Stapes
- Eustachian tube
- Cochlea

- Cranial nerve VIII
- Tympanic membrane
- Incus
- Semicircular canals

Activity C *Match the key terms in Column A with their definitions in Column B.*

1.

Column A

_____ **1.** Arcus senilis

_____ **2.** Entropion

_____ **3.** Ophthalmia neonatorum

_____ **4.** Hordeolum

_____ **5.** Pink eye

_____ **6.** Chalazion

_____ **7.** Ptosis

_____ **8.** Dacryocystitis

_____ **9.** Ectropion

_____ **10.** Sjögren syndrome

Column B

a. Caused by infection of the sebaceous glands

b. An infection of the lacrimal sac

c. Chronic inflammatory granuloma of a meibomian gland

d. Drooping of the eyelid

e. Extracellular lipid infiltration of the cornea

f. Turning in of the lid margin

g. Conjunctivitis that occurs in newborns and is related to sexually transmitted diseases

h. Diminished salivary and lacrimal secretions, resulting in keratoconjunctivitis sicca and xerostomia

i. Eversion of the lower lid margin

j. Inflammation of the conjunctiva

2.

Column A

_____ **1.** Anopia

_____ **2.** Hyperopia

_____ **3.** Cycloplegia

_____ **4.** Scotoma

_____ **5.** Rhegmatogenous detachment

_____ **6.** Tonometry

_____ **7.** Presbyopia

_____ **8.** Myopia

_____ **9.** Direct pupillary light reflex

_____ **10.** Papilledema

Column B

a. The vitreous shrinks and partly separates from the retinal surface

b. A hole in the visual field

c. Anterior-posterior dimension of the eyeball is too short

d. Anterior-posterior dimension of the eyeball is too long

e. Measurement of intraocular pressure

f. Blindness in one eye

g. Paralysis of the ciliary muscle, with loss of accommodation

h. Leakage of fluid results in edema of the optic papilla

i. Rapid constriction of the pupil exposed to light

j. Decrease in accommodation that occurs because of aging

3.

Column A

—— **1.** Otitis media with effusion

—— **2.** Cerumen

—— **3.** Tinnitus

—— **4.** *Streptococcus pneumoniae*

—— **5.** Electrony-stagmography

—— **6.** Presbycusis

—— **7.** Nystagmus

—— **8.** Barotrauma

—— **9.** Cholesteatomas

—— **10.** Frequency

Column B

a. Degenerative hearing loss that occurs with advancing age

b. Cystlike lesions of the middle ear

c. Most common cause of bacterial meningitis that results in sensorineural hearing loss after the neonatal period

d. Injury resulting from the inability to equalize middle ear with ambient pressures

e. Ringing of the ears; it may also assume a hissing, roaring, buzzing, or humming sound

f. Number of waves per unit time

g. Involuntary rhythmic and oscillatory eye movements that preserve eye fixation on stable objects in the visual field during angular and rotational movements of the head

h. Earwax

i. Examination that records eye movements in response to vestibular, visual, cervical, rotational, and positional stimulation.

j. Presence of fluid in the middle ear without signs and symptoms of acute ear infection

Activity D *Briefly answer the following.*

1. Where are tears formed and what purpose(s) do they serve?

——————————————————————

——————————————————————

——————————————————————

2. What is the most common cause of chronic bacterial conjunctivitis and what are the symptoms?

——————————————————————

——————————————————————

——————————————————————

3. How do the different levels of abrasion trauma (less severe to more severe) affect the cornea and how fast to the abrasions heal?

——————————————————————

——————————————————————

——————————————————————

4. What is the mechanism of a primary herpes simplex virus optical epithelial infection?

——————————————————————

——————————————————————

——————————————————————

5. What is the cause of acanthamoeba keratitis and what are the primary symptoms?

——————————————————————

——————————————————————

——————————————————————

6. Explain how the pupil is able to change shape.

——————————————————————

——————————————————————

——————————————————————

7. What is glaucoma? What is primary and secondary glaucoma?

——————————————————————

——————————————————————

——————————————————————

8. What is presbyopia and how does it affect vision?

_____

_____

_____

9. Retinal hemorrhage can occur at many layers. What are the types of retinal bleeding and where do they occur?

_____

_____

_____

10. Why is proliferative diabetic retinopathy a major concern for all diabetic patients?

_____

_____

_____

11. What is the relationship between hypertension and the development of a retinopathy?

_____

_____

_____

12. What is/are the functions of the eustachian tube?

_____

_____

_____

13. What are the complications associated with otitis media?

_____

_____

_____

14. How does otosclerosis lead to progressive deafness?

_____

_____

_____

15. What are the purported causes of subjective tinnitus?

_____

_____

_____

16. What is the cause of hearing loss in conductive hearing loss?

_____

_____

_____

17. How does the vestibular system inform the brain about head and body position?

_____

_____

_____

18. What is the test used to determine vestibular function in an unconscious patient?

_____

_____

_____

SECTION III: APPLYING YOUR KNOWLEDGE

Activity E *Consider the scenario and answer the questions.*

1. **Case study:** The mother of an 18-month-old girl brings her daughter to the clinic for a well-baby check. During the physical examination, the physician notices that the client has a white reflex in her left eye. He suspects retinoblastoma.

   a. What diagnostic measures would the nurse expect the doctor to order?

   _____

   _____

   _____

b. Retinoblastoma is confirmed and a treatment plan is being made. What are the treatment options for retinoblastoma?

_____

_____

_____

2. **Case study:** You are the nurse preparing an educational event for the local junior league, which has asked you to speak on hearing loss and deafness. One of the subjects that you will address is ototoxicity.

a. What drugs would you include when talking about ototoxicity?

_____

_____

_____

SECTION IV: PRACTICING FOR NCLEX

Activity F *Answer the following questions.*

1. Dacryocystitis is an infection in the lacrimal sac. What symptoms indicate dacryocystitis?
   a. Purulent discharge
   b. Swelling
   c. Inflamed conjunctiva
   d. Lack of tears

2. Ophthalmia neonatorum is a conjunctivitis that develops in newborns. It is caused by the agents that cause sexually transmitted diseases. When should ophthalmia neonatorum be suspected?
   a. When a conjunctivitis develops 24 hours after birth
   b. When a conjunctivitis develops 12 hours after birth
   c. When a conjunctivitis develops 48 hours after birth
   d. When a conjunctivitis develops 36 hours after birth

3. Keratitis can be caused by different infectious agents. What is the treatment goal with herpes simplex virus keratitis?
   a. Minimizing pain
   b. Cure for the disease
   c. Eliminating viral replication within the cornea
   d. Minimizing spread of virus to other parts of the eye

4. Corneal transplants are done everyday in hospitals around the world. All of these transplanted corneas come from cadavers. Why do corneal transplants have such a low rejection rate? (Mark all that apply.)
   a. Cornea is very vascular
   b. Antigen-presenting cells are not present in great numbers
   c. The cornea secretes immunosuppressive factors
   d. The cornea has no lymphatics
   e. Corneal cells secrete substances that protect against keratitis

5. Pharmacologic agents can affect dilation of the pupil and the papillary response. What types of drugs produce papillary constriction?
   a. Sympathomimetic agents
   b. Antihistamine agents
   c. Cycloplegic agents
   d. Miotic agents

6. In open-angle glaucoma, there is an increased pressure within the globe of the eye without obstruction at the iridocorneal angle. Usually, this is caused by an abnormality in the trabecular meshwork, which controls the flow or aqueous humor. Where is aqueous humor in a normal eye?
   a. Canal of Schlemm
   b. Ocular canal
   c. Ductus lacrimalis
   d. Behind the pupil

7. Match the terms with their definitions.

Term

1. Presbyopia
2. Cycloplegia
3. Myopia
4. Hyperopia
5. Astigmatism

Definition

a. The anterior-posterior dimension of the eyeball is too long; the focus point for an infinitely distant target is anterior to the retina

b. Paralysis of the ciliary muscle, with loss of accommodation

c. The anterior-posterior dimension of the eyeball is too short; the image is theoretically focused posterior to (behind) the retina

d. Range of focus or accommodation is diminished

e. An asymmetric bowing of the cornea

8. Age-related cataracts are characterized by what?
   a. Everything looking grey
   b. Visual distortion
   c. Narrowing visual field
   d. Blind spots in visual field

9. Vitreous humor occupies the posterior portion of the eyeball. It is an amorphous biologic gel. When liquefaction of the gel occurs, as in aging, what can be seen during head movement?
   a. Blind spots
   b. Meshlike structures
   c. Floaters
   d. Red spots

10. When conditions occur that impair retinal blood flow, such as hyperviscosity of the blood or a sickle cell crisis, what can occur in the eye?
    a. Microaneurysms
    b. Hypertensive retinopathy
    c. Microinfarcts
    d. Neovascularization

11. Age-related macular degeneration that is dry is characterized by what?
    a. Atrophy of the Bruch membrane
    b. Leakage of serous or hemorrhagic fluid
    c. New blood vessels in the eye
    d. Formation of a choroidal neovascular membrane

12. Cortical blindness is the bilateral loss of the primary visual cortex. What is retained in cortical blindness?
    a. Red spots seen behind the eyelids
    b. Pupillary reflexes
    c. Ptosis
    d. Myopia

13. Adult strabismus is almost always of the paralytic variety. What is a cause of adult strabismus?
    a. Huntington disease
    b. Parkinson disease
    c. Graves disease
    d. Addison disease

14. Amblyopia, or lazy eye, occurs at a time when visual deprivation or abnormal binocular interactions occur in visual infancy. Whether or not amblyopia is reversible depends on what?
    a. The child has to be older than 5
    b. The maturity of the visual system at time of onset
    c. The child has to have bilateral congenital cataracts
    d. The child has to be able to wear contact lenses

15. Otitis externa is an inflammation of the outer ear. What fungi cause otitis externa?
    a. *Aspergillus*
    b. *Pseudomonas aeruginosa*
    c. *Staphylococcus aureus*
    d. *Escherichia coli*

16. The eustachian tube connects the nasopharynx and the middle ear. In infants and children with abnormally patent tubes, what are let into the eustachian tube when the infant or child cries or blows the nose?
    a. Air and cerumen
    b. Air and secretions
    c. Secretions and saliva
    d. Cerumen and saliva

17. Acute otitis media is the disorder in children for which antibiotics are most prescribed. What are the risk factors for acute otitis media? (Mark all that apply.)
    a. Ethnicity
    b. Premature birth
    c. Only child in household
    d. Genetic syndromes
    e. Female gender

18. Otosclerosis is a condition in which spongy, pathologic bone grows around the stapes and oval window. It can be treated either medically or surgically. What is the surgical treatment for otosclerosis?
    a. Otosclerotomy
    b. Ovalectomy
    c. Stapedectomy
    d. Amplification surgery

19. What separates the scala vestibule and the scala media?
    a. Corti membrane
    b. Tympani membrane
    c. Modiolus membrane
    d. Reissner membrane

20. Objective tinnitus is tinnitus that someone else can hear. What does the tinnitus that is caused by vascular disorders sound like?
    a. Pulses
    b. Rings
    c. Hums
    d. Roars

21. Conductive hearing loss can occur for a variety of reasons, including foreign bodies in the ear canal, damage to the ear drum, or disease. What disease is associated with conductive hearing loss?
    a. Huntington disease
    b. Paget disease
    c. Alzheimer disease
    d. Parkinson disease

22. Tumors affecting cranial nerve VIII are acoustic neuromas. What are these tumors of?
    a. Inner ear
    b. Organ of Corti
    c. Schwann cells
    d. Labyrinth

23. It is important to differentiate between the kinds of hearing loss so they can be appropriately treated. What is used to test between conductive and sensorineural hearing loss?
    a. Audioscope
    b. Audiometer
    c. Tone analysis
    d. Tuning fork

24. Hearing loss in children can be either conductive or sensorineural, as it is in adults. What is the major cause of sensorineural hearing loss in children?
    a. Genetic causes
    b. Acute otitis media
    c. Paget disease
    d. Ototoxicity

25. Presbycusis is degenerative hearing loss associated with aging. What is the first symptom of this disorder?
    a. Inability to localize sounds
    b. Reduction in ability to understand speech
    c. Inability to detect sound
    d. Reduction in ability to identify sounds

CHAPTER 39

Disorders of the Male Genitourinary System

SECTION I: LEARNING OBJECTIVES

1. State the difference between hypospadias and epispadias.

2. Cite the significance of phimosis.

3. Describe the anatomic changes that occur with Peyronie disease.

4. Explain the physiology of penile erection and relate it to erectile dysfunction and priapism.

5. Describe the appearance of balanitis xerotica obliterans.

6. List the signs of penile cancer.

7. State the physical manifestations and potential risks associated with uncorrected cryptorchidism.

8. Compare the cause, appearance, and significance of hydrocele, hematocele, spermatocele, and varicocele.

9. State the difference between extravaginal and intravaginal testicular torsion.

10. Describe the symptoms of epididymitis.

11. State the manifestations and possible complications of mumps orchitis.

12. Relate environmental factors to development of scrotal cancer.

13. State the cell types involved in seminoma, embryonal carcinoma, teratoma, and choriocarcinoma tumors of the testes.

14. Compare the pathology and symptoms of acute bacterial prostatitis, chronic bacterial prostatitis, and chronic prostatitis/pelvic pain syndrome.

15. Describe the urologic manifestations and treatment of benign prostatic hyperplasia.

16. List the methods used in the diagnosis and treatment of prostatic cancer.

SECTION II: ASSESSING YOUR UNDERSTANDING

Activity A *Fill in the blanks.*

1. _____ and _____ are congenital disorders of the penis resulting from embryologic defects in the development of the urethral groove and penile urethra.

2. _____ involves a localized and progressive fibrosis of unknown origin that affects the tunica albuginea.

3. The manifestations of _____ disease include painful erection, bent erection, and the presence of a hard mass at the site of fibrosis.

4. Erection is under the control of _____ nervous system, and ejaculation and detumescence (penile relaxation) are under the control of the _____ nervous system.

5. Parasympathetic stimulation results in release of _____, which causes relaxation of trabecular smooth muscle of the corpora cavernosa, permitting inflow of blood into the sinuses of the cavernosa at pressures approaching those of the _____ system.

6. _____ is commonly classified as psychogenic, organic, or mixed psychogenic and organic.

7. Erectile dysfunction is now recognized as a marker for _____ disease, and is now considered a component of the _____ syndrome.

8. _____ is caused by impaired blood flow in the corpora cavernosa of the penis.

9. Several risk factors for _____ have been suggested, including increasing age, poor hygiene, smoking, human papillomavirus infections, ultraviolet radiation exposure, and immunodeficiency states.

10. The consequences of _____ include infertility, malignancy, testicular torsion, and the possible psychological effects of an empty scrotum.

11. Sperm concentration and _____ are decreased in men with varicocele.

12. _____ is an inflammation of the epididymis, the elongated cordlike structure that lies along the posterior border of the testis, whose function is the storage, transport, and maturation of spermatozoa.

13. _____ refers to a variety of inflammatory disorders of the prostate gland, some bacterial and some not.

14. The manifestations of _____ include fever and chills, malaise, myalgia, arthralgia, frequent and urgent urination, dysuria, and urethral discharge.

15. As with other cancers, it appears that the development of _____ cancer is a multistep process involving genes that control cell differentiation and growth.

16. Men with _____ typically have recurrent urinary tract infections with persistence of the same strain of pathogenic bacteria in prostatic fluid and urine.

17. The cause of noninflammatory prostatitis is unknown, but because of the absence of inflammation, the search for the cause of symptoms has been directed toward _____ sources.

18. The level of _____ correlates with the volume and stage of prostate cancer.

Activity B *Consider the following figure.*

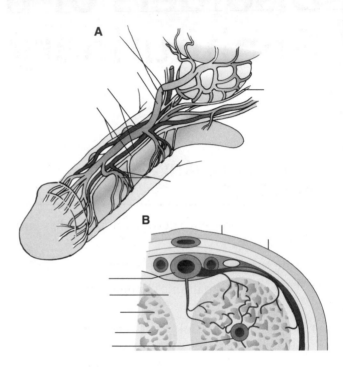

In the figure above, locate and label the structures responsible for penile erection:

- Deep dorsal vein
- Tunica albuginea
- Corpora cavernosa
- Cavernous artery
- Sinusoidal spaces
- Circumflex vein
- Circumflex artery
- Cavernous nerve
- Dorsal nerve
- Dorsal artery
- Subtunical venular plexus

Activity C *Match the key terms in Column A with their definitions in Column B.*

Column A

_____ 1. Balanitis

_____ 2. Smegma

_____ 3. Epispadias

_____ 4. Hydrocele

_____ 5. Cryptorchidism

_____ 6. Orchitis

_____ 7. Prostatitis

_____ 8. Benign prostatic hyperplasia

_____ 9. Phimosis

_____ 10. Priapism

Column B

a. Inflammation of the glans penis

b. Undescended testes

c. Accumulation under the phimotic foreskin

d. Excess fluid collects between the layers of the tunica vaginalis

e. Infection of the testes

f. Inflammation of the prostate

g. Tightening of the penile foreskin

h. Opening of the urethra is on the dorsal surface of the penis

i. Involuntary, prolonged, abnormal and painful erection

j. An age-related, nonmalignant enlargement of the prostate gland

Activity D *Briefly answer the following.*

1. What are some of the known causes of erectile dysfunction?

_____

_____

_____

2. How do drugs like Viagra treat erectile dysfunction?

_____

_____

_____

3. What is testicular torsion? What are the different types?

_____

_____

_____

4. How are testicular cancers staged?

_____

_____

_____

5. How does benign prostatic hyperplasia (BPH) cause obstruction of the urethra?

_____

_____

_____

6. How is prostate cancer diagnosed?

_____

_____

_____

SECTION III: APPLYING YOUR KNOWLEDGE

Activity E *Consider the scenario and answer the questions.*

A 50-year-old man presents at the clinic complaining of a lump on his penis that has progressed over the past 4 months until he can no longer retract his foreskin over his glans. He states the condition is now painful. He is having difficulty urinating, and there is a discharge coming from under his foreskin. He is scheduled for surgery the following day to relieve the phimosis and biopsy the lump. The physician explains the surgery to the client and states that, if the lump is malignant, a partial or total penectomy may be necessary.

1. Before the client leaves, he asks the nurse what causes penile cancer. The nurse correctly responds:

_____

_____

_____

2. The client is admitted to your unit after undergoing a total penectomy for penile cancer with inguinal lymph node involvement. While you are caring for him, the client asks what his prognosis is. What would be your correct response to the client?

_____

_____

_____

SECTION IV: PRACTICING FOR NCLEX

Activity F *Answer the following questions.*

1. In hypospadias, the treatment of choice is surgery to repair the defect. What influences the timing of the surgical repair? (Mark all that apply.)
   a. Penile size
   b. Testicular involvement
   c. Psychological effects on the child
   d. Presence of an abdominal hernia
   e. Anesthetic risk

2. A 75-year-old man presents at the clinic complaining of pain during intercourse and an upward bowing of his penis during erection. The clients' history mentions an inflammation of the penis that was treated 3 months ago. The physician's physical examination of the client notes beads of scar tissue along the dorsal midline of the penile shaft. What would be the suspected diagnosis of this client?
   a. Peyronie disease
   b. Cavernosa disease
   c. Balanitic disease
   d. Paraphimosis disease

3. Priapism (a prolonged painful erection not associated with sexual excitement) can occur at any age. In boys, ages 5 to 10, what are the most common causes of priapism?
   a. Neoplasms or hemophilia
   b. Sickle cell disease or neoplasms
   c. Hemophilia or sickle cell disease
   d. Hypospadias or neoplasms

4. Cryptorchidism, left untreated, is a high risk for testicular cancer and infertility. What are the treatment goals for boys with cryptorchidism?
   a. Prevention of testicular cancer
   b. Prevention of an associated inguinal hernia
   c. Easier cancer detection
   d. Decreased fertility

5. The mother of a 5-year-old boy brings him into the clinic because there is a firm feeling swelling around one of his testes. What would the suspected diagnosis be?
   a. Peyronie disease
   b. Cryptorchism
   c. Priapism
   d. Hydrocele

6. In the neonatal and pediatric population, there can be many physiologic problems with the male genitourinary system. What is the most common acute scrotal disorder in the pediatric population?
   a. Testicular torsion
   b. Hypospadias
   c. Balanitis
   d. Paraphimosis

7. Epididymitis can be sexually transmitted, or it can be caused by a variety of other reasons, including abnormalities in the genitourinary tract. What are the most common causes of epididymitis in young men without underlying genitourinary disease?
   a. *Chlamydia trachomatis* and *Candida albicans*
   b. *Chlamydia trachomatis* and *Neisseria gonorrhoeae*
   c. *Escherichia coli* and *Neisseria gonorrhoeae*
   d. *Candida albicans* and *Escherichia coli*

8. Testicular cancer is highly curable if found and treated early in the disease. What are signs of metastatic spread of testicular cancer? (Mark all that apply.)
   a. Hemoptysis
   b. Back pain
   c. Neck mass
   d. Chest mass
   e. Hoarse voice

9. A 40-year-old man presents at the clinic complaining of painful urination and rectal pain. His vital signs are temperature, 101.7°F; blood pressure, 105/74; pulse, 98; respiration, 22. While taking a history, the nurse notes the client has had chills, malaise, and myalgia. What would the nurse suspect as a diagnosis?

   a. Benign prostatic hyperplasia

   b. Epididymitis

   c. Acute bacterial prostatitis

   d. Orchitis

10. While the cause of BPH is unknown, we do know that the incidence of BPH increases with age. What ethnic group is BPH highest in?

    a. Japanese

    b. White

    c. Native American

    d. African American

CHAPTER 40

Disorders of the Female Genitourinary System

SECTION I: LEARNING OBJECTIVES

1. Compare the abnormalities associated with Bartholin cyst, nonneoplastic epithelial disorders, vulvodynia, and cancer of the vulva.

2. State the role of Döderlein bacilli in maintaining the normal ecology of the vagina.

3. Describe the conditions that predispose to vaginal infections and the methods used to prevent and treat these infections.

4. Describe the importance of the cervical transformation zone in the pathogenesis of cervical cancer.

5. Compare the lesions associated with nabothian cysts and cervical polyps.

6. List the complications of untreated cervicitis.

7. Describe the development of cervical cancer from the appearance of atypical cells to the development of invasive cervical cancer and relate to the importance of the Pap smear in early detection of cervical cancer.

8. Cite the rationale for describing cervical cancer as a sexually transmitted infection and the rationale for use of the human papilloma virus vaccine in prevention of cervical cancer.

9. Compare the pathology and manifestations of endometriosis and adenomyosis.

10. Cite the major early symptom of endometrial cancer and describe the relationship between unopposed estrogen stimulation of the endometrium and development of endometrial cancer.

11. Compare the location and manifestations of intramural and subserosal leiomyomas.

12. List the common causes and symptoms of pelvic inflammatory disease.

13. Describe the risk factors and symptoms of ectopic pregnancy.

14. State the underlying cause of ovarian cysts.

15. Differentiate benign ovarian cyst from polycystic ovary syndrome (PCOS).

16. List the hormones produced by the three types of functioning ovarian tumors.

17. State the reason that ovarian cancer may be difficult to detect in an early stage.

18. Characterize the function of the supporting ligaments and pelvic floor muscles in maintaining the position of the pelvic organs, including the uterus, bladder, and rectum.

19. Describe the manifestations of cystocele, rectocele, and enterocele.

20. Describe the cause and manifestations of uterine prolapse.

21. Define the terms *amenorrhea, hypomenorrhea, oligomenorrhea, menorrhagia, metrorrhagia,* and *menometrorrhagia.*

22. Relate the alteration in estrogen and progesterone levels to the development of dysfunctional menstrual cycles.

23. Differentiate between primary dysmenorrhea and secondary dysmenorrhea.

24. Characterize the manifestations of the premenstrual syndrome, its possible causes, and the methods of treatment.

25. Describe changes in breast function that occur with mastitis.

26. Describe the manifestations of nonproliferative (fibrocystic) breast changes.

27. Cite the risk factors for breast cancer, the importance of clinical breast examination, and recommendations for mammography.

28. Describe the methods used in the diagnosis and treatment of breast cancer.

29. Provide a definition of infertility.

30. List male and female factors that contribute to infertility.

31. Briefly describe methods used in the treatment of infertility.

SECTION II: ASSESSING YOUR UNDERSTANDING

Activity A *Fill in the blanks.*

1. Diseases of the external genitalia are similar to those that affect _____ skin elsewhere in the body.

2. The _____ is particularly prone to skin infections because it is constantly being exposed to secretions and moisture.

3. A _____ is a fluid-filled sac that results from occlusion of the duct system in Bartholin gland.

4. _____ presents as thickened, gray-white plaques with an irregular surface.

5. The normal vaginal _____ depends on the delicate balance of hormones and bacterial flora.

6. _____ represents an inflammation of the vagina that is characterized by vaginal discharge and burning, itching, redness, and swelling of vaginal tissues.

7. The most common symptom of vaginal carcinoma is abnormal _____.

8. During _____, the newly developed squamous epithelial cells of the cervix are vulnerable to development of dysplasia and genetic change if exposed to cancer-producing agents.

9. _____ cancer is readily detected and, if detected early, is the most easily cured of all the cancers of the female reproductive system.

10. Untreated _____ may extend to include the development of pelvic cellulitis, low back pain, dyspareunia, cervical stenosis, dysmenorrhea, and ascending infection of the uterus or fallopian tubes.

11. _____ are the most common lesions of the cervix.

12. A preponderance of evidence suggests a causal link between _____ infection and cervical cancer.

13. _____ is the condition in which functional endometrial tissue is found in ectopic sites outside the uterus.

14. _____ is the condition in which endometrial glands and stroma are found within the myometrium, interspersed between the smooth muscle fibers.

15. _____ and _____, which consists of dilating the cervix and scraping the uterine cavity, is the definitive procedure for diagnosis of endometrial cancer because it provides a more thorough evaluation.

16. Uterine _____ are benign neoplasms of smooth muscle origin.

17. _____ is a polymicrobial infection of the upper reproductive tract associated with the sexually transmitted organisms as well as endogenous organisms.

18. _____ occurs when a fertilized ovum implants outside the uterine cavity, the most common site being the fallopian tube.

19. Disorders of the ovaries frequently cause _____ and _____ problems.

20. _____ syndrome is characterized by varying degrees of menstrual irregularity, signs of hyperandrogenism, and infertility.

21. Most women with PCOS have elevated _____ levels with normal estrogen and follicle-stimulating hormone production.

22. _____ tumors are common; most are benign, but malignant tumors are the leading cause of death from reproductive cancers.

23. The most significant risk factor for ovarian cancer appears to be _____ the length of time during a woman's life when her ovarian cycle is not suppressed by pregnancy, lactation, or oral contraceptive use.

24. The breast cancer susceptibility genes, *BRACA1* and *BRCA2*, which are _____ genes are incriminated in approximately 10% of hereditary ovarian cancers despite being identified as breast cancer genes.

25. _____ is the herniation of the rectum into the vagina.

26. Uterine prolapse is the bulging of the uterus into the vagina that occurs when the _____ ligaments are stretched.

27. Removal of the uterus through the vagina with appropriate repair of the vaginal wall often is done when _____ is accompanied by cystocele or rectocele.

28. Primary _____ is the failure to menstruate by 15 years of age or by 13 years of age if failure to menstruate is accompanied by absence of secondary sex characteristics.

29. _____ is the secretion of breast milk in a nonlactating breast.

30. _____ is inflammation of the breast.

31. _____ are firm, rubbery, sharply defined round masses in breast tissue.

32. _____ changes usually present as nodular granular breast masses that are more prominent and painful during the luteal or progesterone-dominant portion of the menstrual cycle.

33. _____ disease presents as an eczematoid lesion of the nipple and areola.

34. _____ is the inability to conceive a child after 1 year of unprotected intercourse.

Activity B *Consider the following figures.*

In the figure above, locate and label all the common locations of endometriosis within the pelvis and abdomen.

Activity C *Match the key terms in Column A with their definitions in Column B.*

1.

Column A	Column B
____ 1. Papanicolaou smear	a. Insertion of radioactive materials into the body
____ 2. Menorrhagia	b. Commonly called fibroids
____ 3. Vulvodynia	c. Unexplained vulvar pain
____ 4. Leiomyomas	
____ 5. Cystocele	d. Herniation of the bladder into the vagina
____ 6. Curettage	
____ 7. Atrophic vaginitis	e. Inflammation of the vagina that occurs after menopause
____ 8. Lichen sclerosus	
____ 9. Brachytherapy	
____ 10. Cervicitis	

f. Surgical procedure used to scrape out the surface of the endometrium

g. Inflammation of the cervix

h. Excessive menstrual bleeding

i. The vaginal cytology to detect vaginal or cervical cancer

j. Inflammatory disease of the vulva

2.

Column A	Column B
___ **1.** Amenorrhea	**a.** Frequent menstruation
___ **2.** Hypomenorrhea	**b.** Infrequent menstruation
___ **3.** Oligomenorrhea	**c.** Bleeding between periods
___ **4.** Polymenorrhea	**d.** Absence of menstruation
___ **5.** Menorrhagia	**e.** Heavy bleeding during and between menstrual periods
___ **6.** Metrorrhagia	**f.** Scanty menstruation
___ **7.** Menometror-rhagia	**g.** Excessive menstruation

Activity D *Briefly answer the following.*

1. What measures should be taken to avoid vaginal infections?

_____

_____

_____

2. What is the only approved vaccine for cervical cancer and how does it work?

_____

_____

_____

3. What is the normal method of detecting/diagnosing cervical cancer?

_____

_____

_____

4. What are the three most prominent theories of the pathogenesis of endometriosis?

_____

_____

_____

5. What is the mechanism of infection in pelvic inflammatory disease?

_____

_____

_____

6. Why should you be concerned about the future of your patient with PCOS?

_____

_____

_____

7. Describe the functional anatomy of normal pelvic support.

_____

_____

_____

8. Describe the alterations in a normal period and give the hormone that thought to be responsible.

_____

_____

_____

9. What is the genetic component of breast cancer?

_____

_____

_____

SECTION III: APPLYING YOUR KNOWLEDGE

Activity E *Consider the scenario and answer the questions.*

A 23-year-old woman is being seen in her physician's office as a follow-up to an abnormal Pap smear. The physician explains to the client that she may have cervical cancer, and he wants to do a colposcopy so he can diagnose and treat any lesions he may find. The client gives her consent.

1. While the nurse is preparing the client for the procedure, the client asks what a colposcopy is and what it is for. What would the nurse would correctly respond?

_____

_____

_____

2. The colposcopy shows dysplastic lesions, and the physician wants to do a large loop excision of the transformation zone (LEEP procedure). The client gives her consent, but wants to know what this procedure is. How would the procedure be explained to the client?

_____

_____

_____

SECTION IV: PRACTICING FOR NCLEX

Activity F *Answer the following questions.*

1. Bartholin gland obstruction of the ductal system will cause a cyst. Sometimes the cyst becomes infected and an abscess occurs. What is the surgical removal of a Bartholin cyst or abscess when a wedge of vulvar skin is removed along with the cyst wall?
   a. Marsupialization
   b. Vulvectomy
   c. Bartholectomy
   d. Incision and drainage

2. There are two types of vulvar cancer. One type is found in older women, and one type is found in younger women, generally less than 40 years of age. What is the type found in younger women thought to be caused by?
   a. Multiple sexual partners
   b. Human papilloma virus
   c. Nonsquamous cell lesions
   d. Lichen sclerotic lesions

3. Vaginal infections can occur in young girls prior to menarche. These infections generally have nonspecific causes. What are some of the causes of vaginal infections in premenarchal girls? (Mark all that apply.)
   a. Presence of foreign bodies
   b. Intestinal parasites
   c. Poor hygiene
   d. Vaginal deodorants
   e. Tampax

4. The endocervix is covered with large-branched mucous-secreting glands. During the menstrual cycle, they undergo functional changes, and the amount and properties of the mucous that they secret varies as to the stage of the cycle. When one of these glands get blocked, what kind of cyst forms within the cervix?
   a. Bartholin cysts
   b. Bulbourethral cysts
   c. Nabothian cysts
   d. Metaplastic cysts

5. Endometriosis is the condition in which endometrial tissue is found growing outside the uterus in the pelvic cavity. What are risk factors for endometriosis?
   a. Late menarche and regular periods with longer cycles than 27 days
   b. Early menarche and lighter flow
   c. Increased menstrual pain and periods of shorter duration than 7 days
   d. Periods longer than 7 days and increased menstrual pain

6. Leiomyomas, or intrauterine fibroids, are the most common form of pelvic tumor. Approximately half the time leiomyomas are asymptomatic. What are the symptoms of leiomyomas that are not asymptomatic?
   a. Anemia and urinary frequency
   b. Diarrhea and rectal pressure
   c. Menorrhagia and urinary retention
   d. Abdominal distention and diarrhea

7. An 18-year-old woman presents at the clinic complaining new-onset breakthrough bleeding, even though she is taking contraceptives. What contraceptive use, along with new-onset breakthrough bleeding, has been associated with pelvic inflammatory disease?
   a. Intrauterine device
   b. Depo-Provera
   c. Spermicidal foam
   d. Diaphragm

8. Ectopic pregnancies are true gynecologic emergencies and are considered the leading cause of maternal death in the first trimester. What diagnostic test would you expect to have ordered for a suspected ectopic pregnancy?
   a. Transvaginal ultrasound if pregnancy is less than 5 weeks gestation
   b. Serial β-human chorionic gonadotropin (hCG) with higher than normal hCG production
   c. Ultrasonography followed by serial hCG tests
   d. Amniocentesis

9. Polycystic ovary syndrome is an endocrine disorder and a common cause of chronic anovulation. In addition to the clinical manifestations of PCOS, long-term health problems including cardiovascular disease and diabetes have been linked to PCOS. What drug has emerged as an important part of PCOS treatment?
   a. DHEAS
   b. Methotrexate
   c. Mineralocorticoids
   d. Metformin

10. Ovarian cancer, once thought to be asymptomatic, has now been shown to produce nonspecific symptoms, which make the diagnosis of ovarian cancer difficult. What symptoms are believed to have a strong association with ovarian cancer? (Mark all that apply.)
    a. Difficulty eating
    b. Increased intestinal gas
    c. Bloating
    d. Increased appetite
    e. Abdominal or pelvic pain

11. Uterine prolapse is a disorder of pelvic support and uterine position. It can range in severity from a slight descent of the uterus into the vagina, all the way to the entire uterus protruding through the vaginal opening. In women who want to have children, or in older women who are at significant risk if surgery is performed, what device is inserted to hold the uterus in place?
    a. A pessary
    b. A Colpexin sphere
    c. A vesicourethral suspender
    d. A retroversion inducer

12. In primary dysmenorrheal when contraception is not desired, what is the treatment of choice?
    a. Aspirin
    b. Ibuprofen
    c. Acetaminophen
    d. Metformic acid

13. Mastitis is an inflammation of the breast that can occur at any time. What is the treatment for mastitis?
    a. Opioid analgesics
    b. Nonsteroidal anti-inflammatory drugs
    c. Application of heat or cold
    d. Tylenol 3

14. Fibrocystic changes in the breast are not uncommon. How is the diagnosis of fibrocystic changes made?
    a. Physical examination and client history
    b. Galactography and biopsy
    c. Mammography and galactography
    d. Ultrasonography and mammography

15. Cancer of the breast is the most common cancer in women. Many breast cancers are found by women themselves while doing breast self-examination. When should postmenopausal women do breast self-examination?

   a. Any day of the month

   b. 2 days following menses

   c. On the first day of every month

   d. On the 15th of every month

16. The causes of infertility can be in either the male or the female. Male tests for infertility require a specimen of ejaculate that is collected when?

   a. Any time

   b. After 3 days of abstinence

   c. After 3 consecutive days of intercourse

   d. After 3 weeks of abstinence

17. Couples who are being treated for infertility often choose to try in vitro fertilization. When using this technique, the female's eggs are inseminated with the male's sperm in a culture dish. After a period of time, the ova are evaluated for signs of fertilization. If signs of fertilization are present, when are the fertilized eggs placed in the woman's uterus?

   a. 12 to 24 hours after egg retrieval

   b. 36 to 48 hours after egg retrieval

   c. 48 to 72 hours after egg retrieval

   d. 24 to 36 hours after egg retrieval

CHAPTER 41

Sexually Transmitted Infections

SECTION I: LEARNING OBJECTIVES

1. Define what is meant by a sexually transmitted infection (STI).

2. List common portals of entry for STIs.

3. Name the organisms responsible for condylomata acuminata, genital herpes, chancroid, and lymphogranuloma venereum.

4. State the significance of being infected with high-risk strains of the human papillomavirus (HPV).

5. Explain the pathogenesis of recurrent genital herpes infections.

6. State the difference between wet-mount slide and culture methods of diagnosis of STIs.

7. Compare the signs and symptoms of infections caused by *Candida albicans*, *Trichomonas vaginalis*, and *bacterial vaginosis*.

8. Compare the signs and symptoms of gonorrhea in the male and female patient.

9. Describe the three stages of syphilis.

10. State the genital and nongenital complications that can occur with chlamydial infections, gonorrhea, and syphilis.

11. State the treatment for chlamydial urogenital infections, gonorrhea, nonspecific urogenital infections, and syphilis.

SECTION II: ASSESSING YOUR UNDERSTANDING

Activity A *Fill in the blanks.*

1. Sexually transmitted infections can selectively infect the _____ tissues of the external genitalia, primarily cause vaginitis in women, or they can produce both genitourinary and systemic effects.

2. Sexually transmitted infections may be transmitted by an infected mother to a _____, causing congenital defects or death of the child.

3. _____ are caused by the HPV.

4. Genital warts typically present as soft, raised, fleshy lesions on the _____, including the penis, vulva, scrotum, perineum, and perianal skin.

5. _____ is one of the most common causes of genital ulcers in the United States.

6. Herpes simplex virus type-1 and herpes simplex virus type-2 are _____ viruses, meaning that they grow in neurons and share the biologic property of latency.

7. Herpes simplex virus _____ is responsible for more than 90% of recurrent genital herpes infections.

8. The initial symptoms of _____ infections include tingling, itching, and pain in the genital area, followed by eruption of small pustules and vesicles.

9. *Candida albicans* is the most commonly identified organism in vaginal _____ infections, but other *Candida* species, such as *Candida glabrata* and *Candida tropicalis* may also be present.

10. _____ can reside in the paraurethral glands of both sexes.

11. _____ vaginosis is the most prevalent form of vaginal infection seen by health care professionals.

12. _____ exist in two forms: elementary bodies, which are the infectious particles capable of entering uninfected cells, and the initiator or reticulate bodies, which multiply by binary fission to produce the inclusions identified in stained cells.

13. Untreated chlamydial infection results in _____ damage in female patients.

14. The _____ is a pyogenic (i.e., pus-forming) gram-negative diplococcus that evokes inflammatory reactions characterized by purulent exudates.

15. _____ is spread by direct contact with an infectious moist lesion, usually through sexual intercourse.

Activity B *Match the key terms in Column A with their definitions in Column B.*

Column A

____ 1. Transmission of HPV

____ 2. Condylomata acuminata

____ 3. *Trichomonas vaginalis*

____ 4. Chancroid

____ 5. *Treponema pallidum*

____ 6. Candidiasis

____ 7. *Chlamydia trachomatis*

____ 8. Lymphogranuloma venereum

____ 9. Donovan bodies

____ 10. Döderlein cytolysis

Column B

a. Anaerobic protozoan that can be transmitted sexually

b. Development of large, tender, and sometimes fluctuant inguinal lymph nodes called *buboes*

c. Excess of lactobacilli

d. Disease of the external genitalia and lymph nodes

e. Large mononuclear cells filled with intracytoplasmic gram-negative rods

f. Yeast infection

g. Spirochete that is responsible for syphilitic infection

h. Genital warts

i. Obligate intracellular bacterial pathogen that resembles a virus, but like a bacteria has RNA and DNA and is susceptible to some antibiotics

j. Through skin-to-skin contact

Activity C *Briefly answer the following.*

1. What are the risk factors for acquiring the HPV and how is it spread?

_____

_____

_____

2. How do herpes simplex virus type-1 and herpes simplex virus type-2 spread, and where do they reside in the body?

_____

_____

_____

3. What are the risk factors for developing a candidiasis infection?

_____

_____

_____

4. What are the potential complications of trichomoniasis in male and female patients?

_____

_____

_____

5. What are the sex-specific manifestations of gonorrhea?

_____

_____

_____

6. What is the clinical course of syphilis?

_____

_____

_____

SECTION III: APPLYING YOUR KNOWLEDGE

Activity D *Consider the scenario and answer the questions.*

A 35-year-old man presents at the clinic complaining of painful joints of the left leg and pain on urination. He also is noted to have mucocutaneous lesions on the palms of his hands.

1. What would be important for the nurse to note while taking a nursing history?

_____

_____

_____

2. The client is diagnosed with a chlamydial infection. What would be the expected treatment for this client?

_____

_____

_____

SECTION IV: PRACTICING FOR NCLEX

Activity E *Answer the following questions.*

1. After inoculation with HPV, genital warts may begin to grow. They usually manifest as soft, raised fleshy lesions on the external genitalia of either male of female. What is the incubation period for HPV-induced genital warts?

   a. 6 weeks to 8 months

   b. 6 weeks to 8 weeks

   c. 6 months to 8 months

   d. 6 days to 8 days

2. Primary genital herpes is a sexually transmitted disease (STD) caused by either the Herpes simplex virus type-1 or type-2. What are the initial symptoms of primary genital herpes infections? (Mark all that apply.)

   a. Itching

   b. Chancres

   c. Genital pain

   d. Eczemalike lesions

   e. Small pustules

3. There is no known cure for genital herpes, and methods of treatment are often symptomatic. Pharmacologic management of genital herpes includes which drugs?

   a. AZT

   b. Famciclovir

   c. Nonsteroidal anti-inflammatory drugs

   d. Topical corticosteroid compounds

4. Chancroid or soft chancre is a highly contagious STD usually found in the Southeast Asian and North African populations. What is the recommended treatment for Chancroid?

   a. Tetracycline

   b. Sulfamethoxazole

   c. Erythromycin

   d. Acyclovir

5. A male client presents at the clinic with flulike symptoms and reports a weight loss of 10 pounds without trying. On physical examination, the client is found to have splenomegaly and large, tender, fluctuant inguinal lymph nodes. While taking the nursing history, it is discovered that the client prefers male sexual partners, and that 2 weeks ago the client had small, painless papules. What disease would the nurse suspect the client has?

   a. Genital herpes

   b. Chancroid

   c. Syphilis

   d. Lymphogranuloma venereum

6. Candidiasis is a leading cause of vaginal infections. Which antifungal agent is not available without prescription to treat candidiasis?

   a. Terconazole
   b. Clotrimazole
   c. Miconazole
   d. Butaconazole

7. Trichomoniasis is an STD that can occur in either sex. Men carry the protozoan in the urethra and prostate and remain asymptomatic. This anaerobic protozoan can cause a number of complications. What is it a risk factor for in both men and women?

   a. Atypical pelvic inflammatory disease
   b. HIV transmission
   c. Blockage of tubes and ducts
   d. Ovarian and testicular cysts

8. Bacterial vaginosis is the most common vaginal infection seen by health care providers. What is the predominant symptom of bacterial vaginosis?

   a. Thick, cottage cheese–like discharge with a fishy odor
   b. Painless chancres
   c. Grayish-white discharge with a fishy odor
   d. Small, painless papules

9. Gonorrhea is an STD that affects both men and women. When diagnosing gonorrhea, specimens should be collected from the appropriate site and inoculated onto the correct medium. What sites can specimens be collected from when diagnosing gonorrhea? (Mark all that apply.)

   a. Oropharynx
   b. Urethra
   c. Nasal passages
   d. Exocervix
   e. Anal canal

10. Tertiary syphilis is a delayed response of untreated primary syphilis and can occur as long as 20 years after the primary disease. When tertiary syphilis progresses to a symptomatic stage, it can produce localized necrotic lesions. What are these lesions called?

    a. Chancres
    b. Chancroids
    c. Gummies
    d. Gummas

42

Structure and Function of the Skeletal System

SECTION I: LEARNING OBJECTIVES

1. Describe locations and characteristics of compact and cancellous bone.

2. Describe the structure of a long bone.

3. Cite the characteristics and name at least one location of elastic cartilage, hyaline cartilage, and fibrocartilage.

4. Name and characterize the function of the four types of bone cells.

5. State the function of parathyroid hormone, calcitonin, and vitamin D in terms of bone formation and metabolism.

6. State the characteristics of tendons and ligaments.

7. State the difference between synarthroses and synovial joints.

8. Describe the source of blood supply to a synovial joint.

9. Explain why pain is often experienced in all the joints of an extremity when only a single joint is affected by a disease process.

10. Describe the structure and function of a bursa.

11. Explain the pathology associated with a torn meniscus of the knee.

SECTION II: ASSESSING YOUR UNDERSTANDING

Activity A *Fill in the blanks.*

1. The bones of the skeletal system serve as a framework for the attachment of _____, _____, and _____.

2. The bones act as a storage reservoir for _____, and the central cavity of some bones contains the hematopoietic connective tissue in which _____ cells are formed.

3. The skeletal system consists of the _____ and _____ skeleton.

4. _____ bone has a densely packed calcified intercellular matrix that makes it more rigid than cancellous bone.

5. _____ are classified by shape as long, short, flat, and irregular.

6. Bones are covered, except at their articular ends, by a membrane called the _____.

7. Bone _____ occupies the medullary cavities of the long bones throughout the skeleton and the cavities of cancellous bone in the vertebrae, ribs, sternum, and flat bones of the pelvis.

8. The _____ enter the bone through a nutrient foramen and supply the marrow space and the internal half of the cortex.

9. Bone is _____ tissue in which the intercellular matrix has been impregnated with inorganic _____ salts so that it has great tensile and compressible strength but is light enough to be moved by coordinated muscle contractions.

10. The undifferentiated _____ cells are found in the periosteum, endosteum, and epiphyseal plate of growing bone.

11. _____ are "bone-chewing" cells that function in the resorption of bone, removing the mineral content and the organic matrix.

12. _____cartilage is found in areas, such as the ear, where some flexibility is important.

13. _____ is found in the intervertebral disks, in areas where tendons are connected to bone, and in the symphysis pubis.

14. _____ cartilage forms the costal cartilages that join the ribs to the sternum and vertebrae, many of the cartilages of the respiratory tract, the articular cartilages, and the epiphyseal plates.

15. _____ inhibits the release of calcium from bone into the extracellular fluid.

16. _____, which attach skeletal muscles to bone, are relatively inextensible because of their richness in collagen fibers.

17. _____ are fibrous thickenings of the articular capsule that join one bone to its articulating mate.

18. _____ are joints that lack a joint cavity and move a little or not at all.

19. _____ joints are freely movable joints.

20. The purpose of a _____ sac is to prevent friction on a tendon.

Activity B *Consider the following figure.*

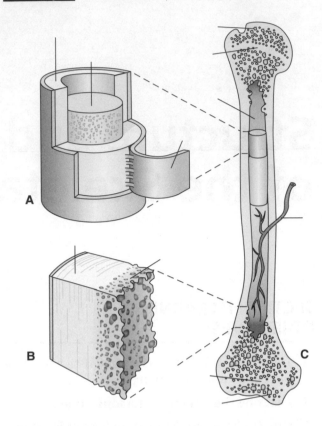

In the figure above, locate and label the following structures:

- Proximal epiphysis
- Medullary cavity
- Periosteum
- Nutrient artery
- Compact bone
- Spongy bone
- Yellow marrow
- Diaphysis

Activity C *Match the key terms in Column A with their definitions in Column B.*

Column A	Column B
____ 1. Trabeculae	a. Connect adjacent haversian canals
____ 2. Appendicular skeleton	b. Prebone that will be ossified
____ 3. Osteoid	c. The bones of the skull, thorax, and vertebral column
____ 4. Lamellar bone	
____ 5. Haversian canal	d. Mature bone found in the adult skeleton

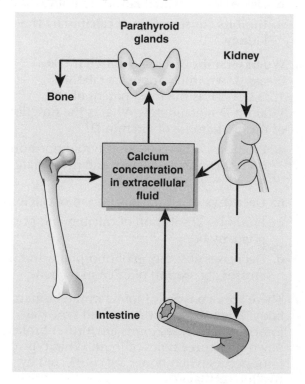

____ **6.** Osteons

____ **7.** Volkmann canals

____ **8.** Axial skeleton

____ **9.** Endosteum

____ **10.** Chondrocytes

e. Contains the blood vessels and nerve supply for the osteon

f. Bones of the upper and lower extremities, including the shoulder and hip

g. Membrane that lines the spaces of spongy bone, the marrow cavities, and the haversian canals

h. Cells that form cartilage

i. Concentric lamellae of bone matrix, surrounding a central canal

j. Lined with osteogenic cells and filled with red or yellow bone marrow

Activity D *In the flow chart shown, put the following in the proper sequence.*

Parathyroid glands

Kidney

Bone

Calcium concentration in extracellular fluid

Intestine

• Reabsorption of calcium via 1,25-dihydroxy vitamin D_3
• Synthesis of 1,25-dihydroxy vitamin D_3
• Release of calcium and phosphate
• Reabsorption of calcium
• Urinary excretion of phosphate

Activity E *Briefly answer the following.*

1. What is the typical structure of a long bone?

_____

_____

_____

2. What are the two types of bone marrow and what are their functions?

_____

_____

_____

3. What is the makeup of the intercellular matrix of bone tissue?

_____

_____

_____

4. What are the similarities and differences between bone and cartilage?

_____

_____

_____

5. How does parathyroid hormone maintain serum calcium levels?

_____

_____

_____

6. What is the action of vitamin D?

_____

_____

_____

SECTION III: APPLYING YOUR KNOWLEDGE

Activity F *Consider the scenario and answer the questions.*

Case study: A 62-year-old woman with multiple sclerosis was referred to the orthopedic clinic by her primary care physician because of pain on movement in her upper arms. Because of the multiple sclerosis, the client's legs were extremely weak, and the client had to lift herself out of a chair with her arms. After a physical examination, the orthopedic physician diagnosed her as having bilateral biceps tendinitis.

1. The client asks what causes tendinitis. What would be the correct answer?

_____

_____

_____

2. The client asks if all tendons are like the biceps tendons. What would be the correct answer?

_____

_____

_____

SECTION IV: PRACTICING FOR NCLEX

Activity G *Answer the following questions.*

1. The metaphysis is the part of the bone that fans out toward the epiphysis. What is the metaphysis composed of?
   a. Trabeculae
   b. Cancellous bone
   c. Red bone marrow
   d. Endosteum

2. We have both red and yellow bone marrow in our bodies. What is yellow bone marrow largely composed of?
   a. Hematopoietic cells
   b. Adipose cells
   c. Cancellous cells
   d. Osteogenic cells

3. Lamellar bone is the bone tissue that is found in the adult body. What is lamellar bone largely composed of?
   a. Hematopoietic cells
   b. Spicules
   c. Osteons
   d. Macrocrystalline cells

4. Our bodies contain three types of cartilage: elastic, hyaline, and fibrocartilage. Which of these types of cartilage is found in the symphysis pubis?
   a. None
   b. Elastic
   c. Hyaline
   d. Fibrocartilage

5. Parathyroid hormone functions to maintain serum calcium levels. How does it fulfill this function? (Mark all that apply.)
   a. Initiates calcium release from bone
   b. Enhances intestinal absorption of calcium
   c. Activates conservation of calcium by the kidney
   d. Decreases intestinal absorption of calcium
   e. Inhibits conservation of calcium by the kidney

6. When vitamin D is metabolized it takes breaks down into various metabolites. $1,25(OH)_2D_3$ is the most potent of the Vitamin D metabolites. What is the function of this metabolite of vitamin D?
   a. Promotes actions of parathyroid hormone on resorption of calcium and phosphate from bone
   b. Decreases intestinal absorption of calcium
   c. Promotes absorption of calcium and phosphate by bone
   d. Decreases absorption of phosphate and increases absorption of calcium by bone

7. There are two types of joints in the human body. They are synarthroses and synovial joints. Synarthroses joints are further broken down into three types of joint. What type of joint occurs when bones are connected by hyaline cartilage?
   a. Synovial
   b. Synchondroses
   c. Syndesmoses
   d. Diarthrodial

8. Rheumatic disorders attack the joints of the body. Which joints are most frequently attacked by rheumatic disorders?
   a. Synchondroses
   b. Articular
   c. Diarthrodial
   d. Synarthroses

9. Each joint capsule has tendons and ligaments? What are the tendons and ligaments of the joint capsule sensitive to?
   a. Position and elevating
   b. Position and lowering
   c. Position and turning
   d. Position and movement

10. Synovial membranes can form sacs, called *bursae*. What is the function of bursae?
    a. Prevent friction on a tendon
    b. Prevent injury to a joint
    c. Prevent friction on a ligament
    d. Cushion the joint

Disorders of the Skeletal System: Trauma, Infections, Neoplasms, and Childhood Disorders

SECTION I: LEARNING OBJECTIVES

1. Describe the physical agents responsible for soft-tissue trauma.

2. Differentiate among the types of soft-tissue injuries.

3. Compare muscle strains and ligamentous sprains.

4. Describe the healing process of soft-tissue injuries.

5. Differentiate open from closed fractures.

6. List the signs and symptoms of a fracture.

7. Explain the measures used in treatment of fractures.

8. Describe the fracture healing process.

9. Differentiate the early complications of fractures from later complications of fracture healing.

10. Explain the implications of bone infection.

11. Differentiate among osteomyelitis due to spread from a contaminated wound, hematogenous osteomyelitis, and osteomyelitis due to vascular insufficiency in terms of etiologies, manifestations, and treatment.

12. Cite the characteristics of chronic osteomyelitis.

13. Describe the most common sites of tuberculosis of the bone.

14. Define *osteonecrosis*.

15. Cite four major causes of osteonecrosis.

16. Characterize the blood supply of bone and relate it to the pathologic features of the condition.

17. Describe the methods used in diagnosis and treatment of the condition.

18. Differentiate between the properties of benign and malignant bone tumors.

19. Contrast osteogenic sarcoma, Ewing sarcoma, and chondrosarcoma in terms of the most common age groups and anatomic sites that are affected.

20. List the primary sites of tumors that frequently metastasize to the bone.

21. State the three primary goals for treatment of metastatic bone disease.

SECTION II: ASSESSING YOUR UNDERSTANDING

Activity A *Fill in the blanks.*

1. A broad spectrum of _____ injuries result from numerous physical forces, including blunt tissue trauma, disruption of tendons and ligaments, and fractures of bony structures.

2. Unintentional _____ are the number-one cause of nonfatal injuries in all age groups.

3. _____ injuries include contusions, hematomas, and lacerations.

4. A _____ is a stretching injury to a muscle or a musculotendinous unit caused by mechanical overloading.

5. A _____ usually is caused by abnormal or excessive movement of the joint.

6. A _____ involves the displacement or separation of the bone ends of a joint with loss of articulation.

7. _____ bodies are small pieces of bone or cartilage within a joint space.

8. _____ injuries and impingement disorders can result from a number of causes, including excessive use, a direct blow, or stretch injury, usually involving throwing or swinging, as with baseball pitchers or tennis players.

9. Meniscus injury commonly occurs as the result of a _____ injury from a sudden or sharp pivot or a direct blow to the knee, as in hockey, basketball, or football.

10. _____ of the hip commonly result from the knee being struck while the hip and knee are in a flexed position.

11. Grouped according to cause, fractures can be divided into three major categories: fractures caused by _____, fatigue or stress fractures, and _____ fractures.

12. A _____ fracture occurs in bones that already are weakened by disease or tumors.

13. The signs and symptoms of a _____ include pain, tenderness at the site of bone disruption, swelling, loss of function, deformity of the affected part, and abnormal mobility.

14. _____ is another method for achieving immobility and maintaining alignment of the bone ends and maintaining the reduction, particularly if the fracture is unstable or comminuted.

15. _____ are skin bullae and blisters representing areas of epidermal necrosis with separation of epidermis from the underlying dermis by edema fluid.

16. Because of inactivity and restrictions in weight bearing, the individual with a lower extremity fracture is at risk for the development of venous _____, which includes pulmonary embolism and deep venous thrombosis.

17. The _____ syndrome refers to a constellation of clinical manifestations resulting from the presence of fat droplets in the small blood vessels of the lung or other organs after a long bone fracture or other major trauma.

18. _____ osteomyelitis symptoms include pain, immobility, and muscle atrophy; joint swelling, mild fever, and leukocytosis also may occur.

19. _____, or death of a segment of bone, is a condition caused by the interruption of blood supply to the marrow, medullary bone, or cortex.

20. Malignant bone tumors, such as _____, grow rapidly and can spread to other parts of the body through the bloodstream or lymphatics.

21. _____ bone tumors usually are limited to the confines of the bone, have well-demarcated edges, and are surrounded by a thin rim of sclerotic bone.

22. A _____ is a tumor composed of hyaline cartilage.

23. _____, a malignant tumor of cartilage that can develop in the medullary cavity or peripherally, is the second most common form of malignant bone tumor.

Activity B *Consider the following figure.*

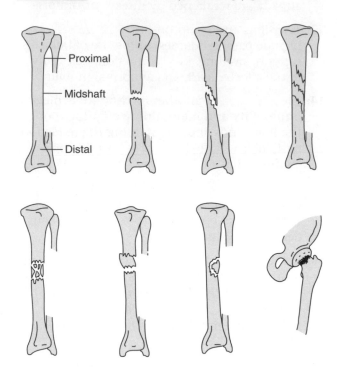

In the figure above, label the type of fracture

- Impacted
- Butterfly
- Comminuted
- Transverse
- Oblique
- Segmental
- Spiral

Activity C *Match the key terms in Column A with their definitions in Column B.*

Column A

___ **1.** Subluxation

___ **2.** Malunion

___ **3.** Contusion

___ **4.** Compound fracture

___ **5.** Menisci

___ **6.** Hematoma

___ **7.** Chondromalacia

___ **8.** Laceration

Column B

a. A partial dislocation

b. Acute or chronic infection of the bone

c. Bone fragments have broken through the skin

d. Injury in which the skin is torn or its continuity is disrupted

___ **9.** Greenstick fracture

___ **10.** Osteomyelitis

e. Healing of bone with deformity, angulation, or rotation

f. Large area of local hemorrhage

g. Softening of the articular cartilage

h. A partial break in bone continuity; resembles what is seen when a young sapling is broken

i. Area becomes ecchymotic (i.e., black and blue) because of local hemorrhage

j. C-shaped plates of fibrocartilage that are superimposed between the condyles of the femur and tibia

Activity D *Put the following events of healing a bone fracture into the proper order in the boxes below.*

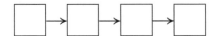

A. Development of fibrin meshwork within the hematoma

B. Replacement of callus with mature bone

C. Formation of fibrocartilaginous callus

D. Remodeling of bone

Activity E *Briefly answer the following.*

1. What joints are most commonly involved in sprain-type injuries?

_____

_____

_____

2. What is the normal healing process of a sprain? What are some of the greatest concerns?

_____

_____

_____

3. What is the structure of rotator cuff and how is it usually injured?

_____

_____

_____

4. When someone "breaks a hip," what is usually occurring?

_____

_____

_____

5. What is compartment syndrome and how does it relate to bone tissue?

_____

_____

_____

6. What are the manifestations of osteomyelitis?

_____

_____

_____

7. What is the pathogenesis of osteonecrosis?

_____

_____

_____

8. What are the general characteristics of bone tumors?

_____

_____

_____

9. What is metastatic bone disease?

_____

_____

_____

SECTION III: APPLYING YOUR KNOWLEDGE

Activity F *Consider the scenario and answer the questions.*

Case study: A 15-year-old boy is brought to the emergency department after an injury playing football. The doctor suspects an injury to the meniscus of the knee.

1. As the nurse, what orders would you expect to receive to confirm the suspected diagnosis?

_____

_____

_____

2. The diagnosis of torn meniscus is confirmed. What would be the first-line treatment for this type of injury?

_____

_____

_____

3. The client asks what will happen if his knee does not heal right. The correct answer would include what?

_____

_____

_____

SECTION IV: PRACTICING FOR NCLEX

Activity G *Answer the following questions.*

1. Athletic injuries fall into two types, acute or overuse injuries. Where do overuse injuries commonly occur?

   a. Knee

   b. Wrist

   c. Neck

   d. Fingers

2. Match the injury to its definition.

Injury	Definition
1. Contusion	**a.** The ligaments may be incompletely torn or, as in a severe sprain, completely torn or ruptured
2. Hematoma	
3. Laceration	
4. Puncture wounds	**b.** An injury in which the skin is torn or its continuity is disrupted
5. Strain	**c.** A stretching injury caused by mechanical overloading
6. Sprain	
7. Dislocation	**d.** Blood accumulates and exerts pressure on nerve endings
	e. Displacement or separation of the bone ends of a joint with loss of articulation
	f. Provide the setting for growth of anaerobic bacteria
	g. The skin overlying the injury remains intact

3. Shoulder and rotator cuff injuries usually occur from trauma or overuse. What orders would be given for conservative treatment of an injured shoulder? (Mark all that apply.)

a. Anesthetic injections

b. Physical therapy

c. Corticosteroid injections

d. Anti-inflammatory agents

e. Pain medicine

4. Hip injuries include dislocations and fractures of the hip. Why is dislocation of a hip considered a medical emergency?

a. The dislocation causes great pain

b. Avascular necrosis may result from the dislocation

c. The longer the hip is dislocated, the less chance of putting it back in place

d. Dislocation interrupts the blood supply to the femoral head

5. There are times when fractures of long bones need enhancement to promote healing. What can be done to induce bone formation and repair bone defects?

a. The use of steroids to induce bone growth

b. The use of growth factors to induce bone growth

c. The use of vibration therapy to induce bone growth

d. The use of physical therapy to induce bone growth

6. Determining the extent of the injury when a fracture occurs is important. It is also important to obtain a thorough history. What is important to determine during the history taking? (Mark all that apply.)

a. Anyone else in family prone to fractures

b. Recognition of symptoms

c. Any treatment initiated

d. Mechanism of injury

e. What patient has eaten

7. Match the complication with the definition.

Complication of Fracture	Definition
1. Fracture blisters	**a.** Areas of epidermal necrosis with separation of epidermis from the underlying dermis by edema fluid
2. Compartment syndrome	
3. Complex regional pain syndrome	**b.** Reflex sympathetic dystrophy
	c. A condition of increased pressure within a limited space (e.g., abdominal and limb compartments) that compromises the circulation and function of the tissues within the space.

8. Fat emboli syndrome can occur after a fracture of a long bone. What are the clinical features of this syndrome?

a. Petechiae on soles of feet and palms of hands

b. Respiratory insufficiency

c. Encephalopathy

d. Global neurologic deficits

9. Osteomyelitis is an infection of the bone. Chronic osteomyelitis is complicated by a piece of infected dead bone that has separated from the living bone. How long does the initial intravenous antibiotic therapy last for chronic osteomyelitis?
   a. 4 weeks
   b. 8 weeks
   c. 12 weeks
   d. 6 weeks

10. Tuberculosis can spread from the lungs into the musculoskeletal system. What is the most common site in the skeletal system for tuberculosis to be found?
    a. Spine
    b. Ankles
    c. Shoulders
    d. Hips

11. Osteonecrosis is a condition in which part of a bone dies because of the interruption of its blood supply. What is the most common cause of osteonecrosis other than fracture?
    a. Vessel injury
    b. Prior steroid therapy
    c. Radiation therapy
    d. Embolism

12. Osteosarcoma is an aggressive malignancy of the bone. What is the primary clinical feature of osteosarcoma?
    a. Pain, worse during the day
    b. Erythema in the overlaying skin
    c. Nighttime awakening
    d. Soreness in nearest joint

13. Metastatic bone disease is a frequent disorder. It occurs at a time when primary tumors in the lungs, breasts, and prostate seed themselves (metastasize) to the musculoskeletal system. What are the primary goals of treatment for metastatic bone disease? (Mark all that apply.)
    a. Prevent pathologic fractures
    b. Cure the disease
    c. Promote survival with maximum functioning
    d. Prevent ischemia to the bone segment
    e. Maintain mobility and pain control

CHAPTER 44

Disorders of the Skeletal System: Metabolic and Rheumatic Disorders

SECTION I: LEARNING OBJECTIVES

1. Characterize the common characteristics of the different systemic autoimmune rheumatic disorders.

2. Describe the pathologic changes that may be found in the joint of a person with rheumatoid arthritis.

3. List the extra-articular manifestations of rheumatoid arthritis.

4. Describe the immunologic process that occurs in systemic lupus erythematosus (SLE).

5. List four major organ systems that may be involved in SLE.

6. Describe the manifestations of systemic sclerosis.

7. Cite a definition of the seronegative spondyloarthropathies.

8. Cite the primary features of ankylosing spondylitis.

9. Describe how the site of inflammation differs in spondyloarthropathies from that in rheumatoid arthritis.

10. Contrast and compare ankylosing spondylitis, reactive arthritis, and psoriatic arthritis in terms of cause, pathogenesis, and clinical manifestations.

11. Compare rheumatoid arthritis and osteoarthritis in terms of joint involvement, level of inflammation, and local and systemic manifestations.

12. Describe the pathologic joint changes associated with osteoarthritis.

13. Characterize the treatment of osteoarthritis.

14. Relate the metabolism and elimination of uric acid to the pathogenesis of crystal-induced arthropathy.

15. State why asymptomatic hyperuricemia is a laboratory finding and not a disease.

16. Describe the clinical manifestations, diagnostic measures, and methods used in the treatment of gouty arthritis.

17. List three types of juvenile arthritis and differentiate among their major characteristics.

18. Name one rheumatic disease that affects only the elderly population.

SECTION II: ASSESSING YOUR UNDERSTANDING

Activity A *Fill in the blanks.*

1. The cause of _____ remains uncertain, but evidence points to a genetic predisposition and the development of joint inflammation that is immunologically mediated.

2. It has been suggested that rheumatoid arthritis is initiated in a genetically predisposed individual by the activation of a _____ response to an immunologic trigger, such as a microbial agent.

3. Systemic lupus erythematosus is a _____ disease that can affect virtually any organ system, including the musculoskeletal system.

4. Almost all persons with _____ develop polyarthritis and Raynaud phenomenon, a vascular disorder characterized by reversible vasospasm of the arteries supplying the fingers.

5. _____ is a chronic, systemic inflammatory disease of the joints of the axial skeleton manifested by pain and progressive stiffening of the spine.

6. The reactive _____ may be defined as sterile inflammatory joint disorders that are distant in time and place from the initial inciting infective process.

7. _____ is considered a clinical manifestation of reactive arthritis that may be accompanied by extra-articular symptoms such as uveitis, bowel inflammation, and carditis.

8. Arthritis that is associated with an inflammatory bowel disease usually is considered an _____ arthritis because the intestinal disease is directly involved in the pathogenesis.

9. _____ is the most prevalent form of arthritis and is a leading cause of disability and pain in the elderly.

10. Popularly known as _____ arthritis, osteoarthritis is characterized by significant changes in both the composition and mechanical properties of cartilage.

11. _____ syndrome includes acute arthritis with recurrent attacks of severe articular and periarticular inflammation; tophi or the accumulation of crystalline deposits in articular surfaces, bones, soft tissue, and cartilage; gouty nephropathy or renal impairment; and uric acid kidney stones.

12. _____ is characterized by synovitis and can influence epiphyseal growth by stimulating growth of the affected side.

13. Children with _____ may present with constitutional symptoms, including fever, malaise, anorexia, and weight loss, just as adults.

14. Juvenile _____ is an inflammatory myopathy primarily involving skin and muscle and associated with a characteristic rash.

15. _____ is the most common complaint of elderly persons.

16. _____ is by far the most common form of arthritis among the elderly.

17. _____ is an inflammatory condition of unknown origin characterized by aching and morning stiffness in the cervical regions and shoulder and pelvic girdle areas.

Activity B *Consider the following figure.*

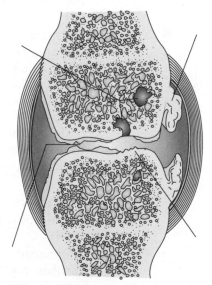

In the figure above, locate the following joint changes seen in osteoarthritis.

- Joint space narrows
- Erosion of cartilage and bone
- Osteophyte development
- Bone cysts

Activity C *Match the key terms in Column A with their definitions in Column B.*

Column A

___ 1. Spondyloarthropathies

___ 2. Reactive arthritis

___ 3. Systemic lupus erythematosus

___ 4. Joint mice

___ 5. Scleroderma

___ 6. Osteophytes

___ 7. Ankylosing spondylitis

___ 8. Baker cyst

___ 9. Polymyalgia rheumatica

___ 10. Gout

Column B

a. Autoimmune disease of connective tissue characterized by excessive collagen deposition

b. Bone spurs

c. Multisystem inflammatory disorders that primarily affect the axial skeleton

d. An inflammatory erosion of the sites where tendons and ligaments attach to bone

e. Result from the presence of a foreign substance in the joint tissue

f. Inflammatory condition marked by antinuclear antibodies

g. Enlargement of the bursa in the popliteal area behind the knee

h. Disorder of the muscles and joints, typically of older persons characterized by pain and stiffness, affecting both sides of the body, and involving the shoulders, arms, neck, and buttock areas

i. Uric acid crystals are found in the joint cavity

j. Fragments of cartilage and bone often become dislodged, creating free-floating osteocartilaginous bodies

Activity D *Put the following processes involved in rheumatoid arthritis in proper sequence.*

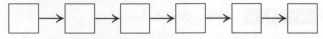

A. Inflammatory response

B. Recruitment of inflammatory cells

C. Destruction of articular cartilage

D. Complement fixation

E. T-cell−mediated response

F. Release of enzymes and prostaglandins

G. RH antigen/immunoglobulin G (IgG) interaction

Activity E *Briefly answer the following.*

1. What is the pathogenesis of rheumatoid arthritis?

_____

_____

_____

2. What causes the degradation of a joint in rheumatoid arthritis?

_____

_____

_____

3. What are the musculoskeletal manifestations of SLE?

_____

_____

_____

4. What are the typical joint changes seen in osteoarthritis?

_____

_____

_____

5. What is the pathogenesis of primary and secondary gout?

_____

_____

_____

SECTION III: APPLYING YOUR KNOWLEDGE

Activity F *Consider the scenario and answer the questions.*

Case study: A 5-year-old girl is brought to the clinic by her mother because she "just isn't feeling well." While taking the history, the nurse notes a weight loss of 5 pounds during the past year and complaints of malaise. The child's growth chart shows she is in the 20th percentile for height. During the physical examination, the physician notes pain in three joints, hepatosplenomegaly, and lymph adenopathy. The suspected diagnosis is juvenile idiopathic arthritis. The mother asks the nurse to explain juvenile idiopathic arthritis.

1. What information would the nurse include in her response?

_____

_____

_____

2. What confirmatory test would the nurse expect to see ordered?

_____

_____

_____

SECTION IV: PRACTICING FOR NCLEX

Activity G *Answer the following questions.*

1. Joint destruction in rheumatoid arthritis occurs by an obscure process. The cellular changes, however, have been documented. Place the process in the correct order.
   a. Vasodilation
   b. Joint swelling
   c. Neutrophils, macrophages, and lymphocytes arrive
   d. Lysosomal enzymes released
   e. Immune complexes phagocytized
   f. Inflammatory response
   g. Reactive hyperplasia of synovial cells and subsynovial tissues
   h. Increased blood flow to joint
   i. Destructive changes in joint cartilage

2. Systemic lupus erythematosus has been called the great imitator because it can affect many different body systems. What is among the most commonly occurring symptoms in the early stages of SLE?
   a. Arthritis
   b. Avascular necrosis
   c. Rupture of the Achilles tendon
   d. Classic malar rash

3. Scleroderma is an autoimmune disease of connective tissue that is characterized by hardening of the skin. What diseases do almost all people with scleroderma develop? (Mark all that apply.)
   a. Dumping syndrome
   b. Chronic diarrhea
   c. Polyarthritis
   d. Raynaud phenomenon
   e. Chronic vasoconstriction

4. Polymyositis and dermatomyositis are chronic inflammatory myopathies that commonly manifest systemically. What is the treatment of choice for these myopathies?
   a. Muscle relaxants
   b. Corticosteroids
   c. IgG
   d. Nonsteroidal anti-inflammatory drugs (NSAIDs)

5. Ankylosing spondylitis is a disease that typically manifests in late adolescence and early adulthood. What is characteristic of the pain in ankylosing spondylitis?
   a. Worse when active
   b. Worse when sitting
   c. Worse when lying
   d. Worse when standing

6. Reiter syndrome is a reactive arthropathy. What disease is Reiter syndrome associated with?
   a. Pelvic inflammatory disease
   b. Gonorrhea
   c. Syphilis
   d. Human immunodeficiency virus (HIV)

7. A seronegative inflammatory arthropathy is psoriatic arthritis. What drug has been found to be beneficial in controlling both the psoriasis and the arthritis in these patients?

   a. Etanercept
   b. Acetaminophen
   c. Interferon B
   d. Econazole

8. Osteoarthritis is the most common cause of arthritis and a significant cause of disability in the elderly. What joint changes occur in osteoarthritis? (Mark all that apply.)

   a. Creation of spurs
   b. Loss of synovial fluid
   c. Loss of articular cartilage
   d. Inflammation of cartilage
   e. Synovitis

9. Gout, or gouty arthritis, cannot be diagnosed on the basis of hyperuricemia. What is the diagnostic criterion for gout?

   a. Finding of tophaceous deposits
   b. Finding of monosodium urate crystals in the synovial fluid
   c. Finding of sodium urate crystals in the tissues
   d. Finding of urate crystal deposits in the synovial fluid

10. The elderly population needs special consideration in the treatment of the arthritic diseases. The NSAIDs, a first-line group of drugs used in the general population for arthritic diseases, may not be well tolerated by the elderly. What side effects of NSAIDs might be seen in the elderly?

    a. Malaise
    b. Lethargy
    c. Sleeplessness
    d. Mania

CHAPTER 45

Structure and Function of the Skin

SECTION I: LEARNING OBJECTIVES

1. Describe the protective functions of skin.

2. Characterize the changes in a keratinocyte from its inception in the basal lamina to its arrival on the outer surface of the skin.

3. List the four specialized cells of the epidermis and describe their functions.

4. Describe the structure and function of the dermis and subcutaneous layers of skin.

5. Describe the following skin appendages and their functions: sebaceous gland, eccrine gland, apocrine gland, nails, and hair.

6. Characterize the skin in terms of sensory and immune functions.

7. Describe the following skin rashes and lesions: macule, patch, papule, plaque, nodule, tumor, wheal, vesicle, bulla, and pustule.

8. Describe the characteristics and causes of blisters, calluses, and corns.

9. Cite two physiologic explanations for pruritus.

10. Describe the causes and treatment of dry skin.

11. State common variations found in dark skin.

SECTION II: ASSESSING YOUR UNDERSTANDING

Activity A *Fill in the blanks.*

1. The skin, also called the _____, is one of the largest organs and most versatile organs of the body, accounting for roughly 16% of the body's weight.

2. Variations are found in the properties of the skin, such as the _____ of skin layers, the distribution of sweat glands, and the number and size of hair follicles.

3. The _____ covers the body, and it is specialized in areas to form the various skin appendages: hair, nails, and glandular structures.

4. The top or surface layer of the skin, the _____, consists of dead, keratinized cells.

5. _____ produce keratin, a complex protein that that forms the surface of the skin, is also the structural protein of the hair, and nails.

6. _____ are pigment-synthesizing cells that are located at or in the basal layer.

7. Exposure to the sun's ultraviolet rays increases the production of _____, causing tanning to occur.

8. _____ cells are potent antigen-presenting cells.

9. The _____ is involved in skin disorders that cause bullae or blister formation.

10. The dermis supports the _____ and serves as its primary source of nutrition.

11. The receptors for touch, pressure, heat, cold, and pain are widely distributed in the _____.

12. The _____ layer of the dermis is supplied with free nerve endings that serve as nociceptors and thermoreceptors.

13. _____ sweat glands are simple tubular structures that originate in the dermis and open directly to the skin surface.

14. _____ sweat glands open through a hair follicle and are found primarily in the axillae and groin.

15. Hair is a _____ structure that is pushed upward from the hair follicle.

16. The nails are hardened _____ plates, called fingernails and toenails, that protect the fingers and toes and enhance dexterity.

17. A _____ is a vesicle or fluid-filled papule.

18. A _____ is a hyperkeratotic plaque of skin due to chronic pressure or friction.

19. _____ are small, well-circumscribed, conical, keratinous thickenings of the skin.

20. Dry skin, also called _____, may be a natural occurrence, as in the drying of skin associated with aging, or it may be symptomatic of underlying systemic disease or skin disorder such as contract dermatitis.

Activity B *Consider the following figures.*

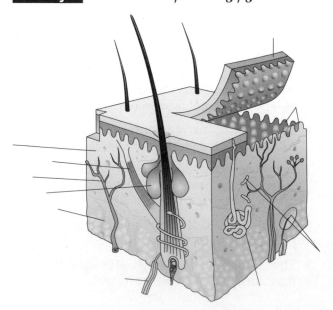

1. In the figure above, locate and label the following structures:

- Nerve
- Sebaceous gland
- Blood vessel
- Arrector pili muscle
- Dermis
- Sweat gland
- Papillae
- Epidermis

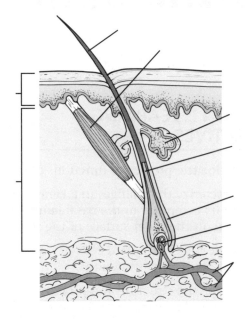

2. In the figure above, locate and label the following structures:

- Epidermis
- Hair papilla
- Dermis
- Hair shaft
- Arrector pili
- Sebaceous gland
- Keratinized cells
- Hair follicle
- Dermal blood vessels

Activity C *Match the key terms in Column A with their definitions in Column B.*

Column A

_____ 1. Keratinocytes

_____ 2. Merkel cells

_____ 3. Keratinization

_____ 4. Epidermis

_____ 5. Papillary dermis

_____ 6. Langerhans cells

_____ 7. Dermis

_____ 8. Ruffini corpuscles

_____ 9. Melanin

_____ 10. Reticular dermis

Column B

a. Consists of collagen fibers and ground substance

b. Responsible for skin color, tanning, and protecting against ultraviolet radiation

c. Outer layer of skin

d. Produce a fibrous protein called keratin, which is essential to the protective function

e. Complex meshwork of three-dimensional collagen bundles interconnected with large elastic fibers and ground substance

f. Inner layer of skin

g. Mechanoreceptors

h. Immune cells

i. Transformation from viable cells to the dead cells of the stratum corneum

j. Provide sensory information

Activity D *Briefly answer the following.*

1. What are the vital functions of the skin?

_____

_____

_____

2. What are the layers of the epidermis?

_____

_____

_____

3. How is it that a person with albinism cannot synthesize melanin?

_____

_____

_____

4. What is the relationship between melanin and different colors of skin?

_____

_____

_____

5. Describe the structure and function of sebaceous glands.

_____

_____

_____

6. How does and itch differ from pain?

_____

_____

_____

SECTION III: APPLYING YOUR KNOWLEDGE

Activity E *Consider the scenario and answer the questions.*

Case study: You are the nurse preparing an educational event for the local chapter of the Daughters of the American Revolution (DAR). You have been asked to speak on skin disorders.

a. What information would you include about dark-skinned people?

_____

_____

_____

SECTION IV: PRACTICING FOR NCLEX

Activity F *Answer the following questions.*

1. Among the skin's protective functions is the fact that it serves as an immunologic barrier. What cells detect foreign antigens?

   a. The Langerhans cells

   b. The Merkel cells

   c. The keratinocytes

   d. The melanocytes

2. Match the cells of the epidermis with their description or function.

Cell	Description or Function
1. Keratinocytes	a. Thought to be neuroendocrine cells
2. Melanocytes	b. Pigment-synthesizing cells
3. Merkel cells	c. Replaces lost skin cells
4. Langerhans cells	d. Immunologic cells

3. The basement membrane separates the epithelium from the underlying connective tissue. It is a major site of what is in skin disease?
   a. Melanocytes
   b. Complement deposition
   c. The lamina lucida
   d. Type IV collagen

4. What is the pars reticularis characterized by?
   a. Dendritic cells
   b. Its color
   c. Three-dimensional collagen bundles
   d. Its immunologic function

5. Why is the subcutaneous tissue considered part of the skin? (Mark all that apply.)
   a. Eccrine glands extend to this layer
   b. The keratinocytes are formed in the subcutaneous tissue
   c. Skin diseases can involve the subcutaneous tissue
   d. The Merkel cells are formed in the subcutaneous tissue
   e. Deep hair follicles can be found in the subcutaneous tissue

6. Cerumen glands excrete a mixture that lubricates the hair and skin. What is this mixture called?
   a. Sweat
   b. Chalasia
   c. Cerumen
   d. Sebum

7. Fingernails and toenails, unlike hair, grow continuously. The nail plate itself is nearly transparent and acts as a window for viewing what?
   a. The amount of oxygen in the blood
   b. The color of the blood in the subcutaneous tissue
   c. The health of the nail plate
   d. The color of the stratum corneum

8. When a degeneration of the epidermal cells occurs, there is separation of the layers of the skin because of a disruption of the intercellular junctions. When this occurs what is formed?
   a. Lichenifications
   b. Vesicles
   c. Petechiae
   d. Pressure ulcer

9. Pruritis, or the itch sensation, is a by-product of almost all skin disorders. However, we can itch without having a skin disorder. Itch then can be local or central in our bodies. Where is it postulated that a central "itch center" exists?
   a. Pons
   b. Medulla oblongata
   c. Somatosensory cortex
   d. Sensory area of the cerebrum

10. The first-line treatment for dry skin is moisturizing agents. How do these agents work?
    a. Decreasing pruritis
    b. Penetrating the lipid barrier of the skin
    c. Increasing transepidermal water loss
    d. Repairing the skin barrier

CHAPTER 46

Disorders of Skin Integrity and Function

SECTION I: LEARNING OBJECTIVES

1. Describe common pigmentary disorders of the skin.

2. Relate the behavior of fungi to the production of superficial skin lesions associated with tinea or ringworm.

3. State the cause and describe the appearance of impetigo and ecthyma.

4. Compare the viral causes, manifestations, and treatments of verrucae, herpes simplex, and herpes zoster lesions.

5. Compare acne vulgaris, acne conglobata, and rosacea in terms of appearance and location of lesions.

6. Describe the pathogenesis of acne vulgaris and relate it to measures used in treating the disorder.

7. Differentiate allergic and contact dermatitis and atopic and nummular eczema.

8. Describe the differences and similarities between erythema multiforme minor, Stevens-Johnson syndrome, and toxic epidermal necrolysis.

9. Define the term *papulosquamous* and use the term to describe the lesions associated with psoriasis, pityriasis rosea, and lichen planus.

10. Relate the life cycle of *Sarcoptes scabiei* to the skin lesions seen in scabies.

11. Describe the three types of ultraviolet radiation and relate them to sunburn, aging skin changes, and the development of skin cancer.

12. Describe the manifestations and treatment of sunburn.

13. State the properties of an effective sunscreen.

14. Compare the tissue involvement in first-degree, second-degree full-thickness, and third-degree burns.

15. State how the rule of nine is used in determining the body surface area involved in a burn.

16. Cite the determinants for grading burn severity using the American Burn Association classification of burns.

17. Describe the systemic complications of burns.

18. Describe the major considerations in treatment of burn injury.

19. Cite two causes of pressure ulcers.

20. Explain how shearing forces contribute to ischemic skin damage.

21. List four measures that contribute to the prevention of pressure ulcers.

22. Describe the origin of nevi and state their relationship to skin cancers.

23. Compare the appearance and outcome of basal cell carcinoma, squamous cell carcinoma, and malignant melanoma.

24. Differentiate a strawberry hemangioma of infancy from a port-wine stain hemangioma in terms of appearance and outcome.

25. Describe the manifestations and probable causes of diaper dermatitis, prickly heat, and cradle cap.

26. Describe the distinguishing features of rashes associated with the following infectious childhood diseases: roseola infantum, rubeola, rubella, and varicella.

27. Characterize the physiologic changes of aging skin.

28. Describe the appearance of skin tags, keratoses, lentigines, and vascular lesions that are commonly seen in the elderly.

SECTION II: ASSESSING YOUR UNDERSTANDING

Activity A *Fill in the blanks.*

1. _____ skin disorders include pigmentary skin disorders, infectious processes, acne, rosacea, papulosquamous dermatoses, allergic disorders and drug reactions, and arthropod infestations.

2. _____ is a genetic disorder in which there is complete or partial congenital absence of pigment in the skin, hair, and eyes is found in all races.

3. _____ are free-living, saprophytic plantlike organisms, certain strains of which are considered part of the normal skin flora.

4. _____ is a yeastlike fungus that is a normal inhabitant of the gastrointestinal tract, mouth, and vagina.

5. Primary _____ infections are superficial skin infections such as impetigo or ecthyma.

6. _____ is common, superficial bacterial infection caused by staphylococci or group A β-hemolytic streptococci that appears as a small vesicle or pustule or as a large bulla on the face or elsewhere on the body.

7. _____ is a deeper infection affecting the dermis and subcutaneous tissues.

8. _____ and _____ occur on the soles of the feet and palms of the hands, respectively.

9. Herpes _____ is an acute, localized vesicular eruption distributed over a dermatomal segment of the skin.

10. _____ is a disorder of the pilosebaceous unit.

11. _____ consists of a mixture of free fatty acids, triglycerides, diglycerides, monoglycerides, sterol esters, wax esters, and squalene.

12. Noninflammatory acne lesions consist of _____; _____ are plugs of material that accumulate in sebaceous glands that open to the skin surface and _____ are pale, slightly elevated papules with no visible orifice.

13. _____ acne lesions consist of papules, pustules, nodules, and, in severe cases, cysts.

14. Hypersensitivity _____ are usually characterized by epidermal edema with separation of epidermal cells; they include irritant contact dermatitis, allergy contact dermatitis, atopic and nummular eczema, urticaria, and drug-induced skin eruptions.

15. _____ dermatitis results from a cell-mediated, type IV hypersensitivity response brought about by sensitization to an allergen.

16. Acute immunologic _____ is commonly the result of an immunoglobulin E-mediated immune reaction that usually occurs within 1 hour of exposure to an antigen.

17. _____ drugs are usually responsible for localized contact dermatitis types of rashes, whereas _____ drugs cause generalized skin lesions.

18. _____ dermatoses are a group of skin disorders characterized by scaling papules and plaques.

19. _____ is a relatively common chronic, pruritic disease that involves inflammation and papular eruption of the skin and mucous membranes.

20. Lichen simplex chronicus is a localized lichenoid, pruritic dermatitis resulting from _____ rubbing and scratching.

21. A mite, *Sarcoptes scabiei*, which burrows into the epidermis, causes _____.

22. _____, commonly referred to as *sunburn rays,* are responsible for nearly all the skin effects of sunlight, including *photoaging*—the wrinkles, pigmentary changes, dryness, and loss of skin tone that occurs with and is enhanced by exposure to sunlight.

23. Some drugs are classified as _____ drugs because they produce an exaggerated response to ultraviolet light when the drug is taken in combination with sun exposure.

24. _____ is caused by excessive exposure of the epidermal and dermal layers of the skin to ultraviolet radiation, resulting in an erythematous inflammatory reaction.

25. _____ are typically classified according to the depth of involvement as first-degree, second-degree, and third-degree.

26. _____ victims often are confronted with hemodynamic instability, impaired respiratory function, hypermetabolic response, major organ dysfunction, and sepsis.

27. Pressure ulcers are _____ lesions of the skin and underlying structures caused by unrelieved pressure that impairs the flow of blood and lymph.

28. Another form of nevi, the _____, is important because of its capacity to transform to malignant melanoma.

29. Malignant melanoma is a malignant tumor of the _____.

30. Severe, blistering sunburns in early childhood and intermittent intense sun exposures contribute to increased susceptibility to _____ in young and middle-aged adults.

31. _____, which is a neoplasm of the nonkeratinizing cells of the basal layer of the epidermis, is the most common skin cancer in white-skinned people.

32. _____ are the second most frequent occurring malignant tumors of the outer epidermis.

33. Pigmented _____ represent abnormal migration or proliferation of melanocytes seen in infants.

34. _____ of infancy are generally benign vascular tumors produced by proliferation of the endothelial cells.

35. _____ represent slow-growing capillary malformations that grow proportionately with a child and persist throughout life.

36. _____ is a form of contact dermatitis that is caused by an interaction with several factors, including prolonged contact of the skin with a mixture of urine and feces.

37. _____ results from constant maceration of the skin because of prolonged exposure to a warm, humid environment.

38. _____ is a greasy crust or scale formation on the scalp that is usually attributed to infrequent and inadequate washing of the scalp.

Activity B *Match the key terms in Column A with their definitions in Column B.*

1.

Column A	Column B
___ 1. Herpes simplex virus	a. Pain that persists longer than 1 to 3 months after the resolution of herpes zoster rash
___ 2. Vitiligo	
___ 3. Postherpetic neuralgia	b. Responsible for cold sore
___ 4. Dermatophytid	c. Superficial mycoses
___ 5. Melasma	d. Warts that are common benign papillomas caused by DNA-containing human papillomaviruses
___ 6. Ecthyma	
___ 7. Verrucae	
___ 8. Dermatophytoses	e. Sudden appearance of white patches on the skin
___ 9. Tinea capitis	f. Darkened macules on the face
___ 10. Shingles	g. Allergic reaction during an acute episode of a fungal infection
	h. Ulcerative form of impetigo
	i. Caused by infection of herpes zoster
	j. Ringworm of the scalp

2.

Column A

_____ **1.** Verrucae

_____ **2.** Acne vulgaris

_____ **3.** Psoriasis

_____ **4.** Acne conglobata

_____ **5.** Decubitus ulcers

_____ **6.** Rosacea

_____ **7.** Urticaria

_____ **8.** Nevi

_____ **9.** Rhinophyma

_____ **10.** Hyper-keratosis

Column B

a. Comedones form primarily on the face and neck and, to a lesser extent, on the back, chest, and shoulders

b. Disorder characterized the development of edematous wheals accompanied by intense itching

c. Thickening of the skin associated with rosacea

d. Bed sore

e. Comedones, papules, pustules, nodules, abscesses, cysts, and scars occur on the back, buttocks, and chest

f. Mole

g. Erythema (flushing and redness) on the central face and across the cheeks, nose, or forehead

h. Benign papillomas caused by the DNA-containing human papillomavirus

i. Increased epidermal cell turnover with marked epidermal thickening

j. Chronic inflammatory skin disease characterized by circumscribed red, thickened plaques with an overlying silvery-white scale

Activity C _Briefly answer the following._

1. What is the cause and symptomology of albinism?

_____

_____

_____

2. What is the mechanism of skin irritation with a fungal infection?

_____

_____

3. What are the types of tinea capitis and what are the mechanisms of irritation?

_____

_____

_____

4. What is the port of entry for cellulitis infections? What are the most common symptoms?

_____

_____

_____

5. Herpes simplex virus type-1 virus will have episodic recurrences. What is the mechanism of recurrence? What are the signs and symptoms of recurrence?

_____

_____

_____

6. What are the factors believed to contribute to the development of acne?

_____

_____

_____

7. What is atopic dermatitis and how does it affect adults differently than infants?

_____

_____

_____

8. What is thought to be the cause of psoriasis?

_____

_____

_____

9. What is the hypothesized mechanism of skin damage brought about by UV-B rays?

_____

_____

_____

10. What are the steps recommended to protect a patient from UV exposure?

_____

_____

_____

11. Why are severe burns an immediate medical emergency?

_____

_____

_____

12. Describe the two main types of basal cell carcinoma.

_____

_____

_____

_____

SECTION III: APPLYING YOUR KNOWLEDGE

Activity D *Consider the scenario and answer the questions.*

A 17-year-old patient with second- and third-degree burns on his trunk, arms, and neck is brought to the emergency department, where he is being stabilized for shipment to the nearest burn unit.

1. The mother asks why her son must be sent to another hospital. The nurse explains that the client is at high risk for complications from his burns. What does the massive loss of skin tissue predispose the client to?

_____

_____

_____

2. The parents ask what specific complication can occur because of the burns their son has. The nurse's correct response would include what?

_____

_____

_____

SECTION IV: PRACTICING FOR NCLEX

Activity E *Answer the following questions.*

1. Match the skin disorder with its description.

Skin Disorder	Description
1. Vitiligo	**A.** Darkened macules on the face
2. Albinism	**B.** Sudden appearance of white patches on the skin
3. Melasma	**C.** A genetic disorder in which there is complete or partial congenital absence of pigment in the skin, hair, and eyes; it is found in all races.

2. Our bodies have, as endemic organisms, both yeast (*Candida albicans*) and molds. When a fungus invades the skin of our body, what is used as a confirmatory diagnostic test?
   a. Potassium hydroxide preparations
   b. The Forest light
   c. Tinea preparations
   d. Sodium chloride preparations

3. Match the bacterial or viral skin infection with its preferred treatment.

Skin Infection	Preferred Treatment
1. Impetigo	**a.** Systemic antibiotics
2. Ecthyma	**b.** Bactroban or systemic antibiotics
3. Cellulitis	**c.** Acyclovir
4. Verrucae	**d.** Oral acyclovir
5. Herpes simplex virus type-1	**e.** Penciclovir cream
6. Herpes simplex virus type-2	**f.** Oral and intravenous antibiotics
7. Herpes zoster	**g.** A keratolytic agent

4. Acne vulgaris is typically an infection in the adolescent population. What topical agent used in the treatment of acne is both an antibacterial and a comedolytic?
   a. Alcohol
   b. Benzoyl peroxide
   c. Bactroban
   d. Resorcinol

5. Rosacea is a chronic inflammatory process that occurs in middle-aged and older adults. What are common manifestations of rosacea? (Mark all that apply.)
   a. Swelling of the eyelid
   b. Heat sensitivity
   c. Burning eyes
   d. Telangiectasia
   e. Erythema

6. Allergic contact dermatitis is a common inflammation of the skin. It produces lesions in the affected areas. What do these lesions look like?
   a. Papules
   b. Papulosquamous pustules
   c. Vesicles
   d. Ulcers

7. Atopic dermatitis, or eczema, occurs at all ages and in all races. What happens in black-skinned people who have eczema?
   a. Hyperpigmentation of skin
   b. Papules cover the area affected
   c. Erythema is a prominent symptom
   d. Loss of pigmentation from lichenified skin

8. In severe Stevens-Johnson syndrome and toxic epidermal necrolysis, hospitalization is required. When large areas of the skin are lost, what intravenous medication may speed up the healing process?
   a. Immunoglobulin
   b. Broad-spectrum antibiotics
   c. Diflucan
   d. Corticosteroids

9. What disease has primary lesions that have a silvery scale over thick red plaques?
   a. Pityriasis rosea
   b. Psoriasis vulgaris
   c. Lichen planus
   d. Lichen simplex chronicus

10. What skin disease manifests with lesions on the skin and oral lesions that look like milky white lacework?
    a. Eczema
    b. Psoriasis
    c. Lichen planus
    d. Pityriasis rosea

11. Scabies infections are caused by mites that burrow under the skin. They are usually easily treated by bathing with a mite-killing agent and leaving it on for 12 hours. When scabies are resistant to the mite-killing agent, what oral drug is prescribed?
    a. Clindamycin
    b. Interferon B
    c. Potassium hydroxide
    d. Ivermectin

12. Pressure ulcers can occur quickly in the elderly and in those who are immobile. What is a method for preventing pressure ulcers?
    a. Preventing dehydration
    b. Frequent position changes
    c. Use of water-based skin moisturizers
    d. Infrequent changing of incontinent clients

13. Nevi are benign tumors of the skin. There is one type of nevi that is important because of its capacity to transform to malignant melanoma. What type of nevus is this?
    a. Nevocellular
    b. Compound nevi
    c. Dysplastic
    d. Dermal

14. Malignant melanomas are metastatic tumors of the skin. In the past decades the incidence of malignant melanoma has grown. This is related to more exposure to UV light, such as tanning salons. What are risk factors for developing malignant melanoma?
    a. Freckles across the bridge of the nose
    b. Blistering sunburns after age 20
    c. Palmar nevi
    d. Presence of actinic keratoses

15. Basal cell carcinoma is the most common skin cancer in white-skinned people. The treatment goal that is most important is elimination of the lesion, but it is also important to maintain the function and cosmetic effect. What treatment is used for basal cell carcinoma?

a. Curettage with electrodesiccation

b. Systemic chemotherapy

c. Topical chemotherapy

d. Simple radiographic radiation

16. Squamous cell carcinoma in light-skinned people is a red, scaling, keratotic, slightly elevated lesion with an irregular border, usually with a shallow chronic ulcer. How do they appear in black-skinned people?

a. Keratotic lesions with rolling, irregular borders

b. Hyperpigmented nodules

c. Hypopigmented nodules

d. Lichenous plaques with silvery scales

17. Hemangiomas of infancy are small, red lesions that are noticed shortly after birth and grow rapidly. What is the treatment of choice for hemangiomas of infancy?

a. Surgical excision

b. Laser surgery

c. No treatment

d. Chemotherapy

18. Rubella, or 3-day measles, is a childhood disease caused by a togavirus. Because rubella can be easily transmitted and because it is dangerous to the fetus if contracted by pregnant women early in their gestational period, immunization is required. What type of vaccine is the rubella vaccine?

a. Attenuated virus vaccine

b. Antibody/antigen vaccine

c. Dead-virus vaccine

d. Live-virus vaccine

19. Lentigines are skin lesions common in the elderly. A type of lentigines is tan to brown in color with benign spots. Lentigines are removed because they are considered precursors to skin cancer. How are lentigines removed?

a. Cryotherapy

b. Chemotherapy

c. Bleaching agents

d. Curettage

Answer Key

CHAPTER 1

SECTION II: ASSESSING YOUR UNDERSTANDING

Activity A

1. Cytoplasm
2. Eukaryotic, prokaryotic
3. DNA, RNA, proteins
4. Protein
5. Rough
6. Golgi
7. Lysosomes
8. Peroxides
9. Respiration, ATP
10. Microtubules
11. microfilaments
12. peripheral
13. epithelial, connective, muscle, neuronal
14. ion
15. muscle, neural

Activity B

1.

1. b	**2.** g	**3.** f	**4.** j	**5.** d
6. a	**7.** e	**8.** g	**9.** i	**10.** c

2.

1. j	**2.** f	**3.** b	**4.** g	**5.** d
6. e	**7.** h	**8.** i	**9.** c	**10.** a

Activity C

1.

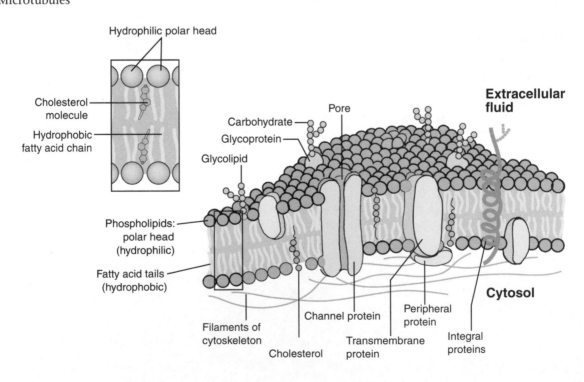

Activity D

1. In ischemia and hypoxia (an anoxia), the cells do not receive enough oxygen. As a result, the electron transport chain cannot pass electrons from complex to complex. Proton pumping slows or is halted and the proton gradient decreases, resulting in a decreased production or a complete lack of ATP. With no ATP, the cell cannot maintain normal functioning (e.g., membrane potential, transport) and begins to malfunction.

2. Individual cells produce extracellular matrix proteins that form a basement membrane where cells can form anchors. Cells will then form connections between each other via cell junctions (tight, gap, desmosome, hemidesmosome). This interaction between cytoskeletal elements, the basement membrane, and cellular adhesion is the basis for tissue formation.

3. First messengers can be neurotransmitters, protein hormones and growth factors, steroids, and/or other chemical messengers. They will bind to receptors either on the cell membrane (hydrophilic first messengers) or in the cytoplasm (hydrophobic first messengers). The activation of a receptor via first messenger results in the activation of a second messenger. Cell surface receptors are transmembrane proteins that will activate an array of second messengers (cAMP, G proteins, and tyrosine kinases) that will have direct effects on membrane potential or a host of other cellular functions. Activation of an intracellular receptor involves the activation of a transcription factor that will directly influence the expression of a gene product. The gene product will then have an effect on cellular function.

4. Endocytosis is the process of bringing in large molecules or substances to a cell. Receptor-mediated endocytosis is triggered by a specific ligand. The inflammatory system contains cells (macrophages, neutrophils) that will endocytose dead cell material, bacteria, or foreign material. This process is known as *phagocytosis*. Exocytosis is the release of large quantities of material, such as the exocytosis of a neurotransmitter.

SECTION III: APPLYING YOUR KNOWLEDGE

Activity E

1. In our bodies, fat is stored in tissue called adipose tissue. Adipose tissue is a special form of connective tissue, so it helps to connect different types of tissue in our body to each other. Adipose cells contain big empty spaces so they can store large quantities of triglycerides and are the largest storage spaces of energy in the body. The subcutaneous fat we store helps to shape our body. It also helps to insulate our body because fat is a poor conductor of heat.

   Adipose tissue exists in two forms: unilocular and multilocular. Unilocular (white) adipose tissue is composed of cells in which the fat is contained in a single, large droplet in the cytoplasm. Multilocular (brown) adipose tissue is composed of cells that contain multiple droplets of fat and numerous mitochondria.

   We have deposits of brown fat when we are born but they decrease over time. White fat is the kind we have most of and it is what we add to our body when we gain weight.

SECTION IV: PRACTICING FOR NCLEX

Activity F

1. **Answer: a**
   RATIONALE: Rough ER is studded with ribosomes attached to specific binding sites on the membrane. Proteins produced by the rough ER are usually destined for incorporation into cell membranes and lysosomal enzymes or for exportation from the cell. The rough ER segregates (rather than combines) these proteins from other components of the cytoplasm and modifies their structure for a specific function. Rough ER does not transport anything through the cell membrane. Rough ER is studded with ribosomes; it does not destroy them.

2. **Answer: b**
   RATIONALE: Recent data suggest that the Golgi apparatus has yet another function: it can receive proteins and other substances from the cell surface by a retrograde transport mechanism. Golgi bodies do not produce bile. They produce secretory, not excretory, granules and they produce large carbohydrate molecules rather than small ones.

3. **Answer: c**
   RATIONALE: Although GM_2 ganglioside accumulates in many tissues, such as the heart, liver, and spleen, its accumulation in the nervous system and retina of the eye causes the most damage.

4. **Answer: d**
   RATIONALE: They do not make energy, but they extract it from organic compounds. Proteasomes are small organelles composed of protein complexes that are thought to be present in both the cytoplasm and the nucleus. They are not formed by mitochondria. Mitochondria contain their own DNA and ribosomes and are self-replicating.

5. **Answer: a**
   RATIONALE: The cell membrane is often called the *plasma membrane*. The nuclear membrane is another type of membrane within the cell. The cell membrane provides receptors for hormones and other biologically active substances; it is not a receptor membrane. A main structural component of the membrane is its lipid bilayer. It is not a bilayer membrane.

6. **Answer: b**
   RATIONALE: At the membrane of the cell nucleus both thyroid and steroid hormones cross into the cell nucleus itself where they influence DNA activity. Ion-channel–linked receptors transiently open or close ion channels. Thyroid and steroid hormones act within the cell nucleus to increase transcription of mRNA to alter cell function.

7. Answer: c
RATIONALE: Each of the two pyruvate molecules formed in the cytoplasm from one molecule of glucose yields another molecule of ATP, which is a special carrier for cellular energy. FAD, or flavin adenine dinucleotide, is a coenzyme of protein metabolism that accepts electrons and is reduced. $NADH + H^+$ is an end product of glycolysis. The electron transport chain oxidizes $NADH + H^+$ and $FADH_2$ and donates the electrons to oxygen, which is reduced to water.

8. Answer: d
RATIONALE: Active transport is what happens when cells use energy to move ions against an electrical or chemical gradient. *Passive transport* is another term for diffusion. There is no such thing as neutral transport. Cotransport is when the sodium ion and the solute are transported in the same direction.

9. Answer: a
RATIONALE: Four categories of tissue exist: (1) epithelium, (2) connective (supportive) tissue, (3) muscle, and (4) nerve. Binding, connecting, and exothelium tissue are not categories of tissue.

10. Answer: b
RATIONALE: These glands are ductless and produce secretions (i.e., hormones) that move directly into the bloodstream. Exocrine glands retain their connection with the surface epithelium from which they originated. This connection takes the form of epithelium-lined tubular ducts through which the secretions pass to reach the surface. Exocytosis occurs when part of the cell membrane ruptures to release particles that are too large to pass through the cell membrane. These cells are ductless, but do not necessarily secrete their contents into the bloodstream.

11. Answer: c
RATIONALE: Thin and thick filaments are the two types of muscle fibers that are responsible for muscle contraction. The thin filaments are composed primarily of actin and the thick filaments are composed of myosin. During muscle contraction, the thick myosin and thin actin filaments slide over each other, causing shortening of the muscle fiber, although the length of the individual thick and thin filaments remains unchanged. When activated by ATP, the cross-bridges swivel in a fixed arc, much like the oars of a boat, as they become attached to the actin filament. During contraction, each cross-bridge undergoes its own cycle of movement, forming a bridge attachment and releasing it, and moving to another site where the same sequence of movement occurs. This pulls the thin and thick filaments past each other. The calcium–calmodulin complex is in smooth muscle. It binds to and activates the myosin-containing thick filaments, which interact with actin.

12. Answer: cytoplasm
RATIONALE: When seen under a light microscope, three major components of the cell become evident: the nucleus, the cytoplasm, and the cell membrane.

13. Answer: jaundice
RATIONALE: When bilirubin collects within the cells, they take on a yellowish color, which is called jaundice.

14. Answers: a, c, d
RATIONALE: The human body has several means of transmitting information between cells. These mechanisms include direct communication between adjacent cells through gap junctions, autocrine and paracrine signaling, and endocrine or synaptic signaling. There is no such thing as express communication between cells.

15. Answers: b, c, d
RATIONALE: Nondividing cells, such as neurons and skeletal and cardiac muscle cells, have left the cell cycle and are not capable of mitotic division in postnatal life. The cells that produce mucous are capable of mitotic division. Smooth muscle is often called *involuntary muscle* because it contracts spontaneously or through activity of the autonomic nervous system.

16. Answer: involuntary
RATIONALE: Three types of muscle tissue exist: skeletal, cardiac, and smooth. Smooth muscle is often called involuntary muscle because it contracts without the person willing it to contract.

CHAPTER 2

SECTION II: ASSESSING YOUR UNDERSTANDING

Activity A

1. size, number, and type
2. size
3. atrophy
4. increase
5. physiologic hypertrophy
6. hyperplasia
7. compensatory
8. Pathologic, nonphysiologic
9. Metaplasia
10. irritation, inflammation
11. dysplasia
12. cancer
13. accumulations
14. Free
15. Hypoxia
16. swelling, fatty
17. Necrosis
18. calcium
19. coagulation

Activity B

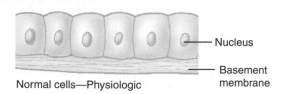

Normal cells—Physiologic

Nucleus

Basement membrane

Atrophy—Pathologic

Hypertrophy—Both

Hyperplasia—Both

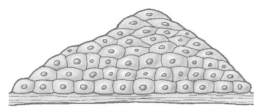

Metaplasia—Both

Dysplasia—Pathologic

Activity C

1. e	2. b	3. e	4. g	5. a
6. c	7. f	8. i	9. h	10. j

Activity D

1. The pathogenesis of dystrophic calcification involves the intracellular and/or extracellular formation of crystalline calcium phosphate. The components of the calcium deposits are derived from the bodies of dead or dying cells as well as from the circulation and interstitial fluid. As tissues die, the calcium crystallizes and deposits form.

2. (1) Injury from physical agents, (2) radiation injury, (3) chemical injury, (4) injury from biologic agents, and (5) injury from nutritional imbalances.

3. The toxicity of lead is related to its multiple biochemical effects. It has the ability to inactivate enzymes, compete with calcium for incorporation into bone, and interfere with nerve transmission and brain development. Lead exposure in children has been demonstrated to result in neurobehavioral and cognitive deficits.

4. The three major mechanisms of cellular damage are free radical formation, hypoxia and ATP depletion, and disruption of intracellular calcium homeostasis. Multiple pathologies, be it mechanical, chemical, biological, or blunt force, will result in a combination of these mechanisms being activated.

5. Oxidative stress leads to the oxidation of cell components, activation of signal transduction pathways, and changes in gene and protein expression. DNA modification and damage can occur because of oxidative stress. In addition, mitochondrial DNA as a target of oxidation and subsequent cause of mitochondrial dysfunction may be the cause of diseases.

6. As oxygen concentrations fall, oxidative metabolism slows down. To make ATP, the cell reverts to anaerobic metabolism. With a decrease in ATP, the ion distribution is altered and cells will swell. The product of anaerobic metabolism is lactic acid, and as lactic acid accumulates, the pH falls. Low pH will change protein conformation, resulting in total loss of enzyme function.

7. Two basic pathways for apoptosis are the extrinsic pathway, which is death receptor–dependent and is under cellular control, and the intrinsic pathway, which is death receptor–independent and results from injury. The execution phase of both pathways is initiated by proteolytic enzymes called *caspases*.

SECTION III: APPLYING YOUR KNOWLEDGE

Activity E

1. In the nervous system, lead toxicity is characterized by demyelination of cerebral and cerebellar white matter and death of cortical cells. The demyelination results in loss of action potential generation and decreased neurotransmitter release.

SECTION IV: PRACTICING FOR NCLEX

Activity F

1. **Answer: a**
   RATIONALE: There are numerous molecular mechanisms mediating cellular adaptation, including factors produced by other cells or by the cells themselves. These mechanisms depend largely on

signals transmitted by chemical messengers that exert their effects by altering gene function. In general, the genes expressed in all cells fall into two categories: "housekeeping" genes that are necessary for normal function of a cell, and genes that determine the differentiating characteristics of a particular cell type. In many adaptive cellular responses, the expression of the differentiation genes is altered, whereas that of the housekeeping genes remains unaffected. Thus, a cell is able to change size or form without compromising its normal function. Once the stimulus for adaptation is removed, the effect on expression of the differentiating genes is removed and the cell resumes its previous state of specialized function.

2. **Answer: b**
RATIONALE: Compensatory hypertrophy is the enlargement of a remaining organ or tissue after a portion has been surgically removed or rendered inactive. The body does not enlarge its major organs during times of malnutrition. Gene expression, not actin expression, stimulates the body to increase the muscle mass of the heart. Hypertrophy is not a progressive decrease in the size of anything.

3. **Answer: c**
RATIONALE: Metastatic calcification occurs in normal tissues as the result of increased serum calcium levels (hypercalcemia). Almost any condition that increases the serum calcium level can lead to calcification in inappropriate sites such as the lung, renal tubules, and blood vessels. The major causes of hypercalcemia are: hyperparathyroidism, either primary or secondary to phosphate retention in renal failure; increased mobilization of calcium from bone as in Paget disease, cancer with metastatic bone lesions, or immobilization; and vitamin D intoxication. Diabetes mellitus and hypoparathyroidism do not cause hypercalcemia; therefore, they cannot be a cause of metastatic calcification.

4. **Answer: d**
RATIONALE: The main source of methyl mercury exposure is from consumption of long-lived fish, such as tuna and swordfish. Although there is mercury in amalgam fillings, the amount of mercury vapor given off by the fillings is very small. Most thermometers today are made without mercury. The same holds true for most blood pressure machines. Lead in paint is a concern, not mercury.

5. **Answer: a**
RATIONALE: Children are exposed to lead through ingestion of peeling lead paint, by breathing dust from lead paint (e.g., during remodeling), or from playing in contaminated soil. The lead danger to potters is from the ceramic glaze before it is fired. You do not have to keep children away from everything ceramic. Newsprint contains lead, but you are not exposed to a significant amount of

lead when you read the newspaper. You have to work directly with ore to be exposed to toxic levels of lead. Walking through part of a mine on a field trip is not a contributing factor to lead poisoning.

6. **Answer: b**
RATIONALE: In a genetic disorder called xeroderma pigmentosum, an enzyme needed to repair sunlight-induced DNA damage is lacking. This autosomal recessive disorder is characterized by extreme photosensitivity and a 2000-fold increased risk of skin cancer in sun-exposed skin. Exposure to sun causes the skin to toughen and become leathery feeling, but not in patches of pink pigmented skin. Vitiligo is a benign acquired skin disease of unknown cause, consisting of irregular patches of various sizes totally lacking in pigment and often having hyperpigmented borders. It can appear in the skin of any race and is not scaly. Photosensitivity is a sign of xeroderma pigmentosum but this disease increases, not decreases, the person's risk of skin cancer.

7. **Answer: c**
RATIONALE: Lightning and high-voltage wires that carry several thousand volts produce the most severe damage. In electrical injuries, the body acts as a conductor of the electrical current.

8. **Answer: d**
RATIONALE: Injury from freezing probably results from a combination of ice crystal formation and vasoconstriction. The decreased blood flow leads to capillary stasis and arteriolar and capillary thrombosis. Edema results from increased capillary permeability. Exposure to low-intensity heat (43°C to 46°C), such as occurs with partial-thickness burns and severe heat stroke, causes cell injury by inducing vascular injury. The process of warming tissue that has been frozen or partially frozen causes pain. If the pain is bad enough, then medication to control the pain is given. Health team members are always concerned about giving pain medication to someone who might be an addict. Asking if this is the first time this person has had an injury induced by the cold is appropriate when taking a health history. However, pointing out that "it is obvious you are a homeless person" is not an appropriate remark for the nurse to make. Also not appropriate is wondering when it will happen again.

9. **Answer: a**
RATIONALE: Destructive changes occur in small blood vessels such as the capillaries and venules. Acute reversible necrosis is represented by such disorders as radiation cystitis, dermatitis, and diarrhea from enteritis. More persistent damage can be attributed to acute necrosis of tissue cells that are not capable of regeneration and chronic ischemia. Hunger is not a sign of radiation injury, nor are muscle spasms.

10. Answer: b

RATIONALE: Gram-negative bacilli release endotoxins that cause cell injury and increased capillary permeability. Certain bacteria excrete elaborate exotoxins that interfere with cellular production of ATP. Gram-negative bacilli do not disrupt a cell's ability to replicate. Many gram-negative bacilli cause harm to cells.

11. Answer: atrophy

RATIONALE: When confronted with a decrease in work demands or adverse environmental conditions, most cells are able to revert to a smaller size and a lower and more efficient level of functioning that is compatible with survival. This decrease in cell size is called atrophy.

12. Answers: 1-a, 2-d, 3-b, 4-c

RATIONALE: Pigments are colored substances that may accumulate in cells. They can be endogenous (i.e., arising from within the body) or exogenous (i.e., arising from outside the body). Icterus, also called *jaundice*, is characterized by a yellow discoloration of tissue due to the retention of bilirubin, an endogenous bile pigment. This condition may result from increased bilirubin production from red blood cell destruction, obstruction of bile passage into the intestine, or toxic diseases that affect the liver's ability to remove bilirubin from the blood. Lipofuscin is a yellow-brown pigment that results from the accumulation of the indigestible residues produced during normal turnover of cell structures (Fig. 2-3). The accumulation of lipofuscin increases with age and is sometimes referred to as the *wear-and-tear pigment*. It is more common in heart, nerve, and liver cells than other tissues and is seen more often in conditions associated with atrophy of an organ. One of the most common exogenous pigments is carbon in the form of coal dust. In coal miners or persons exposed to heavily polluted environments, the accumulation of carbon dust blackens the lung tissue and may cause serious lung disease. The formation of a blue lead line along the margins of the gum is one of the diagnostic features of lead poisoning. Melanin is a black or dark brown pigment that occurs naturally in the hair, skin, and iris and choroid of the eye.

13. Answers: 1-b, 2-c, 3-a, 4-d

RATIONALE: Cell injury can be caused by a number of agents, including physical agents, chemicals, biologic agents, and nutritional factors. Among the physical agents that generate cell injury are mechanical forces that produce tissue trauma, extremes of temperature, electricity, radiation, and nutritional disorders. Chemical agents can cause cell injury through several mechanisms: they can block enzymatic pathways, cause coagulation of tissues, or disrupt the osmotic or ionic balance of the cell. Biologic agents differ from other injurious agents in that they are able to replicate and

continue to produce injury. Among the nutritional factors that contribute to cell injury are excesses and deficiencies of nutrients, vitamins, and minerals.

14. Answers: a, b, c, d

RATIONALE: Many drugs—alcohol, prescription drugs, over-the-counter drugs, and street drugs—are capable of directly or indirectly damaging tissues. Ethyl alcohol can harm the gastric mucosa, liver, developing fetus, and other organs. Antineoplastic (anticancer) and immunosuppressant drugs can directly injure cells. Other drugs produce metabolic end products that are toxic to cells. Acetaminophen, a commonly used over-the-counter analgesic drug, is detoxified in the liver, where small amounts of the drug are converted to a highly toxic metabolite.

CHAPTER 3

SECTION II: ASSESSING YOUR UNDERSTANDING

Activity A

1. Inflammation
2. rubor, tumor, calor, dolor
3. systemic
4. Acute, chronic
5. vascular, cellular
6. leukocytosis
7. Monocyte/macrophages
8. Vascular
9. leukocytes
10. cell-to-cell
11. cell migration
12. chemokines
13. metabolic burst
14. coagulation, complement
15. dilation, permeability
16. eicosanoid
17. prostaglandins
18. cyclooxygenase
19. omega-3 fatty acids
20. Complement
21. kinin, smooth muscle, pain
22. Tumor necrosis factor-α
23. superoxide, hydrogen peroxide, hydroxyl
24. endothelial cell damage
25. exudates
26. penetrate deeply, spread rapidly
27. CRP (C-reactive protein)
28. Fever
29. body temperature
30. arteriovenous (AV) shunts

Activity B

1. The figure depicts the cyclooxygenase and lipoxygenase pathways and sites where the corticosteroids and nonsteroidal anti-inflammatory drugs (NSAIDs) exert their action. Inflammation is essential to the

first phase of wound healing, and immune mechanisms prevent infections that impair wound healing. Among the conditions that impair inflammation and immune function is administration of corticosteroid drugs. Release of arachidonic acid by phospholipases initiates a series of complex reactions that lead to the production of inflammatory mediators. The cyclooxygenase pathway culminates in the synthesis of prostaglandins, and the lipoxygenase pathway culminates in the synthesis of the leukotrienes. Aspirin and the NSAIDs reduce inflammation by inactivating the first enzyme in the cyclooxygenase pathway for prostaglandin synthesis.

Activity C

1. c	**2.** a	**3.** i	**4.** f	**5.** j
6. g	**7.** b	**8.** h	**9.** d	**10.** e

Activity D

Margination and adhesion → transmigration across endothelium → chemotaxis → activation and phagocytosis.

Activity E

1. These signs are *rubor* (redness), *tumor* (swelling), *calor* (heat), and *dolor* (pain). The rubor is the result of increased blood flow due to histamine release. The tumor, or swelling, is due to an increased permeability of blood vessels due to histamine and other long-term vasoactive mediators. The calor, or heat, is the result of increased perfusion of the tissues at the wound site. Dolor, or pain, is due to bradykinin, prostaglandins, and histamines effects on sensory nerve endings.

2. Acute inflammation is the early (almost immediate) reaction of local tissues and their blood vessels to injury. It typically occurs before adaptive immunity becomes established and is aimed primarily at removing the injurious agent and limiting the extent of tissue damage. Acute inflammation can be triggered by a variety of stimuli, including infections, immune reactions, blunt and penetrating trauma, physical or chemical agents, and tissue necrosis from any cause. In contrast to acute inflammation, chronic inflammation is self-perpetuating and may last for weeks, months, or even years. It may develop as the result of a recurrent or progressive acute inflammatory process or from low-grade, smoldering responses that fail to evoke an acute response.

3. The first pattern is an immediate transient response, which occurs with minor injury. It develops rapidly after injury and is usually reversible and of short duration. Typically, this type of leakage affects venules 20 to 60 mm in diameter, leaving capillaries and arterioles unaffected. The second pattern is an immediate sustained response, which occurs with more serious types of injury and continues for several days. It affects all levels of the microcirculation and is usually due to direct damage of the endothelium by injurious stimuli. The third pattern is a delayed hemodynamic response in which the increased permeability begins after a delay of 2 to 12 hours, lasts for several hours or even days, and involves venules as well as capillaries. A delayed response often accompanies radiation types of injuries.

4. Phagocytosis involves three distinct steps: (1) recognition and adherence, (2) engulfment, and (3) intracellular killing. Phagocytosis is initiated by recognition and binding of particles by specific receptors on the surface of phagocytic cells. Microbes can be bound directly to the membrane of the phagocytic cells by several types of pattern recognition receptors or indirectly by receptors that recognize microbes coated with carbohydrate binding-lectins, antibody, and/or complement. Endocytosis is accomplished through cytoplasmic extensions that surround and enclose the particle in a membrane-bound phagocytic vesicle. Intracellular killing of pathogens is accomplished through several mechanisms, including toxic oxygen and nitrogen products, lysozymes, proteases, and defensins.

5. Mediators can be classified by function: (1) those with vasoactive and smooth muscle–constricting properties such as histamine, arachidonic acid metabolites, and platelet-activating factor; (2) plasma proteases that activate members of the complement system, coagulation factors of the clotting cascade, and vasoactive peptides of the kinin system; (3) chemotactic factors such as complement fragments and chemokines; and (4) reactive molecules and cytokines liberated from leukocytes, which when released into the extracellular environment can affect the surrounding tissue and cells.

6. The types of chronic inflammation are nonspecific and granulomatous. Nonspecific chronic inflammation involves a diffuse accumulation of macrophages and lymphocytes at the site of injury. Ongoing chemotaxis causes macrophages to infiltrate the inflamed site, where they accumulate owing to prolonged survival and immobilization. These mechanisms lead to fibroblast proliferation, with subsequent scar formation that in many cases replaces the normal connective tissue or the functional parenchymal tissues of the involved structures. A granulomatous lesion is a small, 1- to 2-mm lesion in which there is a massing of epithelioid cells surrounded by lymphocytes. Granulomatous inflammation is associated with foreign bodies and with microorganisms that are poorly digested and usually not easily controlled by other inflammatory mechanisms.

7. The acute-phase response includes changes in the concentrations of plasma proteins, skeletal muscle catabolism, negative nitrogen balance, elevated erythrocyte sedimentation rate, and increased numbers of leukocytes. These responses are generated by the release of cytokines that affect the

thermoregulatory center in the hypothalamus to produce fever. The metabolic changes provide amino acids that can be used in the immune response and for tissue repair. In general, the acute-phase response serves to coordinate the various changes in body activity to enable an optimal host response.

SECTION III: APPLYING YOUR KNOWLEDGE

Activity F

1. After an injury the body initiates what is called the inflammatory response. This means the body sends cells and fluids that are specific to destroying infectious organisms and healing the injury to the site of the wound. What you are seeing on the bandages is a serous exudate from the plasma in the circulatory system that has responded to the burn injury.
2. The body's response to an injury activates many different types and kinds of cells. This response is called the acute-phase response, and some of the cells that are released during this response act on the central nervous system. Their actions can cause outward manifestations of their work such as anorexia, somnolence, and malaise.

SECTION IV: PRACTICING FOR NCLEX

Activity G

1. **Answer: a**
   RATIONALE: The classic description of inflammation has been handed down through the ages. In the first century AD, the Roman physician Celsus described the local reaction of injury in terms now known as the *cardinal signs* of inflammation. These signs are *rubor* (redness), *tumor* (swelling), *calor* (heat), and *dolor* (pain). In the second century AD, the Greek physician Galen added a fifth cardinal sign, *functio laesa* (loss of function). Altered level of consciousness is not a cardinal sign of inflammation. Sepsis and fever are systemic signs of infection.

2. **Answers: b, c, e**
   RATIONALE: Eosinophils, basophils, and mast cells produce lipid mediators and cytokines that induce inflammation. They are particularly important in inflammation associated with immediate hypersensitivity reactions and allergic disorders. Neutrophils and macrophages are white blood cells that respond to inflammation and destroy invading bacteria. They do not induce inflammation.

3. **Answer: b**
   RATIONALE: Chronic inflammation involves the proliferation of fibroblasts instead of exudates. As a result, the risk of scarring and deformity usually is greater than in acute inflammation. Chronic inflammation is not the persistent destruction of healthy tissue. Typically, agents that cause chronic inflammation are agents that do not penetrate deeply or spread rapidly. Acute inflammation, not chronic, is the result of allergic reactions.

4. **Answer: c**
   RATIONALE: Infection impairs all dimensions of wound healing. It prolongs the inflammatory phase, impairs the formation of granulation tissue, and inhibits proliferation of fibroblasts and deposition of collagen fibers. All wounds are contaminated at the time of injury. Although body defenses can handle the invasion of microorganisms at the time of wounding, badly contaminated wounds can overwhelm host defenses. Trauma and existing impairment of host defenses also can contribute to the development of wound infections.

5. **Answer: c**
   RATIONALE: Histamine causes dilation of arterioles and increases the permeability of venules. It acts at the level of the microcirculation by binding to histamine 1 (H_1) receptors on endothelial cells and is considered the principal mediator of the immediate transient phase of increased vascular permeability in the acute inflammatory response. Arachidonic acid is a 20-carbon unsaturated fatty acid found in phospholipids of cell membranes. Release of arachidonic acid by phospholipases initiates a series of complex reactions that lead to the production of the *eicosanoid* family of inflammatory mediators (prostaglandins, leukotrienes, and related metabolites). Fibroblasts and cytokines are not the principal mediator of the transient phase of an acute inflammatory response.

6. **Answer: a**
   RATIONALE: The most prominent systemic manifestations of inflammation include the acute-phase response, alterations in white blood cell count (leukocytosis or leukopenia), and fever. A widening pulse pressure is not indicative of systemic inflammation, and thrombocytopenia is a hematologic disorder, not an indication of systemic inflammation.

CHAPTER 4

SECTION II: ASSESSING YOUR UNDERSTANDING

Activity A

1. differentiation
   growth
2. proliferation
3. *Differentiation*
4. cyclins
5. phosphorylate
6. progenitor
7. Stem
8. *Embryonic*
9. parenchymal, stromal
10. Labile cells
11. stabile
12. Granulation
13. collagen, fibroblast
14. premature infant

Activity B

1. c   **2.** a   **3.** i   **4.** f   **5.** j
6. g   **7.** b   **8.** h   **9.** d   **10.** e

Activity D

Margination and adhesion to the endothelium →
transmigration across endothelium → chemotaxis →
activation and phagocytosis.

Activity E

1. In terms of cell proliferation, the cells may be divided
   into three groups: (1) the well-differentiated
   neurons and cells of skeletal and cardiac muscle
   that rarely divide and reproduce; (2) the progenitor
   or parent cells, that continue to divide and
   reproduce, such as blood cells, skin cells, and liver
   cells; and (3) the undifferentiated stem cells that
   can be triggered to enter the cell cycle and produce
   large numbers of progenitor cells when the need
   arises.

2. Depending on the extent of tissue loss, wound closure and healing occur by *primary* or *secondary*
   intention. Small or "clean" wounds (such as a surgical incision) are an example of healing by primary
   intention. Larger wounds that have a greater loss of
   tissue and contamination heal by secondary intention. Healing by secondary intention is slower than
   healing by primary intention and results in the formation of larger amounts of scar tissue.

SECTION III: APPLYING YOUR KNOWLEDGE

Activity F

1. After an injury the body initiates what is called the
   inflammatory response. This means the body sends
   cells and fluids that are specific to destroying infectious organisms and healing the injury to the
   site of the wound. What you are seeing on the
   bandages is a serous exudate from the plasma in
   the circulatory system that has responded to the
   burn injury.

2. The body's response to an injury activates many
   different types and kinds of cells. This response is
   called the acute phase response and some of the
   cells that are released during this response act on
   the central nervous system. Their actions can cause
   outward manifestations of their work such as
   anorexia, somnolence, and malaise.

SECTION IV: PRACTICING FOR NCLEX

Activity G

1. **Answers: b, d, e**
   RATIONALE: Wound healing is commonly divided
   into three phases: (1) the inflammatory phase,
   (2) the proliferative phase, and (3) the maturational
   or remodeling phase. There is no activation or
   nutritional phase in wound healing.

2. **Answer: c**
   RATIONALE: An increase in tissue oxygen tension by
   hyperbaric oxygen enhances wound healing by a
   number of mechanisms, including the increased
   killing of bacteria by neutrophils, impaired growth
   of anaerobic bacteria, and the promotion of angiogenesis and fibroblast activity. Eosinophil activity is
   not affected by hyperbaric treatment of wounds.

3. **Answer: c**
   RATIONALE: The child has a greater capacity for
   repair than the adult but may lack the reserves
   needed to ensure proper healing. Such lack is
   evidenced by an easily upset electrolyte balance,
   sudden elevation or lowering of temperature, and
   rapid spread of infection. The neonate and small
   child may have an immature immune system with
   no antigenic experience with organisms that
   contaminate wounds. The younger the child, the
   more likely that the immune system is not fully
   developed. The skin of a neonate or a small child is
   not as fragile as the skin of an elderly person.

4. **Answer: c**
   RATIONALE: Infection impairs all dimensions of
   wound healing. It prolongs the inflammatory
   phase, impairs the formation of granulation tissue, and inhibits proliferation of fibroblasts and
   deposition of collagen fibers. All wounds are
   contaminated at the time of injury. Although
   body defenses can handle the invasion of microorganisms at the time of wounding, badly contaminated wounds can overwhelm host defenses.
   Trauma and existing impairment of host defenses
   also can contribute to the development of wound
   infections.

5. **Answers: a, b, c**

CHAPTER 5

SECTION II: ASSESSING YOUR UNDERSTANDING

Activity A

1. deoxyribonucleic
2. Ribonucleic
3. proteome
4. purine, pyrimidine
5. complementary
6. 23
7. chromosomes
8. triplet
9. mutations
10. haplotype
11. transcription
12. exons
13. Translation
14. chaperones
15. *expression*
16. RNA

17. Transcription
18. phenotype
19. alleles
20. pedigree

Activity B

1.

1. a	**2.** c	**3.** b	**4.** e	**5.** j
6. f	**7.** d	**8.** h	**9.** g	**10.** i

2.

1. d	**2.** a	**3.** c	**4.** b	**5.** e

Activity C

1.

a → c → g → f → b → d → e → h → i

Activity D

1. Mendel discovered the basic pattern of inheritance by conducting carefully planned experiments with garden peas. Experimenting with phenotypic traits in peas, Mendel proposed that inherited traits are transmitted from parents to offspring by means of independently inherited factors, now known as genes, and that these factors are transmitted as recessive and dominant traits from patents to their offspring.
2. Genetic maps use linkage studies to estimate the distances between chromosomal landmarks. They are similar to a road map. Physical maps are similar to a surveyor's map. They make use of cytogenetic and molecular techniques to determine the actual physical locations of genes on chromosomes.
3. While in metaphase I, chromosomes are paired and condensed. Over time an interchange of chromatid segments can occur. This process is called *crossing over*. Crossing over allows for new combinations of genes resulting in an increase in genetic variability. This is a very beneficial process.
4. There are 22 pairs of somatic chromosomes. Half of each pair is received from the female and the other half are from the male. We then have two sex chromosomes, an X from our mother and, in the case of females, an X from the father, for a total of two Xs. Males only have one X chromosome from their mother and one Y chromosome from their father.
5. Gene activator and repressor sites within DNA commonly monitor levels of the synthesized product and regulate gene transcription through a negative feedback mechanism. Expression is also regulated at the transcription level by transcription factors that directly affect protein structure and function.

SECTION III: APPLYING YOUR KNOWLEDGE

Activity E

DNA fingerprinting is a technique for comparing the nucleotide sequences of fragments of DNA from different sources. The fragments are obtained by treating the DNA with various enzymes that break DNA strands at specific sites. There is a chance of 1 in 30 billion that two persons who are not monozygotic twins would have identical DNA fingerprints. Because genetic variations are so distinctive, DNA fingerprinting (analysis of DNA sequence differences) can be used to determine family relationships or help identify persons involved in criminal acts.

SECTION IV: PRACTICING FOR NCLEX

Activity F

1. **Answer: a**
   RATIONALE: The term *proteome* is a relatively new term, created to define the complete set of proteins encoded by a genome. A chromosome is any of the threadlike structures in the nucleus of a cell that function in the transmission of genetic information. The terms *protogene* and *nucleotomics* are not real words.
2. **Answer: b**
   RATIONALE: The two strands of the helix separate and a complementary molecule is duplicated next to each original strand. Two strands become four strands. During cell division, the newly duplicated double-stranded molecules are separated and placed in each daughter cell by the mechanics of mitosis. As a result, each of the daughter cells again contains the meaningful strand and the complementary strand joined together as a double helix.
3. **Answer: c**
   RATIONALE: Of the 23 pairs of human chromosomes, 22 are called autosomes and are alike in both males and females. The double helix is the shape of the DNA molecule. Ribosomes are areas in a cell that synthesize proteins. Haploid have only one complete set of nonhomologous chromosomes.
4. **Answer: d**
   RATIONALE: Rarely, accidental errors in duplication of DNA occur. These errors are called mutations. Ribosomes are areas in a cell that synthesize proteins. Several repair mechanisms exist, and each depends on specific enzymes called endonucleases that recognize local distortions of the DNA helix, cleave the abnormal chain, and remove the distorted region. Four bases—guanine, adenine, cytosine, and thymine (uracil is substituted for thymine in RNA)—make up the alphabet of the genetic code. A sequence of three of these bases forms the fundamental triplet code used in transmitting the genetic information needed for protein synthesis. This triplet code is called a codon.
5. **Answer: a**
   RATIONALE: Polygenic inheritance involves multiple genes at different loci, with each gene exerting a small additive effect in determining a trait. Multifactorial inheritance is similar to polygenic inheritance in that multiple alleles at different loci affect the outcome; the difference is that multifactorial

inheritance includes environmental effects on the genes. Monofactorial inheritance is nonexistent, as is collaborative inheritance.

6. **Answer: b**
RATIONALE: When the deletion is inherited from the mother, the infant presents with Angelman ("happy puppet") syndrome. Turner syndrome is a chromosomal anomaly seen in about 1 in 3000 live female births, characterized by the absence of one X chromosome. Down syndrome is a congenital condition characterized by varying degrees of mental retardation and multiple defects. It is the most common chromosomal abnormality of a generalized syndrome and is caused by the presence of an extra chromosome 21 in the G group. Fragile X syndrome is a reproductive disorder characterized by a nearly broken X chromosome, which has a tip hanging by a flimsy thread. It is the most common inherited cause of mental retardation.

7. **Answer: c**
RATIONALE: A recessive trait is one that is expressed only when a two homozygous people have a child. A dominant trait is one expressed in either a homozygous or a heterozygous pairing. A single-gene trait and a penetrant trait do not exist. However, single-gene inheritance does exist.

8. **Answer: d**
RATIONALE: The establishment of the International HapMap Project was to map the haplotypes of the many closely related single nucleotide polymorphisms in the human genome; and the development of methods for applying the technology of these projects to the diagnosis and treatment of disease. Four bases—guanine, adenine, cytosine, and thymine (uracil is substituted for thymine in RNA)—make up the alphabet of the genetic code. A sequence of three of these bases forms the fundamental triplet code used in transmitting the genetic information needed for protein synthesis. This triplet code is called a codon. Alternate forms of a gene at the same locus are called alleles.

9. **Answer: a**
RATIONALE: Banding patterns are analyzed to see if they match. Four bases—guanine, adenine, cytosine, and thymine (uracil is substituted for thymine in RNA)—make up the alphabet of the genetic code. A sequence of three of these bases forms the fundamental triplet code used in transmitting the genetic information needed for protein synthesis. The small variation in gene sequence (termed a *haplotype*) that is thought to account for the individual differences in physical traits, behaviors, and disease susceptibility. Chromosomes contain all the genetic content of the genome.

10. **Answer: b**
RATIONALE: Cloned DNA sequences are usually the compounds used in gene therapy. Messenger RNA carries the instructions for protein synthesis. Sterically stable liposomes are stable liposomes with long circulation times. Sites in the DNA sequence where individuals differ at a single DNA base are called single nucleotide polymorphisms (SNPs, pronounced "snips").

11. **Answer: *haplotype***
RATIONALE: As the Human Genome Project was progressing it became evident that the human genome sequence is almost exactly (99.9%) the same in all people. It is the small variation (0.01%) in gene sequence (termed a *haplotype*) that is thought to account for the individual differences in physical traits, behaviors, and disease susceptibility.

12. **Answers: b, c, d**
RATIONALE: RNA is a single-stranded rather than a double-stranded molecule. Second, the sugar in each nucleotide of RNA is ribose instead of deoxyribose. Third, the pyrimidine base thymine in DNA is replaced by uracil in RNA. All cells are supposed to have 23 pairs of chromosomes.

13. **Answer: insulin**
RATIONALE: Recombinant DNA technology has also made it possible to produce proteins that have therapeutic properties. One of the first products to be produced was human insulin.

14. **Answers: a, b, c**
RATIONALE: A karyotype is a photograph of a person's chromosomes. It is prepared by special laboratory techniques in which body cells are cultured, fixed, and then stained to display identifiable banding patterns. A centromere is the constricted region of a chromosome that joins the two chromatids to each other and attaches to spindle fibers in mitosis and meiosis. Human chromosomes are classified as one of three types, depending on the position of their centromere. Two types of genes, complementary genes, in which each gene is mutually dependent on the other; and collaborative genes, in which two different genes influencing the same trait interact, play a part in multifactorial inheritance.

15. **Answers: 1-c, 2-a, 3-b, 4-e, 5-d**
RATIONALE: The genotype of a person is the genetic information stored in the base sequence triplet code. The phenotype refers to the recognizable traits, physical or biochemical, associated with a specific genotype. Pharmacogenetics is the variability of drug response due to inherited characteristics in individuals. Somatic cell hybridization involves the fusion of human somatic cells with those of a different species (typically, the mouse) to yield a cell containing the chromosomes of both species. Penetrance represents the ability of a gene to express its function. Seventy-five percent penetrance means 75% of persons of a particular genotype present with a recognizable phenotype.

CHAPTER 6

SECTION II: ASSESSING YOUR UNDERSTANDING

Activity A

1. Congenital
2. DNA, chromosomal
3. codominate
4. mutation
5. inherited, spontaneous
6. carrier
7. Marfan
8. recessive
9. 60
10. structure, abnormal
11. Translocation

Activity B LABELING

1.

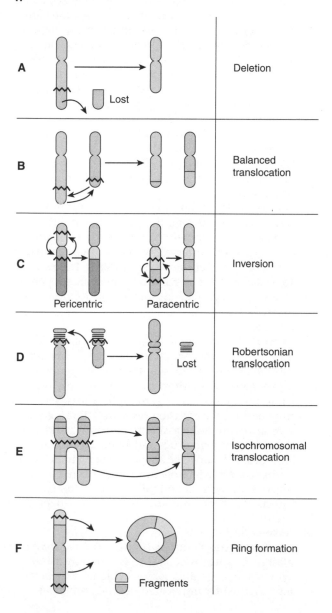

A	Deletion
B	Balanced translocation
C	Inversion
	Pericentric Paracentric
D	Robertsonian translocation
E	Isochromosomal translocation
F	Ring formation

2. The figure represents a simple pedigree for inheritance of an autosomal dominant trait. The colored circle or square represents an affected parent with a mutant gene. An affected parent with an autosomal dominant trait has a 50% chance of passing the mutant gene on to each child regardless of sex.

Activity C

| 1. h | 2. c | 3. e | 4. a | 5. g |
| 6. b | 7. j | 8. d | 9. i | 10. f |

Activity D

1. Conditions are inherited as dominant or recessive on one of the autosomal chromosomes or one of the sex chromosomes. If the trait is dominant, the patient will inherit the condition. For a recessive trait to be expressed, both parents must carry the mutation. If the mutation is on the Y chromosome, all male children will be affected; if it is on the X chromosome, about half of the offspring potentially may be affected.

2. Multifactorial congenital malformations involve a single organ or tissue derived from the same embryonic developmental field. Second, the risk of recurrence in future pregnancies is increased for the same or a similar defect. Third, the risk increases with increasing incidence of the defect among relatives.

3. Structural changes in chromosomes usually results from breakage in one or more of the chromosomes followed by rearrangement or deletion of the chromosome parts. Among the factors believed to cause chromosome breakage are exposure to radiation sources, such as x-rays; influence of certain chemicals; extreme changes in the cellular environment; and viral infections.

4. (1) The inactivation of all but one X chromosome and (2) the modest amount of genetic material that is carried on the Y chromosome.

5. Ova contain the majority of the mitochondria, whereas spermatozoa have very few, if any, so the embryo will inherit most if not all of the mitochondria from the mother. The neural and muscular tissues are most affected by mtDNA mutations because of their great dependence on oxidative phosphorylation. These tissues will have numerous mitochondria and suffer from their malfunction.

SECTION III: APPLYING YOUR KNOWLEDGE

Activity E

1. Alcohol passes freely across the placental barrier so concentrations of alcohol in the fetus are at least as high as in the mother. Unlike other agents harmful to the fetus, the harmful effects of alcohol are not restricted to the sensitive period of early gestation but extend throughout pregnancy. Alcohol consumption during pregnancy can cause fetal alcohol syndrome in the baby.

2. Alcohol has widely variable effects on fetal development, ranging from minor abnormalities to fetal alcohol syndrome. There may be prenatal or postnatal growth retardation; central nervous system involvement, including neurologic abnormalities, developmental delays, behavioral dysfunction, intellectual impairment, and skull and brain malformation; and a characteristic set of facial features that include small eye openings, a thin upper lip, and an elongated, flattened midface and philtrum (i.e., the groove in the middle of the upper lip). Each of these defects can vary in severity, probably reflecting the timing of alcohol consumption in terms of the period of fetal development, amount of alcohol consumed, and hereditary and environmental influences.

SECTION IV: PRACTICING FOR NCLEX

Activity F

1. **Answer: a**
   RATIONALE: If the members of a gene pair are identical (i.e., code the exact same gene product), the person is homozygous, and if the two members are different, the person is heterozygous. The phenotype is the observable expression of a genotype in terms of morphologic, biochemical, or molecular traits. Although gene expression usually follows a dominant or recessive pattern, it is possible for both alleles (members) of a gene pair to be fully expressed in the heterozygote, a condition called codominance. A gene mutation is a biochemical event such as nucleotide change, deletion, or insertion that produces a new allele.

2. **Answer: b**
   RATIONALE: In more than 90% of persons with neurofibromatosis-1, cutaneous and subcutaneous neurofibromas develop in late childhood or adolescence. The cutaneous neurofibromas, which vary in number from a few to many hundreds, manifest as soft, pedunculated lesions that project from the skin. Marfan syndrome affects several organ systems including the ocular system (eyes), the cardiovascular system (heart and blood vessels), and the skeletal system (bones and joints). Down syndrome is a congenital condition characterized by varying degrees of mental retardation and multiple defects. Klinefelter syndrome is a condition that occurs in men who have an extra X chromosome in most of their cells. The syndrome can affect different stages of physical, language, and social development. The most common symptom is infertility.

3. **Answer: c**
   RATIONALE: Cleft lip with or without cleft palate is one of the most common birth defects. This process is under the control of many genes, and the disturbances in gene expression (hereditary or environmental) at this time may result in cleft lip with or without cleft palate (Fig. 6-6). The defect

may also be caused by teratogens (e.g., rubella, anticonvulsant drugs) and is often encountered in children with chromosomal abnormalities.

4. **Answer: d**
   RATIONALE: Occasionally, mitotic errors in early development give rise to two or more cell lines characterized by distinctive karyotypes, a condition referred to as *mosaicism*. A gene mutation is a biochemical event such as nucleotide change, deletion, or insertion that produces a new allele. Referring to someone as a "mutant" is a derogatory expression. Monosomy refers to the presence of only one member of a chromosome pair. It is not a term a person is called. Having an abnormal number of chromosomes is referred to as aneuploidy; it is not a term a person is called.

5. **Answer: a**
   RATIONALE: The risk of having a child with Down syndrome increases with maternal age—it is 1 in 1250 at 25 years of age, 1 in 400 at 35 years, and 1 in 100 at 45 years of age. The reason for the correlation between maternal age and nondisjunction is unknown, but is thought to reflect some aspect of aging of the oocyte. Although males continue to produce sperm throughout their reproductive life, females are born with all the oocytes they ever will have. These oocytes may change as a result of the aging process. With increasing age, there is a greater chance of a woman having been exposed to damaging environmental agents such as drugs, chemicals, and radiation. There is no correlation with maternal age and the other syndromes.

6. **Answer: b**
   RATIONALE: The embryo's development is most easily disturbed during the period when differentiation and development of the organs are taking place. This time interval, which is often referred to as the period of *organogenesis*, extends from day 15 to day 60 after conception. There are no periods of susceptibility, fetal anomalies, or hormonal imbalance.

7. **Answer: c**
   RATIONALE: Teratogenic agents have been divided into three groups: radiation, drugs and chemical substances, and infectious agents. The period of organogenesis, the third trimester, and the second trimester are not teratogenic substances. They are time periods during the pregnancy. Teratogenic substances are not classified as outside, inside, or internal. Although drugs and chemical substances are a class of teratogenic agents, smoking is included in that class as a teratogenic agent. It is not a class unto itself. Bacteria and virus are considered infectious agents and are therefore teratogenic agents.

8. **Answer: d**
   RATIONALE: The acronym TORCH stands for *toxoplasmosis, other, rubella* (i.e., German measles), *cytomegalovirus*, and *herpes*, which are the agents most frequently implicated in fetal anomalies.

Common clinical and pathologic manifestations include growth retardation and abnormalities of the brain (microcephaly, hydrocephalus), eye, ear, liver, hematopoietic system (anemia, thrombocytopenia), lungs (pneumonitis), and heart (myocarditis, congenital heart disorders).

9. **Answer: a**
RATIONALE: The birth of a defective child is a traumatic event in any parent's life. Usually two issues must be resolved. The first deals with the immediate and future care of the affected child, and the second with the possibility of future children in the family having a similar defect.

10. **Answer: b**
RATIONALE: The purpose of prenatal screening and diagnosis is not just to detect fetal abnormalities. Rather, it has the following objectives: to provide parents with information needed to make an informed choice about having a child with an abnormality; to provide reassurance and reduce anxiety among high-risk groups; and to allow parents at risk for having a child with a specific defect, who might otherwise forgo having a child, to begin a pregnancy with the assurance that knowledge about the presence or absence of the disorder in the fetus can be confirmed by testing. It is not the object of genetic counseling and prenatal screening to provide information on where to terminate a pregnancy if that is what the parents choose to do. Prenatal screening cannot be used to rule out all possible fetal abnormalities. It is limited to determining whether the fetus has (or probably has) designated conditions indicated by late maternal age, family history, or well-defined risk factors.

11. **Answers: 1-a, 2-b, 3-c, 4-d, 5-e**
RATIONALE: A single mutant gene may be expressed in many different parts of the body. Marfan syndrome, for example, is a defect in connective tissue that has widespread effects involving skeletal, eye, and cardiovascular structures. In autosomal dominant disorders, a single mutant allele from an affected parent is transmitted to an offspring regardless of sex. In many conditions, the age of onset is delayed, and the signs and symptoms of the disorder do not appear until later in life, as in Huntington's chorea. Tay-Sachs is inherited as an autosomal recessive trait. Fragile X syndrome is a single-gene disorder in which the mutation is characterized by a long repeating sequence of three nucleotides within the fragile X gene.

12. **Answers: a, b, c**
RATIONALE: First, multifactorial congenital malformations tend to involve a single organ or tissue derived from the same embryonic developmental field. Second, the risk of recurrence in future pregnancies is for the same or a similar defect. This means that parents of a child with a cleft palate defect have an increased risk of having another child with a cleft palate, but not with spina bifida.

Third, the increased risk (compared with the general population) among first-degree relatives of the affected person is 2% to 7%, and among second-degree relatives, it is approximately half that amount. The risk increases with increasing incidence of the defect among relatives. Disorders of multifactorial inheritance can be expressed during fetal life and be present at birth, or they may be expressed later in life.

13. **Answer: Phenylketonuria**
RATIONALE: Phenylketonuria (PKU) is a rare metabolic disorder that affects approximately 1 in every 15,000 infants in the United States. The disorder, which is inherited as a recessive trait, is caused by a deficiency of the liver enzyme phenylalanine hydroxylase. As a result of this deficiency, toxic levels of the amino acid phenylalanine accumulate in the blood and other tissues.

14. **Answers: a, d**
RATIONALE: The physiologic status of the mother—her hormone balance, her general state of health, her nutritional status, and the drugs she takes—undoubtedly influences the development of the unborn child. Other agents, such as radiation, can cause chromosomal and genetic defects and produce developmental disorders. Neither the weather nor air pollution has been linked with fetal abnormalities or developmental disorders.

15. **Answer: a**
RATIONALE: In 1983, the U.S. Food and Drug Administration established a system for classifying drugs according to probable risks to the fetus. According to this system, drugs are put into five categories: A, B, C, D, and X. Drugs in category A are the least dangerous, and categories B, C, and D are increasingly more dangerous. Those in category X are contraindicated during pregnancy because of proven teratogenicity.

CHAPTER 7

SECTION II: ASSESSING YOUR UNDERSTANDING

Activity A

1. differentiation growth
2. proliferation
3. *Differentiation*
4. kinases
5. phosphorylate
6. progenitor
7. Stem
8. *Embryonic*
9. *neoplasm*
10. Benign tumors
11. differentiated
12. -oma
13. polyp
14. *carcinoma*

15. solid tumors hematological
16. *anaplasia*
17. growth factors
18. p53
19. protooncogenes suppressor
20. Human T-cell leukemia virus-1
21. *30*
22. anorexia-cachexia
23. ulceration necrosis
24. Anemia
25. biopsy
26. Radiation
27. Chemotherapy

Activity B

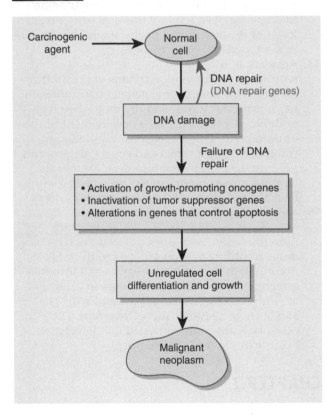

Activity C

1. b	**2.** a	**3.** e	**4.** j	**5.** f
6. c	**7.** d	**8.** h	**9.** g	**10.** i
11. m	**12.** o	**13.** n	**14.** q	**15.** l
16. k	**17.** r	**18.** s	**19.** p	

Activity D

1.

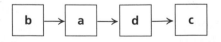

Activity E

1. In terms of cell proliferation, the cells may be divided into three groups: (1) the well-differentiated neurons and cells of skeletal and cardiac muscle that rarely divide and reproduce; (2) the progenitor or parent cells that continue to divide and reproduce, such as blood cells, skin cells, and liver cells; and (3) the undifferentiated stem cells that can be triggered to enter the cell cycle and produce large numbers of progenitor cells when the need arises.

2. Both benign and malignant tumors have lost the ability to suppress growth. As a result, the tumor cells continue to proliferate. Benign tumors are composed of well-differentiated cells and are confined to the area of tissue origin. In contrast, malignant tumors are composed of less differentiated cells that will re-enter circulation and establish secondary tumors in another region of the body.

3. (1) Cell characteristics, (2) rate of growth, (3) manner of growth, (4) capacity to invade and metastasize to other parts of the body, and (5) potential for causing death.

4. Metastasis occurs via lymph channels and blood vessels. When metastasis occurs by way of the lymphatic channels, the tumor cells lodge first in the initial lymph node that receives drainage from the tumor site. If they survive, cancer cells may spread from more distant lymph nodes to the thoracic duct, and then gain access to the blood vasculature. With hematologic spread, the blood-borne cancer cells may enter the venous flow that drains the site of the primary neoplasm. Cancer cells may also enter tumor-associated blood vessels that either infiltrate the tumor or are found at the periphery of the tumor.

5. Cancer cells express abnormal cell surface proteins. Normally, the immune system recognizes these abnormal proteins and destroys the cancerous cell. With a compromised immune system, these abnormalities are missed and allowed to persist in the body.

6. Chemicals will cause cellular transformation either directly (direct reacting agents) or indirectly, only becoming activated via a metabolic process (initiators).

7. Hypermetabolism is the result of the rapidly growing tumor and the increased expression of uncoupling proteins. The tumor uses large quantities of glucose via glycolysis, therefore producing high levels of lactic acid. The lactic acid undergoes the energy-requiring process of gluconeogenesis in order to convert it back to glucose. This uses large amounts of glucose and wastes large amounts of adenosine triphosphate (ATP). The second reason is the presence of uncoupling proteins. The uncoupling proteins uncouple oxidative phosphorylation, thereby reducing the amount of ATP produced.

8. Paraneoplastic syndromes are characterized by manifestations in sites that are not directly affected by the disease. Most commonly, manifestations are caused by the elaboration of hormones by cancer cells, and others from the production of circulating factors that produce hematopoietic, neurologic, and dermatological syndromes.

9. Blood tests for tumor markers, cytologic studies and tissue biopsy, endoscopic examinations, ultrasound, x-ray studies, MRI, computed tomography, and positron-emission tomography.

10. The clinical staging of cancer is intended to group patients according to the extent of their disease. Grading of tumors involves the microscopic examination of cancer cells to determine their level of differentiation and the number of mitoses. Cancers are classified as grades I, II, III, and IV with increasing anaplasia or lack of differentiation. The two basic methods for classifying cancers are *grading* according to the histologic or cellular characteristics of the tumor and *staging* according to the clinical spread of the disease.

SECTION III: APPLYING YOUR KNOWLEDGE

Activity F

1. "To make it better for you, the doctor is going to put a tube just under your skin that the nurses can put your medication in so they won't have to stick you in the hands and arms so many times. You will still get stuck by a needle but it will not be as painful as trying to start an IV in your arms."

2. Since Joe's cancer is found in his blood and bone marrow, you cannot use surgery to cure it. Chemotherapy is the primary treatment for most hematologic and some solid tumors. Chemotherapy is a systemic treatment that enables drugs to reach the site of the tumor as well as other distant sites. Cancer chemotherapeutic drugs exert their effects through several mechanisms. At the cellular level, they exert their lethal action by targeting processes that prevent cell growth and replication. These mechanisms include disrupting the production of essential enzymes; inhibiting DNA, RNA, and protein synthesis; and preventing cell reproduction.

SECTION IV: PRACTICING FOR NCLEX

Activity G

1. **Answer: a**
   RATIONALE: Asking if his tumor will make him die shows lack of understanding of educational material he has been given. For unknown reasons, benign tumors have lost the ability to suppress the genetic program for cell proliferation but have retained the program for normal cell

differentiation. They do not have the capacity to infiltrate, invade, or metastasize to distant sites.

2. **Answer: b**
   RATIONALE: Metastasis occurs by way of the lymph channels (i.e., lymphatic spread) and the blood vessels (i.e., hematogenic spread). In many types of cancer, the first evidence of disseminated disease is the presence of tumor cells in the lymph nodes that drain the tumor area. When metastasis occurs by way of the lymphatic channels, the tumor cells lodge first in the initial lymph node that receives drainage from the tumor site. Once in this lymph node, the cells may die because of the lack of a proper environment, grow into a discernible mass, or remain dormant for unknown reasons. If they survive and grow, the cancer cells may spread from more distant lymph nodes to the thoracic duct, and then gain access to the blood vasculature. Because cancer cells have the ability to shed themselves from the original tumor, they are often found floating in the body fluids around the tumor. Cancer cells are not moved from one place to another by transporter cells. Cancer cells do not form a chain to grow to the new place in the body to form a new tumor.

3. **Answer: c**
   RATIONALE: Cancer occurs because of interactions among multiple risk factors or repeated exposure to a single carcinogenic (cancer-producing) agent. Among the traditional risk factors that have been linked to cancer are heredity, hormonal factors, immunologic mechanisms, and environmental agents such as chemicals, radiation, and cancer-causing viruses. More recently, there has been interest in obesity and type 2 diabetes mellitus as risk factors for a number of cancers. Body type, age, and color of skin have not been identified as risk factors for cancer.

4. **Answer: d**
   RATIONALE: Familial adenomatous polyposis of the colon also follows an autosomal dominant inheritance pattern. It is caused by mutation of another tumor suppressor gene, the *APC* gene. In people who inherit this gene, hundreds of adenomatous polyps may develop, some of which inevitably become malignant. Retinoblastoma is inheritable through an autosomal dominant gene, but only about 40% of retinoblastomas are inherited. Osteosarcoma and ALL are not inheritable through an autosomal dominant process.

5. **Answer: a**
   RATIONALE: Most known dietary carcinogens occur either naturally in plants (e.g., aflatoxins) or are produced during food preparation. Among the most potent of the procarcinogens are the polycyclic aromatic hydrocarbons. The polycyclic aromatic hydrocarbons are of particular interest because they are produced from animal fat in the process of charcoal-broiling meats and are

present in smoked meats and fish. They also are produced in the combustion of tobacco and are present in cigarette smoke. *Initiators* is another term for procarcinogens. Diethylstilbestrol was a drug that was widely used in the United States from the mid-1940s to 1970 to prevent miscarriages.

6. **Answer: b**

   RATIONALE: Lung cancers, breast cancers, and lymphomas account for about 75% of malignant pleural effusions. Complaints of abdominal discomfort, swelling and a feeling of heaviness, and an increase in abdominal girth, which reflect the presence of peritoneal effusions or ascites, are the most common presenting symptoms in ovarian cancer, occurring in up to 65% of women with the disease.

7. **Answer: c**

   RATIONALE: Tumor markers are antigens expressed on the surface of tumor cells or substances released from normal cells in response to the presence of tumor. The serum markers that have proven most useful in clinical practice are the human chorionic gonadotropin (hCG), CA 125, prostate-specific antigen (PSA), alpha-fetoprotein, carcinoembryonic antigen, and CD blood cell antigens. Deoxyribonucleic acid is DNA and is not a serum tumor marker. Cyclin-dependent kinases come from a family of proteins called cyclins, which control entry and progression of cells through the cell cycle. Cyclins act by complexing with (and thereby activating) proteins called cyclin-dependent kinases (CDKs). They are not serum tumor markers.

8. **Answer: d**

   RATIONALE: Growth hormone deficiency in adults is associated with increased prevalence of dyslipidemia, insulin resistance, and cardiovascular mortality. Hypocalcemia is a deficiency of calcium in the serum that may be caused by hypoparathyroidism, vitamin D deficiency, kidney failure, acute pancreatitis, or inadequate amounts of plasma magnesium and protein. It does not result from cancer therapy during childhood. Hyperinsulinemia is associated with syndrome X, which is a condition characterized by hypertension with obesity, type 2 diabetes mellitus, hypertriglyceridemia, increased peripheral insulin resistance, hyperinsulinemia, and elevated catecholamine levels.

9. **Answer: a**

   RATIONALE: Chemotherapy is more widely used in the treatment of children with cancer than in adults because children better tolerate the acute adverse effects, and in general, pediatric tumors are responsive to chemotherapy than adult cancers. Children are very adaptable and tolerate

more forms of cancer treatment than adults do. Children do complain about the nausea and vomiting chemotherapy can cause, just like adults do. And they do not like losing their hair, just like adults.

10. **Answer: b**

    RATIONALE: The combination of selected cytotoxic drugs with radiation has demonstrated a radiosensitizing effect on tumor cells by altering the cell cycle distribution, increasing DNA damage, and decreasing DNA repair. Some radiosensitizers are 5-fluorouracil, capecitabine, paclitaxel, gemcitabine, and cisplatin. Doxorubicin is an antitumor antibiotic; vincristine is a vinca alkaloid; and docetaxel is a taxane.

11. **Answer: *neoplasm***

    RATIONALE: An abnormal mass of tissue in which the growth exceeds and is uncoordinated with that of the normal tissues is called a neoplasm. Unlike normal cellular adaptive processes such as hypertrophy and hyperplasia, neoplasms do not obey the laws of normal cell growth. They serve no useful purpose, they do not occur in response to an appropriate stimulus, and they continue to grow at the expense of the host.

12. **Answers: a, c, e**

    RATIONALE: Malignant neoplasms are less well differentiated and have the ability to break loose, enter the circulatory or lymphatic systems, and form secondary malignant tumors at other sites. Malignant neoplasms frequently cause suffering and death if untreated or uncontrolled. Malignant neoplasms form secondary tumors at sites other than the original tumor site. Malignant neoplasms are not passed out of the body as waste through the alimentary canal.

13. **Answers: b, c, e**

    RATIONALE: Cancer cells differ from normal cells by being immortal with an unlimited life span. Cancer cells often lose cell density-dependent inhibition, which is the cessation of growth after cells reach a particular density. This is sometimes referred to as *contact inhibition* because cells often stop growing when they come into contact with each other. Another characteristic of cancer cells is the ability to proliferate even in the absence of growth factors. Most cancer cells exhibit a characteristic called genetic instability that is often considered to be a hallmark of cancer.

14. **Answers: 1-b, 2-d, 3-c, 4-a**

    RATIONALE: Cancers for which current screening or early detection has led to improvement in outcomes include cancers of the breast (breast self-examination and mammography), cervix (Pap smear), colon and rectum (rectal examination, fecal occult blood test, and flexible sigmoidoscopy and colonoscopy), prostate (PSA testing and transrectal ultrasonography), and malignant melanoma (self-examination).

15. **Answers: a, b, d**

   RATIONALE: With improvement in treatment methods, the number of children who survive childhood cancer is continuing to increase. As these children approach adulthood, there is continued concern that the life-saving therapy they received during childhood may produce late effects, such as impaired growth, cognitive dysfunction, hormonal dysfunction, cardiomyopathy, pulmonary fibrosis, and risk for second malignancies. Liver failure is not viewed as a late effect of childhood cancer therapy.

CHAPTER 8

SECTION II: ASSESSING YOUR UNDERSTANDING

Activity A

1. ICF compartment
2. ECF compartment
3. Electrolytes
4. nonelectrolytes
5. Diffusion
6. Osmosis
7. Osmolarity, osmolality
8. Na^+
9. osmolar gap
10. Osmotically active
11. Na^+-K^+ ATPase
12. Capillary filtration
13. lymphatic system
14. Edema
15. plasma proteins
16. Pitting
17. Third-space fluids
18. insensible water losses
19. kidney
20. effective circulating volume
21. angiotensin II, aldosterone
22. Thirst, ADH
23. Psychogenic polydipsia
24. Diabetes insipidus
25. hyponatremia, hypernatremia
26. *hypovolemia*

27. Third-space losses
28. isotonic
29. Hyponatremia
30. Normovolemic hypotonic
31. ADH
32. Hypernatremia
33. water
34. Na^+-K^+ exchange mechanism
35. resting membrane potential
36. hyperkalemia
37. hypokalemia
38. renal failure
39. excess
40. Vitamin D
41. Magnesium
42. hypocalcemia
43. hypophosphatemia
44. calcium
45. Magnesium
46. 7.35, 7.45
47. pH
48. metabolic
49. volatile, nonvolatile
50. H_2CO_3
51. dietary proteins
52. Henderson-Hasselbalch equation
53. bicarbonate
54. Metabolic alkalosis
55. hypoventilation, hypoxemia
56. acidosis
57. alkalosis

Activity B

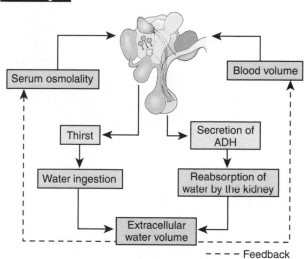

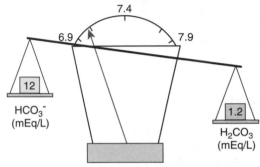

A   Ratio: HCO₃⁻ : H₂CO₃ = 20:1
normal, ph 7.4

$$pH = 6.1 + log_{10} (ratio\ HCO_3^- : H_2CO_3)$$

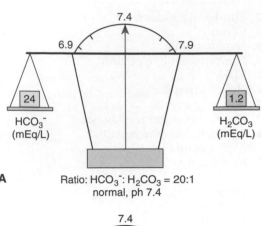

B   Ratio: HCO₃⁻ : H₂CO₃ = 10:1
metabolic acidosis

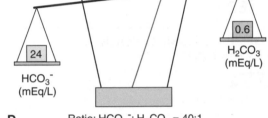

D   Ratio: HCO₃⁻ : H₂CO₃ = 40:1
respiratory alkalosis

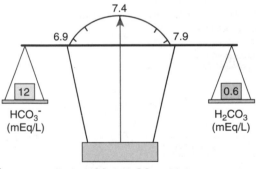

C   Ratio: HCO₃⁻ : H₂CO₃ = 20:1
metabolic acidosis with
respiratory compensation

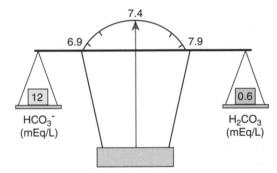

E   Ratio: HCO₃⁻ : H₂CO₃ = 20:1
respiratory alkalosis
with renal compensation

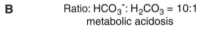

Activity C

1.

1. c	**2.** g	**3.** e	**4.** b	**5.** j
6. f	**7.** a	**8.** h	**9.** d	**10.** i

2.

1. d	**2.** h	**3.** b	**4.** a	**5.** c
6. j	**7.** e	**8.** g	**9.** i	**10.** f

3.

1. e	**2.** a	**3.** i	**4.** h	**5.** c
6. b	**7.** d	**8.** j	**9.** f	**10.** g

Activity D

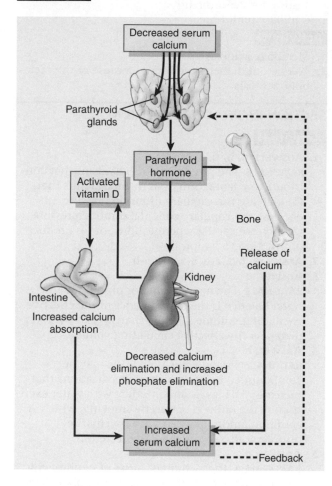

Activity E

1. The ECF, including blood plasma and interstitial fluids, contain large amounts of sodium and chloride, moderate amounts of bicarbonate, but only small quantities of potassium, magnesium, calcium, and phosphate. In contrast to the ECF, the ICF contains almost no calcium; small amounts of sodium, chloride, bicarbonate, and phosphate; moderate amounts of magnesium; and large amounts of potassium.

2. **a.** the capillary filtration pressure, which pushes water out of the capillary into the interstitial spaces
   b. the capillary colloidal osmotic pressure, which pulls water back into the capillary
   c. the interstitial hydrostatic pressure, which opposes the movement of water out of the capillary
   d. the tissue colloidal osmotic pressure, which pulls water out of the capillary into the interstitial spaces

3. Mechanisms that contribute to edema formation include factors that increase the capillary filtration pressure, decrease the capillary colloidal osmotic pressure, increase capillary permeability, or produce obstruction to lymph flow.

4. The major regulator of sodium and water balance is the maintenance of the effective circulating volume, which can described as that portion of the ECF that fills the vascular compartment and is "effectively" perfusing the tissues. A low effective circulating volume results in feedback mechanisms that produce an increase in renal and sodium and water retention and a high circulating volume in feedback mechanisms that decrease sodium and water retention.

5. Three types of polydipsia include (1) symptomatic or true thirst, (2) inappropriate or false thirst that occurs despite normal levels of body water and serum osmolality, and (3) compulsive water drinking.

6. There may be a decrease in BUN and hematocrit because of dilution due to expansion of the plasma volume. An increase in vascular volume may be evidenced by distended neck veins, slow-emptying peripheral veins, a full and bounding pulse, and an increase in central venous pressure. When excess fluid accumulates in the lungs (i.e., pulmonary edema), there are complaints of shortness of breath and difficult breathing, respiratory crackles, and a productive cough. Ascites and pleural effusion may occur with severe fluid volume excess.

7. These changes include prolongation of the PR interval, depression of the ST segment, flattening of the T wave, and appearance of a prominent U wave. Normally, potassium leaves the cell during the repolarization phase of the action potential, returning the membrane potential to its normal resting value. Hypokalemia reduces the permeability of the cell membrane to potassium and thus produces a decrease in potassium efflux that prolongs the rate of repolarization and lengthens the relative refractory period. The U wave normally may be present on the electrocardiogram but should be of lower amplitude than the T wave. With hypokalemia, the amplitude of the T wave decreases as the U-wave amplitude increases.

8. Systemic effects of hypercalcemia are (1) changes in neural excitability, (2) alterations in smooth and cardiac muscle function, and (3) exposure of the kidneys to high concentrations of calcium.

9. Excess H^+ ions can be exchanged for Na^+ and K^+ on the bone surface and dissolution of bone minerals with release of compounds such as sodium bicarbonate ($NaHCO_3$), and calcium carbonate ($CaCO_3$) into the ECF can be used for buffering excess acids. It has been estimated that as much as 40% of buffering of an acute acid load takes place in bone. The role of bone buffers is even greater in the presence of chronic acidosis. The consequences of bone buffering include demineralization of

bone and predisposition to development of kidney stones due to increased urinary excretion of calcium. Persons with chronic kidney disease are at particular risk for reduction in bone calcium because of acid retention.

10. The transcompartmental exchange of H^+ and potassium ions (K^+) provides an important system for regulation of acid-base balance. Both ions are positively charged, and both ions move freely between the ICF and ECF compartments. When excess H^+ is present in the ECF, it moves into the ICF in exchange for K^+, and when excess K^+ is present in the ECF, it moves into the ICF in exchange for H^+. Thus, alterations in potassium levels can affect acid-base balance, and changes in acid-base balance can influence potassium levels.

11. The kidneys play two major roles in regulating acid-base balance. The first is accomplished through the reabsorption of the HCO_3^- that is filtered in the glomerulus so this important buffer is not lost in the urine. The second is through the excretion of H^+ from fixed acids that result from protein and lipid metabolism.

12. There are two types of acid-base disorders: metabolic and respiratory. Metabolic disorders produce an alteration in the plasma HCO_3^- concentration and result from the addition or loss of nonvolatile acid or alkali to or from the extracellular fluids. A reduction in pH due to a decrease in HCO_3^- is called metabolic acidosis, and an elevation in pH due to increased HCO_3^- levels is called metabolic alkalosis. Respiratory disorders involve an alteration in the P_{CO_2}, reflecting an increase or decrease in alveolar ventilation. Respiratory acidosis is characterized by a decrease in pH, reflecting a decrease in ventilation and an increase in P_{CO_2}. Respiratory alkalosis involves an increase in pH, resulting from an increase in alveolar ventilation and a decrease in P_{CO_2}.

SECTION III: APPLYING YOUR KNOWLEDGE

Activity F CASE STUDY

a. When a client has burns over a large area of the body there is a loss of protein in the plasma of the body. In a burn there is also injury to the capillaries in the burned area. When a person is burned, large amounts of albumin are moved out of the blood and are lost in the urine. We are working very hard to infuse fluid that the body needs with our IV solutions.

b. The nurse knows that the diagnosis of fluid volume deficit is based on these factors:
   History of conditions that predispose to sodium and water losses
   Weight loss
   Intake and output
   Heart rate

Blood pressure
Testing for venous refill
Capillary refill time

Activity G

1. Metabolic acidosis
2. To rule out diabetes mellitus as a cause of the metabolic acidosis

---

SECTION IV: PRACTICING FOR NCLEX

Activity H

1. **Answers: a, b, d, e**
   RATIONALE: The physiologic mechanisms that contribute to edema formation include factors that (1) increase the capillary filtration pressure, (2) decrease the capillary colloidal osmotic pressure, (3) increase capillary permeability, or (4) produce obstruction to lymph flow.

2. **Answers: 1-d, 2-e, 3-a, 4-c, 5-b**

3. **Answer: a**
   RATIONALE: The major regulator of sodium and water balance is the maintenance of the effective circulating volume. The other answers are not regulated by the effective circulating volume.

4. **Answer: b**
   RATIONALE: Psychogenic polydipsia may be compounded by antipsychotic medications that increase ADH levels and interfere with water excretion by the kidneys. Cigarette smoking, which is common among persons with psychiatric disorders, also stimulates ADH secretion.

5. **Answer: c**
   RATIONALE: Other acquired causes of nephrogenic DI are drugs such as lithium and electrolyte disorders such as potassium depletion or chronic hypercalcemia. The other answers are not acquired causes of nephrogenic DI.

6. **Answer: c**
   RATIONALE: When this occurs, water moves into the brain cells, causing cerebral edema and potentially severe neurologic impairment. The other cells are not correct.

7. **Answer: a**
   RATIONALE: Changes in nerve and muscle excitability are particularly important in the heart, where alterations in plasma potassium can produce serious cardiac arrhythmias and conduction defects. The other answers are not correct.

8. **Answer: b**
   RATIONALE: The small, but vital, amount of ECF calcium, phosphate, and magnesium is directly or indirectly regulated by vitamin D and parathyroid hormone. The other answers are not correct.

9. **Answer: d**
   RATIONALE: The NPT2 is also inhibited by the recently identified hormone called *phosphatonin*. When this hormone is overproduced, as in tumor-induced osteomalacia, marked hypophosphatemia

occurs. The other conditions are not caused by hypophosphatemia.

10. Answer: a
RATIONALE: Severe hypermagnesemia (>12 mg/dL) is associated with muscle and respiratory paralysis, complete heart block, and cardiac arrest.

11. Answer: a
RATIONALE: The H_2CO_3 content of the blood can be calculated by multiplying the partial pressure of CO_2 (P_{CO_2}) by its solubility coefficient, which is 0.03.

12. Answers: a, c, e
RATIONALE: The pH of body fluids is regulated by three major mechanisms: (1) chemical buffer systems of the body fluids, which immediately combine with excess acids or bases to prevent large changes in pH; (2) the lungs, which control the elimination of CO_2; and (3) the kidneys, which eliminate H^+ and both reabsorb and generate HCO_3^-. None of the other answers are correct.

13. Answer: c
RATIONALE: The renal mechanisms for regulating acid-base balance cannot adjust the pH within minutes, as respiratory mechanisms can, but they continue to function for days, until the pH has returned to normal or near-normal range. It is the respiratory system that responds within minutes to return the body's pH near to its normal limits. The other answers are wrong.

14. Answer: d
RATIONALE: The total base excess or deficit, also referred to as the *whole blood buffer base,* measures the level of all the buffer systems of the blood—hemoglobin, protein, phosphate, and HCO_3^-. For clinical purposes, base excess or deficit can be viewed as a measurement of bicarbonate excess or deficit.

15. Answer: a
RATIONALE: Metabolic disorders produce an alteration in the plasma HCO_3^- concentration and result from the addition or loss of nonvolatile acid or alkali to or from the extracellular fluids. None of the other answers are correct.

16. Answer: b
RATIONALE: Often, compensatory mechanisms are interim measures that permit survival while the body attempts to correct the primary disorder. All of the other answers are wrong.

17. Answer: c
RATIONALE: The anion gap is often useful in determining the cause of the metabolic acidosis. None of the other tests are used to determine the cause of metabolic acidosis.

18. Answer: d
RATIONALE: A fall in pH to less than 7.0 to 7.10 can reduce cardiac contractility and predispose to potentially fatal cardiac dysrhythmias. No other answer is correct.

19. Answers: a, b, c
RATIONALE: Elevated levels of CO_2 produce vasodilation of cerebral blood vessels, causing headache, blurred vision, irritability, muscle twitching, and psychological disturbances. Seizures and psychotic breaks are not signs or symptoms of respiratory acidosis.

20. Answer: a
RATIONALE: One of the most common causes of respiratory alkalosis is hyperventilation syndrome, which is characterized by recurring episodes of overbreathing, often associated with anxiety.

CHAPTER 9

SECTION II: ASSESSING YOUR UNDERSTANDING

Activity A
1. homeostasis, physiologic
2. Homeostasis
3. negative
4. stress
5. disease
6. hypothalamic-pituitary-adrenocortical, adrenomedullary, sympathetic
7. adapting
8. coping strategy
9. Sleep
10. Alcohol

Activity B

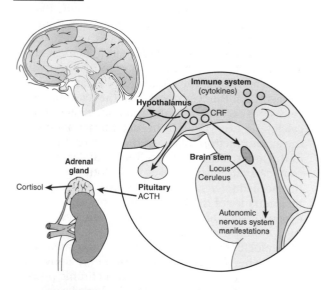

Activity C
1. d	2. j	3. g	4. c	5. f
6. e	7. a	8. h	9. i	10. b

Activity D
1. Negative feedback mechanisms are the primary mechanism used to maintain homeostasis. The negative feedback mechanism that controls blood glucose levels, an increase in blood glucose stimulates an increase in insulin, which enhances the

removal of glucose from the blood. When glucose has been taken up by cells and blood glucose levels fall, insulin secretion is inhibited and glucagon and other counterregulatory mechanisms stimulate the release of glucose from the liver, which causes the blood glucose to return to normal.

2. The stages of general adaptation syndrome are the alarm stage, the resistance stage, and the exhaustion stage. The *alarm stage* is characterized by a generalized stimulation of the sympathetic nervous system and the hypothalamic-pituitary-adrenocortical axis, resulting in the release of catecholamines and cortisol. During the *resistance stage*, the body selects the most effective and economic channels of defense. During this stage, the increased cortisol levels present during the first stage drop because they are no longer needed. If the stressor is prolonged or overwhelms the ability of the body to defend itself, the *exhaustion stage* ensues, during which resources are depleted and signs of "wear and tear" or systemic damage appear.

3. The results of the coordinated release of these neurohormones include the mobilization of energy, a sharpened focus and awareness, increased cerebral blood flow and glucose utilization, enhanced cardiovascular and respiratory functioning, redistribution of blood flow to the brain and muscles, modulation of the immune response, inhibition of reproductive function, and decrease in appetite.

4. Many organs are functioning at much less than maximum capacity, giving the organ a safety margin. The safety margin for adaptation of most body systems is considerably greater than that needed for normal activities. The red blood cells carry more oxygen than the tissues can use, the liver and fat cells store excess nutrients, and bone tissue stores calcium in excess of that needed for normal neuromuscular function. Many of the body organs, such as the lungs, kidneys, and adrenals, are paired to provide anatomic reserve as well. Both organs are not needed to ensure the continued existence and maintenance of the internal environment. As they expend greater amounts of energy, athletes are able to tap into these reserves.

5. Physiologic symptoms arise from exaggerated sympathetic nervous system activation in response to the traumatic event. Persons with chronic posttraumatic stress disorder (PTTSD) have been shown to have increased levels of norepinephrine and increased activity of α_2-adrenergic receptors. The increases in catecholamines, in tandem with increased thyroid levels in persons with PTSD, are thought to explain some of the intrusive and somatic symptoms of the disorder. In the CNS, reactivity of the amygdala and hippocampus and decreased reactivity of the anterior cingulate and orbitofrontal areas and are thought to contribute to PTSD also.

SECTION III: PRACTICING FOR NCLEX
Activity E

1. **Answer: a**
   RATIONALE: The body's control systems regulate cellular function, control life processes, and integrate functions of the different organ systems. Homeostatic control systems do not feed cells when they are under stress, they do not act on invading organisms, and they do not shut down the body at death.

2. **Answer: b**
   RATIONALE: A homeostatic control system consists of a collection of interconnected components that function to keep a physical or chemical parameter of the body relatively constant. Organ systems are a group of organs that function together to accomplish necessary functions in the body; for example, the cardiovascular system provides blood to all the body's components. Biochemical messengers are in the brain; they are not control systems. Neuroendocrine systems are control systems that help to regulate our response to stress. Neurovascular systems do not aid in the control of homeostasis in the body.

3. **Answer: c**
   RATIONALE: Selye contended that many ailments, such as various emotional disturbances, mildly annoying headaches, insomnia, upset stomach, gastric and duodenal ulcers, certain types of rheumatic disorders, and cardiovascular and kidney diseases, appear to be initiated or encouraged by the "body itself because of its faulty adaptive reactions to potentially injurious agents." Psychotic disorders are not caused by stress. Osteogenesis refers to the origin of bone tissue; this is not due to stress. Sarcomas are a type of cancer. There is no such thing as osteogenesis sarcomas. Infections in the head and neck are caused by bacterial or viral invaders of the body; they are not due to stress.

4. **Answer: d**
   RATIONALE: The results of the coordinated release of these neurohormones include the mobilization of energy, a sharpened focus and awareness, increased cerebral blood flow and glucose utilization, enhanced cardiovascular and respiratory functioning, redistribution of blood flow to the brain and muscles, modulation of the immune response, inhibition of reproductive function, and decrease in appetite.

5. **Answer: a**
   RATIONALE: Diseases of the cardiovascular, gastrointestinal, immune, and neurologic systems, as well as depression, chronic alcoholism and drug abuse, eating disorders, accidents, and suicide have all been linked to the chronic and excessive activation of the stress response.

6. **Answer: b**
   RATIONALE: The response to physiologic disturbances that threaten the integrity of the internal

environment is specific to the threat; the body usually does not raise the body temperature when an increase in heart rate is needed. In contrast, the response to psychological disturbances is not regulated with the same degree of specificity and feedback control; instead, the effect may be inappropriate and sustained. No systems in the body are regulated by a positive feedback system. In cardiovascular physiology, the baroreflex or baroreceptor reflex is one of the body's homeostatic mechanisms for maintaining blood pressure. It has nothing to do with the body's response to a psychological threat.

7. **Answer: c**
RATIONALE: The ability of body systems to increase their function given the need to adapt is known as the physiologic reserve. Many of the body organs, such as the lungs, kidneys, and adrenals, are paired to provide anatomic reserve as well. Both organs are not needed to ensure the continued existence and maintenance of the internal environment. Genetic endowment, physiologic reserve, and health status are all coping mechanisms but they do not impact the body's need to survive when one organ of a pair is missing.

8. **Answer: c**
RATIONALE: The configuration of significant others that constitutes the social network functions to mobilize the resources of the person; these friends, colleagues, and family members share the person's tasks and provide monetary support, materials and tools, and guidance in improving problem-solving capabilities. Social networks cannot protect the person from other internal stressors.

9. **Answer: d**
RATIONALE: In persons with limited coping abilities, either because of physical or mental health, the acute stress response may be detrimental. This is true of persons with pre-existing heart disease in whom the overwhelming sympathetic behaviors associated with the stress response can lead to arrhythmias. The acute stress response is not necessarily going to be detrimental to the client who has undergone the resection of a brain tumor or is a schizophrenic client who is off his or her medication, or a client with a broken femur.

10. **Answer: a**
RATIONALE: Posttraumatic stress disorder is an example of chronic activation of the stress response as a result of experiencing a severe trauma. In this disorder, memory of the traumatic event seems to be enhanced. Flashbacks of the event are accompanied by intense activation of the neuroendocrine system. Chronic renal insufficiency, schizophrenia, and postdelivery depression in a new mother are not the result of chronic activation of the stress response following a severe trauma.

11. **Answer: multicellular**
RATIONALE: A multicellular organism is able to survive only as long as the composition of the internal environment is compatible with the survival needs of the individual cells.

12. **Answer: eustress**
RATIONALE: Selye suggested that mild, brief, and controllable periods of stress could be perceived as positive stimuli to emotional and intellectual growth and development. These periods of stress are called eustress.

13. **Answers: b, d**
RATIONALE: The treatment of stress should be directed toward helping people avoid coping behaviors that impose a risk to their health and providing them with alternative stress-reducing strategies. Nonpharmacologic methods used for stress reduction are relaxation techniques, guided imagery, music therapy, massage, and biofeedback.

14. **Answers: 1-b,** Corticotropin-releasing factor is a small peptide hormone found in both the hypothalamus and in extrahypothalamic structures, such as the limbic system and the brain stem. It is both an important endocrine regulator of pituitary and adrenal activity and a neurotransmitter involved in autonomic nervous system activity, metabolism, and behavior.
2-d, The sympathetic nervous system manifestation of the stress reaction has been called the fight-or-flight response. This is the most rapid of the stress responses and represents the basic survival response of our primitive ancestors when confronted with the perils of the wilderness and its inhabitants.
3-c, The term *allostasis* has been used by some investigators to describe the physiologic changes in the neuroendocrine, autonomic, and immune systems that occur in response to either real or perceived challenges to homeostasis. The persistence and/or accumulation of these allostatic changes (e.g., immunosuppression, activation of the sympathetic nervous and renin-angiotensin-aldosterone systems) has been called an "allostatic load," and this concept has been used to measure the cumulative effects of stress on humans.
4-a, The hallmark of the stress response, as first described by Selye, is the endocrine-immune interactions (i.e., increased corticosteroid production and atrophy of the thymus) that are known to suppress the immune response. In concert, these two components of the stress system, through endocrine and neurotransmitter pathways, produce the physical and behavioral changes designed to adapt to acute stress.

15. **Answers: a, b, c**
RATIONALE: The most significant arguments for interaction between the neuroendocrine and immune systems derive from evidence that the immune and neuroendocrine systems share common signal pathways (i.e., messenger molecules and receptors), that hormones and neuropeptides can alter the function of immune cells, and that the immune system and its mediators can modulate neuroendocrine function. These systems do not need each other to function.

CHAPTER 10

SECTION II: ASSESSING YOUR UNDERSTANDING

Activity A

1. Nutritional status
2. Metabolism
3. voluntary physical activity
4. adipose
5. Leptin
6. Recommended Dietary Allowance (RDA)
7. Percent daily value
8. Proteins
9. nitrogen
10. elevate, lower
11. increase, decrease
12. carbohydrates
13. Vitamins
14. Fiber
15. hypothalamus
16. glucose
17. Anthropometric
18. body mass index (BMI)
19. circumference
20. Obesity
21. fat distribution
22. Weight cycling
23. increased
24. Bariatric surgery
25. pediatric
26. Malnutrition, starvation
27. starvation
28. marasmus
29. recurrent

Activity B

1.

1. f	2. d	3. b	4. h	5. i
6. c	7. a	8. g	9. j	10. e

2.

1. f	2. c	3. b	4. a	5. g
6. d	7. e			

Activity C

1. There are two types of adipose tissue: white fat and brown fat. White fat is the prevalent form. At body temperature, the lipid content of fat cells exists as an oil of triglycerides. Triglycerides have the highest caloric content of all nutrients and are an efficient form of energy storage. Fat cells synthesize triglycerides, from dietary fats and carbohydrates. When calorie intake is restricted for any reason, fat cell triglycerides are broken down and the resultant fatty acids and glycerol are released as energy sources. Brown fat differs from white fat in terms of its thermogenic capacity or ability to produce heat. Brown fat, the site of diet-induced thermogenesis and non-shivering thermogenesis, is found primarily in early neonatal life in humans and in animals that hibernate. In humans, brown fat decreases with age but is still detectable in the sixth decade. This small amount of brown fat has a minimal effect on energy expenditure.

2. Bioimpedance is performed by attaching electrodes at the wrist and ankle that send a harmless current through the body. The flow of the current is affected by the amount of water in the body. Because fat-free tissue contains virtually all the water and the conducting electrolytes, measurements of the resistance (i.e., impedance) to current flow can be used to estimate the percentage of body fat present.

3. Family eating patterns, inactivity because of labor-saving devices and time spent on the computer and watching television, reliance on the automobile for transportation, easy access to food, energy density of food, increased consumption of sugar-sweetened beverages, and increasing portion sizes. The obese may be greatly influenced by the availability of food, the flavor of food, time of day, and other cues. The composition of the diet also may be a causal factor, and the percentage of dietary fat independent of total calorie intake may play a part in the development of obesity. Psychological factors include using food as a reward, comfort, or means of getting attention. Eating may be a way to cope with tension, anxiety, and mental fatigue. Some persons may overeat and use obesity as a means of avoiding emotionally threatening situations.

4. The causes of anorexia appear to be multifactorial, with determinants that include genetic influence, personality traits of perfectionism and compulsiveness, anxiety disorders, family history of depression and obesity, and peer, familial, and cultural pressures with respect to appearance. The DSM-IV-TR diagnostic criteria for anorexia nervosa are (1) a refusal to maintain a minimally normal body weight for age and height (e.g., at least 85% of minimal expected weight or BMI $\geq$17.5); (2) an intense fear of gaining weight or becoming fat; (3) a disturbance in the way one's body size, weight, shape is perceived; and (4) amenorrhea (in girls and women after menarche). Other psychiatric disorders often coexist with anorexia nervosa, including major depression or dysthymia, and obsessive-compulsive disorder. Alcohol and substance abuse may also be present, more often among those with binging-purging type of anorexia nervosa.

5. The criteria to diagnose bulimia nervosa are: (1) recurrent binge eating (at least two times per week for 3 months); (2) inappropriate compensatory behaviors such as self-induced vomiting, abuse of laxatives or diuretics, fasting, or excessive exercise that follow the binge-eating episode; (3) self-evaluation that is unduly influenced by body shape and weight; and (4) a determination that the eating disorder does not occur exclusively during episodes of anorexia nervosa.

6. Binge eating is characterized by recurrent episodes of compulsive eating at least 2 days per week for 6 months and at least three of the following: (1) eating rapidly; (2) eating until becoming uncomfortably full; (3) eating large amounts when not hungry; (4) eating alone because of embarrassment; and (5) disgust, depression, or guilt because of eating episodes.

SECTION III: APPLYING YOUR KNOWLEDGE

Activity D

1. Questions include:
   Do you consider yourself a perfectionist?
   Do you do things compulsively?
   Is there a family history of obesity?
   Is anyone in your family overweight?
   Does anyone in your family have an anxiety disorder?
   Does anyone in your family have a history of depression?
2. Criteria include:
   Refusal to maintain a minimally normal body weight for age and height
   An intense fear of gaining weight or becoming fat
   A disturbance in the way one's body size, weight, shape is perceived
   Amenorrhea (in girls and women after menarche)

SECTION IV: PRACTICING FOR NCLEX

Activity E

1. **Answers: a, c, e**
   RATIONALE: The factors secreted by adipose tissue are termed *adipokines* and include leptin, certain cytokines (e.g., tumor necrosis factor-α), growth factors, and adiponectin (important in insulin resistance).
2. **Answer: a**
   RATIONALE: An estimated average requirement is the intake that meets the estimated nutrient need of half of the persons in a specific group. The adequate intake is set when there is not enough scientific evidence to estimate an average requirement. The Recommended Dietary Allowance (RDA) defines the intakes that meet the nutrient needs of almost all healthy persons in a specific age and sex group. The Dietary Reference Intake includes a set of at least four nutrient-based reference values—the recommended dietary allowance, the adequate intake, the estimated average requirement, and the tolerable upper intake level.
3. **Answer: b**
   RATIONALE: The Food and Nutrition Board has set an acceptable macronutrient distribution range for fat of no less than 20% to prevent the fall of HDL cholesterol associated with very low fat diets. The other answers are incorrect.
4. **Answer: c**
   RATIONALE: Centers in the hypothalamus also control the secretion of several hormones (e.g., thyroid and adrenocortical hormones) that regulate energy balance and metabolism. Cholecystokinin (CCK) and glucagon-like peptide-1 (GLP-1) are intestinal hormones. Ghrelin is secreted mostly in the stomach.
5. **Answer: d**
   RATIONALE: The body mass index (BMI) uses height and weight to determine healthy weight (Table 10-2). It is calculated by dividing the weight in kilograms by the height in meters squared (BMI = weight [kg]/height [m^2]). The other answers are incorrect.
6. **Answer: a**
   RATIONALE: The obesity type is determined by dividing the waist by the hip circumference. The other answers are incorrect.
7. **Answer: b**
   RATIONALE: Compared with women, men tend to experience less pressure to engage in behaviors such as self-induced vomiting or laxative use when overeating, less on a subjective sense or loss of control when binge eating, and a greater tendency to use compulsive exercise rather than purging for weight control.
8. **Answer: b**
   RATIONALE: Pediatricians are now beginning to see hypertension, dyslipidemia, type II diabetes, and psychosocial stigma in obese children and adolescents. The other answers are not correct.
9. **Answer: c**
   RATIONALE: The hospitalized patient often finds eating a healthful diet difficult and commonly has restrictions on food and water intake in preparation for tests and surgery. Pain, medications, special diets, and stress can decrease appetite. Even when the patient is well enough to eat, being alone in a room, where unpleasant treatments may be given, is not conducive to eating. The other answers are not correct.

CHAPTER 11

SECTION II: ASSESSING YOUR UNDERSTANDING

Activity A

1. granulocytes
2. thymus
3. plasma
4. natural killer
5. myeloid, lymphoid
6. thymus, spleen
7. CD4$^+$, CD8$^+$
8. aplastic
9. Agranulocytosis
10. neutropenia
11. Infectious mononucleosis
12. Leukemias
13. Lymphomas
14. B

15. nodular, lymphocyte
16. Hodgkin lymphoma
17. leukemias
18. lymphocytic
19. leukemia
20. Acute leukemias
21. lymphocytic, monocytic
22. Chronic leukemias
23. B lymphocytes
24. Kostmann
25. Philadelphia
26. Plasma cell dyscrasias
27. bone
28. *M protein*

Activity B

1. e   **2.** d   **3.** b   **4.** a   **5.** f
6. h   **7.** i   **8.** c   **9.** g   **10.** j

Activity C

1. Neutrophils migrate to sites of infection and engulf, digest, and destroy microorganisms. Thus, a decrease in the number of neutrophils places a person at risk for infection. The risk for and severity of neutropenia-associated infection are directly proportional to the absolute neutrophil count and duration of the neutropenia (defined as a circulating neutrophil count of less than 1500/mL).

2. The Epstein-Barr virus (EBV) initially penetrates the nasopharyngeal, oropharyngeal, and salivary epithelial cells. It then spreads to the underlying oropharyngeal lymphoid tissue and, more specifically, to B lymphocytes, all of which have receptors for EBV. Infection of the B cells may take one of two forms: it may kill the infected B cell or it may become incorporated into its genome. The B cells that harbor the EBV genome proliferate in the circulation and produce the well-known heterophil antibodies that are used for the diagnosis of infectious mononucleosis. The resultant destruction of B cells and production of large T cells result in enlarged lymph nodes, particularly in the cervical, axillary, and groin areas. Hepatitis and splenomegaly are common manifestations of the disease and are thought to be immune-mediated.

3. The manifestations of non-Hodgkin lymphoma (NHL) depend on lymphoma type and the stage of the disease. Persons with indolent or slow-growing lymphomas usually present with painless lymphadenopathy due to increased cell filtering, which may be isolated or widespread. The indolent lymphomas are usually disseminated at the time of diagnosis, and bone marrow involvement is frequent. Many low-grade lymphomas eventually transform into more aggressive forms of lymphoma/leukemia. Persons with intermediate or more aggressive forms of lymphoma usually present with symptoms such as fever, drenching night sweats, or weight loss. Frequently, there are increased susceptibility to bacterial, viral, and fungal infections, and a poor humoral antibody response.

4. First, Hodgkin lymphoma usually arises in a single node or chain of nodes, while NHL frequently originates at extranodal sites and spreads to anatomically contiguous nodes. Second, Hodgkin lymphoma is characterized by the presence of large, atypical, mononuclear tumor cells, called Reed-Sternberg cells. The cells, which frequently constitute less than 1% of the total cell population, are a diagnostic hallmark of the disease.

5. The incidence of leukemia among persons who have been exposed to high levels of radiation is unusually high. An increased incidence of leukemia also is associated with exposure to benzene and the use of antitumor drugs. Leukemia may occur as a second cancer after aggressive chemotherapy for other cancers. The existence of a genetic predisposition to develop acute leukemia is suggested by the increased leukemia incidence among a number of congenital disorders. In individuals with Down syndrome, the incidence of acute leukemia is 10 times that of the general population. Also there are numerous reports of multiple cases of acute leukemia occurring within the same family.

6. Both are characterized by an abrupt onset of symptoms including fatigue resulting from anemia; low-grade fever, night sweats, and weight loss due to the rapid proliferation and hypermetabolism of the leukemic cells; bleeding because of a decreased platelet count; and bone pain and tenderness from bone marrow expansion. Infection results from neutropenia. Generalized lymphadenopathy, splenomegaly, and hepatomegaly caused by infiltration of leukemic cells occur in all acute leukemias but are more common in acute lymphoblastic leukemia (ALL). In addition to the common manifestations of acute leukemia, infiltration of malignant cells in the skin, gums, and other soft tissue is particularly common in the monocytic form of acute myelogenous leukemia (AML). The leukemic cells may also cross the blood-brain barrier and establish sanctuary in the CNS. The CNS involvement is more common in ALL than AML and is more common in children than adults. Signs and symptoms of CNS involvement include cranial nerve palsies, headache, nausea, vomiting, papilledema, and, occasionally, seizures and coma. Leukostasis and blood clotting are seen in severe cases.

7. The early chronic stage is marked by leukocytosis, anemia, and thrombocytopenia. Splenomegaly and hepatomegaly are often present. The accelerated phase of CML is characterized by enlargement of the spleen, resulting in a feeling of abdominal fullness and discomfort. An increase in basophil count and more immature cells in the blood or bone marrow confirm transformation to the accelerated phase. Symptoms such as low-grade fever, night sweats, bone pain, and weight loss develop because

of rapid proliferation and hypermetabolism of the leukemic cells. Bleeding and easy bruising may arise from dysfunctional platelets. The terminal blast crisis phase of CML represents evolution to acute leukemia and is characterized by an increasing number of myeloid precursors, especially blast cells, in the blood. Constitutional symptoms become more pronounced during this period, and splenomegaly may increase significantly. Isolated infiltrates of leukemic cells can involve the skin, lymph nodes, bones, and CNS.

8. The cause of multiple myeloma is unknown. Risk factors are thought to include chronic immune stimulation, autoimmune disorders, exposure to ionizing radiation, and occupational exposure to pesticides or herbicides. Myeloma has been associated with exposure to Agent Orange during the Vietnam War. A number of viruses have been associated with the pathogenesis of myeloma. There is a 4.5-fold increase in the likelihood of developing myeloma for persons with HIV.

SECTION III: APPLYING YOUR KNOWLEDGE

Activity D

1. The causes of leukemia are really unknown. We do know that the event or events causing the leukemias exert their effects through disruption or dysregulation of genes that normally regulate blood cell development, blood cell stability, or both.

2. Treatment of ALL consists of a number of chemotherapeutic agents designed to achieve remission followed by high doses of chemotherapy given to patients who have achieved remission with their induction therapy. This part of Lucy's treatment is designed to reduce the number of cancer cells in her body even more once remission has been achieved. Then she will receive lower doses of chemotherapy given over a long period of time in an attempt to cure her.

SECTION IV: PRACTICING FOR NCLEX

Activity E

1. **Answer: a**
   RATIONALE: A small population of cells called pluripotent stem cells are capable of providing progenitor cells, or parent cells, for myelopoiesis and lymphopoiesis, processes by which myeloid and lymphoid blood cells are made. Unipotent cells are the progenitors for each of the blood cell types and come from pluripotent stem cells. Multipotential progenitor cells act as parent cells for multiple types of blood cells. Myeloproliferative cells do not exist.

2. **Answer: b**
   RATIONALE: The portion of the cortex between the medullary and superficial cortex is called the paracortex. The region contains most of the T cells in the lymph nodes. The B-cell−dependent cortex consists of two types of follicles: immunologically

inactive follicles, called primary follicles, and active follicles that contain germinal centers called secondary follicles. There is no primary cortex in the lymph nodes.

3. **Answer: d**
   RATIONALE: Severe congenital neutropenia, or Kostmann syndrome, is characterized by an arrest in myeloid maturation at the promyelocyte stage of development resulting in an absolute neutrophil count of less than 200 cells/μL. The disorder is characterized by severe bacterial infections. Kostmann syndrome is not characterized by bone marrow disorders, viral infections, or autoimmune disorders.

4. **Answer: a**
   RATIONALE: The incidence of drug-induced neutropenia has increased significantly over the last several decades and is attributed primarily to a wider use of drugs in general and more specifically to the use of chemotherapeutic drugs in the treatment of cancer.

5. **Answer: b**
   RATIONALE: Hepatitis and splenomegaly are common manifestations of infectious mononucleosis and are thought to be immune-mediated. Hepatitis is characterized by hepatomegaly, nausea, anorexia, and jaundice. Although discomforting, it usually is a benign condition that resolves without causing permanent liver damage. The spleen may be enlarged two to three times its normal size, and rupture of the spleen is an infrequent complication. Cranial nerve palsies, not peripheral nerve palsies, can occur. Lymph nodes do not rupture. Severe bacterial infections are complications of Kostmann syndrome.

6. **Answer: c**
   RATIONALE: Non-Hodgkin lymphomas represent the cancer with the second fastest rate of increase in the United States, and the most commonly occurring hematologic cancer. Neoplasms of immature B cells include lymphoblastic leukemia/lymphoma (i.e., ALL). They are not classed as NHLs. Mantle cell lymphoma is one of the mature B-cell lymphomas.

7. **Answer: d**
   RATIONALE: Endemic Burkitt lymphoma is the most common childhood cancer (peak age 3 to 7 years) in central Africa, often beginning in the jaw. It occurs in regions of Africa where both EBV and malaria infection are common. Neither herpes zoster nor streptococcal infections are associated with endemic Burkitt lymphoma.

8. **Answer: a**
   RATIONALE: Although ALL and AML are distinct disorders, they typically present with similar clinical features. Both are characterized by an abrupt onset of symptoms including fatigue resulting from anemia; low-grade fever, night sweats, and weight loss due to the rapid proliferation and hypermetabolism of the leukemic cells; bleeding

because of a decreased platelet count; and bone pain and tenderness due to bone marrow expansion. Polycythemia is an increase in the erythrocytes in the blood. It is not an indication of leukemia.

9. **Answer: b**
   RATIONALE: Diagnosis of multiple myeloma is based on clinical manifestations, blood tests, and bone marrow examination. The classic triad of bone marrow plasmacytosis (more than 10% plasma cells), lytic bone lesions, and either the serum M-protein spike or the presence of Bence-Jones proteins in the urine is definitive for a diagnosis of multiple myeloma. Oligoclonal bands are indicative of multiple sclerosis and BCR-ABL fusion protein is found in CML.

10. **Answer: c**
    RATIONALE: Hypogammaglobulinemia is common in CLL, especially in persons with advanced disease. An increased susceptibility to infection reflects an inability to produce specific antibodies and abnormal activation of complement. The most common infectious organisms are those that require opsonization for bacterial killing, such as *Streptococcus pneumoniae, Staphylococcus aureus,* and *Haemophilus influenzae.* Acne rosacea, *Pseudomonas aeruginosa,* and *Escherichia coli* are not infectious agents common in clients with CLL.

11. **Answer: lyse**

12. **Answer: c**
    RATIONALE: The alimentary canal, respiratory passages, and genitourinary systems are guarded by accumulations of lymphatic tissue that are not enclosed in a capsule. This form of lymphatic tissue is called diffuse lymphatic tissue or mucus-associated lymphatic tissue (MALT) because of its association with mucous membranes. Lymphocytes are found in the subepithelial of these tissues. Lymphomas can arise from MALT as well as lymph node tissue. The cardiovascular system and the central nervous system do not have MALT.

13. **Answers: b, c, d**
    RATIONALE: The existence of a genetic predisposition to develop acute leukemia is suggested by the increased leukemia incidence among a number of congenital disorders, including Down syndrome, neurofibromatosis, and Fanconi anemia. Cushing syndrome is not a genetic disorder, nor is Prader-Willi syndrome.

14. **Answers: a, c, e**
    RATIONALE: Massive necrosis of malignant cells can occur during the initial phase of treatment. This phenomenon, known as *tumor lysis syndrome*, can lead to life-threatening metabolic disorders, including hyperkalemia, hyperphosphatemia, hyperuricemia, hypomagnesemia, hypocalcemia, and acidosis, with the potential for causing acute renal failure.

15. **Answer: radiation**
    RATIONALE: As the cure rate for Hodgkin lymphoma has risen and longer-term follow-up data became

available, the importance of the late effects of treatment, including secondary malignancies, has become more apparent. Because these malignancies have mainly been attributed to radiation therapy, studies are being conducted to determine the lowest effective radiation dose.

CHAPTER 12

SECTION II: ASSESSING YOUR UNDERSTANDING

Activity A

1. *hemostasis*
2. nucleus
3. actin, myosin
4. growth factors
5. ADP, TXA_2
6. coagulation cascade
7. liver
8. disseminated intravascular coagulation (DIC)
9. Hypercoagulability
10. Smoking
11. thrombocytosis
12. protein C
13. coagulation
14. Bleeding
15. *thrombocytopenia*
16. Platelet
17. Immune
18. Thrombocytopathia
19. X-linked.
20. clotting factors
21. scurvy
22. DIC

Activity B

1.

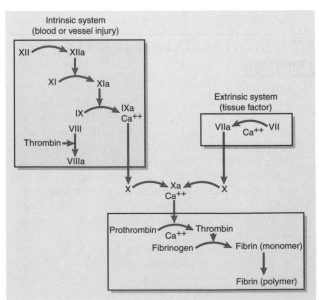

Activity C

1. c   **2.** g   **3.** i   **4.** e   **5.** a
6. f   **7.** j   **8.** h   **9.** d   **10.** c

Activity D

1.

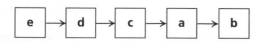

Activity E

1. (1) Vessel spasm, which constricts the vessel and reduces blood flow, (2) formation of the platelet plug initiated platelet contact with subendothelial tissue, (3) blood coagulation via fibrin polymerization, (4) clot retraction in order to squeeze out serum, and (5) clot dissolution by fibrinolysis by plasminogen.

2. Platelets are attracted to a damaged vessel wall, become activated, and change from smooth disks to spiny spheres, exposing glycoprotein receptors on their surfaces. Platelet adhesion requires a protein molecule called von Willebrand factor, which is produced by the endothelial cells of blood vessels and circulates in the blood as a carrier protein for coagulation factor VIII. Adhesion to the vessel subendothelial layer occurs when the platelet receptor binds to von Willebrand factor at the injury site, linking the platelet to exposed collagen fibers.

3. The intrinsic pathway, which is a relatively slow process, begins in the circulation with the activation of factor XII, which is activated as blood comes in contact with collagen in the injured vessel wall. The extrinsic pathway, which is a much faster process, begins with trauma to the blood vessel or surrounding tissues and the release of tissue factor, an adhesive lipoprotein released from the subendothelial cells. The terminal steps in both pathways are the same: the activation of factor X and the conversion of prothrombin to thrombin.

4. These drugs act as haptens and induce antigen–antibody response and formation of immune complexes that cause platelet destruction by complement-mediated lysis (see Chapter 15). In persons with drug-associated thrombocytopenia, there is a rapid fall in the platelet count within 2 to 3 days of resuming a drug or 7 or more days (i.e., the time needed to mount an immune response) after starting a drug for the first time.

5. Activation through the extrinsic pathway occurs with liberation of tissue factors, associated with obstetric complications, trauma, bacterial sepsis, and cancers. The intrinsic pathway may be activated through extensive endothelial damage with activation of factor XII. DIC begins with massive activation of the coagulation sequence as a result of unregulated generation of thrombin,

resulting in systemic formation of fibrin. In addition, levels of all the major anticoagulants are reduced. The microthrombi that result cause vessel occlusion and tissue ischemia. Multiple organ failure may ensue. Clot formation consumes all available coagulation proteins and platelets, and severe hemorrhage results.

SECTION III: PRACTICING FOR NCLEX

Activity F

1. **Answer: a**
   RATIONALE: Platelet adhesion requires a protein molecule called von Willebrand factor. This factor is produced by the endothelial cells of blood vessels and circulates in the blood as a carrier protein for coagulation factor VIII. The release of growth factors results in the proliferation and growth of vascular endothelial cells, smooth muscle cells, and fibroblasts, and is important in vessel repair. Ionized calcium contributes to vasoconstriction. Platelet factor 4 is a heparin-binding chemokine.

2. **Answer: b**
   RATIONALE: The coagulation process results from the activation of what has traditionally been designated the intrinsic or the extrinsic pathways. The intrinsic pathway, which is a relatively slow process, begins in the circulation with the activation of factor XII. The extrinsic pathway, which is a much faster process, begins with trauma to the blood vessel or surrounding tissues and the release of tissue factor, an adhesive lipoprotein released from the subendothelial cells. The terminal steps in both pathways are the same: the activation of factor X and the conversion of prothrombin to thrombin. All other answers do not exist in the formation of clots.

3. **Answer: a**
   RATIONALE: The anticoagulant drugs warfarin and heparin are used to prevent thromboembolic disorders, such as deep vein thrombosis and pulmonary embolism. Warfarin acts by decreasing prothrombin and other procoagulation factors. It alters vitamin K in a manner that reduces its ability to participate in synthesis of the vitamin K–dependent coagulation factors in the liver.

4. **Answer: b**
   RATIONALE: Heparin binds to antithrombin III, causing a conformational change that increases the ability of antithrombin III to inactivate thrombin, factor Xa, and other clotting factors. By promoting the inactivation of clotting factors, heparin ultimately suppresses the formation of fibrin. Heparin does not bind to factors X and Xa. Heparin does not inactivate factor VIII.

5. **Answer: b**
   RATIONALE: Platelets, through the action of their actin and myosin filaments, also contribute to clot

retraction. Clot retraction therefore requires large numbers of platelets and failure of clot retraction is indicative of a low platelet count. Factor Xa is necessary factor in blood coagulation. It does not cause failure of clot retraction.

6. **Answer: c**
   RATIONALE: The common underlying causes of secondary thrombocytosis include tissue damage due to surgery, infection, cancer, and chronic inflammatory conditions such as rheumatoid arthritis and Crohn disease. Lyme disease, caused by a tick bite, does not cause thrombocytosis. Hirschsprung disease and megacolon are the same thing, and they are not inflammatory conditions.

7. **Answer: a**
   RATIONALE: A reduction in platelet number, also referred to as *thrombocytopenia*, is an important cause of generalized bleeding. Thrombocytopenia usually refers to a decrease in the number of circulating platelets to a level less than $100,000/\mu L$. The greater the decrease in the platelet count, the greater the risk of bleeding. Thrombocytopenic can result from a decrease in platelet production, increased sequestration of platelets in the spleen, or decreased platelet survival.

8. **Answer: b**
   RATIONALE: Hemophilia A is an X-linked recessive disorder that primarily affects males. Approximately 90% of persons with hemophilia produce insufficient quantities of the factor VIII. The prevention of trauma is important in persons with hemophilia.

9. **Answer: c**
   RATIONALE: In persons with bleeding disorders caused by vascular defects, the platelet count and results of other tests for coagulation factors are normal. A shift to the left indicates an infectious or inflammatory process, not a clotting disorder. A lack of iron indicates iron deficiency anemia, not a clotting disorder. A normal hematocrit indicates a normal number of packed red blood cells, not a clotting disorder.

10. **Answer: a**
    RATIONALE: Disseminated intravascular coagulation is a paradox in the hemostatic sequence and is characterized by widespread coagulation and bleeding in the vascular compartment. It is not a primary disease but occurs as a complication of a wide variety of conditions such as disease or injury, such as septicemia, acute hypotension, poisonous snake bites, neoplasms, obstetric emergencies, severe trauma, extensive surgery, and hemorrhage.

11. **Answer: c**
    RATIONALE: Hemostasis is divided into five stages: (1) vessel spasm, (2) formation of the platelet plug, (3) blood coagulation or development of an insol-

uble fibrin clot, (4) clot retraction, and (5) clot dissolution.

12. **Answer: intravascular**
13. **Answer: Heparin**
14. **Answers: a, b, c, e**
    RATIONALE: Platelets that adhere to the vessel wall release growth factors that cause proliferation of smooth muscle and thereby contribute to the development of atherosclerosis. Smoking, elevated levels of blood lipids and cholesterol, hemodynamic stress, diabetes mellitus, and immune mechanisms may cause vessel damage, platelet adherence, and, eventually, thrombosis.

15. **Answers: a, c, e**
    RATIONALE: In DIC, microemboli may obstruct blood vessels and cause tissue hypoxia and necrotic damage to organ structures, such as the kidneys, heart, lungs, and brain. As a result, common clinical signs may be due to renal, circulatory, or respiratory failure, acute bleeding ulcers or convulsions and coma. A form of hemolytic anemia may develop as red cells are damaged as they pass through vessels partially blocked by thrombus.

CHAPTER 13

SECTION II: ASSESSING YOUR UNDERSTANDING

Activity A

1. biconcave, cell membrane
2. iron
3. nucleus
4. 4
5. glycolytic
6. methemoglobin
7. red blood cell count (RBC)
8. hematocrit
9. mean corpuscular hemoglobin concentration (MCHC)
10. Anemia
11. hypoxia
12. Hemolytic
13. sickle cell, thalassemias
14. spherocytosis
15. β-Thalassemias, α-thalassemias
16. glucose-6-phosphatase (G6PD)
17. Iron-deficiency
18. chronic blood loss
19. Megaloblastic
20. Pernicious
21. Aplastic anemia
22. Polycythemia
23. oxygen
24. conjugate
25. anemia

Activity B

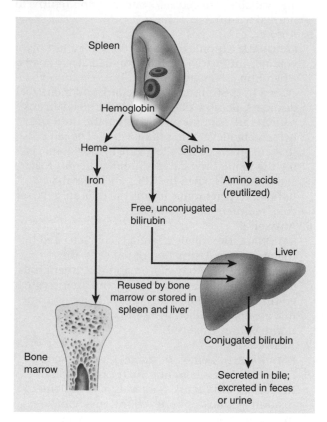

Spleen

Hemoglobin

Heme ——— Globin

Iron

Amino acids (reutilized)

Free, unconjugated bilirubin

Liver

Reused by bone marrow or stored in spleen and liver

Bone marrow

Conjugated bilirubin

Secreted in bile; excreted in feces or urine

Activity C

1. e	**2.** a	**3.** f	**4.** c	**5.** i
6. j	**7.** b	**8.** d	**9.** h	**10.** g

Activity D

1. The hemoglobin molecule is composed of two pairs of structurally different α and β polypeptide chains. Each of the four-polypeptide chains consists of a globin (protein) portion and heme unit, which surrounds an atom of iron that binds oxygen. Thus, each molecule of hemoglobin can carry four molecules of oxygen. The binding that occurs is cooperative, or allosteric. When one oxygen molecule binds, it makes it easier for the next to bind. The process also works in reverse.

2. A group of large phagocytic cells found in the spleen, liver, bone marrow, and lymph nodes facilitates the destruction of RBCs. These phagocytic cells recognize old and defective red cells and then ingest and destroy them in a series of enzymatic reactions. During these reactions, the amino acids from the globulin chains and iron from the heme units are salvaged and reused. The bulk of the heme unit is converted to bilirubin, which is insoluble in plasma and attaches to plasma proteins for transport. Bilirubin is removed from the blood by the liver and conjugated with glucuronide to render it water-soluble so that it can be excreted in the bile.

3. (1) Manifestations of impaired oxygen transport and the resulting compensatory mechanisms, (2) reduction in red cell indices and hemoglobin levels, and (3) signs and symptoms associated with the pathologic process that is causing the anemia.

4. Premature destruction of the cells due to the rigid nondeformable membrane occurs in the spleen, causing hemolysis and anemia due to a decrease in red cell numbers. Secondly, vessel occlusion, a complex process involving an interaction among the sickled cells, endothelial cells, leukocytes, platelets, and other plasma proteins will interrupt blood flow. The adherence of sickled cells to the vessel endothelium causes endothelial activation with liberation of inflammatory mediators and substances that increase platelet activation and promote blood coagulation.

5. Exposure to high doses of radiation, chemicals, and toxins that suppress cellular activity directly or through immune mechanisms are the standard cancer treatments. Chemotherapy and irradiation commonly result in bone marrow depression, which causes anemia, thrombocytopenia, and neutropenia. Identified toxic agents include benzene, the antibiotic chloramphenicol, and the alkylating agents and antimetabolites used in the treatment of cancer will decrease bone marrow of stem cells, thus affecting the production of RBCs.

6. Viscosity rises exponentially with the hematocrit and interferes with cardiac output and blood flow. Hypertension is common and there may be complaints of headache, dizziness, inability to concentrate, and some difficulty with hearing and vision because of decreased cerebral blood flow. Venous stasis gives rise to a plethoric appearance or dusky redness, even cyanosis, particularly of the lips, fingernails, and mucous membranes. Because of the increased concentration of blood cells, the person may experience itching and pain in the fingers or toes, and the hypermetabolism may induce night sweats and weight loss.

7. Hyperbilirubinemia in the neonate is treated with phototherapy or exchange transfusion. Phototherapy is more commonly used to treat jaundiced infants and reduce the risk of kernicterus. Exposure to fluorescent light in the blue range of the visible spectrum (420- to 470-nm wavelength) reduces bilirubin levels. Bilirubin in the skin absorbs the light energy and is converted to a structural isomer that is more water-soluble and can be excreted in the stool and urine.

SECTION III: APPLYING YOUR KNOWLEDGE

Activity E

1. • A sensation of heat along the vein the transfusion is going in
   • Urticaria
   • Headache

- Pain in the low back
- Chills
- Fever
- Chest pain
- Abdominal cramps
- Nausea
- Vomiting
- Tachycardia
- Hypotension
- Dyspnea

RATIONALE: The most feared and lethal transfusion reaction is the destruction of donor red cells by reaction with antibody in the recipient's serum. This immediate hemolytic reaction usually is caused by ABO incompatibility. The signs and symptoms of such a reaction include sensation of heat along the vein where the blood is being infused, flushing of the face, urticaria, headache, pain in the lumbar area, chills, fever, constricting pain in the chest, cramping pain in the abdomen, nausea, vomiting, tachycardia, hypotension, and dyspnea.

2. Most transfusion reactions result from administrative errors or misidentification, and care should be taken to correctly identify the recipient and the transfusion source.

SECTION IV: PRACTICING FOR NCLEX

Activity F

1. **Answer: a**
   RATIONALE: When RBCs age and are destroyed in the spleen, the iron from their hemoglobin is released into the circulation and returned to the bone marrow for incorporation into new RBCs or to the liver and other tissues for storage. Iron is not bound to RBCs in the liver. Iron does not bind with oxygen in the lung without first being incorporated into an RBC. Iron is stored in tissues of the body, but not for strength, only for its oxygen-binding capacity.

2. **Answer: d**
   RATIONALE: The plasma-insoluble form of bilirubin is referred to as *unconjugated bilirubin* and the water-soluble form as *conjugated bilirubin*. Serum levels of conjugated and unconjugated bilirubin can be measured in the laboratory and are reported as direct and indirect, respectively.

3. **Answer: a**
   RATIONALE: Hyperbilirubinemia, an increased level of serum bilirubin, is a common cause of jaundice in the neonate. A benign, self-limited condition, it most often is related to the developmental state of the neonate. Rarely, cases of hyperbilirubinemia are pathologic and may lead to kernicterus and serious brain damage.

4. **Answer: b**
   RATIONALE: It takes about 5 days for the progeny of stem cells to fully differentiate, an event marked by increased reticulocytes in the blood. If the

bleeding is controlled and sufficient, iron stores are available. The red cell concentration returns to normal within 3 to 4 weeks.

5. **Answer: c**
   RATIONALE: Chronic blood loss does not affect blood volume, but instead leads to iron-deficiency anemia when iron stores are depleted. It is commonly caused by gastrointestinal bleeding and menstrual disorders. Because of compensatory mechanisms, patients are commonly asymptomatic until the hemoglobin level is less than 8 g/dL. The red cells that are produced have too little hemoglobin, giving rise to microcytic hypochromic anemia. Macrocytic anemia is when the RBCs are larger than normal. Hyperchromic means the cells are a darker color red then they should be.

6. **Answer: d**
   RATIONALE: Hemolytic anemia is characterized by the premature destruction of red cells, the retention in the body of iron and the other products of hemoglobin destruction, and an increase in erythropoiesis. Almost all types of hemolytic anemia are distinguished by normocytic and normochromic red cells.

7. **Answer: d**
   RATIONALE: In hemolytic anemia, intravascular hemolysis is less common than extravascular hemolysis and occurs as a result of complement fixation in transfusion reactions, mechanical injury, or toxic factors. It is characterized by hemoglobinemia, hemoglobinuria, jaundice, and hemosiderinuria. Spherocytosis is the most common inherited disorder of the red cell membrane and is not associated with hemolytic anemia.

8. **Answer: b**
   RATIONALE: Therapy for aplastic anemia in the young and severely affected includes stem cell replacement by bone marrow or peripheral blood transplantation. Histocompatible donors supply the stem cells to replace the patient's destroyed marrow cells. A liver transplant will not produce new blood cells for the body. Spleen transplants are not done and would not produce new blood cells for the body.

9. **Answer: a**
   RATIONALE: Chronic renal failure almost always results in anemia, primarily because of a deficiency of erythropoietin. Unidentified uremic toxins and retained nitrogen also interfere with the actions of erythropoietin, and red cell production and survival. Hemolysis and blood loss associated with hemodialysis and bleeding tendencies also contribute to the anemia of renal failure. Fibrinogen is essential for blood clotting, not oxygen transportation.

10. **Answer: c**
    RATIONALE: Erythroblastosis fetalis, or hemolytic disease of the newborn, occurs in Rh-positive infants of Rh-negative mothers who have been sensitized. The Rh-negative mother usually

becomes sensitized during the first few days after delivery, when fetal Rh-positive red cells from the placental site are released into the maternal circulation. Because the antibodies take several weeks to develop, the first Rh-positive infant of an Rh-negative mother usually is not affected. There is no such thing as microcytic or macrocytic disease of the newborn, nor is there a hemolytic iron-deficiency anemia.

11. **Answer: vitamin B$_{12}$**
    RATIONALE: Pernicious anemia is believed to result from immunologically mediated, possibly autoimmune, destruction of the gastric mucosa. The resultant chronic atrophic gastritis is marked by loss of parietal cells and production of antibodies that interfere with binding of vitamin B$_{12}$ to intrinsic factor.

12. **Answers: a, b, d**
    RATIONALE: Factors associated with sickling and vessel occlusion include cold, stress, physical exertion, infection, and illnesses that cause hypoxia, dehydration, or acidosis.

13. **Answers: 1-c, 2-a, 3-b**
    RATIONALE: Red cell indices are used to differentiate types of anemias by size or color of red cells. The mean corpuscular volume (MCV) reflects the volume or size of the red cells. The MCV falls in microcytic (small cell) anemia and rises in macrocytic (large cell) anemia. Some anemias are normocytic (i.e., cells are of normal size or MCV). The *mean* corpuscular hemoglobin concentration (MCHC) is the concentration of hemoglobin in each cell.

14. **Answers: a, b**
    RATIONALE: In anemia, the oxygen-carrying capacity of hemoglobin is reduced, causing tissue hypoxia. Tissue hypoxia can give rise to fatigue, weakness, dyspnea, and sometimes angina. Hypoxia of brain tissue results in headache, faintness, and dim vision. The redistribution of the blood from cutaneous tissues or a lack of hemoglobin causes pallor of the skin, mucous membranes, conjunctiva, and nail beds. Tachycardia and palpitations may occur as the body tries to compensate with an increase in cardiac output. Ruddy skin and bradycardia are not signs or symptoms of anemia.

15. **Answers: a, b, e**
    RATIONALE: Primary polycythemia, or polycythemia vera, is a neoplastic disease of the pluripotent cells of the bone marrow characterized by an absolute increase in total RBC mass accompanied by elevated white cell and platelet counts. It most commonly is seen in men with a median age of 62 years, but may occur at any age. In addition, early findings include splenomegaly and depletion of iron stores. Hypertension is common, and there may be complaints of headache, dizziness, inability to concentrate, and some difficulty with hearing and vision because of decreased cerebral blood flow. Venous

stasis gives rise to a plethoric appearance or dusky redness, even cyanosis, particularly of the lips, fingernails, and mucous membranes.

16. **Answer: transfusion**
    RATIONALE: Persons who are homozygous for the trait (thalassemia major) have severe, transfusion-dependent anemia that is evident at 6 to 9 months of age when the hemoglobin switches from HbF to HbA. If transfusion therapy is not started early in life, severe growth retardation occurs in children with the disorder.

CHAPTER 14

SECTION II: ASSESSING YOUR UNDERSTANDING

Activity A

1. commensalism
2. *infection*
3. parasitic
4. opportunistic
5. transmissible neurodegenerative
6. Viruses
7. prokaryotes
8. Staining
9. spirochetes
10. mycoplasmas
11. fungal
12. yeasts, molds
13. feces
14. prodromal stage
15. acute stage
16. convalescent period
17. *itis*
18. *emia*
19. Virulence
20. exotoxins

Activity B

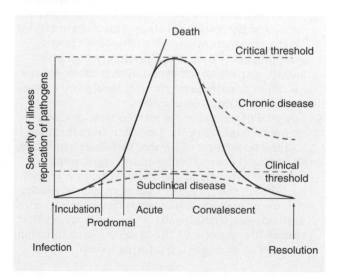

Activity C

1.

1. b	2. f	3. d	4. g	5. a
6. e	7. c	8. h	9. i	10. j

2.

1. f	2. a	3. j	4. e	5. c
6. d	7. b	8. h	9. g	10. i

Activity D

1.

d → e → a → c → f → b

Activity E

1. Viruses are incapable of replication outside a living cell. They must penetrate a susceptible living cell and use the biosynthetic machinery of the cell to produce viral progeny. Not every viral agent causes lysis and death of the host cell during the course of replication. Some viruses enter the host cell and insert their genome into the host cell chromosome, where it remains in a latent, nonreplicating state for long periods without causing disease. Under the appropriate stimulation, the virus undergoes active replication and produces symptoms of disease months to years later.

2. The portal of entry refers to the process by which a pathogen enters the body, gains access to susceptible tissues, and causes disease. Among the potential modes of transmission are penetration, direct contact, ingestion, and inhalation. In terms of pathophysiology, symptoms are the outward expression of the struggle between invading organisms and the retaliatory inflammation and immune responses of the host.

3. The course of any infectious disease can be divided into several distinguishable stages after the point of time in which the potential pathogen enters the host. These stages are the incubation period, the prodromal stage, the acute stage, the convalescent stage, and the resolution stage. The stages are based on the progression and intensity of the host's symptoms over time. The duration of each phase and the pattern of the overall illness can be specific for different pathogens, thereby aiding in the diagnosis of an infectious disease.

4. The goal of treatment for an infectious disease is complete removal of the pathogen from the host and the restoration of normal physiologic function to damaged tissues. When an infectious process gains the upper hand and therapeutic intervention is essential, the choice of treatment may be medicinal, using antimicrobial agents; immunologic, with antibody preparations, vaccines, or substances that stimulate and improve the host's immune function; or surgical, by removing infected tissues.

5. Potential agents of bioterrorism have been categorized into three levels (A, B, and C) based on risk of use, transmissibility, invasiveness, and mortality rate. The agents considered to be in the highest biothreat level—plague, tularemia, smallpox, and hemorrhagic fever—are category A. The category B agents include agents of food-borne and water-borne disease, agents of zoonotic infections, and viral encephalitides. Category C agents are defined as emerging pathogens and potential risks for the future even though many of these organisms are causes of ancient diseases, such as tuberculosis and tick-borne fever viruses.

SECTION III: APPLYING YOUR KNOWLEDGE

Activity F

1. An antibiotic is considered bactericidal if it causes irreversible and lethal damage to the bacterial pathogen, and bacteriostatic if its inhibitory effects on bacterial growth are reversed when the agent is eliminated.

2. The drugs used to treat HIV infections are not antibiotics or antiviral agents. They are classified as antiretroviral agents. These drugs are acyclovir, ganciclovir, vidarabine, ribavirin, zidovudine, lamivudine, didanosine, stavudine, zalcitabine, nevirapine, efavirenz, and delavirdine.

SECTION IV: PRACTICING FOR NCLEX

Activity G

1. **Answer: a**
   RATIONALE: A parasitic relationship is one in which only the infecting organism benefits from the relationship and the host either gains nothing from the relationship or sustains injury from the interaction. If the host sustains injury or pathologic damage in response to a parasitic infection, the process is called an infectious disease. Mutual and commensal relationships do not harm the human body. Communicable diseases can be passed from one human to another; they are not parasitic.

2. **Answer: b**
   RATIONALE: The rickettsiae are accidentally transmitted to humans through the bite of the arthropod (i.e., vector) and produce a number of potentially lethal diseases, including Rocky Mountain spotted fever and epidemic typhus. Viruses, Chlamydiae, and Ehrlichiae do not cause either epidemic typhus or Rocky Mountain spotted fever.

3. **Answer: c**
   RATIONALE: Severe Acute Respiratory Syndrome (SARS) was recognized in the Guangdong province in southern China beginning in November 2002. The illness was highly transmissible as evidenced by the first recognized occurrence in Taiwan. Four days after returning to Taiwan from work in the Guangdong province, a businessman developed a

febrile illness and was admitted to a local hospital. Within 1 month, a large nosocomial outbreak of SARS was documented to have affected ~3000 people in Taipei City, Taiwan. Since the SARS outbreak began in China and crossed continental borders for the first time, it was classified as not only an epidemic but also a pandemic. Regional and endemic mean the same thing, a specific area where the disease occurs. Nosocomial is an infection acquired in a health care facility.

4. **Answer: d**
RATIONALE: The term *symptomatology* refers to the collection of signs and symptoms expressed by the host during the disease course. This is also known as the clinical picture or disease presentation. The virulence of the disease is its power to produce the disease. The source of the disease is the place where it came from. The diagnosis of the disease is the naming of the disease process in the body.

5. **Answer: a**
RATIONALE: The diagnosis of an infectious disease requires two criteria: the recovery of a probable pathogen or evidence of its presence from the infected sites of a diseased host, and accurate documentation of clinical signs and symptoms compatible with an infectious process. Culture and sensitivity are the growing of microorganisms outside the body and the testing to see what kills it. Identifying a microorganism by microscopic appearance and Gram stain reaction are not the criteria for diagnosis. Serology, an indirect means of identifying infectious agents by measuring serum antibodies in the diseased host, and the quantification of those antibodies, an antibody titer, are not criteria for diagnosis.

6. **Answer: b**
RATIONALE: Potential agents of bioterrorism have been categorized into three levels (A, B, and C) based on risk of use, transmissibility, invasiveness, and mortality rate.

7. **Answer: c**
RATIONALE: Aided by a global market and the ease of international travel, the past 5 years has witnessed the importation or emergence of a host of novel infectious diseases. During the late summer and early fall of 1999, West Nile virus (WNV) was identified as the cause of an epidemic involving 56 patients in the New York City area. This outbreak, which led to seven deaths (primarily in the elderly), marked the first time that WNV had been recognized in the Western hemisphere since its discovery in Uganda nearly 60 years earlier. Coxsackie diseases, caused by the coxsackie virus; respiratory syncytial disease, better known as RSV; and hand, foot, and mouth disease are not considered global diseases.

8. **Answer: d**
RATIONALE: The course of any infectious disease can be divided into several distinguishable stages after the point of time in which the potential pathogen enters the host. These stages are the incubation period, the prodromal stage, the acute stage, the convalescent stage, and the resolution stage. There are no postacute, subacute or postdromal stages to a disease.

9. **Answer: a**
RATIONALE: An abscess is a localized pocket of infection composed of devitalized tissue, microorganisms, and the host's phagocytic white blood cells: in essence, a stalemate in the infectious process. A pimple is a small papule or pustule. A lesion is a pathologic change in body tissue. Acne is a disease of the skin.

10. **Answer: c**
RATIONALE: Other exotoxins that have gained notoriety include the Shiga toxins produced by *Escherichia coli* O157:H7 and other select strains. The ingestion of undercooked hamburger meat or unpasteurized fruit juices contaminated with this organism produces hemorrhagic colitis and a sometimes fatal illness called hemolytic uremic syndrome, characterized by vascular endothelial damage, acute renal failure, and thrombocytopenia. *E. coli* does not cause nephritic syndrome or hemolytic thrombocytopenia or neuroleptic malignant syndrome.

11. **Answer: prions**
RATIONALE: Prions, protein particles that lack any kind of a demonstrable genome, have been found to cause pathologic processes in humans. The various prion-associated diseases produce very similar symptoms and pathology in the host and are collectively called transmissible neurodegenerative diseases.

12. **Answer: Congenital**
RATIONALE: When an infectious disease is transmitted from mother to child during gestation or birth, it is classified as a congenital infection.

13. **Answers: 1-c, 2-a, 3-d, 4-b**

14. **Answers: a, c, d, e**
RATIONALE: Virulence factors are substances or products generated by infectious agents that enhance their ability to cause disease. Although the number and type of microbial products that fit this description are numerous, they can generally be grouped into four categories: toxins, adhesion factors, evasive factors, and invasive factors. Prodromal means occurring first or prior to a specific event. It is not a virulence factor.

15. **Answers: a, d, e**
RATIONALE: A number of factors produced by microorganisms enhance virulence by evading various components of the host's immune system. Extracellular polysaccharides including capsules, slime, and mucous layers discourage engulfment and killing of pathogens by the host's phagocytic white blood cells. Phospholipases and collagenases are enzymes that are invasive virulence factors.

CHAPTER 15

SECTION II: ASSESSING YOUR UNDERSTANDING

Activity A

1. immune system
2. allergies, autoimmune
3. innate
4. Adaptive
5. antigens
6. Humoral
7. Cell-mediated
8. macrophages
9. neutrophils, macrophages
10. Neutrophils
11. macrophage
12. B, T
13. Natural killer cells
14. Dendritic
15. Chemokines
16. colony-stimulating factors
17. epithelial
18. pathogens
19. Opsonization
20. Antigens
21. immunoglobulins
22. Humoral
23. CD4$^+$ helper T cell (T$_H$)
24. Regulatory
25. bone marrow, thymus
26. spleen

Activity B

The figure is a schematic model of an immunoglobulin G molecule showing the constant and variable regions of the light and dark chains. Each immunoglobulin is composed of two identical light (L) chains and two identical heavy (H) chains to form a Y-shaped molecule. The two forked ends of the immunoglobulin molecule bind antigen and are called *Fab* (i.e., antigen-binding) fragments, and the tail of the molecule, which is called the *Fc* fragment, determines the bio-logic properties that are characteristic of a particular class of immunoglobulins. The amino acid sequence of the heavy and light chains shows constant (C) regions and variable (V) regions. The *constant regions* have sequences of amino acids that vary little among the antibodies of a particular class of immunoglobulin. The constant regions allow separation of immunoglobulins into classes (e.g., IgM, IgG) and allow each class of antibody to interact with certain effectors cells and mol-ecules. The *variable regions* contain the antigen-binding sites of the molecule. The wide variation in the amino acid sequence of the variable regions seen from anti-body to antibody allows this region to recognize its complementary epitope. A unique amino acid sequence in this region determines a distinctive three-dimensional

pocket that is complementary to the antigen, allowing recognition and binding.

Activity C

1.

1. c	2. j	3. f	4. h	5. e
6. d	7. a	8. b	9. i	10. g

2.

1. g	2. d	3. f	4. e	5. a
6. b	7. c	8. h	9. j	10. i

Activity D

1. Although cells of both the innate and adaptive immune systems communicate critical information by cell-to-cell contact, many interactions and effec-tor responses depend on the secretion of short-act-ing soluble molecules called cytokines. One type of cytokine, chemokines, direct leukocyte movement and migration, and another group of cytokines, the colony-stimulating factors, promote the proliferation and differentiation of bone marrow progenitor cells. Chemokines give the cells of the immune system the ability to act systemically as one.

2. The innate immune system consists of the epithe-lial barriers, phagocytic cells (mainly neutrophils and macrophages), natural killer (NK) cells, and several plasma proteins including those of the com-plement system. These mechanisms are present in the body before an encounter with an infectious agent and are rapidly activated by microbes before the development of adaptive immunity. The activa-tion and regulation of inflammation is also a major job of innate immunity.

3. These phagocytic cells recruited during an inflamma-tory response to recognize and kill infectious invaders. The early-responding innate immune cell is the neutrophil, followed shortly by the more efficient, multifunctional macrophage. They are acti-vated to engulf and digest microbes that attach to their cell membrane. Once the cell is activated and the microbe is ingested, the cell generates digestive enzymes, toxic oxygen, and nitrogen intermediates (i.e., hydrogen peroxide or nitric oxide) through metabolic pathways. The phagocytic killing of microorganisms helps to contain infectious agents.

4. There are three pathways for recognizing microor-ganisms that result in activation of the complement system: the classical, the lectin, and the alternative pathway. The reactions of the com-plement systems are divided into three phases: (1) initiation or activation, (2) amplification of inflammation, and (3) membrane attack response.

5. The <u>major histocompatibility complex</u> (MHC) mol-ecules involved in self-recognition and cell-to-cell communication fall into two classes, class I and class II. Class I MHC molecules are cell surface gly-coproteins that interact with the antigen receptor-foreign peptide complex and the CD8 molecule on T cytotoxic lymphocytes. MHC-I molecules are

found on nearly all nucleated cells in the body and thereby are capable of alerting the immune system of any cell changes due to viruses, intracellular bacteria, or cancer.

6. Macrophages are key members of the mononuclear phagocytic system that engulf and digest microbes and other foreign substances. The monocytes migrate from the blood to various tissues where they mature into the major tissue phagocyte, the macrophages. As the general scavenger cells of the body, the macrophage can be fixed in a tissue or can be free to migrate from an organ to lymphoid tissues. The tissue macrophages are scattered in connective tissue or clustered in organs such as the lung (i.e., alveolar macrophages), liver (i.e., Kupffer cells), spleen, lymph nodes, peritoneum, central nervous system (i.e., microglial cells), and other areas. Macrophages are activated to engulf and break down complex antigens into peptide fragments for association with class II MHC molecules. Macrophages can then present these complexes to the helper T cell so that self–nonself recognition and activation of the immune response can occur.

7. The immunoglobulins have been divided into five classes: IgG, IgA, IgM, IgD, and IgE.
   I. IgG protects against bacteria, toxins, and viruses in body fluids and activates the complement system.
   II. IgA is a primary defense against local infections in mucosal tissues.
   III. IgM is the first circulating immunoglobulin to appear in response to an antigen.
   IV. IgD serves as an antigen receptor for initiating the differentiation of B cells.
   V. IgE is involved in inflammation, allergic responses, and combating parasitic infections.

8. Active immunity is acquired through immunization or actually having a disease. It is active as it depends on a response to the antigen by the person's immune system. Because of memory, the immune system usually is able to react within hours to subsequent exposure to the same agent because of the presence of memory B and T lymphocytes and circulating antibodies. Passive immunity is immunity transferred from another source. An infant receives passive immunity naturally from the transfer of antibodies from its mother in utero and through a mother's breast milk.

SECTION III: APPLYING YOUR KNOWLEDGE
Activity E

1. Every baby is born with passive immunity. Baby receives antibodies from mother through placenta and colostrums. Passive immunity lasts up to 6 months. Passive immunity is replaced by immunity gotten from immunizations.

SECTION IV: PRACTICING FOR NCLEX
Activity F

1. **Answer: a**
   RATIONALE: The major components of innate immunity are the skin and mucous membranes; phagocytic cells (mainly neutrophils and macrophages); specialized lymphocytes called (NK) cells; and several plasma proteins, including the proteins of the complement system. Adaptive, humoral, and cell-mediated immunity do not use NK cells.

2. **Answer: b**
   RATIONALE: The actions of cytokines are often pleiotropic and redundant. Cytokines are not described as rapid and self-limiting, or cell-specific and targeted, or dendritic and morphologic.

3. **Answer: c**
   RATIONALE: The T lymphocytes (T cells) are generated from stem cells in the bone marrow and complete their maturation in the thymus and functions in the peripheral tissues to produce cell-mediated immunity, as well as aiding antibody production.

4. **Answer: d**
   RATIONALE: Activation of macrophages ensures enhanced phagocytic, metabolic, and enzymatic potential, resulting in more efficient destruction of infected cells. This type of defense is important against intracellular pathogens such as *Mycobacterium* species and *Listeria monocytogenes*. Contact dermatitis due to a poison ivy reaction or sensitivity to dyes is an example of delayed or cell-mediated hypersensitivity caused by hapten–carrier complexes. Blood transfusions do not cause hypersensitivity reactions by hapten–carrier complexes.

5. **Answer: a**
   RATIONALE: Passive immunity also can be artificially provided by the transfer of antibodies produced by other people or animals. Some protection against infectious disease can be provided by the injection of hyperimmune serum, which contains high concentrations of antibodies for a specific disease, or immune serum or γ-globulin, which contains a pool of antibodies from many individuals providing protection against many infectious agents. Immunizations and allergy shots are examples of active immunity. Exposure to poison ivy can be the cause of a hypersensitivity reaction; it is not immunity.

6. **Answer: b**
   RATIONALE: Self-regulation is an essential property of the immune system. An inadequate immune response may lead to immunodeficiency, but an inappropriate or excessive response may lead to conditions varying from allergic reactions to autoimmune diseases. All answers are autoimmune diseases except for Huntington disease.

7. Answer: c
RATIONALE: The term *tolerance* is used to define the ability of the immune system to be nonreactive to self-antigens while producing immunity to foreign agents. All other responses have nothing to do with the recognition and tolerance to self-antigens.

8. Answer: d
RATIONALE: Cord blood does not normally contain IgM or IgA. If present, these antibodies are of fetal origin and represent exposure to intrauterine infection.

9. Answer: a
RATIONALE: Aging is characterized by a declining ability to adapt to environmental stresses. One of the factors thought to contribute to this problem is a decline in immune responsiveness. This includes changes in cell-mediated and humoral immune responses. Elderly persons tend to be more susceptible to infections, have more evidence of autoimmune and immune complex disorders than younger persons, and have a higher incidence of cancer. None of the other answers are true or acceptable.

10. Answer: b
RATIONALE: Among the functions of the innate immune system is induction of a complex cascade of events known as the inflammatory response. Recent evidence suggests that inflammation plays a key role in the pathogenesis of a number of disorders such as atherosclerosis and coronary artery disease, bronchial asthma, type 2 diabetes mellitus, rheumatoid arthritis, multiple sclerosis, and systemic lupus erythematosus. Osteoporosis is the abnormal loss of bone tissue and density. Osteogenesis imperfecta is a genetic disease causing multiple bone fractures in a newborn. Hydronephrosis is a condition of the kidney causing distention of the pelvis and calyces because of an obstruction in the ureter causing an inability of urine to pass.

11. Answer: Antigens

12. Answers: 1-d, 2-e, 3-a, 4-c, 5-b

13. Answer: epithelial

14. Answers: bc
RATIONALE: While cells of both the innate and adaptive immune systems communicate critical information about the invading microbe or pathogen by cell-to-cell contact, many interactions and effector responses depend on the secretion of chemical mediators (cytokines, chemokines, and colony-stimulating factors). Virulence factors define how much power an organism has to produce disease. Coxiellas are organisms that cause Q fever.

15. Answers: b, e
RATIONALE: The T and B lymphocytes are the only cells in the body capable of specifically recognizing different antigenic determinants of microbial agents and other pathogens, and therefore responsible for two defining characteristics of adaptive immunity, specificity and memory. Phagocytes, dendritic cells, and NK cells all participate in innate immunity.

CHAPTER 16

SECTION II: ASSESSING YOUR UNDERSTANDING

Activity A

1. immune
2. Immunodeficiency
3. innate
4. adaptive
5. humoral, cellular
6. X
7. pyogenic
8. maternal
9. antibody
10. kidney
11. malignancies
12. $CD4^+$ helper, $CD8^+$ cytotoxic
13. T lymphocytes
14. combined immunodeficiency
15. severe combined immunodeficiency (SCID)
16. boys
17. complement
18. secondary
19. degranulation
20. respiratory burst
21. Hypersensitivity
22. allergic reactions
23. Anaphylaxis
24. atopic
25. rhinitis
26. type II
27. Antibody-dependent cellular cytotoxicity
28. Type III
29. Serum
30. *Arthus reaction*
31. type IV reactions
32. contact dermatitis
33. transplantation
34. autologous, syngeneic, allogeneic
35. Graft-versus-host-disease
36. Autoimmune
37. self-tolerance
38. autoantibodies

Activity B

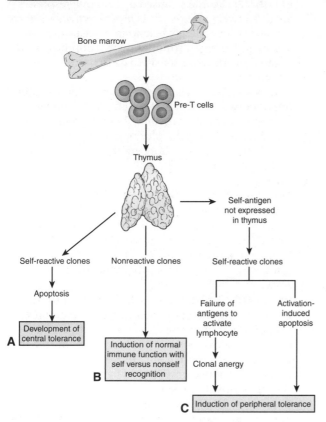

Bone marrow

Pre-T cells

Thymus

Self-antigen
not expressed
in thymus

Self-reactive clones   Nonreactive clones   Self-reactive clones

Apoptosis

Failure of
antigens to
activate
lymphocyte

Activation-
induced
apoptosis

A Development of
central tolerance

Induction of normal
immune function with
self versus nonself
recognition
B

Clonal anergy

C Induction of peripheral tolerance

Activity C

1. e	**2.** h	**3.** l	**4.** a	**5.** f
6. m	**7.** d	**8.** k	**9.** i	**10.** c
11. n	**12.** j	**13.** g	**14.** b	**15.** o

Activity D

1.

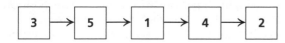

$$3 \rightarrow 5 \rightarrow 1 \rightarrow 4 \rightarrow 2$$

Activity E

1. A primary deficiency or immunodeficiency is congenital or inherited. Secondary immunodeficiency is acquired.

2. During the first few months of life, infants are protected from infection by IgG antibodies that have been transferred from the maternal circulation during fetal life. An infant's level of maternal IgG gradually declines over a period of approximately 6 months. Concomitant with the loss of maternal antibody, the infant's immature humoral immune system begins to function, and between the ages of 1 and 2 years, the child's antibody production reaches adult levels. Once the level of maternal antibodies drops, the infant is susceptible to infection.

3. Type I hypersensitivity reactions begin with mast cell or basophil sensitization. During the sensitization or priming stage, allergen-specific IgE antibodies attach to receptors on the surface of mast cells and basophils. With subsequent exposure, the sensitizing allergen binds to the cell-associated IgE and triggers a series of events that ultimately lead to degranulation of the sensitized mast cells or basophils, causing release of their preformed mediators. Mast cells are also the source of lipid-derived membrane products (e.g., prostaglandins and leukotrienes) and cytokines that participate in the continued response to the allergen.

4. In direct cell-mediated cytotoxicity, $CD8^+$ cytolytic T lymphocytes (CTLs) directly kill the antigen-presenting target cells. In viral infections, CTL responses can lead to tissue injury by killing infected target cells even if the virus itself has no cytotoxic effects. Because CTLs cannot distinguish between cytopathic and noncytopathic viruses, they kill virtually all infected cells, regardless of whether the infection is harmful or not. Delayed-type hypersensitivity reactions occur in response to soluble protein antigens and primarily involve antigen-presenting cells such as macrophages and $CD4^+$ helper T cells of the T_h1 type. During the reaction, T_h1 cells are activated and secrete an array of cytokines that recruit and activate monocytes, lymphocytes, fibroblasts, and other inflammatory cells. These T-cell–mediated responses require the synthesis of effector molecules and take 24 to 72 hours to develop, which is why they are called delayed-type hypersensitivity disorders.

5. Severe combined immunodeficiency (SCID) is the result of genetic mutations that lead to absence of all T-and B-cell function and, in some cases, a lack of natural killer cells. Affected infants have a disease course that resembles AIDS, with failure to thrive, chronic diarrhea, and opportunistic infections. Survival beyond the first year of life is rare without prompt immune reconstitution through bone marrow or hematopoietic stem cell transplantation. Early diagnosis is critical because the chances of successful treatment are highest in infants who have not experienced severe opportunistic infections. There is also hope that gene therapy will someday be available for some, if not all, forms of SCID.

SECTION III: APPLYING YOUR KNOWLEDGE

Activity F

1. Antinuclear antibodies test. The basis for most serologic assays is the demonstration of antibodies directed against tissue antigens or cellular components. For example, a child with chronic or acute history of fever, arthritis, and a macular rash along with high levels of antinuclear antibody has a probable diagnosis of SLE. The detection of autoantibodies in the laboratory usually is accomplished by one of three methods: indirect fluorescent antibody assays

(IFA), enzyme-linked immunosorbent assay (ELISA), or particle agglutination of some kind.

2. Medications used in the treatment of SLE include corticosteroids (prednisone) and immunosuppressive (cytotoxic) agents (azathioprine, cyclophosphamide, methotrexate).

SECTION IV: PRACTICING FOR NCLEX

Activity G

1. **Answer: c**
   RATIONALE: During the first few months of life, infants are protected from infection by IgG antibodies that have been transferred from the maternal circulation during fetal life. IgA, IgM, IgD, and IgE do not normally cross the placenta.

2. **Answers: a, b, c, d**
   RATIONALE: Medications that cause reversible secondary hypogammaglobulinemia include the disease-modifying antirheumatic drugs, corticosteroid agents, and the antiepileptic drugs, phenytoin and carbamazepine. Interferon beta-1a drugs are used in the treatment of autoimmune disorders.

3. **Answer: a**
   RATIONALE: In general, persons with cell-mediated immunodeficiency disorders have infections or other clinical problems that are more severe than antibody disorders. Children with defects in this branch of the immune response rarely survive beyond infancy or childhood, unless immunologic reconstitution is achieved through bone marrow transplantation. In DeGeorge syndrome children who survive the immediate neonatal period may have recurrent or chronic infections because of impaired T-cell immunity. Children also may have an absence of immunoglobulin production, caused by a lack of helper T-cell function. The X-linked immunodeficiency of hyper-IgM, also known as the hyper-IgM syndrome, is characterized by low IgG and IgA levels with normal or, more frequently, high IgM concentrations. X-linked agammaglobulinemia is a primary humeral immunodeficiency disorder. Y-linked agammaglobulinemia does not exist.

4. **Answer: b**
   RATIONALE: Disorders that affect both B and T lymphocytes with resultant defects in both humoral and cell-mediated immunity fall under the broad classification of combined immunodeficiency syndrome. A single mutation in any one of the many genes that influence lymphocyte development or response, including lymphocyte receptors, cytokines, or major histocompatibility antigens, could lead to combined immunodeficiency.

5. **Answer: c**
   RATIONALE: Ataxia-telangiectasia is a complex syndrome of neurologic, immunologic, endocrinologic, hepatic, and cutaneous abnormalities. Pierre-Robin syndrome, Angelman syndrome, and Adair-Dighton syndrome are not immunologic deficiencies.

6. **Answer: a**
   RATIONALE: Disorders caused by immune responses are collectively referred to as *hypersensitivity reactions*. Antigens cause allergic reactions. Mediator response action and allergen stimulating reaction have nothing to do with hypersensitivity reactions.

7. **Answer: b**
   RATIONALE: Anaphylaxis is a systemic life-threatening hypersensitivity reaction characterized by widespread edema, vascular shock secondary to vasodilation, and difficulty breathing. It is not called an antigen reaction, neither is it called an Arthus reaction.

8. **Answer: c**
   RATIONALE: Serum sickness is a systemic immune complex disorder that is triggered by the deposition of insoluble antigen-antibody (IgM, IgG, and occasionally IgA) complexes in blood vessels, joints, heart, and kidney tissue. This is not anti-immune disease, SLE or antigen-antibody sickness.

9. **Answer: d**
   RATIONALE: Cornstarch powder is applied to the gloves during the manufacturing process to prevent stickiness and give the gloves a smooth feel. The cornstarch glove powder has an important role in the allergic response. Latex proteins are readily absorbed by glove powder and become airborne during removal of the gloves. Baking powder is not used inside the gloves. Pieces of latex that become airborne and latex proteins that attach to clothing are not significant contributors to the incidence of latex allergy.

10. **Answer: antidonor**
    RATIONALE: When preformed antidonor antibodies are present, rejection occurs immediately after transplantation.

11. **Answers: a, b, d**
    RATIONALE: Because autoimmunity does not develop in all persons with genetic predisposition, it appears that other factors such as a "trigger event" interact to precipitate the altered immune state. The event or events that trigger the development of an autoimmune response are unknown. It has been suggested that the trigger may be a virus or other microorganism, a chemical substance, or a self-antigen from a body tissue that has been hidden from the immune system during development.

CHAPTER 17

SECTION II: ASSESSING YOUR UNDERSTANDING

Activity A

1. oxygen, waste, hormones
2. pulmonary, systemic
3. pulmonary
4. systemic
5. low

6. atria, ventricles
7. same
8. volume, pressure
9. *hemodynamics*
10. large
11. Viscosity
12. Turbulent
13. thicker
14. distensibility
15. aortic, pulmonic
16. precedes
17. elastic
18. Diastole
19. stroke volume
20. ejection
21. cardiac output
22. cardiac reserve
23. Frank-Starling
24. heart rate
25. tunica adventitia, tunica media, tunica intima
26. arterial pressure pulse
27. decreases
28. central venous pressure
29. Valves
30. Autoregulation
31. hyperemia
32. anastomotic
33. *microcirculation*
34. capillary pores
35. colloidal osmotic
36. medulla oblongata
37. sympathetic, parasympathetic
38. Cushing reflex

Activity B

1.

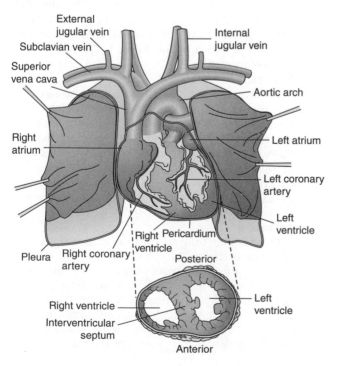

2.

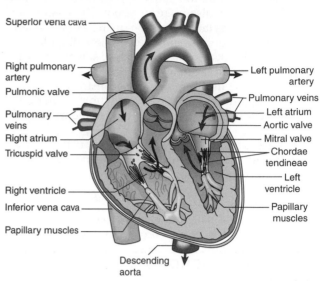

Activity C

| 1. d | 2. b | 3. j | 4. c | 5. i |
| 6. h | 7. e | 8. f | 9. a | 10. g |

Activity D

1. The most important factors governing the flow of blood in the cardiovascular system are pressure, resistance, and flow. Blood flow (F) through a vessel or series of blood vessels is determined by the pressure difference (ΔP) between the two ends of a vessel (the inlet and the outlet) and the resistance (R) that blood must overcome as it moves through the vessel (F = ΔP/R).

2. This is because, even though each individual capillary is very small, the total cross-sectional area of all the systemic capillaries greatly exceeds the cross-sectional area of other parts of the circulation. Because of this large surface area, the slower movement of blood allows ample time for exchange of nutrients, gases, and metabolites between the tissues and the blood.

3. The anatomic arrangement of the actin and myosin filaments in the myocardial muscle fibers is such that the tension or force of contraction depends on the degree to which the muscle fibers are stretched just before the ventricles begin to contract. The maximum force of contraction and cardiac output is achieved when venous return produces an increase in left ventricular end-diastolic filling (i.e., preload) such that the muscle fibers are stretched about two and one-half times their normal resting length. When the muscle fibers are stretched to this degree, there is optimal overlap of the actin and myosin filaments needed for maximal contraction.

4. Sympathetic innervation via α-adrenergic receptors is excitatory in that they produce vasoconstriction; β-adrenergic receptors are inhibitory in that they

produce vasodilation. Smooth muscle contraction and relaxation also occur in response to local tissue factors such as lack of oxygen, increased hydrogen ion concentrations, and excess carbon dioxide. Nitric oxide acts locally to produce smooth muscle relaxation and regulate blood flow.

5. • Norepinephrine—potent vasoconstrictor
   • Epinephrine—mild vasoconstriction or dilation depending on the receptor type found in target tissue
   • Angiotensin II—powerful vasoconstrictor
   • Histamine—powerful vasodilator and can increase permeability
   • Serotonin—vasoconstrictor
   • Bradykinin—vasodilator
   • Prostaglandins—vasodilator or vasoconstrictor depending on type of prostaglandin

SECTION III: PRACTICING FOR NCLEX

Activity E

1. **Answer: a**
   RATIONALE: The total blood volume is a function of age and body weight, ranging from 85 to 90 mL/kg in the neonate and from 70 to 75 mL/kg in the adult.

2. **Answer: b**
   RATIONALE: The blood vessels and the blood vessel itself constitute resistance to flow. A helpful equation for understanding the relationship between resistance, blood vessel diameter (radius), and blood viscosity factors that affect blood flow was derived by the French physician Poiseuille more than a century ago. The other laws do not address resistance to flow.

3. **Answer: b**
   RATIONALE: Compliance refers to the total quantity of blood that can be stored in a given portion of the circulation for each millimeter rise in pressure. Compliance reflects the distensibility of the blood vessel. Wall tension, laminar blood flow, and resistance are not major factors in the distensibility of the blood vessel.

4. **Answer: c**
   RATIONALE: The *Cushing reflex* is a special type of CNS reflex resulting from an increase in intracranial pressure. When the intracranial pressure rises to levels that equal intra-arterial pressure, blood vessels to the vasomotor center become compressed, initiating the CNS ischemic response. The purpose of this reflex is to produce a rise in arterial pressure to levels above intracranial pressure so that the blood flow to the vasomotor center can be re-established. Should the intracranial pressure rise to the point that the blood supply to the vasomotor center becomes inadequate, vasoconstrictor tone is lost, and the blood pressure begins to fall. The elevation in blood pressure associated with the Cushing reflex is usually of short duration and should be considered a protective homeostatic mechanism. The brain and other cerebral structures are located within the rigid confines of the skull, with no room for expansion, and any increase in intracranial pressure tends to compress the blood vessels that supply the brain.

5. **Answer: c**
   RATIONALE: In clinical practice, the measurement of the cardiac forms of troponin T and troponin I are used in the diagnosis of myocardial infarction. Troponin C is not diagnostic of a myocardial infarction. Troponin A is not one of the troponin complexes.

6. **Answer: d**
   RATIONALE: Approximately 60% of the stroke volume is ejected during the first quarter of systole, and the remaining 40% is ejected during the next two quarters of systole. Little blood is ejected from the heart during the last quarter of systole, although the ventricle remains contracted.

7. **Answer: a**
   RATIONALE: With peripheral arterial disease, there is a delay in the transmission of the reflected wave so that the pulse decreases rather than increases in amplitude.

8. **Answer: b**
   RATIONALE: The efficiency of the heart as a pump often is measured in terms of cardiac output (CO) or the amount of blood the heart pumps each minute. The CO is the product of the stroke volume (SV) and the heart rate (HR), and can be expressed by the equation: $CO = SV \times HR$. AV stands for atrioventricular and EF stands for ejection fraction. Neither is part of the equation for CO.

9. **Answers: b, c, d, e**
   RATIONALE: The heart's ability to increase its output according to body needs mainly depends on four factors: the preload, or ventricular filling; the afterload, or resistance to ejection of blood from the heart; cardiac contractility; and the heart rate. Cardiac reserve does not add to the heart's ability to increase its output.

10. **Answer: d**
    RATIONALE: The fact that nitric oxide is released into the vessel lumen (to inactivate platelets) and away from the lumen (to relax smooth muscle) suggests that it protects against both thrombosis and vasoconstriction. Nitroglycerin, which is used in treatment of angina, produces its effects by releasing nitric oxide in vascular smooth muscle of the target tissues. None of the other answers are released by nitroglycerin.

11. **Answer: a**
    RATIONALE: The osmotic pressure caused by the plasma proteins in the blood tends to pull fluid from the interstitial spaces back into the capillary. This pressure is termed *colloidal osmotic pressure* to differentiate the osmotic effects of the plasma proteins, which are suspended colloids, from the osmotic effects of substances such as sodium and glucose, which are dissolved crystalloids.

12. Answer: c
RATIONALE: The lymph capillaries drain into larger lymph vessels that ultimately empty into the right and left thoracic ducts. The thoracic ducts empty into the circulation at the junctions of the subclavian and internal jugular veins. The lymphatic system only joins the vascular system in one place, so no other answer is accurate.

13. Answer: b
RATIONALE: The medullary cardiovascular neurons are grouped into three distinct pools that lead to sympathetic innervation of the heart and blood vessels and parasympathetic innervation of the heart. The first two, which control sympathetic-mediated acceleration of heart rate and blood vessel tone, are called the vasomotor center. The third, which controls parasympathetic-mediated slowing of heart rate, is called the cardioinhibitory center.

CHAPTER 18

SECTION II: ASSESSING YOUR UNDERSTANDING

Activity A

1. blood vessels
2. endothelium
3. vasoconstriction, dilation
4. *ischemia*
5. Infarction
6. cholesterol
7. cholesterol, triglyceride
8. lipoproteins
9. lipolytic
10. small intestine, liver
11. Chylomicrons
12. bad cholesterol
13. LDL receptors, scavenger
14. atherosclerosis
15. good cholesterol
16. coronary heart disease
17. genetic
18. secondary
19. lower, elevate
20. Atherosclerosis
21. hypercholesterolemia
22. Cigarette smoking
23. inflammation
24. C-reactive protein (CRP)
25. Homocysteine
26. free radicals
27. vasculitides
28. embolus
29. Thromboangiitis obliterans
30. Raynaud phenomenon
31. aneurysm
32. asymptomatic, rupture
33. hemorrhage

34. valves
35. deep vein thrombosis
36. Venous insufficiency
37. stasis of blood, increased blood coagulability, vessel wall injury
38. Arterial
39. systolic, diastolic
40. pulse pressure
41. mean arterial pressure
42. cardiac output, peripheral vascular resistance
43. vessel constriction, fluid retention
44. equilibrium
45. kidneys, sodium, water
46. *Primary*, secondary
47. 140 mm Hg, 90 mm Hg
48. constitutional
49. left ventricle
50. nephrosclerosis
51. ischemic, hemorrhage
52. 140/90 mm Hg
53. Diuretics
54. β-adrenergic
55. calcium channel receptor-blocking
56. systole
57. secondary
58. oral contraceptive
59. Preeclampsia-eclampsia
60. orthostatic hypotension

Activity B

1.

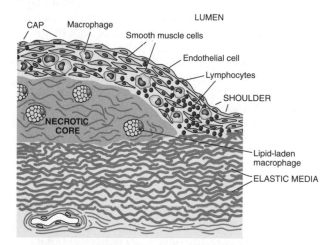

2. Mechanisms of blood pressure regulation. The *solid lines* represent the mechanisms for renal and baroreceptor control of blood pressure through changes in cardiac output and peripheral vascular resistance. The *dashed lines* represent the stimulus for regulation of blood pressure by the baroreceptors and the kidneys.

Activity C

1.

| 1. h | 2. i | 3. g | 4. j | 5. d |
| 6. a | 7. f | 8. c | 9. e | 10. b |

2.

1. i.	**2.** h	**3.** d	**4.** j	**5.** a
6. b	**7.** e	**8.** g	**9.** f	**10.** c

Activity D

1. Decrease in blood pressure
2. Stimulation of juxtaglomerular apparatus
3. Release of renin
4. Conversion of angiotensinogen to angiotensin I
5. Conversion of ANG I to ANG II by angiotensin-converting enzyme
6. Increased vascular resistance, release of aldosterone
7. Na^+ retention, stimulation of ADH release
8. Water retention

Activity E

1. Once thought to be nothing more than a lining for blood vessels, it is now known that the endothelium is a versatile, multifunctional tissue that plays an active role in controlling vascular function. As a semipermeable membrane, the endothelium controls the transfer of molecules across the vascular wall. The endothelium also plays a role in the control of platelet adhesion and blood clotting, modulation of blood flow and vascular resistance, metabolism of hormones, regulation of immune and inflammatory reactions, and elaboration of factors that influence the growth of other cell types, particularly vascular smooth muscle cells.
2. High-calorie diets increase the production of VLDL with triglyceride elevation and high conversion of VLDL to LDL. Excess ingestion of cholesterol may reduce the formation of LDL receptors and thereby decrease LDL removal. Diets that are high in triglycerides and saturated fats increase cholesterol synthesis and suppress LDL receptor activity. In diabetes mellitus and the metabolic syndrome, typical dyslipidemia is seen with elevation of triglycerides, low HDL and minimal or modest elevation of LDL.
3. Lipid-lowering drugs work in several ways including decreasing cholesterol production, decreasing cholesterol absorption from the intestine, or removing cholesterol from the bloodstream. Drugs that act directly to decrease cholesterol levels also have the beneficial effect of further lowering cholesterol levels by stimulating the production of additional LDL receptors.
4. (1) Pistol shot (acute onset), (2) pallor, (3) polar (cold), (4) pulselessness, (5) pain, (6) paresthesia, and (7) paralysis.
5. Ischemia due to vasospasm causes changes in skin color that progress from pallor to cyanosis, a sensation of cold, and changes in sensory perception, such as numbness and tingling. After the ischemic episode, there is a period of hyperemia with intense redness, throbbing, and paresthesias. In severe, progressive cases usually associated with Raynaud phenomenon, trophic changes may develop. The nails may become brittle and the skin over the tips of the affected fingers may thicken. Ulceration and superficial gangrene of the fingers, although infrequent, may occur.
6. During muscle contraction, which is similar to systole, valves in the communicating channels close to prevent backward flow of blood into the superficial system, as blood in the deep veins is moved forward by the action of the contracting muscles. During muscle relaxation, which is similar to diastole, the communicating valves open, allowing blood from the superficial veins to move into the deep veins.
7. Short-term regulation is accomplished through the cardiovascular center of the ANS, baroreceptors, and chemoreceptors. The cardiovascular center transmits parasympathetic impulses to the heart through the vagus nerve and sympathetic impulses to the heart and blood vessels through the spinal cord and peripheral sympathetic nerves. The baroreceptors are pressure-sensitive receptors located in the walls of blood vessels and the heart. They respond to changes in the stretch of the vessel wall by sending impulses to cardiovascular centers in the brain stem to effect appropriate changes in heart rate and vascular smooth muscle tone. The arterial chemoreceptors are chemosensitive cells that monitor the oxygen, carbon dioxide, and hydrogen ion content of the blood.
8. Most acute kidney disorders result in decreased urine formation, retention of salt and water, and hypertension. Renovascular hypertension refers to hypertension caused by reduced renal blood flow and activation of the renin-angiotensin-aldosterone mechanism. The reduced renal blood flow that occurs with renovascular disease causes the affected kidney to release excessive amounts of renin, increasing circulating levels of angiotensin II. Angiotensin II, in turn, acts as a vasoconstrictor to increase peripheral vascular resistance and as a stimulus for increased aldosterone levels and sodium retention by the kidney.

SECTION III: PRACTICING FOR NCLEX

Activity F

1. **Answers: 1-f, 2-e, 3-b, 4-a, 5-d, 6-c**
   RATIONALE: Disturbances in blood flow can result from pathologic changes in the vessel wall (i.e., atherosclerosis and vasculitis), acute vessel obstruction due to thrombus or embolus, vasospasm (i.e., Raynaud phenomenon), or abnormal vessel dilation (i.e., arterial aneurysms or varicose veins).
2. **Answers: a, d**
   RATIONALE: There are two sites of lipoprotein synthesis: the small intestine and the liver. The chylomicrons, which are the largest of the lipoprotein molecules, are synthesized in the wall of the small intestine. The liver synthesizes and releases VLDL and HDL. The large intestine and the pancreas play no part in synthesizing lipoprotein.

3. **Answer: a**
RATIONALE: Many types of primary hypercholesterolemia have a genetic basis. There may be a defective synthesis of the apoproteins, a lack of receptors, defective receptors, or defects in the handling of cholesterol in the cell that are genetically determined. For example, the LDL receptor is deficient or defective in the genetic disorder known as familial hypercholesterolemia (type 2A). This autosomal dominant type of hyperlipoproteinemia results from a mutation in the gene specifying the receptor for LDL. Although heterozygotes commonly have an elevated cholesterol level from birth, they do not develop symptoms until adult life, when they often develop xanthomas (i.e., cholesterol deposits) along the tendons and atherosclerosis appears. Myocardial infarction before 40 years of age is common. Homozygotes are much more severely affected; they have cutaneous xanthomas in childhood and may experience myocardial infarction by as early as 1 to 2 years of age. Homozygotic cutaneous xanthoma and adult-onset hypercholesterolemia (type 1A) are not known diseases. Causes of secondary hyperlipoproteinemia include obesity with high-calorie intake and diabetes mellitus. It does not have a genetic basis.

4. **Answer: b**
RATIONALE: The cause or causes of atherosclerosis have not been determined with certainty. However, epidemiologic studies have identified predisposing risk factors, which include a major risk factor of hypercholesterolemia. Other risk factors include increasing age, family history of premature coronary heart disease, and male sex.

5. **Answer: c**
RATIONALE: Temporal arteritis (i.e., giant cell arteritis), the most common of the vasculitides, is a focal inflammatory condition of medium-sized and large arteries. It predominantly affects branches of arteries originating from the aortic arch, including the superficial temporal, vertebral, ophthalmic, and posterior ciliary arteries. Neither Polyarteritis Nodosa nor Raynaud disease are the most common of the vasculitides. Varicose veins are not vasculitides.

6. **Answer: c**
RATIONALE: Acute arterial occlusion is a sudden event that interrupts arterial flow to the affected tissues or organ. Most acute arterial occlusions are the result of an embolus or a thrombus. Other answers are not appropriate for the nurse to give the client.

7. **Answers: a, d**
RATIONALE: Raynaud disease or phenomenon is a functional disorder caused by intense vasospasm of the arteries and arterioles in the fingers and, less often, the toes. There are two types of Raynaud disease, primary and secondary. The secondary type, called Raynaud phenomenon, is associated with other disease states or known causes of vasospasm. Raynaud phenomenon is associated with previous vessel injury, such as frostbite, occupational trauma associated with the use of heavy vibrating tools, collagen diseases, neurologic disorders, and chronic arterial occlusive disorders. The initial diagnosis is based on history of vasospastic attacks supported by other evidence of the disorder. Treatment measures are directed toward eliminating factors that cause vasospasm and protecting the digits from trauma during an ischemic episode. Abstinence from smoking and protection from cold are priorities. The presenting symptoms of this patient do not support a diagnosis of or treatment for arterial thrombosis or peripheral artery disease.

8. **Answers: c, d**
RATIONALE: Abdominal aortic aneurysms can involve any part of the vessel circumference (saccular) or extend to involve the entire circumference (fusiform). Berry aneurysms typically occur in the circle of Willis. Dissecting aneurysms are false aneurysms and typically occur in the thoracic aorta. Aneurysms can occur at the bifurcation of a blood vessel but are not termed bifurcating aneurysms.

9. **Answer: b**
RATIONALE: Sclerotherapy, which often is used in the treatment of small residual varicosities, involves the injection of a sclerosing agent into the collapsed superficial veins to produce fibrosis of the vessel lumen. Surgical treatment consists of removing the varicosities and the incompetent perforating veins, but it is limited to persons with patent deep venous channels. Sclerotherapy produces fibrosis of the vessel lumen. There is no fibrotherapy for varicose veins. There is no Trendelenburg therapy for varicose veins. There is a Trendelenburg test that is diagnostic for primary or secondary varicose veins.

10. **Answer: d**
RATIONALE: In 1846, Virchow described the triad that has come to be associated with venous thrombosis: stasis of blood, increased blood coagulability, and vessel wall injury. Inflammation is a symptom of venous thrombosis, not a risk factor. Decreased venous blood flow can occur because of venous thrombosis, if the thrombus does not completely obstruct the vein; it is not a risk factor. Hypocoagulability would not cause a thrombus to form.

11. **Answer: c**
RATIONALE: At normal heart rates, mean arterial pressure can be estimated by adding one third of the pulse pressure to the diastolic pressure (i.e., diastolic blood pressure + pulse pressure/3).

12. Answers: a, b, e
RATIONALE: The constitutional risk factors include a family history of hypertension, race, and age-related increases in blood pressure. Another factor that is thought to contribute to hypertension is insulin resistance and the resultant hyperinsulinemia that occurs in metabolic abnormalities such as type 2 diabetes. Lifestyle factors can contribute to the development of hypertension by interacting with other risk factors. These lifestyle factors include high salt intake, excessive calorie intake and obesity, excessive alcohol consumption, and low intake of potassium. Although stress can raise blood pressure acutely, there is less evidence linking it to chronic elevations in blood pressure. Smoking and a diet high in saturated fats and cholesterol, although not identified as primary risk factors for hypertension, are independent risk factors for coronary heart disease and should be avoided.

13. Answer: d
RATIONALE: Like adrenal medullary cells, the tumor cells of a pheochromocytoma produce and secrete the catecholamines epinephrine and norepinephrine. The hypertension that develops is a result of the massive release of these catecholamines. Their release may be paroxysmal rather than continuous, causing periodic episodes of headache, excessive sweating, and palpitations. Headache is the most common symptom and can be quite severe. Nervousness, tremor, facial pallor, weakness, fatigue, and weight loss occur less frequently. Marked variability in blood pressure between episodes is typical.

14. Answer: a
RATIONALE: Because chronic hypertension is associated with autoregulatory changes in coronary artery, cerebral artery, and kidney blood flow, care should be taken to avoid excessively rapid decreases in blood pressure, which can lead to hypoperfusion and ischemic injury. Therefore, the goal of initial treatment measures should be to obtain a partial reduction in blood pressure to a safer, less critical level, rather than to normotensive levels.

15. Answer: b
RATIONALE: Cerebral vasoconstriction probably is an exaggerated homeostatic response designed to protect the brain from excesses of blood pressure and flow. The regulatory mechanisms often are insufficient to protect the capillaries, and cerebral edema frequently develops. As it advances, papilledema (i.e., swelling of the optic nerve at its point of entrance into the eye) ensues, giving evidence of the effects of pressure on the optic nerve and retinal vessels. The patient may have headache, restlessness, confusion, stupor, motor and sensory deficits, and visual disturbances. In severe cases, convulsions and coma follow. Lethargy, nervousness, and hyperreflexia are not signs or symptoms of cerebral edema in malignant hypertension.

16. Answer: c
RATIONALE: Liver damage, when it occurs, may range from mild hepatocellular necrosis with elevation of liver enzymes to the more ominous *h*emolysis, elevated *l*iver function tests, and *l*ow *p*latelet count (HELLP) syndrome that is associated with significant maternal mortality.

17. Answer: d
RATIONALE: Hypertension in infants is associated most commonly with high umbilical catheterization and renal artery obstruction caused by thrombosis. Cerebral vascular bleeds, coarctation of the aorta, and pheochromocytoma all can raise blood pressure; they are not the most common cause of hypertension in an infant.

18. Answer: a
RATIONALE: Among the aging processes that contribute to an increase in blood pressure are a stiffening of the large arteries, particularly the aorta; decreased baroreceptor sensitivity; increased peripheral vascular resistance; and decreased renal blood flow.

19. Answer: b
RATIONALE: Pseudohypertension should be suspected in older persons with hypertension in whom the radial or brachial artery remains palpable but pulseless at higher cuff pressures. The presenting parameters of the patient are not compatible with essential, orthostatic, or secondary hypertension.

20. Answer: c
RATIONALE: The renin-angiotensin-aldosterone system plays a central role in blood pressure regulation. Angiotensin II has two major functions in the rennin-angiotensin-aldosterone system and acts as both a short- and long-term regulation of blood pressure. It is a strong vasoconstrictor, especially of the arterioles regulating blood pressure in the short term. However, its second major action, the stimulation of aldosterone secretion from the adrenal gland, is the end of the rennin-angiotensin-aldosterone loop. The aldosterone that is secreted notifies the kidneys to stop production of renin (the negative feedback in the loop) and contributes to the long-term regulation of blood pressure by increasing salt and water retention by the kidney.

CHAPTER 19

SECTION II: ASSESSING YOUR UNDERSTANDING

Activity A

1. pericardium
2. frictional
3. pericarditis
4. effusion
5. tamponade
6. constrictive

7. atherosclerosis
8. metabolic activity, autoregulatory
9. increased activity
10. 12-Lead ECG
11. Echocardiography
12. Atherosclerosis
13. stable, unstable
14. chronic ischemic heart disease, acute coronary syndrome
15. T-wave inversion, ST-segment elevation, development of an abnormal Q wave
16. resting membrane potential
17. troponin assays
18. Acute ST-segment
19. 20 to 40
20. *ventricular remodeling*
21. vagal
22. nitroglycerin
23. Atherectomy
24. papillary muscle
25. Stable angina
26. exertion, emotional
27. genetic
28. mixed
29. hypertrophic cardiomyopathy
30. Dilated
31. Polyarthritis
32. neurologic
33. valves
34. stenosis
35. regurgitation
36. prolapse
37. stenosis
38. regurgitation
39. fetal heart
40. blood, cyanosis, pulmonary
41. acyanotic
42. ventricular septal
43. Kawasaki

Activity B

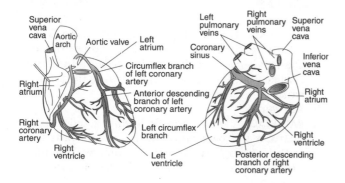

Activity C

1.

1. i	**2.** h	**3.** c	**4.** d	**5.** a
6. f	**7.** g	**8.** b	**9.** e	**10.** j

2.

1. g	**2.** e	**3.** b	**4.** h	**5.** a
6. f	**7.** c	**8.** j	**9.** i	**10.** d

Activity D

1. The pericardial cavity has little reserve volume, so small additions of fluid increase the pericardial pressure. Right heart filling pressures are lower than the left, and increases in pericardial fluid pressure will result in decreased right-side filling.

2. Myocardial oxygen supply is determined by the coronary arteries, capillary inflow, and the ability of hemoglobin to transport and deliver oxygen to the heart muscle. Important factors in the transport and delivery of oxygen include the fraction of inspired oxygen in the blood and the number of red blood cells with normal functioning hemoglobin. There are three major determinants of myocardial oxygen demand (Mvo_2): the heart rate, myocardial contractility, and myocardial wall stress or tension. The heart rate is the most important factor in myocardial oxygen demand for two reasons: (1) as the heart rate increases, myocardial oxygen consumption or demand also increases; and (2) subendocardial coronary blood flow is reduced because of the decreased diastolic filling time with increased heart rates.

3. On rupture, lipid core provides a stimulus for platelet aggregation and thrombus formation. Both smooth muscle and foam cells in the lipid core contribute to the expression of tissue factor in unstable plaques. Once exposed to blood, tissue factor initiates the extrinsic coagulation pathway, resulting in the local generation of thrombin and deposition of fibrin.

4. Biomarkers for ACS include cardiac-specific troponin I (cTnI) and troponin T (cTnT), myoglobin, and creatine kinase MB (CK-MB). As the myocardial cells become necrotic, their intracellular enzymes begin to diffuse into the surrounding interstitium and then into the blood.

5. The pathophysiology is divided into three phases: development of the unstable plaque that ruptures, the acute ischemic event, and the long-term risk of recurrent events that remain after the acute event. Inflammation plays a prominent role in plaque instability, with inflammatory cells releasing cytokines that cause the fibrous cap to become thinner and more vulnerable to rupture. The acute ischemic event can be caused by an increase in myocardial oxygen demand precipitated by tachycardia or hypertension or, more commonly, by a decrease in oxygen supply related to a reduction in coronary lumen diameter due to platelet-rich thrombi or vessel spasm.

6. The extent of the infarct depends on the location and extent of occlusion, amount of heart tissue supplied by the vessel, duration of the occlusion, metabolic needs of the affected tissue, extent of

collateral circulation, and other factors such as heart rate, blood pressure, and cardiac rhythm. An infarct may involve the endocardium, myocardium, epicardium, or a combination of these.

7. The term *reperfusion* refers to re-establishment of blood flow through use of fibrinolytic therapy, percutaneous coronary intervention, or coronary artery bypass grafting. Early reperfusion (within 15 to 20 minutes) after onset of ischemia can prevent necrosis and improve myocardial perfusion in the infarct zone. Reperfusion after a longer interval can salvage some of the myocardial cells that would have died owing to longer periods of ischemia. It also may prevent microvascular injury that occurs over a longer period.

8. A cardiomyopathy is a heterogeneous group of diseases of the myocardium associated with mechanical and/or electrical dysfunction that usually exhibit inappropriate ventricular hypertrophy or dilatation and are due to a variety of causes that frequently are genetic. Cardiomyopathies either are confined to the heart or are part of generalized systemic disorders, often leading to cardiovascular death or progressive heart failure–related disability.

9. Rheumatic heart disease is a complication of immune-mediated response to group A streptococcal throat infection. The acute stage of rheumatic fever includes a history of an initiating streptococcal infection and subsequent involvement of the connective tissue elements of the heart, blood vessels, joints, and subcutaneous tissues. The *recurrent phase* usually involves extension of the cardiac effects of the disease. The *chronic phase* of rheumatic fever is characterized by permanent deformity of the heart valves.

10. Blood typically shunts across the ductus from the higher pressure left side to the lower pressure right side. A murmur is typically detected within days or weeks of birth. The murmur is loudest at the second left intercostal space, continuous through systole and diastole, and has a characteristic machinery sound. A widened pulse pressure is common because of the continuous runoff of aortic blood into the pulmonary artery.

11. Tetralogy of Fallot consists of four associated defects: (1) a ventricular septal defect involving the membranous septum and the anterior portion of the muscular septum; (2) dextroposition or shifting to the right of the aorta; (3) obstruction or narrowing of the pulmonary outflow channel, including pulmonic valve stenosis, a decrease in the size of the pulmonary trunk, or both; and (4) hypertrophy of the right ventricle because of the increased work required to pump blood through the obstructed pulmonary channels.

SECTION III: APPLYING YOUR KNOWLEDGE

Activity E

1. Classic symptoms of a STEMI include:
   • Onset of event that is abrupt and having pain as the significant symptom.
   • Pain is typically severe and crushing and usually substernal
   • The pain can radiate to the left arm, neck, or jaw
   • Pain is not relieved by rest or nitroglycerin
   • Gastrointestinal distress, including nausea and vomiting
   • Fatigue and weakness, especially of the arms and legs
   • Tachycardia, anxiety, restlessness, and feelings of impending doom
   • Pale, cool, moist skin

2. The emergency department goals of management for a patient with a STEMI are:
   • Identification of persons who are candidates for reperfusion therapy
   • Evaluation of the person's chief complaint, typically chest pain, along with other associated symptoms to differentiate ACS from other diagnoses
   • Monitoring should be instituted: a 12-lead ECG should be obtained and read by a physician within 10 minutes of arrival within the emergency department
   • Administration of oxygen, aspirin, nitrates, pain medications, antiplatelet and anticoagulant therapy, β-adrenergic blocking agents, and an angiotensin converting enzyme inhibitor
   • Persons with ECG evidence of infarction should receive immediate reperfusion therapy with a thrombolytic agent or percutaneous coronary intervention

SECTION IV: PRACTICING FOR NCLEX

Activity F

1. **Answer: a**
   RATIONALE: The pain typically is worse with deep breathing, coughing, swallowing, and positional changes because of changes in venous return and cardiac filling. All other answers make the pain worse.

2. **Answer: b**
   RATIONALE: A key diagnostic finding is pulsus paradoxus or an exaggeration of the normal variation in the systemic arterial pulse volume with respiration. None of the other answers occur in cardiac tamponade.

3. **Answer: c**
   RATIONALE: Kussmaul sign is an inspiratory distention of the jugular veins caused by the inability of the right atrium, encased in its rigid pericardium, to accommodate the increase in venous return

that occurs with inspiration. None of the other physiologic signs occur in constrictive pericarditis.

4. **Answers: a, c, e**
RATIONALE: The major determinants of plaque vulnerability to disruption include the size of the lipid-rich core, the stability and thickness of its fibrous cap, the presence of inflammation, and lack of smooth muscle cells. A decrease in blood pressure and coronary blood flow are not determinants of plaque vulnerability to rupture.

5. **Answer: d**
RATIONALE: The troponin assays have high specificity for myocardial tissue and have become the primary biomarker for the diagnosis of myocardial infarction (MI). The troponin complex, which is part of the actin filament, consists of three subunits (i.e., TnC, TnT, and TnI) that regulate calcium-mediated actin-myosin contractile process in striated muscle (see Chapter 1, Fig. 1-19). TnI and TnT, which are present in cardiac muscle, begin to rise within 3 hours after the onset of MI and may remain elevated for 7 to 10 days after the event. This is especially adventitious in the late diagnosis of MI. The other blood work may be ordered, but not to confirm the diagnosis of MI.

6. **Answers: b, d**
RATIONALE: UA/NSTEMI is classified as either low or intermediate risk of acute MI, the diagnosis of which is based on the clinical history, ECG pattern, and serum biomarkers. The other answers are not diagnostic of UA/NSTEMI.

7. **Answer: a**
RATIONALE: The principal biochemical consequence of MI is the conversion from aerobic to anaerobic metabolism with inadequate production of energy to sustain normal myocardial function. As a result, a striking loss of contractile function occurs within 60 seconds of onset. None of the other answers occur.

8. **Answer: b**
RATIONALE: Although a number of analgesic agents have been used to treat the pain of STEMI, morphine is usually the drug of choice. It usually is indicated if chest pain is unrelieved with oxygen and nitrates. The reduction in anxiety that accompanies the administration of morphine contributes to a decrease in restlessness and autonomic nervous system activity, with a subsequent decrease in the metabolic demands of the heart. Morphine does not cause a feeling of depression to the client.

9. **Answer: c**
RATIONALE: If blood flow can be restored within the 20- to 40-minute time frame, loss of cell viability does not occur or is minimal.

10. **Answer: d**
RATIONALE: Angina pectoris usually is precipitated by situations that increase the work demands of the heart, such as physical exertion, exposure to cold, and emotional stress. The pain typically is described as a constricting, squeezing, or suffocating sensation. It usually is steady, increasing in intensity only at the onset and end of the attack. Changing positions abruptly does not cause an attack of angina pectoris.

11. **Answer: a**
RATIONALE: Serum biochemical markers for MI are normal in patients with chronic stable angina. All other answers are tests used in the diagnosis of angina.

12. Hypertrophic cardiomyopathy—genetic
Left ventricular noncompaction—genetic
Myocarditis—acquired
Dilated cardiomyopathy—mixed
Peripartum cardiomyopathy—acquired

13. **Answer: b**
RATIONALE: Alcoholic cardiomyopathy is the single most common identifiable cause of DCM in the United States and Europe. The other answers are incorrect.

14. **Answer: c**
RATIONALE: The intracardiac vegetative lesions also have local and distant systemic effects. The loose organization of these lesions permits the organisms and fragments of the lesions to form emboli and travel in the bloodstream, causing cerebral, systemic, or pulmonary emboli. Preventing the valves of the heart from either opening or closing completely is not a systemic effect of the lesions. Fragmentation of the lesions does not make them larger.

15. **Answer: d**
RATIONALE: It is thought that antibodies directed against the M protein of certain strains of streptococci cross-react with glycoprotein antigens in the heart, joint, and other tissues to produce an autoimmune response through a phenomenon called molecular mimicry. None of the other answers are correct.

16. **Answer: a**
RATIONALE: Persons with palpitations and mild tachyarrhythmias or increased adrenergic symptoms and those with chest discomfort, anxiety, and fatigue often respond to therapy with the β-adrenergic–blocking drugs. None of the other types of drugs are used in the treatment of mitral valve prolapse to relieve symptoms or prevent complications.

17. **Answer: b**
RATIONALE: Heart failure manifests itself as tachypnea or dyspnea at rest or on exertion. For the infant, this most commonly occurs during feeding. The other answers are incorrect.

18. **Answer: c**
RATIONALE: The degree of obstruction may be dynamic and can increase during periods of stress causing hypercyanotic attacks ("tet spells"). None of the other answers occur in association with tetralogy of Fallot or tet spells.

CHAPTER 20

SECTION II: ASSESSING YOUR UNDERSTANDING

Activity A

1. Heart failure
2. coronary artery disease, hypertension, valvular
3. large
4. Cardiac output
5. sympathetic, parasympathetic
6. stroke volume
7. Ejection fraction
8. decrease
9. normal
10. compensatory mechanisms
11. Frank-Starling
12. contractile, volume overload, pressure overload
13. diastolic
14. compress, increase, delay
15. tachycardia
16. side
17. peripheral edema
18. hepatic
19. Left ventricular failure
20. left
21. High-output failure
22. Low-output failure
23. myocardial hypertrophy
24. acute heart failure
25. Paroxysmal nocturnal
26. Acute pulmonary edema
27. brain
28. right
29. oxygenation
30. ventricular
31. brain natriuretic peptide (BNP)
32. left ventricular
33. Circulatory shock
34. myocardial infarction
35. Hypovolemic
36. Vasodilatory
37. neurogenic shock
38. immunologically
39. Structural
40. Aging

Activity B

1.

| 1. j | 2. f | 3. d | 4. i | 5. c |
| 6. b | 7. e | 8. a | 9. g | 10. h |

2.

| 1. g | 2. c | 3. a | 4. d | 5. b |
| 6. f | 7. h | 8. e | | |

3.

| 1. c | 2. e | 3. b | 4. d | 5. a |

Activity C

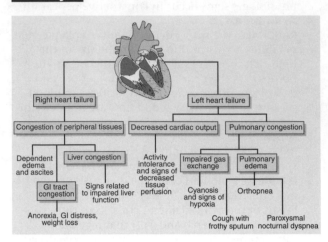

Activity D

1. A number of factors determine cardiac contractility by altering the systolic Ca^{++} levels. Catecholamines increase Ca^{++} entry into the cell by phosphorylation of the Ca^{++} channels via a cAMP-dependent protein kinase. Another mechanism that can modulate inotropy is the sodium ion $(Na^+)/Ca^+$ exchange pump and the ATPase dependent Ca^{++} pump on the myocardial cell membrane. These pumps transport Ca^{++} out of the cell, thereby preventing the cell from becoming overloaded with Ca^{++}. If Ca^{++} extrusion is inhibited, the rise in intracellular Ca^{++} can increase inotropy.

2. With both systolic and diastolic ventricular dysfunction, compensatory mechanisms are usually able to maintain adequate resting cardiac function until the later stages of heart failure. Therefore, cardiac function measured at rest is a poor clinical indicator of the extent of cardiac impairment because cardiac output may be relatively normal at rest.

3. With diastolic dysfunction, blood is unable to move freely into the left ventricle, causing an increase in intraventricular pressure at any given volume. The elevated pressures are transferred backward from the left ventricle into the atria and pulmonary venous system causing a decrease in lung compliance, which increases the work of breathing and evokes symptoms of dyspnea. Cardiac output is decreased because of a decrease in the volume (preload) available for adequate cardiac output. Inadequate cardiac output during exercise may lead to fatigue of the legs and the accessory muscles of respiration.

4. Adaptive responses:
   - Frank-Starling mechanism: increases inotropy but eventually increases metabolic demand of cardiac tissue
   - Activation of the sympathetic nervous system: increases inotropy, but increases wall tension and metabolic demand

- The renin-angiotensin-aldosterone mechanism: increases blood volume and maintains cardiac output, but eventually increases wall tension
- Natriuretic peptides: inhibit sympathetic and renal compensation and decrease work of heart, but inactivation results in decreased cardiac output
- Myocardial hypertrophy and remodeling: cardiomyocyte hypertrophy and increased inotropy, but increase demands more oxygen and increases metabolic needs

5. The signs and symptoms include shortness of breath and other respiratory manifestations, fatigue and limited exercise tolerance, fluid retention and edema, cachexia and malnutrition, and cyanosis. Persons with severe heart failure may exhibit diaphoresis and tachycardia. These signs are the result of decreased tissue perfusion and resultant hypoxia.

6. Diuretics promote the excretion of fluid and help to sustain cardiac output and tissue perfusion by reducing preload and allowing the heart to operate at a more optimal part of the Frank-Starling curve.

7. In severe shock, cellular metabolic processes are essentially anaerobic because of the decreased availability of oxygen. Excess amounts of lactic acid accumulate in the cellular and the extracellular compartment, and limited amounts of ATP are produced and normal cell function cannot be maintained. The sodium-potassium membrane pump is impaired, resulting in cellular edema and an increase in the permeability of cell membranes. Mitochondrial activity becomes severely depressed and lysosomal membranes may rupture, resulting in the release of enzymes that cause further intracellular destruction. This is followed by cell death and the release of intracellular contents into the extracellular spaces. The destruction of the cell membrane activates the arachidonic acid cascade, release of inflammatory mediators, and production of oxygen free radicals that extend cellular damage.

8. (1) Pulmonary injury, (2) acute renal failure, (3) gastrointestinal ulceration, (4) disseminated intravascular coagulation, and (5) multiple organ dysfunction syndrome.

SECTION III: PRACTICING FOR NCLEX

Activity E

1. **Answers: 1-f, 2-a, 3-c, 4-b, 5-e, 6-d**
2. **Answers: a, c**
   RATIONALE: The signs and symptoms of heart failure include shortness of breath and other respiratory manifestations, fatigue and limited exercise tolerance, fluid retention and edema, cachexia and malnutrition, and cyanosis. Persons with severe heart failure may exhibit diaphoresis and tachycardia. A ruddy complexion, bradycardia, and a chronic productive cough are not signs or symptoms of heart failure.

3. **Answers: a, b, d, e**
   RATIONALE: Shock is not a specific disease but a syndrome that can occur in the course of many life-threatening traumatic conditions or disease states. It can be caused by an alteration in cardiac function (cardiogenic shock), a decrease in blood volume (hypovolemic shock), excessive vasodilation with maldistribution of blood flow (distributive shock), or obstruction of blood flow through the circulatory system (obstructive shock). Excessive vasoconstriction and hypervolemia are not causes of shock.

4. **Answers: a, c, e**
   RATIONALE: Signs and symptoms of cardiogenic shock include indications of hypoperfusion with hypotension, although a preshock state of hypoperfusion may occur with a normal blood pressure. The lips, nail beds, and skin may become cyanotic because of stagnation of blood flow and increased extraction of oxygen from the hemoglobin as it passes through the capillary bed. Mean arterial and systolic blood pressures decrease due to poor stroke volume, and there is a narrow pulse pressure and near-normal diastolic blood pressure due to arterial vasoconstriction. Urine output decreases due to lower renal perfusion pressures and the increased release of aldosterone. Elevation of preload is reflected in a rise in CVP and pulmonary capillary wedge pressure. Neurologic changes, such as alterations in cognition or consciousness, may occur due to low cardiac output and poor cerebral perfusion. The other physiologic occurrences are not signs or symptoms of shock.

5. **Answer: c**
   RATIONALE: The treatment of hypovolemic shock is directed toward correcting or controlling the underlying cause and improving tissue perfusion. Ongoing loss of blood must be corrected, such as in surgery. Oxygen is administered to increase oxygen delivery to the tissues. Medications usually are administered intravenously. In hypovolemic shock, the goal of treatment is to restore vascular volume. This can be accomplished through intravenous administration of fluids and blood. The crystalloids (e.g., isotonic saline and Ringer's lactate) are readily available and effective, at least temporarily. Plasma volume expanders (e.g., pentastarch and colloidal albumin) have a high molecular weight, do not necessitate blood typing, and remain in the vascular space for longer periods than the crystalloids, such as dextrose and saline. Blood or blood products (packed or frozen red cells) are administered based on hematocrit and hemodynamic findings. Fluids and blood are best administered based on volume indicators such as CVP and urine output. Vasoactive medications are agents capable of constricting or dilating blood vessels. Considerable controversy exists about the advantages or disadvantages related to the use of these drugs. As a general rule, vasoconstrictor agents are not used as a primary

form of therapy in hypovolemic shock and may be detrimental. These agents are given only when volume deficits have been corrected but hypotension persists.

6. **Answer: a**
   RATIONALE: In contrast to other shock states due to the loss of blood volume or impaired cardiac function, the heart rate in neurogenic shock often is slower than normal, and the skin is dry and warm. This type of distributive shock is rare and usually transitory. The other answers are not correct.

7. **Answer: b**
   RATIONALE: Anaphylaxis is a clinical syndrome that represents the most severe form of systemic allergic reaction. Anaphylactic shock results from an immunologically mediated reaction in which vasodilator substances such as histamine are released into the blood. The vascular response in anaphylaxis is often accompanied by life-threatening laryngeal edema and bronchospasm, circulatory collapse, contraction of gastrointestinal and uterine smooth muscle, and urticaria (hives) or angioedema.

8. **Answer: a**
   RATIONALE: Although activated neutrophils kill microorganisms, they also injure the endothelium by releasing mediators that increase vascular permeability. In addition, activated endothelial cells release nitric oxide, a potent vasodilator that acts as a key mediator of septic shock.

9. **Answer: b**
   RATIONALE: The primary physiologic result of obstructive shock is elevated right heart pressure due to impaired right ventricular function. The other answers are not correct.

10. **Answer: c**
    RATIONALE: The degree of renal damage in shock is related to the severity and duration of shock. None of the other answers relate to the damage to the renal system in shock.

11. **Answer: c**
    RATIONALE: Major risk factors for the development of MODS are severe trauma, sepsis, prolonged periods of hypotension, hepatic dysfunction, infarcted bowel, advanced age, and alcohol abuse. Respiratory dysfunction is not a major risk factor in MODS.

12. **Answer: b**
    RATIONALE: Structural (congenital) heart defects are the most common cause of heart failure in children. The other answers are not correct.

CHAPTER 21

SECTION II: ASSESSING YOUR UNDERSTANDING

Activity A

1. gas exchange
2. conducting, respiratory
3. conducting
4. warmed, filtered, moistened
5. mucus
6. glottis
7. hyaline
8. hilum
9. pulmonary lobule
10. alveoli
11. pulmonary
12. lymphatic
13. parasympathetic
14. sympathetic
15. partial pressure
16. pressure difference
17. intrapleural
18. Valsalva
19. compliance
20. tidal volume (TV)
21. inspiratory reserve volume (IRV), expiratory reserve volume (ERV)
22. inspiratory capacity
23. vital capacity
24. minute volume
25. Pulmonary, alveolar
26. collapse
27. Dead space
28. mismatching
29. blood
30. Hemoglobin
31. cooperatively
32. pH, carbon dioxide, temperature.
33. dissolved carbon dioxide, hemoglobin, bicarbonate
34. pneumotaxic, apneustic
35. chemoreceptors, lung
36. carbon dioxide
37. Dyspnea

Activity B

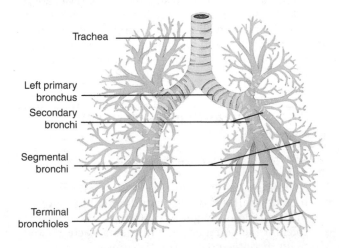

Trachea

Left primary bronchus

Secondary bronchi

Segmental bronchi

Terminal bronchioles

Activity C

1. f **2.** g **3.** h **4.** b **5.** i
6. a **7.** c **8.** j **9.** d **10.** e

Activity D

Activity E

1. The pleural membrane lines the thoracic cavity and encases the lungs. The outer parietal layer lines the pulmonary cavities and adheres to the thoracic wall, the mediastinum, and the diaphragm. The inner visceral pleura closely covers the lung and is adherent to all its surfaces. It is continuous with the parietal pleura at the hilum of the lung, where the major bronchus and pulmonary vessels enter and leave the lung. A thin film of serous fluid separates the two pleural layers, allowing the two layers to glide over each other and yet hold together, so there is no separation between the lungs and the chest wall.

2. During inspiration, the size of the chest cavity increases, the intrathoracic pressure becomes more negative, and air is drawn into the lungs. The diaphragm is the principal muscle of inspiration. When the diaphragm contracts, the abdominal contents are forced downward and the chest expands from top to bottom. The external intercostal muscles, which also aid in inspiration, connect to the adjacent ribs and slope downward and forward. When they contract, they raise the ribs and rotate them slightly so that the sternum is pushed forward; this enlarges the chest from side to side and from front to back. The scalene muscles elevate the first two ribs, and the sternocleidomastoid muscles raise the sternum to increase the size of the chest cavity. Expiration is largely passive. It occurs as the elastic components of the chest wall and lung structures that were stretched during inspiration recoil, causing air to leave the lungs as the intrathoracic pressure increases. When needed, the abdominal and the internal intercostal muscles can be used to increase expiratory effort.

3. Pulmonary surfactant forms a monolayer with its hydrophilic surface binding to liquid film on the surface of the alveoli and its hydrophobic surface facing outward toward the gases in the alveolar air. This monolayer interrupts the surface tension that develops at the air-liquid interface in the alveoli, keeping them from collapsing and allowing equal inflation.

4. Gas diffusion in the lung is described by the Fick law of diffusion. The Fick law states that the volume of a gas diffusing across the membrane per unit time is directly proportional to the partial pressure difference of the gas (P1 – P2), the surface area (SA) of the membrane, and the diffusion coefficient (D), and is inversely proportional to the thickness (T) of the membrane.

5. Arterial blood is commonly used for measuring blood gases. Venous blood is not used because venous levels of oxygen and carbon dioxide reflect the metabolic demands of the tissues rather than the gas exchange function of the lungs.

6. Coughing is a neurally mediated reflex that protects the lungs from accumulation of secretions and from entry of irritating and destructive substances. It is one of the primary defense mechanisms of the respiratory tract. The cough reflex is initiated by receptors located in the tracheobronchial wall; these receptors are extremely sensitive to irritating substances and to the presence of excess secretions. Afferent impulses from these receptors are transmitted through the vagus to the medullary center, which integrates the cough response.

SECTION III: APPLYING YOUR KNOWLEDGE

Activity F

1. When the oxygen levels in the body drop below a specific set-point, the small blood vessels in the lungs go into a vasoconstrictive state; they squeeze down, so very little blood can go through them. This means that no oxygen is exchanged at this point either. This vasoconstriction can occur in a limited part of the lung, or it can occur throughout the lung. This is called generalized hypoxia.

2. Blood gas and pulmonary function tests should be ordered.

SECTION IV: PRACTICING FOR NCLEX

Activity G

1. **Answers: a, c**
   RATIONALE: The lungs are the functional structures of the respiratory system. In addition to their gas exchange function, they inactivate vasoactive substances such as bradykinin; they convert angiotensin I to angiotensin II. They also serve as a reservoir for blood storage. Heparin-producing cells are particularly abundant in the capillaries of the lung, where small clots may be trapped. The other functions do not occur in the lungs.

2. **Answer: a**
   RATIONALE: The bronchial blood vessels are the only ones that can undergo angiogenesis (formation of new vessels) and develop collateral circulation when vessels in the pulmonary circulation are obstructed, as in pulmonary embolism. The development of new blood vessels helps to keep lung tissue alive until the pulmonary circulation can be restored. The blood in the bronchiole blood vessels is unoxygenated, so they neither carry

oxygen-rich blood to the lung tissues nor participate in gas exchange. Bronchiole blood vessels
drain blood into the bronchial veins.

3. **Answers: 1-b, 2-d, 3-c, 4-a**
4. **Answer: b**
   RATIONALE: Specifically, lung compliance (C)
   describes the change in lung volume (ΔV) that
   can be accomplished with a given change in respiratory pressure (ΔP); thus, ($C = \Delta V/\Delta P$). This
   equation has nothing to do with surface tension,
   airway resistance, or a change in peak expiratory
   flow.
5. **Answer: c**
   RATIONALE: The work of breathing is determined by
   the amount of effort required to move air through
   the conducting airways and by the ease of lung
   expansion, or compliance. Expansion of the lungs
   is difficult for persons with stiff and noncompliant
   lungs; they usually find it easier to breathe if they
   keep their TV low and breathe at a more rapid rate
   (e.g., 300 × 20 = 6000 mL) to achieve their
   minute volume and meet their oxygen needs. In
   contrast, persons with obstructive airway disease
   usually find it less difficult to inflate their lungs
   but expend more energy in moving air through
   the airways. As a result, these persons take
   deeper breaths and breathe at a slower rate (e.g.,
   600 × 10 = 6000 mL) to achieve their oxygen
   needs. People with COPD do not have hyperpneic
   breathing under normal conditions.
6. **Answer: c**
   RATIONALE: The distribution of ventilation between
   the apex and base of the lung varies with body
   position and the effects of gravity on intrapleural
   pressure. Intrapleural pressure impacts the
   distribution of ventilation, not intrathoracic or
   alveolar pressures.
7. **Answer: d**
   RATIONALE: Generalized hypoxia occurs at high
   altitudes and in persons with chronic hypoxia due
   to lung disease, and causes vasoconstriction
   throughout the lung. Prolonged hypoxia can lead
   to pulmonary hypertension and increased
   workload on the right heart.
8. **Answer: a**
   RATIONALE: Physiologic shunting of blood usually
   results from destructive lung disease that impairs
   ventilation or from heart failure that interferes
   with movement of blood through sections of the
   lungs. Obstructive lung disease, pulmonary hypertension, and regional hypoxia usually do not
   cause the physiologic shunting of blood.
9. **Answer: b**
   RATIONALE: In the clinical setting, blood gas measurements are used to determine the partial
   pressure of oxygen (P_{O_2}) and carbon dioxide (P_{CO_2})
   in the blood. Arterial blood commonly is used for
   measuring blood gases. Venous blood is not used
   because venous levels of oxygen and carbon dioxide reflect the metabolic demands of the tissues
   rather than the gas exchange function of the
   lungs. The other answers are not correct.
10. **Answers: a, c, e**
    RATIONALE: The automatic and voluntary
    components of respiration are regulated by
    afferent impulses that are transmitted to the respi-
    ratory center from a number of sources. Afferent
    input from higher brain centers is evidenced by
    the fact that a person can consciously alter the
    depth and rate of respiration. Fever, pain, and
    emotion exert their influence through lower brain
    centers.
11. **Answers: d-c-e-a-b**
    RATIONALE: Coughing itself requires the rapid
    inspiration of a large volume of air (usually about
    2.5 L), followed by rapid closure of the glottis and
    forceful contraction of the abdominal and expira-
    tory muscles. As these muscles contract, intratho-
    racic pressures are elevated to levels of 100 mm Hg
    or more. The rapid opening of the glottis at this
    point leads to an explosive expulsion of air.
12. **Answer: d**
    RATIONALE: Dyspnea is observed in at least three
    major cardiopulmonary disease states: primary
    lung diseases, such as pneumonia, asthma, and
    emphysema; heart disease that is characterized by
    pulmonary congestion; and neuromuscular disor-
    ders, such as myasthenia gravis and muscular
    dystrophy that affect the respiratory muscles. Dys-
    pnea is not an identified component of multiple
    sclerosis.

CHAPTER 22

SECTION II: ASSESSING YOUR UNDERSTANDING

Activity A

1. Viruses
2. bronchial, obstruct, bacterial
3. upper
4. rhinoviruses
5. Antihistamines
6. Rhinitis, paranasal
7. oxygen
8. hemagglutinin, neuraminidase
9. upper, viral, bacterial
10. vaccination
11. reassortment
12. *pneumonia*
13. Lobar pneumonia, bronchopneumonia
14. nosocomial
15. *immunocompromised*
16. Legionnaire
17. mycoplasma
18. Tuberculosis
19. waxy

20. Primary
21. tuberculin skin, x-rays
22. Histoplasmosis
23. Fungal
24. smoking
25. 80%
26. Lung cancers
27. small cell lung cancers (SCLCs)
28. non−small cell lung cancers (NSCLCs)
29. Croup
30. 25th to 28th

Activity B

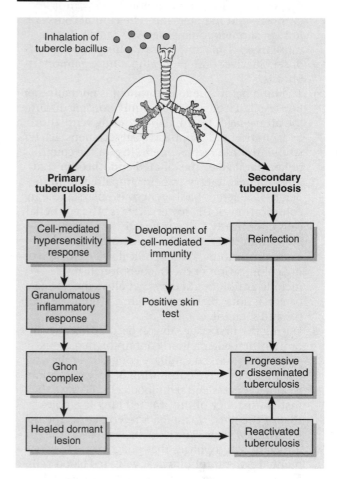

Activity D

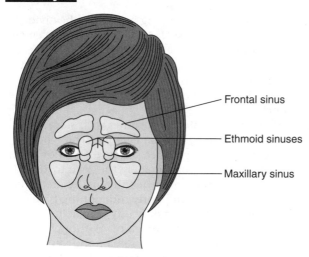

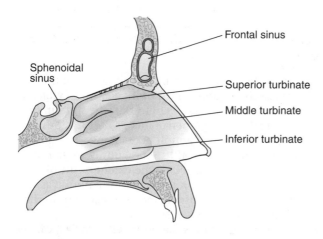

Activity C

1. i	2. c	3. a	4. b	5. d
6. j	7. e	8. g	9. g	10. h

Activity E

1. The fingers are the greatest source of spread, and the nasal mucosa and conjunctival surface of the eyes are the most common portals of entry of the virus. The most highly contagious period is during the first 3 days after the onset of symptoms, and the incubation period is approximately 5 days. Cold viruses have been found to survive for more than 5 hours on the skin and hard surfaces, such as plastic countertops. Aerosol spread of colds, through coughing and sneezing, is much less important than the spread by fingers picking up the virus from contaminated surfaces and carrying it to the nasal membranes and eyes.

2. Contagion results from the ability of the influenza A virus to develop new HA and NA subtypes against which the population is not protected. An antigenic shift, which involves a major genetic rearrangement in either antigen, may lead to epidemic or pandemic infection. Lesser changes, called antigenic drift, find the population partially protected by cross-reacting antibodies.

3. Viral pneumonia occurs as a complication of influenza. It typically develops within 1 day after

onset of influenza and is characterized by rapid progression of fever, tachypnea, tachycardia, cyanosis, and hypotension. The clinical course of influenza pneumonia progresses rapidly. It can cause hypoxemia and death within a few days of onset. Survivors often develop diffuse pulmonary fibrosis.

4. The lung below the main bronchi is normally sterile, despite frequent entry of microorganisms into the air passages by inhalation during ventilation or aspiration of nasopharyngeal secretions. Bacterial pneumonia results due to loss of the cough reflex, damage to the ciliated endothelium that lines the respiratory tract, or impaired immune defenses. Bacterial adherence also plays a role in colonization of the lower airways. The epithelial cells of critically and chronically ill persons are more receptive to binding microorganisms that cause pneumonia. Other clinical risk factors favoring colonization of the tracheobronchial tree include antibiotic therapy that alters the normal bacterial flora, diabetes, smoking, chronic bronchitis, and viral infection.

5. During the first stage, alveoli become filled with protein-rich edema fluid containing numerous organisms. Marked capillary congestion follows, leading to massive outpouring of polymorphonuclear leukocytes and red blood cells. Because the first consistency of the affected lung resembles that of the liver, this stage is referred to as the *red hepatization* stage. The next stage involves the arrival of macrophages that phagocytose the fragmented polymorphonuclear cells, red blood cells, and other cellular debris. During this stage, which is termed the *gray hepatization* stage, the congestion has diminished but the lung is still firm. The alveolar exudate is then removed and the lung returns to normal.

6. *M. tuberculosis hominis* is an airborne infection spread by minute, invisible particles called droplet nuclei that are harbored in the respiratory secretions of persons with active tuberculosis. Coughing, sneezing, and talking all create respiratory droplets; these droplets evaporate, leaving the organisms, which remain suspended in the air and are circulated by air currents. Thus, living under crowded and confined conditions increases the risk for spread of the disease.

7. Inhaled droplet nuclei pass down the bronchial tree without settling on the epithelium and are deposited in the alveoli. Soon after entering the lung, the bacilli are phagocytosed by alveolar macrophages, but resist killing, because cell wall lipids of the *M. tuberculosis* block fusion of phagosomes and lysosomes. Although the macrophages that first ingest *M. tuberculosis* cannot kill the organisms, they initiate a cell-mediated immune response that eventually contains the infection. As the tubercle bacilli multiply, the infected macrophages degrade the mycobacteria and

present their antigens to T lymphocytes. The sensitized T lymphocytes, in turn, stimulate the macrophages to increase their concentration of lytic enzymes and ability to kill the mycobacteria. When released, these lytic enzymes also damage lung tissue. The development of a population of activated T lymphocytes and related development of activated macrophages capable of ingesting and destroying the bacilli constitutes the cell-mediated immune response.

8. Lung cancer is classified as squamous cell lung carcinoma, adenocarcinoma, small cell carcinoma, and large cell carcinoma.

9. The manifestations of lung cancer can be divided into three categories: (1) those due to involvement of the lung and adjacent structures, (2) the effects of local spread and metastasis, and (3) nonmetastatic paraneoplastic manifestations involving endocrine, neurologic, and connective tissue function.

10. Pulmonary immaturity, together with surfactant deficiency, lead to alveolar collapse. The type II alveolar cells that produce surfactant do not begin to mature until approximately the 25th to 28th weeks of gestation; consequently, many premature infants are born with poorly functioning type II alveolar cells and have difficulty producing sufficient amounts of surfactant. Without surfactant, the large alveoli remain inflated, whereas the small alveoli become difficult to inflate, resulting in respiratory distress syndrome.

SECTION III: APPLYING YOUR KNOWLEDGE
Activity F

1. Diagnostic tests for squamous cell cancer of the lung include chest radiography, bronchoscopy, cytologic studies (Papanicolaou [Pap] test) of the sputum or bronchial washings, percutaneous needle biopsy of lung tissue, Scalene lymph node biopsy, computed tomographic scans, MRI studies, ultrasonography to locate lesions and evaluate the extent of the disease, and positron-emission tomography, a noninvasive alternative for identifying metastatic lesions in the mediastinum or distant sites.

2. Treatments used for squamous cell (NSCLC) cancer of the lung include surgery for the removal of small, localized NSCLC tumors; radiation therapy, a definitive or main treatment modality for palliation of symptoms; and chemotherapy, often using a combination of drugs. Often, a combination of these treatments is used.

SECTION IV: PRACTICING FOR NCLEX
Activity G

1. **Answer: a**
   RATIONALE: Decongestant drugs (i.e., sympathomimetic agents) are available in over-the-counter nasal sprays, drops, and oral cold

medications. These drugs constrict the blood vessels in the swollen nasal mucosa and reduce nasal swelling. Rebound nasal swelling can occur with indiscriminate use of nasal drops and sprays. Oral preparations containing decongestants may cause systemic vasoconstriction and elevation of blood pressure when given in doses large enough to relieve nasal congestion. They should be avoided by persons with hypertension, heart disease, hyperthyroidism, diabetes mellitus, or other health problems.

2. **Answer: b**
   RATIONALE: One distinguishing feature of an influenza viral infection is the rapid onset, sometimes in as little as 1 to 2 minutes, of profound malaise. None of the other answers are distinguishing characteristics of an influenza viral infection.

3. **Answer: c**
   RATIONALE: Recently, a highly pathogenic influenza A subtype H5N1 was found in poultry in East and Southeast Asian Countries. Although the H5N1 strain is highly contagious from one bird to another, the transmission from human to human is relatively inefficient and not sustained. The result is only rare cases of person-to-person transmission. Most cases occur after exposure to infected poultry or surfaces contaminated with poultry droppings. Because infection in humans is associated with high mortality, there exists considerable concern that H5N1 strain might mutate and initiate a pandemic.

4. **Answers: a, c, d**
   RATIONALE: Community-acquired pneumonia may be further categorized according to risk of mortality and need for hospitalization based on age, presence of coexisting disease, and severity of illness using physical examination findings and laboratory and radiologic findings. The other answers are not categories used to classify community-acquired pneumonia.

5. **Answer: d**
   RATIONALE: Neutropenia and impaired granulocyte function, as occurs in persons with leukemia, chemotherapy, and bone marrow depression, predispose to infections caused by *S. aureus, Aspergillus*, gram-negative bacilli, and candida. All the other organisms can cause pneumonia, but they are not usually seen in people with neutropenia and impaired granulocyte function.

6. **Answer: a**
   RATIONALE: Pleuritic pain, a sharp pain that is more severe with respiratory movements, is common. With antibiotic therapy, fever usually subsides in approximately 48 to 72 hours, and recovery is uneventful. Elderly persons are less likely to experience marked elevations in temperature; in these persons, the only sign of pneumonia may be a loss of appetite and deterioration in mental status.

7. **Answer: b**
   RATIONALE: The pathogenesis of tuberculosis in a previously unexposed immunocompetent person is centered on the development of a cell-mediated immune response that confers resistance to the organism and development of tissue hypersensitivity to the tubercular antigens. The destructive nature of the disease, such as caseating necrosis and cavitation, results from the hypersensitivity immune response rather than the destructive capabilities of the tubercle bacillus. Tuberculosis does not have rapidly progressing pulmonary lesions, nor does it have purulent necrosis or purulent pulmonary lesions.

8. **Answer: c**
   RATIONALE: The oral antifungal drugs itraconazole and fluconazole are used for treatment of less severe forms of infection. Intravenous amphotericin B is used in the treatment of persons with progressive disease. Long-term treatment is often required. BCG is an attenuated strain of live tubercle vaccine. Rifampin is an oral drug used in the treatment of tuberculosis.

9. **Answer: d**
   RATIONALE: The NSCLCs include squamous cell carcinomas, adenocarcinomas, and large cell carcinomas. As with the SCLCs, these cancers have the capacity to synthesize bioactive products and produce paraneoplastic syndromes. NSCLCs do not neutralize bioactive syndromes. In addition, they neither synthesize ACTH nor produce panneoplastic syndromes.

10. **Answer: a**
    RATIONALE: The infant with BPD often demonstrates a barrel chest, tachycardia, rapid and shallow breathing, chest retractions, cough, and poor weight gain. Other signs and symptoms listed are not those of BPD.

11. Epiglottitis: upper airway
    Acute bronchiolitis: lower airway
    Asthma: lower airway
    Spasmodic croup: upper airway
    Laryngotracheobronchitis: upper airway

12. **Answer: b**
    RATIONALE: The child with bronchiolitis is at risk for respiratory failure resulting from impaired gas exchange. The other answers are not applicable.

CHAPTER 23

SECTION II: ASSESSING YOUR UNDERSTANDING

Activity A
1. carbon dioxide (CO_2), oxygen (O_2)
2. Ventilation
3. oxygenation, removal of CO_2
4. Hypoxemia
5. hypoxia

6. ventilation, vasoconstriction, red blood
7. Hypercapnia
8. pH, acidosis
9. Pleural effusion
10. Hemothorax
11. inflated
12. expiratory
13. asthma
14. T lymphocyte
15. Chronic obstructive
16. inflammation, fibrosis
17. Emphysema, proteases
18. α_1-antitrypsin
19. hypersecretion of mucus
20. *pink puffers*
21. *blue bloaters*
22. Bronchiectasis
23. Cystic fibrosis
24. interstitial
25. collagen, elastic
26. embolism
27. pulmonary embolism
28. Pulmonary hypertension
29. hypoxemia
30. Respiratory failure

Activity B

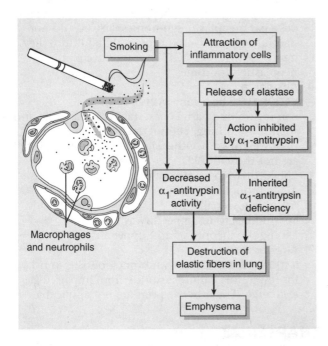

Activity C

1.

1. d	**2.** b	**3.** i	**4.** a	**5.** j
6. e	**7.** f	**8.** g	**9.** h	**10.** c

2.

1. e	**2.** b	**3.** g	**4.** i	**5.** d
6. j	**7.** a	**8.** h	**9.** f	**10.** c

Activity D

1.

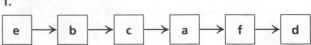

Activity E

1. The mechanisms that result in hypoxemia are hypoventilation, impaired diffusion of gases, inadequate circulation of blood through the pulmonary capillaries, and mismatching of ventilation and perfusion.
2. The clinical manifestations of atelectasis include tachypnea, tachycardia, dyspnea, cyanosis, signs of hypoxemia, diminished chest expansion, absence of breath sounds, and intercostal retractions. Both chest expansion and breath sounds are decreased on the affected area. There may be intercostal retraction over the involved area during inspiration.
3. The symptoms of the acute response are caused by the release of chemical mediators from the presensitized mast cells. Mediator release results in the infiltration of inflammatory cells, opening of the mucosal intercellular junctions, and increased access of antigen to submucosal mast cells. There is bronchospasm caused by direct stimulation of parasympathetic receptors, mucosal edema caused by increased vascular permeability, and increased mucus secretions. The late-phase response involves inflammation and increased airway responsiveness that prolong the asthma attack. An initial trigger in the late-phase response causes the release of inflammatory mediators from mast cells, macrophages, and epithelial cells. These substances induce the migration and activation of other inflammatory cells, which then produce epithelial injury and edema, changes in mucociliary function and reduced clearance of respiratory tract secretions, and increased airway responsiveness.
4. The two processes that are critical to the pathogenesis of bronchiectasis are airway obstruction and chronic persistent infection, causing damage to the bronchial walls, leading to weakening and dilation.
5. Cystic fibrosis is caused by mutations in a single gene on the long arm of chromosome that encodes for the cystic fibrosis transmembrane regulator (CFTR), which functions as a chloride channel in epithelial cell membranes. Mutations in the *CFTR* gene render the epithelial membrane relatively impermeable to the chloride ion. The impaired transport of Cl⁻ ultimately leads to a series of secondary events, including increased absorption of Na⁺ and water from the airways into the blood. This lowers the water content of the mucociliary blanket coating the respiratory epithelium, causing it to become more viscid. The resulting dehydration of the mucous layer leads to defective mucociliary function and accumulation of viscid secretions that obstruct the airways and predispose to recurrent pulmonary infections. The obstruction develops

from the thick mucous and recurrent infections damage lung tissue leading to the development of bronchiectasis.

6. Obstruction of pulmonary blood flow causes reflex bronchoconstriction in the affected area of the lung, wasted ventilation and impaired gas exchange, and loss of alveolar surfactant. Pulmonary hypertension and right heart failure may develop when there is massive vasoconstriction because of a large embolus.

7. Pathologic lung changes include diffuse epithelial cell injury with increased permeability of the alveolar-capillary membrane, which permits fluid, plasma proteins, and blood cells to move out of the vascular compartment into the interstitium and alveoli of the lung. Diffuse alveolar cell damage leads to accumulation of fluid, surfactant inactivation, and formation of a hyaline membrane. The work of breathing becomes greatly increased as the lung stiffens and becomes more difficult to inflate. There is increased intrapulmonary shunting of blood, impaired gas exchange, and hypoxemia despite high supplemental oxygen therapy. Gas exchange is further compromised by alveolar collapse resulting from abnormalities in surfactant production. When injury to the alveolar epithelium is severe, disorganized epithelial repair may lead to fibrosis.

SECTION III: APPLYING YOUR KNOWLEDGE

Activity F

1. Diagnostic tests that the nurse would expect to be ordered to confirm the diagnosis of asthma include spirometry, inhalation challenge tests, and laboratory findings.

2. A plan of care will be developed with the input of both you and your daughter to encourage independence as it relates to the control of her symptoms, along with measures directed at helping her develop and keep a positive self-concept.

SECTION IV: PRACTICING FOR NCLEX

Activity G

1.

Mechanism	Outcome
Decreased oxygen in air	Hypoxemia
Inadequate circulation through pulmonary capillaries	Decreased PO_2
Hypoventilation	Decreased PO_2
Disease in respiratory system	Hypoxemia
Mismatched ventilation & perfusion	Decreased PO_2
Dysfunction of neurologic system	Hypoxemia

RATIONALE: Hypoxemia can result from an inadequate amount of O_2 in the air, disease of the respiratory system, dysfunction of the neurologic system, or alterations in circulatory function. The mechanisms whereby respiratory disorders lead to a significant reduction in PO_2 are hypoventilation, impaired diffusion of gases, inadequate circulation of blood through the pulmonary capillaries, and mismatching of ventilation and perfusion.

2. **Answers: a, b, c, e**
RATIONALE: Hypercapnia refers to an increase in carbon dioxide levels. In the clinical setting, four factors contribute to hypercapnia: alterations in carbon dioxide production, disturbance in the gas exchange function of the lungs, abnormalities in respiratory function of the chest wall and respiratory muscles, and changes in neural control of respiration. A decrease in carbon dioxide production does not cause hypercapnia.

3. **Answer: b**
RATIONALE: One of the complications of untreated moderate or large hemothorax is fibrothorax—the fusion of the pleural surfaces by fibrin, hyalin, and connective tissue—and in some cases, calcification of the fibrous tissue, which restricts lung expansion. Calcification of the lung tissue does not occur because of a hemothorax, neither does pleuritis or an atelectasis.

4. **Answer: c**
RATIONALE: Persons with talc lung are also highly susceptible to the occurrence of pneumothorax. Talc lung may result from inhalation of talc particles, but is more commonly an occurrence of injected or inhaled talc powder that is used as a filler with heroin, methamphetamine, or codeine. A hemothorax is not a complication of talc lung, neither are chylothorax or fibrothorax.

5. **Answer: a**
RATIONALE: Treatment of pleuritis consists of treating the underlying disease and inflammation. Analgesics and nonsteroidal anti-inflammatory drugs (e.g., indomethacin) may be used for pleural pain. Although these agents reduce inflammation, they may not entirely relieve the discomfort associated with deep breathing and coughing. The other answers are not used to treat pleural pain.

6. **Answer: c**
RATIONALE: If the collapsed area is large, the mediastinum and trachea shift to the affected side. In compression atelectasis, the mediastinum shifts away from the affected lung. None of the other answers are correct.

7. **Answer: a**
RATIONALE: For children younger than 2 years of age, nebulizer therapy usually is preferred. Children between 3 and 5 years of age may begin using an MDI with a spacer and holding chamber. The other answers are not correct.

8. **Answer: b**
RATIONALE: The term *chronic obstructive pulmonary disease* encompasses two types of obstructive airway disease: emphysema, with enlargement of air spaces and destruction of lung tissue; and chronic obstructive bronchitis, with increased mucus production, obstruction of small airways, and a chronic productive cough. Persons with COPD often have overlapping features of both disorders. Asthma and chronic bronchitis have not been identified as components of COPD.

9. **Answer: c**
RATIONALE: In the past, bronchiectasis often followed a necrotizing bacterial pneumonia that frequently complicated measles, pertussis, or influenza. Chickenpox has never been linked to bronchiectasis.

10. **Answer: d**
RATIONALE: In addition to airway obstruction, the basic genetic defect that occurs with CF predisposes to chronic infection with a surprising small number of organisms, the most common being *Pseudomonas aeruginosa, Burkholderia cepacia, Staphylococcus aureus,* and *Haemophilus influenzae.* The other disease causing organisms are not linked to CF.

11. **Answers: a, b, e**
RATIONALE: Important etiologic determinants in the development of the pneumoconioses are the size of the dust particle, its chemical nature and ability to incite lung destruction, and the concentration of dust and the length of exposure to it. The density and biologic nature of the dust particles are not linked to their ability to cause pneumoconioses.

12. **Answer: a**
RATIONALE: Drugs can cause a variety of both acute and chronic alterations in lung function. For example, some of the cytotoxic drugs (e.g., bleomycin, busulfan, methotrexate, and cyclophosphamide) used in treatment of cancer cause pulmonary damage as a result of direct toxicity of the drug and by stimulating the influx of inflammatory cells into the alveoli. Amiodarone, a drug used to treat resistant cardiac arrhythmias, is preferentially sequestered in the lung and causes significant pneumonitis in 5% to 15% of persons receiving it. Inderal does not cause a direct toxicity in the lungs.

13. **Answer: b**
RATIONALE: Chest pain, dyspnea, and increased respiratory rate are the most frequent signs and symptoms of pulmonary embolism. Pulmonary infarction often causes pleuritic pain that changes with respiration; it is more severe on inspiration and less severe on expiration. Mediastinal and tracheal shifts are not signs of a pulmonary infarction, and neither is pericardial pain.

14. **Answer: b**
RATIONALE: Continued exposure of the pulmonary vessels to hypoxemia is a common cause of pulmonary hypertension. Unlike blood vessels in the systemic circulation, most of which dilate in response to hypoxemia and hypercapnia, the pulmonary vessels constrict. None of the other answers are correct.

15. **Answer: c**
RATIONALE: Management of cor pulmonale focuses on the treatment of the lung disease and heart failure. Low-flow oxygen therapy may be used to reduce the pulmonary hypertension and polycythemia associated with severe hypoxemia caused by chronic lung disease. Low-flow oxygen used in treating cor pulmonale does not stimulate the body to breathe; it does not act in an inhibitory way on the respiratory center in the brain; nor does it reduce the formation of pulmonary emboli.

16. **Answers: b, d, e**
RATIONALE: Clinically, ALI/ARDS is marked by a rapid onset, usually within 12 to 18 hours of the initiating event, of respiratory distress, an increase in respiratory rate, and signs of respiratory failure. Chest radiography shows diffuse bilateral infiltrates of the lung tissue in the absence of cardiac dysfunction. Marked hypoxemia occurs that is refractory to treatment with supplemental oxygen therapy, which results in a decrease in the PF ratio. Many persons with ARDS have a systemic response that results in multiple organ failure, particularly the renal, gastrointestinal, cardiovascular, and central nervous systems. The other answers are not clinical signs of ARDS.

17. **Answer: d**
RATIONALE: Many of the adverse consequences of hypercapnia are the result of respiratory acidosis. Direct effects of acidosis include depression of cardiac contractility, decreased respiratory muscle contractility, and arterial vasodilation. Raised levels of P_{CO_2} greatly increase cerebral blood flow, which may result in headache, increased cerebral spinal fluid pressure, and sometimes papilledema.

CHAPTER 24

SECTION II: ASSESSING YOUR UNDERSTANDING

Activity A

1. kidneys
2. hilus
3. Nephrons
4. cortex
5. renal pyramids
6. aorta

7. glomeruli
8. glomerulus
9. Peritubular capillaries
10. filtrate
11. glomerular filtration rate (GFR)
12. concentration, basolateral
13. Cotransport
14. proximal
15. renal threshold
16. loop of Henle
17. $Na^+–K^+–2Cl^-$
18. distal convoluted
19. antidiuretic hormone
20. sympathetic
21. clearance
22. Aldosterone
23. sodium
24. bicarbonate, hydrogen
25. Urea
26. erythropoietin
27. Proteinuria
28. specific gravity
29. Creatinine
30. BUN

Activity B

1. e	2. d	3. i	4. a	5. j
6. g	7. b	8. h	9. f	10. c

Activity C

1. Decreased GFR → juxtaglomerular release of renin → conversion of angiotensinogen to angiotensin I by renin → conversion of angiotensin I to angiotensin II by angiotensin converting enzyme → angiotensin II stimulates release of ADH and aldosterone → sodium and water retention.

Activity D

1. The glomerular capillary membrane is composed of three layers: the capillary endothelial layer, the basement membrane, and the single-celled capsular epithelial layer. The endothelial layer contains many small perforations, called fenestrations. The epithelial layer that covers the glomerulus is continuous with the epithelium that lines Bowman's capsule. The cells of the epithelial layer have unusual octopus-like structures that possess a large number of extensions, or foot processes. These foot processes form slit pores through which the glomerular filtrate passes. The basement membrane consists of a homogeneous acellular meshwork of collagen fibers, glycoproteins, and mucopolysaccharides. The spaces between the fibers that make up the basement membrane represent the pores of a filter and determine the size-dependent permeability barrier of the glomerulus.
2. The basic mechanisms of transport across the tubular epithelial cell membrane include active and passive transport mechanisms. Water and urea are passively absorbed along concentration gradients. Sodium, K^+, chloride, calcium, and phosphate ions, as well as urate, glucose, and amino acids, are reabsorbed using primary or secondary active transport mechanisms to move across the tubular membrane. Some substances, such as hydrogen, potassium, and urate ions, are secreted into the tubular fluids.
3. The juxtaglomerular complex is a feedback control system that links changes in the GFR with renal blood flow. It is located at the site where the distal tubule extends back to the glomerulus and then passes between the afferent and efferent arteriole. The distal tubular site that is nearest the glomerulus is characterized by densely nucleated cells called the macula densa. In the adjacent afferent arteriole, the smooth muscle cells of the media are modified as special secretory cells called juxtaglomerular cells. These cells contain granules of inactive renin, an enzyme that functions in the conversion of angiotensinogen to angiotensin. Renin functions by means of angiotensin II to produce vasoconstriction of the efferent arteriole as a means of preventing serious decreases in GFR. Angiotensin II also increases sodium reabsorption indirectly by stimulating aldosterone secretion from the adrenal gland and directly by increasing sodium reabsorption by the proximal tubule cells. The increase in sodium will result in an increase in water retention, which will increase blood volume and in turn increase GFR.
4. The actions of ANP include vasodilation of the afferent and efferent arterioles, which results in an increase in renal blood flow and GFR. ANP inhibits aldosterone secretion by the adrenal gland and sodium reabsorption from the collecting tubules through its action on aldosterone and through direct action on the tubular cells. It also inhibits ADH release from the posterior pituitary gland, thereby increasing excretion of water by the kidneys. ANP also has vasodilator properties.
5. The kidneys function as an endocrine organ in that they produce chemical mediators that travel through the blood to distant sites where they exert their actions. The kidneys participate in control of blood pressure by way of the renin-angiotensin mechanism, in calcium metabolism by activating vitamin D, and in regulating red blood cell production through the synthesis of erythropoietin.
6. By blocking the reabsorption of these solutes, diuretics create an osmotic pressure gradient within the nephron that prevents the passive reabsorption of water. Thus, diuretics cause water and sodium to be retained within the nephron, thereby promoting the excretion of both. The increase in urine flow that a diuretic produces is related to the amount of sodium and chloride reabsorption that it blocks.

SECTION III: APPLYING YOUR KNOWLEDGE

Activity E

1. Tests that the nurse would expect to be ordered to either confirm or deny the diagnosis include urine specific gravity, urinalysis with culture and sensitivity, urine osmolality, GFR, BUN, and serum electrolytes.
2. A simple flat-plat radiograph will show the kidneys, ureters, and any radio-opaque stones that may be in the kidney pelvis or ureters.

SECTION IV: PRACTICING FOR NCLEX

Activity F

1. **Answer: a**
   RATIONALE: The plasma level at which the substance appears in the urine is called the renal threshold. Renal clearance, renal filtration rate, and renal transport levels are not the right answers.
2. **Answer: b**
   RATIONALE: With ingestion of a high-protein diet, renal blood flow increases 20% to 30% within 1 to 2 hours. Although the exact mechanism for this increase is uncertain, it is thought to be related to the fact that amino acids and sodium are absorbed together in the proximal tubule (secondary active transport). The same mechanism is thought to explain the large increases in renal blood flow and GFR that occur with high blood glucose levels in persons with uncontrolled diabetes mellitus.
3. **Answers: a, b**
   RATIONALE: With inulin, after intravenous injection, the amount that appears in the urine is equal to the amount that is filtered in the glomeruli (i.e., the clearance rate is equal to the GFR). Because of these properties, inulin can be used as a laboratory measure of the GFR. The other answers are not correct.
4. **Answer: c**
   RATIONALE: Small doses of aspirin compete with uric acid for secretion into the tubular fluid and reduce uric acid secretion, and large doses compete with uric acid for reabsorption and increase uric acid excretion in the urine.
5. **Answer: d**
   RATIONALE: Alkaline or acid diuresis may be used to increase elimination of drugs in the urine, particularly in situations of drug overdose. The other answers are incorrect.
6. **Answer: a**
   RATIONALE: Persons with end-stage kidney disease often are anemic because of an inability of the kidneys to produce erythropoietin. This anemia usually is managed by the administration of a recombinant erythropoietin (epoetin alfa), produced through DNA technology, to stimulate erythropoiesis.
7. **Answer: b**
   RATIONALE: The increase in urine flow that a diuretic produces is related to the amount of sodium and chloride reabsorption that it blocks. The other answers are not correct.
8. **Answer: b**
   RATIONALE: With diminished renal function, there is a loss of renal concentrating ability, and the urine specific gravity may fall to levels of 1.006 to 1.010 (usual range is 1.010 to 1.025 with normal fluid intake). These low levels are particularly significant if they occur during periods that follow a decrease in water intake (e.g., during the first urine specimen on arising in the morning). The other answers are incorrect.
9. **Answer: d**
   RATIONALE: Creatinine is freely filtered in the glomeruli, is not reabsorbed from the tubules into the blood, and is only minimally secreted into the tubules from the blood; therefore, its blood values depend closely on the GFR. A normal serum creatinine level usually indicates normal renal function. In addition to its use in calculating the GFR, the serum creatinine level is used in estimating the functional capacity of the kidneys. If the value doubles, the GFR—and renal function—probably has fallen to half of its normal state. A rise in the serum creatinine level to three times its normal value suggests that there is a 75% loss of renal function. A BUN, 24-hour urine test, and urine test of first void in the morning do not tell you about serum creatinine levels.
10. **Answer: a**
    RATIONALE: The actions of ANP include vasodilation of the afferent and efferent arterioles, which results in an increase in renal blood flow and GFR. ANP inhibits aldosterone secretion by the adrenal gland and sodium reabsorption from the collecting tubules through its action on aldosterone and through direct action on the tubular cells. It also inhibits ADH release from the posterior pituitary gland, thereby increasing excretion of water by the kidneys. ANP also has vasodilator properties.

CHAPTER 25

SECTION II: ASSESSING YOUR UNDERSTANDING

Activity A

1. shape, position
2. agenesis
3. *Potter syndrome*
4. hypoplasia
5. dysplasia
6. multicystic
7. Polycystic

8. autosomal dominant
9. destructive
10. Stagnation
11. Hydronephrosis
12. distention
13. calculi
14. nidus
15. calcium
16. pain
17. second
18. *Escherichia coli*
19. urethra
20. more
21. anatomic, functional
22. Catheter
23. cystitis
24. Glomerulonephritis
25. nephritic, nephrotic
26. Acute nephritic
27. deposition
28. hypercellularity
29. Goodpasture
30. Nephrotic
31. Membranous
32. Berger disease
33. basement membrane
34. Renal tubular acidosis
35. HCO_3^-
36. Acute pyelonephritis
37. Wilms tumor
38. hematuria, mass

Activity B

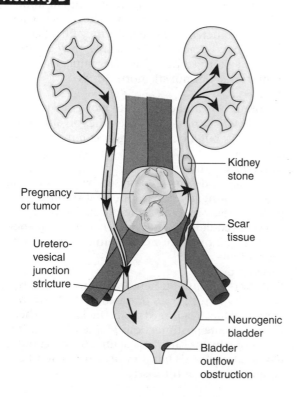

Activity C

1. c	2. a	3. f	4. g	5. e
6. i	7. d	8. h	9. b	10. j

Activity D

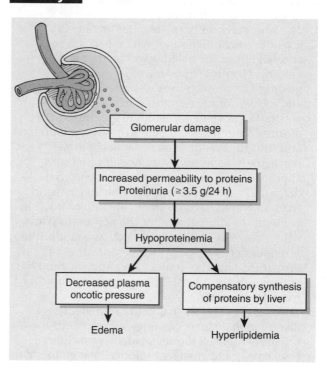

Activity E

1. The destructive effects of urinary obstruction on kidney structures are determined by the degree (i.e., partial versus complete, unilateral versus bilateral) and the duration of the obstruction. The two most damaging effects of urinary obstruction are stasis of urine, which predisposes to infection and stone formation, and progressive dilation of the renal collecting ducts and renal tubular structures, which causes destruction and atrophy of renal tissue.

2. Kidney stone formation requires supersaturated urine and an environment that allows the stone to grow. The risk for stone formation is increased when the urine is supersaturated with stone components (e.g., calcium salts, uric acid, magnesium ammonium phosphate, cystine). Supersaturation depends on urinary pH, solute concentration, ionic strength, and complexation. The greater the concentration of two ions, the more likely they are to precipitate. Complexation influences the availability of specific ions.

3. The risk factors for UTI are higher:
   a. in persons with urinary obstruction and reflux
   b. in people with neurogenic disorders that impair bladder emptying

c. in women who are sexually active
d. in postmenopausal women
e. in men with diseases of the prostate
f. in elderly persons.
g. in those who have undergone catheterization
h. in women with diabetes

4. The host defenses of the bladder include the washout phenomenon, in which bacteria are removed from the bladder and urethra during voiding; the protective mucin layer that lines the bladder and protects against bacterial invasion; and local immune responses. In the ureters, peristaltic movements facilitate the movement of urine from the renal pelvis through the ureters and into the bladder. Immune mechanisms, particularly secretory immunoglobulin (Ig) A, appear to provide an important antibacterial defense. Phagocytic blood cells further assist in the removal of bacteria from the urinary tract. In women, the normal flora of the periurethral area, which consists of organisms such as lactobacillus, provides defense against the colonization of uropathic bacteria. In men, the prostatic fluid has antimicrobial properties that protect the urethra from colonization.

5. The cellular changes that occur with glomerular disease include increases in glomerular and/or inflammatory cell number, basement membrane thickening, and changes in noncellular glomerular components.

6. The development of glomerulonephritis follows a streptococcal infection by approximately 7 to 12 days, the time needed for the production of antibodies. The primary infection usually involves the pharynx. Oliguria, which develops as the GFR decreases, is one of the first symptoms. Proteinuria and hematuria follow because of increased glomerular capillary wall permeability. The red blood cells are degraded by materials in the urine, and cola-colored urine may be the first sign of the disorder. Sodium and water retention gives rise to edema (particularly of the face and hands) and hypertension.

7. Widespread thickening of the glomerular capillary basement membrane occurs in almost all persons with diabetes and can occur without evidence of proteinuria. This is followed by a diffuse increase in mesangial matrix, with mild proliferation of mesangial cells. As the disease progresses, the mesangial cells impinge on the capillary lumen, reducing the surface area for glomerular filtration.

8. Drug-related nephropathies involve functional or structural changes in the kidneys that occur after exposure to a drug. Because of their large blood flow and high filtration pressure, the kidneys are exposed to any substance that is in the blood. The kidneys also are active in the metabolic transformation of drugs and therefore are exposed to a number of toxic metabolites. Drugs and toxic substances can damage the kidneys by causing a decrease in renal blood flow, obstructing urine flow, directly damaging tubulointerstitial structures, or producing hypersensitivity reactions.

SECTION III: APPLYING YOUR KNOWLEDGE

Activity F

1. Urine analysis, urine culture and sensitivity, and broad-spectrum antibiotic given intravenously.

SECTION IV: PRACTICING FOR NCLEX

Activity G

1. **Answers: a, b; c, e**
   RATIONALE: Bilateral renal dysplasia causes oligohydramnios and the resultant Potter facies, pulmonary hypoplasia, and renal failure. Multicystic kidneys are a disorder, not the result of a congenital problem.

2. **Answers: 1-b, 2-a, 3-d, 4-c**

3. **Answer: a**
   RATIONALE: Urinary tract obstruction encourages the growth of microorganisms and should be suspected in persons with recurrent UTIs. The other answers can cause lower UTIs, but an obstruction would be considered because of the frequency of the infections.

4. **Answer: b**
   RATIONALE: Phosphate levels are increased in alkaline urine and magnesium, always present in the urine, and combine to form struvite stones. These stones can increase in size until they fill an entire renal pelvis. Because of their shape, they often are called staghorn stones. The other minerals can form stones, but not staghorn stones.

5. **Answer: c**
   RATIONALE: Most uncomplicated lower UTIs are caused by *Escherichia coli*. The other organisms can cause UTIs, but are not the most common cause of infection.

6. **Answers: b, c, d**
   RATIONALE: Toddlers often present with abdominal pain, vomiting, diarrhea, abnormal voiding patterns, foul-smelling urine, fever, and poor growth. Toddlers do not typically have frequency in voiding, nor do they complain of burning when they urinate.

7. **Answer: d**
   RATIONALE: Group A β-hemolytic streptococci have the ability to seed from one area of the body to another. One area it seeds to is the kidney, where it causes acute postinfectious glomerulonephritis. Other organisms can cause acute postinfectious glomerulonephritis but they are not the most common cause of the disease.

8. Answer: a
RATIONALE: The lesions of diabetic nephropathy most commonly involve the glomeruli and are associated with three glomerular syndromes: nonnephrotic proteinuria, nephrotic syndrome, and chronic renal failure. The other answers are not commonly associated with diabetic nephropathy.

9. Answer: b
RATIONALE: The most common causative agents of acute pyelonephritis are Gram-negative bacteria, including *E. coli* and *Proteus, Klebsiella, Enterobacter,* and *Pseudomonas.* The other answers are not considered a common causative agent of acute pyelonephritis.

10. Answer: c
RATIONALE: The tolerance to drugs varies with age and depends on renal function, state of hydration, blood pressure, and the pH of the urine. None of the other answers are correct.

11. Answer: d
RATIONALE: The common presenting signs of a Wilms tumor are a large asymptomatic abdominal mass and hypertension. The tumor is often discovered inadvertently, and it is not uncommon for the mother to discover it while bathing the child. Some children may present with abdominal pain, vomiting, or both. Hypotension, oliguria, and diarrhea are not common presenting signs of a Wilms tumor.

CHAPTER 26

SECTION II: ASSESSING YOUR UNDERSTANDING

Activity A

1. Acute renal failure
2. prerenal, intrinsic, postrenal
3. Prerenal
4. tubular epithelial
5. blood urea nitrogen
6. Postrenal
7. cause
8. chronic kidney disease
9. 120 to 130
10. creatinine
11. tubulointerstitial, albumin
12. uremic
13. dehydration, overload
14. sodium
15. bone
16. *osteodystrophy*
17. Hypertension
18. uremia
19. atrophy, demyelination
20. GFR

Activity B

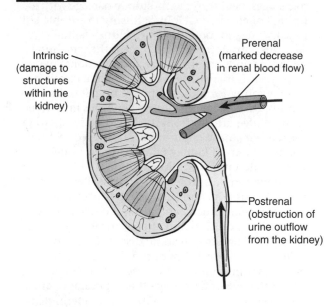

Intrinsic (damage to structures within the kidney)

Prerenal (marked decrease in renal blood flow)

Postrenal (obstruction of urine outflow from the kidney)

Activity C

1. b	**2.** j	**3.** d	**4.** g	**5.** a
6. e	**7.** h	**8.** i	**9.** f	**10.** c

Activity D

1. Acute tubular necrosis (ATN) is characterized by the destruction of tubular epithelial cells with acute suppression of renal function. ATN can be caused by a variety of conditions, including acute tubular damage due to ischemia, sepsis, nephrotoxic effects of drugs, tubular obstruction, and toxins from a massive infection. Tubular epithelial cells are particularly sensitive to ischemia and are vulnerable to toxins. The tubular injury that occurs in ATN frequently is reversible.

2. The onset or initiating phase, which lasts hours or days, is the time from the onset of the precipitating event until tubular injury occurs. The maintenance phase of ATN is characterized by a marked decrease in the glomerular filtration rate (GFR), causing sudden retention of endogenous metabolites, such as urea, potassium, sulfate, and creatinine that normally are cleared by the kidneys. Fluid retention gives rise to edema, water intoxication, and pulmonary congestion. If the period of oliguria is prolonged, hypertension frequently develops and, with it, signs of uremia. The recovery phase is the period during which repair of renal tissue takes place. Its onset usually is heralded by a gradual increase in urine output and a fall in serum creatinine, indicating that the nephrons have recovered to the point at which urine excretion is possible.

3. GFR is used to classify chronic kidney disease into five stages, beginning with kidney damage with normal or elevated GFR, progressing to chronic kidney disease and, potentially, to kidney failure.

4. As kidney structures are destroyed, the remaining nephrons undergo structural and functional hypertrophy, each increasing its function as a means of compensating for those that have been lost. In the process, each of the remaining nephrons must filter more solute particles from the blood. It is only when the few remaining nephrons are destroyed that the manifestations of kidney failure become evident.

5. The manifestations of CKD include an accumulation of nitrogenous wastes; alterations in water, electrolyte, and acid-base balance; mineral and skeletal disorders; anemia and coagulation disorders; hypertension and alterations in cardiovascular function; gastrointestinal disorders; neurologic complications; disorders of skin integrity; and disorders of immunologic function. The point at which these disorders make their appearance and the severity of the manifestations are determined largely by the extent of renal function that is present and the coexisting disease conditions.

6. The anemia of CKD is due to several factors including chronic blood loss, hemolysis, bone marrow suppression due to retained uremic factors, and decreased red cell production due to impaired production of erythropoietin and iron deficiency. The kidneys are the primary site for the production of the hormone erythropoietin, which controls red blood cell production. In renal failure, erythropoietin production usually is insufficient to stimulate adequate red blood cell production by the bone marrow.

7. People with CKD tend to have an increased prevalence of left ventricular dysfunction, with both depressed left ventricular ejection fraction, as in systolic dysfunction, and impaired ventricular filling, as in diastolic failure. Multiple factors lead to development of left ventricular dysfunction, including extracellular fluid overload, shunting of blood through an arteriovenous fistula for dialysis, and anemia. Coupled with the hypertension that often is present, they cause increased myocardial work and oxygen demand, with eventual development of heart failure. Congestive heart failure and pulmonary edema tend to occur in the late stages of kidney failure. Coexisting conditions that have been identified as contributing to the burden of cardiovascular disease include hypertension, anemia, diabetes mellitus, dyslipidemia, and coagulopathies. Anemia, in particular, has been correlated with the presence of left ventricular hypertrophy.

SECTION III: APPLYING YOUR KNOWLEDGE
Activity E

1. Description of the disease process; prognosis; manifestations of the disease, including physical growth and developmental delays; medication regimen, including side effects; and dietary restrictions including protein, caloric, sodium, and fluid restrictions.

2. Chronic kidney disease is a progressive disorder that can be slowed by adherence to dietary restrictions and medication regimen. The disorder usually progresses to the point where the child needs either hemodialysis or peritoneal dialysis or a kidney transplant. All forms of renal replacement therapy are considered safe in the pediatric population, and renal transplantation is considered the best treatment for a child.

SECTION IV: PRACTICING FOR NCLEX
Activity F

1. **Answer: a**
   RATIONALE: The most common indicator of acute renal failure is azotemia, an accumulation of nitrogenous wastes (urea nitrogen, uric acid, and creatinine) in the blood and a decrease in the GFR. The other answers are not common indicators of acute renal failure.

2. **Answers: a, c, d**
   RATIONALE: Ischemic ATN occurs most frequently in persons who have major surgery, severe hypovolemia, overwhelming sepsis, trauma, and burns. Hypervolemia and hypertension are not considered contributing factors to ischemic ATN.

3. **Answer: b**
   RATIONALE: In clinical practice, GFR is usually estimated using the serum creatinine concentration. The other answers are not used to estimate the GFR.

4. **Answer: c**
   RATIONALE: The number one hematologic disorder that accompanies CKD is anemia. The other answers are incorrect.

5. **Answers: a, b, c**
   RATIONALE: Uremic pericarditis resembles viral pericarditis in its presentation. This includes all potential complications, up to and including cardiac tamponade. The presenting signs include mild to severe chest pain with respiratory accentuation and a pericardial friction rub. Fever is variable in the absence of infection and is more common in dialysis than uremic pericarditis. Shortness of breath and thromboangiitis are not indicative of uremic pericarditis.

6. **Answer: d**
   RATIONALE: Restless legs syndrome is a manifestation of peripheral nerve involvement and can be seen in as many as two-thirds of patients on dialysis. The other answers are not correct.

7. **Answer: a**
   RATIONALE: Many persons with CKD fail to mount a fever with infection, making the diagnosis more difficult. All of the other answers occur.

8. **Answers: a, b, c**
   RATIONALE: The cause of sexual dysfunction in men and women with CKD is unclear. The cause probably is multifactorial and may result from high levels of uremic toxins, neuropathy, altered endocrine function, psychological factors, and medications (e.g., antihypertensive drugs). The other answers do not apply in this situation.

9. **Answer: b**
   RATIONALE: Access to the vascular system is accomplished through an external arteriovenous shunt (i.e., tubing implanted into an artery and a vein) or, more commonly, through an internal arteriovenous fistula (i.e., anastomosis of a vein to an artery, usually in the forearm). The other answers are incorrect.

10. **Answer: c**
    RATIONALE: At least 50% of the protein intake for clients with CKD should consist of proteins of high biologic value, such as those in eggs, lean meat, and milk, which are rich in essential amino acids. The other sources of protein contribute to high levels of nitrogen.

CHAPTER 27

SECTION II: ASSESSING YOUR UNDERSTANDING

Activity A

1. bladder
2. retroperitoneally, symphysis
3. prostate
4. ureters
5. epithelial lining
6. external sphincter
7. parasympathetic, sympathetic
8. sacral, pelvic nerve
9. pons
10. Cortical
11. β_2-adrenergic
12. α_1 receptors
13. obstruction, incontinence
14. prostate gland
15. store, empty
16. micturition reflex
17. stroke
18. Atony
19. Stress incontinence
20. neurogenic, myogenic
21. transitional
22. hematuria

Activity B

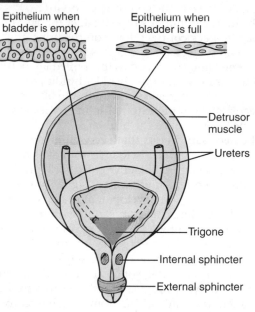

Epithelium when bladder is empty

Epithelium when bladder is full

Detrusor muscle

Ureters

Trigone

Internal sphincter

External sphincter

Activity C

1. i	2. f	3. a	4. d	5. j
6. g	7. b	8. e	9. h	10. c

Activity D

1. The bladder is composed of four layers. The first is an outer serosal layer, which covers the upper surface and is continuous with the peritoneum; the second is a network of smooth muscle fibers called the *detrusor muscle*; the third is a submucosal layer of loose connective tissue; and the fourth is an inner mucosal lining of transitional epithelium.

2. The pelvic nerve carries sensory fibers from the stretch receptors in the bladder wall; the pudendal nerve carries sensory fibers from the external sphincter and pelvic muscles; and the hypogastric nerve carries sensory fibers from the trigone area.

3. As bladder filling occurs, ascending spinal afferents relay this information to the micturition center, which also receives important descending information from the forebrain concerning behavioral cues for bladder emptying and urine storage. Descending pathways from the pontine micturition center produce coordinated inhibition or relaxation of the external sphincter. Cortical brain centers enable inhibition of the micturition center in the pons and conscious control of urination. Neural influences from the subcortical centers in the basal ganglia modulate the contractile response. They modify and delay the detrusor contractile response during filling

and then modulate the expulsive activity of the bladder to facilitate complete emptying.

4. The detrusor muscle of the bladder fundus and bladder neck contract down on the urine; the ureteral orifices are forced shut; the bladder neck is widened and shortened as it is pulled up by the globular muscles in the bladder fundus; the resistance of the internal sphincter in the bladder neck is decreased; and the external sphincter relaxes as urine moves out of the bladder.

5. The necessary factors that every child must possess in order to attain conscious control of bladder function are (1) normal bladder growth, (2) myelination of the ascending afferents that signal awareness of bladder filling, (3) development of cortical control and descending communication with the sacral micturition center, (4) ability to consciously tighten the external sphincter to prevent incontinence, (5) and motivation of the child to stay dry.

6. During the early stage of obstruction, the bladder begins to hypertrophy and becomes hypersensitive to afferent stimuli arising from stretch receptors in the bladder wall. The ability to suppress urination is diminished, and bladder contraction can become so strong that it virtually produces bladder spasm. There is further hypertrophy of the bladder muscle, the thickness of the bladder wall may double, and the pressure generated by detrusor contraction will increase to overcome the resistance from the obstruction. As the force needed to expel urine from the bladder increases, compensatory mechanisms may become ineffective, causing muscle fatigue before complete emptying can be accomplished. The inner smooth surface of the bladder is replaced with coarsely woven structures called *trabeculae*. Small pockets of mucosal tissue commonly develop between the trabecular ridges. These pockets form diverticula, making the patient more susceptible to secondary infections. Along with hypertrophy of the bladder wall, there is hypertrophy of the trigone area and the interureteric ridge, which is located between the two ureters. This causes backpressure on the ureters, the development of hydroureters and eventually, kidney damage.

7. The angle between the bladder and the posterior proximal urethra normally is 90 to 100 degrees, with at least one-third of the bladder base contributing to the angle when not voiding. During the first stage of voiding, this angle is lost as the bladder descends. In women, diminution of muscle tone associated with childbirth can cause weakness of the pelvic floor muscles and result in stress incontinence by obliterating the critical posterior urethrovesical angle. In these women, loss of the posterior urethrovesical angle, descent and fun-

neling of the bladder neck, and backward and downward rotation of the bladder occur, so that the bladder and urethra are already in an anatomic position for the first stage of voiding. Any activity that causes downward pressure on the bladder is sufficient to allow the urine to escape involuntarily.

8. The neurogenic theory for overactive bladder postulates that the CNS functions as an on-off switching circuit for voluntary control of bladder function. Therefore, damage to the CNS inhibitory pathways may trigger bladder overactivity owing to uncontrolled voiding reflexes. Neurogenic causes of overactive bladder include stroke, Parkinson disease, and multiple sclerosis.

9. The overall capacity of the bladder is reduced, as is the urethral closing pressure. Detrusor muscle function also tends to decline with aging; thus, there is a trend toward a reduction in the strength of bladder contraction and impairment in emptying that leads to larger postvoid residual volumes.

SECTION III: APPLYING YOUR KNOWLEDGE

Activity E

1. In people who have multiple sclerosis, the demyelination of the nerves can cause an interruption in the messages from the brain and the spinal cord in reaching the bladder. This causes a condition known as a neurogenic bladder.

2. The nurse would expect the client to be given an antimuscarinic drug, such as oxybutynin, tolterodine, or propantheline, to decrease detrusor muscle tone and increase bladder capacity.

SECTION IV: PRACTICING FOR NCLEX

Activity F

1. **Answers: a, c, e**
   RATIONALE: Disruption of pontine control of micturition, as in spinal cord injury, results in uninhibited spinal reflex-controlled contraction of the bladder without relaxation of the external sphincter, a condition known as *detrusor-sphincter dyssynergia*. The other answers are not true.

2. **Answer: a**
   RATIONALE: As the child grows, the bladder gradually enlarges, with an increase in capacity, in ounces, that approximates the age of the child plus 2. The other answers are not true.

3. **Answer: b**
   RATIONALE: Sphincter EMG allows the activity of the striated (voluntary) muscles of the perineal area to be studied. Cystometry measures the ability of the bladder to store urine as well as the pressure of the bladder during filling and emptying. Uroflowmetry measures the flow rate during urination.

4. Answer: b

RATIONALE: During the early stage of obstruction, the bladder begins to hypertrophy and becomes hypersensitive to afferent stimuli arising from stretch receptors in the bladder wall. The ability to suppress urination is diminished, and bladder contraction can become so strong that it virtually produces bladder spasm. There is urgency, sometimes to the point of incontinence, and frequency during the day and at night. The other answers are wrong.

5. Answer: c

RATIONALE: The most common causes of spastic bladder dysfunction are spinal cord lesions such as spinal cord injury, herniated intervertebral disk, vascular lesions, tumors, and myelitis. The other answers are wrong.

6. Answer: d

RATIONALE: With acute overdistention of the bladder, usually no more than 1,000 mL of urine is removed from the bladder at one time. The other answers are incorrect.

7. Answer: a

RATIONALE: In women, the angle between the bladder and the posterior proximal urethra (i.e., urethrovesical junction) is important to continence. This angle normally is 90 to 100 degrees. The other answers are incorrect.

8. Answers: b, c, e

RATIONALE: Among the transient causes of urinary incontinence are recurrent urinary tract infections, medications that alter bladder function or perception of bladder filling and the need to urinate, diuretics and conditions that increase bladder filling, stool impaction, restricted mobility, and confusional states. The other answers are not associated with transient urinary incontinence.

9. Answer: b

RATIONALE: Habit training with regularly scheduled toileting—usually every 2 to 4 hours—often is effective. The other answers are incorrect.

10. Answer: c

RATIONALE: The intervesicular administration of bacillus Calmette-Guérin (BCG) vaccine, made from a strain of *Mycobacterium bovis* that formerly was used to protect against tuberculosis, causes a significant reduction in the rate of relapse and prolongs relapse-free interval in persons with cancer in situ. The other drugs are used to treat bladder cancer, but not cancer in situ.

CHAPTER 28

SECTION II: ASSESSING YOUR UNDERSTANDING

Activity A

1. gastrointestinal (GI) system
2. pharyngoesophageal
3. gastroesophageal
4. stomach
5. duodenum, jejunum, ileum
6. jejunum
7. epithelial, mucus
8. Serous
9. mesentery
10. pacemaker
11. enteric
12. Mechanoreceptors, chemoreceptors
13. vagovagal
14. oral, pharyngeal, esophageal
15. small intestine
16. Defecation
17. hormones
18. gastrin
19. Ghrelin
20. Cholecystokinin
21. parietal, vitamin B_{12}
22. pepsinogen
23. gastrin
24. Brunner glands
25. bacteria
26. indigestible dietary residue
27. Digestion
28. Absorption
29. enterocytes
30. brush border enzymes
31. lipase
32. Anorexia
33. Nausea
34. Vomiting

Activity B

1.

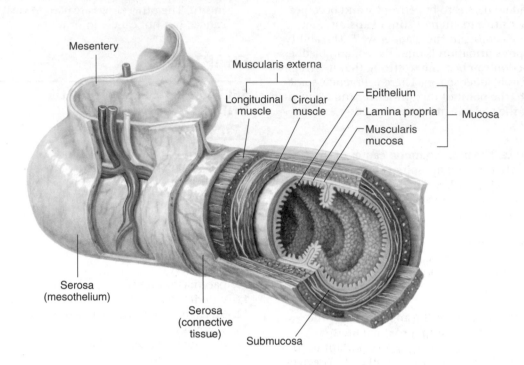

2.

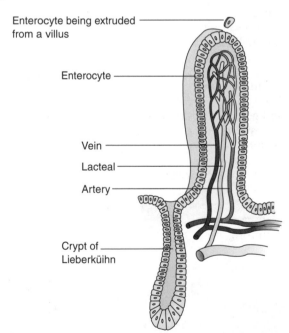

Activity C

1. c	**2.** d	**3.** b	**4.** f	**5.** e
6. i	**7.** h	**8.** d	**9.** a	**10.** j

Activity D

1. The upper part—the mouth, esophagus, and stomach—acts as an intake source and receptacle through which food passes and in which initial digestive processes take place. The middle portion—the duodenum, jejunum, and ileum—is the place where most digestive and absorptive processes occur. The lower segment—the cecum, colon, and rectum—serves as a storage channel for the efficient elimination of waste.

2. The emptying of the stomach is regulated by hormonal and neural mechanisms. The hormones cholecystokinin and glucose-dependent insulinotropic polypeptide are thought to partly control gastric emptying, which are released in response to the pH and the osmolar and fatty acid composition of the chyme. Afferent receptor fibers synapse with the neurons in the intramural plexus or trigger intrinsic reflexes by means of vagal or sympathetic pathways that participate in extrinsic reflexes.

3. With segmentation waves, slow contractions of the circular muscle layer occlude the lumen and drive the contents forward and backward. Most of the contractions that produce segmentation waves are local events involving only 1 to 4 cm of intestine at a time. They function mainly to mix the chyme with the digestive enzymes from the pancreas and to ensure adequate exposure of all parts of the

chyme to the mucosal surface of the intestine, where absorption takes place. Peristaltic movements are rhythmic propulsive movements designed to propel the chyme along the small intestine toward the large intestine.

4. The incretin effect is the increase in insulin release after an oral glucose load. The two hormones that account for about 90% of the incretin effect are GLP-1, which is released from L cells in the distal small bowel, and GIP, which is released by K cells in the upper gut (mainly the jejunum). Because increased levels of GLP-1 and GIP can lower blood glucose levels by augmenting insulin release in a glucose-dependent manner (i.e., at low blood glucose levels no further insulin is secreted, minimizing the risk of hypoglycemia), these hormones have been targeted as possible antidiabetic drugs. Moreover, GLP-1 can exert other metabolically beneficial effects, including suppression of glucagon release, slowing of gastric emptying, augmenting of net glucose clearance, and decreasing appetite and body weight.

5. The first function of saliva is protection and lubrication. Saliva is rich in mucus, which protects the oral mucosa and coats the food as it passes through the mouth, pharynx, and esophagus. The sublingual and buccal glands produce only mucus-type secretions. The second function of saliva is its protective antimicrobial action. The saliva cleans the mouth and contains the enzyme lysozyme, which has an antibacterial action. Third, saliva contains ptyalin and amylase, which initiate the digestion of dietary starches.

6. The cellular mechanism for hydrochloric acid (HCl) secretion by the parietal cells in the stomach involves the hydrogen (H^+)/potassium (K^+) adenosine triphosphatase (ATPase) transporter and chloride (Cl^-) channels located on their luminal membrane. During the process of HCl secretion, carbon dioxide (CO_2) produced by aerobic metabolism combines with water (H_2O), catalyzed by carbonic anhydrase, to form carbonic acid (H_2CO_3), which dissociates into H^+ and bicarbonate (HCO_3^-). The H^+ is secreted with Cl^- into the stomach, and the HCO_3^- moves out of the cell and into blood from the basolateral membrane. At the luminal side of the membrane, H^+ is secreted into the stomach via the H^+-K^+ ATPase transporter and chloride follows H^+ into the stomach by diffusing through Cl^- channels in the luminal membrane.

7. Digestion of starch begins in the mouth with the action of amylase. Pancreatic secretions also contain an amylase. Amylase breaks down starch into several disaccharides, including maltose, isomaltose, and α-dextrins. The brush border enzymes convert the disaccharides into monosaccharides that can be absorbed.

8. Protein digestion begins in the stomach with the action of pepsin. Proteins are broken down further by pancreatic enzymes, such as trypsin, chymotrypsin, carboxypeptidase, and elastase. The pancreatic enzymes are secreted as precursor molecules. Trypsinogen, which lacks enzymatic activity, is activated by an enzyme located on the brush border cells of the duodenal enterocytes. Activated trypsin activates additional trypsinogen molecules and other pancreatic precursor proteolytic enzymes. The amino acids are liberated on the surface of the mucosal surface of the intestine by brush border enzymes that degrade proteins into peptides that are one, two, or three amino acids long. Similar to glucose, many amino acids are transported across the mucosal membrane in a sodium-linked process that uses ATP as an energy source. Some amino acids are absorbed by facilitated diffusion processes that do not require sodium.

SECTION III: APPLYING YOUR KNOWLEDGE

Activity E

1. The gastrointestinal tract is the largest endocrine gland in the body. Many nerves make the GI tract work. The stomach begins digestion by kneading and churning the food we eat. Food then progresses to the small intestine, where most of the food is digested and absorbed. Our food then goes into the large intestine, where it is compacted into the feces that we expel from our bodies.

SECTION IV: PRACTICING FOR NCLEX

Activity F

1. **Answer: a**
   RATIONALE: At the end of the pyloric channel, the circular layer smooth muscle thickens to form the pyloric sphincter. This muscle serves as a valve that controls the rate of stomach emptying and prevents the regurgitation of intestinal contents back into the stomach. There is no cardiac sphincter in the GI tract. The antrum is a portion of the stomach that is the wider, upper portion of the pyloric region. The cardiac orifice is the opening between the esophagus and the stomach.

2. **Answer: b**
   RATIONALE: It is in the jejunum and ileum that food is digested and absorbed. The other answers are incorrect.

3. **Answer: c**
   RATIONALE: No contraction can occur without an action potential and an action potential cannot occur unless the slow wave brings the membrane potential to threshold. The other answers are incorrect.

4. **Answer: d**
   RATIONALE: The external sphincter is controlled by nerve fibers in the pudendal nerve, which is part of the somatic nervous system and therefore under voluntary control. The other answers are incorrect.

5. **Answer: a**
   RATIONALE: Ghrelin is a newly discovered peptide hormone produced by endocrine cells in the

mucosal layer of the fundus of the stomach. It displays potent growth hormone-releasing activity and has a stimulatory effect on food intake and digestive function, while reducing energy expenditure. The isolation of this hormone has led to new insights into the gut-brain regulation of growth hormone secretion and energy balance. The other hormones are secreted elsewhere in the GI tract.

6. **Answers: a, b, c, d**
   RATIONALE: Saliva has three functions. The first is protection and lubrication. Saliva is rich in mucus, which protects the oral mucosa and coats the food as it passes through the mouth, pharynx, and esophagus. The second function of saliva is its protective antimicrobial action. Third, saliva contains ptyalin and amylase, which initiate the digestion of dietary starches. The other answer is incorrect.

7. **Answer: b**
   RATIONALE: The major metabolic function of colonic microflora is the fermentation of undigestible dietary residue and endogenous mucus produced by the epithelial cells. The other answers are not their main function.

8. **Answer: c**
   RATIONALE: Absorption is accomplished by active transport and diffusion. The other answers are incorrect.

9. **Answer: d**
   RATIONALE: A common cause of nausea is distention of the duodenum or upper small intestinal tract. The other answers are not associated with nausea.

10. **Answer: d**
    RATIONALE: Serotonin is believed to be involved in the nausea and emesis associated with cancer chemotherapy and radiation therapy. Serotonin antagonists (e.g., granisetron and ondansetron) are effective in treating the nausea and vomiting associated with these stimuli. The other answers are incorrect.

CHAPTER 29

SECTION II: ASSESSING YOUR UNDERSTANDING

Activity A
1. esophagus
2. Congenital
3. Dysphagia
4. Hiatal hernia
5. GERD
6. asthma
7. Reflux esophagitis
8. infant
9. alcohol, tobacco
10. impermeable
11. prostaglandins
12. Gastritis

13. Acute gastritis
14. Chronic gastritis
15. autoantibodies
16. *Peptic ulcer*
17. hemorrhage, obstruction
18. bleeding ulcers
19. Histamine
20. stress ulcers
21. carcinoma
22. Irritable bowel syndrome
23. Crohn, ulcerative colitis
24. Crohn
25. colon, rectum
26. Nutritional
27. Lieberkühn
28. Cancer
29. bacterial enterocolitis
30. Diverticulosis
31. Diverticulitis
32. appendicitis
33. diarrhea
34. noninflammatory diarrhea
35. Chronic
36. Inflammatory diarrhea
37. Constipation
38. Fecal impaction
39. cephalocaudal
40. Paralytic
41. serous membrane
42. gluten
43. Colonoscopy

Activity B
1.

| 1. g | 2. f | 3. a | 4. e | 5. j |
| 6. h | 7. d | 8. i | 9. c | 10. b |

2.

| 1. c | 2. g | 3. a | 4. b | 5. e |
| 6. j | 7. d | 8. f | 9. i | 10. h |

Activity C
1. GERD is gastroesophageal reflux disease. It is thought to be associated with a weak or incompetent lower esophageal sphincter that allows reflux to occur, the irritant effects of the refluxate, and decreased clearance of the refluxed acid from the esophagus after it has occurred. In most cases, reflux occurs during transient relaxation of the esophagus. Gastric distention and meals high in fat increase the frequency of relaxation. Delayed gastric emptying also may contribute to reflux by increasing gastric volume and pressure with greater chance for reflux. Esophageal mucosal injury is related to the destructive nature of the refluxate and the amount of time it is in contact with mucosa. Acidic gastric fluids (pH <4.0) are particularly damaging.

2. Several factors contribute to the protection of the gastric mucosa, including an impermeable epithelial cell surface covering, mechanisms for the selective transport of hydrogen and bicarbonate ions, and the

characteristics of gastric mucus. The gastric epithelial cells are connected by tight junctions that prevent acid penetration, and they are covered with an impermeable hydrophobic lipid layer that prevents diffusion of ionized water-soluble molecules. The secretion of hydrochloric acid by the parietal cells of the stomach is accompanied by secretion of bicarbonate ions (HCO_3^-). For every hydrogen ion (H^+) that is secreted, an HCO_3^- is produced, and as long as HCO_3^- production is equal to H^+ secretion, mucosal injury does not occur. Water-insoluble mucus forms a thin, stable gel that adheres to the gastric mucosal surface and provides protection from the proteolytic (protein-digesting) actions of pepsin. It also forms an unstirred layer that traps bicarbonate, forming an alkaline interface between the luminal contents of the stomach and its mucosal surface. The water-soluble mucus is washed from the mucosal surface and mixes with the luminal contents; its viscid nature makes it a lubricant that prevents mechanical damage to the mucosal surface.

3. A peptic ulcer can affect one or all layers of the stomach or duodenum. The ulcer may penetrate only the mucosal surface, or it may extend into the smooth muscle layers. Occasionally, an ulcer penetrates the outer wall of the stomach or duodenum. Spontaneous remissions and exacerbations are common. Healing of the muscularis layer involves replacement with scar tissue; although the mucosal layers that cover the scarred muscle layer regenerate, the regeneration often is less than perfect, which contributes to repeated episodes of ulceration.

4. Chronic infection with *H. pylori* appears to serve as a cofactor in some types of gastric carcinomas. The bacterial infection causes gastritis, followed by atrophy, intestinal metaplasia, and carcinoma. This sequence of cellular events depends on both the presence of the bacterial proteins and the host immune response; the latter being influenced by the host genetic background. However, most people with *H. pylori* infection will not develop gastric cancer, and not all *H. pylori* infections increase the risk of gastric cancer, suggesting that other factors must be involved.

5. The condition is believed to result from deregulation of intestinal motor and sensory functions modulated by the CNS. Irritable bowel disease is characterized by persistent or recurrent symptoms of abdominal pain, altered bowel function, and varying complaints of flatulence, bloatedness, nausea and anorexia, constipation or diarrhea, and anxiety or depression. A hallmark of irritable bowel syndrome is abdominal pain that is relieved by defecation and associated with a change in consistency or frequency of stools. Abdominal pain usually is intermittent, cramping, and in the lower abdomen.

6. According to the currently accepted hypothesis, this normal state of homeostasis is disrupted in inflammatory bowel disease leading to unregulated and exaggerated immune responses against bacteria in the normal intestinal flora of genetically susceptible individuals. Thus, as in many other autoimmune disorders, the pathogenesis of Crohn disease and ulcerative colitis involves a failure of immune regulation, genetic predisposition, and an environmental trigger, especially microbial flora.

7. In a manner similar to the small intestine, bands of circular muscle constrict the large intestine. As the circular muscle contracts at each of these points (approximately every 2.5 cm), the lumen of the bowel becomes constricted, so that it is almost occluded. The combined contraction of the circular muscle and the lack of a continuous longitudinal muscle layer cause the intestine to bulge outward into pouches called *haustra*. Diverticula develop between the longitudinal muscle bands of the haustra, in the area where the blood vessels pierce the circular muscle layer to bring blood to the mucosal layer. An increase in intraluminal pressure in the haustra provides the force for creating these herniations. The increase in pressure is thought to be related to the volume of the colonic contents. The scantier the contents, the more vigorous are the contractions and the greater is the pressure in the haustra.

8. The pathophysiology of constipation can be classified into three broad categories: normal-transit constipation, slow-transit constipation, and disorders of defecatory or rectal evacuation. Normal-transit constipation (or functional constipation) is characterized by perceived difficulty in defecation and usually responds to increased fluid and fiber intake. Slow-transit constipation, which is characterized by infrequent bowel movements, is often caused by alterations in intestinal innervation. Hirschsprung disease is an extreme form of slow-transit constipation in which the ganglion cells in the distal bowel are absent because of a defect that occurred during embryonic development; the bowel narrows at the area that lack ganglionic cells. Although most persons with this disorder present in infancy or early childhood, some with a relatively short segment of involved colon do not have symptoms until later in life. Defecatory disorders are most commonly due to dysfunction of the pelvic floor or anal sphincter.

9. The cause of colon cancer is unknown, but attention has focused on dietary fat intake, refined sugar intake, fiber intake, and the adequacy of such protective micronutrients as vitamins A, C, and E in the diet. It has been hypothesized that a high level of fat in the diet increases the synthesis of bile acids in the liver, which may be converted to potential carcinogens by the bacterial flora in the colon. Bacterial organisms in particular are suspected of converting bile acids to carcinogens; their proliferation is enhanced by a high dietary level of refined sugars. Dietary fiber is thought to increase stool bulk and thereby dilute and remove potential carcinogens. Refined diets often contain reduced amounts of vitamins A, C, and E, which may act as oxygen free radical scavengers.

SECTION III: APPLYING YOUR KNOWLEDGE

Activity D

1. The doctor wants to try giving you the chemotherapy medicine to try to reduce the size of your tumor so the surgery will not be as extensive as it would be if the surgery were done today.
2. Even though your cancer has already spread, removing the tumor in your esophagus will make you more comfortable and, hopefully, allow you to live longer than you would without the surgery.

SECTION IV: PRACTICING FOR NCLEX

Activity E

1. **Answer: b**
   RATIONALE: Esophageal acid clearance can be retarded in cases of severe erosive esophagitis where gastroesophageal reflux and a large hiatal hernia coexist. The other answers are incorrect.

2. **Answer: c**
   RATIONALE: Tilting of the head to one side and arching of the back may be noted in children with severe reflux. Early satiety is another indication of gastroesophageal reflux, but not coupled with consolable crying. The other answers are not correct.

3. **Answers: a, c, e**
   RATIONALE: The stomach lining usually is impermeable to the acid it secretes, a property that allows the stomach to contain acid and pepsin without having its wall digested. Several factors contribute to the protection of the gastric mucosa, including an impermeable epithelial cell surface covering, mechanisms for the selective transport of hydrogen and bicarbonate ions, and the characteristics of gastric mucus. These mechanisms are collectively referred to as the *gastric mucosal barrier*. The other answers are incorrect.

4. **Answer: d**
   RATIONALE: *Helicobacter pylori* gastritis can be a chronic infection that can lead to gastric atrophy, peptic ulcer, and is associated with increased risk of gastric adenocarcinoma and low-grade B-cell gastric lymphoma (mucosa-associated lymphoid tissue [MALToma]). The other answers are incorrect.

5. **Answer: a**
   RATIONALE: Diagnostic procedures for peptic ulcer include history taking, laboratory tests, radiologic imaging, and endoscopic examination. The other answers are not expected orders for a suspected peptic ulcer.

6. **Answers: a, c**
   RATIONALE: Diagnosis of gastric cancer is accomplished by means of a variety of techniques, including barium radiographic studies, endoscopic studies with biopsy, and cytologic studies (e.g., Papanicolaou smear) of gastric secretions. Cytologic studies can prove particularly useful as routine screening tests for persons with atrophic gastritis or gastric polyps. Computed tomography and endoscopic ultrasonography often are used to delineate the spread of a diagnosed stomach cancer. Papanicolaou smears are done on gastric secretions but not by the nurse. A lower gastrointestinal study would be of no value in diagnosing this client. A technician does not do an endoscopic ultrasound.

7. **Answer: b**
   RATIONALE: A hallmark of irritable bowel syndrome is abdominal pain that is relieved by defecation and associated with a change in consistency or frequency of stools. Nausea, altered bowel function, and diarrhea are also symptoms of irritable bowel syndrome but not combined with abdominal pain that is unrelieved by defecation. A bowel impaction is not a symptom of irritable bowel syndrome.

8. **Answer: c**
   RATIONALE: A characteristic feature of Crohn disease is the sharply demarcated, granulomatous lesions that are surrounded by normal-appearing mucosal tissue. When the lesions are multiple, they often are referred to as *skip lesions* because they are interspersed between what appear to be normal segments of the bowel.

9. **Answer: d**
   RATIONALE: Rotavirus infection typically begins after an incubation period of less than 24 hours, with mild to moderate fever, and vomiting, followed by onset of frequent watery, stools. The fever and vomiting usually disappear on about the second day, but the diarrhea continues for 5 to 7 days. Dehydration may develop rapidly, particularly in infants. The other answers are incorrect.

10. **Answer: a**
    RATIONALE: One of the most common complaints of diverticulitis is pain in the lower left quadrant, accompanied by nausea and vomiting, tenderness in the lower left quadrant, a slight fever, and an elevated white blood cell count. Both B and D describe a suspected appendicitis, and C describes symptoms of a peptic ulcer.

11. **Answers: b, c, d**
    RATIONALE: Noninflammatory diarrhea is associated with large-volume watery and nonbloody stools, periumbilical cramps, bloating, and nausea and/or vomiting. The other answers are incorrect.

12. **Answer: b**
    RATIONALE: One of the most important manifestations of peritonitis is the translocation of extracellular fluid into the peritoneal cavity (through weeping or serous fluid from the inflamed peritoneum) and into the bowel as a result of bowel obstruction. The other answers are incorrect.

13. **Answer: c**
    RATIONALE: The primary treatment of celiac disease consists of removal of gluten and related proteins from the diet. No other answer is correct.

14. Answer: d
   RATIONALE: To reduce the likelihood of false-
   positive tests, persons are instructed to avoid nonsteroidal anti-inflammatory drugs such as
   ibuprofen and aspirin for 7 days prior to testing, to
   avoid vitamin C in excess of 250 mg from either
   supplements or citrus fruits for 3 before testing,
   and to avoid red meats for 3 days before testing.
   The other answers are incorrect.

CHAPTER 30

SECTION II: ASSESSING YOUR UNDERSTANDING

Activity A

1. accessory
2. artery, portal vein
3. hepatic portal vein
4. bile
5. albumin
6. cholesterol, bile
7. fat
8. triglycerides
9. emulsifying, micelles
10. Cholestasis
11. bile
12. Hemolytic
13. Conjugation
14. Phase 1 reactions
15. CYP or cytochrome P450 gene
16. Phase 2 reactions
17. toxic metabolites
18. Cholestatic
19. Hepatitis
20. injection drug, blood transfusions, high-risk sexual behavior
21. Autoimmune
22. Intrahepatic
23. Secondary
24. fatty
25. Cirrhosis
26. Portal hypertension
27. increased, dilatation
28. Ascites
29. Spontaneous bacterial peritonitis
30. hepatorenal
31. encephalopathy
32. liver cancer
33. gallbladder
34. Cholecystokinin
35. cholesterol, bilirubin
36. cholecystitis
37. exocrine
38. pancreatitis
39. Chronic pancreatitis
40. cigarette smoking

Activity B

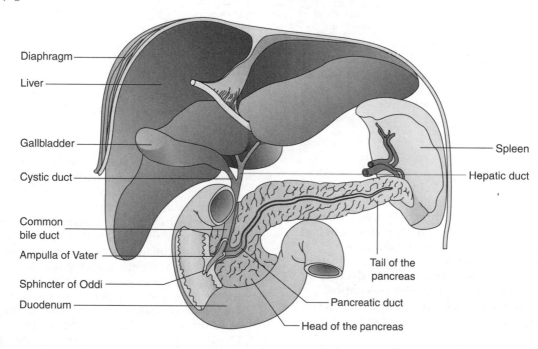

Activity C

1.

1. c	**2.** f	**3.** h	**4.** b	**5.** e
6. g	**7.** a	**8.** d	**9.** i	**10.** j

2.

1. d	**2.** c	**3.** e	**4.** a	**5.** b

Activity D

1.

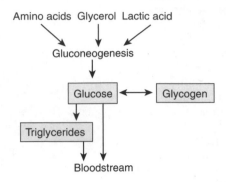

2.

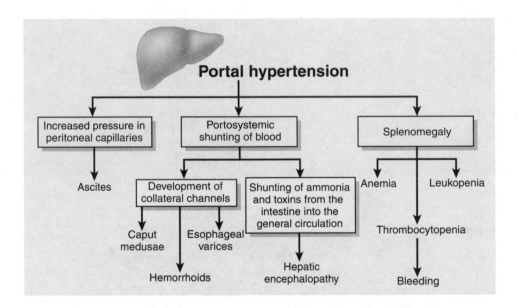

Activity E

1. The liver is one of the most versatile and active organs in the body. It produces bile; metabolizes hormones and drugs; synthesizes proteins, glucose, and clotting factors; stores vitamins and minerals; changes ammonia produced by deamination of amino acids to urea; and converts fatty acids to ketones. The liver degrades excess nutrients and converts them into substances essential to the body. In its capacity for metabolizing drugs and hormones, the liver serves as an excretory organ.

2. A number of mechanisms are implicated in the pathogenesis of cholestasis. Primary biliary cirrhosis and primary sclerosing cholangitis are caused by disorders of the small intrahepatic canaliculi and bile ducts. In the case of extrahepatic obstruction, such as that caused by conditions such as cholelithiasis, common duct strictures, or obstructing

neoplasms, the effects begin with increased pressure in the large bile ducts. Genetic disorders involving the transport of bile into the canaliculi also can result in cholestasis.

3. The four major causes of jaundice are excessive destruction of red blood cells, impaired uptake of bilirubin by the liver cells, decreased conjugation of bilirubin, and obstruction of bile flow in the canaliculi of the hepatic lobules or in the intrahepatic or extrahepatic bile ducts. From an anatomic standpoint, jaundice can be categorized as prehepatic, intrahepatic, and posthepatic.

4. Elevated serum enzyme tests usually indicate liver injury earlier than other indicators of liver function. The key enzymes are alanine aminotransferase (ALT) and aspartate aminotransferase (AST), which are present in liver cells. Alanine aminotransferase is liver specific, whereas AST is derived from organs other than the liver. In most cases of liver damage, there are parallel rises in ALT and AST. The most dramatic rise is seen in cases of acute hepatocellular injury.

5. The clinical course of viral hepatitis involves a number of syndromes, including asymptomatic infection with only serologic evidence of disease, acute hepatitis, the carrier state without clinically apparent disease or with chronic hepatitis, chronic hepatitis with or without progression to cirrhosis, with rapid onset of liver failure. Not all hepatotoxic viruses provoke each of the clinical syndromes.

6. The metabolic end products of alcohol metabolism (e.g., acetaldehyde, free radicals) are responsible for a variety of metabolic alterations that can cause liver injury. Acetaldehyde, for example, has multiple toxic effects on liver cells and liver function. The metabolism of alcohol leads to chemical attack on certain membranes of the liver. Acetaldehyde is known to impede the mitochondrial electron transport system, which is responsible for oxidative metabolism and generation of ATP; as a result, the hydrogen ions that are generated in the mitochondria are shunted into lipid synthesis and ketogenesis. Binding of acetaldehyde to other molecules impairs the detoxification of free radicals and synthesis of proteins. Acetaldehyde also promotes collagen synthesis and fibrogenesis.

7. Fatty liver is characterized by the accumulation of fat in hepatocytes, a condition called *steatosis*. The liver becomes yellow, enlarges owing to excessive fat accumulation, and is characterized by inflammation and necrosis of liver cells. Alcoholic hepatitis is the intermediate stage between fatty changes and cirrhosis. It often is seen after an abrupt increase in alcohol intake and is common in "spree" drinkers. Alcoholic cirrhosis is the result of repeated bouts of drinking-related liver injury and designates the onset of end-stage alcoholic liver disease. The gross appearance of the early cirrhotic liver is one of fine, uniform nodules on its surface.

8. Cirrhosis is characterized by diffuse fibrosis and conversion of normal liver architecture into nodules containing proliferating hepatocytes encircled by fibrosis. The formation of nodules represents a balance between regenerative activity and constrictive scarring. The fibrous tissue that replaces normally functioning liver tissue forms constrictive bands that disrupt flow in the vascular channels and biliary duct systems of the liver. The disruption of vascular channels predisposes to portal hypertension and its complications; obstruction of biliary channels and exposure to the destructive effects of bile stasis; and loss of liver cells, leading to liver failure.

9. An increase in capillary pressure due to portal hypertension and obstruction of venous flow through the liver, salt and water retention by the kidney, and decreased colloidal osmotic pressure due to impaired synthesis of albumin by the liver lead to the development of ascites. Diminished blood volume (i.e., underfill theory) and excessive blood volume (i.e., overfill theory) have been used to explain the increased salt and water retention by the kidney.

10. With the gradual obstruction of venous blood flow in the liver, the pressure in the portal vein increases, and large collateral channels develop between the portal and systemic veins that supply the lower rectum. The dilation of the collaterals between the inferior and internal iliac veins may give rise to hemorrhoids.

SECTION III: APPLYING YOUR KNOWLEDGE

Activity F

1. Serum aminotransferase, liver biopsy, complete blood count, and complete metabolic panel.
2. Interferons, nucleotide and nucleotide analog antiretroviral agents, and pegylated interferon alfa-2a.

SECTION IV: PRACTICING FOR NCLEX

Activity G

1. **Answer: a**
   RATIONALE: Kupffer cells are reticuloendothelial cells that are capable of removing and phagocytizing old and defective blood cells, bacteria, and other foreign material from the portal blood as it flows through the sinusoid. Langerhans cells are stellate dendritic cells found mostly in the stratum spinosum of the epidermis. Epstein cells do not exist. Davidoff cells are large granular epithelial cells found in intestinal glands.

2. **Answer: b**
   RATIONALE: The morphologic features of cholestasis depend on the underlying cause. Common to all types of obstructive and hepatocellular cholestasis is the accumulation of bile pigment in the liver. The other answers are incorrect.

3. **Answer: c**
   RATIONALE: Usually, only a small amount of bilirubin is found in the blood; the normal level of total serum bilirubin is 0.1 to 1.2 mg/dL. The other answers are incorrect.

4. **Answer: d**
   RATIONALE: Because of the greater activity of the drug-metabolizing enzymes in the central zones of the liver, these agents typically cause centrilobular necrosis. The other answers are incorrect.

5. **Answer: a**
   RATIONALE: The earliest symptoms are unexplained pruritus or itching, weight loss, and fatigue, followed by dark urine and pale stools. The other answers are not indicative of primary biliary cirrhosis.

6. **Answer: b**
   RATIONALE: When the capacity of the liver to export triglyceride is saturated, excess fatty acids contribute to the formation of fatty liver.

7. **Answer: c**
RATIONALE: Because of the many limitations in sodium restriction, the use of diuretics has become the mainstay of treatment for ascites. A paracentesis may be done if the diuretics do not correct the problem. A thoracentesis would never be done for ascites. DDAVP is given to decrease urine output, not increase it.

8. **Answer: d**
RATIONALE: Diagnostic methods include ultrasound, CT scans, and MRI. Liver biopsy may be used to confirm the diagnosis. The serum α-fetoprotein can be indicative of liver cancer but it is not confirmatory. An endoscopy is of no value. An ultrasound of the liver is not confirmatory for liver cancer.

9. **Answer: a**
RATIONALE: Gallbladder sludge (thickened gallbladder mucoprotein with tiny trapped cholesterol crystals) is thought to be a precursor of gallstones. The other answers are incorrect.

10. **Answer: b**
RATIONALE: Serum amylase and lipase are the laboratory markers most commonly used to establish a diagnosis of acute pancreatitis. Cholesterol and triglycerides are not used as laboratory markers for acute pancreatitis.

11. **Answer: c**
RATIONALE: In pancreatic cancer, the most significant and reproducible environmental risk factor is cigarette smoking. The other answers are incorrect.

CHAPTER 31

SECTION II: ASSESSING YOUR UNDERSTANDING

Activity A

1. hormones
2. nervous, immune
3. paracrine
4. autocrine
5. free, bound
6. high-affinity receptors
7. receptors
8. Lipid-soluble
9. hypothalamus
10. master gland
11. metabolites, hormone levels

Activity B

1. c   2. a   3. e   4. d   5. b
6. f   7. g

Activity C

1. Hormones generally are thought of as chemical messengers that are transported in body fluids. They are highly specialized organic molecules produced by endocrine organs that exert their action on specific target cells. Hormones do not initiate reactions but function as modulators of cellular and systemic responses. Most hormones are present in body fluids at all times, but in greater or lesser amounts depending on the needs of the body.

2. Hormones are divided into three categories: (1) amines and amino acids; (2) peptides, polypeptides, proteins, and glycoproteins; and (3) steroids. The first category, the amines, includes norepinephrine and epinephrine, which are derived from a single amino acid, and the thyroid hormones, which are derived from two iodinated tyrosine amino acid residues. The second category, the peptides, polypeptides, proteins, and glycoproteins, can be as small as only to contain three amino acids, and as large and complex to consist of approximately 200 amino acids. The third category consists of the steroid hormones, which are derivatives of cholesterol.

3. The response of a target cell to a hormone varies with the number of receptors present and with the affinity of these receptors for hormone binding. The number of hormone receptors on a cell may be altered for any of several reasons. Antibodies may destroy or block the receptor proteins. Increased or decreased hormone levels often induce changes in the activity of the genes that regulate receptor synthesis. For example, decreased hormone levels often produce an increase in receptor numbers by means of a process called *up-regulation*; this increases the sensitivity of the body to existing hormone levels. Likewise, sustained levels of excess hormone often bring about a decrease in receptor numbers by down-regulation, producing a decrease in hormone sensitivity.

4. The intracellular signal system is termed the *second messenger*, and the hormone is considered the first messenger. The most widely distributed second messenger is cyclic adenosine monophosphate (cAMP). Adenylate cyclase is functionally coupled to various cell surface receptors by the regulatory actions of G proteins. The second major cell surface receptor involves the binding of a hormone or neurotransmitter to a surface receptor acts directly to open an ion channel in the cell membrane. The influx of ions, then, serves as an intracellular signal to convey the hormonal message to the interior of the cell.

5. Hormones produced by the anterior pituitary control body growth and metabolism (growth hormone, GH), function of the thyroid gland (thyrotropin, TSH), glucocorticoid hormone levels (corticotropin, ACTH), function of the gonads

(follicle-stimulating hormone, FSH, and luteinizing hormone, LH), and breast growth and milk production (prolactin). Melanocyte-stimulating hormone, which is involved in the control of pigmentation of the skin, is produced by the pars intermedia of the pituitary gland.

6. The level of hormones in the body is regulated by negative feedback mechanisms. Sensors detect a change in the hormone level and adjust hormone secretion so that body levels are maintained within an appropriate range. When the sensors detect a decrease in hormone levels, they initiate changes that cause an increase in hormone production; when hormone levels rise above the set point of the system, the sensors cause hormone production and release to decrease the level.

SECTION III: APPLYING YOUR KNOWLEDGE

Activity D

1. The nurse would expect a dual electron x-ray absorptiometry (DEXA) to be ordered as the nurse knows that this test is used routinely for the diagnosis and monitoring of osteoporosis and metabolic bone diseases.
2. The nurse would expect an assessment of insulin function through a blood glucose level.

SECTION IV: PRACTICING FOR NCLEX

Activity E

1. **Answer: a**
   RATIONALE: Neurotransmitters such as epinephrine can act as neurotransmitters or as hormones. The other answers are not correct.
2. **Answer: b**
   RATIONALE: When hormones act locally on cells other than those that produced the hormone, the action is called paracrine. Hormones also can exert an autocrine action on the cells from which they were produced. The other terms are incorrect.
3. **Answer: c**
   RATIONALE: Hormones that are synthesized by non–vesicle-mediated pathways include the glucocorticoids, androgens, estrogens, and mineralocorticoids—all steroids derived from cholesterol. The other answers are incorrect.
4. **Answer: d**
   RATIONALE: Unbound adrenal and gonadal steroid hormones are conjugated in the liver, which renders them inactive, and then excreted in the bile or urine. Adrenal and gonadal steroid hormones are not excreted in the feces, cell metabolites, or the lungs.
5. **Answer: a**
   RATIONALE: The hypothalamus and pituitary (i.e., hypophysis) form a unit that exerts control over many functions of several endocrine glands as well as a wide range of other physiologic functions.

These two structures are connected by blood flow in the hypophyseal portal system, which begins in the hypothalamus and drains into the anterior pituitary gland, and by the nerve axons that connect the supraoptic and paraventricular nuclei of the hypothalamus with the posterior pituitary gland. The other answers are not correct.

6. **Answer: b**
   RATIONALE: The level of many of the hormones in the body is regulated by negative feedback mechanisms. The other answers are incorrect.
7. **Answer: c**
   RATIONALE: Real progress in measuring plasma hormone levels came more than 40 years ago with the use of competitive binding and the development of radioimmunoassay methods. The other answers are incorrect.
8. **Answer: d**
   RATIONALE: The advantages of a urine test include the relative ease of obtaining urine samples and the fact that blood sampling is not required. The other answers are not true.
9. **Answer: a**
   RATIONALE: A suppression test may be useful to confirm this situation. The other answers are incorrect.
10. **Answer: b**
    RATIONALE: Isotopic imaging includes radioactive scanning of the thyroid. The other answers are all examples of nonisotopic imaging.

CHAPTER 32

SECTION II: ASSESSING YOUR UNDERSTANDING

Activity A

1. hypofunction, hyperfunction
2. Congenital
3. growth
4. insulinlike growth factors
5. Growth hormone
6. *Constitutional short stature*
7. *constitutional tall stature*
8. gigantism
9. acromegaly
10. overstimulation
11. Precocious
12. Thyroid
13. metabolism, protein
14. metabolism
15. immunoassay
16. preventable mental retardation
17. *myxedema*
18. Thyrotoxicosis
19. Graves
20. oxygen, metabolic
21. Thyroid storm

22. adrenal cortex
23. Aldosterone
24. glucocorticoid
25. Cortisol

26. Addison
27. *Cushing syndrome*

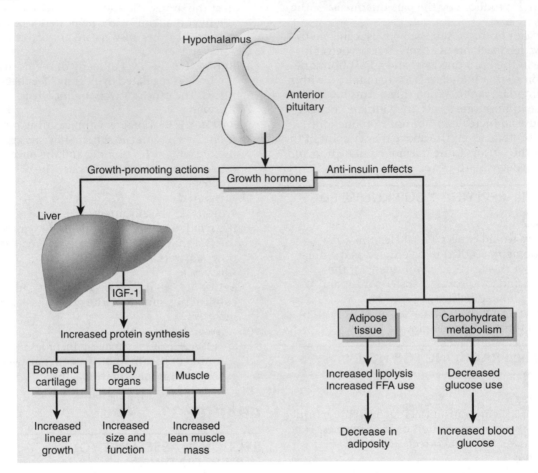

1. i	**2.** j	**3.** d	**4.** e	**5.** b
6. g	**7.** f	**8.** c	**9.** a	**10.** h

1. *Primary defects* in endocrine function originate in the target gland responsible for producing the hormone. In secondary disorders of endocrine function, the target gland is essentially normal, but its function is altered by defective levels of stimulating hormones or releasing factors from the pituitary system. A *tertiary disorder* results from hypothalamic dysfunction.

2. Hormones directly affected by hypopituitarism are ACTH, thyrotropin, growth hormone, the gonadotrophic hormones, and prolactin. Hypopituitarism is characterized by a decreased secretion of pituitary hormones, which affects many of the other endocrine systems by under stimulation.

3. Growth hormone is necessary for growth and contributes to the regulation of metabolic functions. All aspects of cartilage growth are stimulated by growth hormone; one of the most striking effects of growth hormone is on linear bone growth, resulting from its action on the epiphyseal growth plates of long bones. The width of bone increases because of enhanced periosteal growth; visceral and endocrine organs, skeletal and cardiac muscle, skin, and connective tissue all undergo increased growth in response to growth hormone. In many instances, the increased growth of visceral and endocrine organs is accompanied by enhanced functional capacity.

4. Growth hormone secretion is stimulated by hypoglycemia, fasting, starvation, increased blood levels of amino acids (particularly arginine), and stress conditions such as trauma, excitement, emotional stress, and heavy exercise. Growth hormone is inhibited by increased glucose levels, free fatty acid release, cortisol, and obesity. Impairment of secretion, leading to growth retardation, is common in children with severe emotional deprivation.

5. The secretion of thyroid hormone is regulated by the hypothalamic-pituitary-thyroid feedback system. In this system, thyrotropin-releasing hormone (TRH) controls the release of thyrotropin (TSH) from the anterior pituitary gland. TSH increases the overall activity of the thyroid gland by increasing thyroglobulin breakdown and the release of thyroid hormone from follicles into the bloodstream, activating the iodide pump (by increasing Na^+/I Symporter [NIS] activity), increasing the oxidation of iodide and the coupling of iodide to tyrosine, and increasing the number and the size of the follicle cells. Increased levels of thyroid hormone act in the feedback inhibition of TRH or TSH.

6. The manifestations of the disorder are related largely to two factors: the hypometabolic state resulting from thyroid hormone deficiency, and myxedematous involvement of body tissues. The hypometabolic state associated with hypothyroidism is characterized by a gradual onset of weakness and fatigue, a tendency to gain weight despite a loss of appetite, and cold intolerance. As the condition progresses, the skin becomes dry and rough and acquires a pale yellowish cast, which primarily results from carotene deposition, and the hair becomes coarse and brittle. There can be loss of the lateral third of the eyebrows. Gastrointestinal motility is decreased, producing constipation, flatulence, and abdominal distention. Nervous system involvement is manifested in mental dullness, lethargy, and impaired memory.

7. Addison disease is a relatively rare disorder in which all the layers of the adrenal cortex are destroyed. Autoimmune destruction is the most common cause. Because of a lack of glucocorticoids, the person with Addison disease has poor tolerance to stress. Hyperpigmentation results from elevated levels of ACTH. The skin looks bronzed or suntanned in exposed and unexposed areas, and the normal creases and pressure points tend to become especially dark. The gums and oral mucous membranes may become bluish-black. Mineralocorticoid deficiency causes increased urinary losses of sodium, chloride, and water, along with decreased excretion of potassium. The result is hyponatremia, loss of extracellular fluid, decreased cardiac output, and hyperkalemia.

8. The major manifestations of Cushing syndrome represent an exaggeration of the many actions of cortisol. Altered fat metabolism causes a peculiar deposition of fat characterized by a protruding abdomen, subclavicular fat pads or "buffalo hump" on the back, and a round, plethoric "moon face." There is muscle weakness, and the extremities are thin because of protein breakdown and muscle wasting.

SECTION III: APPLYING YOUR KNOWLEDGE

Activity E

1. We are testing the baby for a disorder called *congenital hypothyroidism*. This means that the baby's thyroid gland is not functioning normally, and it is not producing thyroid hormone.

2. Thyroid hormone is necessary for the brain to grow and develop. If the baby's thyroid gland is not working correctly, the doctor will order thyroid medicine for the baby. As long as the baby receives the medication as the doctor orders, the baby's brain will grow and develop just as it is supposed to.

SECTION IV: PRACTICING FOR NCLEX

Activity F

1. **Answer: a**
   RATIONALE: When further information regarding pituitary function is required, combined hypothalamic-pituitary function tests are undertaken (although these are performed less often today). These tests consist mainly of hormone stimulation tests (e.g., rapid ACTH stimulation test) or suppression tests (e.g., GH suppression test). The other answers are incorrect.

2. **Answer: b**
   RATIONALE: The secretion of GH fluctuates over a 24-hour period, with peak levels occurring 1 to 4 hours after onset of sleep. The other answers are incorrect.

3. **Answers: a, b, c**
   RATIONALE: In addition to its effects on growth, GH facilitates the rate of protein synthesis by all of the cells of the body, enhances fatty acid mobilization and increases the use of fatty acids for fuel, and maintains or increases blood glucose levels by decreasing the use of glucose for fuel. Growth hormone has an initial effect of increasing insulin levels. Growth hormone does not decrease the production of ACTH.

4. **Answer: b**
   RATIONALE: When the production of excessive GH occurs after the epiphyses of the long bones have closed, as in the adult, the person cannot grow taller, but the soft tissues continue to grow. Enlargement of the small bones of the hands and feet and of the membranous bones of the face and skull results in a pronounced enlargement of the hands and feet, a broad and bulbous nose, a protruding lower jaw, and a slanting forehead. The other answers are incorrect.

5. **Answer: c**
   RATIONALE: Persons with precocious puberty usually are tall for their age as children, but short as adults because of the early closure of the epiphyses. The other answers are incorrect.

6. **Answer: d**
   RATIONALE: The assessment of thyroid autoantibodies (e.g., antithyroid peroxidase antibodies in Hashimoto thyroiditis) is important in the diagnostic workup and consequent follow-up of thyroid patients.

7. **Answer: a**
   RATIONALE: As a result of myxedematous fluid accumulation, the face takes on a characteristic puffy look, especially around the eyes. The tongue is

enlarged, and the voice is hoarse and husky. The other answers are incorrect.

8. **Answers: a, c, e**
   RATIONALE: Thyroid storm is manifested by a very high fever, extreme cardiovascular effects (i.e., tachycardia, congestive failure, and angina), and severe CNS effects (i.e., agitation, restlessness, and delirium). The mortality rate is high. Very low fever and bradycardia are not manifestations of a thyroid storm.

9. **Answer: b**
   RATIONALE: Chronic suppression causes atrophy of the adrenal gland, and the abrupt withdrawal of drugs can cause acute adrenal insufficiency. The other answers are incorrect.

10. **Answer: c**
    RATIONALE: In female infants, an increase in androgens is responsible for creating the virilization syndrome of ambiguous genitalia with an enlarged clitoris, fused labia, and urogenital sinus. The other answers are incorrect.

11. **Answer: d**
    RATIONALE: Hydrocortisone usually is the drug of choice. The other answers are not drugs; they are naturally occurring steroids.

12. **Answers: a, b, c, e**
    RATIONALE: If Addison disease is the underlying problem, exposure to even a minor illness or stress can precipitate nausea, vomiting, muscular weakness, hypotension, dehydration, and vascular collapse.

13. **Answer: a**
    RATIONALE: The major manifestations of Cushing syndrome represent an exaggeration of the many actions of cortisol (see Table 32-2). Altered fat metabolism causes a peculiar deposition of fat characterized by a protruding abdomen, subclavicular fat pads or "buffalo hump" on the back, and a round, plethoric "moon face." There is muscle weakness, and the extremities are thin because of protein breakdown and muscle wasting. The other answers are incorrect.

CHAPTER 33

SECTION II: ASSESSING YOUR UNDERSTANDING

Activity A

1. glucose
2. brain
3. hypoglycemia
4. glycogen
5. glycogenolysis
6. gluconeogenesis
7. 9, 4
8. Proteins
9. fatty acids, proteins
10. *glucose transporter*
11. GLUT-4
12. Glucagon
13. glycogenolysis, gluconeogenesis
14. insulin
15. Diabetes
16. <100 mg/dL, 140 mg/dL
17. Type 1
18. *idiopathic*
19. Type 2
20. resistance
21. obesity, physical inactivity
22. obesity
23. Gestational
24. fasting
25. casual, greater than (>)
26. glycated hemoglobin
27. insulin
28. ketoacidosis
29. hyperosmolar hyperglycemic
30. Advanced glycation end products
31. *diabetic nephropathy*
32. Diabetic retinopathy
33. macrovascular disease

Activity B

1. d	2. c	3. f	4. e	5. h
6. a	7. j	8. i	9. b	10. g
11. k				

Activity C

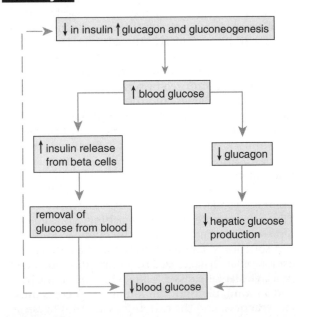

Activity D

1. The actions of insulin are threefold: (1) it promotes glucose uptake by target cells and provides for glucose storage as glycogen, (2) it prevents fat and glycogen breakdown, and (3) it inhibits gluconeogenesis and increases protein synthesis

2. The release of insulin from the pancreatic beta cells is regulated by blood glucose levels, increasing as blood glucose levels rise and decreasing when blood glucose levels decline. Blood glucose enters the beta cell by means of the glucose transporter, is phosphorylated by an enzyme called *glucokinase*, and metabolized to form the adenosine triphosphate (ATP) needed to close the potassium channels and depolarize the cell. Depolarization, in turn, results in opening of the calcium channels and insulin secretion.

3. The absolute lack of insulin in people with type 1 diabetes mellitus means that they are particularly prone to the development of ketoacidosis. One of the actions of insulin is the inhibition of lipolysis and release of free fatty acids (FFA) from fat cells. In the absence of insulin, ketosis develops when these fatty acids are released from fat cells and converted to ketones in the liver.

4. Type 1A diabetes is thought to be an autoimmune disorder resulting from a genetic predisposition; an environmental triggering event, such as an infection; and a T-lymphocyte–mediated hypersensitivity reaction against some beta cell antigen. Much evidence has focused on the inherited major histocompatibility complex (MHC) genes on chromosome 6. In addition to the MHC susceptibility genes for type 1 diabetes on chromosome 6, an insulin gene regulating beta cell replication and function has been identified on chromosome 11.

5. The metabolic abnormalities that lead to type 2 diabetes include (1) insulin resistance, (2) deranged secretion of insulin by the pancreatic beta cells, and (3) increased glucose production by the liver.

6. Specific causes of beta cell dysfunction include an initial decrease in the beta cell mass related to genetic or prenatal factors, increased apoptosis and/or decreased beta cell regeneration, beta cell exhaustion due to long-standing insulin resistance, glucotoxicity, lipotoxicity, and amyloid deposition or other conditions that have the potential to reduce beta cell mass.

7. The manifestations include obesity, high levels of plasma triglycerides, and low levels of high-density lipoproteins, hypertension, systemic inflammation, abnormal fibrinolysis, abnormal function of the vascular endothelium, and macrovascular disease.

8. This has several consequences: first, excessive and chronic elevation of FFAs can cause beta cell dysfunction (lipotoxicity); second, FFAs act at the level of the peripheral tissues to cause insulin resistance and glucose underutilization by inhibiting glucose uptake and glycogen storage; and third, the accumulation of FFAs and triglycerides reduce hepatic insulin sensitivity, leading to increased hepatic glucose production and hyperglycemia, especially fasting plasma glucose levels. Thus, an increase in FFAs that occurs in obese individuals with a genetic predisposition to type 2 diabetes may eventually lead to beta cell dysfunction, increased insulin resistance, and greater hepatic glucose production.

9. The most commonly identified signs and symptoms of diabetes are referred to as the three polys: (1) polyuria (i.e., excessive urination), (2) polydipsia (i.e., excessive thirst), and (3) polyphagia (i.e., excessive hunger). These three symptoms are closely related to the hyperglycemia and glycosuria of diabetes.

10. Weight loss despite normal or increased appetite is a common occurrence in people with uncontrolled type 1 diabetes. First, loss of body fluids results from osmotic diuresis. Second, body tissue is lost because the lack of insulin forces the body to use its fat stores and cellular proteins as sources of energy.

11. This technique involves the insertion of a small needle or plastic catheter into the subcutaneous tissue of the abdomen. Tubing from the catheter is connected to a syringe set into a small infusion pump worn on a belt or in a jacket pocket. The computer-operated pump then delivers one or more set basal amounts of insulin. In addition to the basal amount delivered by the pump, a bolus amount of insulin may be delivered when needed (e.g., before a meal) by pushing a button.

12. The three major metabolic derangements in diabetic ketoacidosis (DKA) are hyperglycemia, ketosis, and metabolic acidosis. Hyperglycemia leads to osmotic diuresis, dehydration, and a critical loss of electrolytes. Serum potassium levels may be normal or elevated, despite total potassium depletion resulting from protracted polyuria and vomiting. Metabolic acidosis is caused by the excess ketoacids that require buffering by bicarbonate ions; this leads to a marked decrease in serum bicarbonate levels.

13. The chronic complications of diabetes include disorders of the microvasculature (i.e., neuropathies, nephropathies, and retinopathies), macrovascular complications (i.e., coronary artery, cerebral vascular, and peripheral vascular disease), and foot ulcers. In the sorbitol pathway, glucose is transformed first to sorbitol and then to fructose. Although glucose is converted readily to sorbitol, the rate at which sorbitol can be converted to fructose and then metabolized is limited. Sorbitol is osmotically active, and it has been hypothesized that the presence of excess intracellular amounts may alter cell function in those tissues that use this pathway.

14. Pathologic changes include thickening of the walls of the nutrient vessels that supply the nerve, leading to the assumption that vessel ischemia plays a major role in the development of neural changes. In addition, segmental demyelinization process that affects the Schwann cell. This demyelinization process is accompanied by a slowing of nerve conduction.

15. Various glomerular changes may occur in people with diabetic nephropathy, including capillary basement membrane thickening, diffuse glomerular sclerosis, and nodular glomerulosclerosis. Changes in the capillary basement membrane take the form of thickening of basement membranes along the length of the glomeruli. Diffuse glomerulosclerosis consists of thickening of the basement membrane and the mesangial matrix. Nodular glomerulosclerosis, Kimmelstiel-Wilson disease, is a form of glomerulosclerosis that involves the development of nodular lesions in the glomerular capillaries of the kidneys, causing impaired blood flow with progressive loss of kidney function and, eventually, renal failure. Changes in the basement membrane in diffuse glomerulosclerosis and Kimmelstiel-Wilson syndrome allow plasma proteins to escape in the urine, causing proteinuria and the development of hypoproteinemia, edema, and others signs of impaired kidney function.

SECTION III: APPLYING YOUR KNOWLEDGE

Activity E

1. Type 1A diabetes mellitus is thought to be a chronic autoimmune disease that has a genetic predisposition. Type 1A diabetes mellitus is characterized by a total lack of insulin, an elevation of blood glucose, and a breakdown of body fats and proteins. Type 1A diabetics are prone to the development of ketoacidosis. Type 1A diabetics require daily injections of exogenous insulin to control blood glucose levels and prevent ketosis.
2. Presently, there is no cure for diabetes mellitus. There is research being conducted into prevention of the disease, but none has been successful to date.

SECTION IV: PRACTICING FOR NCLEX

Activity F

1. **Answer: b**
   RATIONALE: Each islet is composed of beta cells that secrete insulin and amylin, alpha cells that secrete glucagon, and delta cells that secrete somatostatin. In addition, at least one other type of cell, the PP cell, is present in small numbers in the islets and secrets a hormone of uncertain function called pancreatic polypeptide.
2. **Answers: a, b, c, e**
   RATIONALE: These hormones, along with glucagon, are sometimes called counterregulatory hormones because they counteract the storage functions of insulin in regulating blood glucose levels during periods of fasting, exercise, and other situations that either limit glucose intake or deplete glucose stores. Mineralocorticoids are not considered counterregulatory hormones.
3. **Answer: c**
   RATIONALE: In predisposed persons, the prolonged elevation of glucocorticoid hormones can lead to

hyperglycemia and the development of diabetes mellitus and starvation. They stimulate gluconeogenesis by the liver, sometimes producing a 6- to 10-fold increase in hepatic glucose production. A prolonged increase in glucocorticoid hormones does not cause hepatomegaly, portal hypertension, or adrenal hyperplasia.

4. **Answer: a**
   RATIONALE: Type 1A diabetes is thought to be an autoimmune disorder resulting from a genetic predisposition (i.e., diabetogenic genes); an environmental triggering event, such as an infection; and a T-lymphocyte–mediated hypersensitivity reaction against some beta cell antigen. The other answers are incorrect.
5. **Answers: a, c, d**
   RATIONALE: The metabolic abnormalities that lead to type 2 diabetes include (1) insulin resistance, (2) deranged secretion of insulin by the pancreatic beta cells, and (3) increased glucose production by the liver. The other answers are incorrect.
6. **Answer: a**
   RATIONALE: Such diabetes can occur with pancreatic disease or the removal of pancreatic tissue and with endocrine diseases, such as acromegaly, Cushing syndrome, or pheochromocytoma. Endocrine disorders that produce hyperglycemia do so by increasing the hepatic production of glucose or decreasing the cellular use of glucose. Dwarfism, hepatomegaly, and pancreatic hyperplasia do not cause secondary diabetes.
7. **Answer: b**
   RATIONALE: Diagnosis and careful medical management are essential because women with gestational diabetes mellitus are at higher risk for complications of pregnancy, mortality, and fetal abnormalities. Fetal abnormalities include macrosomia (i.e., large body size), hypoglycemia, hypocalcemia, polycythemia, and hyperbilirubinemia. Microsomia and hypercalcemia are not fetal abnormalities are associated with gestational diabetes mellitus.
8. **Answer: c**
   RATIONALE: The most commonly identified signs and symptoms of diabetes are referred to as the three polys: (1) polyuria (i.e., excessive urination), (2) polydipsia (i.e., excessive thirst), and (3) polyphagia (i.e., excessive hunger). Pheochromocytoma and polycythemia are not hallmark signs of diabetes mellitus.
9. **Answers: 1-d, 2-c, 3-e, 4-b, 5-f, 6-a**
10. **Answer: d**
    RATIONALE: The definitive diagnosis of DKA consists of hyperglycemia (blood glucose levels >250 mg/dL), low bicarbonate (<15 mEq/L), and low pH (<7.3), with ketonemia (positive at 1:2 dilution) and moderate ketonuria. The other answers are not diagnostic for DKA.
11. **Answer: a**
    RATIONALE: Alcohol decreases liver gluconeogenesis, and people with diabetes need to be cautioned

about its potential for causing hypoglycemia, especially if alcohol is consumed in large amounts or on an empty stomach.

12. Answer: b

RATIONALE: The signs and symptoms of hypoglycemia can be divided into two categories: (1) those caused by altered cerebral function and (2) those related to activation of the autonomic nervous system. Because the brain relies on blood glucose as its main energy source, hypoglycemia produces behaviors related to altered cerebral function. Headache, difficulty in problem solving, disturbed or altered behavior, coma, and seizures may occur. Muscle spasms are not one of the signs or symptoms of hypoglycemia.

13. Answer: c

RATIONALE: The Somogyi effect describes a cycle of insulin-induced posthypoglycemic episodes. In 1924, Joslin and associates noticed that hypoglycemia was associated with alternate episodes of hyperglycemia. The other answers are not correct.

14. Answer: d

RATIONALE: The loss of feeling, touch, and position sense, which increases the risk of falling. Impairment of temperature and pain sensation increases the risk of serious burns and injuries to the feet. Denervation of the small muscles of the foot result in clawing of the toes and displacement of the submetatarsal fat pad anteriorly. These changes together with joint and connective tissue changes alter the biomechanics of the foot, increasing plantar pressure and predisposing to development of foot trauma and ulcers. The other answers are incorrect.

15. Answer: a

RATIONALE: Diabetic nephropathy is the leading cause of chronic kidney disease, accounting for 40% of new cases. Also, diabetes is the leading cause of acquired blindness in the United States. The liver and pancreas are not organs that diabetes attacks.

16. Answer: a

RATIONALE: Multiple risk factors for macrovascular disease, including obesity, hypertension, hyperglycemia, hyperinsulinemia, hyperlipidemia, altered platelet function, endothelial dysfunction, systemic inflammation (as evidenced by increased C-reactive protein), and elevated fibrinogen levels, frequently are found in people with diabetes. Hypotension, hypoinsulinemia and decreased fibrinogen levels are not risk factors for macrovascular disease in diabetics.

17. Answer: b

RATIONALE: Foot problems have been reported as the most common complication leading to hospitalization among people with diabetes.

18. Answer: c

RATIONALE: Pyelonephritis and urinary tract infections are relatively common in persons with diabetes, and it has been suggested that these infections may bear some relation to the presence of a neurogenic bladder or nephrosclerotic changes in the kidneys. Urinary retention and urinary incontinence can both be the result of a neurogenic bladder. Nephrotic syndrome is not thought to be related to a neurogenic bladder in diabetics.

CHAPTER 34

SECTION II: ASSESSING YOUR UNDERSTANDING

Activity A

1. neurons
2. Schwann cells, neuroglial
3. body, dendrites, axons, synapses
4. Dendrites
5. Schwann, satellite
6. Satellite
7. myelin
8. nodes of Ranvier, saltatory conduction
9. oligodendrocytes
10. Glucose
11. action potentials
12. resting membrane potential
13. synapses
14. Chemical
15. synaptic cleft
16. depolarization, hyperpolarization
17. excitatory postsynaptic
18. neurotransmission
19. Neuromodulator
20. Neurotrophic
21. reticular activating system
22. pia mater
23. spinal nerves
24. paired segmental spinal nerves
25. *plexuses*
26. reflex
27. withdrawal
28. hindbrain, midbrain, forebrain
29. hypoglossal
30. vagus
31. spinal accessory nerve
32. glossopharyngeal nerve
33. vestibulocochlear nerve
34. facial nerve
35. abducens
36. trigeminal nerve
37. cerebellum
38. thalamus
39. gyrus, *sulcus*
40. basal ganglia
41. primary somatosensory cortex
42. meninges
43. CSF
44. autonomic nervous system.
45. parasympathetic nervous system

Activity B

1.

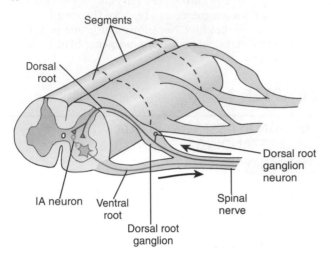

Segments

Dorsal root

IA neuron   Ventral root

Dorsal root ganglion

Dorsal root ganglion neuron

Spinal nerve

2.

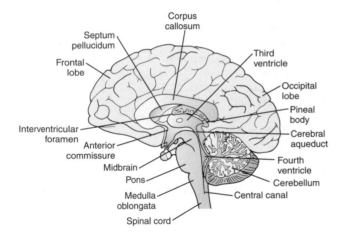

Corpus callosum

Septum pellucidum

Frontal lobe

Third ventricle

Occipital lobe

Pineal body

Cerebral aqueduct

Interventricular foramen

Anterior commissure

Midbrain

Pons

Medulla oblongata

Spinal cord

Fourth ventricle

Cerebellum

Central canal

Activity C

1.

1. f	**2.** h	**3.** e	**4.** b	**5.** d
6. c	**7.** a	**8.** j	**9.** g	**10.** i

2.

1. b	**2.** i	**3.** e	**4.** g	**5.** f
6. a	**7.** h	**8.** c	**9.** d	

Activity D

1. Myelin formation is essentially the same in both the peripheral nervous system (PNS) and CNS; both contain myelin basic protein and both involve the winding of plasma membranes around the nerve fiber. During the wrapping of myelin, the cytoplasm between two adjacent inner leaflets of the plasma membrane is expelled. The two adjacent inner leaflets and any remaining cytoplasm appear as a dark line called the *major dense line*. Likewise, during the wrapping of the plasma membranes to form myelin, adjacent outer plasma membrane leaflets become opposed creating the interperiod or minor dense line. Linking proteins, proteolipid protein (PLP) found only in the CNS and myelin protein zero (MPZ) found only in the PNS, help stabilize adjacent plasma membranes of the myelin sheath.

2. Nervous tissue has a high rate of metabolism. Although the brain comprises only 2% of the body's weight, it receives approximately 15% of the resting cardiac output and consumes 20% of its oxygen. Despite its substantial energy requirements, the brain cannot store oxygen or effectively engage in anaerobic metabolism. An interruption in the blood or oxygen supply to the brain rapidly leads to clinically observable signs and symptoms. Without oxygen, brain cells continue to function for approximately 10 seconds. Unconsciousness occurs almost simultaneously with cardiac arrest, and the death of brain cells begins within 4 to 6 minutes.

3. The local currents resulting from an excitatory postsynaptic potential (EPSP, sometimes called a *generator potential*) are usually insufficient to reach threshold and cause depolarization of the axon's initial segment. However, if several EPSPs occur simultaneously, the area of depolarization can become large enough and the currents at the initial segment can become strong enough to exceed the threshold potential and initiate an action potential. This summation of depolarized areas is called *spatial summation*. Excitatory postsynaptic potentials also can summate and cause an action potential if they occur in rapid succession. This temporal aspect of the occurrence of two or more EPSPs is called *temporal summation*. Inhibitory postsynaptic potentials (IPSPs) also can undergo spatial and temporal summation with each other and with EPSPs, reducing the effectiveness of the latter by a roughly algebraic summation. If the sum of EPSPs and IPSPs keeps the depolarization at the initial segment below threshold levels, no action potential occurs.

4. (1) They can be broken down into inactive substances by enzymes; (2) they can be taken back up into the presynaptic neuron in a process called *reuptake*; or (3) they can diffuse away into the intercellular fluid until its concentration is too low to influence postsynaptic excitability.

5. The nervous system appears very early in embryonic development. At the beginning of week 3, the ectoderm begins to invaginate and migrates between the two layers, forming a third layer called the *mesoderm*. Mesoderm along the entire midline of the embryo forms a specialized rod of embryonic tissue called the *notochord*. The notochord and adjacent mesoderm provide the necessary induction signal for the overlying ectoderm to differentiate and form a thickened structure called the *neural plate*. Within the neural plate an axial groove develops and sinks into the underlying mesoderm, allowing its walls to fuse across the top and form an ectodermal tube called the *neural tube*. As the neural tube closes, ectodermal cells called *neural crest cells* migrate away from the dorsal surface of the neural tube to become the progenitors of the neurons and supporting cells of the PNS. During development, the more rostral portions of the embryonic neural tube—approximately 10 segments—undergoes extensive modification and enlargement to form the brain.

6. Four columns of afferent (sensory) neurons in the dorsal root ganglia directly innervate four corresponding columns of input association neurons in the dorsal horn. These columns are categorized as special and general afferents: special somatic afferent, general somatic afferent, special visceral afferent, and general visceral afferent. The ventral horn contains three longitudinal cell columns: general visceral efferent, pharyngeal efferent, and general somatic efferent (Fig. 34-9). Each of these cell columns contains output association and efferent neurons. The output association neurons coordinate and integrate the function of the efferent motor neurons cells of its column.

7. Maintenance of a chemically stable environment is essential to the function of the brain. In most regions of the body, extracellular fluid undergoes small fluctuations in pH and concentrations of hormones, amino acids, and potassium ions during routine daily activities such as eating and exercising. If the brain were to undergo such fluctuations, the result would be uncontrolled neural activity because some substances such as amino acids act as neurotransmitters, and ions such as potassium influence the threshold for neural firing. Two barriers, the blood-brain barrier and the CSF-brain barrier, provide the means for maintaining the stable chemical environment of the brain. Only water, carbon dioxide, and oxygen enter the brain with relative ease; the transport of other substances between the brain and the blood is slower and more controlled.

8. The blood-brain barrier prevents many drugs from entering the brain. Most highly water-soluble compounds are excluded from the brain, especially molecules with high ionic charge such as many of the catecholamines. In contrast, many lipid-soluble molecules cross the lipid layers of the blood-brain barrier with ease. Some drugs, such as the antibiotic chloramphenicol, are highly lipid-soluble and therefore enter the brain readily. Other medications have a low solubility in lipids and enter the brain slowly or not at all. Alcohol, nicotine, and heroin are very lipid-soluble and rapidly enter the brain. Some substances that enter the capillary endothelium are converted by metabolic processes to a chemical form incapable of moving into the brain.

SECTION III: APPLYING YOUR KNOWLEDGE
Activity E

1. Your baby has a meningomyeloceles.
2. Most children with meningomyeloceles have clinical dysfunction in both the motor and sensory nerves of the lower extremities. Dysfunction usually extends to bowel and bladder control. The extent of the dysfunction cannot be determined until the infant is born and can be better assessed.

SECTION IV: PRACTICING FOR NCLEX
Activity F

1. **Answer: a**
   RATIONALE: The supporting cells, such as Schwann cells in the PNS and the neuroglial cells in the CNS, protect the nervous system and provide metabolic support for the neurons. The other answers are incorrect.

2. **Answer: b**
   RATIONALE: These membrane channels are guarded by voltage-dependent gates that open and close with changes in the membrane potential. The other answers are incorrect.

3. **Answer: c**
   RATIONALE: The most common type of synapse is the chemical synapse. The other answers are incorrect.

4. **Answer: d**
   RATIONALE: Neurotransmitters are synthesized in the cytoplasm of the axon terminal. The other answers are incorrect.

5. **Answer: a**
   RATIONALE: Neuromodulator molecules react with presynaptic or postsynaptic receptors to alter the release of or response to neurotransmitters. The other answers are incorrect.

6. **Answer: b**
   RATIONALE: With rare exceptions, peripheral nerves including the cranial nerves contain afferent and efferent processes of more than one of the four afferent and three efferent cell columns. This provides the basis for assessing the function of the any peripheral nerve. The other answers are incorrect.

7. **Answer: c**
   RATIONALE: On the lateral sides of the spinal cord, extensions of the pia mater, the denticulate ligaments, attach the sides of the spinal cord to the bony walls of the spinal canal. Thus, the cord is suspended by both the denticulate ligaments and the segmental nerves. The posterior vertebra and vertebral blood vessels do not support the spinal cord.

8. **Answer: d**
   RATIONALE: The myotatic or stretch reflex controls muscle tone and helps maintain posture. Specialized sensory nerve terminals in skeletal muscles and tendons relay information on muscle stretch and joint tension to the CNS. This information, which drives postural reflex mechanisms, also is relayed to the thalamus and the sensory cortex and is experienced as *proprioception*, the sense of body movement and position.

9. **Answer: a**
   RATIONALE: The cerebellum compares what is actually happening with what is intended to happen. It then transmits the appropriate corrective signals back to the motor system, instructing it to increase or decrease the activity of the participating muscle

groups so that smooth and accurate movements can be performed. Answer B describes the trigeminal nerve, which exits the brain stem. Answer C describes the pons. Answer D describes midbrain.

10. **Answer: b**
   RATIONALE: Parkinson disease, Huntington chorea, and some forms of cerebral palsy, among other dysfunctions involving the basal ganglia, result in a frequent or continuous release of abnormal postural or axial and proximal movement patterns. If damage to the basal ganglia is localized to one side, the movements occur on the opposite side of the body. The other answers are incorrect.

11. **Answer: c**
   RATIONALE: The sympathetic and parasympathetic nervous systems are continually active. The effect of this continual or basal (baseline) activity is referred to as *tone*.

12. **Answer: d**
   RATIONALE: Dopamine, which is an intermediate compound in the synthesis of norepinephrine, also acts as a neurotransmitter. It is the principal inhibitory transmitter of internuncial neurons in the sympathetic ganglia. It also has vasodilator effects on renal, splanchnic, and coronary blood vessels when given intravenously and is sometimes used in the treatment of shock.

CHAPTER 35

SECTION II: ASSESSING YOUR UNDERSTANDING

Activity A

1. somatosensory
2. General
3. Special
4. visceral
5. trigeminal
6. dermatome
7. discriminative
8. anterolateral
9. modalities
10. action potentials
11. acuity
12. tactile
13. Thermal
14. pain
15. sensory, perception
16. Neuropathic
17. neuromatrix
18. Nociceptive
19. C fibers
20. neospinothalamic
21. paleospinothalamic
22. periaqueductal gray
23. enkephalins, endorphins, dynorphins

24. threshold
25. Cutaneous
26. Deep somatic
27. warning
28. analgesic
29. hyperalgesia
30. Analgesia
31. Neuralgia
32. Cluster
33. tension-type
34. temporomandibular joint

Activity B

1.

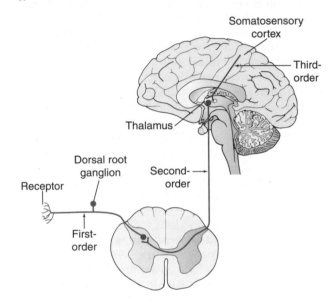

2. • Lips
   • Trunk/back
   • Lips

Activity C

1.

| 1. f | 2. a | 3. d | 4. i | 5. j |
| 6. e | 7. g | 8. c | 9. h | 10. b |

2.

| 1. d | 2. f | 3. c | 4. a | 5. b |
| 6. e | | | | |

Activity D

1. Sensory systems are organized in a serial succession of neurons consisting of first-order, second-order, and third-order neurons. First-order neurons transmit sensory information from the periphery to the CNS. Second-order neurons communicate with various reflex networks and sensory pathways in the spinal cord and travel directly to the thalamus. Third-order neurons relay information from the thalamus to the cerebral cortex. This organizing framework corresponds with the three primary levels of neural integration in the somatosensory

system: the sensory units, which contain the sensory receptors; the ascending pathways; and the central processing centers in the thalamus and cerebral cortex.

2. These somatosensory receptors monitor four major types or modalities of sensation: discriminative touch, which is required to identify the size and shape of objects and their movement across the skin; temperature sensation; sense of movement of the limbs and joints of the body; and nociception, or pain.

3. A pinpoint pressed against the skin of the sole of the foot that results in a withdrawal reflex and a complaint of skin pain confirms the functional integrity of the afferent terminals in the skin, the entire pathway through the peripheral nerves of the foot, leg, and thigh to the sacral (S1) dorsal root ganglion, and through the dorsal root into the spinal cord segment. It confirms that the somatosensory input association cells receiving this information are functioning and that the reflex circuitry of the cord segments (L5 to S2) is functioning. In addition, the lower motor neurons of the L4 to S1 ventral horn can be considered operational, and their axons through the ventral roots, the mixed peripheral nerve, and the motor neuron to the muscles producing the withdrawal response can be considered intact and functional. The communication between the lower motor neuron and the muscle cells is functional, and these muscles have normal responsiveness and strength. Observation of a normal withdrawal reflex rules out peripheral nerve disease, disorders of the dorsal root and ganglion, diseases of the myoneural junction, and severe muscle diseases. Normal reflex function also indicates that many major descending CNS tract systems are functioning within normal limits. If the person is able to report the pinprick sensation and accurately identify its location, many ascending systems through much of the spinal cord and brain also are functioning normally, as are basic intellect and speech mechanisms.

4. According to the gate control theory, the internuncial neurons involved in the gating mechanism are activated by large-diameter, faster-propagating fibers that carry tactile information. The simultaneous firing of the large-diameter touch fibers has the potential for blocking the transmission of impulses from the small-diameter myelinated and unmyelinated pain fibers. Pain therapists have long known that pain intensity can be temporarily reduced during active tactile stimulation.

5. Referred pain is pain that is perceived at a site different from its point of origin but innervated by the same spinal segment. It is hypothesized that visceral and somatic afferent neurons converge on the same dorsal horn projection neurons (Fig. 35-10). For this reason, it can be difficult for the brain to identify the original source of pain. Pain that origi-

nates in the abdominal or thoracic viscera is diffuse, poorly localized, and often perceived at a site far removed from the affected area.

6. Heat dilates blood vessels and increases local blood flow; it also can influence the transmission of pain impulses and increase collagen extensibility. An increase in local circulation can reduce the level of nociceptive stimulation by reducing local ischemia caused by muscle spasm or tension, increase the removal of metabolites and inflammatory mediators that act as nociceptive stimuli, and help to reduce swelling and relieve pressure on local nociceptive endings. It also may trigger the release of endogenous opioids. Heat also alters the viscosity of collagen fibers in ligaments, tendons, and joint structures so that they are more easily extended and can be stretched further before the nociceptive endings are stimulated.

7. The pain often begins as sensations of tingling, heat and cold, or heaviness, followed by burning, cramping, or shooting pain. It may disappear spontaneously or persist for many years. Several theories have been proposed as to the causes of phantom pain. One theory is that the end of a regenerating nerve becomes trapped in the scar tissue of the amputation site. It is known that when a peripheral nerve is cut, the scar tissue that forms becomes a barrier to regenerating outgrowth of the axon. The growing axon often becomes trapped in the scar tissue, forming a tangled growth of small-diameter axons, including primary nociceptive afferents and sympathetic efferents. It has been proposed that these afferents show increased sensitivity to innocuous mechanical stimuli and to sympathetic activity and circulating catecholamines. A related theory moves the source of phantom limb pain to the spinal cord, suggesting that the pain is due to the spontaneous firing of spinal cord neurons that have lost their normal sensory input from the body. In one hypothesis, the pain is caused by changes in the flow of signals through somatosensory areas of the brain.

8. Migraine without aura is a pulsatile, throbbing, unilateral headache that typically lasts 1 to 2 days and is aggravated by routine physical activity. The headache is accompanied by nausea and vomiting, which often is disabling, and sensitivity to light and sound. Visual disturbances occur quite commonly and consist of visual hallucinations such as stars, sparks, and flashes of light. Migraine with aura has similar symptoms, but with the addition of reversible visual symptoms including positive features (e.g., flickering lights spots, or lines) and/or negative features (loss of vision); fully reversible sensory symptoms including positive features (feeling of pins or needles) or negative features (numbness); and fully reversible speech disturbance.

9. Activation of the trigeminal sensory fibers may lead to the release of neuropeptides, causing painful

neurogenic inflammation within the meningeal vasculature characterized by plasma protein extravasation, vasodilation, and mast cell degranulation. Another possible mechanism implicates neurogenic vasodilation of meningeal blood vessels as a key component of the inflammatory processes that occur during migraine. Activation of trigeminal sensory fibers evokes a neurogenic dural vasodilation mediated by calcitonin gene-related peptide. It also has been observed that calcitonin gene-related peptide level is elevated during migraine.

SECTION III: APPLYING YOUR KNOWLEDGE

Activity E

1. It is difficult to assess pain and discomfort in someone suffering with dementia. In our facility we use *The Assessment for Discomfort in Dementia Protocol* as it has been shown to improve pain management in this population.
2. Acetaminophen is the drug of choice to manage this client's discomfort. You can also place ice on the cast at the point of fracture for 20 minutes, each hour, to help reduce the discomfort.

SECTION IV: PRACTICING FOR NCLEX

Activity F

1. Answers: 1-e, 2-a, 3-g, 4-b, 5-c, 6-h, 7-d, 8-f
2. Answers: 1-c, 2-g, 3-i, 4-d, 5-h, 6-a, 7-f, 8-j, 9-b, 10-k, 11-e
3. **Answer: a**
   RATIONALE: Clinically, neurologic assessment of somatosensory function can be done by testing the integrity of spinal segmental nerves. The other answers are incorrect.
4. **Answer: b**
   RATIONALE: Stimuli used include pressure from a sharp object, strong electric current to the skin, or application of heat or cold of approximately 10°C above or below normal skin temperature. The other answers are incorrect.
5. **Answer: c**
   RATIONALE: The amino acid glutamate is a major excitatory neurotransmitter released from the central nerve endings of the nociceptive neurons. The other answers are incorrect.
6. **Answer: d**
   RATIONALE: The paleospinothalamic tract is a slower-conducting, multisynaptic tract concerned with the diffuse, dull, aching, and unpleasant sensations that commonly are associated with chronic and visceral pain. The other answers are incorrect.
7. Answers: 1-c, 2-d, 3-f, 4-g, 5-e, 6-b, 7-a
8. **Answers: a, c**
   RATIONALE: Assessment includes such things as the nature, severity, location, and radiation of the pain. Spinal reflex involvement and spinal tract involvement are not assessed when assessing pain.

9. **Answer: a**
   RATIONALE: Part of the reluctance of health care workers to provide adequate relief for acute pain has been fear of addiction. However, addiction to opioid medications is thought to be virtually nonexistent when these drugs are prescribed for acute pain. The other answers are not the major concern.
10. **Answer: b**
    RATIONALE: The World Health Organization has created an analgesic ladder for cancer pain that assists clinicians in choosing the appropriate analgesic. The other answers are incorrect.
11. **Answers: a, b, c**
    RATIONALE: The ideal analgesic would be effective, nonaddictive, and inexpensive. In addition, it would produce minimal adverse effects and not affect the person's level of consciousness.
12. **Answer: c**
    RATIONALE: Surgery for severe, intractable pain of peripheral or central origin has met with some success. It can be used to remove the cause or block the transmission of intractable pain from phantom limb pain, severe neuralgia, inoperable cancer of certain types, and causalgia. The other answers are incorrect.
13. **Answer: d**
    RATIONALE: Primary hyperalgesia describes pain sensitivity that occurs directly in damaged tissues. The other answers are incorrect.
14. Answers: 1-d, 2-b, 3-a, 4-c
15. **Answer: a**
    RATIONALE: Treatment of phantom limb pain has been accomplished by the use of sympathetic blocks, transcutaneous electrical nerve stimulation of the large myelinated afferents innervating the area, hypnosis, and relaxation training.
16. **Answer: b**
    RATIONALE: Based on clinical trials, first-line agents include acetylsalicylic acid, combinations of acetaminophen, acetylsalicylic acid, and caffeine and nonsteroidal anti-inflammatory drug analgesics (e.g., naproxen sodium, ibuprofen), serotonin ($5\text{-}HT_1$) receptor agonists (e.g., sumatriptan, naratriptan, rizatriptan, zolmitriptan), ergotamine derivatives (e.g., dihydroergotamine), and antiemetic medications (e.g., ondansetron, metoclopramide). Morphine, tramadol, and syrup of ipecac are not first-line drugs in the treatment of migraine.
17. **Answer: c**
    RATIONALE: Cluster headache is a type of primary neurovascular headache that typically includes severe, unrelenting, unilateral pain located, in order of decreasing frequency, in the orbital, retroorbital, temporal, supraorbital, and infraorbital region. The other answers are incorrect.
18. **Answer: d**
    RATIONALE: With children 3 to 8 years old, scales with faces of actual children or cartoon faces can

be used to obtain a report of pain. The other pain rating scales are inappropriate in this age group.

19. Answer: a
RATIONALE: The overriding principle in all pediatric pain management is to treat each child's pain on an individual basis and to match the analgesic agent with the cause and the level of pain. The other answers are incorrect.

CHAPTER 36

SECTION II: ASSESSING YOUR UNDERSTANDING

Activity A

1. Motor function
2. spinal cord
3. polysynaptic
4. posture
5. cortex
6. motor
7. cerebellum, basal ganglia
8. circuits
9. muscle spindles
10. Golgi tendon organs
11. peripheral
12. motor
13. atrophy
14. muscle tone
15. UMN
16. Hyporeflexia
17. lower motor neuron disorders, peripheral, myopathies
18. *dystrophy*
19. fibrillations
20. Duchenne
21. neuromuscular junction
22. acetylcholine
23. Myasthenia gravis
24. spinal cord, cranial nerve
25. peripheral nerve
26. Mononeuropathies
27. Polyneuropathies
28. herniated disk
29. cerebellar
30. basal ganglia
31. tremor
32. Parkinson
33. bradykinesia
34. Amyotrophic lateral sclerosis
35. Multiple sclerosis (MS)
36. demyelination
37. spinal cord injury
38. loss
39. Tetraplegia
40. Paraplegia
41. vasovagal
42. Orthostatic
43. deep venous thrombosis

Activity B

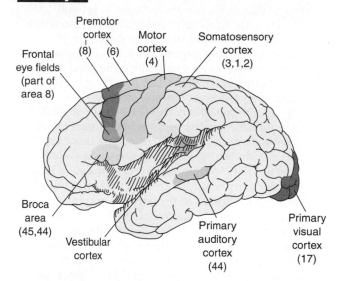

Premotor cortex (8)
Frontal eye fields (part of area 8)
Motor cortex (4)
Somatosensory cortex (3,1,2)
Broca area (45,44)
Vestibular cortex
Primary auditory cortex (44)
Primary visual cortex (17)

Activity C

1.

| 1. d | 2. c | 3. i | 4. e | 5. a |
| 6. f | 7. j | 8. h | 9. g | 10. b |

2.

| 1. c | 2. e | 3. f | 4. i | 5. b |
| 6. j | 7. g | 8. a | 9. h | 10. d |

Activity D

1.

2 → 5 → 4 → 3 → 1

Activity E

1. The lowest level of the hierarchy occurs at the spinal cord, which contains the basic reflex circuitry needed to coordinate the function of the motor units involved in the planned movement. Above the spinal cord is the brain stem, and above the brain stem is the cerebellum and basal ganglia, structures that modulate the actions of the brain stem systems. Overseeing these supraspinal structures are the motor centers in the cerebral cortex. The highest level of function, which occurs at the level of the frontal cortex, is concerned with the purpose and planning of the motor movement. The efficiency of movement depends on input from sensory systems that operate in parallel with the motor systems.

2. The motor neuron and the group of muscle fibers it innervates in a muscle is called a *motor unit*. When the motor neuron develops an action potential, all of the muscle fibers in the motor unit it innervates develop action potentials, causing them to contract simultaneously. Thus, a motor neuron and the muscle fibers it innervates function as a single unit—the basic unit of motor control. Each motor neuron undergoes multiple branching, making it

possible for a single motor neuron to innervate a few to thousands of muscle fibers. In general, large muscles—those containing hundreds or thousands of muscle fibers and providing gross motor movement—have large motor units. This sharply contrasts with those that control the hand, tongue, and eye movements, for which the motor units are small and permit very precise control.

3. The muscle spindles consist of a group of specialized miniature skeletal muscle fibers called *intrafusal fibers* that are encased in a connective tissue capsule and attached to the extrafusal fibers of a skeletal muscle. In the center of the receptor area, a large sensory neuron spirals around the intrafusal fiber forming the so-called primary or annulospiral ending. The intrafusal muscle fibers function as stretch receptors. When a skeletal muscle is stretched, the spindle and its intrafusal fibers are stretched, resulting in increased firing of their afferent nerve fibers. Segmental branches make connections, along with other branches, that pass directly to the anterior gray matter of the spinal cord and establish monosynaptic contact with each of the LMNs that have motor units in the muscle containing the spindle receptor. This produces an opposing muscle contraction. Another segmental branch of the same afferent neuron innervates an internuncial neuron that is inhibitory to motor units of antagonistic muscle groups. This disynaptic inhibitory pathway is the basis for the reciprocal activity of agonist and antagonist muscles (i.e., when an agonist muscle is stretched, the antagonists relax).

4. Coordination of muscle movement requires that four areas of the nervous system function in an integrated manner—the motor system for muscle strength, the cerebellar system for rhythmic movement and steady posture, the vestibular system for posture and balance, and the sensory system for position sense.

5. Duchenne muscular dystrophy is caused by mutations in a gene located on the short arm of the X chromosome that codes for a protein called *dystrophin*. Dystrophin is a large cytoplasmic protein located on the inner surface of the sarcolemma or muscle fiber membrane. The dystrophin molecules are concentrated over the Z-bands of the muscle, where they form a strong link between the actin filaments of the intracellular contractile apparatus and the extracellular connective tissue matrix. Abnormalities in the dystrophin-associated protein complex compromise sarcolemma integrity, particularly with sustained contractions. This disruption in integrity may be responsible for the observed increased fragility of dystrophic muscle, excessive influx of calcium ions, and release of soluble muscle enzymes such as creatine kinase into the serum. The degenerative process in Duchenne muscular dystrophy consists of a relentless necrosis of muscle fibers, accompanied by a continuous

process of repair and regeneration, and progressive fibrosis.

6. Segmental demyelination occurs when there is a disorder of the Schwann cell (as in Guillain-Barré syndrome) or damage to the myelin sheath (e.g., sensory neuropathies), without a primary abnormality of the axon. It typically affects some Schwann cells while sparing others. Axonal degeneration is caused by primary injury to a neuronal cell body or its axon. Damage to the axon may be due either to a focal event occurring at some point along the length of the nerve (e.g., trauma or ischemia) or to a more generalized abnormality affecting the neuronal cell body (neuropathy).

7. The condition can be caused by a variety of events that produce a reduction in the capacity of the carpal tunnel (i.e., bony or ligament changes) or an increase in the volume of the tunnel contents (i.e., inflammation of the tendons, synovial swelling, or tumors). Carpal tunnel syndrome is an example of a compression-type mononeuropathy that is relatively common. It is caused by compression of the median nerve as it travels with the flexor tendons through a canal made by the carpal bones and transverse carpal ligament.

8. Guillain-Barré syndrome is an acute immune-mediated polyneuropathy that is characterized by rapidly progressive limb weakness and loss of tendon reflexes. The disorder is marked by progressive ascending muscle weakness of the limbs, producing a symmetric flaccid paralysis. Symptoms of paresthesia and numbness often accompany the loss of motor function. Paralysis may progress to involve the respiratory muscles. Autonomic nervous system involvement that causes postural hypotension, arrhythmias, facial flushing, abnormalities of sweating, and urinary retention is common. Pain is another common feature.

9. The primary brain abnormality found in all persons with Parkinson disease is degeneration of the nigrostriatal dopamine neurons. On microscopic examination, there is loss of pigmented substantia nigra neurons. Some residual nerve cells are atrophic, and few contain *Lewy bodies*, which are visualized as spherical, eosinophilic cytoplasmic inclusions. Although the cause of Parkinson disease is still unknown, it is widely believed that most cases are caused by an interaction of environmental and genetic factors. Over the past several decades, several pathologic processes (e.g., oxidative stress, apoptosis, and mitochondrial disorders) that might lead to degeneration have been identified. One theory is that the auto-oxidation of catecholamines such as dopamine during melanin synthesis injures neurons in the substantia nigra. There is increasing evidence that the development of Parkinson disease may be related to oxidative metabolites of this process and the inability of neurons to render these products harmless.

10. In amyotrophic lateral sclerosis, the death of LMNs leads to denervation, with subsequent shrinkage of musculature and muscle fiber atrophy. It is this fiber atrophy, called *amyotrophy*, which appears in the name of the disease. The loss of nerve fibers in lateral columns of the white matter of the spinal cord, along with fibrillary gliosis, imparts a firmness or sclerosis to this CNS tissue; the term *lateral sclerosis* designates these changes.

11. The primary neurologic injury occurs at the time of mechanical injury and is irreversible. It is characterized by small hemorrhages in the gray matter of the cord, followed by edematous changes in the white matter that lead to necrosis of neural tissue. This type of pathology results from the forces of compression, stretch, and shear associated with fracture or compression of the spinal vertebrae, dislocation of vertebrae, and contusions due to jarring of the cord in the spinal canal. Secondary injuries follow the primary injury and promote the spread of injury. Although there is considerable debate about the pathogenesis of secondary injuries, the tissue destruction that occurs ends in progressive neurologic damage. After spinal cord injury, several pathologic mechanisms come into play, including vascular damage, neuronal injury that leads to loss of reflexes below the level of injury, and release of vasoactive agents and cellular enzymes.

SECTION III: APPLYING YOUR KNOWLEDGE

Activity F

1. "The medicine that we are giving your husband is methylprednisolone, a short-acting corticosteroid. In a case of spinal cord injury, the drug is thought to enhance the generation of impulses down the spinal cord and improve the blood flow around the site of the injury."

2.
   1. Bed rest with log rolling only
   2. Continuous pulse oximetry
   3. Vital signs hourly until stable
   4. Methylprednisolone intravenously
   5. Monitor for gastric bleeding, venous thrombosis, and steroid myopathy

SECTION IV: PRACTICING FOR NCLEX

Activity G

1. **Answer: a**
   RATIONALE: The highest level of function, which occurs at the level of the frontal cortex, is concerned with the purpose and planning of the motor movement. The other answers are incorrect.
2. **Answers: 1-b, 2-a, 3-d, 4-c**
3. **Answer: b**
   RATIONALE: The anatomic basis of a reflex consists of an afferent neuron, which synapses either directly with an effector neuron that innervates a muscle or with an interneuron that synapses with an effector neuron.

4. **Answers: a, b, c, e**
   RATIONALE: These signs and symptoms include changes in muscle characteristics (strength, bulk, and tone), spinal reflex activity, and motor coordination. Muscle innervation is incorrect.
5. **Answer: c**
   RATIONALE: The postural muscles of hip and shoulder are usually the first to be affected. The other answers are incorrect.
6. **Answer: d**
   RATIONALE: The aminoglycoside antibiotics (e.g., gentamicin) may produce a clinical disturbance similar to botulism by preventing the release of acetylcholine from nerve endings. These drugs are particularly dangerous in persons with pre-existing disturbances of neuromuscular transmission, such as myasthenia gravis. The other answers are incorrect.
7. **Answer: a**
   RATIONALE: Myasthenia crisis occurs when muscle weakness becomes severe enough to compromise ventilation to the extent that ventilatory support and airway protection are needed. The other answers are incorrect.
8. **Answer: b**
   RATIONALE: Carpal tunnel syndrome is an example of a compression-type mononeuropathy that is relatively common. The other answers are not mononeuropathies.
9. **Answer: c**
   RATIONALE: The straight-leg test is an important diagnostic maneuver for a herniated disk in the lumbar area. The other answers are incorrect.
10. **Answers: 1-a, 2-b, 3-c**
11. **Answer: d**
    RATIONALE: The function of the striatum also involves local cholinergic interneurons and their destruction is thought to be related to the choreiform movements of Huntington disease, another basal ganglia-related syndrome. The other answers do not involve the cholinergic interneurons of the striatum.
12. **Answer: a**
    RATIONALE: In Parkinson disease, also known as idiopathic parkinsonism, dopamine depletion results from degeneration of the dopamine nigrostriatal system. The other answers are incorrect.
13. **Answer: b**
    RATIONALE: The most common clinical presentation is slowly progressive weakness and atrophy in distal muscles of one upper extremity. The other answers do not describe the clinical presentation of amyotrophic lateral sclerosis.
14. **Answer: c**
    RATIONALE: A large percentage of patients with multiple sclerosis have elevated immunoglobulin G (IgG) levels, and some have oligoclonal patterns

(i.e., discrete electrophoretic bands) even with normal IgG levels.

15. **Answer: d**
    RATIONALE: A functional C7 injury allows full elbow flexion and extension, wrist plantar flexion, and some finger control. At the C8 level, finger flexion is added. The other answers are incorrect.

16. **Answer: a**
    RATIONALE: Cord injuries involving C1 to C3 result in a lack of respiratory effort, and affected patients require assisted ventilation. The other answers involve injuries further down the spinal column.

17. **Answers: a, c, e**
    RATIONALE: Autonomic dysreflexia is characterized by vasospasm, hypertension ranging from mild (20 mm Hg above baseline) to severe (as high as 240/120 mm Hg or higher), skin pallor, and gooseflesh associated with the piloerector response. Fever and vasoconstriction are not manifestations of autonomic dysreflexia.

18. **Answer: b**
    RATIONALE: Even though the enteric nervous system innervation of the bowel remains intact, without the defecation reflex, peristaltic movements are ineffective in evacuating stool. The other answers are incorrect.

CHAPTER 37

SECTION II: ASSESSING YOUR UNDERSTANDING

Activity A

1. brain's
2. 20
3. hypoxia
4. focal, global
5. sodium
6. Laminar necrosis
7. amino acids, proteases
8. intracranial
9. herniation
10. edema
11. vasogenic
12. Cytotoxic
13. primary, cerebral hypoxia
14. Epidural hematomas
15. tear
16. Consciousness
17. brain
18. vegetative
19. autoregulation
20. carbon dioxide, hydrogen ion, oxygen
21. Stroke
22. Ischemic, hemorrhagic

23. ministroke, angina
24. Thrombi
25. Lacunar
26. embolic
27. hemorrhage
28. cerebral artery
29. cerebral aneurysm
30. Arteriovenous
31. Encephalitis
32. Vomiting
33. chemotherapy
34. seizure
35. Simple partial
36. Complex partial
37. muscle contractions
38. Tonic-clonic
39. *status epilepticus*

Activity B

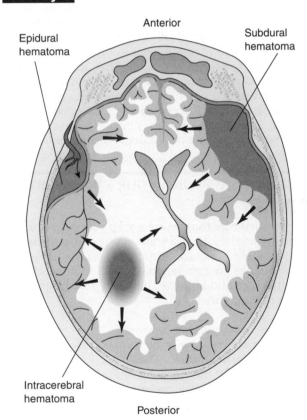

Epidural hematoma

Anterior

Subdural hematoma

Intracerebral hematoma

Posterior

Activity C

| 1. f | 2. g | 3. d | 4. j | 5. b |
| 6. c | 7. e | 8. h | 9. a | 10. i |

Activity D

1.

5 → 1 → 3 → 7 → 2 → 6 → 4 → 8

2.

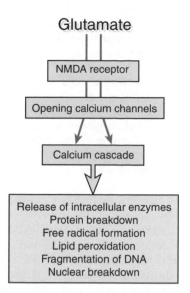

Glutamate

NMDA receptor

Opening calcium channels

Calcium cascade

Release of intracellular enzymes
Protein breakdown
Free radical formation
Lipid peroxidation
Fragmentation of DNA
Nuclear breakdown

Activity E

1. Global ischemia occurs at a time when blood flow is inadequate to meet the metabolic needs of the entire brain. The result is a spectrum of neurologic disorders reflecting global brain dysfunction. Unconsciousness occurs within seconds of severe global ischemia, such as that resulting from complete cessation of blood flow, as in cardiac arrest, or with marked decrease in blood flow, as in serious cardiac arrhythmias. If cerebral circulation is restored immediately, consciousness is regained quickly. However, if blood flow is not promptly restored, severe pathologic changes take place. Energy sources, glucose and glycogen, are exhausted in 2 to 4 minutes, and cellular ATP stores are depleted in 4 to 5 minutes. When ischemia is sufficiently severe or prolonged, infarction or death of all the cellular elements of the brain occurs. Even if blood flow is restored, if ischemic thresholds for injury were exceeded, then permanent cell death ensues.

2. Watershed infarcts are concentrated in anatomically vulnerable border zones between the overlapping territories supplied by the major cerebral arteries, notably the middle, anterior, and posterior cerebral arteries. The overlapping territory at the distal ends of these vessels forms extremely vulnerable areas in terms of global ischemia, called *watershed zones*. During events such as severe hypotension, these distal territories undergo a profound lowering of blood flow, predisposing to focal ischemia and infarction of brain tissues. Therefore, global ischemia can result in focal infarcts that occur in the border zones between major vascular territories.

3. During prolonged ischemia, the glutamate transport mechanisms become immobilized, causing extracellular glutamate to accumulate.

Additionally, intracellular glutamate is released from the damaged cells. This glutamate excess then drives the uncontrolled opening of N-methyl-D-aspartate (NMDA) receptor–operated channels producing an increase in intracellular calcium. Excess intracellular calcium leads to a series of calcium-mediated processes called the *calcium cascade* (Fig. 37-2), including the release of intracellular enzymes that cause protein breakdown, free radical formation, lipid peroxidation, fragmentation of DNA, mitochondrial injury, nuclear breakdown, and eventually cell death.

4. Although recovery usually takes place within 24 hours, mild symptoms, such as headache, irritability, insomnia, and poor concentration and memory, may persist for months. The memory loss usually includes an interval of time preceding the accident (retrograde amnesia) and following the injury (anterograde amnesia).

5. Global brain injury, whether due to head trauma, stroke, or other pathologies, is manifested by alterations in sensory, motor, and cognitive function and by changes in the level of consciousness. In contrast to focal injury, which causes focal neurologic deficits without altered consciousness, global injury nearly always results in altered levels of consciousness ranging from inattention to stupor or coma. Severe injury that seriously compromises brain function may result in brain death.

6. The two components of consciousness are (1) arousal and wakefulness, and (2) content and cognition. The content and cognition aspects of consciousness are determined by a functioning cerebral cortex. Arousal and wakefulness requires the concurrent functioning of both cerebral hemispheres and an intact reticular activating system in the brain stem. The earliest signs of diminution in level of consciousness are inattention, mild confusion, disorientation, and blunted responsiveness. With further deterioration, the delirious person becomes markedly inattentive and variably lethargic or agitated. The person may progress to become obtunded and may respond only to vigorous or noxious stimuli.

7. A bilateral loss of the pupillary light response is indicative of lesions of the brain stem. A unilateral loss of the pupillary light response may be due to a lesion of the optic or oculomotor pathways. The oculocephalic reflex (doll's-head eye movement) can be used to determine whether the brain stem centers for eye movement are intact and the oculovestibular may be used to elicit nystagmus.

8. During the evolution of a stroke, there usually is a central core of dead or dying cells, surrounded by an ischemic band or area of minimally perfused cells called the *penumbra*. Brain cells of the penumbra receive marginal blood flow, and their metabolic activities are impaired; although the area undergoes an "electrical failure," the structural integrity of

the brain cells is maintained. Whether the cells of the penumbra continue to survive depends on the successful timely return of adequate circulation, the volume of toxic products released by the neighboring dying cells, the degree of cerebral edema, and alterations in local blood flow. If the toxic products result in additional death of cells in the penumbra, the core of dead or dying tissue enlarges, and the volume of surrounding ischemic tissue increases.

9. First, blood is shunted from the high-pressure arterial system to the low-pressure venous system without the buffering advantage of the capillary network. The draining venous channels are exposed to high levels of pressure, predisposing them to rupture and hemorrhage. Second, the elevated arterial and venous pressures divert blood away from the surrounding tissue, impairing tissue perfusion.

10. Seizures may be caused by alterations in cell membrane permeability or distribution of ions across the neuronal cell membranes. Another cause may be decreased inhibition of cortical or thalamic neuronal activity or structural changes that alter the excitability of neurons. Neurotransmitter imbalances such as an acetylcholine excess or α-aminobutyric acid (GABA, an inhibitory neurotransmitter) deficiency have been proposed as causes. Certain epilepsy syndromes have been linked to specific genetic mutations causing ion channel defects.

SECTION III: APPLYING YOUR KNOWLEDGE

Activity F CASE STUDY

a. 1. Family history of stroke
    2. History of hypertension
    3. History of smoking
    4. History of diabetes mellitus
    6. History of sickle cell disease
    7. History of hyperlipidemia
    8. History of atrial fibrillation
    9. Weight
    10. Alcohol and drug use
    11. Hormone replacement therapy
    12. Oral contraceptive use
    13. Activity level
b. 1. Administration of tissue plasminogen activator to be given within 3 hours of onset
    2. Administration of neuroprotective drugs
    3. Hypothermia treatment

SECTION IV: PRACTICING FOR NCLEX

Activity G

1. Answers: 1-g, 2-c, 3-a, 4-f, 5-b, 6-e, 7-d
2. Answers: 1-e, 2-a, 3-b. 4-g, 5-c, 6-d, 7-f

3. **Answers: a, b, d, e**
   RATIONALE: The direct brain injuries include diffuse axonal injury and the focal lesions of laceration, contusion, and hemorrhage. A hypoxic brain injury is considered a secondary type of injury.

4. **Answer: a**
   RATIONALE: In contrast to focal injury, which causes focal neurologic deficits without altered consciousness, global injury nearly always results in altered levels of consciousness ranging from inattention to stupor or coma. The other answers are manifestations of different types of brain injury, not a global injury.

5. **Answer: b**
   RATIONALE: Decorticate (flexion) posturing is characterized by flexion of the arms, wrists, and fingers, with abduction of the upper extremities, internal rotation, and plantar flexion of the lower extremities. Decerebrate and extensor posturing are the same thing and are incorrect. Diencephalon posturing does not exist, so it is incorrect.

6. **Answer: c**
   RATIONALE: Clinical examination must disclose at least the absence of responsiveness, brain stem reflexes, and respiratory effort. Brain death is a clinical diagnosis, and a repeat evaluation at least 6 hours later is recommended. An electrocardiogram is not assessed in an examination for brain death.

7. **Answers: a, c, e**
   RATIONALE: The criteria for diagnosis of vegetative state include the absence of awareness of self and environment and an inability to interact with others; the absence of sustained or reproducible voluntary behavioral responses; lack of language comprehension; sufficiently preserved hypothalamic and brain stem function to maintain life; bowel and bladder incontinence; and variably preserved cranial nerve (e.g., pupillary, gag) and spinal cord reflexes. People in a persistent vegetative state can open their eyes and have enough hypothalamic function to maintain life.

8. **Answer: d**
   RATIONALE: If blood pressure falls below 60 mm Hg, cerebral blood flow becomes severely compromised, and, if it rises above the upper limit of autoregulation, blood flow increases rapidly and overstretches the cerebral vessels. The other answers are incorrect.

9. **Answer: a**
   RATIONALE: The diagnosis of subarachnoid hemorrhage and intracranial aneurysms is made by clinical presentation, CT scan, lumbar puncture, and angiography. An MRI is not necessary for the diagnosis of subarachnoid hemorrhage and intracranial aneurysm. Loss of cranial nerve reflexes is not diagnostic of subarachnoid hemorrhage and intracranial aneurysm and neither is venography.

10. Answer: b

RATIONALE: Two assessment techniques can help determine whether meningeal irritation is present. Kernig sign is resistance to extension of the knee while the person is lying with the hip flexed at a right angle. Brudzinski sign is elicited when flexion of the neck induces flexion of the hip and knee. The other answers are incorrect.

11. Answer: c

RATIONALE: Intracranial tumors give rise to focal disturbances in brain function and increased ICP. Focal disturbances occur because of brain compression, tumor infiltration, disturbances in blood flow, and brain edema. Blood pressure, either increased or decreased, is not a manifestation of a brain tumor.

12. Answers: 1-f, 2-e, 3-d, 4-a, 5-b, 6-c

13. Answer: d

RATIONALE: The most common surgery consists of removal of the amygdala and an anterior part of the hippocampus and entorhinal cortex, as well as a small part of the temporal pole, leaving the lateral temporal neocortex intact. Only a portion of the hippocampus and entorhinal cortex, and temporal pole are removed.

14. Answer: a

RATIONALE: Treatment consists of appropriate life-support measures. Medications are given to control seizure activity. Intravenously administered diazepam or lorazepam is considered first-line therapy for the condition. Lorazepam is not given intramuscularly in status epilepticus. Cyclobenzaprine and cyproheptadine are not used to treat status epilepticus.

CHAPTER 38

SECTION II: ASSESSING YOUR UNDERSTANDING

Activity A

1. eyeball
2. sclera
3. levator palpebrae superioris, orbicularis oculi
4. conjunctivitis
5. Hyperacute
6. cornea
7. Keratitis
8. keratitis
9. ophthalmicus
10. iris
11. uveitis
12. pupils
13. Glaucoma

14. degenerative
15. Congenital
16. astigmatism
17. Accommodation
18. cataract
19. retina
20. color-blind
21. Retinitis pigmentosa
22. Macular
23. visual field
24. inferior recti, lateral recti, obliques
25. Conjugate
26. Strabismus
27. Amblyopia
28. ear
29. cerumen
30. Otitis externa
31. temporal
32. eustachian
33. abnormally patent
34. Otitis media
35. Acute otitis media
36. Otosclerosis
37. cochlea
38. Sensorineural
39. bacterial meningitis
40. cranial nerve VIII
41. cytomegalovirus
42. vestibular
43. vertigo
44. Motion sickness
45. paroxysmal positional
46. vestibular neuronitis
47. Ménière
48. cerebellum

Activity B

1.

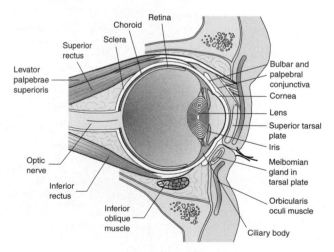

2.

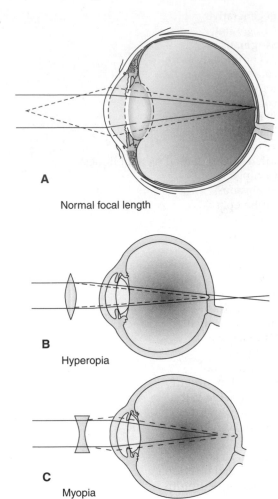

A

Normal focal length

B

Hyperopia

C

Myopia

3.

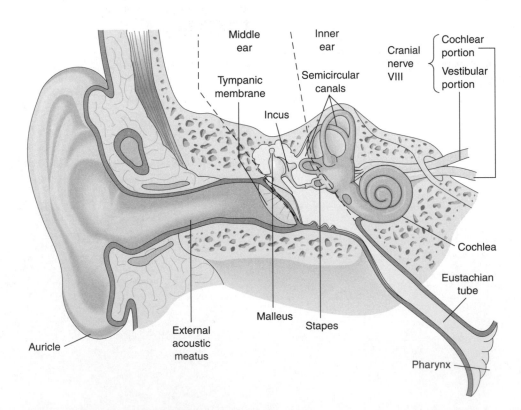

Activity C

1.

1. e	**2.** f	**3.** g	**4.** a	**5.** j
6. c	**7.** d	**8.** b	**9.** i	**10.** h

2.

1. f	**2.** c	**3.** g	**4.** b	**5.** a
6. e	**7.** j	**8.** d	**9.** i	**10.** h

3.

1. j	**2.** h	**3.** e	**4.** c	**5.** i
6. a	**7.** g	**8.** d	**9.** b	**10.** f

Activity D

1. The lacrimal system includes the major lacrimal gland, which produces the tears, the puncta, canaliculi, and tear sac, which collect the tears, and the nasolacrimal duct, which empties the tears into the nasal cavity. Tears contain approximately 98% water, 1.5% sodium chloride, and small amounts of potassium, albumin, and glucose. The function of tears is to provide a smooth optical surface by abolishing minute surface irregularities. Tears also wet and protect the delicate surface of the cornea and conjunctiva. They flush and remove irritating substances and microorganisms, and provide the cornea with necessary nutrient substances. Tears also contain lysozymes and immunoglobulin A (IgA), IgG, and IgE, which synergistically act to protect against infection.

2. *Chronic bacterial conjunctivitis* most commonly is caused by *Staphylococcus* species, although other bacteria may be involved. It is often associated with blepharitis and bacterial colonization of eyelid margins. The symptoms of chronic bacterial conjunctivitis vary and can include itching, burning, foreign body sensation, and morning eyelash crusting. Other symptoms include flaky debris and erythema along the lid margins, eyelash loss, and eye redness. Some people with chronic bacterial conjunctivitis also have recurrent styes and chalazia of the lid margins.

3. Trauma that causes abrasions of the cornea can be extremely painful, but if minor, the abrasions usually heal in a few days. The epithelial layer can regenerate, and small defects heal without scarring. If the stroma is damaged, healing occurs more slowly, and the danger of infection is increased. Injuries to Bowman membrane and the stromal layer heal with scar formation and permanent opacification. Opacities of the cornea impair the transmission of light. A minor scar can severely distort vision because it disturbs the refractive surface.

4. Primary epithelial infections are the optical counterpart of labial herpes with similar immunologic and pathologic features as well as a similar time course. During childhood, mild primary herpes simplex virus infection may go unnoticed. After the initial primary infection, the virus may persist in a quiescent or latent state that remains in the trigeminal ganglion and possibly in the cornea without causing signs of infection.

5. Acanthamoeba keratitis is a rare but serious and sight-threatening complication caused by wearing soft contact lenses, particularly when they are worn overnight beyond doctor-recommended periods or when poor disinfection techniques are used. It also may occur in non–contact lens wearers after exposure to contaminated water or soil. It is characterized by pain that is disproportionate to the clinical manifestations, redness of the eye, and photophobia.

6. Changes in pupil size are controlled by contraction or relaxation of the sphincter and radial muscles of the iris. The pupillary reflex, which controls the size of the pupillary opening, is controlled by the autonomic nervous system, with the parasympathetic nervous system producing pupillary constriction or miosis and the sympathetic nervous system producing pupillary dilation or mydriasis. The sphincter muscle that produces pupillary constriction is innervated by postganglionic parasympathetic neurons of the ciliary ganglion and other scattered ganglion cells between the scleral and choroid layers. The pupillary reflex is controlled by a region in the midbrain called the pretectum.

7. Glaucoma usually results from congenital or acquired lesions of the anterior segment of the eye that mechanically obstruct aqueous outflow. Primary glaucoma occurs without evidence of preexisting ocular or systemic disease. Secondary glaucoma can result from inflammatory processes that affect the eye, from tumors, or from blood cells of trauma-produced hemorrhage that obstruct the outflow of aqueous humor.

8. The term *presbyopia* refers to decrease in accommodation that occurs because of aging. The lens consists of transparent fibers arranged in concentric layers, of which the external layers are the newest and softest. No loss of lens fibers occurs with aging; instead, additional fibers are added to the outermost portion of the lens. As the lens ages, it thickens, and its fibers become less elastic, so that the range of focus or accommodation is diminished to the point where reading glasses become necessary for near vision.

9. Hemorrhage can be preretinal, intraretinal, or subretinal. Preretinal hemorrhages occur between the retina and the vitreous. These hemorrhages are usually large because the blood vessels are only loosely restricted; they may be associated with a subarachnoid or subdural hemorrhage and are usually regarded as a serious manifestation of the disorder. They usually reabsorb without complications unless they penetrate into the vitreous. Intraretinal hemorrhages occur because of abnormalities of the retinal vessels, diseases of the blood, increased pressure in the retinal vessels, or vitreous traction on the vessels. Systemic causes include diabetes mellitus, hypertension, and blood

dyscrasias. Subretinal hemorrhages are those that develop between the choroid and pigment layer of the retina. A common cause of subretinal hemorrhage is neovascularization. Photocoagulation may be used to treat microaneurysms and neovascularization.

10. Proliferative diabetic retinopathy represents a more severe retinal change than background retinopathy. It is characterized by formation of new fragile blood vessels (i.e., neovascularization) at the disk and elsewhere in the retina. These vessels grow in front of the retina along the posterior surface of the vitreous or into the vitreous. They threaten vision in two ways. First, because they are abnormal, they often bleed easily, leaking blood into the vitreous cavity and decreasing visual acuity. Second, the blood vessels attach firmly to the retinal surface and posterior surface of the vitreous, such that normal movement of the vitreous may exert a pull on the retina, causing retinal detachment and progressive blindness.

11. Persistently elevated blood pressure results in the compensatory thickening of arteriolar walls, which effectively reduces capillary perfusion pressure. With severe uncontrolled hypertension, there is disruption of the blood-retinal barrier, necrosis of smooth muscle and endothelial cells, exudation of blood and lipids, and retinal ischemia. These changes are manifested in the retina by microaneurysms, intraretinal hemorrhages, hard exudates, and cotton-wool spots.

12. The eustachian tube serves three basic functions: (1) ventilation of the middle ear, along with equalization of middle ear and ambient pressures; (2) protection of the middle ear from unwanted nasopharyngeal sound waves and secretions; and (3) drainage of middle ear secretions into the nasopharynx.

13. Hearing loss, which is a common complication of otitis media, usually is conductive and temporary based on the duration of the effusion. Hearing loss that is associated with fluid collection usually resolves when the effusion clears. Permanent hearing loss may occur as the result of damage to the tympanic membrane or other middle ear structures. Cases of sensorineural hearing loss are rare. Persistent and episodic conductive hearing loss in children may impair their cognitive, linguistic, and emotional development.

14. During active bone resorption, the bone structure appears spongy and softer than normal. The resorbed bone is replaced by an overgrowth of new, hard, sclerotic bone. The process is slowly progressive, involving more areas of the temporal bone, especially in front of and posterior to the stapes footplate. As it invades the footplate, the pathologic bone increasingly immobilizes the stapes, reducing the transmission of sound. Pressure of otosclerotic bone on middle ear structures or the vestibulocochlear nerve (CN VIII) may

contribute to the development of tinnitus, sensorineural hearing loss, and vertigo.

15. A number of causes and conditions have been associated with subjective tinnitus. Intermittent periods of mild, high-pitched tinnitus lasting for several minutes are common in normal-hearing persons. Impacted cerumen is a benign cause of tinnitus, which resolves after the earwax is removed. Medications such as aspirin and stimulants such as nicotine and caffeine can cause transient tinnitus. Conditions associated with more persistent tinnitus include noise-induced hearing loss, presbycusis (sensorineural hearing loss that occurs with aging), hypertension, atherosclerosis, head injury, and cochlear or labyrinthine infection or inflammation.

16. Conductive hearing loss occurs when auditory stimuli are not adequately transmitted through the auditory canal, tympanic membrane, middle ear, or ossicle chain to the inner ear. Temporary hearing loss can occur as the result of impacted cerumen in the outer ear or fluid in the middle ear. Foreign bodies, including pieces of cotton and insects, may impair hearing. More permanent causes of hearing loss are thickening or damage of the tympanic membrane or involvement of the bony structures (ossicles and oval window) of the middle ear due to otosclerosis or Paget disease.

17. The hair cells in both utricular and saccular maculae are embedded in a flattened gelatinous mass, the otolithic membrane, which is studded with tiny stones called otoliths. Although they are small, the density of the otoliths increases the membrane's weight and its resistance to change in motion. When the head is tilted, the gelatinous mass shifts its position because of the pull of the gravitational field, bending the stereocilia of the macular hair cells. While each hair cell becomes more or less excitable depending on the direction in which the cilia are bending, the hair cells are oriented in all directions, making these sense organs sensitive to static or changing head position in relation to the gravitational field. In a condition called *benign positional vertigo* (to be discussed), the otoliths become dislodged from their gelatinous base, causing positional vertigo.

18. Caloric testing involves elevating the head 30 degrees and irrigating each external auditory canal separately with 30 to 50 mL of ice water. The resulting changes in temperature, which are conducted through the petrous portion of the temporal bone, set up convection currents in the endolymph that mimic the effects of angular acceleration. In an unconscious person with a functional brain stem and intact oculovestibular reflexes, the eyes exhibit a jerk nystagmus lasting 2 to 3 minutes, with the slow component toward the irrigated ear followed by rapid movement away from the ear (see Fig. 37-10). With impairment of brain stem function, the response becomes perverted and eventually disappears.

SECTION III: APPLYING YOUR KNOWLEDGE

Activity E CASE STUDY

1.
   a. Ophthalmoscopic examination under anesthesia by an ophthalmologist; CT or MRI scans are used to evaluate the extent intraocular disease and extraocular spread.
   b. Laser thermotherapy, cryotherapy, chemotherapy, and nucleation

2.
   a. Aminoglycosides, antimalarial drugs, chemotherapeutic drugs, loop diuretics, and salicylates.

SECTION IV: PRACTICING FOR NCLEX

Activity F

1. **Answer: b**
   RATIONALE: The symptoms include tearing and discharge, pain, swelling, and tenderness. The other answers are incorrect.

2. **Answer: c**
   RATIONALE: Infection should be suspected when conjunctivitis develops 48 hours after birth. The other answers are not correct.

3. **Answer: c**
   RATIONALE: The treatment of herpes simplex virus keratitis focuses on eliminating viral replication within the cornea while minimizing the damaging effects of the inflammatory process. The other answers are not goals in the treatment of herpes simplex virus keratitis.

4. **Answers: b, c, d**
   RATIONALE: The low rejection rate is due to several factors: the cornea is avascular, including lymphatics, thereby limiting perfusion by immune elements; major histocompatibility complexes (class II) are virtually absent in the cornea; antigen-presenting cells are not present in great numbers; the cornea secretes immunosuppressive factors, and corneal cells secrete substances (e.g., Fas ligand) that protect against apoptosis, thereby minimizing inflammation. The other answers are incorrect.

5. **Answer: d**
   RATIONALE: Miotic drugs (e.g., pilocarpine), which are used in the treatment of angle-closure glaucoma (to be discussed), produce pupil constriction and, in that manner, facilitate aqueous humor circulation. The other answers are classes of drugs that do not affect papillary constriction.

6. **Answer: a**
   RATIONALE: Primary open-angle glaucoma usually occurs because of an abnormality of the trabecular meshwork that controls the flow of aqueous humor into the canal of Schlemm. The other answers are incorrect.

7. **Answers: 1-d, 2-b, 3-a, 4-c, 5-e**

8. **Answer: b**
   RATIONALE: Age-related cataracts, which are the most common type, are characterized by increasingly blurred vision and visual distortion. The other answers are incorrect.

9. **Answer: c**
   RATIONALE: With the loss of gel structure, fine fibers, membranes, and cellular debris develop. When this occurs, floaters (images) can often be noticed as these substances move within the vitreous cavity during head movement. Blind spots, meshlike structures, and red spots are not seen during head movement with a loss of the gel structure of the vitreous humor.

10. **Answer: d**
    RATIONALE: Neovascularization occurs in many conditions that impair retinal blood flow, including stasis because of hyperviscosity of blood or decreased flow, vascular occlusion, sickle cell disease, sarcoidosis, diabetes mellitus, and retinopathy of prematurity. The other answers are incorrect.

11. **Answer: a**
    RATIONALE: Nonexudative age-related macular degeneration is characterized by various degrees of atrophy and degeneration of the outer retina, Bruch membrane, and the choriocapillary layer of the choroid. It does not involve leakage of blood or serum; hence, it is called dry age-related macular degeneration. The other answers are characterizations of the "wet" form of macular degeneration.

12. **Answer: b**
    RATIONALE: Crude analysis of visual stimulation at reflex levels, such as eye-orienting and head-orienting responses to bright moving lights, pupillary reflexes, and blinking at sudden bright lights, may be retained even though vision has been lost. The other answers are incorrect.

13. **Answer: c**
    RATIONALE: Paralytic strabismus is uncommon in children but accounts for nearly all cases of adult strabismus. It can be caused by infiltrative processes including: Graves disease, myasthenia gravis, stroke, and direct optical trauma. The other diseases have nothing to do with adult strabismus.

14. **Answer: b**
    RATIONALE: The reversibility of amblyopia depends on the maturity of the visual system at the time of onset and the duration of the abnormal experience. The other answers are incorrect.

15. **Answer: a**
    RATIONALE: The most common bacterial pathogens are gram-negative rods (*Pseudomonas aeruginosa, proteus* sp) and fungi (*Aspergillus*) that grow in the presence of excess moisture. The other answers are not fungi.

16. Answer: a
RATIONALE: The abnormally patent tube does not close or does not close completely. In infants and children with an abnormally patent tube, air and secretions often are pumped into the eustachian tube during crying and nose blowing. Cerumen and saliva are not let into the eustachian tube.

17. Answers: a, b, d
RATIONALE: Risk factors include premature birth, male gender, ethnicity (Native American, Inuit), family history of recurrent otitis media, presence of siblings in the household, genetic syndromes, and low socioeconomic status. Being an only child and being a female are not risk factors for acute otitis media.

18. Answer: c
RATIONALE: Because much of the conductive hearing loss associated with otosclerosis is caused by stapedial fixation, surgical treatment involves stapedectomy with stapedial reconstruction using the patient's own stapes or a stapedial prosthesis. The other answers are incorrect.

19. Answer: d
RATIONALE: The scala vestibuli and scala media are separated from each other by the vestibular membrane, also known as Reissner membrane. The other answers are incorrect.

20. Answer: a
RATIONALE: In some vascular disorders, for example, sounds generated by turbulent blood flow (e.g., arterial bruits or venous hums) are conducted to the auditory system. Vascular disorders typically produce a pulsatile form of tinnitus. The other answers are incorrect.

21. Answer: b
RATIONALE: More permanent causes of hearing loss are thickening or damage of the tympanic membrane or involvement of the bony structures (ossicles and oval window) of the middle ear due to otosclerosis or Paget disease. Huntington, Alzheimer, and Parkinson disease are not associated with conductive hearing loss.

22. Answer: c
RATIONALE: Acoustic neuromas are benign Schwann cell tumors affecting CN VIII. The other answers are incorrect.

23. Answer: d
RATIONALE: Tuning forks are used to differentiate conductive and sensorineural hearing loss. Audioscope, audiometer, and tone analysis do not differentiate between conductive and sensorineural hearing loss.

24. Answer: a
RATIONALE: Genetic causes are probably responsible for as much as 50% of sensorineural hearing loss in children. The other diseases are not the correct answer.

25. Answer: b
RATIONALE: The disorder first reduces the ability to understand speech and, later, the ability to detect, identify, and localize sounds.

CHAPTER 39

SECTION II: ASSESSING YOUR UNDERSTANDING

Activity A

1. Hypospadias, epispadias
2. Peyronie disease
3. Peyronie
4. parasympathetic, sympathetic
5. nitric oxide, arterial
6. Erectile dysfunction
7. cardiovascular, metabolic
8. Priapism
9. penile cancer
10. cryptorchidism
11. motility
12. Epididymitis
13. Prostatitis
14. acute bacterial prostatitis
15. prostate
16. chronic bacterial prostatitis
17. extraprostatic
18. prostate-specific antigen (PSA)

Activity B

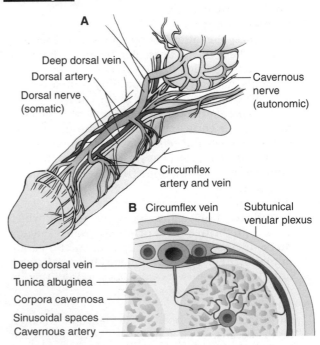

Activity C

1. a **2.** c **3.** h **4.** d **5.** b
6. e **7.** f **8.** j **9.** g **10.** i

Activity D

1. Neurogenic disorders such as Parkinson disease, stroke, and cerebral trauma often contribute to erectile dysfunction by decreasing libido or preventing the initiation of erection. In spinal cord injury, the extent of neural impairment depends on the level, location, and extent of the lesion. Hormonal causes of erectile dysfunction include a decrease in androgen levels due to both primary and secondary hypogonadism. Common risk factors for generalized penile arterial insufficiency include hypertension, hyperlipidemia, cigarette smoking, diabetes mellitus, and pelvic irradiation.

2. Sildenafil (Viagra) is a selective inhibitor of phosphodiesterase type 5, the enzyme that inactivates cyclic guanosine monophosphate. This acts by facilitating corporeal smooth muscle relaxation in response to sexual stimulation.

3. Testicular torsion is a twisting of the spermatic cord that suspends the testis. Extravaginal torsion, which occurs almost exclusively in neonates, is the less common form. It occurs when the testicle and the fascial tunicae that surround it rotate around the spermatic cord at a level well above the tunica vaginalis. The torsion probably occurs during fetal or neonatal descent of the testes before the tunica adheres to the scrotal wall. Intravaginal torsion is considerably more common than extravaginal torsion. It occurs when the testis rotates on the long axis in the tunica vaginalis. In most cases, congenital abnormalities of the tunica vaginalis or spermatic cord exist. The tunica vaginalis normally surrounds the testes and epididymis, allowing the testicle to rotate freely in the tunica. Patients usually present in severe distress within hours of onset and often have nausea, vomiting, and tachycardia. The affected testis is large and tender, with pain radiating to the inguinal area.

4. The clinical staging for testicular cancer is as follows: stage I, tumor confined to testes, epididymis, or spermatic cord; stage II, tumor spread to retroperitoneal lymph nodes below the diaphragm; and stage III, metastases outside the retroperitoneal nodes or above the diaphragm.

5. The anatomic location of the prostate at the bladder neck contributes to the pathophysiology and symptomatology of benign prostatic hyperplasia (BPH). There are two prostatic components to the obstructive properties of BPH and development of lower urinary tract symptoms: dynamic and static. The static component of BPH is related to an increase in prostatic size, and gives rise to symptoms such as a weak urinary stream, postvoid dribbling, frequency of urination, and nocturia. The dynamic component of BPH is related to prostatic smooth muscle tone. α_1-Adrenergic receptors are the main receptors for the smooth muscle component of the prostate.

6. The diagnosis of prostate cancer is based on history and physical examination and confirmed through biopsy methods. Transrectal ultrasonography is used to guide a biopsy needle and document the exact location of the biopsied tissue. Radiologic examination of the bones of the skull, ribs, spine, and pelvis can be used to reveal metastases. PSA levels are important in the staging and management of prostatic cancer. In untreated cases, the level of PSA correlates with the volume and stage of disease.

SECTION III: APPLYING YOUR KNOWLEDGE

Activity E

1. The cause of penile cancer is not known, although several risk factors are thought to be linked to this cancer.

2. Research data has shown that the most important prognostic indicator is the status of your lymph nodes. The more lymph nodes that are involved, the more advanced your cancer has become. It is important that you ask your physician what your prognosis is.

SECTION IV: PRACTICING FOR NCLEX

Activity F

1. Answers: a, c, e
RATIONALE: Factors that influence the timing of surgical repair include anesthetic risk, penile size, and the psychological effects of the surgery on the child. In mild cases, the surgery is done for cosmetic reasons only. In more severe cases, repair becomes essential for normal sexual functioning and to prevent the psychological sequelae of having malformed genitalia. Testicular involvement and presence of an abdominal hernia have no bearing on the timing of the surgery.

2. Answer: a
RATIONALE: Peyronie disease involves a localized and progressive fibrosis of unknown origin that affects the tunica albuginea (i.e., the tough, fibrous sheath that surrounds the corpora cavernosa) of the penis. The disorder is characterized initially by an inflammatory process that results in dense fibrous plaque formation. The plaque usually is on the dorsal midline of the shaft, causing upward bowing of the shaft during erection. The other answers are incorrect.

3. **Answer: b**
   RATIONALE: Priapism can occur at any age, in the newborn as well as other age groups. Sickle cell disease or neoplasms are the most common cause in boys between 5 and 10 years of age. Hemophilia and hypospadias are not linked to priapism in any age group.

4. **Answer: c**
   RATIONALE: The treatment goals for the boys with cryptorchidism include measures to enhance future fertility potential, placement of the gonad in a favorable place for cancer detection, and improved cosmetic appearance. The other answers are incorrect.

5. **Answer: d**
   RATIONALE: Hydroceles are palpated as cystic masses that may attain massive proportions. If there is enough fluid, the mass may be mistaken for a solid tumor. Transillumination of the scrotum (i.e., shining a light through the scrotum for the purposes of visualizing its internal structures) or ultrasonography can help to determine whether the mass is solid or cystic and whether the testicle is normal. The other answers are incorrect.

6. **Answer: a**
   RATIONALE: The most common acute scrotal disorder in the pediatric population is testicular torsion. The other answers are incorrect.

7. **Answer: b**
   RATIONALE: Sexually transmitted acute epididymitis occurs mainly in young men without underlying genitourinary disease and is most commonly caused by *Chlamydia trachomatis* and *Neisseria gonorrhoeae*. *Candida albicans* and *Escherichia coli* are not the most common causes of epididymitis in young men without underlying genitourinary disease.

8. **Answers: a, b, c**
   RATIONALE: Signs of metastatic spread include swelling of the lower extremities, back pain, neck mass, cough, hemoptysis, or dizziness. Gynecomastia (breast enlargement) may result from human chorionic gonadotropin-producing tumors and occurs in about 5% of men with germ cell tumors. The other answers are not signs of metastatic spread of a testicular cancer.

9. **Answer: c**
   RATIONALE: The manifestations of acute bacterial prostatitis include fever and chills, malaise, myalgia, arthralgia, frequent and urgent urination, dysuria, and urethral discharge. Dull, aching pain often is present in the perineum, rectum, or sacrococcygeal region. The other answers are incorrect.

10. **Answer: d**
    RATIONALE: The incidence of BPH increases with advanced age and is highest in African Americans and lowest in native Japanese. The other answers are incorrect.

CHAPTER 40

SECTION II: ASSESSING YOUR UNDERSTANDING

Activity A

1. hair-covered
2. vulva
3. Bartholin gland cyst
4. Chronic dermatitis
5. ecology
6. Vaginitis
7. bleeding
8. metaplasia
9. Cervical
10. cervicitis
11. Polyps
12. Human papilloma virus (HPV)
13. Endometriosis
14. Adenomyosis
15. Dilatation, curettage
16. leiomyomas
17. Pelvic inflammatory disease
18. Ectopic pregnancy
19. menstrual, fertility
20. Polycystic ovary
21. luteinizing hormone
22. Ovarian
23. ovulatory age
24. tumor suppressor
25. Rectocele
26. cardinal
27. uterine prolapse
28. amenorrhea
29. Galactorrhea
30. Mastitis
31. Fibroadenomas
32. Fibrocystic
33. Paget
34. Infertility

Activity B

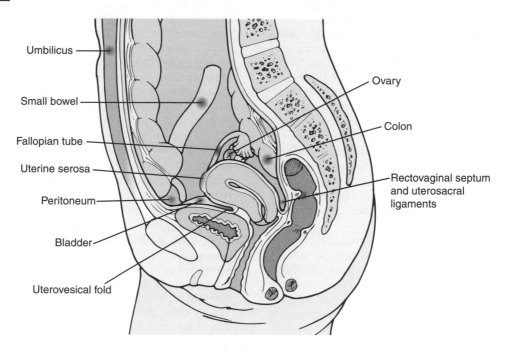

Umbilicus

Small bowel

Fallopian tube

Uterine serosa

Peritoneum

Bladder

Uterovesical fold

Ovary

Colon

Rectovaginal septum and uterosacral ligaments

Activity C

1.

1. i	**2.** h	**3.** c	**4.** b	**5.** d
6. f	**7.** e	**8.** i	**9.** a	**10.** g

2.

1. d	**2.** f	**3.** b	**4.** a	**5.** g
6. c	**7.** e			

Activity D

1. The prevention and treatment of vaginal infections depend on proper health habits and accurate diagnosis and treatment of ongoing infections (see Chapter 41). Measures to prevent infection include measures that keep the genital area clean and dry, maintenance of normal vaginal flora and healthy vaginal mucosa, and avoidance of contact with organisms known to cause vaginal infections. Perfumed products, such as feminine deodorant sprays, douches, bath powders, soaps, and even toilet paper, can be irritating and may alter the normal vaginal flora. Tight clothing prevents the dissipation of body heat and evaporation of skin moisture and promotes favorable conditions for irritation and the growth of pathogens. Cotton undergarments that can withstand hot water and bleach (a fungicide) may be preferable for women to prevent such infections.

2. A quadrivalent vaccine (Gardasil) to prevent infection with the HPV subtypes 16, 18, 6, and 11 was licensed by the Food and Drug Administration (FDA) in June 2006. The vaccine targets the two strains of HPV (HPV 16 and 18), which are responsible for 70% of cervical cancer, and the two most common benign strains (HPV 6 and 11), which account for up to 90% of genital warts. The target population for the vaccine is females between the ages of 9 and 26 years, optimally prior to initiating sexual activity. Clinical studies provided to the FDA have confirmed that the vaccine appears safe and effective in inducing long-term immunity to HPV.

3. Diagnosis of cervical cancer requires pathologic confirmation. Pap smear results demonstrating a squamous intraepithelial lesion often require further evaluation by colposcopy, during which a biopsy sample may be obtained from suspect areas and examined microscopically. An alternate diagnostic tool in areas where colposcopy is not readily available is a noninvasive photographic technique, in which a cervicography camera is used to take photographs of the cervix. The projected cervicogram (a slide made from the film) is then sent for expert evaluation. In one study, the cervicogram was found to give a greater yield of cervical intraepithelial neoplasia (CIN) than Pap smear alone in patients with previous abnormal pap smears.

4. The first theory, the regurgitation/implantation theory, suggests that menstrual blood containing fragments of endometrium is forced upward through the fallopian tubes into the peritoneal cavity. Retrograde menstruation is not an uncommon phenomenon, and it is unknown why endometrial cells implant and grow in some women but not in others. A second theory, the metaplastic theory, proposes that dormant, immature cellular elements, spread over a wide area during embryonic development, persist into adult life and then differentiate into endometrial tissue. A third theory, the vascular or lymphatic theory, suggests that the endometrial tissue may metastasize through the lymphatics or vascular system. Genetic and immune factors also have been studied as contributing factors to the development of endometriosis.

5. The organisms ascend through the endocervical canal to the endometrial cavity, and then to the tubes and ovaries. The endocervical canal is slightly dilated during menstruation, allowing bacteria to gain entrance to the uterus and other pelvic structures. After entering the upper reproductive tract, the organisms multiply rapidly in the favorable environment of the sloughing endometrium and ascend to the fallopian tube.

6. There is also concern that women with PCOS who are anovulatory do not produce significant amounts of progesterone. This may, in turn, subject the uterine lining to an unopposed estrogen environment, which is a significant risk factor for development of endometrial cancer. Although is there also a reported association with breast cancer and ovarian cancer, PCOS has not been conclusively shown to be an independent risk factor for either malignancy.

7. The uterus and the pelvic structures are maintained in proper position by the uterosacral ligaments, round ligaments, broad ligament, and cardinal ligaments. The two cardinal ligaments maintain the cervix in its normal position (Fig. 40-13A). The uterosacral ligaments hold the uterus in a forward position and the broad ligaments suspend the uterus, fallopian tubes, and ovaries in the pelvis (see Fig. 40-4). The vagina is encased in the semirigid structure of the strong supporting fascia. The muscular floor of the pelvis is a strong, slinglike structure that supports the uterus, vagina, urinary bladder, and rectum.

8. Dysfunctional menstrual cycles are related to alterations in the hormones that support normal cyclic endometrial changes. Estrogen deprivation causes retrogression of a previously built-up endometrium and bleeding. Such bleeding often is irregular in amount and duration, with the flow varying with the time and degree of estrogen stimulation and with the degree of estrogen withdrawal. A lack of progesterone can cause abnormal menstrual bleeding; in its absence, estrogen induces development of a much thicker endometrial layer with a richer blood supply. The absence of progesterone results

from the failure of any of the developing ovarian follicles to mature to the point of ovulation, with the subsequent formation of the corpus luteum and production and secretion of progesterone.

9. Approximately 5% to 10% of all breast cancers are hereditary, with genetic mutations causing up to 80% of breast cancers in women under age 50. Two breast cancer susceptibility genes—*BRCA1* on chromosome 17 and *BRCA2* on chromosome 13—may account for most inherited forms of breast cancer (see Chapter 7). *BRCA1* is known to be involved in tumor suppression. A woman with known mutations in *BRCA1* has a lifetime risk of 60% to 85% for breast cancer and an increased risk of ovarian cancer. *BRCA2* is another susceptibility gene that carries an elevated cancer risk similar to that of *BRCA1*.

SECTION III: APPLYING YOUR KNOWLEDGE

Activity E

1. A colposcopy is the examination of the vagina and cervix with an optical magnifying instrument. It is usually done after a Pap smear shows abnormal cells.

2. The LEEP procedure uses a thin, rigid, wire loop that is attached to a generator. It blends high-frequency, low-voltage current for cutting with a higher voltage current for coagulation. The wire loop allows the physician to remove the entire transformation zone of the cervix. This removes the entire lesion while providing a specimen for further histologic evaluation. The procedure is done under local anesthesia in the physician's office at a lower cost than a cone biopsy, which is done in the hospital or outpatient surgery clinic.

SECTION IV: PRACTICING FOR NCLEX

Activity F

1. **Answer: a**
   RATIONALE: Surgical treatment of a Bartholin cyst that has abscessed or blocks the introitus is called *marsupialization*, a procedure that involves removal of a wedge of vulvar skin and the cyst wall. The other answers are incorrect.

2. **Answer: b**
   RATIONALE: One-third to one-half of vulvar intraepithelial neoplasia (VIN) cases appear to be caused by the cancer-promoting potential of certain strains (subtypes 16 and 18) of HPV that are sexually transmitted and are associated with the type of vulvar cancer found in younger women. The other answers are not thought to be associated with vulvar cancer in younger women.

3. **Answers: a, b, c**
   RATIONALE: In premenarchal girls, most vaginal infections have nonspecific causes, such as poor hygiene, intestinal parasites, or the presence of foreign bodies. Vaginal deodorants and Tampax are not associated with vaginal infections in premenarchal girls.

4. **Answer: c**
RATIONALE: Blockage of the mucosal glands results in trapping of mucus in the deeper glands leading to the formation of dilated cysts within the cervix, called *nabothian cysts*. The other answers are incorrect.

5. **Answer: d**
RATIONALE: Risk factors for endometriosis may include early menarche; regular periods with shorter cycles (less than 27 days), longer duration (greater than 7 days), or heavier flow; increased menstrual pain; and other first-degree relatives with the condition. Late menarche, light flow, and periods shorter than 7 days are not risk factors for endometriosis.

6. **Answer: a**
RATIONALE: Leiomyomas are asymptomatic approximately half of the time and may be discovered during a routine pelvic examination, or they may cause menorrhagia (excessive menstrual bleeding), anemia, urinary frequency, rectal pressure/constipation, abdominal distention, and, infrequently, pain. Diarrhea and urinary retention are not symptoms of leiomyomas.

7. **Answer: b**
RATIONALE: New-onset breakthrough bleeding in women who are taking oral contraceptives or medroxyprogesterone contraceptive injection (Depo-Provera) has been associated with pelvic inflammatory disease. The other forms of contraception have not been associated with pelvic inflammatory disease.

8. **Answer: c**
RATIONALE: Diagnostic tests for ectopic pregnancy include a urine pregnancy test, ultrasonography, and β-hCG (hormone produced by placental cells) levels. Serial β-hCG tests may detect lower-than-normal hCG production. Transvaginal ultrasound studies after 5 weeks' gestation may demonstrate an empty uterine cavity or presence of the gestational sac outside the uterus. In a comparison of various protocols for diagnosing ectopic pregnancy, ultrasound followed by serial hCG levels was found to yield the best results. The other answers are incorrect.

9. **Answer: d**
RATIONALE: Metformin, an insulin-sensitizing drug, used with or without ovulation-inducing medications, is emerging as an important component of PCOS treatment. DHEAS is often found in the blood of women with PCOS; Methotrexate is used in ectopic pregnancies; Spironolactone, an antimineralocorticoid, is used in treating PCOS, not mineralocorticoids.

10. **Answers: a, c, e**
RATIONALE: Symptoms that are believed to have a strong correlation to ovarian cancer include abdominal or pelvic pain, increased abdominal size or bloating, and difficulty eating or feeling full quickly after ingesting food. Increased intestinal gas and an increased appetite are not highly correlated with ovarian cancer.

11. **Answer: a**
RATIONALE: A pessary may be inserted to hold the uterus in place and may stave off surgical intervention in women who want to have children or in older women for whom the surgery may pose a significant health risk. The other answers are incorrect.

12. **Answer: b**
RATIONALE: Although analgesic agents such as aspirin and acetaminophen may relieve minor uterine cramping or low back pain, prostaglandin synthetase inhibitors (e.g., ibuprofen, naproxen, mefenamic acid, indomethacin) are more specific for dysmenorrhea and the treatment of choice, if contraception is not desired. Metformic acid is incorrect.

13. **Answer: c**
RATIONALE: Treatment for mastitis symptoms include application of heat or cold, excision, aspiration, mild analgesics, antibiotics, and a supportive brassiere or breast binder. The other answers are incorrect.

14. **Answer: d**
RATIONALE: Diagnosis of fibrocystic changes is made by physical examination, mammography, ultrasonography, and biopsy (i.e., aspiration or tissue sample). Client history and galactography are not used to diagnose fibrocystic changes in the breast.

15. **Answer: a**
RATIONALE: Postmenopausal women and women who have had a hysterectomy can perform the examination any day of the month. The other answers are incorrect.

16. **Answer: b**
RATIONALE: The specimen is best collected by masturbation into a sterile container after 3 days of abstinence. The other answers are incorrect.

17. **Answer: c**
RATIONALE: Between 12 and 24 hours after insemination, the ova are evaluated for signs of fertilization. If signs are present, the ova are returned to the incubator, and 48 to 72 hours after egg retrieval, the fertilized eggs are placed into the woman's uterus by means of a transcervical catheter. The other answers are incorrect.

CHAPTER 41

SECTION II: ASSESSING YOUR UNDERSTANDING

Activity A

1. mucocutaneous
2. fetus or newborn
3. Genital warts
4. external genitalia
5. Genital herpes
6. *neurotropic*

7. type-2
8. primary genital herpes
9. yeast
10. Trichomonads
11. Bacterial
12. Chlamydiae
13. fallopian tube
14. gonococcus
15. Syphilis

Activity B

1. j	2. h	3. a	4. d	5. g
6. f	7. i	8. b	9. e	10. c

Activity C

1. Risk factors for acquiring HPV include young age (<25 years), early age of first intercourse (<16 years), increasing numbers of sex partners, and having a male partner with multiple sex partners. The HPV infection can occur with any type of vaginal or anal penetration and is common in men having sex with men and women having sex with women. Oral-genital and manual-genital contact are less likely means of spreading this infection.

2. Herpes simplex virus type is transmitted by contact with infectious lesions or secretions. Herpes simplex virus type-1 is transmitted by oral secretions, and infections frequently occur in childhood. Herpes simplex virus type-1 may be spread to the genital area by autoinoculation after poor hand washing or through oral-genital contact. Herpes simplex virus type-2 usually is transmitted by sexual contact but can be passed to an infant during childbirth if the virus is actively being shed from the genital tract. In genital herpes, the virus ascends through the peripheral nerves to the sacral dorsal root ganglia. The virus can remain dormant in the dorsal root ganglia or it can reactivate, in which case the viral particles are transported back down the nerve root to the skin, where they multiply and cause a lesion to develop.

3. Reported risk factors for the overgrowth of *Candida albicans* include recent antibiotic therapy, which suppresses the normal protective bacterial flora; high hormone levels owing to pregnancy or the use of oral contraceptives, which cause an increase in vaginal glycogen stores; and uncontrolled diabetes mellitus or human immunodeficiency virus (HIV) infection, because they compromise the immune system.

4. It is a risk factor for HIV transmission and infectivity in both men and women. In women, it increases the risk of tubal infertility and atypical pelvic inflammatory disease (see Chapter 40), and it is associated with adverse outcomes such as premature birth in pregnant women. Trichomonads attach easily to mucous membrane. They may serve as vectors for

the spread of other organisms, carrying pathogens attached to their surface into the fallopian tubes. In men, it is a common cause of nongonococcal urethritis and is a risk factor for infertility, altering sperm motility and viability. It has also been associated with chronic prostatitis.

5. Men are more likely to be symptomatic than women. In men, the initial symptoms include urethral pain and a creamy yellow, sometimes bloody, discharge. The disorder may become chronic and affect the prostate, epididymis, and periurethral glands. Rectal infections are common in homosexual men. In women, recognizable symptoms include unusual genital or urinary discharge, dysuria, dyspareunia, pelvic pain or tenderness, unusual vaginal bleeding (including bleeding after intercourse), fever, and proctitis. Symptoms may occur or increase during or immediately after menses because the bacterium is an intracellular diplococcus that thrives in menstrual blood but cannot survive long outside the human body. There may be infections of the uterus and development of acute or chronic infection of the fallopian tubes, with ultimate scarring and sterility.

6. The clinical disease is divided into three stages: primary, secondary, and tertiary. Primary syphilis is characterized by the appearance of a chancre at the site of exposure. These lesions usually are painless and located at the site of sexual contact. The timing of the second stage of syphilis varies even more than that of the first, lasting from 1 week to 6 months. The symptoms of a rash, fever, sore throat, stomatitis, nausea, loss of appetite, and inflamed eyes may come and go for a year but usually last for 3 to 6 months. Secondary manifestations may include alopecia and genital condylomata latum. Condylomata latum are elevated, red-brown lesions that may ulcerate and produce a foul discharge. They are 2 to 3 cm in diameter; they contain many spirochetes and are highly infectious. Tertiary syphilis is a delayed response of the untreated disease. It can occur as long as 20 years after the initial infection. When syphilis does progress to the symptomatic tertiary stage, it commonly takes one of three forms: development of localized destructive lesions called *gummas*, development of cardiovascular lesions, or development of central nervous system lesions.

SECTION III: APPLYING YOUR KNOWLEDGE

Activity D

1. The nurse, while taking the nursing history, would find it important to note the following: urethral itching, meatal erythema and tenderness, urethral discharge, history of sexual relations with someone

being treated for a chlamydial infection, and history of recent conjunctivitis.

2. The expected treatment for chlamydial infection includes: pharmacologic treatment with either azithromycin or doxycycline, simultaneous treatment of both sexual partners, and abstinence from sexual activity to facilitate cure.

SECTION IV: PRACTICING FOR NCLEX

Activity E

1. **Answer: a**
    RATIONALE: The incubation period for HPV-induced genital warts ranges from 6 weeks to 8 months, with a mean of 2 to 3 months. The other answers are incorrect.

2. **Answers: a, c, e**
    RATIONALE: The initial symptoms of primary genital herpes infections include tingling, itching, and pain in the genital area, followed by eruption of small pustules and vesicles. Chancres and eczemalike lesions are not indicative of genital herpes.

3. **Answer: b**
    RATIONALE: The antiviral drugs acyclovir, valacyclovir, and famciclovir have become the cornerstone for management of genital herpes. The other drugs are not used in the treatment of genital herpes.

4. **Answer: c**
    RATIONALE: The organism has shown resistance to treatment with sulfamethoxazole alone and to tetracycline. The Centers for Disease Control and Prevention recommends treatment with azithromycin, erythromycin, or ceftriaxone. The other answers are incorrect.

5. **Answer: d**
    RATIONALE: An important characteristic of lymphogranuloma venereum is the early (1 to 4 weeks later) development of large, tender, and sometimes fluctuant inguinal lymph nodes called *buboes*.

6. **Answer: a**
    RATIONALE: Antifungal agents such as clotrimazole, miconazole, butaconazole, and terconazole, in various forms, are effective in treating candidiasis. These drugs, with the exception of terconazole, are available without prescription for use by women who have had a previously confirmed diagnosis of candidiasis.

7. **Answer: b**
    RATIONALE: Trichomoniasis can cause a number of complications. It is a risk factor for HIV transmission and infectivity in both men and women. In women, it increases the risk of tubal infertility and

atypical pelvic inflammatory disease, and it is associated with adverse outcomes such as premature birth in pregnant women. The other answers are incorrect.

8. **Answer: c**
    RATIONALE: The predominant symptom of bacterial vaginosis is a thin, grayish-white discharge that has a foul, fishy odor. The other answers are incorrect.

9. **Answers: a, b, e**
    RATIONALE: A specimen should be collected from the appropriate site (i.e., endocervix, urethra, anal canal, or oropharynx), inoculated onto a suitable medium, and transported under appropriate conditions. The nasal passages and the exocervix are not sites that would be used for the collection of *Neisseria gonorrhoeae*.

10. **Answer: d**
    RATIONALE: The syphilitic gumma is a peculiar, rubbery, necrotic lesion that is caused by noninflammatory tissue necrosis. Gummas can occur singly or multiply and vary in size from microscopic lesions to large, tumorous masses. They most commonly are found in the liver, testes, and bone. Chancres occur in primary syphilis. Chancroid is an STD. Gummies are candy.

CHAPTER 42

SECTION II: ASSESSING YOUR UNDERSTANDING

Activity A

1. muscles, tendons, ligaments
2. calcium, blood
3. axial, appendicular
4. Compact
5. Bones
6. periosteum
7. marrow
8. nutritional arteries
9. connective, calcium
10. osteoprogenitor
11. Osteoclasts
12. Elastic
13. Fibrocartilage
14. Hyaline
15. Calcitonin
16. Tendons
17. Ligaments
18. Synarthroses
19. Synovial
20. bursa

Activity B

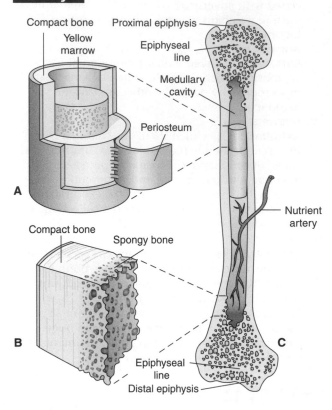

Compact bone
Yellow marrow
Proximal epiphysis
Epiphyseal line
Medullary cavity
Periosteum
A

Compact bone
Spongy bone
Nutrient artery
B
C
Epiphyseal line
Distal epiphysis

Activity C

1. j	**2.** f	**3.** b	**4.** d	**5.** e
6. i	**7.** a	**8.** c	**9.** g	**10.** h

Activity D

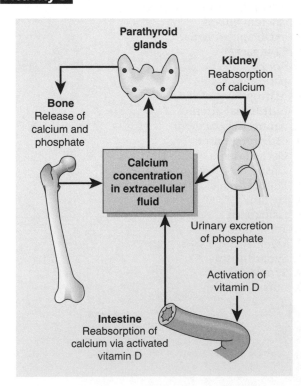

Parathyroid glands

Kidney
Reabsorption of calcium

Bone
Release of calcium and phosphate

Calcium concentration in extracellular fluid

Urinary excretion of phosphate

Activation of vitamin D

Intestine
Reabsorption of calcium via activated vitamin D

Activity E

1. A typical long bone has a shaft, or diaphysis, and two ends, called epiphyses. Long bones usually are narrow in the midportion and broad at the ends so that the weight they bear can be distributed over a wider surface. The shaft of a long bone is formed mainly of compact bone roughly hollowed out to form a marrow-filled medullary canal. The ends of long bones are covered with articular cartilage.

2. Red bone marrow contains developing red blood cells and is the site of blood cell formation. Yellow bone marrow is composed largely of adipose cells. At birth, nearly all of the marrow is red and hematopoietically active. As the need for red blood cell production decreases during postnatal growth, red marrow is gradually replaced with yellow bone marrow in most of the bones. In the adult, red marrow persists in the vertebrae, ribs, sternum, and ilia.

3. The intercellular matrix is composed of two types of substances: organic matter and inorganic salts. The organic matter, including bone cells, blood vessels, and nerves, constitutes approximately one third of the dry weight of bone; the inorganic salts make up the other two-thirds. The organic matter consists primarily of collagen fibers embedded in an amorphous ground substance. The inorganic matter consists of hydroxyapatite, an insoluble macrocrystalline structure of calcium phosphate salts, and small amounts of calcium carbonate and calcium fluoride.

4. Both of these types of connective tissue consist of living cells, nonliving intercellular fibers, and an amorphous (shapeless) ground substance. The tissue cells are responsible for secreting and maintaining the intercellular substances in which they are housed. However, cartilage consists of more extracellular substance than bone, and fibers are embedded in a firm gel rather a calcified cement substance. Hence, cartilage has the flexibility of a firm plastic material rather than the rigid characteristics of bone.

5. Parathyroid hormone maintains serum calcium levels by initiation of calcium release from bone, by conservation of calcium by the kidney, by enhanced intestinal absorption of calcium through activation of vitamin D, and by reduction of serum phosphate levels. Parathyroid hormone also increases the movement of calcium and phosphate from bone into the extracellular fluid.

6. The most potent of the vitamin D metabolites is $1,25\text{-}(OH)_2D_3$. This metabolite increases intestinal absorption of calcium and promotes the actions of parathyroid hormone on resorption of calcium and phosphate from bone. Bone resorption by the osteoclasts is increased and bone formation by the osteoblasts is decreased; there is also an increase in acid phosphatase and a decrease in alkaline phosphatase. Intestinal absorption and bone resorption increase the amount of calcium and phosphorus available to the mineralizing surface of the bone.

SECTION III: APPLYING YOUR KNOWLEDGE

Activity F CASE STUDY

1. Tendinitis occurs because of overuse of the tendon, which causes inflammation of the tendon.
   b. Some tendons are enclosed in sheaths, and they slide inside the sheath and are cushioned by synovial fluid. Other tendons are not encased in a sheath. All tendons attach muscles to bone and they do not stretch very much.

SECTION IV: PRACTICING FOR NCLEX

Activity G

1. **Answer: a**
   RATIONALE: The metaphysis is composed of bony trabeculae that have cores of cartilage. The other answers are incorrect.
2. **Answer: b**
   RATIONALE: Yellow bone marrow is composed largely of adipose cells. Hematopoietic cells are in red bone marrow. Cancellous cells are in spongy bone. Osteogenic cells line the latticelike pattern that forms bone marrow.
3. **Answer: c**
   RATIONALE: Lamellar bone is composed largely of cylindrical units called osteons or haversian systems. Hematopoietic cells, spicules, and macrocrystalline cells do not make up lamellar bone.
4. **Answer: d**
   RATIONALE: Fibrocartilage is found in the intervertebral disks, in areas where tendons are connected to bone, and in the symphysis pubis. The other answers are incorrect.
5. **Answers: a, b, c**
   RATIONALE: Parathyroid hormone maintains serum calcium levels by initiation of calcium release from bone, by conservation of calcium by the kidney, by enhanced intestinal absorption of calcium through activation of vitamin D, and by reduction of serum phosphate levels.
6. **Answer: a**
   RATIONALE: The most potent of the vitamin D metabolites is $1,25(OH)_2D_3$. This metabolite increases intestinal absorption of calcium and promotes the actions of parathyroid hormone on resorption of calcium and phosphate from bone. None of the other answers are correct.

7. **Answer: b**
   RATIONALE: Synchondroses are joints in which bones are connected by hyaline cartilage and have limited motion. The other answers are incorrect.
8. **Answer: c**
   RATIONALE: Diarthrodial joints are the joints most frequently affected by rheumatic disorders. The other types of joint are not the ones most frequently affected by rheumatic disorders.
9. **Answer: d**
   RATIONALE: The tendons and ligaments of the joint capsule are sensitive to position and movement, particularly stretching and twisting. The other answers are incorrect.
10. **Answer: a**
    RATIONALE: These sacs, or bursae, contain synovial fluid. Their purpose is to prevent friction on a tendon. Bursae do not prevent injury to a joint, nor do they cushion joints. Bursae do not prevent friction on a ligament.

CHAPTER 43

SECTION II: ASSESSING YOUR UNDERSTANDING

Activity A

1. musculoskeletal
2. falls
3. Soft-tissue
4. strain
5. sprain
6. dislocation
7. Loose
8. Rotator cuff
9. rotational
10. Dislocations
11. sudden injury, pathologic
12. pathologic
13. fracture
14. Traction
15. Fracture blisters
16. thromboemboli
17. fat embolism
18. Tuberculosis
19. Osteonecrosis
20. osteosarcoma
21. Benign
22. chondroma
23. Chondrosarcoma

Activity B

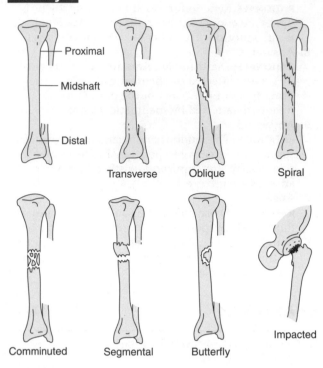

Transverse	Oblique	Spiral
Comminuted	Segmental	Butterfly

Impacted

Proximal
Midshaft
Distal

Activity C

1. a	**2.** e	**3.** i	**4.** c	**5.** j
6. f	**7.** g	**8.** d	**9.** h	**10.** b

Activity D

1.

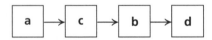

Activity E

1. Any joint may be sprained, but the ankle joint is most commonly involved, especially in fast-moving injuries in which an ankle or knee can be suddenly twisted. Most ankle sprains occur in the lateral ankle when the foot is turned inward under a person, forcing the ankle into inversion beyond the structural limits. Other common sites of sprain are the knee (the collateral ligament and anterior cruciate ligament) and elbow (the ulnar side). As with a strain, the soft-tissue injury that occurs with a sprain is not evident on the radiograph. Wrist sprains most often occur with a fall on an outstretched hand.

2. If properly treated, injuries usually heal with the restoration of the original tensile strength. Repair is accomplished by fibroblasts from the inner tendon sheath or, if the tendon has no sheath, from the loose connective tissue that surrounds the tendon. Capillaries infiltrate the injured area during the initial healing process and supply the fibroblasts with the materials they need to produce large amounts of collagen. Formation of the long collagen bundles occurs within the first 2 weeks, and although tensile strength increases steadily thereafter, it is not sufficient to permit strong tendon pulls for 6 to 8 weeks. There is a danger that muscle contraction will pull the injured ends apart, causing the tendon to heal in the lengthened position. There is also a danger that adhesions will develop in areas where tendons pass through fibrous channels, such as in the distal palm of the hands, rendering the tendon useless.

3. Motion of the arm involves the coordinated movement of muscles of the rotator cuff (supraspinous, teres minor, infraspinatus, and subscapularis) and their musculotendinous attachments. These muscles are separated from the overlying coracoacromial arch by two bursae, the subdeltoid and subcoracoid. These two bursae, sometimes referred to as the *subacromial bursa*, often communicate and are affected by lesions of the rotator cuff. Rotator cuff injuries and impingement disorders can result from a number of causes, including excessive use, a direct blow, or stretch injury, usually involving throwing or swinging, as with baseball pitchers or tennis players. Overuse and degenerative disorders have a slower onset and are seen in older persons with minor or no trauma. The tendons of the rotator cuff fuse together near their insertions into the tuberosities of the humerus to form the musculotendinous cuff.

4. A hip fracture is generally a fracture of the proximal femur. Such fractures are commonly categorized according to the anatomic site in which they occur. Femoral-neck fractures are located in the area distal to the femoral head but proximal to the greater and lesser trochanters and are considered intracapsular because they are located within the capsule of the hip joint. Intertrochanteric fractures occur in the metaphyseal region between the greater and lesser trochanter. Subtrochanteric fractures are those that occur just below the greater trochanter. Femoral-neck and intertrochanteric fractures account for over 90% of hip fractures, occurring in approximately equal proportions.

5. The compartment syndrome has been described as a condition of increased pressure within a limited space (e.g., abdominal and limb compartments) that compromises the circulation and function of the tissues within the space. The muscles and nerves of an extremity are enclosed in a tough, inelastic fascial envelope called a muscle compartment. If the pressure in the compartment is sufficiently high, tissue circulation is compromised, causing death of nerve and muscle cells. Permanent loss of function may occur. The amount of pressure required to produce a compartment syndrome depends on many factors, including the duration of the pressure elevation, the metabolic rate of the tissues, vascular tone, and local blood pressure. Compartment syndrome can result from a decrease in compartment size, an increase in the volume of its contents, or a combination of the two factors.

6. Osteomyelitis after trauma or bone surgery usually is associated with persistent or recurrent fevers, increased pain at the operative or trauma site, and poor incisional healing, which often is accompanied by continued wound drainage and wound separation. Prosthetic joint infections often present with joint pain, fever, and cutaneous drainage.

7. The pathologic features of bone necrosis are the same, regardless of cause. The site of the lesion is related to the vessels involved. There is necrosis of cancellous bone and marrow. The cortex usually is not involved because of collateral blood flow. In subchondral necrosis, a triangular or wedge-shaped segment of tissue that has the subchondral bone plate as its base and the center of the epiphysis as its apex, undergoes necrosis. When medullary infarcts occur in fatty bone marrow, the death of bone cells causes calcium release and necrosis of fat cells, with the formation of free fatty acids. Released calcium forms an insoluble "soap" with free fatty acids. Because bone lacks mechanisms for resolving the infarct, the lesions remain for life.

8. There are three major manifestations of bone tumors: pain, presence of a mass, and impairment of function. Pain is a feature common to almost all malignant tumors, but may or may not occur with benign tumors. A mass or hard lump may be the first sign of a bone tumor. A malignant tumor is suspected when a painful mass exists that is enlarging or eroding the cortex of the bone. The ease of discovery of a mass depends on the location of the tumor; a small lump arising on the surface of the tibia is easy to detect, whereas a tumor that is deep in the medial portion of the thigh may grow to a considerable size before it is noticed. Benign and malignant tumors may cause the bone to erode to the point at which it cannot withstand the strain of ordinary use. In such cases, even a small amount of bone stress or trauma precipitates a pathologic fracture. A tumor may produce pressure on a peripheral nerve, causing decreased sensation, numbness, a limp, or limitation of movement.

9. Metastatic lesions are seen most often in the spine, femur, pelvis, ribs, sternum, proximal humerus, and skull, and are less common in anatomic sites that are further removed from the trunk of the body that are secondary tumors. Tumors that frequently spread to the skeletal system are those of the breast, lung, prostate, kidney, and thyroid, although any cancer can ultimately involve the skeleton. More than 85% of bone metastases result from primary lesions in the breast, lung, or prostate.

SECTION III: APPLYING YOUR KNOWLEDGE

Activity F CASE STUDY

1. Magnetic resonance imaging of the injured knee.
2. Place the knee in a removable knee immobilizer and prescribe isometric quadriceps exercises.

3. An arthroscopic meniscectomy may be performed if there is recurrent or persistent locking, recurrent fluid buildup in the knee, or disabling pain.

SECTION IV: PRACTICING FOR NCLEX

Activity G

1. **Answer: a**
   RATIONALE: Overuse injuries have been described as chronic injuries, including stress fractures that result from constant high levels of physiologic stress without sufficient recovery time. They commonly occur in the elbow ("Little League elbow" or "tennis elbow") and in tissue in which tendons attach to the bone, such as the heel, knee, and shoulder. The other answers are incorrect.

2. **Answers: 1-g, 2-d, 3-b, 4-f, 5-c, 6-a, 7-e**

3. **Answers: b, c, d**
   RATIONALE: Conservative treatment with anti-inflammatory agents, corticosteroid injections, and physical therapy often is undertaken. A period of rest is followed by a customized exercise and rehabilitation program to improve strength, flexibility, and endurance. Pain medicine and anesthetic injections are not usually prescribed for conservative treatment of a shoulder or rotator cuff injury.

4. **Answer: b**
   RATIONALE: Hip dislocation is an emergency. In the dislocated position, great tension is placed on the blood supply to the femoral head, and avascular necrosis may result. Pain caused by a dislocated hip is not considered an emergency. The longer the hip is dislocated, the more time it takes to heal and remain in place, but this does not make the situation an emergency, and dislocation of the hip does not interrupt the blood supply to the femoral head.

5. **Answer: b**
   RATIONALE: Various growth factors, such as bone morphologic protein, are thought to induce bone formation and repair bone defects. The other answers are not used to induce healing in fractures.

6. **Answers: b, c, d**
   RATIONALE: A thorough history includes the mechanism, time, and place of the injury; first recognition of symptoms; and any treatment initiated. It is unimportant if anyone else in the family is prone to fractures. It is also unimportant what the patient has eaten. If surgery were indicated than it would be important to find out *if* the patient has eaten.

7. **Answers: 1-a, 2-c, 3-b**

8. **Answer: c**
   RATIONALE: The main clinical features of fat emboli syndrome are respiratory failure, cerebral dysfunction, and skin and mucosal petechiae. Cerebral manifestations include encephalopathy, seizures, and focal neurologic deficits unrelated to head injury. The other answers are incorrect.

9. **Answer: d**
   RATIONALE: Intravenous therapy is usually needed for up to 6 weeks. Initial antibiotic therapy is

followed by surgery to remove foreign bodies (e.g., metal plates, screws) or sequestra and by long-term antibiotic therapy. The other answers are incorrect.

10. Answer: a
RATIONALE: Any bone, joint, or bursa may be affected, but the spine is the most common site, followed by the knees and hips. The ankles and shoulders are not common sites for tuberculosis to be found.

11. Answer: b
RATIONALE: Besides fracture, the most common causes of bone necrosis are idiopathic (i.e., those of unknown cause) and prior steroid therapy. Vessel injury, radiation therapy, and embolism can cause osteonecrosis, but not as commonly as the others mentioned.

12. Answer: c
RATIONALE: The primary clinical feature of osteosarcoma is deep localized pain with nighttime awakening and swelling in the affected bone. In osteosarcoma, the pain is worse at night. There may be erythema in the overlaying skin, but that is not the primary clinical feature of the disease. Osteosarcoma does not cause soreness in the nearest joint; it may impede range of motion.

13. Answers: a, c, e
RATIONALE: The primary goals in treatment of metastatic bone disease are to prevent pathologic fractures and promote survival with maximum functioning, allowing the person to maintain as much mobility and pain control as possible. Cure of the disease and preventing bone segment ischemia are not primary goals of treatment in metastatic bone disease.

CHAPTER 44

SECTION II: ASSESSING YOUR UNDERSTANDING

Activity A

1. rheumatoid arthritis
2. T-cell–mediated
3. chronic inflammatory
4. scleroderma
5. Ankylosing spondylitis
6. arthropathies
7. Reiter syndrome
8. enteropathic
9. Osteoarthritis
10. wear and tear
11. Gout
12. Juvenile idiopathic arthritis
13. systemic lupus erythematosus
14. dermatomyositis
15. Arthritis
16. Osteoarthritis
17. Polymyalgia rheumatica

Activity B

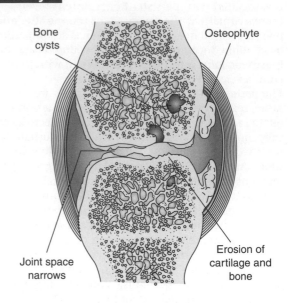

Bone cysts

Osteophyte

Joint space narrows

Erosion of cartilage and bone

Activity C

1. c	2. e	3. f	4. j	5. a
6. b	7. d	8. g	9. h	10. i

Activity D

1.

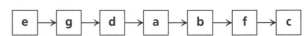

e → g → d → a → b → f → c

Activity E

1. The pathogenesis of rheumatoid arthritis (RA) can be viewed as an aberrant immune response that leads to synovial inflammation and destruction of the joint architecture. It has been suggested that the disease is initiated by the activation of helper T cells, release of cytokines, and antibody formation. Approximately 70% to 80% of those with the disease have a substance called the *rheumatoid factor (RF)*, which is an autologous (self-produced) antibody (Ig RF) that reacts with a fragment of immunoglobulin G (IgG) to form immune complexes. Immune complexes (IgG RF + IgG) and complement components are found in the synovium, synovial fluid, and extra-articular lesions of persons with RA.

2. At the cellular level, neutrophils, macrophages, and lymphocytes are attracted to the area. The neutrophils and macrophages phagocytize the immune complexes and, in the process, release lysosomal enzymes capable of causing destructive changes in the joint cartilage. The inflammatory response that follows attracts additional inflammatory cells, setting into motion a chain of events that perpetuates the condition. As the inflammatory process progresses, the synovial cells and subsynovial

tissues undergo reactive hyperplasia. Vasodilation and increased blood flow cause warmth and redness. The joint swelling that occurs is the result of the increased capillary permeability that accompanies the inflammatory process.

3. Arthralgias and arthritis are among the most commonly occurring early symptoms of SLE. The polyarthritis of SLE initially can be confused with other forms of arthritis, especially rheumatoid arthritis, because of the symmetric arthropathy. Flexion contractures, hyperextension of the interphalangeal joint, and subluxation of the carpometacarpal joint contribute to the deformity and subsequent loss of function in the hands. Other musculoskeletal manifestations of SLE include tenosynovitis, rupture of the intrapatellar and Achilles tendons, and avascular necrosis, frequently of the femoral head.

4. The joint changes associated with osteoarthritis, which include a progressive loss of articular cartilage and synovitis, result from the inflammation caused when cartilage attempts to repair itself, creating osteophytes or spurs. These changes are accompanied by joint pain, stiffness, limitation of motion, and, in some cases, joint instability and deformity.

5. The pathogenesis of gout resides in an elevation of the serum uric acid levels. Uric acid is the end product of purine (adenine and guanine from DNA and RNA) metabolism. The elevation of uric acid and the subsequent development of gout can result from overproduction of purines, decreased salvage of free purine bases, augmented breakdown of nucleic acids because of increased cell turnover, or decreased urinary excretion of uric acid. Primary gout, which constitutes 90% of cases, may be a consequence of enzyme defects, which result in an overproduction of uric acid, inadequate elimination of uric acid by the kidney, or a combination of the two. In secondary gout, the hyperuricemia may be caused by increased breakdown in the production of nucleic acids, as occurs with rapid tumor cell lysis during treatment for lymphoma or leukemia. Other cases of secondary gout result from chronic renal disease.

SECTION III: APPLYING YOUR KNOWLEDGE
Activity F　CASE STUDY

1. Juvenile idiopathic arthritis can be regarded not as a single disease, but as a category of diseases with three principle types of onset: (1) systemic onset disease, (2) pauciarticular arthritis, and (3) polyarticular disease.

2. The nurse would expect blood work for rheumatoid factor and a complete metabolic panel along with a complete blood count to be ordered.

SECTION IV: PRACTICING FOR NCLEX
Activity G

1. **Answers: c, e, d, i, f, g, a, h, b**
   RATIONALE: The role of the autoimmune process in the joint destruction of RA remains obscure. At the cellular level, neutrophils, macrophages, and lymphocytes are attracted to the area. The neutrophils and macrophages phagocytize the immune complexes and, in the process, release lysosomal enzymes capable of causing destructive changes in the joint cartilage. The inflammatory response that follows attracts additional inflammatory cells, setting into motion a chain of events that perpetuates the condition. As the inflammatory process progresses, the synovial cells and subsynovial tissues undergo reactive hyperplasia. Vasodilation and increased blood flow cause warmth and redness. The joint swelling that occurs is the result of the increased capillary permeability that accompanies the inflammatory process.

2. **Answer: a**
   RATIONALE: Arthralgias and arthritis are among the most commonly occurring early symptoms of SLE. The other answers are symptoms of SLE in differing stages of the disease.

3. **Answers: c, d**
   RATIONALE: Almost all persons with scleroderma develop polyarthritis and Raynaud phenomenon, a vascular disorder characterized by reversible vasospasm of the arteries supplying the fingers. Dumping syndrome, chronic diarrhea, and chronic vasoconstriction are not diseases developed by people with scleroderma.

4. **Answer: b**
   RATIONALE: Corticosteroids are the mainstay of treatment for these conditions. The other drug types are not the treatment of choice for polymyositis and dermatomyositis.

5. **Answer: c**
   RATIONALE: The pain, which becomes worse when resting, particularly when lying in bed, initially may be blamed on muscle strain or spasm from physical activity. The other answers are incorrect.

6. **Answer: d**
   RATIONALE: Reiter syndrome was the first rheumatic disease to be recognized in association with HIV infection. Symptoms of arthritis may precede any overt signs of HIV disease. The other sexually transmitted diseases have not been associated with Reiter syndrome.

7. **Answer: a**
   RATIONALE: The biologic response modifiers, specifically the tumor necrosis factor inhibitors (e.g., etanercept, infliximab, and adalimumab) have been found to be beneficial in controlling the arthritis as well as the psoriasis in patients with psoriatic arthritis. The other drugs have not been found to be beneficial in psoriatic arthritis.

8. Answers: a, c, e
RATIONALE: The joint changes associated with osteoarthritis, which include a progressive loss of articular cartilage and synovitis, result from the inflammation caused when cartilage attempts to repair itself, creating osteophytes or spurs. These changes are accompanied by joint pain, stiffness, limitation of motion, and, in some cases, joint instability and deformity. The other answers are incorrect.

9. Answer: b
RATIONALE: A definitive diagnosis of gout can be made only when monosodium urate crystals are in the synovial fluid or in tissue sections of tophaceous deposits. The other answers are not diagnostic of gout.

10. Answer: c
RATIONALE: In terms of medications, the selection of drugs used in the treatment of arthritic disorders and their dosages may need to be considered when prescribing for the elderly. For example, the NSAIDs may be less well tolerated by the elderly, and their side effects are more likely to be serious. In addition to bleeding from the gastrointestinal tract and renal insufficiency, there may be cognitive dysfunction, manifested by forgetfulness, inability to concentrate, sleeplessness, paranoid ideation, and depression. Malaise, lethargy, and mania are not side effects of NSAIDs.

CHAPTER 45

SECTION II: ASSESSING YOUR UNDERSTANDING

Activity A

1. integumentum
2. thickness
3. epidermis
4. *stratum corneum*
5. Keratinocytes
6. Melanocytes
7. eumelanin
8. Langerhans
9. basement membrane
10. epidermis
11. dermis
12. papillary
13. Eccrine
14. Apocrine
15. keratinized
16. keratinized
17. blister
18. callus
19. Corns
20. *xerosis*

Activity B

1.

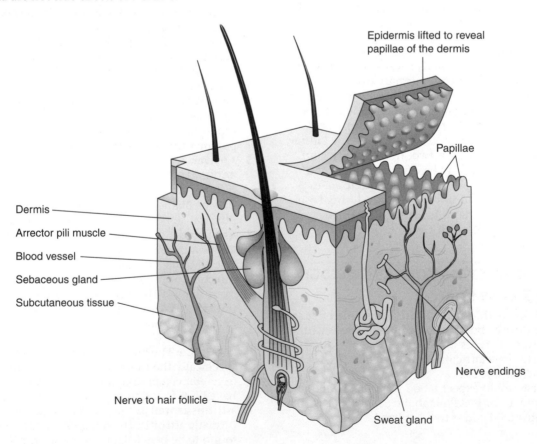

Epidermis lifted to reveal papillae of the dermis

Papillae

Dermis

Arrector pili muscle

Blood vessel

Sebaceous gland

Subcutaneous tissue

Nerve endings

Nerve to hair follicle

Sweat gland

2.

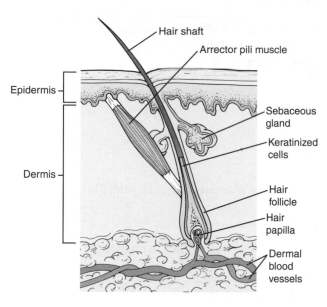

Hair shaft
Arrector pili muscle
Epidermis
Sebaceous gland
Keratinized cells
Dermis
Hair follicle
Hair papilla
Dermal blood vessels

Activity C

1. d	**2.** j	**3.** i	**4.** c	**5.** a
6. h	**7.** f	**8.** g	**9.** b	**10.** e

Activity D

1. The skin serves several other vital functions, including somatosensory function, temperature regulation, and vitamin D synthesis. The skin is richly innervated with pain, temperature, and touch receptors. Skin receptors relay the numerous qualities of touch, such as pressure, sharpness, dullness, and pleasure to the central nervous system for localization and fine discrimination. The rate at which heat is dissipated from the body is determined by constriction or dilation of the arterioles that supply blood to the skin and through evaporation of moisture and sweat from the skin surface. Vitamin D_3 is the most important of these and is formed in the skin as the result of irradiation of 7-dehydrocholesterol, a substance normally found in the skin, by ultraviolet rays from the sun.

2. The epidermis is composed of stratified squamous keratinized epithelium, which, when viewed under the microscope, is seen to consist of five distinct layers, or strata, that represent a progressive differentiation or maturation of the keratinocytes: the stratum germinativum, or basal layer; the stratum spinosum; the stratum granulosum; the stratum lucidum; and the stratum corneum.

3. The ability to synthesize melanin depends on the ability of the melanocytes to produce an enzyme called *tyrosinase*, which converts the amino acid tyrosine to a precursor of melanin. A genetic lack of this enzyme results in a clinical condition called *albinism*. Persons with this disorder lack pigmentation in the skin, hair, and iris of the eye.

4. Dark-skinned and light-skinned people have approximately the same number of melanocytes, but the production and packaging of pigment is different. In dark-skinned people, *larger* melanin-containing melanosomes are produced and transferred individually to the keratinocyte; whereas, in light-skinned people, *smaller* melanosomes are produced and then packaged together in a membrane before being transferred to the keratinocyte. Although the number of melanosomes in dark and white skin is the same, black skin produces more melanin and produces it faster than white skin.

5. The sebaceous glands are located over the entire skin surface except for the palms, soles, and sides of the feet. They are part of the *pilosebaceous unit*. They secrete a mixture of lipids, including triglycerides, cholesterol, and wax. This mixture is called *sebum*; it lubricates hair and skin. Sebum is not the same as the surface lipid film. Sebum prevents undue evaporation of moisture from the stratum corneum during cold weather and helps to conserve body heat. Sebum production is under the control of genetic and hormonal influences.

6. It is generally agreed that itch is a sensation that originates in free nerve endings in the skin, is carried by small myelinated type C nerve fibers to the dorsal horn of the spinal cord, and is then transmitted to the somatosensory cortex via the spinothalamic tract, differing from the pain pathways.

SECTION III: APPLYING YOUR KNOWLEDGE

Activity E CASE STUDY

a. Skin color is determined by the melanin produced by the melanocytes. Black skin produces more melanin and produces it faster than white skin. Because of their skin color, dark-skinned persons are better protected against skin cancer, premature wrinkling, and aging of the skin that occurs with sun exposure. Dry or "ashy" skin also can be a problem for people with dark skin. It often is uncomfortable, and it also is easily noticed because it gives the skin an ashen or grayish appearance. The darker pigmentation can make skin pallor, cyanosis, and erythema more difficult to observe. Changes in skin color; in particular hypopigmentation and hyperpigmentation, often accompany disorders of dark skin and are very important signs to observe when diagnosing skin conditions.

SECTION IV: PRACTICING FOR NCLEX

Activity F

1. **Answer: a**
   RATIONALE: The skin also serves as an immunologic barrier. The Langerhans cells detect foreign antigens, playing an important part in allergic skin

conditions and skin graft rejections. The other cell types are not part of the immunologic barrier.

2. **Answers: 1-c, 2-b, 3-a, 4-d**
3. **Answer: b**
   RATIONALE: The basement membrane is also a major site of immunoglobulin and complement deposition in skin disease. The other answers are incorrect.
4. **Answer: c**
   RATIONALE: The reticular dermis (pars reticularis) is the thicker area of the dermis and forms the bulk of the dermal layer. The other three answers are part of the reticular dermis but it is not characterized by them.
5. **Answers: a, c, e**
   RATIONALE: Because the eccrine glands and deep hair follicles extend to this layer and several skin diseases involve the subcutaneous tissue, the subcutaneous tissue may be considered part of the skin. The keratinocytes and the Merkel cells are not part of the subcutaneous tissue.
6. **Answer: d**
   RATIONALE: This mixture is called sebum; it lubricates hair and skin. Sweat comes from sweat glands. Chalasia is an abnormal relaxation or the cardiac sphincter of the stomach. Cerumen is found in the ear.
7. **Answer: a**
   RATIONALE: The nearly transparent nail plate provides a useful window for viewing the amount of oxygen in the blood, providing a view of the color of the blood in the dermal vessels. The other answers are incorrect.
8. **Answer: b**
   RATIONALE: When a blister occurs, histologically, there is degeneration of the epidermal cells and a disruption of the intercellular junctions that causes the layers of the skin to separate. Lichenifications are thickened areas of the skin. Petechiae are pinpoint rashes on the skin. A pressure ulcer is sometimes referred to as a "bed sore" and is caused by continuous pressure on a bony prominence.
9. **Answer: c**
   RATIONALE: Given these new findings, it has been postulated that itch exists both locally and centrally, that, in addition to localized itch, an "itch center" exists in the somatosensory cortex. The other answers are incorrect.
10. **Answer: d**
    RATIONALE: Moisturizing agents are the cornerstone of treatment for dry skin. These agents exert their effects by repairing the skin barrier, increasing the water content of the skin, reducing transepidermal water loss, and restoring the lipid barrier's ability to attract, hold, and redistribute water. The other answers are incorrect.

CHAPTER 46

SECTION II: ASSESSING YOUR UNDERSTANDING

Activity A

1. Primary
2. Melanin
3. Fungi
4. Candidiasis
5. bacterial
6. Impetigo
7. Cellulitis
8. Verrucae plantaris, verrucae palmaris
9. zoster
10. Acne
11. Sebum
12. comedones, blackheads, whiteheads
13. Inflammatory
14. dermatoses
15. Allergic contact
16. urticaria
17. Topical, systemic
18. Papulosquamous
19. Lichen planus
20. repeated
21. scabies
22. UV-B rays
23. photosensitive
24. Sunburn
25. Burns
26. Burn
27. ischemic
28. *dysplastic nevus*
29. melanocytes
30. melanoma
31. Basal cell carcinoma
32. Squamous cell carcinomas
33. birthmarks
34. Hemangiomas
35. Port-wine stains
36. Irritant diaper dermatitis
37. Prickly heat
38. Cradle cap

Activity B

1.

1. b	2. e	3. a	4. g	5. f
6. h	7. d	8. c	9. j	10. i

2.

1. h	2. a	3. j	4. e	5. d
6. g	7. b	8. f	9. c	10. i

Activity C

1. The most common type is recessively inherited oculocutaneous albinism, in which there are a normal number of melanocytes, but they lack tyrosinase, the enzyme needed for synthesis of

melanin. Individuals have pale or pink skin, white or yellow hair, and light-colored or sometimes pink eyes. Persons with albinism have ocular problems, such as extreme sensitivity to light, refractive errors, lack of stereopsis, and nystagmus.

2. The fungi that cause superficial mycoses live on the dead keratinized cells of the epidermis. They emit an enzyme that enables them to digest keratin, which results in superficial skin scaling, nail disintegration, or hair breakage, depending on the location of the infection. Deeper reactions involving vesicles, erythema, and infiltration are caused by the inflammation that results from exotoxins liberated by the fungus. Fungi also are capable of producing an allergic or immune response.

3. There are two common types of tinea capitis: primary (noninflammatory) and secondary (inflammatory). The infection is spread most often among household members who share combs and brushes on which the spores are shed and remain viable for long periods. Depending on the invading fungus, the lesions of the noninflammatory type can vary from grayish, round, hairless patches to balding spots, with or without black dots on the head. The individual usually is asymptomatic, although pruritus may exist. The inflammatory type of tinea capitis is caused by virulent strains. The onset is rapid, and inflamed lesions usually are localized to one area of the head. The inflammation is believed to be a delayed hypersensitivity reaction to the invading fungus. The initial lesion consists of a pustular, scaly, round patch with broken hairs. A secondary bacterial infection is common and may lead to a painful, circumscribed, boggy, and indurated lesion called a *kerion*.

4. Pre-existing wounds (e.g., ulcers, erosions) and tinea pedis are often portals of entry. Legs are the most common sites, followed by the hands and pinnas of the ears, but cellulitis may be seen on many body parts. The lesion consists of an expanding red, swollen, tender plaque with an indefinite border, covering a small to wide area. Cellulitis is frequently accompanied by fever, erythema, heat, edema, and pain. Cellulitis often involves the lymph system and, once compromised, repeat infections may impair lymphatic drainage, leading to chronically swollen legs, and eventually dermal fibrosis and lymphedema.

5. The recurrent lesions of HSV-1 usually begin with a burning or tingling sensation. Umbilicated vesicles and erythema follow and progress to pustules, ulcers, and crusts before healing. Lesions are most common on the lips, face, mouth, nasal septum, and nose. When a lesion is active, HSV-1 is shed and there is risk of transmitting the virus to others. Pain is common, and healing takes place within 10 to 14 days. Precipitating factors may be stress, menses, or injury. In particular, UV-B exposure seems to be a frequent trigger for recurrence.

Individuals who are immunocompromised may have severe attacks.

6. Factors that are believed to contribute to the development of acne are (1) increased sebum production, (2) increased proliferation of the keratinizing epidermal cells that form the sebaceous cells, (3) the colonization and proliferation of *Propionibacterium acnes*, and (4) inflammation.

7. Atopic dermatitis (atopic eczema) is an itchy, inflammatory skin disorder that is characterized by poorly defined erythema with edema, vesicles, and weeping at the acute stage and skin thickening (lichenification) in the chronic stage. The infantile form of atopic dermatitis is characterized by vesicle formation, oozing, and crusting with excoriations. The skin of the cheeks may be paler, with extra creases under the eyes. Adolescents and adults usually have dry, red patches affecting the face, neck, and upper trunk, but without the thickening and discrete demarcation associated with psoriasis. The bends of the elbows and knees are usually involved. In chronic cases, the skin is dry, leathery, and lichenified.

8. It is thought that activated T lymphocytes (mainly CD4 helper cells) produce chemical messengers that stimulate abnormal growth of keratinocytes and dermal blood vessels. Accompanying inflammatory changes are caused by infiltration of neutrophils and monocytes. Skin trauma (i.e., prepsoriasis) is a common precipitating factor in people predisposed to the disease. The reaction of the skin to an original trauma of any type is called the *Koebner reaction*. Stress, infections, trauma, xerosis, and use of medications such as angiotensin-converting enzyme inhibitors, β-adrenergic blocking drugs, lithium, and the antimalarial agent, hydroxychloroquine (Plaquenil), may precipitate or exacerbate the condition.

9. Skin damage induced by UV-B is believed to be caused by the generation of reactive oxygen species and by damage to melanin. Cellular proteins and DNA are primarily damaged because of their abundance and ability to absorb UV radiation. Both UV-A and UV-B also deplete Langerhans cells and immune cells. It is believed that these effects prevent immune cells from detecting and removing sun-damaged cells with malignant potential.

10. A patient should: (1) wear a wide-brimmed hat, (2) cover up in the sun, (3) seek shade, (4) wear wraparound sunglasses, and (5) avoid the sun during the hours of 10 AM to 4 PM, while using a broad-spectrum sunscreen with an sun protection factor of 15 or higher. It is also important to avoid sun-tanning booths, perform a self-assessment of the skin every month, and obtain a professional skin examination every year.

11. The massive loss of skin tissue not only predisposes to attack by microorganisms that are present in the environment but it allows for the massive loss

of body fluids and their contents, it interferes with temperature regulation, it challenges the immune system, and it imposes excessive demands on the metabolic and reparative processes that are needed to restore the body's interface with the environment.

12. Basal cell carcinoma usually is a nonmetastasizing tumor that extends wide and deep if left untreated. Nodular ulcerative basal cell carcinoma is the most common, accounting for 60% of all basal cell carcinomas. It has a nodulocystic structure that begins as a small, flesh-colored or pink, smooth, translucent nodule that enlarges over time. Telangiectatic vessels frequently are seen beneath the surface. Over the years, a central depression forms that progress to an ulcer surrounded by the original shiny, waxy border. The second most common form is superficial basal cell carcinoma, which is seen most often on the chest or back. It begins as a flat, nonpalpable, erythematous plaque. The red, scaly areas slowly enlarge, with nodular borders and telangiectatic bases. This type of skin cancer is difficult to diagnose because it mimics other dermatologic problems.

SECTION III: APPLYING YOUR KNOWLEDGE
Activity D
1. Attack by microorganisms in the environment; massive loss of body fluids; interferes with temperature regulation; imposes excessive demands on the metabolic system; and challenges the immune system.
2. Hemodynamic instability due to fluid loss; smoke inhalation and postburn lung injury; hypermetabolism, characterized by increased oxygen consumption, increased glucose use, and protein and fat wasting; impaired function of the kidneys; hypovolemic shock and impaired organ perfusion; and sepsis.

SECTION IV: PRACTICING FOR NCLEX
Activity E
1. **Answers: 1-a, 2-c, 3-b**
2. **Answer: a**
   RATIONALE: Treatment of fungal infections usually follows diagnosis confirmed by potassium hydroxide preparation or culture. The other answers are incorrect.
3. **Answers: 1-b, 2-a, 3-f, 4-g, 5-e, 6-d, 7-c**
4. **Answer: b**
   RATIONALE: Benzoyl peroxide is a topical agent that has both antibacterial and comedolytic properties. It is the topical agent most effective in reducing the *P. acnes* population. The other topical agents do not act both as comedolytic and antibacterial agents.
5. **Answers: a, c, e**
   RATIONALE: Prominent symptoms include eyes that are itchy, burning, or dry; a gritty or foreign sensation; and erythema and swelling of the eyelid.

Heat sensitivity and telangiectasia occur later in the disease and are not considered prominent symptoms.
6. **Answer: c**
   RATIONALE: The lesions of allergic contact dermatitis range from a mild erythema with edema to vesicles or large bullae. The other answers are incorrect.
7. **Answer: d**
   RATIONALE: In persons with black skin, pigmentation may be lost from lichenified skin. The other answers do not occur in people with black skin who have eczema.
8. **Answer: a**
   RATIONALE: Intravenous immunoglobulin may hasten the healing response of the skin. Broad-spectrum antibiotics and corticosteroids may be given but they do not hasten the healing response of the skin. Diflucan is given for vaginal candidiasis.
9. **Answer: b**
   RATIONALE: In psoriasis vulgaris the primary lesions are sharply demarcated, thick, red plaques with a silvery scale that vary in size and shape. The other answers are incorrect.
10. **Answer: c**
    RATIONALE: Most persons with lichen planus who have skin lesions also have oral lesions, appearing as milky white lacework on the buccal mucosa or tongue. The other answers are incorrect.
11. **Answer: d**
    RATIONALE: Oral ivermectin, a broad-spectrum antiparasitic agent, has been used for treatment-resistant scabies. The other drugs are not used for treatment-resistant scabies.
12. **Answer: b**
    RATIONALE: Methods for preventing pressure ulcers include frequent position change, meticulous skin care, and frequent and careful observation to detect early signs of skin breakdown. The other answers are incorrect.
13. **Answer: c**
    RATIONALE: Another form of nevi, the dysplastic nevus, is important because of its capacity to transform to malignant melanoma. The other answers are incorrect.
14. **Answer: d**
    RATIONALE: Other risk factors include a family history of malignant melanoma, presence of marked freckling on the upper back, history of three or more blistering sunburns before 20 years of age, and presence of actinic keratoses. The other answers are incorrect.
15. **Answer: a**
    RATIONALE: The most important treatment goal is complete elimination of the lesion. Also important is the maintenance of function and optimal cosmetic effect. Curettage with electrodesiccation, surgical excision, irradiation, laser, cryosurgery, and chemosurgery are effective in removing all cancerous cells. The other answers are incorrect.

16. **Answer: b**
    RATIONALE: In black persons, the lesions may appear as hyperpigmented nodules and occur more frequently on non–sun-exposed areas. The other answers do not describe squamous cell carcinoma in black-skinned people.

17. **Answer: c**
    RATIONALE: Hemangiomas of infancy typically undergo an early period of a proliferation during which they enlarge, followed by a period of slow involution where the growth is reversed until complete resolution. Surgical excision, laser surgery, and chemotherapy are not used on hemangiomas of infancy.

18. **Answer: d**
    RATIONALE: Immunization is accomplished by live-virus injection. Rubella vaccination has nearly 100% immunity response in immunized children. The other answers are incorrect.

19. **Answer: a**
    RATIONALE: Lentigines can be removed surgically (cryotherapy, laser therapy, liquid nitrogen). Topical creams and lotions containing adapalene, tretinoin, have been used. The other answers are incorrect.